ANCIENT NAPLES
A DOCUMENTARY HISTORY
ORIGINS TO C. 350 CE

RABUN M. TAYLOR

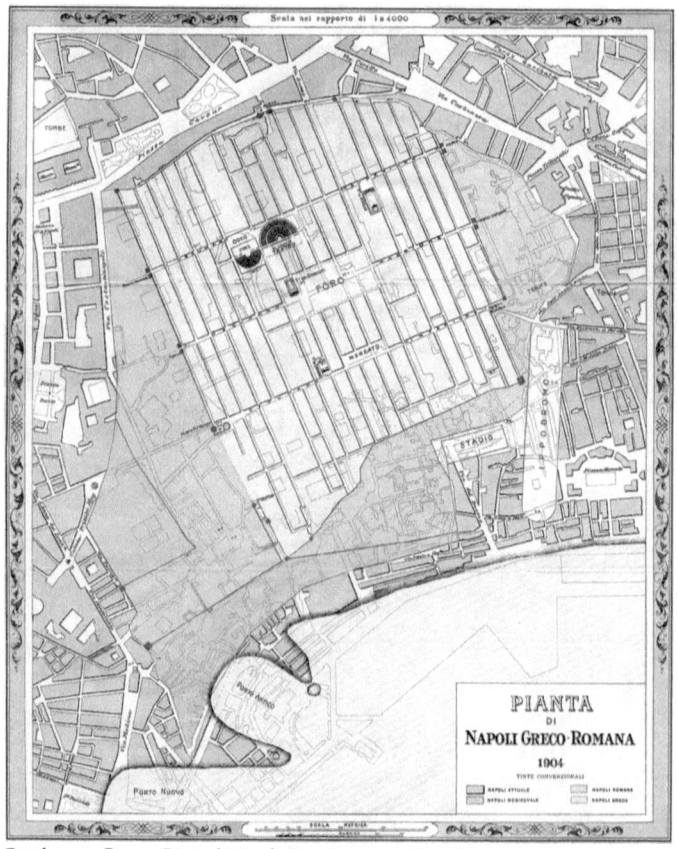

Bartolommeo Capasso, *Pianta di Napoli Greco-Romana* in Napoli greco-romana *(Naples: Società Napoletana di Storia Patria, 1905), insert.*

ANCIENT NAPLES
A DOCUMENTARY HISTORY
ORIGINS TO C.350 CE

RABUN M. TAYLOR

ITALICA PRESS
NEW YORK & BRISTOL
2021

Copyright © 2021 by Rabun M. Taylor
A Documentary History of Naples Series
Visit our website at: http://www.italicapress.com/index128.html.

ITALICA PRESS, INC.
99 Wall Street, Suite 650
New York, New York 10005
inquiries@italicapress.com

All rights reserved. No part of this publication may be reproduced, stored in a retrieval system, or transmitted, in any form or by any means, electronic, mechanical, photocopying, recording, or otherwise, without prior permission of Italica Press. It may not be used in a course-pack or any other collection without prior permission of Italica Press.

Library of Congress Cataloging-in-Publication Data
Names: Taylor, Rabun M., author.

Title: Ancient Naples : a documentary history, origins to c. 350 CE / Rabun M. Taylor.

Description: New York ; Bristol : Italica Press, Inc., 2021. | Series: A documentary history of Naples | Includes bibliographical references and index. | Summary: "Drawing on historical, literary, and archaeological sources, this volume provides a cultural, economic, material, and political history of the city of Naples, Italy from its beginnings as a Greek settlement in the eighth century BCE to the reign of the emperor Constantine in the fourth century CE"— Provided by publisher.

Identifiers: LCCN 2021002260 (print) | LCCN 2021002261 (ebook) | ISBN 9781599102214 (hardcover) | ISBN 9781599102221 (trade paperback) | ISBN 9781599102238 (kindle edition) | ISBN 9781599104072 (pdf)

Subjects: LCSH: Naples (Italy)—History—To 1503. | Greeks—Italy—Naples. | Naples (Italy)—Civilization.

Classification: LCC DG70.N35 T39 2021 (print) | LCC DG70.N35 (ebook) | DDC 937/.7251—dc23

LC record available at https://lccn.loc.gov/2021002260

LC ebook record available at https://lccn.loc.gov/2021002261

Cover Illustration: Remains of the Temple of the Dioscuri. Naples, S. Paolo Maggiore, facade. Photo: R. Taylor.

CONTENTS

ILLUSTRATIONS	viii
READINGS	xiv
COMMENTARIES	xvii
ABBREVIATIONS	xviii
PREFACE & ACKNOWLEDGMENTS	xxii
INTRODUCTION	1
Disasters and opportunities	3
Recent Archaeology	6
A Word on Style and Language	7
References	8
CHAPTER 1. THE PHYSICAL SETTING	9
Geography and Geology	9
Climate and Agriculture	21
The Territory of Neapolis	23
The Specter of Calamity	27
References	29
CHAPTER 2. THE GREEK CITY	31
Prehistory	31
Naples within Remotest Memory	35
Parthenope and Early Neapolis in Literature	38
The Foundation Myth	42
Parthenope, Neapolis, and Cumae	46
Syracuse and Ischia	54
The Athenian Connection	55
The Rise of the Samnites	59
City Organization and Administration	63
Archaeology	66
References	82
CHAPTER 3. EARLY COINAGE OF NEAPOLIS	85
Die Studies: Neapolis' Contact with Samnite Cities	86
Neapolitan Coins in Context	88
Parthenope and the Bull-Man	89
The Winged Spirit of Tereina and Neapolis	96
Athena on Neapolitan Coinage	99

Other Early Types — 101
Bronze in the Fourth and Third Centuriesm BCE — 102
Silver Coinage: Fourth and Third Centuries BCE — 104
Who Put Control Marks on Coins, and Why? — 107
Neapolitan Coinage under Rome — 109
References — 110

CHAPTER 4. NEAPOLIS AND THE RISE OF ROME — 113
Introduction — 113
The Second Samnite War — 114
Romano-Campanian Coinage — 122
Neapolis and Rome after 327/6 BCE — 126
The Crisis of 216–211 BCE and the Last Neapolitan Coinage — 132
Neapolis as a Commercial Power in the Second Century BCE — 135
Sulla — 142
References — 149

CHAPTER 5. FROM REPUBLIC TO EMPIRE — 151
The Landscape of Disaster — 155
The High Empire — 168
Population and Demographics — 171
City Government — 173
The Phratries in the Roman Period — 174
Conclusion — 176
References — 183

CHAPTER 6. A GLIMPSE OF ROMAN NEAPOLIS — 185
Introduction — 185
Forum Duplex — 188
The Odeion and Theater — 191
The Temple of the Dioscuri — 196
The Complex at S. Lorenzo Maggiore — 205
The Sebasta Games and the Kaisareion — 211
The Harbor — 218
The Honorific Arch at Piazza Bovio — 226
Neapolis and the Food Supply for Italy — 230
Outside the Walls: Cemeteries — 236
Suburbs — 238
Hedging Her Bets — 243
References — 246

CONTENTS

CHAPTER 7. THE CULTURE OF WATER	249
Gods of the Water	250
The Thermo-Mineral Baths	253
The Roman Hydraulic Infrastructure	262
The Serino Aqueduct	262
The Bolla Aqueduct	272
Conventional Baths	275
References	288
CHAPTER 8. HAVEN OF HELLENISM: GREEK CULTURE IN ROMAN NEAPOLIS	291
The Landscape of the Mind	296
The Villa Culture under the Republic	298
The Cult and Tomb of Virgil	303
Pausilypon and Other Imperial Villas	306
Statius	313
The Games at Neapolis	316
Roots of the Games	322
Visual Arts	330
References	344
CHAPTER 9. THE THIRD CENTURY AND CONSTANTINE	347
The Third Century	347
Constantine and the City	356
References	371
BIBLIOGRAPHY	373
INDEX	419

ILLUSTRATIONS

Frontispiece. Bartolommeo Capasso, Pianta di Napoli Greco-Romana, in *Napoli Greco-Romana* (Naples: Società Napoletana di Storia Patria, 1905), insert. ii
Map of ancient Naples with its furthest expansion in the Roman imperial age. From Mario Napoli, "Napoli greco-romana: Topografia e archeologia," *SN* 1. xxiv

CHAPTER 1. THE PHYSICAL SETTING
Fig. 1.1. Map of Neapolis and its western suburbs in antiquity. 10
Fig. 1.2. Map of the Bay of Naples and its vicinity in antiquity. 11
Fig. 1.3. Capri, with a panoramic view to the Anacapri headland. Photo:
P. Costa Baldi / Wikimedia Commons GFDL/CC BY-SA 3.0. 12
Fig. 1.4. View of the Roman *macellum* at Pozzuoli. Photo: Doktorpixel14 /
Wikimedia Commons CC BY-SA 4.0. 15
Fig. 1.5. Lago d'Averno. Gouache by Jacob Philipp Hackert, 1794. Munich, Neue Pinakothek. Wikimedia Commons. 17
Fig. 1.6. Ischia, the town of Lacco Ameno. Photo: C. Marra / Wikimedia Commons CC BY 2.0. 19
Fig. 1.7. La Solfatara, near Pozzuoli. Photo: D. Reiskoffer / Wikimedia Commons. 25
Fig. 1.8. View of Mt.Vesuvius from Pizzofalcone, Naples. Anonymous hand-colored engraving, 1858. Archiv "Deutschland und die Welt." Wikimedia Commons. 27

CHAPTER 2. THE GREEK CITY
Fig. 2.1. Map of Neapolis and vicinity in the Greek period. 30
Fig. 2.2. Italo-Geometric oinochoe from the Pizzofalcone necropolis. Second quarter of the seventh century BCE. Naples, Museo Archeologico Nazionale. Photo: R. Taylor. 37
Fig. 2.3. Roman fresco from Pompeii. Mid-first century CE. British Museum. © Trustees of the British Museum. 44
Fig. 2.4. Votive female busts from excavations at S. Aniello a Caponapoli. By permission of the Ministero per i Beni e le Attività Culturali e per il Turismo, Museo Archeologico Nazione di Napoli. Photo: R. Taylor. 51
Fig. 2.5. Greek fortification walls at Piazza Bellini. Photo: R. Taylor. 67
Fig. 2.6. View of Castel S. Elmo from Spaccanapoli. Photo: Kalamita / Wikimedia Commons CC BY-SA 2.0. Modified. 69
Fig. 2.7. Excavations at the necropolis of Sta. Teresa. Plate 4 from A. de Jorio, *Metodo per rinvenire e frugare i sepolcri degli antichi*, Naples 1824. 70

CHAPTER 3. EARLY COINAGE OF NEAPOLIS
Fig. 3.1. Silver didrachm of Neapolis. Paris, Bibliothèque Nationale de France, Cabinet des Médailles. 90
Fig. 3.2. Silver didrachm of Neapolis. Photo courtesy of American Numismatic Society. CC BY-NC 4.0. Modified. 91
Fig. 3.3. Detail from an Attic red-figure column crater from Agrigento, c.450 BCE. Paris, Musée du Louvre. Photo: Marie-Lan Nguyen / Wikimedia Commons CC PD-Mark 1.0. 92

ILLUSTRATIONS

Fig. 3.4. Silver obol of Neapolis. Photo courtesy of Numismatica Ars Classica. 93
Fig. 3.5. Silver didrachm of Gela. Ex P.H. Gerrie collection. Photo courtesy of Classical Numismatic Group. 93
Fig. 3.6. Silver obol of Neapolis. By permission of the Ministero per i Beni e le Attività Culturali e per il Turismo, Museo Archeologico Nazione di Napoli. 95
Fig. 3.7. Silver didrachm of Tereina. Ex C.R.J. Spencer-Churchill collection. Photo courtesy of Classical Numismatic Group. 97
Fig. 3.8. Attic red-figure stamnos, 480-460 BCE. British Museum. © Trustees of the British Museum. 98
Fig. 3.9. Silver didrachm of Neapolis. Ex R. Jameson and Sir A. Evans collections. Photo courtesy of Nomos AG, Zürich. 99
Fig. 3.10. Silver didrachm of Hyria. Ex R.C. Lockett collection. Photo courtesy of Classical Numismatic Group. 100
Fig. 3.11. Silver didrachm of Hyria. Ex P. Tichant and R.J. Graham collections. Photo courtesy of LHS Numismatik, AG, Zürich. 103
Fig. 3.12. Bronze coin of Neapolis. Photo courtesy of Numismatica Ars Classica. 104
Fig. 3.13. Silver didrachm of Neapolis. Photo courtesy of Numismatica Ars Classica. 105
Fig. 3.14. Silver didrachm of Neapolis. Ex P.H. Gerrie collection. Photo courtesy of Classical Numismatic Group. 107

CHAPTER 4. NEAPOLIS AND THE RISE OF ROME
Fig. 4.1. Romano-Campanian bronze hemiobol. Photo courtesy of Classical Numismatic Group. 123
Fig. 4.2. Romano-Campanian silver didrachm. Photo courtesy of Numismatica Ars Classica. 124
Fig. 4.3. Interior of Tomb C at Via Cristallini. Photo courtesy of M. Jodice. 127
Fig. 4.4. Entrance of Tomb C at Via Cristallini. Photo courtesy of M. Jodice. 128
Fig. 4.5. Bronze trias of Neapolis. By permission of the Ministero per i Beni e le Attività Culturali e per il Turismo, Museo Archeologico Nazione di Napoli. 132
Fig. 4.6. Funerary reliefs from tombs of Neapolis. By permission of the Ministero per i Beni e le Attività Culturali e per il Turismo, Museo Archeologico Nazione di Napoli. Photo: R. Taylor. 136
Fig. 4.7. Pottery recovered from the Piazza Municipio excavations. In foreground, "Campana A" vessels. By permission of the Ministero per i Beni e le Attività Culturali e per il Turismo, Museo Archeologico Nazione di Napoli. Photo: R. Taylor. 139
Fig. 4.8. Map of the western Mediterranean representing the diffusion of "Campana A" pottery. After Morel 1985. 140

CHAPTER 5. FROM REPUBLIC TO EMPIRE
Fig. 5.1. Map indicating the extent of the six surges of the eruption of 79 CE. After Sigurdsson and Carey 2002. 158
Fig. 5.2. Reconstructed cadastral grid of the territory of Neapolis. Background © 2020 Google. After Chouquer and Favory 1987. 159
Fig. 5.3. Cadastral grids of the Vesuvian area. Illustration courtesy of G.F. De Simone. 160

CHAPTER 6. A GLIMPSE OF ROMAN NEAPOLIS

Fig. 6.1. Map of Roman Neapolis featuring the major known monuments and excavated areas. 188

Fig. 6.2. Axonometric reconstruction of the forum area with the theater and odeion. Greco 1985a, 1986. 189

Fig. 6.3. Anonymous sketch of the façade of S. Paolo Maggiore. Cabinet des Estampes. Courtesy of Bibliothèque Nationale de France. 190

Fig. 6.4. Ravine and escarpments west of the ancient walled city. Satellite image © 2020 Google. 192

Fig. 6.5. Barrel-vaulted corridor of the Roman theater. Photo: R. Taylor. 195

Fig. 6.6. Theater and odeion of Pompeii. Photo: ElfQrin. Wikimedia Commons CC SA-4.0. Modified. 195

Fig. 6.7. Façade of the church of S. Paolo Maggiore with remaining Roman columns and column bases in situ. Photo: R. Taylor. 197

Fig. 6.8. Ink drawing of the pediment at S. Paolo Maggiore. Fol. 45 v from the manuscript of *Os desenhos das antiqualhas* by Francisco de Holanda, Real Biblioteca del Monasterio de El Escorial. © Patrimonio Nacional (Spain). 199

Fig. 6.9. Details of Fig. 6.8. 200

Fig. 6.10. Fragmentary remains of the statues of the Dioscuri from S. Paolo Maggiore. By permission of the Ministero per i Beni e le Attività Culturali e per il Turismo, Museo Archeologico Nazione di Napoli. Photo: R. Taylor. 203

Fig. 6.11. Model of the Temple of the Dioscuri in its forum context on display at the church of S. Lorenzo Maggiore. Photo: R. Taylor 204

Fig. 6.12. Eastern sector of the excavations at S. Lorenzo Maggiore, looking south. Photo: R. Taylor. 206

Fig. 6.13. Isometric view of the excavated area under S. Lorenzo Maggiore. Illustration by Francesco Corni. 207

Figs. 6.14a, 6.14b. Complete and cutaway models at the church of S. Lorenzo Maggiore representing the Roman *macellum* and commercial precinct excavated under the church. 208

Fig. 6.15. Southern sector of the excavations under S. Lorenzo Maggiore, looking west. Photo: R. Taylor. 209

Fig. 6.16. Western sector of the excavations under S. Lorenzo Maggiore, looking north-northeast. Photo: R. Taylor. 210

Fig. 6.17. Roman imperial statue of Nike. By permission of the Ministero per i Beni e le Attività Culturali e per il Turismo, Museo Archeologico Nazione di Napoli. Photo: R. Taylor. 212

Fig. 6.18. Fragments of the columns and roof of the Kaisareion. By permission of the Ministero per i Beni e le Attività Culturali e per il Turismo, Museo Archeologico Nazione di Napoli. Photo: R. Taylor. 214

Fig. 6.19. Map of Roman Neapolis highlighting known cemetery zones and bathing establishments. 216

Fig. 6.20. Map of the harbor excavations at Piazza Municipio with remains of

ILLUSTRATIONS

Roman architecture and ships. After Boetto 2019. 219
Fig. 6.21. Selection of pottery recovered from the harbor excavations. By permission of the Ministero per i Beni e le Attività Culturali e per il Turismo, Museo Archeologico Nazione di Napoli. Photo: R. Taylor. 220
Fig. 6.22. Model of the ships A, B, and C from the harbor excavations at Piazza Municipio. By permission of the Ministero per i Beni e le Attività Culturali e per il Turismo, Museo Archeologico Nazione di Napoli. Photo: R. Taylor. The pilings and rubble to the left formed a jetty; just to its left are the scooped recesses in the tuff bedrock formed by a rotary dredge. 220
Fig. 6.23. First-century-CE bath building beside the harbor, before demolition. Photo: R. Taylor. 224
Fig. 6.24. Reconstruction of a dismantled Severan honorific arch with hypothetical placement of several key components. From Cavalieri and Hesberg 2010. Courtesy of Electa. 226
Fig. 6.25. The two finished sides of a corner fragment from the Severan arch. By permission of the Ministero per i Beni e le Attività Culturali e per il Turismo, Museo Archeologico Nazione di Napoli. Photo: R. Taylor. 227
Fig. 6.26. Frieze fragment of the Severan arch representing a scene of imperial disembarkment and sacrifice. By permission of the Ministero per i Beni e le Attività Culturali e per il Turismo, Museo Archeologico Nazione di Napoli. Photo: R. Taylor. 228
Fig. 6.27. Frieze fragment of the Severan arch representing a scene of imperial address. By permission of the Ministero per i Beni e le Attività Culturali e per il Turismo, Museo Archeologico Nazione di Napoli. Photo: R. Taylor. 229
Fig. 6.28. Aerial view of the Via Celle necropolis at Pozzuoli. Courtesy of Electa. 237
Fig. 6.29. Western entrance of the "Grotta di Seiano" at the villa of Pausilypon. Photo: R. Taylor. 240
Fig. 6.30. Aerial view of the Pausilypon villa. Photo: S. Capuano / Wikimedia Commons CC BY-SA 2.0. 242

CHAPTER 7. THE CULTURE OF WATER

Fig. 7.1. Relief from Ischia representing Apollo and two of the Nitrodes nymphs. One nymph delivers spring water from a basin with which the nude dedicant, Capellina, washes her hair. By permission of the Ministero per i Beni e le Attività Culturali e per il Turismo, Museo Archeologico Nazione di Napoli. 248
Fig. 7.2. The Roman thermo-mineral baths at Baiae. By permission of the Ministero per i Beni e le Attività Culturali e per il Turismo, Museo Archeologico Nazione di Napoli. Photo: R. Taylor. 254
Fig. 7.3. The Roman bath of Tritoli. Illustration by G. B. Natali, in Paoli 1768. 256
Fig. 7.4. "I Pisciarelli." Illustration by P. Fabris, in W. Hamilton, *Campi Phlegraei* (Naples 1776). 258
Fig. 7.5. Illumination from Peter of Eboli's *De balneis Puteolanis*. Biblioteca Angelica, Rome. Denghiù / Wikimedia Commons. 259
Fig. 7.6. Baths of Agnano in the early twentieth century. Anonymous photo. CC BY-SA. 260

XI

Fig. 7.7. Plan of the Roman baths at Agnano. Macchioro 1912. 261
Fig. 7.8. Map of the course of the Serino Aqueduct. Background © 2020 Google. 263
Fig. 7.9. Remains of the Serino Aqueduct known as the Ponti Rossi.
Photo: R. Taylor. 264
Fig. 7.10. View of the eastern end of the Crypta Neapolitana. Photo: R. Taylor. 265
Fig. 7.11. View of the western end of the Crypta Neapolitana. Photo: R. Taylor. 266
Fig. 7.12. The Grotto of Posillipo at Naples, oil painting by A.S. Pitloo, 1826.
Rijksmuseum. 267
Fig. 7.13. Cross-section of the Crypta Neapolitana, eastern end. Günther 1913,
after Paoli 1768. 268
Fig. 7.14. Satellite view of Pizzofalcone highlighting the ancient rock-cut
nymphaeum at Palazzo Carafa di S. Severino. Satellite imagery: © 2020 Google,
CNES / Airbus, Maxar Technologies. Inset photo: R. Taylor. 269
Fig. 7.15. Rear slab of a marble fountain basin from Via del Cerriglio. By permission of
the Ministero per i Beni e le Attività Culturali e per il Turismo, Museo Archeologico
Nazione di Napoli. Photo: R. Taylor. 270
Fig. 7.16. Plan of known rock-cut underground features in the area northwest of
Piazza Dante. Esposito 2018. 272
Fig. 7.17. Roman bath under the church of Sta. Chiara. Photo: R. Taylor. 276
Fig. 7.18. Multi-use Roman complex at Via Carminiello ai Mannesi.
Photo: R. Taylor. 277
Fig. 7.19. Isometric cutaway reconstruction by Sheila Gibson of the complex of
Carminiello ai Mannesi in the second century CE. Arthur, ed. 1994.
Courtesy of Paul Arthur. 277
Fig. 7.20. Fountain in the complex at Via Carminiello ai Mannesi. Photo: R. Taylor. 279
Fig. 7.21. Baths of the Via Terracina. Photo: R. Taylor. 280
Fig. 7.22. View and elevations of the circular bathing pool at Pausilypon. Günther 1913. 281

CHAPTER 8. HAVEN OF HELLENISM

Fig. 8.1. Analytical reconstruction of the Villa of the Papyri at Herculaneum.
Illustration by Rocío Espín Piñar. 301
Fig. 8.2. Plan of the ruins in the vicinity of Pausilypon. Günther 1913. 304
Fig. 8.3. The "Scuola di Virgilio." Illustration by G. B. Natali, in Paoli 1768. 304
Fig. 8.4. Interior of the so-called Tomb of Virgil. Illustration by G. B. Natali,
in Paoli 1768. 304
Fig. 8.5. Villa of Pausilypon, seen from the west. Photo: R. Taylor. 309
Fig. 8.6. Eastern end of the "Grotta di Seiano." Photo: R. Taylor. 310
Fig. 8.7. Early imperial marble statue of a Nereid and *pistrix*. By permission of the
Ministero per i Beni e le Attività Culturali e per il Turismo, Museo Archeologico
Nazione di Napoli. Photo: R. Taylor. 312
Fig. 8.8. Marble statues of an African fisherman (second century CE) and a
Muse (uncertain date). By permission of the Ministero per i Beni e le
Attività Culturali e per il Turismo, Museo Archeologico Nazione di Napoli.
Photos: R. Taylor. 313

ILLUSTRATIONS

Fig. 8.9. Marble agonistic inscription of Hermagoras. By permission of the Ministero per i Beni e le Attività Culturali e per il Turismo, Museo Archeologico Nazione di Napoli. Photo: R. Taylor. 321

Fig. 8.10. Impression from a gem once in the British Museum; now presumed lost. From F. Imhoof-Blumer, *Tier- und Pflanzenbilder auf Münzen und Gemmen des klassischen Altertums*. Leipzig 1889. 324

Figs. 8.11. Room 14 at the Villa of Oplontis near Pompeii, featuring elaborate Second-Style architectural frescos. Photo: R. Taylor; 331

Fig. 8.12. Room 15 at the Villa of Oplontis. Photo: R. Taylor. 331

CHAPTER 9. THE THIRD CENTURY AND CONSTANTINE

Fig. 9.1. Catacomb of S. Gennaro. Photo: Peppe Guida / Wikimedia Commons CC BY-SA 4.0. Modified. 353

Fig. 9.2. Plan of the excavations under Sta. Restituta and dependencies of the cathedral. Base plan from Amodio 2015; overlay providing the approximate layout of the earlier Roman structures by R. Taylor. 359

Fig. 9.3. Small vaulted chamber in the excavated area under S. Gennaro with a Roman *opus reticulatum* wall projecting from a Greek ashlar retaining wall. Photo: R. Taylor. 360

Fig. 9.4. Roman gutter bounding the peristyle of area A in Fig. 9.3, running under the apse of Sta. Restituta. Photo: R. Taylor. 360

Fig. 9.5. General view of the excavated area under S. Gennaro and Sta. Restituta. Photo courtesy of M. Jodice. 361

Fig. 9.6. Late Roman lead pipe in the excavated area under S. Gennaro. Photo: R. Taylor. 363

READINGS

1. Statius, *Silvae* 3.5.72–105	9
2. Seneca, *Moral Epistles* 57.1–2	13
3. Strabo, *Geography* 5.4.6	14
4. *Apocryphal Acts of Peter and Paul* 12	16
5. Virgil, *Aeneid* 6.237–42	17
6. Diodoros of Sicily, *Historical Library* 4.21.1–2	18
7. Strabo, *Geography* 5.4.9	20
8. Strabo, *Geography* 5.4.3	22
9. Dio Cassius, *Roman History* 66.22–23	28
10. Cup of Nestor Inscription, *SEG* 14.604	33
11. Velleius Paterculus, *Compendium of Roman History* 1.4.1	39
12. Pseudo-Skymnos, *Periegesis* 252–53	39
13. Pliny, *Natural History* 3.62	39
14. Strabo, *Geography* 5.4.7	39
15. *Scholia Bernensia*, on Virgil's *Georgics* 4.564	39
16. Philargyrios, scholium on Virgil's *Georgics* 4.564	39
17. Tzetzes, scholium of Lykophron, *Alexandra* 732	40
18. Livy, *History of Rome* 8.22.5–6	41
19. Lykophron, *Alexandra*, 712–38	42
20. Philargyrios, scholium on Virgil's *Georgics* 4.564	48
21. Strabo, *Geography* 5.4.9	54
22. Diodoros of Sicily, *Historical Library* 12.76.4	60
23. Dionysios of Halikarnassos, *Roman Antiquities* 15.6.4	61
24. Strabo, *Geography* 5.4.7	62
25. Velleius Paterculus, *Compendium of Roman History* 1.4.2	73
26. Strabo, *Geography* 14.2.10	75
27. Lykophron, *Alexandra* 724–31	98
28. Livy, *History of Rome* 8.22.7	115
29. Dionysios of Halikarnassos, *Roman Antiquities* 15.5.1–15.6.5	115
30. Livy, *History of Rome* 8.22.8–10	116
31. Dionysios of Halikarnassos, *Roman Antiquities* 15.7.3–5	118
32. Dionysios of Halikarnassos, *Roman Antiquities* 15.8.3–5	119
33. Livy, *History of Rome* 8.23, 25–26	119
34. Livy, *History of Rome* 35.16.8	130

READINGS

35. Cicero, *For Balbus* 21	142
36. Livy, *History of Rome* 22.32.4–9	146
37. Livy, *History of Rome* 23.1.5–10	146
38. Livy, *History of Rome* 23.15.1–2	147
39. Pliny the Younger, *Epistles* 4.20	156
40. Suetonius, *Titus* 8.4	163
41. Dio Cassius, *Roman History* 66.24.3	163
42. *Liber coloniarum*, ed. Lachmann 1.235	164
43. Pliny the Elder, *Natural History* 2.197	177
44. Pliny the Elder, *Natural History* 15.94	177
45. Pliny the Elder, *Natural History* 17.122	177
46. Fronto, *Correspondence* 2.6 = LCL 1.143	178
47. Petronius, *Satyricon* 6–7	180
48. L. Munatius Hilarianus to the Phrateres Artemisioi, *SEG* 39.1055	182
49. Seneca, *Moral Epistles* 76.3–4	193
50. Pediment inscription, Temple of the Dioscuri, *IG* 14.714	198
51. Dio Chrysostom, *Discourse* 28.1	213
52. Piazza Bovio inscription, *NSc* 1892:479–81	221
53. *Historia Augusta, Septimius Severus* 18.3; 23.2	233
54. Plutarch, *Table Talk* 4.4.1 (667c)	239
55. Plutarch, *Sulla* 26.3	239
56. Pliny the Elder, *Natural History* 31.4	249
57. Statius, *Silvae* 1.2.262–65	249
58. Strabo, *Geography* 5.4.7	257
59. Gregory I, *Dialogue* 4.40	261
60. Pliny the Elder, *Natural History* 31.4–5	284
61. Pausanias, *Description of Greece* 8.7.3	285
62. Vitruvius, *Ten Books on Architecture* 2.6.1–4	285
63. *CIL* 10.1805	285
64. *Theodosian Code* 15.2.8	286
65. Serino Aqueduct tunnel inscription, Colonna 1898:72	286
66. Strabo, *Geography* 5.4.7	291
67. Silius Italicus, *Punica* 12.31–32	291
68. Homer, *Odyssey* 5.377–78	293
69. Dio Chrysostom, *Discourse* 64.11–13	294

70. Dio Chrysostom, *Discourse* 29.5–6 — 295
71. Cicero, *For Archia* 5, 10 — 299
72. Fragment of Philodemos from one of the Herculaneum papyri, *PHerc* 312 — 302
73. Fragment from Villa of the Papyri, *PHerc Paris* 2.21–23 — 302
74. Statius, *Silvae* 2.2.1–13 — 315
75. Statius, *Silvae* 3.5.72–105 — 316
76. Suetonius, *Nero* 40.4–41.1 — 318
77. Lykophron, *Alexandra* 220–22 — 322
78. Lykophron, *Alexandra* 733–36 — 322
79. Tzetzes, scholium of Lykophron 733 — 323
80. Strabo, *Geography* 5.4.7 — 325
81. Suetonius, *Augustus* 98.4 — 328
82. Philostratos, *Images* I.pr. — 330
83. Virgil, *Georgics* 4.559–66 — 333
84. *Appendix Virgiliana*, Catalepton 5 — 333
85. *Appendix Virgiliana*, Catalepton 8 — 334
86. Velleius Paterculus, *Compendium of Roman History* 2.33.4 — 335
87. Pliny the Elder, *Natural History* 9.170 — 335
88. An Epicurean Funerary Epigram, *CIL* 10.2971 — 335
89. Dio Cassius, *Roman History* 54.23.1–6 — 336
90. Ausonius, *Moselle* 208–19 — 337
91. An Inscription from the Sebasta Games, Miranda de Martino 2014 — 340
92. Suetonius, *Nero* 20 — 341
93. Tacitus, *Annals* 15.34 — 342
94. A Personal Agonistic Inscription, *IG* 14.739 = Miranda 1990–1995 no. 49 — 342
95. A Public Inscription Honoring a Prominent Musician, *IG* 14.737 = Miranda 1990–1995 no. 47 — 343
96. *Historia Augusta*, *Severus Alexander* 26.9–10. — 347
97. San Gennaro Catacomb inscription, *IG* 14.823 — 354
98. Inscription on resoration of Aqua Augusta, *CIL* 10.1805 — 357
99. John the Lydian, *On Powers* 3.70 — 358
100. Sta. Restituta baths inscription, *CIL* 10.1757 — 362
101. *Acts of the Apostles* 28.13–14 — 366
102. *Liber pontificalis* 34.32 — 369

COMMENTARIES

2.1. A Rhodian Connection?	75
2.2. Neapolis and Capri	77
2.3. The Origins of Pozzuoli	78
2.4. The Phratries of Neapolis	79
3.1. Coinage and Prosperity	109
4.1. Neapolis Remains Faithful to Rome	146
4.2. Hannibal's Attempts to Seize Neapolis	146
4.3. The Pottery Workshop of Corso Umberto	147
5.1. Neapolis' Anomalous Earthquake Dynamics	176
5.2. Neapolitan Chestnut Production	177
5.3. The Herculanean District	177
5.4. A Letter from Marcus Aurelius to Fronto	178
5.5. The Site of Trimalchio's Feast	179
5.6. The Phratry Inscription of the Artemisioi	181
6.1. The Kaisareion's Decoration	244
6.2. The Ships of Neapolis	244
6.3. Sea-Level Change in the Tyrrhenian	245
7.1. The Spas of Ischia	283
7.2. Ancient Authors on the Phlegraean Fields	284
7.3. Serino Aqueduct Documents	285
7.4. The Aqueduct Tunnel Inscriptions	286
8.1. Virgil's Epicurean Awakening	333
8.2. Lucullus' Neapolitan Villa	334
8.3. An Epicurean Funerary Epigram	335
8.4. Vedius Pollio	336
8.5. A View of the Sebasta from Late Antiquity	337
8.6. An Inscription from the Games	339
8.7. Nero's Stage Debut	341
8.8. A Personal Agonistic Inscription	342
8.9. A Public Inscription Honoring a Prominent Musician	343
9.1. Constantine's Gifts to Neapolis	369

ABBREVIATIONS

Short titles not included in this list follow the style of the *Archäologische Bibliographie*.

Acqua e architettura	Starace, F., ed. 2002. *L'acqua e l'architettura: Acquedotti e fontane del regno di Napoli.* Lecce: Edizioni del Grifo
AIIN	*Annali dell'Istituto Italiano di Numismatica*
AION (archeol)	*Annali di archeologia e storia antica, Università degli Studi di Napoli "L'Orientale"*
AION (or)	*Annali dell'Università degli Studi di Napoli "L'Orientale," sezione orientale*
AJA	*American Journal of Archaeology*
Ambiente geologico	Vallario, A., ed. 2001. *L'ambiente geologico della Campania.* Naples: CUEN
Apoikia	D'Agostino, B. and D. Ridgway, ed. 1994. ΑΠΟΙΚΙΑ: *I più antichi insediamenti greci di occidente. Funzioni e modi dell'organizzazione politica e sociale. Scritti in onore di Giorgio Buchner. AION (archeol)* n.s. 1
Apolline Project	De Simone, G.F. and R.T. Macfarlane, ed. 2009. *Apolline Project.* 1: *Studies on Vesuvius' North Slope and the Bay of Naples.* Naples and Provo, Utah: Università degli Studi Suor Orsola Benincasa and Brigham Young University
Archäologie und Seismologie	*Archäologie und Seismologie: La regione vesuviana dal 62 al 79 d.C. Problemi archeologici e sismologici.* 1995 Munich: Biering & Brinkmann
ArchClas	*Archeologia classica*
ASPN	*Archivio storico per le province napoletane*
ASub	*Archeologia subacquea*
ATTA	*Atlante tematico di topografia antica*
AttiAccPontan	*Atte dell'Accademia Pontaniana*
AttiTaranto	*Atti del Convegno di studi sulla Magna Grecia, Taranto*
BABesch	*Bulletin Antieke Beschaving*
BHL	*Bibliotheca hagiographica Latina*
Campania romana	*Campania romana: Studi e materiali* 1. 1938. Naples: Rispoli
Campi Flegrei	*I Campi Flegrei nell'archeologia e nella storia.* 1977. Rome: Accademia Nazionale dei Lincei

ABBREVIATIONS

CIL	Corpus inscriptionum Latinarum
Crise et transformation	Crise et transformation des sociétés archaïques de l'Italie antique au Ve siècle av. J.C. 1990. Rome: École Française de Rome
Crossroads	Hackens, T. et al., ed. 1984. *Crossroads of the Mediterranean*. Louvain and Providence, RI: Université Catholique de Louvain and Brown University
Cuma	*Cuma. Atti Taranto* 48. 2009
Greek Colonists	J.-P. Descoeudres, ed. *Greek Colonists and Native Populations*. 1990. Oxford: Clarendon
Greek Identity	Lomas, K., ed. 2004. *Greek Identity in the Western Mediterranean: Papers in Honour of Brian Shefton* Leiden: Brill
Destino	Amalfitano, P., ed. 1986. *Il destino della Sibilla: Mito, scienza e storia dei Campi Flegrei*. Naples: Bibliopolis
Euboica	Bats, M. and B. D'Agostino, ed. 1998. *Euboica: L'Eubea e la presenza euboica in Calcidica e in Occidente. Atti del Convegno Internazionale di Napoli, 13–16 novembre 1996. AION (archeol) quaderno* 12. Naples: Centre Jean Bérard
IG	Inscriptiones Graecae
ILS	Inscriptiones Latinae Selectae
LIMC	Lexicon iconographicum mythologiae classicae
JRS	Journal of Roman Studies
Magna Grecia	*Magna Grecia e mondo miceneo. Atti Taranto* 22. 1983
MÉFRA	Melanges de l'École Française de Rome (antiquité)
MemLinc	Atti della Accademia Nazionale dei Lincei Memorie. Classe di scienze morali, storiche e filologiche
MemNap	Memorie della Reale Accademia di Archeologia, Lettere e Belle Arti
MGR	Miscellanea greca e romana
Modalità insediative	Lo Cascio, E. and A Storchi Marino, ed. *Modalità insediative e strutture agrarie nell'Italia meridionale in età romana*. 2001. Bari: Edipuglia
MonAnt	Monumenti antichi dell'Accademia Nazionale dei Lincei
Monetazione di Neapolis	Stazio, A. et al., ed. 1986. *La monetazione di Neapolis nella Campania antica: Atti del VII Convegno del Centro Internazionale di Studi Numismatici, Napoli, 20–24 aprile 1980*. Naples: Arte tipografica

Monetazione romano-campana	La monetazione romano-campana: Atti del X Convegno del Centro Internazionale di Studi Numismatici, Napoli, 18–19 giugno 1993. 1998. Rome: Istituto Italiano di Numismatica
Napoli antica	Napoli antica. 1985. Naples: Macchiaroli
Napoli, la città e il mare	Napoli, la città e il mare: Piazza Bovio tra romani e bizantini. Napoli, Museo Archeologico Nazionale, 21 maggio – 20 settembre 2010. 2010. Naples: Electa
Natural History	Jashemski, W.F. and F.G. Meyer, ed. The Natural History of Pompeii. 2002. Cambridge: Cambridge University Press
Neapolis	Neapolis. Atti Taranto 25. 1986
NSc	Notizie degli scavi di antichità
NN	Napoli nobilissima: Rivista di arti figurative, archeologia e urbanistica
PHerc	Papyri herculanenses or Herculaneum Papyri
Pompei, Capri	Senatore, F., ed. 2004. Pompei, Capri e la Penisola Sorrentina. Capri: Oebalus
PP	La parola del passato
RBNum	Revue belge de numismatique
RE	Pauly–Wissowa. Paulys Real-Encyclopädie der classischen Altertumswissenschaft
Remembering Parthenope	J. Hughes and C. Buongiovanni, ed. 2015. Remembering Parthenope: The Reception of Classical Naples from Antiquity to the Present. Oxford: Oxford University Press
RendNap	Rendiconti [Atti] della Accademia di Archeologia, Lettere e Belle Arti, Napoli
RendPont	Rendiconti della Pontificia Accademia Romana di Archeologia
RIA	Rivista dell'Istituto Nazionale d'Archeologia e Storia dell'Arte
RIN	Rivista italiana di numismatica e scienze affini
RivStudPomp	Rivista di studi pompeiani
RM	Mitteilungen des Deutschen Archäologisches Instituts, Römische Abteilung
Roman Baths	J. DeLaine and D.E. Johnston, eds. 1999. Roman Baths and Bathing: Proceedings of the First International Conference on Roman Baths. Portsmouth, RI: Journal of Roman Archaeology

ABBREVIATIONS

Romanizzazione	Franciosi, G., ed. 2002. *La romanizzazione della Campania antica*. Naples: Jovene
San Lorenzo Maggiore	*San Lorenzo Maggiore: Guida al museo e al complesso.* 2005. Naples: Edizioni Scientifiche Italiane
Sebastà Isolympia	Vito, G., ed. 2017. *Sebastà Isolympia: Il patrimonio riscoperto, l'eredità culturale da valorizzare*. Naples: Enzo Albano
SIFC	*Studi italiani di filologia classica*
SN	*Storia di Napoli* 1. *Età classica, alto medioevo*. 1967. E. Pontieri, gen. ed. Naples: Società Editrice Storia di Napoli
Sottosuoli	Varriale, R., ed. 2009. *Undergrounds in Naples / I sottosuoli napoletani*. Rome: Consiglio Nazionale delle Ricerche, Istituto degli Studi sulle Società del Mediterraneo
TAPA	*Transactions of the American Philological Association*
Terremoti	Guidoboni, E., ed. 1989. *I terremoti prima del mille in Italia e nell'area mediterranea*. Bologna: Storia-Geofisica-Ambiente
Tremblements	C. Albore Livadie, ed. 1986. *Tremblements de terre, éruptions volcaniques et vie des hommes dans la Campanie antique*. Naples: Centre Jean Bérard
Vergil, Philodemus	Armstrong, D. et al., ed. 2004. *Vergil, Philodemus, and the Augustans*. Austin: University of Texas Press
Volcanology and Archaeology	Albore-Livadie, C. and F. Widemann, ed. *Volcanology and Archaeology: Proceedings of the European Workshops of Ravello, November 19–27, 1987, and March 30–31, 1989*. Strasbourg: Council of Europe
Zevi, Campi	Zevi, F., ed. 1987. *I Campi Flegrei*. Naples: Macchiaroli
Zevi, Neapolis	Zevi, F., ed. 1994. *Neapolis*. Naples: Banco di Napoli
Zevi, Puteoli	Zevi, F., ed. 1993. *Puteoli*. 2 vols. Naples: Banco di Napoli
ZPE	*Zeitschrift für Papyrologie und Epigraphik*

PREFACE & ACKNOWLEDGMENTS

The prolonged and unusual history of this volume's formation comprises two periods of concentrated activity closer to the beginning (2006) and end (2021) of the process, while the intervening hiatus was punctuated by a few brief bursts of activity related to my collateral publications on ancient Naples in journals and collection volumes.

For their assistance at the front end of the project I wish to extend special thanks to Daniela Giampaola, Vittoria Carsana, and Francesca Longobardo for sharing their time and knowledge about the recent and ongoing excavations in the city during site visits in 2008. Pier Giovanni Guzzo, Superintendent of Naples and Pompeii at the time, granted access to the sites. Most of the book was written in the early phases before the hiatus; during that period I benefited greatly from long conversations about the ancient city with Joseph Alchermes, a collaborator on the project in the early phase.

Several colleagues read sections of the manuscript at different stages of its development; of these, I am especially grateful to David Armstrong and Kathleen Coleman for their perspicacity and polymathy on the literary, artistic, and agonistic culture on the Bay of Naples in antiquity; and to Ferdinando De Simone and Duncan Keenan-Jones for their insights into the history, archaeology, and infrastructure on ancient Neapolis and its surrounding territory. With their edited volume *Remembering Parthenope,* Jessica Hughes and Claudio Buongiovanni offered me a sounding board with which to test some of my hypotheses on Neapolis' self-refashioning during the Roman imperial period. Other ideas incubated in other laboratories; for example, those related to Neapolis' bull-man imagery and its early Siren cult developed in the context of two conferences and their published proceedings: *The Nature and Function of Water, Baths, and Hygiene from Antiquity through the Renaissance* at Northern Arizona University, and *Attitudes towards the Past in Antiquity: Creating Identities* at Stockholm University. I assigned two recensions of this manuscript in a graduate seminar at the University of Texas at Austin entitled "Greeks and Romans on the Bay of Naples," once in 2011 and

PREFACE & ACKNOWLEDGEMENTS

again in 2020, thereby putting it to the acid test of graduate student appraisal.

At several stages in the process I have been grateful for the multilingual technical, administrative, and scholarly assistance of Natsumi Nonaka. Finally, I wish to thank Ronald Musto and Eileen Gardiner of Italica Press for their flexible approach to the project, alternately attentive and patient as circumstances shifted.

Austin, Texas
February 18, 2021

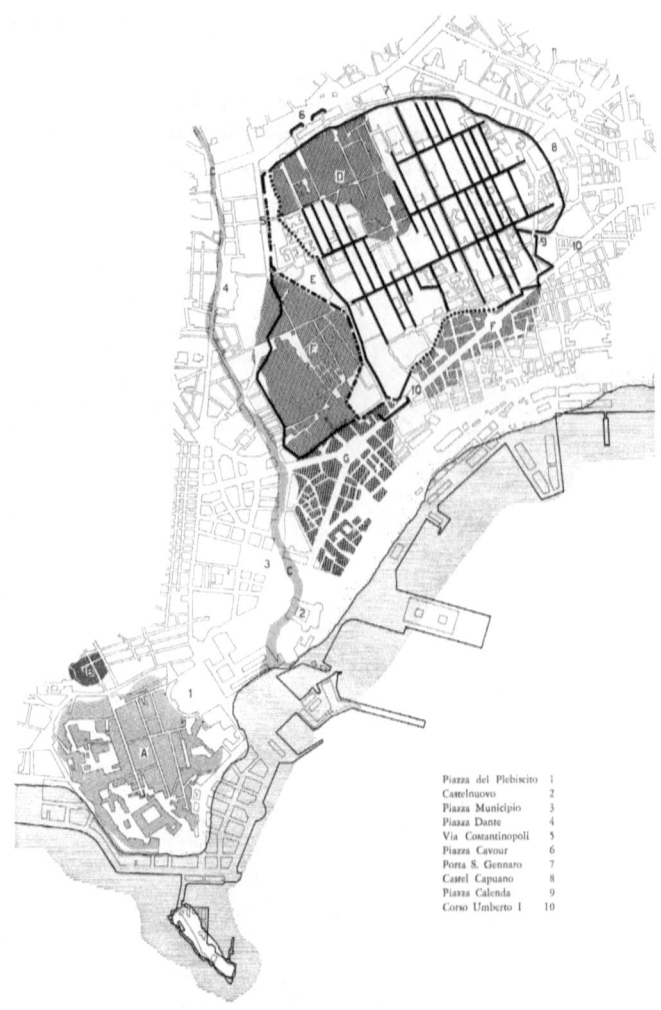

Map of ancient Naples with its furthest expansion in the Roman imperial age. From Mario Napoli, "Napoli greco-romana: Topografia e archeologia," SN 1.

INTRODUCTION

This volume of the Italica Press Documentary History of Naples series is unique in the extent to which it builds a narrative around the merest fragments of testimonial evidence. Such is the nature of the city's history: as we strain to read backward through time, the documentary record diminishes. By the Classical Greek period we are completely bereft of written sources, except to the extent that a handful of later texts draw on lost older sources. Even the surviving testimony of Romans, who placed abundant stock in the Bay of Naples as a physical and cultural retreat for the power elite, tends to disappoint. Indeed, apart from a few long inscriptions of fairly formulaic character, some potted speeches in Livy, a brief geographical foray by Strabo, and a single poem by Statius, no sustained passage of poetry, prose, or administrative record-keeping survives from the ancient world that places the city of Neapolis, as we call ancient Naples, at its center of interest. What do survive in significant numbers are random or passing references to Neapolitan history, monuments, institutions, and daily life; and it is on this miscellany of sources, ranging widely by genre and dating overwhelmingly to the Roman imperial period, that I will draw. In consequence, it can be said justly that my task on the textual side is just as oblique and fragmentary as on the material side — perhaps even more so, for while genuine artifacts of Greek Neapolis extend back to the turn of the seventh century BCE, not a single surviving text relating to the city — not even a short public inscription — can be dated earlier than the second century BCE.

In parallel with the texts, then, this volume will give careful attention to archaeology and material objects as documents of the city's life and times fully as important and informative as the literary sources. Sometimes these genres are complementary, sometimes they are dialectical, and occasionally they threaten contradiction. Neither kind of evidence will be given priority, but I will strive to interpret each individual source on its own terms and without prejudice to genre or methodology. With some documents I will be satisfied to summarize the *status quaestionis,* but in many others I will advance new arguments. And arguments they will be, subject to instant revision if and when better evidence emerges.

The opportunities for archaeology at Naples have always been meager. Unlike Rome, which shrank to the size of a village in the Middle Ages and whose historic center thereafter remained a patchwork of settlements, vineyards, and meadows into the nineteenth century, Naples never contracted away from its ancient urban center. Its forum was never a cow pasture, as was the forum at Rome at the time of its first organized excavations under Napoleon. Its monuments were never so temptingly situated as the Baths of Caracalla, whose bulk languished among farms and grassy wilderness in the sixteenth century when it was first systematically looted for sculpture under popes Clement VII and Paul III.

Even in its leanest centuries (the seventh and eighth CE in particular) the city on the Bay functioned as a Byzantine naval base and remained dense at its core. Whatever misfortunes befell the population in that period, the continuation of that physical density remained unbroken through the centurties. Except for a few pinpricks of illumination here and there, that means that long sectors of the ancient defensive walls —and the entire grid of Greek streets and buildings enclosed within them — all lie unseen, indeed, undiscovered, under the visible city. Though the street grid of the fifth century BCE is instantly recognizable in the street pattern today, we literally don't even know whether the buildings hemming in these narrow streets mark the full width of their Greek predecessors. Nor do we know whether (as seems more likely) the ancient streets were wider, and the visible buildings (mostly early modern, some medieval) encroach on their sidewalks. Today the city's density has spread far out into the countryside, generating a megalopolis of impermeable concrete, asphalt, and basalt. Almost by definition, Neapolitan archaeology is salvage archaeology, conducted in cramped urban quarters on tight schedules. Archaeologists in Naples do not choose where to dig; the places are chosen for them by the vagaries of politics, commerce, or — ever so occasionally — disaster.

INTRODUCTION

DISASTERS AND OPPORTUNITIES

It has now been four decades since the Irpina Earthquake of November 1980, which spread damage over 26,000 square kilometers of south-central Italy. The initial tremor and scores of aftershocks killed hundreds, leaving some towns in ruins. It leveled dozens of buildings in Naples and other municipalities in Campania. The earthquake didn't just fray the nerves of all who lived within the seismic zone. It also rattled the sooty windows of Neapolitan antiquarianism.

For centuries, students of Neapolis' history had relied more on lamplight than spadework to shape their understanding of the city's ancient topography. Certainly medieval and early modern texts (and occasionally maps or illustrations) elucidating the city's antiquities have invited profitable scholarly forays into its past. The Neapolitan habit of writing or record-keeping had rarely advanced the ancient city as an entity of historical interest. Even in the Renaissance, however, a spike in antiquarian enthusiasm could temper, but not obviate, the realization that great volumes of physical information had already been lost forever. The enthusiasm of Renaissance antiquarians for text-based urban topography and history marked a genuine advancement in Italian letters. But when spadework was possible, it only aggravated the worst impulses of the era. Early modern Naples, like so many other Italian cities, was sporadically subjected to plunder-hunting excavations when the opportunity emerged. Easy targets like Pausilypon were ransacked early and often. At nearby Herculaneum, Pompeii, and Stabiae royally sponsored excavations proceeded sporadically from the late 1730s with little regard for the sites themselves but intense interest in the finest objects extracted from them. Initially little more than treasure hunts meant to adorn the palaces of the Bourbons or the Bonapartes, these projects evolved only much later into enterprises that we would recognize as archaeology.

Only with the arrival of an incipient kind of scientific archaeology at nearby Pompeii in the 1860s under the direction of Giuseppe Fiorelli, and soon thereafter with the efflorescence of urban salvage archaeology in the early years of Italian independence, did Naples reach a kind of awakening of its own. The episode of urban renewal known as the Risanamento ("Remediation") sprang up after a deadly cholera epidemic in 1884. Tragic as it was, the epidemic served as a convenient pretext to remake Naples in a manner resembling the Haussmannization of many other European cities in that era, including Rome. The result was an orgy of demolition and drawing-board renewal that did more to erase the city's precious ancient heritage than to reveal it. Even so, as in Rome and elsewhere, a clutch of newly professionalized archaeologists set to work documenting antiquities as they were unearthed, even publishing them in emerging scientific journals such as *Notizie degli scavi di antichtà*. From tragedy came an opportunity to glimpse the ancient city afresh.

The 1980 earthquake also presented an opportunity. By then professional archaeologists had long operated comfortably in Naples, but generally out of the limelight. While excavations at other sites around the Bay under the direction of Amedeo Maiuri, Giorgio Buchner, Alfonso De Franciscis, and others were making archaeological discoveries of global significance — and not just at Pompeii and Herculaneum but also at other sites, such as Baiae, Cumae, and Ischia — Neapolitan archaeology remained small-scale, low-voltage stuff. Not that it lacked for talent. Ettore Gabrici and Werner Johannowsky, for example, were among the best archaeologists working in Campania in their day (the early and mid-twentieth century, respectively); and their published work on Neapolis remains essential reading. Mario Napoli's *Napoli Greco-romana*, published in a second edition in 1959, is another touchstone, but it relied, to a considerable extent, on the author's instinctive feel for the city at surface level. Napoli left no stone in his namesake city unexamined, but circumstances compelled him to leave most unturned. Allied bombing of occupied Naples in World War II had, however, caused serious damage to some urban neighborhoods, as it had at Pompeii too. This regrettable destruction did lead to some remarkable discoveries, such as the bath complex under the church of Sta. Chiara[1] and the unique Roman multi-use complex at Carminiello ai Mannesi.[2]

1. See p. 276.
2. See pp. 277–79, 355.

🏛 INTRODUCTION

But the slow pace of recovery after the war left the excavation and interpretation of these sites to a younger generation of archaeologists, among them Paul Arthur and Giuseppe Vecchio. As late as the 1970s, when he was laboring at his monumental study of Campania, the historian Martin Frederiksen felt so stymied by the lack of advancement in archaeological knowledge at Naples that he declined to devote a special chapter to the city as he did to Pozzuoli and Capua. First published in 1970, John D'Arms' *Romans on the Bay of Naples* focused on a later period with more abundant literary and epigraphic sources, but this work too gives the impression of looking in from a distance, and in flickering lamplight.

To the benefit of subsequent scholarship, the earthquake happened at a time of great ferment in Italian archaeology. Long an entirely male preserve, the state-financed archaeological apparatus had begun to put women in charge of excavations in the 1960s, a turn that greatly accelerated in the ensuing decades and has brought rich rewards to the discipline. Methodologies were also changing, and by the late 1970s modern stratigraphic techniques were de rigueur among younger archaeologists. In the wake of the tremor's destruction, flush with funds for relief and restoration, national and regional authorities took the opportunity to examine and reassess the ancient city to a degree never seen before, not even during the Risanamento. Ongoing excavations were completed; new ones (like those under the direction of Anna Maria D'Onofrio at S. Aniello a Caponapoli[3]) were begun. Many were published promptly. Legacy material — including the massive holdings of pottery, coins, and other finds in the Museo Archeologico Nazionale di Napoli — were subjected to fresh scrutiny. (Unfortunately, the archives at the archaeological superintendency headquartered there seem to have preserved few useful excavation reports from Naples itself.) From all this work, dozens of articles and several monographs appeared. Three important thematic collections, two dedicated to the general archaeology and history of ancient Neapolis and one to its coinage, came out in quick succession around a flurry of conferences, exhibits, and publications in

3. See pp. 51–52, 68, 202.

the mid-1980s. Established institutions of classical studies at Naples, such as its great universities (Federico II, Suor Orsola Benincasa, "L'Orientale"), the Centre Jean Bérard (the French institute for the study of antiquity in southern Italy), the Museo Archeologico, and the (now evidently defunct) Centro Internazionale di Studi Numismatici all got a temporary boost in publicity.

RECENT ARCHAEOLOGY

The second great impetus for archaeological investigation in the last half-century was the introduction of a new line for the Metropolitana subway in the early 2000s. All the Neapolitan subway lines have avoided surface work directly inside the *centro storico*, i.e., the area corresponding to the ancient walled Greek city. But stations are now situated just outside the circuit to the east (Garibaldi), west (Dante), north (Cavour), and south (Duomo). As of 2021, the project remains unfinished, though archaeological excavations under the general direction of Daniela Giampaola are more or less complete at the three new stations skirting the waterfront: Municipio, Università (Piazza Bovio), and Duomo (Piazza Nicola Amore). Not only have the station excavations yielded many notable finds and features, as several chapters in the book will demonstrate; but coring campaigns in advance of excavations, and then in collaboration with them, have also greatly advanced our understanding of the geomorphology of the coastal region, the flora and fauna that occupied it at various phases of history, and even the concentration and provenance of lead in the ancient city's water supply.[4]

The Metropolitana excavations too have yielded many publications, several of which inform later chapters in this book. They include a volume centered on an exhibit of finds from the Piazza Bovio (Stazione Università) excavations entitled *Napoli: La città e il mare*. The discovery and study of a rich deposit of Greco-Italic amphoras at Piazza Nicola Amore (Stazione Duomo) has led to monographs on the topic by Lydia Pugliese and, by way of the amphora production centers on the island of Ischia, by Gloria Olcese. Olcese's wide-ranging *Immensa aequora* project has invigorated the study of

4. On the lead isotopes, see pp. 274, 364–65.

the production and distribution of ceramics produced in south-central Italy along the Tyrrhenian littoral between the fourth century BCE and the first century CE. Her work, along with Pugliese's, has brought attention to the importance of the local wine industry during the Hellenistic period, and particularly the wines transported in Greco-Italic amphoras.

More or less independently of these trends, other scholarly projects on ancient Neapolis have also advanced. A catalog of the ancient Neapolitan sculpture in the Museo Archeologico was published in 2012 by Armando Cristilli. Maria Amodio has published prolifically on early Christian Neapolis, with particular emphasis on the city's cemeteries and catacombs. Amodio too has initiated a project centered on ancient ceramics, but in this case specifically those of Neapolis, in an online archaeological map of catalogued and dated ceramics with documented find-spots around the city. For now, however, the project remains in limbo.

It is high time for a general monograph on the pre-medieval city that takes account of the two great waves of discovery and knowledge production from the last forty years. Though its tone may often be hypothetical and its errors undoubtedly frequent, the present volume aims to fill a longstanding need for a rigorously researched urban history of the ancient city. It will be the first since Napoli's 1959 edition of *Napoli greco-romana,* and the first ever in English.

A WORD ON STYLE AND LANGUAGE

Throughout this book, I use the name "Naples" to refer to the modern city and "Neapolis" for the ancient one. By necessity, the latter name greatly predominates. Following conventions used throughout the series to which this book belongs, certain frequently mentioned places retain their modern names (Ischia, Capri, and Pozzuoli, for example), but with periodic reminders of their ancient names. Places with less prominence or proximity, however, are generally given their ancient names — but again, alongside initial reference to their modern nomenclature, often in parentheses. For the names of well-known gods, I generally follow English convention (Athena for Athene, Dioscuri for Dioskouroi, etc.). I do the same for famous places, authors, and personages (Livy, Pliny, Strabo, Athens, Euboea, Rhodes, Cumae, Rome, etc.). Otherwise I adhere to the contemporary preference for transliterating Greek words in general, and proper nouns in particular, in a manner closely approximating original spellings (Herakles, Lykophron, Hekataios of Miletos, etc.).

With some exceptions, translations of primary texts are drawn from the popular editions of the Loeb Classical Library. In these translations I adapt the spellings of proper names to the rule established above, and occasionally I modify the text slightly when I feel that it elides, blurs, or misinterprets some point that I deem important. I have also modernized certain locutions and Americanized the spellings.

REFERENCES

Neapolis' urban density and international connections in the early Middle Ages: Arthur 2002: 21–22; Bruzelius and Tronzo 2011: 41–44; Musto 2013: 39–50. **Neapolitan antiquarianism in the Renaissance:** Nichols and McGregor 2019: 377–93; 464–66. **The Risanamento:** Santore 2001: 204–17. **Broad historico-topographical studies and collections of ancient Neapolis:** Castagnoli 1977; Capasso 1978 [1905]; *Napoli antica*; *Neapolis*; Beloch 1989 [1890]; Napoli 1997 [1959]; Arthur 2002. **Important monographs, essay collections, or catalogs:** *Monetazione* [1986]; D'Onofrio and D'Agostino 1987; Miranda 1990–1995; Arthur 1994; Baldassare 2010b; *Napoli città e mare* [2010]; Olcese 2010; Cristilli 2012; Amodio 2014. **Immensa aequora project:** https://www.immensaaequora.org. **Archaeological map of ancient Neapolitan pottery:** Amodio 2017.

CHAPTER 1. THE PHYSICAL SETTING

1. This is the spot — for neither barbarous Thrace nor Libya is my native land — to which I would bring you; mild winters and cool summers temper its climate, its shores are lapped by the sluggish waters of a harmless sea. Peace untroubled reigns there, and life is leisurely and calm, with quiet undisturbed and sleep unbroken.... Nor are there lacking all around the amusements that a varied life affords: whether it pleases you to visit Baiae with its steaming springs and alluring coast, or the prophetic Sibyl's inspired abode, or the hill made memorable by the Ilian oar; whether you prefer the flowing vineyards of Bacchic Gaurus, or the dwellings of the Teleboi, where the Pharos raises aloft the beacon that rivals the night-wandering moon and is welcomed by affrighted sailors, or the Sorrentine hills beloved of fiery Bacchus, which my friend Pollius before all men honors by his dwelling, or the health-giving lakes of Aenaria and Stabiae reborn. [Statius, *Silvae* 3.5.72–105]

GEOGRAPHY AND GEOLOGY

The city of Naples — Neapolis ("New City"), as we shall call it in its ancient phase — occupies the northern rim of its eponymous bay on the coast of Campania in southern Italy. Home to one of the most important natural ports in the world, the site has enjoyed success as an urban and commercial center since the age of Greek expansion around the Mediterranean. In this respect, it is unique among all the cities of the ancient Greek West. Nautically, the city's location is auspicious, occupying a central position on a crucial marine trade route. For centuries Greek Neapolis controlled the west coast of Italy, and thereby a significant sector of Mediterranean trade and movement.

The earliest settlement, named Parthenope after one of the fabled Sirens worshiped there, was on the easily defended promontory of Pizzofalcone only a few hundred meters southwest of a natural inlet that served as the ancient port. Later a larger walled town, Neapolis, emerged north of the harbor and quickly eclipsed its predecessor. Visitors to modern Naples are struck by the stark contrast between the precipitous tufaceous cliffs, hills, and ravines of its westerly neighborhoods — the terrain of Parthenope — and the far more

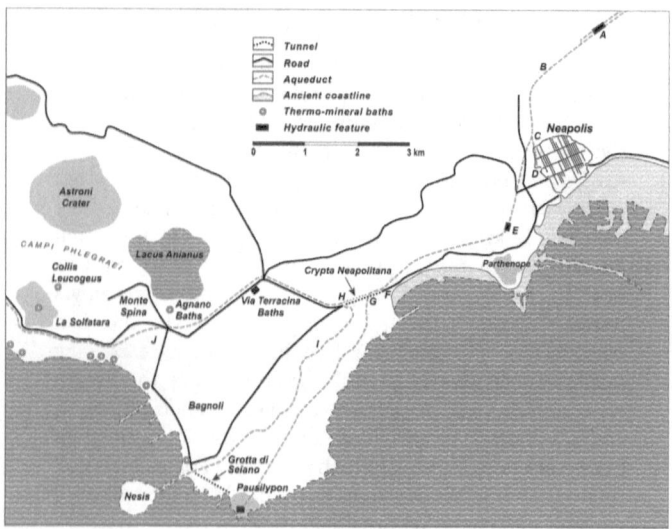

Fig. 1.1. Map of Neapolis and its western suburbs in antiquity.

gently sloping prospect of the city's central area, on which Neapolis was built.

East and south of the ancient city a fertile plain, now mostly urbanized, ambled gently to the foot of Mt. Vesuvius, whose semiforested cone culminates no more than fifteen kilometers from the center of town [Fig. 1.2]. Halfway there, along the coastal road, the modern town of Ercolano lies partly superimposed over its ancient predecessor, Herculaneum, separated from it by a massive stratum of pyroclastic rock laid down during the calamitous eruption of Vesuvius in 79 CE. We know nothing of the early history of this "place of Hercules"; the ancient geographer Strabo (*Geography* 5.4.8) thinks the town predated the Greek presence, asserting that both it and Pompeii had exchanged hands among numerous tribes and peoples who preceded the Greeks in Italy. But if its formal origins are Greek, as the name might suggest, then it would be the only such settlement of any size on the Bay south of Neapolis.

This entire southeastern sector of the Bay, though engulfed in a chaotic megalopolis today, was sparsely populated in antiquity. Near

CHAPTER 1 🏛 THE PHYSICAL SETTING

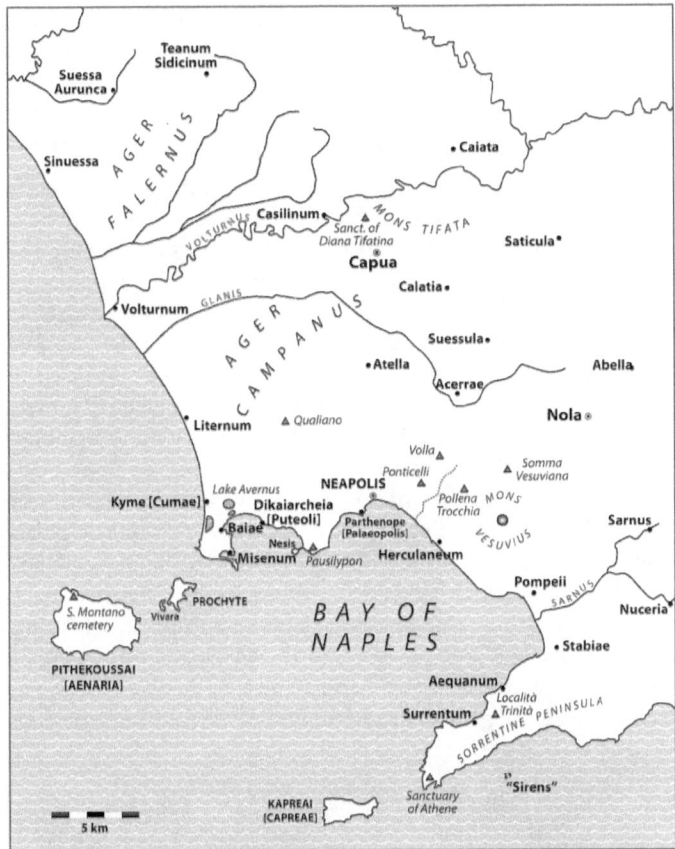

Fig. 1.2. Map of the Bay of Naples and its vicinity in antiquity.

the mouth of the Sarno (Sarnus) River stood its largest town, home to maybe 8,000 souls at the time of the eruption: Pompeii, longstanding custodian of two important cult centers from at least the sixth century BCE. Strabo's conviction about the town's age and indigenous character has been vindicated recently. High concentrations of phosphates in the soil have revealed that Pompeii was inhabited ever since the Avellino eruption around 1360 BCE. The river, which was at least partially navigable, led inland to the towns of Sarno and Nocera (ancient Nuceria), and from there to the interior. Nola, lying northeast of Vesuvius, exploited the mantle of prime agricultural land around the volcano. It too, probably, has been settled in some form since the Bronze Age. Guarding an important route to Italy's rugged interior, Nola was easily reached by highway from either Sarno or Neapolis.

The coastline follows the plain southeast to Castellamare di Stabia (Roman Stabiae) and then veers right as it encounters the precipitous limestone mass of the Sorrentine Peninsula. Home to many villas and two small towns in the Roman period, this towering promontory was barely settled by the Greeks. Yet the two important sanctuaries situated here suggest that the Euboean settlements of the west Bay had a controlling interest in this coastline from a fairly early date. On the inner coast was the sanctuary of the Sirens, to whom Neapolis in particular gave homage. We would like to know more about this place, probably the only sanctuary of its kind, and the logical culmination of a local myth-making process that found a site for every event, documented or inferred, in Odysseus' westernmost wanderings. At the very tip of the promontory stood a shining landmark to sailors, the sanctuary of Athena — founded by Odysseus, Strabo dutifully informs us. The dolomitic limestone ridge on which the sanctuary perched then plunges into the Mediterranean, emerging again at the spectacular isle of Capri: Kapreai to the Greeks, Capreae to the Romans [Fig. 1.3]. The easternmost of the two island gateposts

Fig. 1.3. Capri, with a panoramic view to the Anacapri headland. Photo: P. Costa Baldi / Wikimedia Commons GFDL/CC BY-SA 3.0.

CHAPTER 1 🏛 THE PHYSICAL SETTING

of the Bay, and thus a point of strategic importance, it probably came into the possession of Neapolis in the fifth century BCE.

West of Naples, the weathered terrain of yellow tuff, emplaced by an eruption about 15,000 years ago, is so rugged that intercity access has relied since Roman times on tunnels. The most famous of these, the Crypta Neapolitana [see Figs. 1.1; 7.10–13], greatly facilitated east–west traffic; but traversing it was a trying experience, as Seneca memorably complained:

> **2.** No place could be longer than that prison; nothing could be dimmer than those torches, which enabled us, not to see amid the darkness, but to see the darkness. But, even supposing that there was light in the place, the dust, which is an oppressive and disagreeable thing even in the open air, would destroy the light; how much worse the dust is there, where it rolls back upon itself, and, being shut in without ventilation, blows back in the faces of those who set it going! [*Epistulae morales* 57.1–2]

Beyond the tunnel begins one of the most striking landscapes in the Mediterranean basin. Known in antiquity as the Campi Phlegraei (today Campi Flegrei, or Phlegraean Fields), the rough coastal triangle between Naples, Cumae, and Misenum is actually the northern rim of a great caldera of collapsed craters enveloping the Bay of Pozzuoli. Unlike Vesuvius, whose tuffs are principally leucitic, this family of volcanoes is trachytic. In its relatively brief existence it has produced massive deposits of tuff ranging from the hard, gray, cinder-flecked *piperno* that remains a favored building material in Naples today, to the soft, sensuous yellow stone upon which the old city itself rests. Strabo calls this coastal arc the Lucrine Gulf, a lesser concavity constituting the western extreme of the Bay of Naples. In Roman times its inner part, from Pozzuoli to Baiae, was protected by an artificial mole. The entire coastline from the western reaches of Naples to land's end at Misenum is defined by this ragged, pockmarked basin. Seething with geothermal energy, the Phlegraean landscape came to be regarded as the place where Herakles had battled down the Giants,[1] or where some of these sons of the Earth still lay imprisoned below. Strabo's description follows below.

1. Diodoros of Sicily, *Historical Library* 4.21.5–7.

3. The Lucrine Gulf broadens out as far as Baiae; and it is shut off from the outer sea by a mole eight stades [4,800 feet] in length and broad as a wagon-road. This mole is said to have been brought to completion by Herakles, when he was driving the cattle of Geryon. But since it admitted the waves over its surface in times of storm, so that it could not easily be traversed on foot, Agrippa built it up higher. The gulf affords entrance to light boats only; it affords most abundant catches of oysters. And some say that this gulf itself is Lake Acherousia, while Artemidoros says that Avernus itself is that lake. But Baiae is said to be named after one of the companions of Odysseus, Baios; and also Misenum. Next in order come the headlands that are in the neighborhood of Dikaiarcheia [Pozzuoli], and then the city itself. In earlier times it was only a port-town of the Cumaeans, situated on the brow of a hill, but at the time of Hannibal's expedition the Romans settled a colony there, and changed its name to Pozzuoli from the wells there — though some say that it was from the foul smell of the waters, since the whole district, as far as Baiae and Cumae, has a foul smell, because it is full of sulfur and fire and hot waters. And some believe that it is for this reason that the Cumaean country was called "Phlegra," and that it is the wounds of the fallen giants, inflicted by the thunderbolts, that pour forth those streams of fire and water. And the city has become a very great emporium, since it has havens that have been made by the hand of man — a thing made possible by the natural qualities of the sand, for it is in proper proportion to the lime, and takes a firm set and solidity. And therefore, by mixing the sand-ash with the lime, they can run jetties out into the sea and thus make the wide-open shores curve into the form of bays, so that the greatest merchant-ships can moor therein with safety. Immediately above the city lies the Forum of Hephaistos, a plain shut in all round by exceedingly hot ridges, which in numerous places have fumaroles that are like chimneys and that have a rather noisome smell; and the plain is full of drifted sulfur. [Strabo, *Geography* 5.4.6]

Around the cliffy bend of Capo di Posillipo — named for Pausilypon, villa of the Roman bon vivant Vedius Pollio — a small

CHAPTER 1 🏛 THE PHYSICAL SETTING

crater rises just offshore to form the island of Nisida, ancient Nesis, once the villa refuge of Brutus [see Fig. 1.1].[2] On the mainland, as one moves north and west, the hilly terrain yields to a small plain at Bagnoli. Beginning here and extending around the caldera, a series of copious thermo-mineral spas drew visitors and renown to the region in antiquity; their known positions in Neapolitan territory are marked on Fig. 1.1. The next cape marks the town of Pozzuoli. Called Dikaiarcheia by the Greeks, a place of little consequence, it was reborn as the bustling Roman port town of Puteoli and eventually eclipsed even Neapolis. Whereas the coast near Vesuvius has advanced over the centuries due to thick deposits of volcanic ash and stone, Pozzuoli has experienced the curious effects of bradyseism, causing its shoreline to retreat. Associated with active calderas, this geological phenomenon causes marked shifts in the ground elevation. These are often attended by tremors — and in one notorious case, by the formation and eruption of a small volcano, Monte Nuovo, over the course of a few days in September 1538. At its lowest point in the tenth century CE the ground at Pozzuoli had descended by 17–18 meters, leaving unmistakable water marks on the three standing columns in the Roman marketplace [Fig. 1.4]. The city has regained some of that deficit but still lies 11 meters or more below its elevation in antiquity, as the submerged but visible remains of the Roman harbor buildings

Fig. 1.4. View of the Roman macellum at Pozzuoli. Photo: Doktorpixel14 / Wikimedia Commons CC BY-SA 4.0.

2. See pp. 75–76, 151–52, 266, 268–69.

attest. Naples too shows evidence of bradyseism, but on a smaller scale; its recently discovered ancient harbor between Parthenope and Neapolis experienced subsidence,[3] and submerged Roman remains some 5 meters below water have been mapped off the shore of Capo di Posillipo [see Fig. 8.2]. Clear evidence has also emerged of dramatic subsidence at Herculaneum's waterfront not long before the eruption of 79 CE; this interred the lowest story of the House of the Relief of Telephos and parts of the Suburban Baths. Martin Frederiksen[4] has brought attention to an account in the medieval *Acts of Peter and Paul* in which the local geology serves as a convenient send-up of the wicked Romans and Jews of Pozzuoli who opposed St. Paul's arrival on Italian shores:

> 4. And going out of Pontioli [sic] with them that believed the word of the Lord, [Paul and his companions] came to a place that is called Baiae, and looking out with their eyes they all saw that town which is called Pontioli sinking to the floor of the sea to the depth of about a fathom. And there it remains to this day as a memorial, under the sea. [*Apocryphal Acts of Peter and Paul* 12 (Lipsius and Bonnet), trans. Frederiksen]

West of Pozzuoli are two famous crater lakes, Lucrinus and Avernus — the former now a tiny lagoon much reduced from its size in the Roman era, when it served both as a famous oyster farm and as the outer harbor of a naval base during Octavian's and Agrippa's operations against Sextus Pompey.[5] Writing some decades later, Strabo comments on the extreme shallowness of the waters behind the harbor mole.[6] Given the known downward trend of the ground level over time, his observation seems counterintuitive: why was the harbor getting shallower, not deeper? Frederiksen believes, with reason, that local subsidence was entirely a postclassical phenomenon; Strabo's evidence may suggest that a temporary uplift took place at the Lucrine Lake before the gradual and inexorable sinking began. Bradyseism is unpredictable

3. See pp. 222–25, 245–46, 313.
4. Frederiksen 1984 15–17.
5. Dio Cassius, *Roman History* 48.49–51.
6. See reading 3 above.

CHAPTER 1 ⛫ THE PHYSICAL SETTING

Fig. 1.5. Lago d'Averno. *Gouache by Jacob Philipp Hackert, 1794. Munich, Neue Pinakothek. Wikimedia Commons.*

and sometimes self-reversing; indeed, two subsequent periods of uplift can be identified at Pozzuoli, in the seventh and sixteenth centuries.

Lake Avernus, immediately north, hardly needs introduction. It was wooded and virtually uninhabited before Agrippa annexed it to his port by means of a canal dug to the Lucrine Lake and another to the Bay beyond. In the high Empire, a hydrothermal spa was built on Avernus' eastern shore with an impressive domed hall [Fig. 1.5, left]. But more famously, this was Aeneas' (and, some claimed, Odysseus') legendary gateway to the underworld — a dismal, reeking place full of ill omen:

> 5. A deep cave there was, yawning wide and vast, shingly, and sheltered by dark lake and woodland gloom, over which no flying creatures could safely wing their way; such a vapor from those black jaws poured into the overarching heaven — whence the Greeks spoke of Aornos, the Birdless Place.
> [Virgil, *Aeneid* 6.237–42]

Diodoros of Sicily, writing almost contemporaneously with Virgil, was also aware of the lake's baleful reputation. To Agrippa's massive engineering works, probably under way or completed as he wrote, he provided a worthy predecessor, Herakles fresh from the battle with the Giants:

> 6. From the Phlegraean plain Herakles went down to the sea, where he constructed works about the lake which bears the name Lake Aornos and is held sacred to Persephone.... And the myths record that in ancient times there had been on its shores an oracle of the dead which, they say, was destroyed in later days. Lake Aornos once had an opening into the sea, but Herakles is said to have filled up the outlet and constructed the road which runs at this time along the sea and is called after him the "Way of Herakles." [Diodoros, *Historical Library* 4.21.1–2]

From here it was a mere two kilometers overland due west to Cumae, the mother city of Neapolis and seat of the Sibyl, on the outer edge of the Bay's western peninsula. Yet only the most extravagant applications of Roman know-how allowed easy passage through that punishing terrain — first a tunnel fashioned by Cocceius, the architect of the Crypta Neapolitana,[7] who may well have operated on Agrippa's behalf; and later the Via Domitiana, a road of stupendous engineering.[8]

The peninsula, ever contrary and corrugated, bends south. On its inner crescent there developed the spa of Baiae, which by the late Republic had grown famous as a resort and a haunt of Rome's fashionable elite. A cluster of thermo-mineral springs on its steeply rising littoral was clad in a continuous crust of Roman bathing establishments.[9] Their ruins — like those of the harbor mole at Pozzuoli and the bathing pavilion at Lake Avernus — are of imperial-era Roman concrete, a material associated with this region on account of the abundant local presence of *pozzolana*, the wondrous volcanic "sand of Pozzuoli" that lends Roman concrete its strength and hydraulic properties.[10] Baiae has suffered from bradyseism on a par with Pozzuoli. The submerged remains of its coastal plain extend out at least 800 meters from the modern shoreline and lie as much as eighteen meters below water.

7. Strabo, *Geography* 5.4.5.
8. Statius, *Silvae* 4.3.72–89. See pp. 168–69, 229, 231, 232–33.
9. See pp. 238–43, 253–62.
10. Vitruvius, *Ten Books on Architecture* 2.6.

CHAPTER 1 ☗ THE PHYSICAL SETTING

Fig. 1.6. Ischia, the town of Lacco Ameno. Photo: C. Marra / Wikimedia Commons CC BY 2.0.

Finally, at land's end, is Capo Miseno. Like Baiae, it reputedly took its name from Greek myth, thereby enriching this storied landscape's longstanding associations with the wanderings of heroes of the Trojan War.[11] Thus, in Statius' words, the cape was "made memorable by the Ilian oar." According to local tradition, Baiae was the burial site of Odysseus' pilot, Baios.[12] Another story identifies Misenus as Aeneas' battle-trumpeter. He had challenged Triton to a musical contest with the conch shell and been drowned for his presumption. Aeneas buried him on the shores of the cape as prologue for entering the underworld at Lake Avernus.[13] To Misenum, after Augustus decommissioned the Julian port at the Lucrine Lake, the Roman navy came to stay. It remained the single active naval base on the west coast of Italy into late antiquity. From this spot the elder Pliny, admiral of the home fleet, departed on his fateful rescue mission across the Bay during the eruption of Vesuvius in 79 CE.

Like the Sorrentine Peninsula at the opposite end of the Bay, Cape Miseno terminates with an island: modern Ischia, Pithekoussai to the Greeks, Aenaria to the Romans [Fig. 1.6], separated from the cape by two lesser islands, Procida and Vivara. Procida too was given a connection

11. See reading 3 above and 75 below.
12. Lykophron, *Alexandra* 694.
13. Virgil, *Aeneid* 6.156–82.

to Troy, as the burial place of the eponymous Prochyte, kinswoman of Aeneas.[14] Geologically distinct from the Bay of Pozzuoli caldera, Ischia looms large in the history of the Euboean Greek colonization of this region. Strabo offers an extended chorography of the area.[15]

> 7. The island of Prochyta lies off Cape Miseno, and it is a fragment broken off of Pithekoussai [Ischia]. Pithekoussai was once settled by Eretrians and also Chalkidians, who, although they had prospered there on account of the fruitfulness of the soil and on account of the gold industry, forsook the island as the result of a quarrel; later on they were also driven out of the island by earthquakes, and by eruptions of fire, sea, and hot waters; for the island has "fistulas" of this sort, and it was these that caused also the people sent there by Hieron the tyrant of Syracuse [478–467 BCE] to forsake the island and the fortress they had erected there; and then the Neapolitans came over and took possession. Hence, also, the myth according to which Typhon lies beneath this island, and when he turns his body the flames and the waters, and sometimes even small islands containing boiling water, spout forth. But what Pindar says is more plausible, since he starts with the actual phenomena; for this whole channel, beginning at the Cumaean country and extending as far as Sicily, is full of fire, and has caverns deep down in the earth that form a single whole, connecting not only with one another but also with the mainland; and therefore, not only Mount Aitne [Etna] clearly has such a character as it is reported by all to have, but also the Lipari Islands, and the districts round about Dikaiarcheia [Pozzuoli], Neapolis, and Baiae, and the island of Pithekoussai. This, I say, is Pindar's thought when he says that Typhon lies beneath this whole region: "Now, however, both Sicily and the sea-fenced cliffs beyond Kyme [Cumae] press hard upon his shaggy breast." And Timaios, also, says that many marvelous things are told by the ancients about Pithekoussai, and that only shortly before his own time [born c.350 BCE] the hill called Epopeus, in the center of the island, on being shaken by earthquakes, cast forth fire and shoved the part between

14. Servius Auctus, Commentary on Virgil, *Aeneid* 9.715; Pseudo-Aurelius Victor, *De origine gentis Romanae* 10.

15. See also chapter 2.

CHAPTER 1 ▥ THE PHYSICAL SETTING

it and the sea back to the open sea; and the part of the land that had been burned to ashes, on being lifted high into the air, crashed down again upon the island like a whirlwind; and the sea retreated for three stades [1,800 feet], but not long after retreating turned back and with its reverse current deluged the island; and consequently, the fire in the island was quenched, but the noise was such that the people on the mainland fled from the coast into Campania. The hot springs in the island are thought to cure those who have gallstones. Kapreai [Capri] had two small towns in ancient times, though later on only one. The Neapolitans took possession of this island too; and although they lost Pithekoussai in war, they got it back again, Augustus Caesar giving it to them, though he appropriated Kapreai to himself personally and erected buildings on it. [Strabo, *Geography* 5.4.9]

It also has an active volcanic history, preserving the memory of several eruptions and earthquakes, while retaining more of its ancient thermal springs than the mainland. Like Capri, the island was a strategic possession of Neapolis from the fifth century BCE; it also contributed to an important phase in the city's economic history by providing massive deposits of clay for the famous "Campana A" tableware manufactured by the Neapolitans in the Hellenistic period, as well as other mass-produced wares.[16]

CLIMATE AND AGRICULTURE

The pleasant, temperate climate of Naples is quintessentially Mediterranean. There is little reason to believe that it differs appreciably today from its Greek and Roman phases, although global warming is widening the gap. The average high temperature in July is 29.3° C (84.7° F) and 12.5° C (54.5° F) in January. 77.7 percent of annual precipitation — which totals 1006.6 mm, or 39.6 inches — falls between September and March, and it is not unusual for this region to endure a virtually rainless summer. Before they were canalized in modern times, the small regional rivers ran low in the summer, rendering large-scale irrigation impracticable. In these circumstances, soils with high water retention — such as those in the arable eastern

---

16. See pp. 129, 138–42, 143, 147–48, 206, 217.

part of Neapolitan territory — had a natural advantage over similar but less retentive soils in other parts of southern Italy.

Campanian soil was renowned for its fertility and the intensity of farming that it could support. As Strabo wrote:

> 8. A proof of the fruitfulness of the country is that it produces the finest grain — I mean the wheat from which groats are made, which is superior, not only to every kind of rice, but also to almost every kind of grain-food. It is reported that, in the course of one year, some of the plains are seeded twice with spelt, the third time with millet, and others still the fourth time with vegetables." [5.4.3]

In antiquity the whole region of Campania was synonymous with agricultural abundance. The distinctive gravelly loam around Vesuvius, which encompassed most of Neapolis' truly arable territory, was in no way inferior to the famous croplands of the Ager Campanus around Capua to the north. It was demonstrably capable of producing three or even four crops in a season, as it does today. Being in an active volcanic zone, the soil in this region is highly stratified. Over the millennia, eruptions have blanketed the countryside in pumice, ash, and other tephra; gradually, overlying layers of soil, or paleosols, have accumulated in turn. Rich in organic content as well as nutrients such as nitrogen, potassium, and phosphorus, and lacking deterrents to root formation such as clay, these soils provide excellent aeration and water retention when they are mixed with the light and absorbent pumice of the underlying volcanic strata.

Campania's most famous farmland lay well north of the Bay of Naples, in the breadbasket of the Volturnus Valley. It brought wealth and power to the city of Capua, and was deemed so valuable by Rome in the Second Punic War that it was designated public land under direct control of the Roman state. The Ager Falernus beyond it produced several of the most distinguished vintages in Italy.[17] Pompeii too was prolific in wine, even if its product was more pedestrian. This was the town on the Bay of Naples with a territory most capable of a substantial export economy — not only wine, but also garum (fish sauce) and

---

17. Strabo 5.3.6, 5.4.3.

CHAPTER 1 ☖ THE PHYSICAL SETTING

wool. Each of these presupposed a connection to a different domain: the intensively farmed local territory, Tyrrhenian fisheries, and pasturage, perhaps in the upper Sarno Valley. The towns clustered around the western caldera — Pozzuoli, Baiae, Misenum (Cumae excepted) — were built on service economies and had at best a limited agricultural base; their most famous farmed commodity was shellfish, especially oysters.[18]

Neapolis, however, possessed the broadest economic base of the Bay towns, supporting on the one hand a robust commercial and industrial life, and on the other a compact but productive hinterland that yielded grain, olive oil, several varieties of wine, flowers for perfume production, and chestnuts of great renown.[19] One Roman source, to which we will return in the next chapter, reports that in the classical Greek period many residents of Cumaean territory were drawn to the Neapolitan territory "on account of the fertility and pleasantness of the precinct."[20] As we shall see in chapter 5, the eruption of Vesuvius took a severe toll on the territory, but not a fatal one. Wine production on a healthy scale had reclaimed parts of the region by the late second century CE.[21] Stabiae was gaining fame for its milk production,[22] and even earlier in that century the poet Dionysios Periegetes praised "chaste Parthenope [i.e., Neapolis], heavy under the weight of grain-sheaves."[23]

THE TERRITORY OF NEAPOLIS

The sheer obscurity of earliest Naples, which for two centuries after 700 BCE survives in the record only as a name (Parthenope) and a place (the promontory of Pizzofalcone), defies any attempt to situate it within a human landscape. Discussion of the development of a *chora*, or territory, around the town begins with the systematization of the New City, Neapolis, around 490 BCE. Before that time Parthenope was probably little more than a coastal outpost

18. See reading 3 above.
19. See pp. 138, 177.
20. Philargyrius, scholium on Virgil's *Georgics* 4.564. See pp. 39–40, 48.
21. Dio Cassius, *Roman History* 66.21.3.
22. Galen 10.363–66 Kühn.
23. *Description of the World* 358 Müller.

of Cumae, her attention and meager resources directed toward the Bay, not inland. Yet the fertile hinterland lying to the north and east, and those who already populated it, must have attracted interest from the earliest moment of Greek presence.

No solid evidence for the town's influence on its surrounding territory emerges until the late fifth century BCE, when patterns of coin distribution and a proliferation of Attic imported pottery in Campania, probably funneled through Neapolis, offer a semblance of geographical cohesion. Werner Johannowsky therefore believes that the territory of Neapolis was defined only after the fall of Cumae to the Campani in 421 BCE, before which, he conjectures, Neapolis was merely part of Cumaean territory. My own reading of the early history of the city, presented in the next chapter, pivots upon deep divisions that had arisen between the mother city and her satellite nearly a century before. Thus I date the establishment of a territorial boundary to the era of Neapolis' formal elaboration, with street grid and city wall, around 490 or 485 BCE. The most decisive evidence that Neapolitans understood themselves as custodians of a *chora* is their annexation of the island of Ischia shortly after 474 BCE,[24] a full half-century before Greek Cumae fell. The island of Capri probably came into Neapolitan possession at about the same time. These acquisitions suggest that Neapolis already had, or was building, a territorial administrative apparatus.

Apart from the eventual loss of the islands, the city's territorial boundaries may have changed little through the entire Greco-Campanian and Roman periods. Admittedly, evidence for physical boundaries in any period is largely circumstantial. The Greek historian Polybios[25] writes that during the Second Punic War the coastal territories of Campania, in sequence from west to east, belonged to Sinuessa, Cumae, Dikaiarcheia (Pozzuoli), Neapolis, and Nuceria. The approximate boundary between Pozzuoli (refounded as a Roman colony and renamed in 194 BCE) and Neapolis can be established with some confidence. The two jurisdictions controlled

24. See pp. 47, 54–55.
25. 3.91.4.

CHAPTER 1 🏛 THE PHYSICAL SETTING

Fig. 1.7. *La Solfatara, near Pozzuoli. Photo: D. Reiskoffer / Wikimedia Commons.*

the western and eastern Phlegraean Fields respectively, the boundary between them lying just west of the Collis Leucogaeus, and so probably bisecting the sulfurous wasteland of La Solfatara [Fig. 1.7. See Fig. 1.1.]. Northeast of the Astroni Crater (Lago Grande), the discovery of Greek inscriptions, both Hellenistic and Roman in date, at Pianura suggest that this area fell within the Neapolitan domain, where Greek language and culture were retained long after they had dwindled at Pozzuoli.

The Glanis (Clanis, Clanius) River, flowing northwest from Acerrae and gradually arcing west and southwest toward the coast, is the most likely candidate for the northern boundary of both the Neapolitan and Cumaean territories, at least in the early years of Greek occupation before the Samnite invasions in the 420s BCE [Fig. 1.2]. A marshy no-man's-land serving as a natural boundary throughout antiquity and the Middle Ages, it was finally canalized into the Regi Lagni system in the seventeenth century. However, Neapolitan territory may have retreated south of the marshes at some point during the Italian wars of the fourth and third centuries BCE. The town of Atella lies between Neapolis and the river, and there is no doubt that it acted

25

against Neapolis' interests when siding with Capua to enter an alliance with Hannibal.[26] The fact that Rome took control of the town after Hannibal's withdrawal rather than ceding it to Neapolis suggests that by 210 BCE, at least, Neapolis had no claim on the Glanis Valley.[27]

The eastern boundary of Neapolitan territory, dividing it from Nola's *chora*, lacks any visible definition today but it probably possessed a small river in antiquity. Numerous scholars and antiquarians believe this to be Neapolis' proprietary river, the Sebethos, celebrated in poetry and on the city's coinage.[28] The modern Sebeto, which runs in approximately the same area but has been culverted under the urban sprawl, was given this name by Renaissance antiquarians and probably bears no relation to its ancient namesake. Yet it is likely that an ancient stream ran roughly in the same area, northeast–southwest through the fertile plain between Neapolis and Mt. Vesuvius [Fig. 1.2]. In the post-classical period this area was beset by pestilential marshes known as *Le Paludi*, but unlike the perennially boggy Glanis this stream was gradually annihilated by cumulative volcanic deposits.[29] Its disappearance was abetted by the reappropriation of its spring sources for other uses and land reclamation in the nineteenth century.

Thus we have good reason to believe that a river, probably the Sebethos, ran through the eastern territory of ancient Neapolis. The boundary dividing Neapolitan from Nola's territory, however, cannot have been the river alone: a land dispute between the two cities was arbitrated in the 180s BCE, and unexpectedly parts of the area in question ended up in Roman hands.[30] The Neapolitan domain may have expanded along the coast to encompass Herculaneum, which offers no evidence of a territory of its own. On the lower slopes north of Vesuvius, it certainly included the region of Volla (Bolla), the source of one of the city's early aqueducts [Fig. 1.2].[31]

26. Livy, *History of Rome* 26.16.5; Silius Italicus, *Punica* 11.14–15.
27. Livy 26.33.12–14, 26.34.11, 26.36.6–13, 27.3.7.
28. See pp. 94–96, 99, 250.
29. See p. 161.
30. Cicero, *De officiis* 1.33.
31. See pp. 272–75.

CHAPTER 1 🏛 THE PHYSICAL SETTING

Fig. 1.8. View of Mt. Vesuvius from Pizzofalcone, Naples. Anonymous hand-colored engraving, 1858. Archiv "Deutschland und die Welt." Wikimedia Commons.

THE SPECTER OF CALAMITY

Again and again, Vesuvius returns to our narrative. It is a presence to conjure with: the geographic fulcrum of the Bay, the elephant in the room. In elaborating the geography and history of Naples, one can never stray far from it. Vesuvius surges from the surrounding plains at roughly the halfway point around the rim of the Bay, solitary and menacing [Fig. 1.8]. It is the world's most famous volcano, and the most dangerous on account of the mass of humanity living in its shadow. Minor disturbances are common, but eruptions on a genuinely lethal scale are "black swans," phenomena of such rarity — and well-documented intensity — that some claim that they channel the psychology of Neapolitans toward unhealthy extremes. A looming specter in the background of the millennia-old human drama on the Bay, the volcano's double-decker cone — the old collapsed out and a new one suppurating within — speaks to the arbitrary violence of its past. Around 1360 BCE, then in 79 CE, again in 472 CE, and soon after in the early sixth century, massive Plinian or subplinian eruptions erased the human presence in the surrounding countryside. Every time, humans chose to return. Eruptions have continued into modern times, though nothing so colossal as the 79 event, which buried Pompeii and Herculaneum altogether and left the rest of the Bay in limbo for decades thereafter. During that dreadful calamity it seemed to some that the long-tormented prisoners of the Earth had been released to the surface:

> **9.** Numbers of huge men quite surpassing any human stature — such creatures, in fact, as the Giants are pictured to have been — appeared, now on the mountain, now in the surrounding country, and again in the cities, wandering over the earth day and night and also flitting through the air.... Some thought that the Giants were rising again in revolt (for at this time also many of their forms could be discerned in the smoke and, moreover, a sound as of trumpets was heard), while others believed that the whole universe was being resolved into chaos or fire. [Dio Cassius, *Roman History* 66.22–23]

We cannot blame the regional mythology for tending to such extremes. Apocalyptic battle, a massive jailbreak of Titans wreaking fiery revenge — these were appropriate metaphors for the horrors of Vesuvius at its worst. Coming from a rather different point of view, the Sirens too are apt representatives of Neapolis and her surroundings, a landscape so seductive that every Roman of means and standing was drawn almost irresistibly to stake a claim to its beauty and bounty. Beneath the dulcet melody in their ears ground notes of danger and entrapment were audible for any who cared to hear. The natural beauties of the Bay are fewer in number today, and smaller in scope, though perhaps intensified thereby. The danger rumbles on with undiminished menace.

In fact, both horns of the Bay inspired cautionary tales grounded in music, each resolved by expiation. At the eastern end dwelt the Sirens, dire and tempting songstresses. Defeated by the wiles of Odysseus, they drowned themselves in the sea only to be reborn as benign goddesses, far removed from their earlier incarnation. First among these was Parthenope, patroness of Neapolis. At the western end, the unburied body of drowned Misenus, the overreaching trumpeter, threatened to thwart Aeneas' mission to father the Roman nation. Only by properly burying his companion could the hero proceed to Lake Avernus, the underworld, and his destiny. It is

CHAPTER 1 🏛 THE PHYSICAL SETTING

the nature of geographic endpoints and turning points to be coiled in the semiotics of danger, to which music so often lends its meaning. When we interpose between those headlands the volatility of volcanism, the result is a landscape of unparalleled evocative potential.

REFERENCES

For references on the geology of Mount Vesuvius and ancient earthquakes in the region, see chapter 5.

Geography of the region: Napoli 1967b; 1967d; 1997 [1959]: 111–20; Frederiksen 1984: 1–53. **Geology, geomorphology, and paleobotany of the region:** Scherillo 1967, 1977; Cinque et al. 1991; Cinque and Romano 2001; Cocco 2001; Luongo 2001; Pagliaro 2001; Arthur 2002: 1–2; Aulinas et al. 2007; Giampaola and Carsana 2007; Amato et al. 2009; Allevato et al. 2010; Russo Ermolli et al. 2013; Aucelli et al. 2017. **Bradyseism at Herculaneum:** Wallace-Hadrill 2011: 18–25, 249. **Nesis:** Cardone 1992: 13–21. **Phlegraean Fields:** Castagnoli 1977; Carapezza and Carapezza 1986; Ippolito 1986; Celico et al. 2001: 241–42; Mele 2014: 263–73. **Geology of Ischia:** Rittmann and Gottini 1981; Vezzoli 1988; Celico et al. 2001: 239–41; Cocco 2001: 154–57. **Clay and pottery of Ischia:** Olcese 2010; 2011; 2017. **Climate:** De Vita 2001. **Territory of Neapolis:** Lepore 1967a: 141–50; Johannowsky 1985a; Giampaola and D'Henry 1986; *Napoli antica* 300–39 (various authors). **Sebethos River:** Napoli 1997 [1959]: 130–34; Frederiksen 1984: 19; Brillante 2000. **Road system:** Johannowsky 1952; 1985a.

🏛

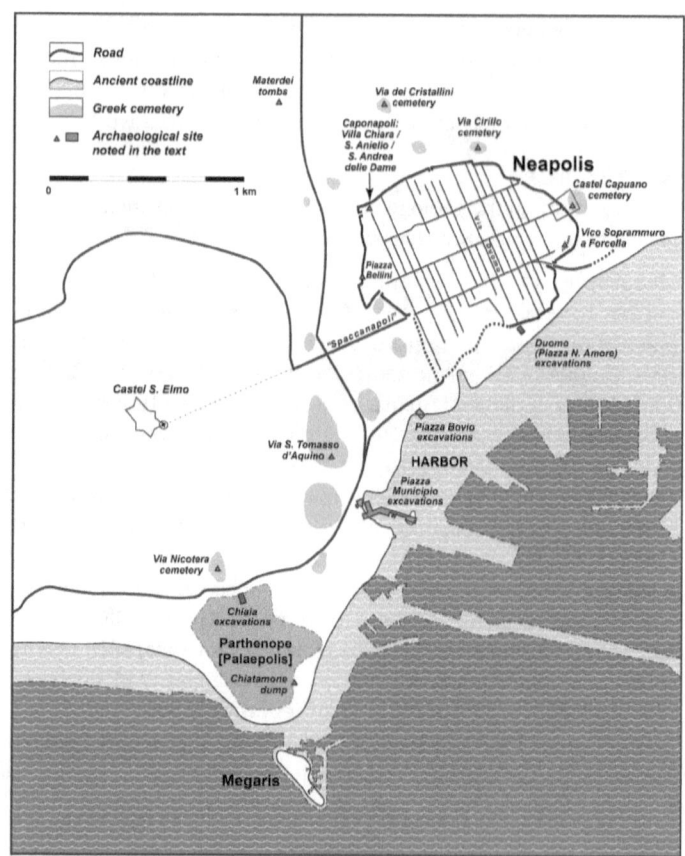

Fig. 2.1. Map of Neapolis and vicinity in the Greek period.

CHAPTER 2. THE GREEK CITY: FROM PARTHENOPE TO NEAPOLIS

PREHISTORY

Naples and its vicinity have seen human occupation since at least the late Neolithic period. Careful excavation, aided by the preservative effect of volcanic events in antiquity, has shown that the earliest residents here were not herdsmen, as previously believed, but farmers. As we learn more about prehistoric Campania, it is becoming clear that farming in late-Neolithic times was a sophisticated and widespread undertaking throughout the region's fertile plains, involving irrigation, drainage, intensive cultivation — even regular, orthogonal land division. Equally intriguing is the evidence that the people of this period contended with frequent volcanic eruptions. In the words of Stefano De Caro,

> the road that led to this stunning revelation was the discovery that almost the entire northern territory of Campania was involved in many eruptions of the Phlegraean volcanoes and Vesuvius; these, with their particular levels of ash and pumice, have sealed up true and proper fossil landscapes, as if there had been a Pompeii of 79 CE every three quarters of a century.

Lacking permanent buildings, the local Neolithic peoples were able to return to the fields as soon as they became cultivable again. The event that led to these discoveries was the preparation for a new high-speed rail line between Cassino and Naples. In Naples itself, a separate project — the excavation for a new line of the Metropolitana subway — has yielded similar results. Delicate networks of furrows plowed by inhabitants of the mid-third millennium BCE have turned up at several sites, and in at least two layers separated by volcanic strata. The first evidence of this kind in the city was discovered in the mid-2000s, during subway excavations at Via Díaz at Piazza Bovio [Fig. 2.1]. More came to light at the church of S. Andrea delle Dame, near the acropolis of ancient Neapolis, and again at Piazza Sta. Maria degli Angeli and Fuorigrotta. These furrows — which must have been ubiquitous in the area — attest the lifeways of a people who, characteristically of the region's early inhabitants, are best known by their funerary customs.

But in Naples proper, burials from this period have been elusive. In the mid-twentieth century two characteristic late-Neolithic "oven" tombs were found on the north slopes of the hill of Materdei [Fig. 2.1]. They had been blanketed by four strata of volcanic material, probably from minor eruptions of the Phlegraean Fields. Cut into the tufaceous hillside, each was sealed with a large stone block. Within the single undisturbed tomb of the pair, the skeleton of a young man lay in the flexed position, on its right side; a crudely forged dagger of arsenical bronze was at his side. The assemblage of hand-built terracotta vessels has been dated to the late third millennium BCE, which in Italy falls within a transitional phase between the Neolithic and the full-fledged Bronze Age.

In 2005, during public-transit excavations at Piazzale Tecchio in Fuorigrotta (south of the Via Terracina baths; see Fig. 1.1), archaeologists recovered a large deposit of pottery dating to roughly the same time, along with post holes for a wood-frame shelter. These are relics of the Protoapennine culture, whose presence elsewhere in Campania is well documented — for example, on the tiny islet of Vivara, aligned between Procida and Ischia (Prochyte and Pithekoussai) just off the northern spur of the Bay of Naples [see Fig. 1.2]. The Apennine culture in general, structured around pastoralism, was distinctly Italic. Originating in the mountainous interior and spreading toward the coasts, it had little in common, at least initially, with its seafaring, palace-building contemporaries of the Aegean Bronze Age. The culture was highly permeable; the variability in assemblages at different Bronze-Age sites around south Italy has led prehistorians to refer to each distinctive pattern of artifacts as a *facies*, or "face," of a manifold ethnographic creature with various identities. The two tombs of Materdei have been classified with the so-called Gaudo *facies*, named for a site near Paestum where it was first identified. We do not know if these peoples were related to the farmers who plowed the territory a few centuries earlier.

As havens along a busy prehistoric trade route, Naples and other sites on the northern Bay witnessed much cultural movement and

CHAPTER 2 ☰ THE GREEK CITY

exchange. The stories of Odysseus' adventures along the Tyrrhenian coast of Italy have always stirred the imagination, and many have wished to find traces of the Aegean Age of Heroes imprinted in the local archaeological record. Certainly this was true in antiquity. Quite apart from the *Aeneid*, even Virgil's no-nonsense contemporary, the geographer Strabo,[1] claimed that "from the time of the Trojan War" Greeks had occupied most of Italy, including its interior. Local mythologies capitalized on the convention. Thus, for example, the city of Capua, north of Neapolis, preserved a replica of the famous cup of Nestor.[2] Modern interest was fired by the discovery in 1953 of another "Cup of Nestor," an eighth-century-BCE ceramic drinking vessel from a tomb on Ischia that proclaimed, in an early Greek script:

> 10. I AM THE CUP OF NESTOR, A JOY TO DRINK FROM, BUT ANYONE DRINKING FROM THIS CUP WILL IMMEDIATELY BE STRUCK WITH DESIRE FOR LOVELY-CROWNED APHRODITE.[3]

A seal on a near-contemporary amphora from another tomb probably represents Ajax carrying the body of Achilles. Here was material testimony of the Homeric stories rendered on vessels that were roughly coeval with Homer himself. Old debates were rekindled. Were the Trojan myths influenced by colonization in the West? To what extent had Aegean peoples wandered or even settled in the West in precolonial times?

In a manner of speaking, Aegeans (Greek or not) *were* here before the age of colonization, in at least two major phases, if only by proxy of their export wares. Like Odysseus himself, they seem to have had no interest in putting down roots. Cycladic and Anatolian peoples may have established contact along the coasts of Italy and Sicily in the third millennium BCE. Their influence is evident in the Gaudo *facies*. Certain ceramics found at Gaudo sites in south Italy are identical to contemporary wares made on the Greek islands and in Troy (!). Then in the sixteenth century BCE, Mycenaean artifacts began to appear among Apennine assemblages in the region; by the fourteenth they were on the islet of Vivara.

1. *Geography* 6.1.2.
2. Athenaeus, *Deipnosophists* 11.466e, 489b-c.
3. *SEG* 14.604, trans. Malkin.

But are Aegean goods anything more than mere imports? Do they mark a point of cultural interface? Giovanni Pugliese Carratelli postulated that Mycenaean traders, seeking ores and alum, established "precolonies" in Italy half a millennium before the great age of colonization. In truth, there is no evidence of such precocity — let alone evidence that the exchange of goods or techniques developed into an exchange of beliefs and behaviors long before Greek settlements arrived. But Nicolas Coldstream, David Ridgway, Bruno D'Agostino, and others offer a more modest and refined notion of precolonialism, in which Euboeans actively traded in the West at least some decades before settling there. Apart from the profit motive, Coldstream believes, "they needed also to prospect for a forward base" (Ischia), perhaps with an eye to colonizing the sparsely inhabited regions of the northern Bay.

For the period between the thirteenth century and the end of the Italian Bronze Age in the tenth century (or eleventh, if we follow the contemporary revisionist chronology), archaeological evidence of human occupation of any kind around the Bay is vanishingly thin. The causes of this sparsity are unknown, but probably have to do with a general decline in security. Coastal peoples retreated to more defensible positions in hills and caves, perhaps to avoid piracy, and cremation replaced inhumation as the preferred method of disposal of the dead. A significant segment of this period (c. 1150–800 BCE) corresponds to an era of widespread instability around the eastern Mediterranean.

In the Iron Age, Campania hosted a single well-defined culture, the cremating Villanovan (sometimes called proto-Etruscan), mainly in the north and far south, and various ill-defined groups who inhumed their dead (the so-called *Fossakultur*). Little material from this age has been found in the vicinity of Naples; but to its west at Cumae (Greek Kyme, or "Wave"; see Fig. 1.2), and southeast in the Sarno Valley, burials signal a human presence on the Bay just before the age of Greek colonization. The peoples in coastal Campania did not gather in large settlements; they seem to have participated in small, localized pastoral economies that sometimes were extended by transhumance along river valleys. Toward the end of this pre-Hellenic

CHAPTER 2 ⛩ THE GREEK CITY

period, the Etruscans began to manifest themselves as the new cultural hegemon of northern and central Italy. They persistently tested their power in Campania as well, and for a while were masters of the whole Tyrrhenian Sea. The rise of the Euboean colonies at Ischia and Cumae took place in a landscape dominated by the Etruscans; the emergence of the colonies' daughter-city, Neapolis, coincided with the long decline of Etruria and the gradual arrival of waves of Samnites from the interior.

The chronology of the European Early Iron Age, we must note, is facing substantial revision. When all is said and done, and relative chronologies are painstakingly matched to emerging dendrochronological and isotopic benchmarks, we may have to push back most of the Italian Early Iron Age, which encompasses early Greek settlement in the West. This further complicates the already uneasy relationship between artifacts and the literary record of events, the latter available to us mostly through Hellenistic or Roman sources. But for the moment, any reassessment of absolute dates is premature. For what ensues, we will follow the traditional chronology, which may be skewed forward by as much as several decades in the eighth century BCE, but converges into near-alignment with the old chronology by the seventh.

NAPLES WITHIN REMOTEST MEMORY

Memory, mother of the Muses, has slighted the Greek founders of Neapolis. On the matter of the origins of a *city* — as opposed to a mere settlement — there is no easy road to the truth, only fragmentary and variably compatible snatches of hearsay culled centuries after the fact. Archaeology generates its own data, which rarely fit the narratives transmitted by the written or spoken word so snugly as to constitute confirmation. The pattern of activity that we call Greek colonization seems to have become possible only with the emergence of the *polis,* the Greek city-state, in the eighth century BCE; but even this conventional notion may be in dispute as the concept of colonization is deconstructed and the implications of the new chronology are realized. Still, it can be said with some confidence that Greek settlement in the West began on the northern Bay of Naples — initially, as one might expect, on an island, and only thereafter in locations along the Italian and Sicilian coast. The sheer distance from the homeland forced western Greek settlements into self-sufficiency from the start. They could do this in either of two ways: by subsisting on trade; or by controlling relatively large and productive territories. The earliest Greek settlers chose the first option.

The first Greek settlement in this region was founded by Euboeans and Phoenicians on Ischia in the mid-eighth century. Shortly thereafter, or even concurrently, the Euboean presence was extended to Cumae on a mainland promontory just north of the Bay. Ischia, which was never a conventional colony, may (doubtfully) have been able to support itself on island agriculture, as Strabo claims,[4] but it operated principally on the first, and earliest, model of Greek expansion, survival by trade. The main shipping lane in the Tyrrhenian Sea probably ran along the coast between the island and Cumae. The harbors of Ischia and Cumae must have become important staging or trading posts for merchant vessels plying this busy corridor. Blessed with excellent clay deposits, the island soon developed an export trade in pottery. Pliny the Elder[5] even submits that its name is derived from large storage jars (*pithoi*) produced there. Strabo[6] claims the colonists also excelled at *chryseia*, "gold-work," usually interpreted as goldsmithing. Whatever the accuracy of this claim — and it has not been confirmed archaeologically — the Ischians worked other metals (iron from Elba, copper and silver from Etruria) expertly.

Early Cumae may have been principally a strategic outpost serving as a buffer to Ischia on land. This is not to say that it had a military role per se. Irad Malkin and others have emphasized the predominantly benign relations, at least initially, obtaining among the Euboeans, the local tribes, and the Etruscans who dominated the mainland and coastal routes. The French and Italian archaeologists excavating at Cumae, however, give credence to the testimony of Roman sources,

4. *Geography* 5.4.9.
5. *Natural History* 3.82.
6. 5.4.9.

CHAPTER 2 🏛 THE GREEK CITY

Fig. 2.2. Italo-Geometric oinochoe from the Pizzofalcone necropolis. Second quarter of the seventh century BCE. Naples, Museo Archeologico Nazionale. Photo: R. Taylor.

which assert that the Greek islanders seized Cumae by force.[7] First, though, some of them seem to have dwelt among the natives, who already had a long-established settlement there; then, in the latter eighth century, a hiatus has been noted in settlement activity, after which an urbanized core in the Greek manner developed. The new construction encroached on indigenous burial grounds, suggesting a radical cultural dissociation, even a conquest.

There can be little doubt that the Greeks of Cumae were seeking material advantage by consolidating surveillance and control over the straits between the island and the mainland. It has been observed in other contexts that Euboean colonists were natural masters of strategic narrows (most notably the Hellespont, which they colonized heavily) because of their experience with the important straits that divided their home island from mainland Greece. Over time, Cumae developed fisheries and a productive agricultural territory, along with all the interests and insecurities of a mainland settlement.

It was only a matter of time before the Greeks in this area secured a foothold on the Bay itself. A colony named Neapolis ("New City"; see Fig. 1.1) cannot have been, and was not, the first settlement to be planted in this place. In 1949, on the heights of Pizzofalcone at Via Nicotera, roughly 1.5 km southwest of the walls of ancient Neapolis, workers discovered a necropolis that yielded ceramics ranging from about 675 to 550 BCE [Figs. 2.1; 2.2]. These assemblages included wares manufactured at Cumae or Ischia. The discovery confirmed

7. Breglia Pulci Doria 1983 frag. B 54; Livy, *History of Rome*, 8.22.5–6. For Livy, see reading 18 below.

an existing hypothesis that the early colony, which ancient literary sources name Parthenope or Palae[o]polis, was situated on the easily defended promontory just south of the necropolis. For its harbor, the citadel town must have had easy access to an inlet about 600 meters to the northeast, now somewhat inland from the shore. Archaeologists and geomorphologists working in concert with Naples' subway expansion have identified the inlet and its dimensions and confirmed a Greek presence there in the late eighth and seventh centuries BCE [see Fig. 2.1]. Extending under the modern city from Piazza Municipio to Piazza Bovio, it was dredged and systematized into a medium-depth harbor only in the fourth or third century BCE, but the finds signal its earlier use. Among the recent discoveries at the harbor are Protocorinthian and Italo-Geometric wares contemporary with the ones found at Pizzofalcone, and more ceramics from Ischia.

As Filippo Càssola has observed, the handful of arbitrarily discovered tomb groups on Via Nicotera may help us establish limited time horizons of Greek presence, but they cannot offer definitive proof that gaps in the record constitute an *absence*. Too often it has been assumed that a long hiatus in the Pizzofalcone necropolis ceramics beginning about 550 BCE represents the abandonment of Parthenope. This assumption is probably mistaken. An ancient dump at Chiatamone at the eastern foot of Pizzofalcone, excavated in the late nineteenth century, adds perspective to the picture from Via Nicotera [see Fig. 2.1]. The ceramic found in it indicate continuous habitation from the late eighth to the early fifth century BCE; then a hiatus of half a century, followed by a resumption of activity until the third century BCE. From these two data sets, then, we may establish a composite presence at Parthenope, in round numbers (give or take a decade), from 700 to 490 BCE; an abandonment lasting until about 450; then resumption of activity until roughly 300 BCE.

PARTHENOPE AND EARLY NEAPOLIS IN LITERATURE

In outline, the material evidence comports reasonably well with the literary sources. These, unfortunately, are meager. The most important history composed in antiquity chronicling Magna Graecia in this period, by Timaios of Tauromenion, is lost, along with the influential

CHAPTER 2 ☖ THE GREEK CITY

geographies of Hekataios of Miletos and Eratosthenes of Kyrene. These are believed to have been important sources for the later authors, such as Dionysios of Halikarnassos and Strabo, who chronicled early Greek history in the West for a Roman audience. Probably because of the widely acknowledged authority of Timaios, most of the references to the earliest history of Neapolis can be patched together into a reasonably consistent narrative. We begin with seven references, most or all of them dating to the Roman period:

> 11. The Chalkidians, who... were of Attic origin, founded Cumae in Italy.... At a considerably later period, a portion of the citizens of Cumae founded Neapolis. [Velleius Paterculus, *Compendium* 1.4.1]
>
> 12. From Cumae, which lies before Avernus, Neapolis was founded, according to an oracle. [Pseudo-Skymnos, *Periegesis* 252–53, trans. Taylor]
>
> 13. On the coast stands Neapolis, itself also a colony of the Chalkidians, named Parthenope from the tomb of one of the Sirens.... [Pliny, *Natural History* 3.62].
>
> 14. After Dikaiarcheia [Pozzuoli] comes Neapolis, a city of the Cumaeans. At a later time it was recolonized by Chalkidians, and also by some Ischians and Athenians, and hence, for this reason, was called Neapolis. A monument of Parthenope, one of the Sirens, is pointed out in Neapolis, and in accordance with an oracle an athletic contest is celebrated there. [Strabo, *Geography* 5.4.7]
>
> 15. Suetonius Tranquillus says that the Siren Parthenope was buried on the coast of Campania; from her name Neapolis, also called Parthenope, is thought to be derived. [Scholia Bernensia, on Virgil's *Georgics* 4.564, trans. Taylor]
>
> 16. Book four [of the history of Lutatius] says that [some] inhabitants of Cumae, leaving behind their ancestors, founded the city of Parthenope — called Parthenope from the Siren, whose body also [is buried there]. Later, on account of the fertility and pleasantness of the precinct, it began to be more heavily populated. Fearing that Cumaean territory would be deserted, [the Cumaeans] contrived to destroy Parthenope; but later, beset by a pestilence, on the

strength of an oracle, they restored the city and took up the rites of Parthenope with great religious vigor. [Philargyrios, scholium on Virgil's *Georgics* 4.564, trans. Taylor]

17. Timaios says that Diotimos, admiral of the Athenians, came to Neapolis; and, according to an oracle, he sacrificed to Parthenope and founded a torch race; wherefore even up to [Timaios'] own time, a torch race was taking place among the Neapolitans. [Tzetzes, scholium of Lykophron, *Alexandra* 732, trans. Taylor]

These sources, though imperfectly aligned, seem to establish a rough chronology of events:

- Greek colonization on the site of Naples existed in two phases with an interval dividing them.
- In its first phase the colony was named Parthenope, derived from the city's tutelary spirit, the Siren, whose tomb was established here.
- The second foundation, named Neapolis ("New City") was the result of an oracle.
- Both Parthenope and Neapolis were foundations of Cumae, itself a colony of Chalkis and Eretria on the island of Euboea. (Ancient authors often call Neapolis and Cumae "Euboean" or "Chalkidian.")
- A cult was maintained around Parthenope after the second foundation, including a torch race in her honor; this race too may have been dictated by the oracle.
- The race was introduced by an Athenian admiral, Diotimos.

The agreement among the seven sources is admittedly tenuous. None of these events is confirmed by all. Some details appear only in a single source. Only Tzetzes, for example, mentions the Athenian Diotimos. Philargyrios, quoting a certain Lutatius (his identity is disputed), alone claims (or so it seems) that Parthenope was destroyed by its mother city, evidently out of fear or jealousy. Only Strabo attributes the second foundation to three peoples: Chalkidians, Ischians, and Athenians.

CHAPTER 2 ⛫ THE GREEK CITY

Writing about a later phase, the outbreak of the Second Samnite War in 327/6 BCE, the Roman historian Livy observes — crucially, and rather unexpectedly — that the two settlements existed concurrently, and were separated by some distance; in fact, the Romans briefly cut off communications between them. He calls the early town Palaepolis ("Old City"):

> 18. Palaepolis was not far from the spot where Neapolis is now, and the two cities were inhabited by one people. Cumae was their mother city, and the Cumeans derive their origin from Chalkis in Euboea. Thanks to the fleet in which they had sailed from their home, they enjoyed much power on the coast of that sea by which they dwell; having landed first on the island of Aenaria [Ischia] and the Pithecusae,[8] they afterwards ventured to transfer their seat to the mainland. [Livy, *History of Rome* 8.22.5–6]

The detail of two settlements appears to be confirmed geographically by the presence of the early necropolis on the promontory of Pizzofalcone. Palaepolis, in effect, was on this headland. Neapolis was the walled city to its northeast [see Fig. 2.1]. But what about the instability of nomenclature? Why do some sources, including Strabo, have no name for the proto-Neapolis, while others call it Parthenope? And why does Livy refer to it as Palaepolis, while he and other Roman authors use Parthenope as a variant name for Neapolis?

Place names can be fluid and fungible, and it is dangerous to extrapolate too much from such limited source material. Despite an energetic attempt by Flavio Raviola to phase the nomenclature of this settlement, I accept the traditional scholarly position that its original name was Parthenope, just as several ancient authors say, and that this name evolved into a quaint and archaizing metonym for the entire urban area, as it remains even today.[9] Livy's "Palaepolis," a name that also appears in the triumphal calendar from the Roman Forum referencing these very events,[10] is simply a retronym of the

---

8. These must be nearby islands with the same family name as the main island (Pithekoussai/Pithecusae–Aenaria–Ischia), probably Vivara and Procida.

9. See Pliny, *Natural History* 3.62; Suetonius, *Virgil* 36.

10. *Fasti Capitolini* 95 Degrassi.

kind frequently encountered at municipalities with two successively settled sites, like Emporion (Ampurias, Spain) or Samothrake.

THE FOUNDATION MYTH

Like Greek colonists everywhere, Neapolitans fashioned a story to explain the origins of their city and justify their intrusion. The oldest and most important surviving document concerning the etiological myth of Neapolis is the *Alexandra* of Lykophron, written around 190 BCE. This long poem is presented as a prophecy delivered by the Trojan princess Cassandra foretelling events in Greek myth and history, with particular attention to the Trojan War and Odysseus' subsequent adventures. The city to be known as Neapolis, according to the narrative, will be established at the tomb of Parthenope, one of the three Sirens who will die after being foiled by Odysseus as he sails up the Tyrrhenian coast of Italy. Each of these creatures will wash ashore at a different place: the future sites of Leukosia (near Poseidonia–Paestum), Tereina, and Neapolis; and each will be honored with a tomb and with newly acquired divine status. Among the three, Parthenope is the "first goddess of the sisterhood."

> **19.** And he [Odysseus] shall slay the triple daughters of Tethys' son [Acheloös], who imitated the strains of their melodious mother [Melpomene]: self-hurled from the cliff's top, they dive with their wings into the Tyrrhenian sea, where the bitter thread spun by the Fates shall draw them. One of them washed ashore the tower of Phaleros shall receive, and Glanis wetting the earth with its streams. There the inhabitants shall build a tomb for the maiden and with libations and sacrifice of oxen shall yearly honor the bird goddess Parthenope. And Leukosia shall be cast on the jutting strand of Enipeos and shall long haunt the rock that bears her name, where rapid Is and neighbouring Laris pour forth their waters. And Ligeia shall come ashore at Tereina spitting out the wave. And her shall sailormen bury on the stony beach nigh to the eddies of Okinaros; and an ox-horned Ares shall lave her tomb with his streams, cleansing with his waters the bird-child's home. And there one day in the honor of the first goddess of the sisterhood shall the ruler of all the navy of Mopsops [i.e., Athens] array for his

CHAPTER 2 ▣ THE GREEK CITY

mariners a torch race, in obedience to an oracle, which one day the people of the Neapolitans shall celebrate, even they who shall dwell on bluff crags beside Misenum's sheltered haven untroubled by the waves. [712–38]

Lykophron's version of the fate of the Sirens seems to have dominated mythological discourse in this part of Italy.[11] It relates that each of the wave-tossed Sirens, in effect, gave rise to a local cult and, by extension, a community. Parthenope was first among these; her city became the greatest. (The island of Leukosia, we may note, also took the name of its founder–Siren.) We also know that the Sirens as a group were worshiped at a sanctuary on the north side of the Sorrentine Peninsula, perhaps at Località Trinità [See Fig. 1.2]. The straits between this peninsula and the island of Capri would most logically be where the Sirens had encountered Odysseus.[12]

The poet also draws our attention to two topographical features associated with Neapolis: the Glanis River and a tower of Phaleros. As we have seen, the Glanis probably marked the northern boundary of the territories of Neapolis and Cumae,[13] and so was thoroughly "Euboeanized." Phaleros or Phaleron was the name of an Athenian hero on the voyage of the Argo.[14] The Athenians named one of their harbors after him and maintained an altar and cult in his honor.[15] He cannot otherwise be attached to this place, or anywhere in Magna Graecia, for that matter. But Lykophron, for all his pedantic obscurity, should be taken seriously as a uniquely valuable source of local mythological knowledge in this area; for, as a native Chalkidian, he had a special interest in his compatriots' doings in this region. The hero Phaleros, born in Athens and exiled to Chalkis,[16] has precisely the right dual ethnicity to be attached to the foundation myth of the proto-Neapolis.

11. Eustathius, commentary on Dionysios Periegetes 358.
12. Strabo, *Geography* 1.2.12–13.
13. See pp. 25–26.
14. Apollonios, *Voyage of the Argo* 1.95–96; Valerius Flaccus 4.654.
15. Pausanias, *Description of Greece* 1.1.4.
16. Scholiast of Apollonios, *Voyage of the Argo* 1.96.

Fig. 2.3. *Roman fresco from Pompeii. Mid-first century CE. British Museum.* © *Trustees of the British Museum.*

I suggest, tentatively, that Phaleros was presented as the discoverer of Parthenope's body, and thus as the human founder of her cult — much as King Sisyphos discovered, honored, and deified Melikertes–Palaimon, a boy whose body washed ashore at Isthmia — and for whom honorary games were founded; one thinks of Diotimos' torch races. Phaleros may also have been, from the Athenians' perspective, the town's mythic founder. Such was his role in the origins of at least one Athenian colony, Soloi on Cyprus.[17] Possibly, as Càssola suggests, the Athenian immigrants at Neapolis even gave the hero's name to the harbor in recollection of their own harbor district dedicated to Phaleros, as Athenians did elsewhere.[18]

17. Strabo 14.6.3.
18. Strabo 12.3.14.

CHAPTER 2 🏛 THE GREEK CITY

As for Lykophron's "tower of Phaleros," the headland of Pizzofalcone could not have lacked a lighthouse, most logically on its furthest seaward extension: the causeway-connected islet of Megaris (modern Megaride, or Castel dell'Ovo; see Fig. 2.1).[19] If such a monument indeed memorialized the founder/finder, then it would have been a suitable starting-point, or ignition-station, for the Athenian-style torch race honoring the goddess—presuming, of course, that there was a causeway to the island, as there is today.

The cult of the Sirens is a curious thing. Casting aside outdated notions that these creatures are derived from Eastern gods, Maurizio Giangiulio has shrewdly characterized their cult as a phenomenon that emerged exclusively among Greeks in the West. As objects of veneration, the Sirens fall within a class of beings that control points of passage, such as straits, headlands, and mountain passes [Fig. 2.3]. Often they belong equally to the liminal zone at the meeting of two geographic realms, such as land and sea. In this respect, Parthenope is akin to another bird goddess worshiped at Neapolis, Ino–Leukotheia — or even her stepdaughter Helle, who drowned in the narrows of the eponymous Hellespont. Giangiulio observes that these figures often fit into a particular mytheme: the *katapontismos*, deification by drowning in the sea. One can hardly imagine a more appropriate class of gods for a people whose lives depended on taming the collision between land and sea, and whose well-being depended on controlling promontories and narrow passages. Cumaean tradition placed the main cult of the Sirens on the Sorrentine Peninsula, which lies across the strait from the island of Capri. Given the Sirens' proclivity to ensnare mariners from the shore, it is no coincidence that the strait was notorious for pirate ambushes from the island, and eventually — under Neapolitan control — for the likely imposition of duties on merchant ships [Commentary 2.2, p. 77]. Palaimon, the god of Isthmia, conforms perfectly to the type, both as the guardian of a narrow passageway (the Isthmus of Corinth) and as a victim of *katapontismos:* indeed, his mother was none other than Ino–Leukotheia, who held him as she leapt into the sea. And like Parthenope, he washed to a grateful shore.

19. See Musto 2013, xxxviii–xxxix.

Significantly, according to Euboean tradition,[20] the Sirens were daughters of Acheloös, a hybrid river god who belongs to another class of liminal water deities. Taking the form of bull-men, and most popular in Sicily and Magna Graecia, they fit a similar mytheme in which a hero drowns in a river or spring and is reborn as the attendant spirit of the body of water. Neapolis honored its own river god, Sebethos, in precisely this form.[21] These gods' combination of sacrificial, expiatory properties (they tend to undergo a death and rebirth) and geographic suitability exercised a powerful hold on the imaginations of western Greeks.

PARTHENOPE, NEAPOLIS, AND CUMAE

Since Parthenope was reputedly a Cumaean town, its date of foundation must have fallen between that of Cumae and roughly 700 BCE, when the earliest pottery among the refuse at Chiatamone was manufactured. A date close to 700 is usually proposed; this situates the settlement comfortably within the narrative of Euboean colonization in the West. As Alfonso Mele has remarked, the Cumaean presence at nearby Dikaiarcheia, modern Pozzuoli [Commentary 2.3, pp. 78–79], dates to about the same time, suggesting that Cumae was expanding its coastal holdings at two sites simultaneously.

Initially, both were probably *epineia*, satellite ports with no independence from the mother city. The Cumaeans understood the long-term advantage of controlling not only the best natural harbors on the entire Tyrrhenian coast, but the bay that enclosed them. In due time, the Bay of Naples was to be known as the Cumaean Gulf.[22] But despite the proximity of the busy north-south sea route that had served pan-Mediterranean traders for well over a millennium, Parthenope probably was *not* envisioned to be a center of trade. Ancient Tyrrhenian traders had no business along the rocky and sparsely populated northern rim of the Bay, with its puny rivers and limited access to the interior. To the extent that Greeks sought

20. Lykophron, *Alexandra* 712–13.
21. See pp. 94–96.
22. Eratosthenes, scholium of Strabo 1.2.12; Stephanos of Byzantion, s.v. *Seirenoussai*.

CHAPTER 2 🏛 THE GREEK CITY

to trade with the Etruscans in northern Campania, they could do so more easily from Cumae itself. Yet in later years tiny Parthenope would grow into one of the greatest ports in the Mediterranean, a distinction Naples has retained ever since. In a word, Parthenope and Pozzuoli were harbors too good to concede to some foreign power; by seizing them, Cumae denied a beachhead to others. The settlement of Parthenope proved highly defensible, enjoying a natural barrier to incursions from inland, and prudently strategic, bringing back-door protection to the mother city. From the heights of Pizzofalcone, which commands a view of the entire southern bay and the north shore of Capri, Parthenope could monitor and deter threats from the south.

As for Parthenope's decline, unfortunately we can say little for sure. Livy[23] asserts straightforwardly that both Palaepolis and Neapolis were founded by Cumae, though he gives no details or motives. So what are we to make of Strabo's claim that the New City was a refoundation by Chalkidians along with Ischians and Athenians? Are these Chalkidians the chastened Cumaeans cited by Lutatius? Probably not, since the Ischians, themselves Chalkidian in origin, are called by their own name. Surely Cumaean co-founders would have merited the same treatment. Perhaps Cumae had indeed called on Chalkis, her Euboean mother city, for new settlers, but with little independent evidence to corroborate this, we must leave the question open. An Ischian migration is much easier to justify, and indeed a cause is ready to hand: the crescendo of earthquakes and eruptions on the island that eventually forced its complete evacuation sometime after 474 BCE, at which time perhaps the only remaining inhabitants were a Syracusan garrison.[24] That leaves the Athenians to consider. Of them we will have more to say below; suffice it to say here that the case for their presence in the region when Neapolis was first founded, around 500–480 BCE, is feeble.

From Strabo we lurch to an equally problematic source on the opposite end of the ideological spectrum. Are we really to believe

23. See reading 18 above.
24. See p. 55.

Lutatius, who supposedly claims that a jealous Cumae sought to destroy its own settlement because of its unanticipated success? Certainly there is no shortage of evidence that Greek colonies could vex their mother cities. But this account, even if true, is undoubtedly much distorted, simplified, or misunderstood. The same can be said about Lutatius' account of the restoration. This (he claims) the Cumaeans undertook on the instructions of an oracle, seeking to quell a chastening pestilence. Implicitly, at least, they had been punished by their oracular god Apollo for destroying their own colony in anger; now, they sought expiation by refounding it. This episode is sometimes cited as evidence for the early presence of the Sibylline oracle at Cumae, who would become famous under Roman dominion. But as we shall see below, it has been badly misinterpreted.

Let us review Lutatius' text, paraphrased by Virgil's scholiast Philargyrios.

> **20.** Book four... says that [some] inhabitants of Cumae, leaving behind their ancestors, founded the city of Parthenope — called Parthenope from the Siren, whose body also [is buried there]. Later, on account of the fertility and pleasantness of the precinct, it began to be more heavily populated. Fearing that Cumaean territory would be deserted, [the Cumaeans] contrived to destroy Parthenope; but later, beset by a pestilence, on the strength of an oracle they restored the city and took up the rites of Parthenope with great religious vigor.

If we can trust Lutatius, the first settlement proved to be a greater success than Cumae had bargained for, quickly rising to threaten her dominance. The superior port, along with access to fertile territory at the western foot of Vesuvius, may have proved a winning combination. Still, did this really lead Cumae to take such a drastic measure as to destroy its colony, and then leave it unpopulated and exposed to usurpation by external forces?

Pugliese Carratelli and Càssola contend that Cumae did nothing so drastic. Cooptation of the site, whether by force or by diplomacy, is the likely scenario during the later sixth century or early fifth, when the Etruscans were threatening Greek power along the Tyrrhenian

CHAPTER 2 🏛 THE GREEK CITY

seaways and probing weaknesses in the Euboean defenses. While we may disagree with the historical frameworks they advance, their instincts in dismissing the scenario of an absolute destruction and abandonment of Parthenope are borne out archaeologically. Daniela Giampaola and Bruno D'Agostino report abundant finds of sixth-century pottery along several segments of the defensive wall of Neapolis. Moreover, the oldest part of the wall seems to date between 500 and 480 BCE — before the moment traditionally assigned to the foundation of Neapolis. The ceramic record from recent excavations, taken with that of Pizzofalcone and Chiatamone, suggest the following chronology:

- Parthenope existed continuously through the entire seventh and sixth centuries BCE; despite an arbitrary lacuna in *burial* evidence starting around 550, the continuity beyond that moment is assured by the evidence in the dump at Chiatamone.
- During the second half of the sixth century BCE, activity at the harbor and the future site of Neapolis increased.
- Parthenope was abandoned, or practically abandoned, around 490 BCE.
- At roughly (even precisely?) the same time, the earliest defensive walls of Neapolis, and presumably the beginnings of a city plan, were established.
- Parthenope again had inhabitants around 450 BCE, and for the following century and a half.

This sequence is important, because it directly undermines the traditional chronology. It was long believed that Neapolis was founded *de novo* shortly after the Battle of Cumae in 474 BCE. According to this view, conditions favored the new colony only after that historic naval conflict, in which the Syracusans, with the help of Cumae, permanently crushed Etruscan hegemony over the Tyrrhenian Sea. In truth, scholars have been moving away from the old consensus for some time. Elaborating on Càssola's ideas set forth in the mid-1980s, Raviola contended that the battle of 474 BCE and its aftermath had little bearing on the foundation of Neapolis, and that the real motive for it should be sought in the internal affairs of Cumae in the preceding decades. By his reckoning, the "new city" was so named because it consisted of political dissidents from the "old city" of Cumae, who chose (or were forced) to make a fresh start after the fall of Aristodemos' tyranny at Cumae around 485 BCE. Along the same lines, D'Agostino suggests that even during the tyranny, which began in 505/4, the site of Neapolis (whether or not it was so called at the time) served as the refuge of dispossessed former oligarchs and their supporters.

Some Cumaean oligarchs fled to Capua,[25] but from there they may soon have hatched a plan to seize Parthenope and establish a beachhead for their ambitions. Dionysios,[26] our principal source of information on the tyranny, says only that these exiles joined forces with a ragtag army of youths — the sons of the councilmen whom Aristodemos had slain, and who had been scattered in the countryside as slaves of their fathers' murderers. Nino Luraghi has shown this account to be more myth than fact. (The patent distortions of Dionysios are manifold; he neglects even to mention the founding of Neapolis.) An alternative scenario goes as follows: the oligarchs, probably with the help of Capua and other Campanian cities alarmed by the radical populism of Aristodemos, seized Parthenope as a staging-post for the revolt against him. In effect, we may suppose that the exiled Cumaean aristocracy sought to found a new Cumae in their own image, resurrecting the old political, religious, and social institutions of the mother city that had been hijacked by Aristodemos. This population of exiles may have included the leading citizens of nearby Dikaearcheia (Pozzuoli), who had fled their home of Samos in 531 BCE to avoid precisely the scenario playing out under Aristodemos. As Fausto Zevi has suggested, they were likely to be of an oligarchic persuasion. Echoes of the conservatism of Neapolis' leadership may have reemerged later in the fifth century BCE, when the city's Greek aristocracy was forced to endure first an influx of Samnites into their territory, and then a wave of Greek refugees from Cumae.

If the foundation of Neapolis is to be deemed contemporary with its earliest defensive wall, then the chronological window for this

25. Dionysios of Halikarnassos, *Roman Antiquities* 7.10.3.
26. 7.7–11.

CHAPTER 2 🏛 THE GREEK CITY

Fig. 2.4. *Votive female busts from excavations at S. Aniello a Caponapoli. Naples, Museo Archeologico Nazionale. Photo: R. Taylor.*

event can now be set at c. 500–480 BCE. The founding seems to be more or less concurrent with the temporary abandonment or drastic diminution of Parthenope. If there was a gap between these two events, it did not span several decades, as previously thought. In fact, it is now easy to envision direct contiguity between them, perhaps even causality: the abandonment of one led quickly to the founding of the other. If we accept Raviola's and D'Agostino's historical framework, then it can be suggested that the oligarchic faction seized and temporarily occupied Parthenope before they overthrew Aristodemos, and then founded Neapolis immediately after it as a thank-offering. We can place these events in the mid-480s BCE.

Yet the site of the future Neapolis was not a tabula rasa. The widespread incidence of pottery from the second half of the sixth century signals a robust human presence here for several decades before the formal foundation of the New City. The discovery of a midsixth-century architectural terracotta fragment at Villa Chiara on Caponapoli [see Fig. 2.1], very close to a later deposit of terracotta busts indicating a cult center of Demeter [Fig. 2.4], even suggests that a sanctuary district had developed here well before the walled city was built. It may have functioned as a mediatory sanctuary in the manner proposed by François de Polignac — i.e., as a cult site created by Greek settlers to resolve tensions with indigenous peoples during the process of synoecism or urbanization; or, more specifically, as a Thesmophorion, a periurban sanctuary where women, as agents and guardians of fertility, took symbolic control of both the urban and rural components of the *polis*. The continuity of activity both before and after the critical moment indicates that the foundation of Neapolis merely formalized an urbanizing trend on the site that was already well under way. And it would seem to lend credence to Lutatius' testimony of the gathering strength of Parthenope, which he claims was attracting people away from Cumaean territory.

Can our revised understanding of the events be reconciled with other aspects of the narrative of Lutatius? After all, archaeologists rightly question the oft-presumed primacy of written texts. Further, Mele has observed just how biased this perspective is against Cumae. But let us briefly reverse the usual approach — i.e., taking archaeological finds as illustration of textual information — and see if we can fit Lutatius' text into the emerging archaeological model. A reasonable interpretation of the archaeology would suggest that contrary to the *favored reading* of Lutatius, there was no destruction of Parthenope at all. The inhabitants gradually moved, of their own volition, down to the site of the future Neapolis; then, at a certain moment at the beginning of the fifth century BCE, the new walled city was laid out, and the remaining population on the hill was swiftly relocated to it. In point of fact, Lutatius does *not* say that the Cumaeans destroyed Parthenope; he says that, at some unspecified time, they *considered* destroying it (*iniisse consilium Parthenopen diruendi*) because of its success. A destruction is usually presumed, because the text goes on to say that they "restored the city" (*urbem restituisse*), along with its cult of the Siren, after the onset of a pestilence. But that restoration may simply have been a resettlement *as a result of depopulation from the pestilence*. That is, Parthenope may have been decimated by the same plague that Lutatius says beset Cumae and instigated the founding of Neapolis. Since the tomb of the Siren was probably on the shore below the old town, the new settlers would have had no difficulty reviving her cult even if the citadel above was abandoned. Only around the mid-fifth century BCE, when Etruscan piracy flared up again[27] and the Samnites began to threaten the coastal cities of Campania,

27. Diodoros, *Historical Library* 11.88.4–5.

CHAPTER 2 ⛪ THE GREEK CITY

did the Neapolitans choose to reoccupy Parthenope, a place of considerable strategic importance that must have remained garrisoned even through the lean years.

Colonization (if that is the appropriate term) is always, in some sense, a political act. The pestilence — malaria, perhaps, which had been a scourge during Aristodemos' years in power[28] — may well have weakened the Cumaean tyranny in ways that Dionysios, in his zeal to tell a moralizing tale, suppressed or never knew. For all we know, it could have figured in the demise of Aristodemos himself, perhaps by decimating the armed guard at Cumae. A plague would also have created an opening for an influx to Parthenope of the oligarchic party, perhaps chafing under their exile at Capua. Whatever the precise nature of the new enterprise, as we shall see, the new settlement of Neapolis quickly eclipsed the mother city, even as it honored Cumaean traditions.

Let us then summarize our necessarily sketchy narrative, which accounts for both the revolt and the plague:

- At some point in the late sixth century BCE, maybe before Aristodemos' rise to power, or maybe during the campaign that led to it, the oligarchy of Cumae had considered wiping out the upstart Parthenope.
- But other events intervened: in 505/4 BCE Aristodemos seized power, murdering some of Cumae's aristocracy and driving others into exile at Capua. His tyranny lasted about twenty years.
- Toward the end of the tyranny, a pestilence weakened Aristodemos' hold on power. Sensing an opening, the exiles — probably with assistance from their host city — probed the Cumaean territory for vulnerabilities.
- They sought out an oracle to guide them, and they were directed to Parthenope.
- The citadel town of Parthenope admitted the newcomers, perhaps partly because of decimation from the plague and partly out of local ties of patronage and kinship to the oligarchs.

---

28. Lutatius F7 P.

- From their base at Parthenope, and maybe Capua too, the oligarchic party invaded Cumae and assassinated Aristodemos.
- As a thank-offering to the gods (Apollo? Parthenope?) they founded Neapolis on the site of the growing settlement. For now, the citadel of Parthenope was abandoned, but the goddess' cult thrived at the site of her tomb.
- Ranks of settlers in the New City included refugees from Ischia's volcanism[29] and possibly an infusion of Chalkidians from the mother country.

SYRACUSE AND ISCHIA

Whatever slump the plague had engendered, Neapolis emerged from it in fine fettle. While the New City must initially have operated in the shadow of Cumae and the great new regional power, Syracuse, there is little to suggest that these cities impeded her growth. If anything, Neapolis demonstrated autonomy by seizing the stricken island of Ischia after the war between Syracuse and Etruria. Strabo recounts this episode:

> **21.** [the Ischians] were... driven out of the island by earthquakes, and by eruptions of fire, sea, and hot waters; for the island has "fistulas" of this sort [thermal spring vents], and it was these that caused also the people sent thither by Hieron the tyrant of Syracuse [478–467 BCE] to forsake the island and the fortress they had erected there; and then the Neapolitans came over and took possession. [*Geography* 5.4.9]

Raviola astutely observes that the distribution of oil and wine amphoras around Tyrrhenian sites indicates that throughout the 470s BCE, despite periodic Syracusan blockades, the region maintained a robust trade relationship with many production centers. So either the principal combatants — the Etruscans on one side, Syracuse and Cumae on the other — were less powerful, or more permissive, than previously believed. Well before 474 BCE, Cumae had gained control of Ischia, and the island continued to thrive as a center of maritime trade. Cumae participated in the naval battle of 474 that broke the back of Etruscan domination on its doorstep. But Syracuse, perhaps demanding further payment for its majority role in the battle, had

29. See the following section.

been granted permission to garrison the island. All this developed during a sequence of geological upheavals on Ischia that prompted a complete evacuation. Meanwhile, Cumae's fortunes were declining. For reasons unknown (perhaps a resurgence of its internal class strife) the city could not capitalize on its military victory. It was in no shape to repopulate Ischia, and an invigorated Neapolis sprang into the void. The New City probably made a friendly accommodation with the Syracusans, who would have been pleased, on the one hand, with the decline of Cumae and, on the other, with the opportunity to delegate a task that they themselves no longer relished: policing the northern end of the Bay against piracy.

The island became a valuable resource for Neapolis, giving the city complete control over the Bay, augmenting the landmass of its territory, and offering limitless deposits of high-quality clay that would eventually support a massive homegrown industry in export ceramics.

THE ATHENIAN CONNECTION

What role did Athenians play in the history of Neapolis? Although the Euboean ethnicity always dominated Greek identity there, the Athenians too, or so Strabo claims, had a formative presence in Neapolis' history. Noting Strabo's ambiguous chronology (Neapolis "was recolonized by Chalkidians, and also by some Ischians and Athenians"), most scholars have doubted an Athenian presence in Neapolis' *beginnings* altogether. They prefer to see Athenians here in later decades, only after the legation of Diotimos and his mariners, when Athens' foreign policy in the West gained greater visibility. Indeed, it is hard to verify an Athenian presence in the West (apart from its ubiquitous export pottery) before 480/79 BCE, when Athens overcame the Persian threat and began to expand its sphere of influence beyond the Aegean. But for uncertain reasons, Athens seems to have held a significant stake in Neapolitan foundation myth and its cult of Parthenope. As noted above, the mythic Athenian hero Phaleros had a dual ethnic identity, for he later settled in Euboea. This duality seems to reflect a concocted ethnological tradition, perhaps originating in Campania, that claimed the Chalkidians who founded Cumae were of Attic descent.[30]

30. Velleius Paterculus, *Compendium* 1.4.1–2.

Càssola, following the traditional chronology of a foundation after 474, has proposed that an Athenian contingent of settlers joined the Cumaeans shortly thereafter as the result of a policy hinted at by Themistocles, the famous Athenian general and statesman. Herodotus[31] reports that in 480, on the eve of the Battle of Salamis, Themistocles threatened the wavering Spartan commander that if the Spartans did not join him in battle against the Persians, the Athenians would abandon Greece to the enemy and move to their colony at Siris (usually understood as Sybaris in south Italy). Themistocles is said to have named two of his daughters after places in Magna Graecia, Italia and Sybaris[32] — a gesture that seemingly demonstrates a deep personal commitment to the region. Yet there is ample reason for skepticism. First, nothing indicates that Themistocles had any actual dealings in the West, or that Athens had any reason to make good on his threat. Second, neither Siris nor Sybaris, both in Italy's far south, had any clear connection to Neapolis. So even if Athens could be tied to either, there is no hint of interests farther north. Athens, like other cities, did cultivate a mythology of colonization in the West attached to the Age of Heroes, and was undeniably involved in some limited colonizing exploits elsewhere in the second half of the fifth century BCE. But none of the surviving accounts of events before the 450s gives the slightest hint that Athens was colonizing at that time.

I prefer the majority view that the Athenian "colonization" of Neapolis consisted of a modest, but important, injection of citizens in the mid-fifth century BCE, several decades after the founding of the walled city. This would have coincided, probably, with another important event: the arrival of the Athenian navarch Diotimos and his dedication of torch races to Parthenope. As we saw above, Lykophron and his scholiast Tzetzes are our principal sources for this information. Tzetzes adds that Diotimos went to Neapolis "when as an Athenian general he was at war with the Sikels."[33] The dates of Diotimos' embassy to Neapolis and of the Athenian engagement

31. *Histories* 8.62.
32. Plutarch, *Themistocles* 32.2.
33. Scholium of verse 733.

CHAPTER 2 ☗ THE GREEK CITY

with the Sikels (indigenous peoples of Sicily) have stirred ongoing controversy, but most scholars now would place the event somewhere between 454/3 BCE and 440/39 BCE.

In our present state of knowledge it would be unwise to refine this chronological penumbra surrounding the event. Still, it is remarkable — and rarely observed — that the penumbra intersects perfectly with the period of renewed activity attested by the ceramics recovered from the Chiatamone dump. At this moment, the old town of Parthenope was reconstituted after roughly half a century of dereliction. The synchronicity of events is compelling enough to suggest contingency. What could be a more natural than tying Diotimos' enhancement of the cult of Parthenope to the resuscitation of the old town to which she was inexorably linked by name and proximity? The torch races, whose first competitors were Diotimos' own mariners, served to ingratiate the Athenians to the goddess of their adopted home. In such a context a refounding of the old neighborhood of Parthenope — presumably to accommodate the new Athenian colonists — makes perfect sense as an attendant gesture of piety. Greek torch races were traditionally extraurban events, connecting significant places outside the walls to the city. In this case, whether or not the race began or ended in Neapolis, it may have traced a course through the old citadel town in order to create a ritual bond between it and the New City.

If we accept de Polignac's theory of Greek cult distribution, we may regard the revival of this cult, which seems to have been chthonic in nature, as a mediatory strategy to allay real or potential conflicts between the original Greek settlers and the newcomers — a middle ground in both the real and the figurative sense. As to the precise causes of Diotimos' visit, or the circumstances surrounding it, we remain utterly ignorant. Ettore Lepore frames the episode broadly within the context of a surge in Athenian diplomacy in the West from around 480 to 425 BCE, during which Athens sought, among other things, to diversify its grain imports. Indeed Athenians, who had no obvious reason to settle at Neapolis, must have done so in expectation of some mercantile advantage in return. One possible scenario behind this singular episode is that Athens, now the greatest sea power in the Mediterranean, sent immigrants to Neapolis to augment the Neapolitan navy in exchange for favored trading status. Both cities needed the other's resources. The acquisition of the island of Ischia had expanded not only Neapolis' territory, but also its strategic mandate. As an ascendant regional power with growing interests to defend, it would have felt pressed to upgrade its naval forces. And as the international conduit for Cumaean grain (Capua and its fertile territory were still in Etruscan hands), it held a valuable card in its dealings with Athens.

The steadiest indicators of an Athenian imprint on life at Neapolis are, on the one hand, the city's coinage, and on the other, imported Attic pottery. At various times in the fifth and fourth centuries BCE, the head of Athena, usually clad in an Attic helmet, appeared on Neapolitan coins.[34] Because Athena constitutes one of a very limited number of types on the city's coinage, she is generally thought to have held special significance for the residents of the city. The mere presence of Attic painted ceramics at Neapolis does not in itself say much about a relationship between that city and Athens. Attic export wares were immensely popular throughout Italy and Sicily in the sixth and fifth centuries BCE. What it suggests, however, is Neapolis' success as a *conduit* to this trade. Vast quantities of Attic ceramics that made their way to such places as Nola, Nuceria, Acerrae, Capua, and many inland sites further afield came either directly through Neapolis, or by secondary ports and routes within its sphere of control, such as Pozzuoli or the Sarno River — by which time the Neapolitans may have exacted tariffs at Capri. [See Commentary 2.2, p. 77]. The volume of closely datable Attic pottery increased throughout Magna Graecia and Sicily around 480 BCE and continued at this level until about 425 — precisely the time horizon of Athens' age of expansion in foreign relations. There followed a sharp decline attributable to the Peloponnesian War and, most pointedly, to the calamitous Athenian expedition to Sicily in 415. A modest recovery was seen in Campania after the turn of the fourth century BCE. Neapolis' contact with Athens surely vacillated over the fourth century, but its growing status as the entrepôt of choice in the region guaranteed it a profit on goods flowing in both directions.

34. See pp. 92–102.

CHAPTER 2 🏛 THE GREEK CITY

THE RISE OF THE SAMNITES
Between the three major Neapolitan events in the fifth century — the foundation, the arrival of the Athenians, and the Samnite invasion — the screen of narrative history goes dark. For social conditions in this period, and for grounding in the continuities of everyday life, we rely largely on the archaeological evidence, which will be surveyed presently. Now we turn to the third and final great event.

Throughout the period of Greek occupation, Campania was home to successive and overlapping populations of peoples who spoke a range of Italic dialects known collectively as Oscan. By the end of the fifth century BCE, they dominated large inland centers such as Capua, Acerrae, Nola, and Nuceria, as well as Cumae, Pompeii, and Surrentum (modern Sorrento), creating a virtually continuous crescent-shaped bloc around Neapolitan territory. Their various tribes (Sabelli, Campani, Osci, Pentri, Caudini, Hirpini, etc.) have proved impossible to distinguish, and we will make no attempt to do so here except when the primary sources warrant it. For the time being, we will use the umbrella term favored by modern scholars, "Samnites," to identify them as a totality — hardly adequate, admittedly, given the variations in tribal identities, fortunes, customs, and objectives that lurk in the umbrella's shadow. We cannot be sure whether the Samnites of this period regarded themselves loosely as a nation bound by ethnicity, rather like the Greeks. But in times of duress or opportunity, they acted with a cohesion and unity that bespeak strong bonds of kinship, language, and heritage transcending tribal differences.

The Samnites of northern Campania were deemed cohesive enough that our principal Greek sources for the events of this period, Diodoros of Sicily and Dionysios of Halikarnassos, considered them a single people, whom they called by the Italic name Campani.[35] Probably the region is named for them, rather than vice versa. The popular etymology claiming that this name meant originally "people of the fields" (from Latin *campus*) is fanciful, as Martin Frederiksen has argued. More likely it simply meant "people of Capua," a city whose name is of uncertain meaning but greater antiquity than is

---

35. Diodoros, *Historical Library* 12.31.1.

usually granted. Roman geographers distinguished the Campani, who settled in northern Campania, from the Samniti, who settled in the south. Following modern convention, I will make no distinction until we deal with the Samnite Wars, when the Campani severed ties with the Samnite League.

One proto-Samnite tribe, the Opici, had occupied the coastal territory of the Bay before the arrival of the Euboeans. They probably blend into the Cumaean *facies* of the Iron Age, the so-called *Fossakultur.* Their presence in the coastal territories seems to have been unobtrusive to the Greeks even as inland Campania gradually absorbed more of their ethnic brethren to fill the void created by the dwindling Etruscan presence. As early as the late sixth century BCE, Samnites were a distinct presence in the agricultural heartland of the region. When the Cumaean oligarchs were exiled to Capua at this time, they sought the assistance of mercenaries among them.[36] Thenceforth these peoples had a reputation as fierce and reliable horsemen for hire.[37]

Some kind of a modus vivendi among the Samnites, Etruscans, and Greeks existed for several decades in Campania after 474 BCE. But in 438, Diodoros reports,[38] "the nation of the Campani was formed, deriving their name from the fertility of the plain about them." Presumably this constituted an enduring alliance among the Samnite tribes in the region. Suddenly, in 423/2 BCE, they began to move against the lowland cities held by Greeks and Etruscans. That year they seized Capua, slaughtering its Etruscan inhabitants by treachery.[39] Two years later they took Cumae:

> 22. In the course of this year in Italy the Campani advanced against Cumae with a strong army, defeated the Cumaeans in battle, and destroyed the larger part of the opposing forces. And settling down to a siege, they launched a number

36. Dionysios of Halikarnassos, *Roman Antiquities* 7.10.3.
37. Diodoros, *Historical Library* 13.62.5; 13.80.4; 16.8.1.
38. Diodoros 12.31.1.
39. Livy, *History of Rome* 4.37.1–2, 10.38.6; Dionysios of Halikarnassos, *Roman Antiquities* 15.3.7.

CHAPTER 2 🏛 THE GREEK CITY

of assaults upon the city and took it by storm. They then plundered the city, sold into slavery the captured prisoners, and selected an adequate number of their own citizens. [Diodoros 12.76.4]

The Greek men were sold as slaves, and the Campani took the Greek women for wives.[40] But evidently not all the Cumaeans were killed or enslaved; according to Dionysios, an unspecified number of refugees were "received by the Neapolitans and made sharers of all their own blessings."[41] Their descendants were still living in Neapolis and hoping for restitution nearly a century later.

Lepore has interpreted Greek–Samnite relations in Campania from this time onward as a phenomenon inseparable from the Greek class struggle, which had already been expressed by the tyranny and uprising at Cumae. The core passage supporting this reading comes from Dionysios of Halikarnassos, which refers back to the event from the perspective of later developments, the run-up to the Second Samnite War in 327:

> **23.** Furthermore, when the Neapolitans had repulsed the Roman army, [the Samnites promised they] would not only recover Cumae for them, which the Campani had occupied... earlier after expelling the Cumaeans, but would also restore to their possessions those of the Cumaeans who still survived — these, when driven out of their own city, had been received by the Neapolitans and made sharers of all their own blessings — and they would also grant to the Neapolitans some of the land the Campani were then holding — the part without cities. [15.6.4]

For "the Cumaeans" Lepore reads the propertied aristocracy of Cumae. He reasons that the lower classes, if they had not been killed or sold into slavery at the outset, had nothing to lose from remaining in Cumaean territory. Accordingly, Neapolis inherited a population of disaffected aristocrats. A decade later, in 411 BCE, the Samnites of Capua and Cumae were curtailing grain exports, perhaps because of augmented demand within their own territories. Specifically, those

---

40. Strabo, *Geography* 5.4.4.
41. 15.6.4.

controlling Capua and Cumae refused to sell grain to the Romans, who were suffering a shortage.[42] Any such curtailment of trade, especially if it became a matter of policy, would have cut deeply into Neapolis' profits. Circumstances may thus have been ripe for unrest, perhaps even class warfare. It is this moment, Lepore believes, to which a passage from Strabo refers:

> 24. As the result of a dissension, [the Neapolitans] admitted some of the Campani as fellow-inhabitants, and thus they were forced to treat their worst enemies as their best friends, now that they had alienated their proper friends. This is disclosed by the names of their demarchs, for the earliest names are Greek only, whereas the later are Greek mixed with Campanian. [*Geography* 5.4.7]

As with Lutatius, we must look past a strong bias in Strabo's source here, but this time against Neapolis. Lepore argues that by 421/0, Neapolis would have been in the process of democratizing, like so many other Greek cities at the time — Syracuse, for example.[43] The influx of old-line plutocrats could have threatened the benefits that a robust trade with Athens and other Greek cities had bestowed upon a growing mercantile class. That trade was being compromised by the restriction of Campanian grain exports. Meanwhile, the Samnites were settling in Neapolitan territory, threatening to do unto Neapolis as they had done to Cumae. In effect, the merchant class, breaking with the aristocracy, aligned itself with the Samnites and facilitated the interlopers' peaceful entrance into Neapolitan territory and society: this is what Strabo meant by the Neapolitans alienating their proper friends. Although there was no dramatic siege or invasion, the subsequent Samnite imprint on country and city life was profound. From the viewpoint of the embittered aristocrats, the new residents were "worst enemies." But discretion being the better part of valor, they kept their own counsel and endured the inevitable.

In outline it is a sound hypothesis. Bitter class divisions had contributed to the long decline of Greek Cumae, and the great internal

---

42. Livy, *History of Rome* 4.52.6.
43. Diodoros, *Historical Library* 13.34.6.

CHAPTER 2 🏛 THE GREEK CITY

crisis at Neapolis in 327/6 BCE[44] may indicate continuity with the conditions that developed a century earlier. Circumstances suggest that the broad outlines of his hypothesis are correct — i.e., that the Samnites gained entrance to Neapolitan society not by main force but by participating in a broad coalition, probably including elements of the smallholding, merchant, and career military classes, which shared few of the oligarchs' interests. Neapolitan society had diversified over the decades since the city's founding by an earlier group of exiled oligarchs. Certainly the influx of Athenians during the maturity of Athens' democracy had contributed to this diversity. And Neapolis would have exhibited the natural cosmopolitanism expected of a major port city. Moreover — this must not be forgotten — Cumae had exchanged hands for good, and no longer provided comfort to the local Greek aristocracy. It was in league with the newcomers.

CITY ORGANIZATION AND ADMINISTRATION

Most of what can be said about the civic structure of Neapolis through the first century and a half of its existence must be extrapolated from much later evidence, particularly inscriptions from the Roman period. The urban institutions of this era show evidence of a conservatism that persists even through periods of social upheaval. That is not to say that the institutions did not change, even profoundly. But the evident continuity of nomenclature over many centuries is extraordinary. When every other Italian city had converted to the Roman municipal system with its *aediles, duumviri, quattuorviri,* and *decuriones,* Neapolis retained its *demarchoi, archontes, antarchontes,* and the puzzling *laukelarchoi.* Founded by an oligarchic party from Cumae, the city continued for centuries to shelter a reactionary demographic which, when confronted with an influx of Samnites and a more inclusive, quasi-participatory government, would have maintained a clannish, aristocratic insularity.

There is no evidence that Neapolis ever became a proper democracy. Its deliberative bodies probably were, at most, a compromise forced upon the aristocracy. The upper class was represented by the

---

44. See chapter 4.

boule or *synkletos,* the city council. This may well have been modeled on Cumae's *boule*.[45] The *archontes* would likely have provided some checks and balances against it. Lepore notes that in Rhegion (Reggio Calabria), another Chalkidian colony in Italy, *archontes* represented the mercantile and military class. Neapolis may have followed a similar pattern. If there was a popular assembly in the fifth century BCE, we have no clear evidence of it. But by 327/6 BCE an independent assembly was in place. At this time the city council consisted of "the men at the head of the state," and thus seems to have had priority in state decisions. But in the crucial dilemma over whether to back the Romans or the Samnites, it granted the assembly the decisive vote.[46] An inscription of 242 BCE found on the island of Kos refers to a resolution "of the archontes, the council, and the people" (*demos*) of Neapolis.[47] Doubtless the assembly of Neapolis resembled the *ekklesia* of many Greek democracies, or the *eskletos* of western cities like Rhegion, Syracuse, and Akragas. To the extent that the Samnites exercised political influence at Neapolis, they would have done so through the entities representing the mercantile, smallholding, and military interests of the territory. Each had a somewhat different ethnic makeup by the end of the fifth century BCE. The rural smallholders would have been dominated by Samnites; the navy, probably by Athenian colonists and their descendants.

In the Roman period, the demarch of Neapolis was a single magistrate.[48] By then, the post had become strictly honorific; even the emperor Hadrian held the title at one time.[49] But in the fifth century BCE the title *demarchos* referred to a group of leaders of *demoi* (demes), geographical districts of a city and its territory, who together formed a kind of council of mayors. Demarchates were rare in the Greek world. But as it happens, two of the best-known examples belonged to municipalities with close ties to Neapolis, Athens–Attica and Eretria on

45. Dionysios of Halikarnassos, *Roman Antiquities* 7.4.4, 7.5.3, 7.7.2–3.
46. Dionysios of Halikarnassos, *Roman Antiquities* 15.6.1–3. See chapter 4.
47. *SEG* 12.378.
48. *IGR* 1.452=*ILS* 6460; *AE* 1913, 134.
49. *Historia Augusta, Hadrian* 19.1.

CHAPTER 2 — THE GREEK CITY

Euboea. One or both surely influenced the Neapolitan model. As we have seen, Strabo[50] had access to lists of Neapolitan demarchs from before and after the Samnite invasion of the second half of the fifth century BCE. Campanian names began to creep into the lists after the invasion, indicating that Neapolis was becoming a genuinely bicultural city. We may postulate that the Samnites, who were principally farmers and herdsmen, established their power base, at least initially, on Neapolis' agricultural land, represented by its own demes.

Once we recognize that the Neapolitan demarchate provided some form of representative government to the population of the entire territory, and not just to the urban core, then we can understand how important it was to the ascendancy of Samnite political power. The lack of direct evidence for the existence of Neapolitan demes stems from the lack of inscriptions dated before the great reorganization of the city in the 90s and 80s BCE. At that time, the demes probably were dissolved or converted into Roman-style *pagi* and the demarchate compressed into a single honorific title. But in the fifth and fourth centuries BCE, demarchs represented real constituencies, many of them nonelite or Samnite, and wielded real power.

Apart from geography, the principal units of civic self-definition in Greek Neapolis were the phratries ("brotherhoods"), identity groups organized around families or religious cults [Commentary 2.4, pp. 79–81]. They had proprietary gods, the *theoi phretores*, some of which were ancestral, others broadly canonical. In the early centuries most Neapolitan citizens would have belonged to one of these organizations, some of which seem to have cherished long histories extending far back beyond the beginnings of Neapolis, even Parthenope, to the Euboean homeland, to which several refer onomastically. By the mid-first century BCE, all other phratries in Italian towns of Greek origin had disappeared, presumably engulfed by the voting tribes of Rome. Only at Neapolis did they persist. At least, that is what we conclude from Varro's taciturn definition of a phratry as "a part of the people, as at Neapolis even now."[51] They lasted into the third century CE at least.

50. 5.4.7. See Reading 24 above.
51. *Latin Language* 5.8a.

ARCHAEOLOGY

So far, the limited opportunities for excavation in Naples have yielded no monumental civic buildings, inscriptions, or meaningful household assemblages from the early phases of occupation. The city's coinage is a special case, since most of it has been found elsewhere. We will discuss it in chapter 3. We are left, then, with two domains of archaeological data to evoke the life and times of pre-Roman Neapolis. The first, ceramics, can be divided into two kinds: utilitarian and fine wares. The second is architecture, particularly that of tombs, the city wall, and the fragmentary remains of a few utilitarian structures. The two domains are intertwined inextricably, and in many ways. Pottery is studied principally as a diagnostic tool for dating other archaeological features and for identifying and differentiating certain cultural practices. But the fine wares adorned with figural painting are the subject of an entire subfield of art history. This analysis, particularly of individual painters' styles and preferred subject matter, often allows for unparalleled precision of dating. The patient and careful work of ceramics specialists serves as the foundation upon which we build, on the one hand, relative and absolute chronologies, and on the other, patterns of cultural diffusion.

The only prominent traces of Greek Neapolis identified in the modern city fabric are the defensive wall and the orthogonal street grid [see Fig. 2.1]. The grid has numerous gaps, and from its anomalies many untested hypotheses have been drawn. In the 1950s Mario Napoli hypothesized that Neapolis was inhabited in phases, the earliest zone of occupation being the "acropolis," Caponapoli in the northwest of the walled city. But the continuing discovery of abundant quantities of sixth-century-BCE pottery in the foundation trenches of almost every excavated segment of the city wall has demonstrated that virtually the entire area of Neapolis was inhabited before its formal urbanization. So in the early fifth century BCE, when that urbanization was put into effect and the city was laid out on a grid within a defensive wall, many potential residents were already available to occupy it, augmented by the influx of Cumaean and Ischian refugees and the few remaining denizens of Parthenope. There is no Neapolitan analogue of Pompeii, where the street grid was plainly laid out in multiple phases. Neapolis' grid is evidently all

CHAPTER 2 ☗ THE GREEK CITY

of a piece, and it appears to be contemporary with the wall. In the extreme elongation of the city blocks the grid most resembles the layouts of cities formed in the sixth century BCE.

That said, the city was not built in a day. Nor was it fully peopled instantaneously thereafter. If a plague afflicted the region at the time of its foundation, as Lutatius reports, the expected completion date and occupation rate may have been compromised. Many segments of the wall have been investigated over the centuries, of which a few — mostly from a second phase of the late fourth century BCE — are visible today, as at Piazza Bellini in the far west [Figs. 2.1; 2.5]. The first phase of the wall went up in sections over the course of one or two decades; in places, its compass was expanded by the later rebuilding. The oldest segment yet investigated, along the Vico Sopramuro a Forcella at the city's eastern end, has been dated by Giampaola and D'Agostino between 500 and 480 BCE [see Fig. 2.1]. The fifth-century wall inscribed a natural plateau that slopes upward to Caponapoli in the northwest, which already accommodated a cult center. To some extent this sanctuary may have determined the position, size, and shape of the city that grew up to host it, rather in the manner of

Fig. 2.5. Greek fortification walls at Piazza Bellini. Photo: R. Taylor.

67

Pompeii's Triangular Forum and sanctuary of Apollo. The wall consists of large orthostates of friable local tuff that in lower areas form a double curtain, and on escarpments a retaining structure made accessible on the city side, where necessary, by cut-and-fill terracing. Inwardly projecting spurs set at regular intervals create a bond with the rubble and earth fill. The fourth-century-BCE augmentation, of horizontally laid ashlars of denser tuff, is generally built against the older wall, but in places it follows a new path. It is recognizable by the prominent masons' marks on almost every block [see Fig. 2.5]. The gates and some angles of the wall seem to have been turreted. Emanuele Greco envisions a total of seven gates, but probably there were more.

The orthogonal street grid, still visible in the modern city overlying it, follows the classic Hippodameian principles so commonly encountered in Greek colonies [see Fig. 2.1]. It consists of three east-west thoroughfares *(plateiai)* arranged 185 meters apart (600 Italian feet, or one stade) intersecting orthogonally with at least 21 narrower north–south streets *(stenopoi)* set at intervals of 35 meters (about 114 Italian feet). Although the stade is clearly the base unit for determining the length of the blocks, the ratio of axial length to width, 1:5.25, is not neatly resolved.

Another anomaly in comparison to other Greek orthogonal city plans is the narrow width of the *plateiai*. Today the modern avenues overlying them are only about 6 meters wide, whereas in antiquity they typically measured 12 to 20 meters across. Greco hypothesizes that the current dimensions mark the width of the ancient street only, whereas the sidewalks, which may have broadened these avenues by as much as 10 meters, were engulfed in the medieval period. Quite apart from the disposition of the city wall, which follows the physical topography of the site, the single most salient feature of the grid is the southernmost surviving *plateia*, known today informally as Spaccanapoli ("Naples-Splitter," Via Scura–Croce–S. Biagio dei Librai–Forcella). It aligns perfectly with Castel S. Elmo, the fortress on the summit of an imposing hill west of the ancient city [Figs. 2.1; 2.6]. Clearly the top of this hill served as a visual focal point and surveying benchmark for the Greek city. From this definitive point of departure, the best that can be said is that the surveying is approximate. For

CHAPTER 2 ☖ THE GREEK CITY

Fig. 2.6. View of Castel S. Elmo from Spaccanapoli. Photo: Kalamita / Wikimedia Commons CC BY-SA 2.0. Modified.

example, the second and third *plateiai* converge perceptibly toward the eastern end.

The intensive investigative work of the 1980s in preparation for the *Napoli antica* exhibit included an exhaustive reexamination of all the scattered evidence for ancient burials at Neapolis after centuries of often careless excavation and indifferent record keeping. The results have brought a chaotic body of evidence into sharper focus. The known tomb complexes of Neapolis are clustered around the city walls and along the ancient roads leading to the city [Figs. 2.1; 2.7]. Rosaria Borriello, Angela Pontrandolfo, Giuseppe Vecchio, and others have revealed four principal clusters, each of them accumulating around a core of fifth- and fourth-century-BCE tombs. The first, and

Fig. 2.7. Excavations at the necropolis of Sta. Teresa. Plate 4 from A. de Jorio, Metodo per rinvenire e frugare i sepolcri degli antichi, Naples 1824.

oldest, is on the east side, centered on the fifth-century tombs under Castel Capuano. It is the only group of the four that can definitively be called a necropolis. The other clusters — to the north, northwest, and west — are less coherent and somewhat younger; their oldest tombs are from the fourth century BCE. Another feature, a series of tombs extending southwest toward Pizzofalcone, is equally striking. These trace the course of the highway running between Neapolis and Parthenope. One of them, a rare cremation burial at S. Tomasso d'Aquino, dates from the fifth century BCE. Since the publication of the tombs, a burial ground with no local parallel has come to light in the excavations of the Duomo Metropolitana station just outside the city wall on the south side of town. Dating to the late fifth century BCE, it comprises burials of small children, either cremated or inhumed in clay vessels. Even the complete skeleton of a fetus was found carefully deposited in a jar.

Strikingly, both the oldest sector of the city wall and the oldest tombs are at the eastern extremity of the city. If we suppose that Neapolis was populated incrementally, then it would appear that its earliest population clustered at this end. The time horizon for the

CHAPTER 2 🏛 THE GREEK CITY

earliest segment of wall is 500–480 BCE, perhaps toward the later end; that of the earliest tombs at Castel Capuano, 475–450 BCE. The time lag seems unobjectionable. On the one hand, we are dealing with relatively formalized burial zones that would have developed only after the city of the living was established. The New City would not have been inhabited immediately upon commencement of construction, of course, but only after some years of work. On the other hand, earlier burials *must* have taken place somewhere in the vicinity, due to the sheer abundance of the living who occupied the *centro storico* through the final years of the sixth century BCE. Either we have not found these burials, or (just as likely) they are too scattered and too poor in diagnostic ceramics to be identified or dated. As with most colonies, we should envision the residents in a kind of limbo throughout the city's planning and construction period, during which the colonists-to-be lived provisionally, perhaps in temporary housing in the surrounding countryside, with few opportunities to accumulate or display wealth.

Yet prosperity, if not wealth, is in full evidence even in the earliest known tombs of the fifth century BCE. A typical unit held a plain tuff-slab sarcophagus; one or two achromous amphorettes of local production; red-figure *skyphoi*, either Attic imports or south Italian; black-glaze *kylikes;* and, sporadically, red-figure vases of various sizes and shapes, some Attic. Beginning in the tombs of the third quarter of the century, a different standard emerges. Now another vase type, the red-figure *krater* (wine-mixing bowl) begins to appear, first in association with the amphorette, and later with a *kylix* (shallow drinking cup) or *stamnos* (fineware storage vessel). Unfortunately, the arrangement of the tomb assemblages at Castel Capuano was never recorded; but a similar tomb on Via Cirillo was found intact [see Fig. 2.1]. Here the *krater* stood at the feet of the deceased, and a *kylix* and *pyxis* (cosmetics box) were deposited inside. This arrangement — with emphasis placed on a lone *krater* — is not seen in Greek tombs of the fifth century BCE. But it is well attested at Etruscan and Samnite centers — most notably Caudium, lying between Capua and Beneventum.

Assuming the evidence has not been over-interpreted (always a danger with small samples), we seem to be confronting a Samnite tradition that was selectively introduced into Neapolis even before the regional invasion of the 420s BCE. The nature and significance of this tradition are hard to assess. But the more we learn about Greek colonization, especially in port cities, the less this kind of hybridity should surprise us. The emphasis is clearly on the consumption of wine, and one thinks of the widespread south-Italian attachment to the cult of Dionysos, especially in funerary contexts. But it must also be admitted that more purely Greek assemblages feature plenty of Dionysiac imagery too, and frequently include wine cups. Attic wares completely ceased to be imported in the final decade and a half of the fifth century BCE. As these imports were revived around 400 BCE, they faced increasing competition from a now robust trade of home-grown wares within Italy. Quantities of this "Italiote" ware, much of it originating in Campania, naturally showed up in Neapolitan tombs.

It is worth considering whether the newly demarcated territory of Neapolis had been dominated by non-Greeks even through Cumae's peak years. On the future site of Neapolis itself, Etruscans, Osco-Samnite peoples, and Greeks may have rubbed elbows in a classic multilingual and multiethnic middle-ground community after the manner of Emporion on the Spanish coast, which diversified as it expanded from an island *palaipolis* to a mainland *neapolis*. But the high Hellenic tone of the Cumaean revanchists in the 480s BCE, followed by the influx of Osco-Samnite Campanians in the 420s, may have unsettled this balance, leading to the balkanization of rival ethnic communities we will examine in chapter 4.

Despite the vicissitudes of the late fifth century BCE, buildings — not just tombs — began to accumulate outside the walls, at least toward the shore. Among these is a large orthogonal structure of uncertain function excavated at the Duomo Metropolitana station, which apparently intersects both in time and space with the child burials. Built on foundations that alternate between stone ashlars and rubble fill, it was modified later with partition walls and several terracotta wells. In the mid-second century BCE it was destroyed and

CHAPTER 2 🏛 THE GREEK CITY

backfilled to create a more monumental space eventually destined for a ceremonial district associated with the Roman imperial games.[52]

From the late fifth through the fourth century BCE rural settlements grew up throughout Neapolis' territory, each with its own necropolis. A number of these were hastily excavated over the course of the twentieth century — most notably, Ponticelli and Caivano. These too were subjected to a reassessment in advance of the *Napoli antica* exhibit. A careful analysis of the assemblages has led Gabriella d'Henry and Daniela Giampaola to conclude that they resemble those found in the territories of Samnite Capua and Atella, as well as indigenous Campanian sanctuaries, much more closely than those of the tombs clustered around Neapolis. Here the evidence of parallels is more substantial than at Castel Capuano. Numerous types of ceramics, as well as a particular form of fibula, find direct analogues in Samnite contexts. Every bit as distinctive as this noted difference between center and periphery is the relative uniformity of the peripheral finds. For now, at least, it seems that Lepore's vision of greater Samnite homogeneity in the hinterland than in Neapolis itself has been vindicated. It is against this horizon that we must reexamine the next great event that shook Neapolis, the Samnite Wars.

For a century the situation remained thus: the Greeks of Neapolis living in an uneasy balance with their more numerous Samnite neighbors — holding their island possessions of Capri and Ischia, giving and taking as necessary, but maintaining a cultural difference. Over this time they remained "a friend and ally" of the Samnites by means of "many great services."[53] Velleius Paterculus remarked on this unique situation, comparing the city's character to that of Cumae, the Greek city called "Wave" that had been totally engulfed by the Samnite tsunami:

> **25.** The remarkable and unbroken loyalty to the Romans of both these cities [Cumae and Neapolis] makes them well worthy of their repute and of their charming situation. The

52. See pp. 129, 211–18.
53. Dionysios of Halikarnassos, *Roman Antiquities* 15.8.3.

Neapolitans, however, continued the careful observance of their ancestral customs; the Cumaeans, on the other hand, were changed in character by the proximity of their Oscan neighbors. The extent of their walls at the present day serves to reveal the greatness of these cities in the past. [*Compendium of Roman History* 1.4.2]

The defensive walls of Neapolis may indeed have expressed greatness, but their extensive reinforcement in the fourth century BCE also conveys a sense of insecurity and vulnerability. Whether this came about as the result of a crisis, or merely of a policy of prudence, we do not know. By the final quarter of the century, a new political conflict would give the Neapolitans cause to welcome the reinforcements, but it would also mark the beginnings of an inexorable realignment of power in Italy that no walls could withstand.

CHAPTER 2 🏛 THE GREEK CITY

Commentary 2.1: A Rhodian Connection?

Strabo is one of our principal sources for the "majority" account of the Cumaean origins of the proto-Neapolis. Yet he himself, much later in his *Geography*, turns the whole foundation narrative on its head:

26. It is also related of the Rhodians that they have been prosperous by sea, not merely since the time when they founded the present city, but that even many years before the establishment of the Olympian Games they used to sail far away from their homeland to insure the safety of their people. Since that time, also, they have sailed as far as Iberia; and there they founded Rhodes, of which the Massaliotes later took possession; among the Opici they founded Parthenope; and among the Daunians they, along with the Koans, founded Elpiai. [*Geography* 14.2.10]

This is an entirely alien tradition, attributing the foundation of Parthenope to Rhodes rather than Cumae. The Opici were a Samnite people dwelling in Campania at the time of colonization. Apart from Strabo's testimony, there is very little real evidence of a Rhodian presence in this area. Some eighth-century-BCE Rhodian pottery has been found on Ischia, but that is to be expected, given the wide diffusion of export wares from Rhodes. The origins of the Neapolitan cult of Aphrodite Euploia have also been sought by way of this island, but the hypothesis seems to be driven largely by an urge to justify Strabo. Nor should we countenance Pugliese Carratelli's tenacious theory that the cult of the Sirens arrived from Anatolia by way of Rhodes. There is simply no reason to prefer this "Rhodocentric" account to the earlier one in Strabo's *Geography* that professes a Euboean–Cumaean foundation.

Filippo Càssola offers an ingenious but ultimately inadequate solution. According to Ptolemy,[54] Parthenope appears among a list of Tyrrhenian *islands*. Within the sequence, it appears with three others in the Bay of Naples: Ischia, Procida, and Capri [see Fig. 1.2]. Càssola identifies Parthenope as Nesis (Nisida), the only remaining island of

54. *Geography* 3.1.69.

any size in the vicinity that is not included in Ptolemy's list. He would have the early Rhodians occupying and naming the island, then moving northeast to the promontory on the mainland, which they gave the same name; whereupon the Cumaeans simply applied the existing name to this place when they colonized it.

Really, there is no way to excuse Strabo's inconsistency, but one may at least try to trace the origins of the minority tradition. Flavio Raviola accepts the historicity of a Cumaean foundation without any trace of a Rhodian presence. But he suggests that at roughly the same time that Timaios and Lykophron were transmitting this tradition — the late fourth or early third century BCE — the Rhodians were consciously introducing an alternate mythology. This was done at the height of their power in the Mediterranean, and they were seeking to burnish the reputation of Rhodes in the distant Age of Heroes before the great wave of colonization in the Geometric and Archaic periods. The idea was to apply an extremely early Rhodian pedigree to far-flung Greek settlements whose origins were genuinely very old — though not so old as Rhodes sought to claim — and whose origins had been blurred by a discontinuity in occupation. But because proto-Neapolis was back in business at this time (as Livy makes clear by his references to Palaepolis in 327 BCE), Rhodian mythmakers had to be especially crafty. Rather than focus on the physical settlement, they adduced a vaporous *construct* of a town and gave it the name Parthenope. Rather than anchor it in space, they merely situated it "among the Opici."

It is surely right to attribute the tradition of early Rhodian colonization to Rhodes itself. But in the particulars, Raviola's hypothesis is too refined. Strabo's carelessness with his source material about the Bay of Naples is rather obvious, and it is simply impossible to extract such subtleties from it as a floating Rhodian construct of Parthenope that was kept carefully distinct from the existing settlement. Neapolis in the fourth century BCE, with its pan-Mediterranean connections, was hardly as remote or mysterious as Raviola suggests; and its Cumaean origins surely were widely known and hard to deny. The Rhodian tradition was probably much earlier.

Commentary 2.2: *Neapolis and Capri*

The circumstances by which Neapolis gained control of the island of Capri are unknown. Yet the relationship forged between the island and the city must have been fundamental, for it was sealed in myth. Telon, the hero of Capri and ancestor of the Teleboi, was the husband of Sebethis, nymph of the Neapolitan river of the same name.[55] Among their most illustrious descendants were Oibalos, and, through him, the Dioscuri,[56] whose cult was popular in Neapolis. It is generally believed that Neapolis inherited the island from Cumae at about the time it acquired Ischia in the years following 474 BCE. Our first definitive evidence that the island lay under Neapolis' jurisdiction comes from a Roman source. Suetonius[57] notes that Augustus acquired the island from Neapolis in exchange for Ischia (which had been in Roman hands probably since the days of Sulla). We may reasonably suppose that Cumae had taken control of Capri during a period of Euboean expansion, perhaps around the time that Parthenope was being founded in the late eighth or early seventh century BCE. The island was strategic from both a military and an economic standpoint. Serving as the southern doorpost to the Bay of Naples, it was an excellent lookout and staging point for policing the Bay and watching the coast to its south. It was also a convenient customs station at a bottleneck along the coastal shipping lane.

Understandably, given its strategic location, Capri had historical and mythic associations with piracy — all the more reason why any dominant force in the Bay should want to control it. Alfonso Mele submits that the names Telon and Teleboi, themselves a mythic clan of pirates, are derived from the Greek *telos*, "tax" — suggesting that

---

55. Virgil, *Aeneid* 7.734.
56. Hesiod, fr. 199 Merkelbach-West.
57. *Augustus* 92. See Reading 7 above.

Neapolis or its Euboean predecessors had long used the island as a customs station for coastal commerce.

Commentary 2.3: The Origins of Pozzuoli

Before the construction of a harbor at Ostia, the city known to the Romans as Puteoli (Pozzuoli today), lying on the Bay between Neapolis and Baiae, had the greatest port on the entire Tyrrhenian coast of Italy. Known to Greeks as Dikaiarcheia, the place was occupied by about 650 BCE. In its early life it must have fallen under the control of Cumae, whose territory encompassed it. According to Statius, Pozzuoli was founded under the auspices of the Cumaean Apollo.[58] Strabo[59] claims that it was a port serving Cumae. Dionysios[60] confirms this, noting that Cumae under Greek control was "mistress of the most convenient havens round about Misenum." Yet there is no report of the town's formal status before 530 BCE. In that year, Samians founded a settlement here. (Thus says the chronicle of St. Jerome; dates on either side of this have also been proposed). Only then, evidently, did the place acquire the utopian name Dikaiarcheia, "City of just rule." Most likely, the settlers were Samian aristocrats fleeing Polykrates, who had installed himself as tyrant at Samos. The mathematician and philosopher Pythagoras, one of their fellow exiles, fled to Kroton in the far south of Italy; but his influence has been seen in the naming of the new settlement. Evidently the town never had the independent status of a *polis*. Fausto Zevi suggests that it was always controlled by Cumae, which had ties to Samos before the tyranny of Polykrates. Accordingly, the "just rule" was a mirror image of the oligarchy in place at Cumae, and must have been cut short upon the ascent of Cumae's own tyrant, Aristodemos, in 505/4.

Dikaiarcheia remains a puzzle. It is absent from the narratives of the Samnite invasion, nor can its existence be consistently verified thereafter until its refounding as

58. *Silvae* 3.5.74–75.
59. *Geography* 5.4.6.
60. *Roman Antiquities* 7.3.2.

CHAPTER 2 🏛 THE GREEK CITY

Puteoli by the Romans in 194 BCE. Archaeology has not verified a significant Greek presence there after the Archaic period. Hannibal unsuccessfully tried to seize the port,[61] but we learn little of its condition at the time. The prosaic new name of the Roman colony, Puteoli, refers to the local hot springs or fumaroles, revealing no trace of an earlier identity. Zevi is most struck by the evident lack of a local mythology or collective memory:

In a land like the Parthenopean bay, notable for its mythological density and the confluence of all legends of the West, from the Gigantomachy to the return of Herakles, to the adventures of Odysseus and those of Aeneas, where there is no important city or site that does not find a way to be connected to myth, a divine ancestor, or founder hero, Dikaiarcheia possesses not a single tradition that elucidates its antiquity or origins.

That is an anomaly indeed; and it probably indicates that Dikaiarcheia, feeble in life, was hastened to an early death. Because this region is prone to geological upheavals, I conjecture that the town was abandoned gradually or suddenly, for the same reason and at the same time as nearby Ischia (in the decades around 474 BCE), and was not recolonized until the Roman period. If so, then we may suppose that some of the refugees resettled at Neapolis.

Commentary 2.4: The Phratries of Neapolis

Twelve phratries are attested in Neapolitan inscriptions. Six are clan groups taking the form of patronymics (the stem ends in *-id* or *-d*) that refer back to a founding father. These are the *Eumeleidai, Eunostidai, Euereidai, Kretondai, Pankleidai,* and *Theotadai*. Only the first three hold any meaning for us. The clan of Eumelos, a Thessalian hero, may have come to Cumae (Greek Kyme) by way of the Euboean colony in Aeolia also named Kyme.[62] He was worshiped as a hero at Neapolis even in Roman times.[63] The cult of the Dioscuri,

61. Livy, *History of Rome* 24.12.4–5; 13.6–7.
62. *Vita Homeri Herodotea* p. 193 Allen.
63. *IG* 14.715.

classed among the founding gods of Neapolis by Statius,[64] was strong among the Eumeleidai. Eunostos was a hero of Tanagra in eastern Boeotia, which had close cultural ties to its neighbor Euboea. Eueres is a name given to several figures in mythology. Elena Miranda, who identified his eponymous phratry after reexamining a published inscription,[65] suggests that the founder of this clan was either a son of Herakles by that name, or (more likely) Eueres son of Pterelaos, king of the Teleboi–Taphioi.[66] Telon was the hero of Capri [See Commentary 2.2, p. 77.] and his clan, the piratical Teleboi, were closely associated with the Bay of Naples.

Four other phratries bear the names of gods: the *Aristaioi, Artemisioi, Hermaioi,* and (possibly) *Herakleidai.* Usually classed with the religious phratries, the latter properly belongs to the previous group; for it is a clan phratry, meaning "Sons of Herakles." All of the eponymous gods listed here — Aristaios, Artemis, Hermes, Herakles — were widely worshiped in the Greek world, and their names alone carry little explanatory value. These theophoric phratries (at least the first three) probably began not as clans, but as cult groups. The final two names are ethnics: *Euboeis* and *Kymaioi* (Euboeans and Cumaeans). Somewhat puzzlingly, their names refer globally to the citizenry from which the phratries were drawn. The Kymaioi are believed to have consisted of exiles driven from Cumae in 421/0 BCE. Why a single phratry styled itself as Euboeans we do not know, but it may reference the "Chalkidians" Strabo[67] recognizes as cofounders of Neapolis along with the Ischians and Athenians. Such a partitioned nomenclature is not unique to Neapolitan phratries. Argos, for example, had forty-eight phratries in the fifth century BCE, some named for local heroes, others for tribes, and still others for Greek peoples such as the Achaioi and Doriadai (Achaeans and Dorians). These latter were partitioned across the four Argive tribes.

64. 4.8.52–53.
65. *IG* 14.730.
66. Apollodoros, *Voyage of the Argo* 2.4.6.
67. 5.4.7. See Reading 14 above.

CHAPTER 2 🏛 THE GREEK CITY

That brings us back to the phratry of the Herakleidai. This name sometimes referred generically to Dorians or Peloponnesians, the seed of Herakles. As such, it would represent an otherwise unattested Peloponnesian element in the population of Neapolis. But the influence of Argos may be evident here in a different way. The myth of the Heraklids was home-grown in the Argolid, but it would also have resonated powerfully with the displaced Cumaean oligarchs. It relates how the descendants of Herakles were denied their rightful succession to the Argive crown and exiled for over a century. Deprived of the kingship first by their cousin Eurystheus and then by a plague, the Heraklids consulted the oracle at Delphi, who advised that they should return to power after "three crops." Originally misinterpreted as years, these "crops" turned out to be full generations. Their tale of unjust exile, pestilence, oracular quest, and long-delayed but triumphant return would have appealed to the likely founders of Neapolis, the exiled aristocracy of Cumae, just as it did to the returning Messenians in the 360s BCE after the end of their 300-year exile.[68] Is it mere coincidence that around the time of the overthrow of the tyranny, Cumae issued a new coin type representing symbols of two of Herakles' conquests — the Nemean Lion and the Erymanthian Boar — or that the tusks of this boar went on display in the Cumaean sanctuary of Apollo?

---

68. Pausanias 4.27.5–7.

REFERENCES

Prehistory of Naples and region: Dall'Osso 1906; Pugliese Carratelli 1967; Buchner et al. 1978; D'Agostino 1979; Marzocchella 1980, 1985; Monti 1980: 29–46; various articles in *Magna Grecia* (1983); Bietti Sestieri 1984: 55–65, 85–92; Albore Livadie 1985a, 1985b, 1999; Damiani et al. 1985; Marazzi and Re 1985; Peroni 1985; Marazzi and Tusa 1991; Ridgway 1992: 1–10, 122–38; 2004; Napoli 1997 [1959]: 37; Papadopoulos 1997; Nijboer et al. 1999–2000; De Caro 2002; Monaco 2002: 93; Wijngaarden 2002; Nava 2006a; Cervasio 2007; Vecchio et al. 2007; Salvatore and Nava 2011: 708–9; Sampaolo 2012: 1328–29, 1334–36. **Problems with Iron Age chronology:** Nijboer et al. 1999–2000; Ridgway 2004; Nijboer and Plicht 2008. **Greek colonization, foundation myths, and identity:** Bérard 1957: 301–508; Malkin 1987; 1998; 2002; Dougherty 1993; 1998; Snodgrass 1994; de Polignac 1995: 89–127; Hall 1997; Lomas 2004; Mele 2007b; 2009b; 2014. **Early Greeks in the West:** Bérard 1959; Dunbabin 1968; Johannowsky 1978; Monti 1980: 47–54; Ridgway 1985; 1990; 1992; D'Agostino 1990; Graham 1990; Purcell 1990; Greco 1992: 3–96; various articles in *Apoikia* (1994) and *Euboica* (1998); Osborne 1998; Mele 2007b; 2014. **Odysseus, other Greek heroes, and Italian identity:** Bérard 1959: 303–22; Malkin 1998: 156–209; 2002. **Early Ischia, Cumae, and the Bay:** Pugliese Carratelli 1952a; 1979; La Rocca 1974-1975; Buchner 1975; 1977; 1985; 1987; Johannowsky 1975; Ridgway 1979; 1985; 1990; 1992; 2004; Monti 1980: 54–121; Frederiksen 1984: 54–84; Tocco Sciarelli 1985; Di Sandro 1986; Giangiulio 1986: 135–54; Gras 1986; Zevi 1987; Buchner and Ridgway 1993; Coldstream 1994; De Caro 1994; Scatozza Höricht 2007; D'Agostino 2009; 2011; Mele 2009a; 2014: 1–139; Munzi and Brun 2011. **Coastline and harbor:** Giampaola et al. 2005; 2006; Amato et al. 2009; Carsana et al. 2009; Di Donato et al. 2018. **Pizzofalcone necropolis and Parthenope:** Cardona 1880; De Petra 1905; Pirro 1905; De Petra and Capasso 1912; Napoli 1952; 1967b: 379–84; Pugliese Carratelli 1952a: 243–51; 1967; De Caro 1974; 1985; Frederiksen 1984: 85–87; Giangiulio 1986; Raviola 1990; 1991; 1995: 147–48; 1997. **Chiatamone:** Giampaola and D'Agostino 2005: 51–52. **Phaleros:** Trowbridge 1938; Ciaceri 1966 [1924]: 1.328–30; Càssola 1986: 64–65; Giangiulio 1986: 135–38; Raviola 1990: 57–60;

CHAPTER 2 ☖ THE GREEK CITY

1995: 58–60; 1997. **Cults of the Sirens, Parthenope, and Ino–Leukotheia:** De Petra 1908; Peterson 1919: 174–81, 302–6; Pugliese Carratelli 1952b; 1967: 119–22; Sbordone 1967a; Frederiksen 1984: 105; Giangiulio 1986: 110–40; Breglia Pulci Doria 1987; Raviola 1990; 1995: 173–81; Greco 1992; Napoli 1997 [1959]: 159–65; Federico and Miranda 1998: 388–89; Mele 2009b; 2014: 151–60; Taylor 2014. **Other Greek cults at Neapolis:** Peterson 1919: 165–73, 182–206; Napoli 1967c: 417–32; 1997 [1959]: 137–57; Pugliese Carratelli 1979: 227–28; Miranda 1985a: 392–95; 1990–1995: 1.11–31, 52–54, 2.42–43; Giangiulio 1986: 101–16, 140–54. **The sanctuary at S. Aniello a Caponapoli:** Borriello and De Simone 1985; D'Onofrio and D'Agostino 1985; 1987; Carafa 2008: 48–52; Greco 2013. **The foundation and early history of Neapolis:** Lepore 1967a; 1990; Napoli 1967b: 384–98; 1997 [1959]: 21–31; Frederiksen 1984: 90–95, 104–7; 1986; Mele 1985; 2009b; Càssola 1986; Raviola 1995: 151–207; Arthur 2002: 2–6; Giampaola and D'Agostino 2005; Cerchiai 2010; Mele 2014: 141–96. **Tyranny at Cumae:** Frederiksen 1984: 95–99; Luraghi 1994: 79–118; Raviola 1995: 153–64; Mele 2009a; 2014: 97–135. **The Etruscans in Campania:** Frederiksen 1984: 117–33. **Syracusans in the Tyrrhenian:** Dunbabin 1968: 410–34; De Sensi Sestito 1981; Asheri 1988: 766–75; 1992: 147–56; Luraghi 1994: 273–373. **Syracuse and the acquisition of Ischia** Lepore 1967a: 150–64; Monti 1980: 122–27; Càssola 1986: 58–60; Raviola 1995: 100–23, 181–95. **Athens and Neapolis:** Lepore 1967a: 170–91; 1990: 293–96; Mattingly 1969; Rutter 1979: 5–6, 49; Frederiksen 1984: 103–7; Cantilena 1985b: 353–55; Càssola 1986: 62–65; Maurizi 1993–95; Raviola 1993; 1995: 59, 67–73, 87–91, 166, 169; Mariotta 2003; Mele 2007a; 2014: 180–87. **Territory of early Neapolis:** Lepore 1967a: 141–51; Johannowsky 1985a. **Samnites and early Neapolis:** Lepore 1967b; 1985a; Frederiksen 1984: 137–39, 144; Càssola 1986: 65–73; D'Agostino 1992. **City walls and grid:** Santoro 1984; Greco 1985b; 1986: 199–208; Vecchio 1985b; D'Onofrio and Agostino 1987: 11–28; Pani Ermini 1994; Scarpati et al. 1996; Napoli 1997 [1959]: 33–110; Giampaola 2004; De Caro and Giampaola 2008. **Phratries and political institutions:** Guarducci 1938; Latte 1941; De Martino 1952; Sartori 1953: 42–55; Napoli 1960; 1967c: 433–35; 1997 [1959]: 167–81; Lepore 1967b: 202–16; Pinsent

1969; Roussel 1976: 91–157; Càssola 1986: 51–55; Mele 1985: 105; 2014: 177–78; Miranda 1988b; 1990–95: 1.61–74; Beloch 1989 [1890]: 55–58; Lomas 1993: 147–51; 1995; Raviola 1995: 164–73; Bresson 2013. **Demes of Eretria and Athens:** Wallace 1947; Cairns 1984; 1986; Whitehead 1986; Knoepfler 2017. **The physical remains of early Greek Neapolis:** Baldassarre 1985: 122–27; D'Onofrio 1985; Greco 1985b; 1986; Vecchio 1985b; D'Onofrio and D'Agostino 1987: 11–28, 206–11; Beloch 1989 [1890]: 82–86; Napoli 1997 [1959]: 33–110; Giampaola and D'Agostino 2005; Giampaola and Carsana 2007. **Tombs of Greek Neapolis and its territory:** Ruggiero 1888: passim; Colonna 1898: passim; De Petra 1898; Pesce 1935; De Caro 1974; 1985; D'Henry et al. 1985; Baldassarre 1985: 123–25; 1998; 2010a; Borriello et al. 1985a; 1985b; Greco Pontrandolfo and Vecchio 1985; Morel 1986b: 309–10; Pontrandolfo 1986. **Rhodes and Neapolis:** Pugliese Carratelli 1952a: 245, 248; 1952b; 1967: 116–22; Frederiksen 1984: 86–87; Càssola 1996: 41–46; Giangiulio 1986: 110–13; Raviola 1990; 2005: 29, 38–46, 209–17; Mele 2014: 147–49. **Greek Capri:** Mele 1985: 105–6; 2007a: 256–57; Federico and Miranda 1998: 375–415; Federico 2004. **Greek Pozzuoli:** De Franciscis 1971; Adinolfi 1977; 1987; Accame 1980; Frederiksen 1984: 87–88; Zevi 1987: 27–30; Zevi, *Puteoli:* 1.9–15.

CHAPTER 3. EARLY COINAGE OF NEAPOLIS

Any study of an ancient Greek city's identity, self-perception, and sphere of influence must take account of its coinage. What motivated a city to issue coins? What were their patterns of distribution, and what historical significance did those patterns have? What was their role in the regional economy? What was the meaning of their imagery and inscriptions? And how do we date and sequence the sometimes bewildering array of coin issues from a city, most of which offer up no obvious clues about the historical circumstances in which they were minted? The Neapolitan coinage invites all these questions. Not only was the mint of Neapolis one of the most important in all Italy between the fifth and third centuries BCE; it probably also gave birth, sometime late in the fourth century BCE, to the coinage of Rome.

Issued by autonomous city-states, Greek coinages tend to reflect situational politics rather than long-term policy. New issues, it is believed, were generally undertaken for expensive and prominent projects, such as military campaigns or building programs. Although we know far too little about Greek Neapolis to divine the specific reasons for most of its issues, larger patterns of heavy minting activity interspersed with periods of relative idleness can sometimes be mapped onto major events of the time. But only hypothetically. Although I will argue that certain Neapolitan coin issues made specific historical references, not a single one can be *definitively* attached to an event or initiative; in fact, many issues leave us struggling to find a cause.

Let me suggest, by way of conventional guesswork, a possible but indemonstrable instance of cause and effect. As events in the next chapter will suggest, a significant part of this maritime city's coinage after 327/6 BCE, and up through the First Punic War (264–241 BCE), must have gone to paying for ships and sailors, which Neapolis was obligated by treaty to provide to Rome as needed. It may be no accident, then, that Neapolis was furiously minting in the years shortly after 310 BCE, just when Rome was conducting amphibious operations against Nuceria and its allies in the Sarno Valley in southern Campania.[1] Yet sporadic operations of this sort cannot have accounted entirely for a

---

1. See p. 89.

phenomenon happening on a much broader scale: the greater flow of money in the regional economy throughout this period and beyond. Scholars sometimes rely too heavily on wars to explain sudden spasms of minting in antiquity, when other political or economic considerations — peacetime projects, monetary policy, an increase in the volume of commerce, even civic pride or sheer grandiosity — may have played an equal or greater part [Commentary 3.1, pp. 109–10].

DIE STUDIES:
NEAPOLIS' CONTACT WITH SAMNITE CITIES

Direct traces of minting operations in Magna Graecia have eluded archaeological discovery. It is now generally agreed, however, that apart from the Second Punic War (218–201 BCE), when Capua minted coinage for itself and for the Carthaginians during its brief rebellion from Rome between 216 and 211 BCE,[2] only two mints ever existed in ancient Campania: in Cumae and Neapolis. The Neapolitan mint alone survived beyond the fifth century BCE. Most of this chapter will focus on Neapolis' own coinage. But as it happens, the city also served as the clearinghouse for coinages throughout the region until the rise of the mint in Rome put an end to regional Italian money production. This was an unusual relationship, indeed so unusual that it was not even recognized until the 1970s. And since it illuminates Neapolitan–Samnite relations more broadly, as discussed at the end of the previous chapter, I begin this chapter with it.

The painstaking progress in modern numismatic knowledge would be impossible if not for the tendency of cities to inscribe their names (or more often, the ethnic adjective of their citizens) on their coinage — and it is from this single certainty that all further knowledge follows. Most of Neapolis' coins, from the very first issue in the mid-fifth century BCE, bear a one-word inscription identifying the city of origin.

But at a somewhat later date, other Campanian towns and tribes — in some cases, quite obscure ones — also issued coinage in their own names. Apart from these inscribed names — Hyria, Nola, Allifae, Fisteli, Fenserni, Campani (Capuans?), even Samnite Cumae — the

2. See pp. 132–35.

CHAPTER 3 ⛫ EARLY COINAGE OF NEAPOLIS

coins looked exactly like the Neapolitan ones. For this reason it was long assumed that these cities and tribes operated their own mints and were simply imitating the more prestigious Neapolitan coinage. But the study of dies — the cylindrical metal stamps from which the coins were minted — has proved otherwise.

First a word of explanation about die studies. Every ancient coin die (essentially a metal cylinder roughly the diameter of the coin it would strike) was engraved on one circular end with intricate hand tools. A single coin issue typically required the production of many thousands of coins, each struck on a blank metal disk inserted between two dies. After hundreds of strikes with a heavy hammer, a die would begin to crack; the cracks opened slightly, strike after strike, until the die was discarded and replaced with a fresh replica. For each side of the coin, then, an issue of any size would run through a series of hand-engraved dies, all of them *almost* but *not quite* identical. On the basis of their detectable differences, a coin's obverse and reverse impressions, analyzed under magnification, can be identified with particular dies in the series. Traces of the die cracks in a coin can even offer clues about its place in the sequence. Because the cracks widened slightly with each strike, it is often possible to sequence coins struck by a single die.

By conducting an exhaustive die study of the coin issues in question, Keith Rutter determined that the various coins issued under the names of other Campanian cities and ethnicities in the fourth and third centuries BCE were actually minted at Neapolis. The inscribed sides of the coins, of course, were original to the issues; some of them even advertised their names in the Oscan rather than the Greek alphabet. But in many cases, the *uninscribed* sides were struck with the very same dies as self-identifying Neapolitan coins. This provides a valuable glimpse into Neapolitan relations with these Samnite communities during a period when Neapolis itself was becoming more bicultural. That Neapolis was contracting out its mint to Samnites indicates, first and foremost, a productive and peaceful relationship with its neighbors. Our improved knowledge of just how "Campanized" Neapolis had become by the fourth century BCE might even suggest that this service developed out of strong

87

bonds of kinship. But we will return to the question of causes below. We will also see an example of a Hyrian coin, chosen because it illustrates a Neapolitan coin type as well as, or better than, any of the surviving Neapolitan examples.

NEAPOLITAN COINS IN CONTEXT

From the perspective of archaeological context, there are four categories of ancient coins: undocumented finds, documented but sporadic finds, deposits, and hoards. The first group, which constitutes the majority of coins in known collections, is useful for such non-contextual matters as die studies and statistical analysis, but virtually useless in helping to establish patterns of money diffusion within a given region. Casually scattered coins documented under controlled archaeological circumstances are far more useful from this perspective. They can also help to refine relative and absolute dating sequences. The study of votive coins in sanctuaries, abundantly and sometimes densely deposited by pilgrims and worshipers from many points of origin, has proven especially fruitful in this respect.

Perhaps the most useful category of all, and the rarest, consists of coin hoards. At least forty-eight ancient hoards, discovered under various circumstances in Italy and Sicily, are known to have contained Neapolitan coins. Hoards can be dated by various means, but one of the most useful methods is by establishing which coins among them demonstrate the least wear. If, say, a particular coin type is known by independent evidence to have been issued around 450 BCE, and particular examples of that type show up in a hoard looking fresher than their companion coins, then that knowledge can help not only to date the deposit of the hoard itself (shortly after 450), but also, potentially, to refine the dating of other coin types in the hoard.

Hoards are not necessarily representative of the general diffusion of coinage. Being what they are — i.e., stashes of money deemed valuable enough to hide — they may favor higher denominations in silver or even gold, though some hoards have consisted mostly or entirely of bronze. (Neapolis itself minted no gold coinage.) Whatever their shortcomings as evidence, hoards have shown that over the

CHAPTER 3 🏛 EARLY COINAGE OF NEAPOLIS

fourth and the first half of the third century BCE Neapolis was the economic fulcrum of its region, its influence growing ever wider over time both among coastal Greek cities and in the interior of Campania and central Italy.

By analyzing both hoards discovered around Italy and coin deposits found in sanctuaries around Campania, Renata Cantilena has demonstrated that Neapolitan economic influence shadowed that of Rome from the late fourth century BCE onward. When Roman military action created a money vacuum — as perhaps happened during the campaign against Nuceria of 310 BCE mentioned above — Neapolitan bronze and silver probably helped to fill it. After 270, Neapolitan coins proliferated in sanctuaries outside Campania, a clear sign of the widespread presence of Roman and allied forces during the First Punic War. By the mid-third century BCE, however, this abundance of Neapolitan coins began to give way to a surge in Romano-Campanian money, also probably minted at Neapolis but issued in the name of Rome.[3] Before long the orbit of Neapolis' mint had contracted to the city itself, its tiny hinterland, and its island possessions, Ischia and Capri. By 200 BCE, the archaeological record of new Neapolitan coinage ceases, submerged in a flood of Roman money.

PARTHENOPE AND THE BULL-MAN

We now turn to our chronological survey and analysis. If, as it would seem, Neapolis was born in the early years of the fifth century BCE, then its coinage emerged only after some decades. When, exactly, is a matter of debate. We may presume that in its early years the new colony relied on the coinage of its mother city, Cumae. From the beginning, Neapolis seems to have adopted the Campanian weight standard (based on the Phocaean in Greece), which would eventually prevail throughout Campania and even in Rome itself. Phocaean– (Some variability of weight was expected, and coins often fell slightly short of the standard.)

The very first coin issue attributed to the new colony of Neapolis is represented by a single surviving example, a silver didrachm in the

3. See pp. 122–26.

Fig. 3.1. *Silver didrachm of Neapolis. Paris, Bibliothèque Nationale de France, Cabinet des Médailles.*

Greek Severe Style from the De Luynes Collection, now in Paris [Fig. 3.1]. Its date is uncertain but probably falls within the 460s or 450s BCE. This issue established an iconographic pairing that would dominate the city's coinage thereafter. On the obverse appeared the profile bust of a jeweled and coiffed female in the manner of the famous images of Arethousa, the local water nymph of Syracusan coinage. Cumae too had already adopted this motif to represent her own nymph, who shared the city's Greek name (Kyme). Though never identified by an inscription, the female on Neapolitan coins is universally recognized to be Neapolis' imported water-goddess, the Siren Parthenope. On this early example, the bust is encircled by a crown of olive.

On the reverse appeared another motif that would be repeated almost obsessively on later Neapolitan coins: the image of a man-headed bull. Borrowing again from regional traditions (this time perhaps from Gela in Sicily), the coin depicts the forward half — or protome — of the bull in a kneeling posture of sacrifice. The usual claim that this figure is swimming or running contradicts the fact that sacrificial bulls having no associations with water are often represented in the same way; the silver coinage of Thourioi and Katane in Sicily, for example, demonstrates how representations of kneeling terrestrial bulls and riverine bull-men may have influenced each other. Also on this side, never again to be repeated in precisely the same way, is the Ionic Greek legend *Neepolis*. It is the only

CHAPTER 3 ☗ EARLY COINAGE OF NEAPOLIS

Fig. 3.2. Silver didrachm of Neapolis. Photo courtesy of American Numismatic Society. CC BY-NC 4.0. Modified.

direct invocation of the city's name on Neapolitan coinage. The more popular designations are ethnics: *Neopolites,* "Neapolitan" in the nominative singular (probably masculine, like Cumae's *Kymaios*), or the genitive plural *Neopoliton:* "of the Neapolitans." The coins do not use our own Attic standard of Greek orthography, which would spell the city "Nea-polis." The preferred spelling is "Neo-."

Soon after the city's debut coin issue — and so perhaps around 450 BCE — the bull-man began to appear with his body in full profile, usually striding forward, his bearded head also in profile. Above him sometimes appeared the hovering figure of Nike, goddess of victory, holding a crown over his head [Fig. 3.2]. This hybrid creature has been variously identified. The favored hypothesis today, and for more than a century, asserts that he is a personification of the Thessalian river Acheloös. Best known as the unsuccessful rival of Herakles for the hand of Deianeira, this river god was, according to one tradition, the father of the Sirens — and therefore of Parthenope herself. A shape-shifter like Nereus and Proteus, he frequently appears in Greek art as the very man-faced bull that adorns Neapolitan coinage. On vases he is shown battling Herakles, and sometimes losing one of his horns in the struggle [Fig. 3.3].

There can be no doubt that Acheloös imagery, popular throughout Magna Graecia, inspired these coin types. But is the Neapolitan figure

Fig. 3.3. Detail from an Attic red-figure column crater from Agrigento, c.450 BCE. Paris, Musée du Louvre. Photo: Marie-Lan Nguyen / Wikimedia Commons CC PD-Mark 1.0.

meant to represent Acheloös *specifically?* To be sure, his cult was brought to Sicily and the Tyrrhenian coast by settlers or traders in the early centuries of Greek colonization, particularly the Rhodians, and it seems to have flourished in some western colonies. Perhaps it is right, then, to conjecture that Neapolitans retained a reverence for the father of their adored Parthenope. But of this reverence there is no independent evidence whatever; in fact, there are difficulties with the association. The cult of Herakles–Hercules was particularly strong in this region. Evidence of his worship is abundant at Cumae, Capua, and Neapolis. He is even featured on Neapolitan silver obols of c.330–310 BCE wrestling the Nemean Lion [Fig. 3.4]. The coastal road running from Baiae to Puteoli was later called Via Herculanea, and the eponymous Herculaneum was just a few miles to the southeast of Neapolis. The "Rock of Hercules" (Scoglio di Rovigliano) on the coast near Pompeii, was reportedly where the hero had landed after his adventures in Spain; the "Herculean salt pans" were nearby.[4] Thus it seems inapt that Acheloös, a bitter rival of the region's favorite superhero, should have outstripped his nemesis as an object of attention. And it would be downright strange that

4. Pliny, *Natural History* 32.17; Columella, *On Agriculture* 10.130.

CHAPTER 3 ⛫ EARLY COINAGE OF NEAPOLIS

Fig. 3.4 (above). Silver obol of Neapolis. Photo courtesy of Numismatica Ars Classica. Fig. 3.5 (below). Silver didrachm of Gela. Ex P.H. Gerrie collection. Photo courtesy of Classical Numismatic Group.

the river god, who lost the struggle against Herakles, should have appeared as a crowned victor on the coinage of Neapolis. (Much later, the hero's victory over the river god would be commemorated in a fresco in the "College of the *Augustales*" at Herculaneum.) More probably, the man–bull hybrid was abstracted from the particulars of Acheloös and his mythic origins, and like another, later formal type — the reclining human figure — was easily replicated to represent local water deities. A few other western Greek colonies also adopted this mascot on their coins, and in at least one case his identity was demonstrably shifted to that of a local river god. On the coinage of Gela, the man-faced bull is identified by the legends as the Gelas River in the nominative singular *Gelas* [Fig. 3.5]. The attribution is confirmed by the historian Timaios of Tauromenion.[5] If this city could adapt an old motif to a new purpose, why not Neapolis too?

From the fifth century BCE, the creature's hybridity may have developed a special meaning in Neapolis that had little to do with

5. Scholiast of Pindar, *Pythian Ode* 1.185.

the origins of tauriform river gods. As we saw in chapter 2, the city's population and governing bodies were shared between the Greeks and the indigenous Samnites. Did this composite of man and ox now symbolize a city of two peoples — indeed, two towns, Parthenope and Neapolis — united into one? Cults or symbols of civic unity were not uncommon in antiquity. One need look no further than the cult of Concordia in Rome, which celebrated (however artificially) the comity between social classes. It is tempting, in fact, to associate the very first Roman silver didrachm, probably minted in Neapolis, with the political events surrounding the establishment of the cult of Concordia in 304 BCE.[6] In the wake of the Samnite invasion of the late fifth century, and the ensuing years when Neapolitans were forced to "treat their worst enemies as their best friends,"[7] it may have been the very duality, not the individuality, of this symbol that was most important. There was little reason to invoke its Classical prototype, Acheloös, unless that god had a living cult in Neapolis — an unproven proposition.

To ascribe to this symbol such an abstract concept as synoecism — the cohabitation of different peoples — may seem far-fetched, until one settles upon the most likely identity of the man-faced bull at Neapolis: the Sebethos River. This watercourse was deified in the customary fashion, as the Acheloös-like god venerated at small shrines.[8] The old cult site of Parthenope, referenced on the obverse by the female bust, joins forces with the local river, symbol of unity and more generally of the new colony's broader claim on the Campanian landscape. The river's location is uncertain, but recent opinion has favored the notion that it ran through the fertile plain between Neapolis and Mount Vesuvius. Samnites and Greek homesteads may well have mingled in the fertile fields surrounding this river, lending an ethnic tinge to the god's symbolic duality. Not once is the striding or kneeling bull-man identified by name. But as it happens, the city's coinage features another bull-man hybrid with an established identity. A silver obol series of about

6. See p. 125.
7. Strabo, *Geography* 5.4.7. See Reading 24 above.
8. *CIL* 10 1480.

CHAPTER 3 🏛 EARLY COINAGE OF NEAPOLIS

Fig. 3.6. Silver obol of Neapolis. Naples, Museo Archeologico Nazionale.

400–380 BCE represents on its obverse the bust of a young man in profile, the horns of a bull sprouting from his forehead. Inscribed around the bust, in retrograde Greek, is the legend *Sepeithos* [Fig. 3.6]. No doubts here: the ox-man is the Sebethos River, identified in the nominative singular, just like Gelas, who also appears in both forms, youthful and mature, on Gelaian coins. On the reverse appears a winged female figure seated on a recumbent water jar; we will return to her momentarily.

The bull-man was the most popular subject to appear in nearly every phase of the 250-year life of the Neapolitan mint. As we have suggested, he was more than just a *genius loci* for Neapolis. Did his symbolism extend beyond coinage alone? We have no specific evidence that it did. But an inscription from the island of Kos, dating to 242 BCE, indicates that the Neapolitans were using as an emblem for their civic identity "a figure of a male animal."[9] When a single image of the Sebethos appears to us next, on the Roman imperial temple of the Dioscuri, he has taken the Roman form of a reclining bearded man.[10]

Finally there is the matter of the hovering Nike, crowning the Sebethos as a victor [see Fig. 3.2]. The earliest Neapolitan didrachm did not represent this, but Parthenope's bust itself was shown encircled by a wreath of olive [see Fig. 3.1]. Soon the wreath motif would move to the reverse, and its recipient would become the Sebethos. The circumstances surrounding the symbolism are

9. SEG 12.378.
10. See pp. 200–201.

obscure, but Rutter suggests a cause for its introduction: the Nike and the crown denote not military victory, but the Athenian torch races introduced at Neapolis around the mid-fifth century BCE. It is even possible to suppose that the cash prizes were paid out using the local higher-denomination currency, hence the confinement of the Nike symbolism to the silver coinage. Rutter's hypothesis is defensible, but the generalized use of a crown-bearing Nike in almost every imaginable context on western Greek coins softens the focus of the reference. The kneeling bull-man of Gela is sometimes shown being crowned by Nike, as are occasionally the submissive bulls of Thourioi. Even inanimate objects can get crowned. On the other hand, the motif is extraordinarily persistent on coinage of Naples, to the extent that the presence of Parthenope's bust on the obverse obligates Nike to appear crowning the Sebethos on the reverse. We may tentatively call this the agonistic class of Neapolitan coinage — not so different, perhaps, from coins of Roman Elis, which administered the Olympic Games. These showed the local river of Olympia, the Alpheios, as a reclining male figure holding a wreath, while a palm and an upright urn (a prize?) rest at his feet.

THE WINGED SPIRIT OF TEREINA AND NEAPOLIS

It is generally presumed that the winged female figure seated on an overturned water urn on the reverse of the Neapolitan *Sepeithos* obol [see Fig. 3.6] represents a local water deity, specifically the "nymph Sebethis" mentioned by Virgil[11] — in short, the female equivalent of the bull-horned youth on the obverse labeled as the Sebethos River. The image of a seated or reclining figure with an overturned urn was a common Greek allegory for a local source of water. But no such figure was ever shown with wings, as she appears here. Two other western Greek cities, Morgantina and Tereina, featured this unusual motif too. We focus here on the more prominent of the two issues, probably the source of this type. The coastal city of Tereina in Bruttium (modern Calabria) first issued this type sometime in the second half of the fifth century BCE, before the Neapolis issue [Fig. 3.7]. A Parthenope-like female bust is featured consistently on the obverse; the winged figure, however,

11. *Aeneid* 7.735.

CHAPTER 3 🏛 EARLY COINAGE OF NEAPOLIS

Fig. 3.7. Silver didrachm of Tereina. Ex C.R.J. Spencer-Churchill collection. Photo courtesy of Classical Numismatic Group.

has several variants. At first she was simply a standing Nike figure, and then she was represented seated on an altar or pedestal, holding any of a number of objects — bird, caduceus, olive branch, olive crown, etc. But the most striking variation, dating to the late fifth century BCE, represents her seated on a recumbent water urn, as on the Neapolitan coin, which clearly copies it. A much less generic, more specifically denotative symbol than the others, the urn signifies a river or spring. What connection, if any, could have inspired these two coastal cities to adopt such an unusual image — a winged water spirit — on their coins?

Ettore Gabrici, who identified the figure on all three coinages as a local nymph, could not entirely square his hypothesis with those troublesome wings, so he proposed that the nymph was assimilated to Nike, the popular winged goddess of victory. The assimilation cannot be denied, as far as it goes; but in fact the female figure, so obviously Nike at one level, can be hybridized more precisely. I contend (with Mario Napoli and others) that she is to be identified, just as in Naples, with an imported Siren. Like Furies and Harpies, Sirens belonged to a class of birdlike female spirits whose original character was malicious [Fig. 3.8. See Fig. 2.3]. Western Greeks associated them with the coastal waters of southern Italy, where they had putatively harassed Odysseus. In time, their reputation for mischief gave way to a cult of active veneration. This evolution has a certain logic, for the mortal Sirens, within Greek memory, were already dead. Like cult heroes, they would have acquired a new character upon deification. As we have seen, Tereina is one of the three

Fig. 3.8. Attic red-figure stamnos, 480-460 BCE. British Museum. © Trustees of the British Museum.

sites on the Tyrrhenian coast that hosted a Siren cult.[12] But why would a creature of the seacoast be shown with a water jug, which usually signals a body of *terrestrial* water, and not the sea?

Presenting the mythic origins of Neapolis as an oracle of Cassandra, the Hellenistic poet Lykophron declares that the dead Parthenope, cast ashore by the sea, would be worshiped at a site watered by a stream: the Glanis, a river that formed the northern boundary of Cumaean territory, and which may be a mistake for the Sebethos (the poem's text is notoriously nettlesome). He then addresses in turn the second Siren sister, Leukosia, who washed ashore south of Paestum; and finally, the third:

> **27.** To Tereina shall Ligeia drift, spitting out the surge. Sailors shall bury her in the shingle of the shore, by the eddies of the Okinaros [River]. And an ox-horned Ares shall bathe her tomb with his waters, cleansing the bird-child's home with his quenching stream."
> [*Alexandra* 724–31]

Tereina too claimed a Siren as a patron deity. Evidently the citizens of that Tyrrhenian city chose to depict her on both sides of her most distinctive coin type. In both cities, the Siren's tomb adjoins a nearby river — in the case of Tereina, the Okinaros (modern Fiume dei Bagni?); in the case of Neapolis, the Sebethos–Glanis. Following Greek tradition, the poet envisions the Okinaros in the form of an oxman ("Ares" is obscure). Neapolis does the same with the Sebethos on its coinage. In both cities, then, there seems to have been a significant bond between the Siren cult and the local watercourse. In Neapolis,

12. See pp. 42–43.

CHAPTER 3 🏛 EARLY COINAGE OF NEAPOLIS

Fig. 3.9. Silver didrachm of Neapolis. Ex R. Jameson and Sir A. Evans collections. Photo courtesy of Nomos AG, Zürich.

this bond was celebrated by pairing them on its coinage in two mirroring types: bust of Parthenope with full-body Sebethos (many coin issues); and bust of Sebethos with full-body Parthenope (silver obol).

ATHENA ON NEAPOLITAN COINAGE

Among the earliest Neapolitan silver coin issues, the one alternative to Parthenope on the obverse was the helmeted bust of Athena in profile. The introduction of Athena may have been encouraged, in part, by her abundant presence on Cumaean coinage of the mid-fifth century. But Cumae's goddess, who commonly wears a Corinthian helmet, is rather distinct in style and iconography. The first Athena didrachms of Neapolis can be divided into two groups. The earliest, representing a profile bust of the goddess in a close-fitting, uncrested helmet, have been variously dated from the 460s to the 440s BCE. The best-known early series is quite rare and bears the ethnic *Neopolitikon* on both sides. A locust hovers above the bull-man [Fig. 3.9]. The early group should be ascribed, as Rutter advises, to the later end of the date range, for it was probably intended to reference the arrival of the Athenians. Other explanations of this goddess' robust presence on Neapolitan silver coinage have been advanced: for example, a local attachment to the famous cult of Athena on the Sorrentine Peninsula [see Fig. 1.2]. While it is certainly possible that Neapolis administered that cult, Diotimos the Athenian's arrival not only provides a more proximate cause for the new coin iconography, but can even account for the practical need to issue coinage at the time, that is, if we are correct in conjecturing that Neapolis admitted the Athenians

Fig. 3.10. Silver didrachm of Hyria. Ex R.C. Lockett collection. Photo courtesy of Classical Numismatic Group.

in order to augment its navy.[13] The second group, dating roughly to 420–400 BCE, is far more abundant and more purely Athenian in inspiration: it represents the goddess' bust in profile, wearing a crested Attic helmet crowned with an olive wreath upon which an owl is occasionally perched. The type quickly proliferated on the flood of coinage sponsored by Campanian towns, such as Nola and Hyria, all of which (as we just saw) was produced at the Neapolitan mint. Hyria's coinage most often features the owl [Fig. 3.10]. The style and motif of the second Athena group were influenced by coins from Thourioi (a colony in which Athens had a stake). But those coins never included the owl, the most iconic of Athenian symbols. Later Neapolitan issues represent Athena in various guises, sometimes with the Corinthian rather than the Attic helmet.

Athena's image was especially popular on the Neapolitan bronze obols of the later fifth century BCE. These proliferated after 421, the year that Cumae, stricken by the Samnite occupation, gave up minting obols. On the reverse there appeared the kneeling bull-man protome, or sometimes the oyster shell borrowed from Cumae. Again, the Athenian motifs dominate on the obverse. Yet not a single Neapolitan coin features *both* of the notionally Athenian elements together: the bust of Athena on the obverse, and Nike, representing the torch races introduced by the Athenians, crowning the bull-man on the reverse. The coronation is featured almost exclusively on

13. See pp. 55–59.

CHAPTER 3 ⛩ EARLY COINAGE OF NEAPOLIS

Parthenope issues; the bull-man on the reverse of the Athena coins goes uncrowned. Perhaps this can be explained by the evident fact that the torch races were dedicated to the Siren and her cult. Nothing suggests that the patron goddess of Athens had any connection to the games.

Let us briefly review the most important points about the Parthenope and Athena types. Although the Athenian intervention was not necessarily the catalyst for early Neapolitan coinage, it nonetheless seems to have profoundly influenced all but the very first issue [see Fig. 3.1]. Arguably, then, it gave Neapolis the incentive to develop each of the two main silver didrachm types in the years between 450 and 440 BCE. Consistent across both types is Neapolis' unique identity, expressed either in terms of foundation myth (Parthenope), geography (Sebethos), or both. However, the iconic Parthenope–bull-man type, which after the first issue always included the hovering Nike on the reverse, may have been minted initially to celebrate the torch races introduced by Diotimos and his men — and perhaps even to serve as cash prizes for the winners. The Athena / bull-man type never included the hovering Nike, and so was minted as a conscious counterpoint to the agonistic symbolism of the first type. It may have been meant to honor — and to pay for — the other likely Athenian service to the Neapolitans, the augmentation of the navy. That is not to say that either event had a long-term hold on the economics or even the conscious reception of later issues featuring these types; I only mean to suggest that they constituted a plausible beginning. Nor can any of the discrete iconographic elements be called original in their own right. That they were borrowings goes without saying. As on most Greek coinage, it is the particular combination and emphasis of the borrowings that creates new meaning.

OTHER EARLY TYPES

The late 420s BCE, when the Samnites overran Campania, witnessed a dramatic change in coinage. Syracusan types disappeared from Neapolitan coins, to be replaced by models from the south-Italian cities of Tereina and Thourioi. It was during the final years of Syracusan influence that a number of ethnically Samnite cities and tribes began to mint coins on the Neapolitan model by arrangement with the

Neapolitan mint itself. By about 400 BCE the cities of Hyria and Nola, and the "Campani," probably the Capuans, were producing coinage prolifically, borrowing engravers, ideas, and even dies from Neapolis. Rutter has hypothesized that the demand for this money can be linked to the rise of Campania as an exporter of mercenaries. Modern social-network and middle-ground theory, however, would suggest the ties were more intricate and socially embedded. Within one or two decades, other Samnite towns or groups joined in: Fisteli, Allifae, Fenserni. Athena, Parthenope, and the bull-man continued to predominate on their coins. Whatever the difficulties of mutual assimilation, the general satisfaction with the old Neapolitan symbolism may suggest that the Samnites appreciated its pluralistic message, celebrating a river that embodied and embraced the multiethnicity of the region. What is most interesting about these coinages, perhaps, is the wildly diverging range of letterforms, spellings, and misspellings of the ethnics. Evidently the engravers were not always fully literate, let alone proficient in Greek.

The bust of Parthenope itself was inspired originally by the famous profile heads of Arethousa on Syracusan coins. Another memorable type borrowed from Syracuse in the fifth century BCE features on the obverse a female head in three-quarters view, her loosened hair radiating dramatically from her head. This type, like the Athena obverses, was borrowed by Hyria, with the addition of a kind of flat basket *(kalathos)* for a crown [Fig. 3.11]. Any kind of relationship between Syracuse and Neapolis is hard to define in this period, although it is well to remember that after 474 BCE Syracuse had held the island of Ischia for some years before ceding it to Neapolis. In the event, there is no need whatever to postulate an affinity between these cities. The Syracusan silver coinage was admired around the Mediterranean in the fifth century BCE, prompting countless spinoffs from dozens of mints.

BRONZE IN THE FOURTH AND THIRD CENTURIES

For several decades after 380 BCE Neapolis and other Samnite centers minted very little coinage, though a few series of didrachms have been placed hypothetically around the middle of the century. The reasons for this hiatus are obscure. In the early fourth century BCE Samnite mercenaries were working mostly for Syracusan tyrants in Sicily. Luigi

CHAPTER 3 🏛 EARLY COINAGE OF NEAPOLIS

Fig. 3.11. Silver didrachm of Hyria. Ex P. Tichant and R.J. Graham collections. Photo courtesy of LHS Numismatik, AG, Zürich.

Pedroni conjectures that the sudden influx of Gauls in Italy in the early 380s, and their employment by Syracuse in subsequent years, suddenly left the Samnite mercenaries out in the cold. Without their customary jobs or booty, there was no need — or metal — for coinage. It is a rather precarious hypothesis, given how little we know about the Gauls in Italy over these decades. Perhaps it is enough to observe, with Martin Frederiksen, that Samnite cities needed little new coinage because they exported soldiers instead of hiring them. Whether or not barter systems favored by non-Greek mercenaries had any effect on the hiatus of coinage must remain an open question.

This situation lasted at least until a new and more urgent call to arms, the First Samnite War in 343 BCE, perhaps even longer. After its resumption the Neapolitan mint turned out bronze coinage more or less continually for the next century and a half. Denominations came and went. Around 280 BCE, the weight standard shifted dramatically downward. But through all these vicissitudes, the bull-man retained his dominance on coin reverses. On smaller denominations he appeared in the kneeling-protome format. On obols he was in the full-figure striding pose, and from about 270 onward the hovering Nike again appeared above him. At times, the bronze coinage was destined for a smaller, more localized circulation than the silver, and so its iconography — which certainly demonstrates much greater variety — may have been intended less for broad propagandistic gestures than for local or regional politico-economic messages. New

Fig. 3.12. Bronze coin of Neapolis. Photo courtesy of Numismatica Ars Classica.

types emerged, particularly on the obverses. Parthenope ceded her dominance to Apollo. On some series this god's bust appeared in a deliberately archaizing form, as if it were replicating a venerated cult statue. On others his form was more classicizing, with a prominent crown of laurel. From the mid-third century BCE he was often accompanied on the reverse by his distinctive symbols: a cithara resting beside the *omphalos,* a mound-shaped, reticulated cult object [Fig. 3.12]. Another Apolline symbol, the tripod, also appeared on reverses of this period, but paired with an unidentified male bust on the obverse, lacking Apollo's features.

The cult of Apollo was strong in Neapolis in the Roman period. Statius[14] implies that the god had been revered there since the earliest days of Euboean colonization as one of the "parent gods." His famous sanctuary at Cumae, only a dozen miles to the west, was probably administered by the Samnites after 421 BCE. If we accept that Neapolis maintained a degree of continuity in the pre-Roman period with Cumae and its Euboean roots, we should not be surprised that Apollo was a dominant presence in local myth and devotion.

SILVER COINAGE: FOURTH AND THIRD CENTURIES BCE

From the late fourth century into the third BCE, Neapolis minted several denominations of silver coins, including obols, triobols,

---

14. *Silvae* 4.8.45-49.

CHAPTER 3 🏛 EARLY COINAGE OF NEAPOLIS

Fig. 3.13. Silver didrachm of Neapolis. Photo courtesy of Numismatica Ars Classica.

drachms, and didrachms. The first three of these were of minor importance; the didrachms are far more numerous. Between 327/6 and about 280 BCE, Neapolitan didrachms featured but a single type: the familiar agonistic pairing of Parthenope on the obverse, the striding bull-man with Nike on the reverse. On the earlier coins of this period, the Siren faces right [Fig. 3.13]; on the later ones, left. (This rule has some exceptions, as do the rules outlined below.) Study of this group would seem a monotonous task, were it not for an accompanying multitude of symbols, names, monograms, and letters known collectively as control marks. In the first period, any one of ten symbols appears behind Parthenope's neck. An eleventh, a ring of dolphins, encircles her entire head in the manner of Syracusan coins of the same period, 317–310 BCE. A whole or partial Greek name (such as "Charileos" or "Chari") appears below the bust. A letter or monogram — again probably referring to a man's name — may appear in the exergue on the reverse, accompanying the ethnic. There seems to be no clear pattern of interrelationship among these control marks, which have yet to be fully decoded — nor do they follow patterns identical to the coinages of other cities that used control marks in this period, such as Taras (Tarentum, modern Taranto) and Corinth. However, careful study of the bronzes — particularly by Renata Cantilena — has advanced our understanding. One of the most interesting features of didrachms of this period is that coins of different series sometimes share a die either on the obverse or the reverse. Obviously in such cases the variability is manifested on the sides that do *not* share the die: a change in symbol, name, or monogram. Sometimes two of the three elements change, sometimes only one. Charileos / -aos is a resonant name in the history of this period. Livy informs us that the foremost citizens of Neapolis at the time were a man of this name and a certain Nymphius, whose name may also appear on Neapolitan coins (as N or NY). Together they engineered the Roman occupation in 327/6 BCE that led to a long-standing alliance with Rome.[15] Ever since Arthur Sambon identified these historical figures with the coin legends over a century ago, historians have taken seriously the proposition that both men, after resolution of the crisis with Rome, were rewarded with magistracies of the mint. One of the responsibilities of such officials, no doubt, was to plan and oversee the volume of each coin series. Cantilena and her colleagues believe the symbols appearing in the first period were assigned as control marks designating the amount of metal used for a given series. Possibly, however, they represent different workshops of coin engravers.

The first phase of the final period of the agonistic didrachms ended around 280 BCE, the year that Pyrrhus of Epirus invaded Italy. From this time until the end of Neapolitan silver coinage, all the didrachms shared a single type: on the obverse, the bust of Parthenope facing left, a variable symbol behind her head; on the reverse, the bull striding right, one or two letters appearing between his legs, and the ethnic in the exergue below [Fig. 3.14]. A different set of rules seems to have governed the use of control marks in this period. Suddenly there are only four single or paired letters: A, BI, E, and IΣ. Now, the function previously filled by the symbol seems to have been given to the letters on the reverse. The symbols, on the other hand, vary widely within each group, and seem to designate sequences within series.

Silver drachms of this period, or shortly thereafter, follow the same pattern. Now, however, the IΣ group is followed by a letter that varies among A, B, Γ, and Δ — the first four letters of the Greek alphabet. Neapolitan bronze coins also appear with an IΣ group. As if to

15. See chapter 4.

CHAPTER 3 🏛 EARLY COINAGE OF NEAPOLIS

Fig. 3.14. Silver didrachm of Neapolis. Ex P.H. Gerrie collection. Photo courtesy of Classical Numismatic Group.

continue the same control system, these appear with an additional letter that cycles through almost the entire alphabet, from B to T. Roberto Lippi has argued that the four cycling letters of the alphabet represent sequential years — in each case, beginning with the year 272 BCE, when Rome seized Tarentum. The four years of drachms may represent the last gasp of Neapolitan silver coinage. According to this hypothesis, in 269 BCE Rome began minting her own silver at home to the exclusion of all other Italian silver. Neapolitan bronze coinage, as we have said, continued on for some time, through the First and Second Punic Wars. But by this time local cities had been relieved of their obligation to mint pay-grade silver for the men they provided to Rome's war effort. Rome had undertaken to pay them herself.

WHO PUT CONTROL MARKS ON COINS, AND WHY?

Neapolitan coinage is an especially rich source of control marks, which often vary considerably even within a single series, or can be carried over to multiple series. It is postulated that a control mark — which, when in the form of letters, often seems to represent a Greek name — is meant to represent either the magistrate responsible for the issue or the engraver who made the dies of the coin bearing it. In the case of Neapolis, Patrick Marchetti favors the second hypothesis. Names may recur over multiple series covering many years, even decades; and it would seem unlikely that a single man would hold a magistracy of the mint for so long.

Some engravers worked for more than one city. Suessa in particular, a town of the Campanian interior, shared its craftsmen with Neapolis. Marchetti has even suggested that the distant city of Tarentum employed some engravers who also worked on the Neapolitan coinage. Whereas double employment by two Campanian towns would not have required any travel (towns like Suessa had no mint of their own), the metropolis of Tarentum was over 300 kilometers to the southeast, requiring that the engravers "ΔΙ" and "**EYX TAP**" (Euch--- the Tarentine?) reside alternately in the two cities.

Quite apart from letters, forty-nine different symbols have also been identified on Neapolitan coins, most from the third century BCE. These range from animals (elephant, dove, eagle, etc.) to gods (Helios, Artemis, Athena) to objects (tripod, cuirass, ship's prow, etc.) to geometric forms (crescent, star, etc.). The Campanian towns of Suessa and Cales overlap extensively with Neapolis in the symbols appearing on their coinage. Tarentum too shares many symbols with Neapolis, as does a common Romano-Campanian type featuring Roma–Victoria. These symbols, Marchetti believes, function independently of the letter "signatures." Embedded in the heart of the third century BCE, all these series would have been under the control of Rome: those of Campania, by virtue of the Samnite Wars of the previous century; those of Tarentum, by virtue of her capture by Rome in 272 BCE. Each symbol, he proposes, designated a separate initiative by Rome to control the monetary standards across all the participating towns. In effect, then, each *signature* represents an individual, whereas each *symbol* designates a discrete point in time.

Marchetti's hypotheses remain controversial because they do not account for such matters as coins that share a monogram but bear obvious stylistic differences; nor have they been carefully tested against the patterns of control marks produced by other cities and at other times — particularly the second half of the fourth century BCE, when symbols proliferated on certain Greek coinages well outside of the sphere of Roman influence.

CHAPTER 3 🏛 EARLY COINAGE OF NEAPOLIS

NEAPOLITAN COINAGE UNDER ROME

In the late fourth and early third centuries BCE, Neapolis probably minted coins on behalf of Rome itself. This so-called Romano-Campanian coinage, which we will essay briefly in the next chapter, is iconographically distinct from Neapolis' own coinage. Yet it would be naïve to presume that Neapolis' independent coinage somehow escaped Roman influence — especially in its final decades around the Second Punic War, when the city on the Bay was deeply implicated in Roman political affairs. Also in the next chapter, we will provide a case study of a seemingly innocent incongruity of types on an ostensibly insignificant bronze fraction which may have carried a political message for Rome. It is safe to say that the coinage conveyed an abundance of such messages, more or less subtle in their expression, that elude us completely today. We see the familiar vocabulary — iconographic clichés such as gods, animals, ritual objects, symbols of abundance — but we miss the grammar and syntax that combined them in meaningful ways.

Commentary 3.1: Coinage and Prosperity

Andrew Burnett has observed that Neapolis and other mints of Magna Graecia enjoyed a massive increase of silver coinage between about 320 and 300 BCE. Some began to mint gold too; even minor mints were active at this time. By 270, this trend was definitively over. The stage was set for the rise of Rome.

Burnett sees a correspondence between the abundance of coinage in this period and other kinds of archaeological evidence of prosperity throughout south Italy: in Neapolis, for example, the profusion of late-fourth-century-BCE pottery in the cemetery at Pizzofalcone. Nola, Capua, and Poseidonia (Paestum) all show greater wealth and abundance in funerary practices; and the same can be said of other cities further afield. Prosperity, however, should not be confused with peace: much of this coinage was probably minted for various military expeditions attached to the second and third Samnite Wars, the Pyrrhic War, and ongoing conflicts with the Lucani.

It seems a dubious proposition to find prosperity in the midst of war. But with regard to Neapolis at least, a few distinguished historians, most notably Martin Frederiksen, have arrived at precisely that conclusion. Relying both on its maritime might and its compact but fertile territory, the city was ideally positioned to play the part of the war profiteer. It was precisely at this time that the Neapolitan wine trade began to flourish in the western Mediterranean.[16] Yet this modestly scaled export business says little about the city's overall well-being. It is wise to maintain, with Ross Holloway, a healthy skepticism about *general* prosperity when dealing with archaeological evidence weighted toward tomb treasures and coin hoards, the residue of the rich — or at least the comfortable. Grandiosity is often a benchmark of tyranny and says little about the fortunes of the majority. The perceived prosperity seems more a cultural than an economic phenomenon, especially when framed against the rise of the royal house of Macedonia. Famous for its conspicuous consumption and vast military expenditures, Macedonian royalty may have encouraged a trend of imitation among elites throughout the Greek world.[17]

REFERENCES

Coinage of Italy before the Romans, with material relevant to Neapolis: Sambon 1903; Gabrici 1959; Burnett 1977; Rutter and Burnett 2001; Cantilena 2004. **General treatments of the coinage of Neapolis:** Sambon 1903; Breglia 1952b; Rutter 1979: 42–59, 142–58; 1986; 1997: 63–65, 72–76, 83–93; Cantilena 1985a; Pozzi 1986; Valenza Mele 1993: 172–78; Rutter and Burnett 2001: 68–71. **Historical context:** Lepore 1967a: 164–68; Burnett 1986; Frederiksen 1986; Raviola 1995: 124–38, 173–74. **Dialect and orthography of coin legends:** Càssola 1986: 55–58. **Sirens:** De Petra 1908; Pugliese Carratelli 1952b; Gabrici 1959: 90–97; Sbordone 1967a; Giangiulio 1986: 116–40; Breglia Pulci Doria 1987; Raviola 1990; Greco 1992;

16. See pp. 6–7, 129, 138–39.
17. See pp. 127–29.

CHAPTER 3 🏛 EARLY COINAGE OF NEAPOLIS

Napoli 1997 [1959]: 159–65; Taylor 2014a. **The man-faced bull, Acheloös, and river gods:** Peterson 1919: 203–4; Imhoof-Blumer 1923; Lacroix 1953; Gabrici 1959: 75–97; Isler 1970; 1981; Gais 1978; Rutter 1979: 46–47; Weiss 1984; 1988; Taylor 2009; Molinari and Sisci 2016. **The winged figure with water jug:** Gabrici 1959: 111–20; Napoli 1997 [1959]: 160–61; Rutter 1997: 61–62. **Coinage and local cults:** Peterson 1919: 165–221 et passim. **Athena on Neapolitan and Campanian coinage:** Sambon 1903: 207–13; Lepore 1967a: 164–66, 181–86; Rutter 1979: 47–63, 81–82, 92–95; Cantilena 1985b: 353–54; Rutter 1986; Mele 2007a; Cantilena 2008. **Chronology:** Breglia 1952a; Caccamo Caltabiano 1981; Cantilena et al. 1986; Pozzi 1986; Taliercio Mensitieri 1986; Lippi 2002. **The minting hiatus of the fourth century:** Caccamo Catalbiano 1981; Frederiksen 1986: 19–20; Pedroni 1996. **Iconography and symbols:** Breglia 1942; Rutter 1979: passim; Holloway 1986. **Neapolis and the coinage of other cities:** Breglia 1946–1948; Rutter 1979: 60–100; Cantilena 1985a; Stazio 1986; Burnett and Crawford 1998. **Circulation:** Cantilena 1985a, 1985b, 2004; Giove 1985; Taliercio Mensitieri 1999. **Bronze coinage of Neapolis:** Caccamo Caltabiano 1981; Taliercio Mensitieri 1986; Molinari and Sisci 2016. **Coin legends and control marks:** Gabrici 1959: 59–73; Cantilena et al. 1986; Marchetti 1986; Taliercio Mensitieri 1987. **Weight standards:** Hackens 1986; Pedroni 1996: 11–16; Lippi 2002.

🏛

CHAPTER 4. NEAPOLIS AND THE RISE OF ROME

INTRODUCTION

Our lens on Neapolis grows clearer from the moment that Rome began to take an interest in dominating Campania in the fourth century BCE. We owe this improvement to a handful of Roman and pro-Roman authors who documented the rise of the city's imperial fortunes, most notably Polybios, Dionysios of Halikarnassos, and Livy. As one might expect, their interest in Naples and Campania at large was confined to Rome's geopolitical interests, with the consequence that Neapolis made few appearances in their narratives except by way of her relationship to the rising hegemon—or to the hegemon's allies and enemies.

The second half of the fourth century BCE in south Italy saw the rise of two great forces in opposition, Rome and the Samnite League. We must readjust our definition of the Samnites once we turn to the wars that took their name in the fourth century. No longer can our narrative categorize the Campani, the Oscan-speaking people of Capua, Cumae, Nola, and Neapolis, among them. For by mid-century, these lowland tribes had, at least in some quarters, become alienated from their Samnite brethren in the League, who were growing more menacing by the year. Perhaps partly by kinship and partly by intimidation, Neapolis and Nola remained allied to the Samnites. But so threatened was Capua by Samnite designs on Falernian territory to its immediate north that in 345 BCE it sought protection from Rome by *deditio,* a temporary and complete surrender of power and territory, to which Rome responded by garrisoning the town. Capua's act of supplication led to a *foedus aequum,* a standard type of treaty by which sovereignty was soon restored to Capua. In 338 BCE Roman citizenship (*sine suffragio,* without the vote) was granted to Capua, Cumae, and Suessula — all cities dominated by the Campani.[1] By collaborating with the Campani, Rome was renouncing a treaty with the Samnite League it had signed nine years earlier. This was tantamount to a declaration of war.

1. Livy, *History of Rome* 8.14.10–12.

Thus was Roman influence extended to Campania by invitation. Livy[2] considers this moment the crux of Rome's glorious destiny, when a regional power chose to oppose the most formidable federation in Italy. As for Neapolis, her role in these events, and her relations with Rome over the previous century or more, are obscure. Livy relates that the two cities had enjoyed "friendly relations" and "old ties of duty" — a bond that the Samnites, in Dionysios' text,[3] mysteriously call enslavement. One seed of this relationship may have been planted in 411 BCE when Rome, suffering famine, sought grain from "all the peoples round about who dwelt on the Tyrrhenian Sea or by the Tiber."[4] Whatever the complexities of diplomatic relations between Neapolis and Rome, they must have centered upon Rome's growing need for imported food and goods, which suited Neapolis' role as importer, exporter, and broker.

THE SECOND SAMNITE WAR

If tensions had indeed so escalated between Rome and Neapolis that they could be characterized (by a hostile source, admittedly) as those between master and slave, their specific cause and explanation elude us. Yet tensions certainly there were, not only between the cities, but within the Neapolitan populace itself. Since the 340s BCE, Rome had been ruthlessly consolidating power in Falernian territory northwest of Campania; and, as we have seen, she was making alliances of protection in Campania, even with Cumae. Such aggressive expansion must have alarmed many Neapolitans, and indeed during this period the city walls were strengthened and augmented. By the fateful year of 327/6 BCE Neapolis was allied with the Samnite League and was skirmishing with Romans in Campanian and Falernian territory. At this point in the narrative, Livy and Dionysios are able to draw upon detailed sources. They vividly depict the bitter divisions among the Neapolitans, who seem to have been geographically and perhaps politically divided into enclaves at Palaepolis (Parthenope) and Neapolis.

2. 7.29.
3. Dionysios of Halikarnassos, *Roman Antiquities* 15.8.4.
4. Livy 4.52.4–6.

CHAPTER 4 🏛 NEAPOLIS AND THE RISE OF ROME

28. This community [Palaepolis], relying on their own strength and on the lax observance of treaty obligations which the Samnites were showing towards the Romans, or possibly trusting to the effect of the pestilence which they had heard was now attacking Rome, committed many acts of aggression against the Romans who were living in Campania and the Falernian country. [Livy 8.22.7]

29. The Roman Senate, when the Campanians made repeated charges and complaints against the Neapolitans, voted to send ambassadors to the latter to demand that they should do no wrong to the subjects of the Roman empire...; but in particular, the envoys, if they could do so by courting the favor of the influential men, were to get the city ready for revolt from the Samnites and become friendly to the Romans. It chanced that at this same time ambassadors sent by the Tarentines had come to the Neapolitans...; others had also come, sent by the Nolans, who were their neighbors and greatly admired the Greeks, to ask the Neapolitans on the contrary neither to make an agreement with the Romans or their subjects nor to give up their friendship with the Samnites. If the Romans should make this their pretext for war, the Neapolitans were not to be alarmed or terrified by the strength of the Romans in the belief that it was some invincible strength, but to stand their ground nobly and fight as befitted Greeks, relying both on their own army and the reinforcements which would come from the Samnites, and, in addition to their own naval force, being sure to receive a large and excellent one which the Tarentines would send them in case they should require that also.

When the [Neapolitan] council had convened and many speeches had been made there by both the embassies and their supporters, the opinions of the councilors were divided, though the most enlightened [*hoi chariestatoi*] seemed to favor the Roman cause. On that day, accordingly, no preliminary decree was passed, but the decision with regard to the embassies was postponed to another session, at which time the most influential of the Samnites came in large numbers to Neapolis, and winning over the men at the head of the state [*hoi dynatotatoi*] by means of some favors, persuaded the council to leave to the popular assembly the decision regarding the best interests of the state. And appearing before the assembly, they first recounted their own services, then made many accusations against the Roman state, charging it with being faithless and treacherous; and at the end of their speech they made some remarkable promises to the Neapolitans if they would enter the war. They would send an army, they announced, as large as the Neapolitans should require, to guard their walls, and would also furnish marines for their ships as well as all the rowers, providing all the expenses of the war not only for their own armies, but for the others too. Furthermore, when the Neapolitans had repulsed the Roman army, they would not only recover Cumae for them, which the Campanians had occupied for two generations earlier after expelling the Cumaeans, but would also restore to their possessions those of the Cumaeans who still survived — these, when driven out of their own city, had been received by the Neapolitans and made sharers of all their own blessings — and they would also grant to the Neapolitans some of the land the Campanians were then holding — the part without cities. The element among the Neapolitans that was reasonable and able to foresee long in advance the disasters that would come upon the city from the war, wished to remain at peace; but the element that was fond of innovations and sought the personal advantages to be gained from turmoil joined forces for the war. There were mutual recriminations and skirmishes, and the strife was carried to the point of hurling stones; in the end the worse element overpowered the better, so that the ambassadors of the Romans returned home without having accomplished anything. For these reasons the Roman Senate resolved to send an army against the Neapolitans. [Dionysios 15.5.1–15.6.5]

30. In consequence of this, the [Roman] consuls, L. Cornelius Lentulus and Q. Publilius Philo, sent the fetials to Palaepolis to demand redress. On hearing that the Greeks, a people valiant in words rather than in deeds, had sent a defiant reply, the [Roman] people, with the sanction of the Senate, ordered war to be made on Palaepolis. The consuls arranged their

CHAPTER 4 🏛 NEAPOLIS AND THE RISE OF ROME

respective commands; the Greeks were left for Publilius to deal with; Cornelius, with a second army, was to check any movement on the part of the Samnites. As, however, he received intelligence that they intended to advance into Campania in anticipation of a rising there, he thought it best to form a standing camp there. [Livy 8.22.8–10]

In light of the much larger relative size and manpower of Neapolis, Livy's insistence that these events were centered on Palaepolis–Parthenope is striking. The famous inscription from the Roman Forum known as the Fasti Capitolini confirms the centrality of the older town in these events, recording that Publilius Philo celebrated a triumph "over the matter of the Samnites and Palaeopolitans."[5] Scholars have conjectured that Palaepolis had become the stronghold of the local Campani, and thus of a pro-Samnite faction, while Neapolis remained more Hellenocentric and pro-Roman. Certainly this makes sense in light of the testimony that Palaepolis was leading the skirmishes against Romans. Yet both narratives of these affairs are scrubbed clean of any taint of ethnic division. The whole community is treated as if it had a uniformly Greek sensibility riven not by culture or tribe, but by outlooks and personalities: the wise and peace-loving Greeks (those who supported the Romans) opposing the foolish, warmongering Greeks (those who supported the Samnites). Livy, no expert in the history of Neapolis, may be forgiven this whitewash. But Dionysios was well aware of the deep Samnite roots in the community (he, more than our other sources, chronicled it). So under the circumstances, his simplistic characterization of local motivations must be read with a keen and skeptical eye — even if the events he relates are broadly correct.

In his narrative the Samnite legates, seeing no chance of a clear outcome in the council, sought a vote in the popular assembly.[6] This could suggest that pro-Roman Greek aristocrats *(hoi chariestatoi?)* still influenced the council, whereas Campani, reflexively inclined toward the Samnite cause, dominated the assembly. Yet the Samnites

---

5. *Fasti Capitolini* 95 Degrassi. I use Livy's spelling of Palae[o]polis, without the interpolated "o."

6. On the Neapolitan assemblies, see pp. 64, 173–74, 356.

addressing the assembly seem to appeal to a strictly Hellenocentric mentality. They promise to restore Cumae to the Cumaean Greek families that have been exiled in Neapolis since 421 BCE — nearly a century before, much longer than the two generations asserted in the text (the author has forgotten his own chronology). From the standpoint of Dionysios' Greek source, such a slant was sensible. But the real incentives behind the offer would have been quite different. It is hard to reconstruct the factions' motivations, but the notion of a Samnite-led conquest of Cumae disguised as Greek revanchism is patently absurd. Since Cumae had become a Roman municipality in 338 BCE, it is more likely that the Greeks had welcomed the concomitant weakening of Campanian influence and that the Campani had opposed it for the same reason; or, equally plausible, that the aristocracy — Greek and Campanian — supported Romanization in opposition to the lower classes. A real factor underlying the offer was the presence at Neapolis of the Cumaean community in exile. Host nations often tire of such burdens over time, and the Samnite legates may have perceived that to the Neapolitans, these "sharers of all their blessings" had become an obnoxious deadweight. Under the circumstances, any plan to resettle them, however quixotic, would fall on receptive ears.

Rebuffed by Neapolis, the Romans sent ambassadors to the Samnite League. It became abundantly clear that the Samnites were spoiling for a fight. Attempts at arbitration were brushed aside. Soldiers were being conscripted throughout Samnium, and an unwelcome garrison of six thousand had just been stationed at Palaepolis. Presumably others were assigned to Neapolis, but again the Old City is presented as the geographic flashpoint.

> **31.** [Romans, addressing the Samnites]: ...When the Neapolitans were afraid to declare war against us, you devoted all your zeal and efforts to encouraging them, or rather compelling them, to do so, and are paying all the expenses and are holding their city with your own forces.... First, we wish you to withdraw the armed assistance you have sent to the Neapolitans, and second, not to send out any army against our colonists nor to invite our subjects to all your encroachments. [Dionysios 15.7.3–5]

CHAPTER 4 🏛 NEAPOLIS AND THE RISE OF ROME

32. [Samnites, responding]: As for the city of Neapolis, in which there are some of our troops, far from wronging you, if we as a state contribute some aid toward the safety of those who are in danger, it is rather we ourselves who seem to be greatly wronged by you. For, though this city had become our friend and ally, not just recently nor from the time when we made our compact with you [354 BCE], but two generations earlier, in return for many great services, you enslaved it, though you had been wronged in no respect. Yet not even in this action has the Samnite state wronged you; rather it is some men connected by private ties of hospitality, as we learn, and friends of the Neapolitans who are aiding that city of their own free will, together with some also who through lack of a livelihood, perhaps, are serving as mercenaries. [Dionysios 15.8.3–5]

Neapolis had a military alliance with Taras [Tarentum], which it hoped would provide assistance. Livy's narrative, just as colored by Roman bias as that of Dionysios, emphasizes the harshness of the Samnites who claimed to be the protectors of Neapolis. And again, to a fault, he stresses the Greekness of the Neapolitans:

33. Both consuls sent word to the Senate that there were very slender hopes of the Samnites remaining at peace. Publilius informed them that 2000 troops from Nola and 4000 Samnites had been admitted into Palaepolis, more under pressure from Nola than from any great desire for their presence on the part of the Greeks.... Publilius meantime had taken up a suitable position between Palaepolis and Neapolis in order to prevent them from rendering each other the mutual assistance they had hitherto given....

Not only were the two towns Palaepolis and Neapolis cut off from all communication with each other by the enemy's lines, but the townsfolk within the walls were practically prisoners to their own defenders, and were suffering more from them than from anything which the outside enemy could do; their wives and children were exposed to such extreme indignities as are only inflicted when cities are stormed and sacked. A report reached them that succors were coming from Taras and from the Samnites.

They considered that they had more Samnites than they wanted already within their walls, but the force from Taras, composed of Greeks, they were prepared to welcome, being Greeks themselves, and through their means they hoped to resist the Samnites and the Nolans no less than the Romans.

At last, surrender to the Romans seemed the less of the two evils. Charilaos and Nymphios, the leading men in the city,[7] arranged with one another the respective parts they were to play. One was to desert to the Roman commander, the other to remain in the city and prepare it for the successful execution of their plot. Charilaos was the one who went to Publilius Philo. After expressing the hope that all might turn out for the good and happiness of Palaepolis and Rome, he went on to say that he had decided to deliver up the fortifications. Whether in doing this he should be found to have preserved his country or betrayed it depended upon the Roman sense of honor. For himself he made no terms and asked for no conditions, but for his countrymen he begged rather than stipulated that if his design succeeded the people of Rome should take into consideration the eagerness with which they sought to renew the old friendly relations, and the risk attending their action rather than their folly and recklessness in breaking the old ties of duty. The Roman commander gave his approval to the proposed scheme and furnished him with 3000 men to seize that part of the city which was in the occupation of the Samnites. Lucius Quinctius, a military tribune, was in command of this force.

Nymphios at the same time approached the Samnite praetor and persuaded him, now that the whole of the Roman fighting force was either round Palaepolis or engaged in Samnium, to allow him to sail round with the fleet to the Roman seaboard and ravage not only the coastal districts but even the country close to the city. But to ensure secrecy he pointed out that it would be necessary to start by night, and that the ships should be at once launched. To expedite matters the whole of the Samnite troops, with the exception of those who were mounting guard in the city,

7. See p. 106.

CHAPTER 4 ☖ NEAPOLIS AND THE RISE OF ROME

were sent down to the shore. Here they were so crowded as to impede one another's movements and the confusion was heightened by the darkness and the contradictory orders which Nymphios was giving in order to gain time. Meantime Charilaos had been admitted by his confederates into the city.

When the Romans had completely occupied the highest parts of the city, he ordered them to raise a shout, on which the Greeks, acting on the instructions of their leaders, kept quiet. The Nolans escaped at the other end of the city and took the road to Nola. The Samnites, shut out as they were from the city, had less difficulty in getting away, but when once out of danger they found themselves in a much more sorry flight. They had no arms, there was nothing they possessed which was not left behind with the enemy; they returned home stripped and destitute, an object of derision not only to foreigners but even to their own countrymen. I am quite aware that there is another view of this transaction, according to which it was the Samnites who surrendered, but in the above account I have followed the authorities whom I consider most worthy of credit. Neapolis became subsequently the chief seat of the Greek population, and the fact of a treaty being made with that city renders it all the more probable that the reestablishment of friendly relations was due to them. As it was generally believed that the enemy had been forced by the siege to come to terms, a triumph was decreed to Publilius. [Livy 8.23, 25–26]

Judging by their names, the co-conspirators Charilaos and Nymphius were a Greek and a Campanus, respectively. This unremarkable fact has led some to question the importance of ethnicity in the Neapolitan troubles. Yet it could just as easily confirm it. After all, the pro-Roman cause had no hope of succeeding unless a few sympathetic Campani — a fifth column, in effect — had been recruited to gain the trust of the occupying Samnites. In either case, Kathryn Lomas is right to caution that social class must be regarded as a powerful factor distinct from ethnicity. The aristocrats among the Campani, having longstanding ties with Roman elites, would likely have sympathized with the Roman cause more than their humbler kin. It may be by their agency that Neapolis acquired such favorable terms, among which (evidently) was a virtual exemption from service in Roman land forces — a burden that characteristically fell to the upper-class cavalry in Campanian towns.

As Martin Frederiksen observes, Neapolis resorted to the same two-step process in repairing its relations with Rome as Capua had done earlier: first, a *deditio,* or supplication; and quickly thereafter, a *foedus aequum,* or treaty of equals, which granted full sovereignty to Neapolis with the added advantage of Roman *civitas sine suffragio.* Neapolis now had the status of *municipium,* just like Capua and Cumae. This relationship proved profitable over time, ensuring that Neapolis would retain political and diplomatic autonomy. The city never again made the mistake of crossing Rome; in effect, it retired any remaining aspirations for undue power or influence in Italian affairs. A.N. Sherwin-White's characterization of such "federated cities" abroad applies equally to Neapolis at home. In later years, Rome's willingness to tolerate them as "equals" demonstrated, in effect, their inequality, for such cities almost by definition posed no threat. But there was a difference, too. The *foederati* overseas gradually became subject states. Neapolis, by contrast, continued to enjoy not only an extraordinary degree of independence, but a distinctive, almost hyperreal Hellenistic culture to which Romans contributed and responded with delight.[8]

ROMANO-CAMPANIAN COINAGE

Probably around the time of the First Samnite War, but arguably as late as 327/6 BCE, Neapolis resumed minting silver coinage after a long hiatus — initially, perhaps, to support the war effort, and soon (it would seem) to provide coinage for Rome herself. There is very little consensus about the so-called Romano-Campanian coinage, including the usefulness of its name. This is derived from the perception that, although the coinage was sponsored by Rome, its obverses and control marks borrow heavily from Campanian motifs. Campanian influence does not prove that this coinage was *produced* in Campania. But the majority view has long held that the earliest issues, at least,

8. See chapter 8.

CHAPTER 4 ☗ NEAPOLIS AND THE RISE OF ROME

Fig. 4.1. Romano-Campanian bronze hemiobol. Photo courtesy of Classical Numismatic Group.

were minted at Neapolis. Certainly the Neapolitan influence is felt in all early Roman coinage, for the Romans borrowed their weight standard from this city. Whatever the truth about their Campanian origins, the legend inscribed on the early series makes no secret of who sponsored them: it reads *Romano*, an abbreviation of the genitive plural *Romanorum*, "of the Romans," rendered in the Latin alphabet. Later coins switched to *Roma*. Given the difficulty of attaching the later issues to Neapolis, we will pass them by, focusing instead on the earliest issues.

Probably the first coin series bearing the name of the Romans is a bronze fraction (at about 3.20 grams, its precise denomination is uncertain) that blends almost seamlessly into several Neapolitan bronze series featuring an archaizing Apollo on the obverse with a distinctive crescent-shaped "flip" of hair behind his neck and the bull–man protome on the reverse with a star on his flank [Fig. 4.1]. As such, it corresponds to Marina Taliercio's phase Ic of Neapolitan bronzes, which fits comfortably in the third quarter of the fourth century BCE. Uniquely, the ethnic ΡΩΜΑΙΩΝ (*Rhomaion*) is in Greek, the equivalent of the Latin *Romanorum*. The volume and denomination of the issue are too modest to account for military pay (there is no companion silver series). Probably, it was more an expression of formative identity than a response to a serious monetary need. Either it was issued by Greeks or Hellenized locals to acknowledge Rome's growing presence in the region, or it was issued at the initiative of Romans themselves. But when?

Fig. 4.2. Romano-Campanian silver didrachm. Photo courtesy of Numismatica Ars Classica.

Many, such as Arthur Sambon and Keith Rutter, have associated it with the *foedus aequum* of 327/6 BCE; others, such as Rudi Thomsen, with events as late as the Pyrrhic War (280–275 BCE). Various dates have been proposed in between these two extremes, and earlier as well. Maria Caccamo Caltabiano makes a meticulous case for the years immediately following Capua's *deditio* in 338 BCE. Immigrant Romans settling in Campania, she believes, issued the coin series from the Neapolis mint on their own behalf, just as Campanian towns had done earlier on a much larger scale. The new settlements would have led to the "friendly relations" between Rome and Neapolis cited by Livy above. The main difficulty with this interpretation is that the Neapolitans' treatment of the Romans in the run-up to 327/6 BCE was far from friendly. Another is that it is hard to envision a group of recent immigrants, with no civic base or government apparatus operating locally, minting coins. More probably, as Andrew Burnett proposes, Neapolis minted this modest series shortly after 327/6 at Rome's bidding and expense. It was issued in a small quantity for local circulation and probably for no special purpose except to ingratiate Neapolis to the new regional hegemon.

The very first Romano-Campanian silver coin issue, by contrast, departs entirely from Neapolitan imagery, boldly adopting an alien Roman theme — but again, exclusively for a local clientele: this coin did not circulate in Rome [Fig. 4.2]. Although it has been sequenced by its isolation from the later Romano-Campanian issues in coin

CHAPTER 4 ⚏ NEAPOLIS AND THE RISE OF ROME

hoards, its absolute date remains contested, falling between 327/6 BCE (the Neapolitan treaty with Rome) and 260 BCE (the construction of the first Roman fleet). Burnett's examination of the coin within the context of the hoards in which it appears situates it around 300 BCE. It is quite rare in both its denominations: a didrachm, surviving in only a handful of examples, and a silver obol, of which only two examples are known. On the obverse is the helmeted head of Mars; on the reverse, the head of a bridled horse resting on a plinth inscribed with the ethnic *Romano[rum]*. The reference is probably to the October Horse, dedicated each autumn in Rome to Mars. As the rightmost of the victorious team of horses in a special chariot race (hence the bridle), it was beheaded (and set on a plinth?); teams of Romans then fought ritually for possession of the head.[9] An oak spray and an ear of grain appear behind Mars and the horse respectively. Their significance is uncertain; the ear appears prominently on the coinage of Metapontion, but that slight coincidence is no guarantee of a connection. Nor is there any obvious historical catalyst for the issue, which was quite small and isolated by several decades from the next Romano-Campanian issues. Michael Crawford has proposed the construction of the Via Appia from Rome to Campania, begun in 312 BCE but presumably completed many years later. Burnett instead points to the struggle between the social classes of Rome, punctuated by the dedication of the shrine of Concordia in the Roman Forum in 304 BCE. Close analysis of Tarentine coins found with this type, however, may take it into the 390s or 380s.

On the basis of its circulation and weight standard, which is Neapolitan, many specialists attribute this first Romano-Campanian silver issue to Neapolis. Though rare, examples of it have been found in the abundant company of Neapolitan didrachms, including those with the datable "circle of dolphins" control mark — suggesting that the two coinages circulated in similar patterns. The next issues of Romano-Campanian didrachms, however, are more controversial. Their incidental gold content is higher than that of the first issue. Because sophisticated minting operations were fully capable of higher fineness ratios, and extracting gold from silver would seem an

9. Festus 190 L; Plutarch, *Roman Questions* 97.

obvious economic benefit, Burnett concludes that production after the first issue was moved from Neapolis to some other city with inferior metallurgical technology, probably Rome itself. Each of the three subsequent issues was reduced in weight, beginning with an average of 7.21 grams and ending at 6.60 grams, a standard that persisted until the Second Punic War.

The iconography of these third-century-BCE coins has been variously interpreted and will not concern us here. It is worth noting, however, that the fourth issue has control marks, including a sequence of letters on the reverse in the Greek alphabet probably intended to identify individual dies. An almost identical control system appears on Alexandrian coins minted after 270 BCE, but careful comparative study of the two systems has not entirely decoded them. At any rate, it would be a mistake to insist that Greek letters on Roman coins must point to a mint outside Rome itself. First, Romans would logically have hired Greek artisans to do what they could not yet do themselves. Second, this is a numbering system, and Greek numbers are more compact than Roman numerals. Neapolis was using a similar system at about the same time on its ΙΣ coins, both in silver and bronze.[10] Again, this is not to suggest that Neapolis was still minting on Rome's behalf. By this time, the two weight standards had diverged. But we may at least acknowledge the possibility of continued Neapolitan influence on the Roman mint, facilitated by the strong alliance of the two cities through the Pyrrhic and Punic Wars.

NEAPOLIS AND ROME AFTER 327/6 BCE

On the whole, the subsequent fortunes of ancient Neapolis appear to have been auspicious. Velleius Paterculus[11] writes of the city's "remarkable and unbroken loyalty to the Romans," an initial risk that paid rich dividends for centuries to come. The city's gain is history's loss: steadfastness and quiet stability rarely attract inquiry. After 327/6 BCE, the record of events there recedes into the background until the Second Punic War. Perhaps as a condition of the treaty with Rome, Palaepolis was largely abandoned at this time. There is no evidence that it was ever again resurrected as a community, and it

10. See p. 107.
11. *Compendium* 1.4.2.

CHAPTER 4 🏛 NEAPOLIS AND THE RISE OF ROME

Fig. 4.3. Interior of Tomb C at Via Cristallini. Photo courtesy of M. Jodice.

may even have fallen prey to the plutocrat Lucullus when he came looking for a suitably grandiose setting for a seaside villa in the late 80s BCE.

The most striking material legacy of the century following the *foedus aequum* at Neapolis consists of the Macedonian-style chamber tombs cut into the tuff escarpments in the ancient city's outskirts. Today they are buried deep beneath modern Naples and encumbered by later structures; but in antiquity they were street tombs, probably adorned with Greek-style facades. In the second half of the fourth century BCE the new discourse of Hellenism invented under Philip II, Alexander the Great, and Alexander's successors, the Diadochoi, swept through Magna Graecia, inspiring local and regional aristocracies to borrow a little of the Macedonian magic.

Fig. 4.4. View of the entrance of Tomb C at Via Cristallini. Photo courtesy of M. Jodice.

These upper-class tombs seem to be modeled on types at Vergina and other Macedonian aristocratic necropoleis. Typically the tombs consist of small barrel-vaulted chambers lined with stone sarcophagi. In the Roman period, niches for cinerary urns were often added. The finest of them, four two-story chamber tombs beneath Via dei Cristallini, date to the mid-third century BCE. In the lower chambers the sarcophagi are carved in the form of Greek couches, each complete with stone cushions. In Tomb C, the finest of the four, the walls are adorned with relief pilasters and a cornice. Frescoed panels between the pilasters depict hanging garlands and shields [Figs. 4.3; 4.4]. Axially positioned under the vault is an apotropaic gorgon head. Many of these tombs continued in use until the Roman imperial era, as inscriptions and alterations indicate. But to our knowledge, no

CHAPTER 4 ■ NEAPOLIS AND THE RISE OF ROME

new tombs of this kind were built after the late third century BCE. Their efflorescence corresponds to the century of relative stability between the Second Samnite War and the Second Punic War.

Sometimes Samnite influence is seen in these tombs and their assemblages, as in the more modest tombs of the fifth century BCE. That may be true among aristocrats at Neapolis, who often had complicated, multiethnic heritages. But in general the animosity between Oscan-speaking peoples and Greeks in Italy continued to simmer over the ensuing decades. Campanian cities contributed limited numbers of their famed cavalry to Roman campaigns in the third century. During the Pyrrhic War (280–275 BCE), when Rome called on Campanian mercenaries to garrison Greek towns in south Italy, their presence often incited resentment. Notoriously, around 280 BCE a garrison of Campani under Roman command in the Greek colony of Rhegion (Reggio Calabria) mutinied and slaughtered the inhabitants.[12] Yet we hear nothing of ethnic divisions at Neapolis, where Greek cultural identity (at least in the urban area) gradually but inexorably subsumed the Campanian. The torch races of Parthenope continued; or so it is conjectured, at least, on the basis of a mass of Greco-Italic wine amphoras of local manufacture found in third-century-BCE contexts at the Duomo Metropolitana station. Directly above these remains, a "Wall of Fame" later arose commemorating victors in the Roman version of the games.[13] Some of these amphoras bore stamps marked with the symbol of a vegetal crown. This is taken to refer to the races, for which the vessels may have been expressly manufactured.

By about 211 BCE, Neapolis was stable enough to have acquired the status of a safe haven for citizens condemned for capital offenses at Rome.[14] Presumably this arrangement was designed with prominent political figures in mind. Polybios notes that two other cities federated with Rome, Praeneste (Palestrina), and Tibur (Tivoli), enjoyed

---

12. Orosius, *History against the Pagans* 4.3.4–5; Livy, *History of Rome* epitomes 12, 15; Polybios, *Histories* 1.7.7–11.

13. See pp. 326, 339–40.

14. Polybios 6.14.8.

the same status. These three towns all had territories that were beginning to effloresce with the country villas of Rome's political elite; and significantly, the privilege of safe haven within them extended to their territories as well. A political exile, though banished from Rome itself, could thus retire comfortably to his country estates. It is even possible that the safe-haven status was approved by general senatorial agreement as a preemptive measure of self-preservation, since political fortunes were liable to shift unpredictably in Rome. A tainted politician like Sulla could retire to the Bay of Naples to forestall any possible legal action against him after his retirement. But there was also a very Greek component to Neapolis' liberality, tied to the age-old concepts of *xenia,* hospitality to travelers, and possibly *asylia,* territorial inviolability granted by general agreement.

As part of their treaty obligation to Rome, Neapolis and other port cities were required to provide ships and their crews during times of war; but the number of ships, it seems, was modest.[15] In the early years of the treaty, as J.H. Thiel argues, Rome was unlikely to have demanded too much from Neapolis, given the political instability within the city. In later times, Livy has the Romans claiming that:

> **34.** from the people of Rhegion [Reggio Calabria] and Neapolis and Tarentum [Taranto, formerly Taras] we demand what they owe [i.e., ships] in accordance with the treaty from the time they came under our sovereignty, with one unbroken continuity of right, always recognized, never interrupted. [Livy 35.16.8]

But this generality crudely conflates three very distinct treaties, the harshest of which was with Tarentum. That city may rightly have been understood to lie under Roman "sovereignty" — but Neapolis, never — or at least not until the Social War. Evidently the first time Neapolis was called upon to provide ships to Rome was at the onset of the First Punic War (264–241 BCE), specifically for transporting troops across the straits of Sicily.[16]

---

15. Livy 26.39.5, 35.16.3, 36.42.1–2.
16. Polybios 1.20.13–14.

CHAPTER 4 🏛 NEAPOLIS AND THE RISE OF ROME

It was probably as an expert transporter of troops and provisions, rather than as shipbuilder or combatant, that Neapolis made her greatest contributions to Rome's wars in the third century. Thiel contends that from 311 BCE, when Rome established the office of *duoviri navales*, Rome's maritime allies, not the Romans themselves, operated the expanding Roman navy. Neapolis probably provided crews to navigate Roman ships as well as her own, just as Sicilian cities did during the Second Punic War (218–201 BCE). Now undeniably the foremost port on the Tyrrhenian, Neapolis would have contributed men in their capacity as mariners, not warriors; yet this would not have insulated them from peril. Diodoros[17] claims that in the Second Punic War "the Romans and their allies lost a multitude of ships and no fewer than one hundred thousand men [in naval operations alone], including those who perished by shipwreck" — an astounding figure, doubtless exaggerated to emphasize the truly international scope of the effort undertaken by the maritime powers allied with Rome. Of course Neapolis' geography played a role in Roman conflicts too. Her preexisting control of the Bay and its approaches ensured a reliable Tyrrhenian harborage. In 191 and 171 BCE, for example, the fleets of Rome and her allies gathered there before sailing to Greece;[18] and in 180, seven thousand Ligurian captives disembarked here.[19]

Neapolis was essential to Rome's seaborne provisioning and transport but seems to have had no role in Roman land campaigns. In the Second Punic War, numerous Campanian cities contributed cavalry to the Roman cause. Capua sent three hundred officers of the horse to garrison Sicilian cities and Campanian cavalry participated in the battles of Lake Trasimene and Cannae.[20] Yet in late 217 BCE, some months after the calamity at Lake Trasimene, Neapolitan ambassadors made a spontaneous offer of gold vessels to the Roman treasury, which they characterized as a substitute for "their own persons" — a gesture intimating that even in that moment of dire alarm, Neapolis was contributing no soldiers to Rome [Commentary 4.1, p. 146].

17. *Historical Library* 23.15.4.
18. Livy, *History of Rome* 36.42.1–2, 42.48.9.
19. Livy 40.41.3.
20. Livy 23.4.8, 23.31.10, 22.13.2, 22.42.11.

THE CRISIS OF 216–211 BCE AND THE LAST NEAPOLITAN COINAGE

The following year marked a convulsion in the Roman alliance in Campania. First came Hannibal's victory at Cannae, and then his first attempt to seize Neapolis to gain a seaport on the Tyrrhenian [Commentary 4.2, pp. 146–47]. There ensued a potentially fatal disaster to Rome's fortunes: the Capuans broke with Rome and sided with Hannibal. The praetor Marcellus rushed to Neapolis, finding its citizens in no danger of revolt. But Nola, whose grain supply was almost as important to Rome as Capua's, was wavering and required political intervention.[21] The loss of Capua's fertile territory to the Carthaginians had an immediate effect. The following year, Rome had to requisition grain from Nola and Neapolis for the war effort.[22] The situation cannot have failed to magnify the importance of Neapolis. Suddenly she was on the doorstep of Hannibal's power base, and suddenly her contribution to the food supply was greatly magnified. Yet for all we know about Capua's affairs in this period, Neapolis remains an enigma.

Of course Neapolis' magnification must be viewed against the gathering strength of Rome, whose power had already been manifest for a century. As Rome began to centralize control of money in Italy in the third century BCE, many of her allies stopped minting altogether. Neapolis gave up making silver coins first; its final issues, all bronze, probably date to the Second Punic War. We discussed

Fig. 4.5. Bronze trias of Neapolis. Naples, Museo Archeologico Nazionale.

21. Plutarch, *Marcellus* 10–11.
22. Livy 23.46.9.

CHAPTER 4 🏛 NEAPOLIS AND THE RISE OF ROME

Neapolitan coinage at length in chapter 3, but here we consider a few seemingly insignificant bronze issues that have drawn little attention. One group features Apollo on the obverse, his lyre and *omphalos* on the reverse. A second, half-weight group represents, respectively, a male bust with a star behind the neck and a horseman, probably one of the Dioscuri in each case. Finally, a one-third-weight group depicts Artemis–Diana and a cornucopia [Fig. 4.5]. All of these include a handful of series that represent crowns of laurel around the border as an alternative to the more usual circle of dots. This has led Taliercio to suggest that the entire category of bronzes issued at this time celebrates a victory. But whose victory, achieved when?

The Apollo and Dioscuri imagery fits the cultic context of Neapolis as we know it. Much more puzzling is the Artemis–cornucopia pairing. To be sure, the cornucopia motif, though not a staple of coin iconography in this region, is a thoroughly suitable symbol of abundance under the circumstances. After all, Neapolis had long been a major entrepôt of food shipments and seems to have gained temporary importance as a producer of grain after Capua's change of sides. But there is no evidence of a Neapolitan cult of Artemis–Diana outside the limited scope of the phratry of the Artemisioi [Commentary 5.3, pp. 177–78]. Nor was the hunter-goddess often affiliated with the bounty of agriculture. In truth, this coin seems more appropriate for nearby Capua, with its fertile and productive fields. The only attested cult site of Artemis–Diana in all of ancient Campania — and easily the most venerable and prestigious sanctuary in the region — was on Mons Tifata, administered by Capua [see Fig. 1.2]. A coinage bearing the legend "Campani," minted in Neapolis itself and sponsored by Capua, had featured this goddess prominently. But what event would have led Neapolis to celebrate the favors of another city, let alone one with which it had never had close ties?

The answer, I believe, lies in Capua's decision in 216 BCE to cast its lot with the Carthaginians. In the ensuing years Hannibal garrisoned the city and took the adjacent Mons Tifata as his citadel and base of operations. When in 211 Roman forces took Capua after a long siege, retribution was swift and ruthless. The old city institutions were dismantled and Capua's fabled fields were declared Roman public territory. Rome seized the city, the Campanian plains, and Capua's most potent religious asset, the sanctuary of Diana Tifatina, for its own, establishing a magistracy for maintaining the sanctuary.

During these years of desperate warfare, grain shortages in Italy were a constant worry. Neapolis, still in control of its port and the southern Tyrrhenian Sea, did what it could to provision the Roman army. In 215 BCE, Q. Fabius transported grain from Nola and Neapolis to the Roman camp above Suessula, which was protecting the crucial Nolan territory.[23] On their own, such relief efforts would not have inspired any commemorative coins; but the enormous psychological victory at Capua in 211 is a different matter. Mons Tifata must have seemed a prize of great political potency, its famous goddess having suffered the outrage of Hannibal's occupation. Consciously avoiding the Carthaginian's scorched-earth policies, the Romans carefully preserved the vanquished city and its fertile fields: the cornucopia was not an empty promise. At this time, whether out of fear or gratitude, it must have seemed a politically astute gesture for Rome's loyal ally and vassal state, Neapolis, to issue a coin — the Diana–cornucopia type — celebrating the refashioning of the once-independent Capua into a profitable Roman possession. Numerous mints had sprung up in previous years, some working on Rome's behalf, some on Hannibal's; so Neapolis was working in an improvisatory environment in which partisan symbolism would hardly be unexpected. The companion Dioscuri series also had resonance with Rome: more or less contemporaneously, a variety of coins in the name of Rome prominently featured the mythic twins, Kastor and Polydeukes (Castor and Pollux in Latin), recalling their heroism against the enemies of Rome at the dawn of the Republic. These undertakings would have been part of a concerted effort by Neapolis to press her advantage with the Romans, while simultaneously sending a message to Campanians at large.

Taliercio is correct to conjecture that a victory stood behind the final bronze coins of Neapolis, but the city's agency in that victory was secondary at best. In essence, this is the numismatic manifestation of a *Roman* achievement. A similar impulse may have driven Neapolis' only known native historian, Eumachos, to compose a history of the

23. Livy 23.46.9.

CHAPTER 4 🏛 NEAPOLIS AND THE RISE OF ROME

Hannibalic War.[24] The coinage sent a simple and powerful message of the twofold glory redounding to Rome, and thus, by extension, to Neapolis itself. On the one hand, there was the recovery of the great sanctuary of Diana. Rome could be seen as a liberator of a revered Italian deity. This liberation was simultaneously an act of *pietas* that would have resonated not only in Campania, but in Rome itself, which harbored the third-most-important Diana sanctuary in Italy, after those at Aricia and Capua. On the other hand, the bounty of the land had been wrested from the grip of Hannibal, and now it was the permanent property of Rome. The theme encompasses a double restitution, religious and alimentary. One represents a return to the status quo ante, while the other bespeaks radical new conditions under Roman hegemony.

These coins seem to distill the unique interdependency of Neapolis and Rome. But the symbolism is not overtly Roman, for Neapolis retained its identity and its civic independence. Its congratulation of the hegemon, though clear enough, was nevertheless veiled behind a symbolism of more local significance. The Roman message, in essence, was connotative. The surface, denotative message was thoroughly consonant with it. But because bronze coinage was principally for regional circulation, Neapolis wished to communicate that it was, first and foremost, a Campanian city, attendant to the interests of the region — while gently pressing the advantage of having a powerful external friend.

NEAPOLIS AS A COMMERCIAL POWER IN THE SECOND CENTURY BCE

After the war, northern Campania was a solid bloc of Roman municipalities. A prefecture of ten territories was established: along the inland plain, Casilinum, Capua, Calatia, Suessula, Acerrae, and Atella; along the coast, Cumae, Pozzuoli, Liternum, and Volturnum.[25] The final three were refounded as colonies between 197 and 194 BCE. Neapolis, however, remained independent and autonomous. For the time being, her status as the most important port on the Tyrrhenian

---

24. Athenaeus, *Deipnosophists* 13.577a. No text of this work survives.
25. Festus p. 262 L.

remained unchallenged. But a new, Rome-centered world order was now firmly in place, and Neapolis went in search of opportunities. Neapolitan merchants and brokers seem to have flourished in the wake of expanded Roman power. By the second century BCE Italian exports, especially wine and oil, were enjoying a much amplified scale and reach. Imports of foodstuffs increased as well, along with luxury goods. The steady urbanization of Italian towns, the growth of *latifundia,* or large-scale, slave-powered farms, and Rome's aggressive policy of imperialism fueled a robust slave trade. Neapolis would have participated in all these markets and probably continued her central role in grain imports too. The names of Neapolitan merchants and

Fig. 4.6. *Funerary reliefs from tombs of Neapolis. Naples, Museo Archeologico Nazionale.* Photo: R. Taylor.

CHAPTER 4 ▥ NEAPOLIS AND THE RISE OF ROME

middlemen appear in numerous places around the Mediterranean at this time, sometimes on public inscriptions, and often on control marks of pottery and amphoras. They were particularly active on the island of Delos in the second and early first centuries BCE. More Neapolitans are attested among Italians at Delos than any other citizens except those of Elea–Velia. The Neapolitan financiers Trebius Loesius and Marcus Anterius were particularly prominent. Another, Philostratos of Askalon, gained Neapolitan citizenship sometime between 106 and 97 BCE — though for what reason, we do not know. Loesius, active in the 160s BCE, was an entrepreneur as well as a banker. Stamped pots from his factory on Ischia appear in Sicily and Carthage, among other destinations.

In one tangible form, Delos — or properly speaking, the adjoining cemetery island, Rhenaia — left its mark on the culture of Neapolis. In the first century BCE, in the various cemeteries around the city, tombs were adorned with relief plaques or stelae featuring formulaic, Atticizing representations of the dead, seated and draped — women often in classical Greek fashion, men in contemporary Italian clothing — either alone or clasping the right hand of a relative [Fig. 4.6]. Greek, Oscan, and Latin names consort together in the inscriptions, which, however, are always in Greek. These reliefs have no analogue elsewhere in Italy except at the Adriatic port of Ancona. Delos, it seems, was the inspiration for both cities. Recent petrographic analysis demonstrates that the marble for some of the Neapolitan plaques came from the famous white-marble quarries on the island of Paros, just 25 kilometers south of Delos. In other cases, the marble has been traced to Carrara in Italy, where the quarries began operations only under Julius Caesar [d. 44 BCE]. Initially Neapolitans of the mercantile class brought the idea to their homeland. Whether made of marble or terracotta, such reliefs seem to have remained popular at Neapolis deep into the imperial era.

The modest Neapolitan territory supported oil and wine production of high quality. We have already seen that in the Hellenistic period Neapolis was evidently producing wine of prize quality for the games. Pliny the Elder cites a newfangled grape hybrid called Trebellian produced four miles from Neapolis, presumably in the rich plains east of the city.[26] Other varieties, such as Cauline and Trifoline, were also widespread in the region by the first century CE, and the Aminaean, developed in the famous Ager Falernus north of Campania, flourished here too.[27] Pliny cites other, more specialized produce for which the Neapolitan territory was noted: chestnuts,[28] quinces,[29] and roses cultivated for perfume.[30] And as the fame of the region grew among Romans in the second and first centuries BCE, the city benefited immeasurably from the culture of therapeutic bathing that developed around the abundant thermal spas west of the city and on Ischia.[31]

Neapolis' founders probably never envisioned their colony as a center of production and export. The city's early economic success relied instead on its function as a maritime entrepôt along the lucrative Tyrrhenian trade routes. But as early as the mid-fifth century BCE, Neapolis was manufacturing pottery for the regional market and wine for export. From the fourth century BCE, multiple potteries along the waterfront were producing amphora types known as Greco-Italic IV–VI, including the "crown" amphoras mentioned above.[32] Ischia had been exporting wine since the seventh century BCE, and continued to do so under Neapolitan control. The scope of the local wine trade is only just coming into focus; it appears to have grown significantly in the late fourth century BCE, after Rome and Neapolis had established their *foedus aequum*. Initially it targeted Carthaginian centers in Corsica, Sicily, and Africa, but by the mid-third century, when Rome and Neapolis were at war with Carthage, exports shifted to the northwest Mediterranean, particularly Gaul and Spain. Throughout the three Punic Wars, Neapolis seems to have maintained a brisk export business with these regions.

26. *Natural History* 14.69.
27. Galen, *De methodo medendi* 12.4.
28. 15.94, 17.122.
29. 15.38.
30. 13.5.
31. See chapter 7.
32. See pp. 129–30.

CHAPTER 4 ◾ NEAPOLIS AND THE RISE OF ROME

Fig. 4.7. Pottery recovered from the Piazza Municipio excavations. In foreground, "Campana A" vessels. Naples, Museo Archeologico Nazionale. Photo: R. Taylor.

Around 220 BCE or even earlier, Neapolis began to export a cheap, mass-produced fineware made from the granular, light-brown clay quarried on Ischia. The finish is a simple black or charcoal-colored gloss with a metallic sheen [Fig. 4.7]. Known as "Campana A" pottery, these Neapolitan wares have been extensively studied by Nino Lamboglia and J. Paul Morel [Commentary 4.3, pp. 147–48].

The forms are simple and elegant. Tablewares such as plates, bowls, cups, and fish platters predominate. Lamps, as well as *gutti* (implements for pouring oil into lamps), were produced too. Simple decorations, either in the form of white painted glaze or stamped patterns, were sometimes applied to the surface. Producers' stamps on the wares reveal Greek, Osco-Samnite, and Roman names. Standards of production are strikingly uniform for "Campana A." This fact above all has suggested the existence in Neapolis of a rigid, fairly

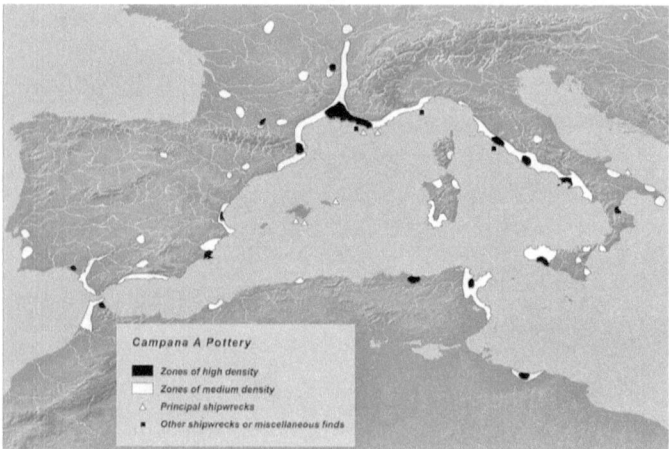

Fig. 4.8. Map of the western Mediterranean representing the diffusion of "Campana A" pottery. After Morel 1985.

centralized, slave-reliant model of production that discouraged innovation and confined the reach of prosperity to a fairly small merchant elite. "Campana A" pottery was transported in enormous quantities all around the western Mediterranean [Fig. 4.8]. At its height annual production amounted, at the very least, to hundreds of thousands of units per year. It is abundant in shipwrecks of the period. Castoffs form thick deposits at many sites, some measured in hundreds of cubic meters. In Carthage, this class of pottery represents half of all fine ceramic used in the first half of the second century BCE, and similar statistics can be extracted from other North African cities.

The key to the astonishing success of this enterprise was the perfection of mass-production techniques and exclusive distribution by sea. The vast majority of "Campana A" has been found within a few miles of the seacoast. Even in Italy this pottery barely penetrated the interior. To the extent that it reached inland elsewhere, particularly in Gaul and North Africa, it probably did so by means of independent middlemen *(negotiatores, navicularii)* who bought shipments wholesale at the ports and transported them overland or upriver. Whereas the old coastal colonies consumed "Campana A" with careless abandon, consumers in the hinterland — faced with higher prices from the

CHAPTER 4 ⬛ NEAPOLIS AND THE RISE OF ROME

additional costs of transport — treated the wares with proportionally greater care.

What convergence of accident, opportunity, and initiative motivated this model of production and distribution — one of the most intensive commercial enterprises in all antiquity? It was not a matter of the sudden happy discovery of a natural resource. The clay deposits on Ischia had been exploited since the eighth century BCE. One factor in this fairly sudden phenomenon may have been the unique marriage in Neapolis of the Greek genius for sea trade with Campanian networks of regional influence. Even more important to its success, however, was the blessing of Rome. In return for loyalty, Rome not only allowed Neapolis to keep her sovereignty but also endorsed — openly or tacitly — the city's ambitious regime of economic expansion. In the West, wherever Roman influence advanced, "Campana A" often followed.

From the end of the second century BCE, the production and diffusion of "Campana A" pottery began to taper off. In 91 BCE, a volcanic eruption occurred on Ischia;[33] and although the Neapolitan industry did not cease production altogether until about 40 BCE, its fate was sealed in 82 BCE when Sulla's soldiers seized Neapolis — and, implicitly, Ischia as well. By curtailing the flow of cheap fine ware from Neapolis, Sulla fortuitously set the stage for the future success of one of his veteran colonies to the north, probably founded in the following year: Arretium (modern Arezzo), which would soon establish itself as the foremost center for the production of fine tableware in the Roman West. The fiery orange sheen of the Arretine red slipware, endlessly imitated around the Roman world, would remain the favored aesthetic for centuries to come.

Neapolitan export pottery did not die out with "Campana A." Investigations of two discard heaps near the churches of Sta. Maria Maggiore and the Girolamini seem to suggest that in the Roman period a widely exported variety of red slipware from the Vesuvian region was produced at least partly in Neapolis. Production began in the mid-first century BCE, just as the old black-gloss industry

33. Julius Obsequens 54.

was expiring. The new forms of tableware, which were produced for about a century, have been found not only around the Bay of Naples, but also in Apulia, Sicily, North Africa, and Spain. From the Augustan period through the mid-Empire, the city seems to have produced a significant amount of thin-walled slipware. Of the examples recovered from the Metropolitana excavations, 39 percent fit the mineralogical profile of the older "Campana A" pottery.

SULLA

We know nothing of Neapolis' role in the Social War (91–88 BCE) except that it remained a faithful ally of Rome. In 90, after the outbreak of hostilities, Rome passed a *lex Iulia*, a law that extended the option of full citizenship to Italian allied communities. Cicero characterizes it as the culmination of a long series of Roman laws that had been freely offered to allies as models for their own legislation.

> 35. Last of all came the Julian Law itself under which citizenship was offered to the federated cities and the Latins on condition that those states which had not "given consent," should not hold citizenship. This was the cause of a lively dispute among the citizens of Herakleia [in Lucania] and of Neapolis, since a great part of the inhabitants of those states preferred to our citizenship the freedom enjoyed under their own treaty. [*Pro Balbo* 21]

Elsewhere, Cicero makes clear that Neapolis accepted the offer,[34] thereby abrogating the old *foedus aequum* of 327/6 BCE. The form of Roman citizenship the Neapolitans had held since that time, *civitas sine suffragio*, which had been extended widely to allied cities and their territories, allowed them to keep their own sovereign systems of government but also to enjoy the privileges of Roman citizenship with the important exception of the vote. The *lex Iulia* granted full enfranchisement, including voting rights, but at a price: any city accepting it would relinquish its own laws and constitution. It was this shift in legal standing that would later impel Strabo[35] to say that although Neapolis preserved many Greek traditions, the

---

34. *Letters to His Friends* 13.30, *Letters to Atticus* 10.13.1.
35. *Geography* 5.4.7. See Reading 80 below.

CHAPTER 4 ■ NEAPOLIS AND THE RISE OF ROME

people themselves were Romans. At the time, it seems, a majority of Neapolitans resisted the Roman franchise; yet in this "lively dispute" they did not prevail. A minority won the day — whether by procedural maneuver, deceit, or intimidation, we cannot say. Heavy Roman influence would have played a part in the outcome. Also, the eruption on Ischia in the previous year may have disrupted "Campana A" production and trade, weakening Neapolis' resistance to Roman will. Interestingly, in the following year of 89 BCE, nearby Herculaneum succumbed to a Sullan siege.[36] The fall of this town, linked closely to its more powerful neighbor, seems to have cemented Neapolis' hostility to Sulla, even as it paid obeisance to Rome.

Less than a decade later, as civil war engulfed Italy, raw Roman power was again exercised on Neapolis — this time, in the starkest terms. What must have been a transformative event for the community receives the merest mention in a single written source, almost an afterthought in the awful narrative of Sulla's ruthless Italian offensive in 82 BCE upon his return from the Mithridatic War. According to Appian,[37] not long after their landing at Brundisium (Brindisi), Sulla's forces gained entrance to Neapolis by treachery, killing all who could not escape and seizing the triremes in the harbor. These were probably removed to Pozzuoli, which thenceforth would enjoy primacy over Tyrrhenian maritime affairs for a century and a half. Sulla's offensive against Neapolis may have turned upon a grudge: six years earlier, in 88 BCE, Ischia, still under Neapolitan control, had served as a refuge for his archenemy Marius as he fled to Africa.[38] But the situation as described by Appian signals open opposition to Sulla from Neapolis, manifested by use of the triremes. And again, there is the shadow of divisiveness within: as in 327 BCE, the city was breached by treachery. The legal maneuvers that followed can only be guessed. Ischia seems to have been confiscated from Neapolis altogether and absorbed into Roman state property. That, at least, is my inference from Strabo's report[39] that Neapolis lost the island in a war and that

36. Velleius Paterculus, *Compendium* 2.16.
37. *Civil Wars* 1.89.
38. Plutarch, *Marius* 40.
39. 5.4.9.

Augustus later returned it. Capri too may have been seized at this time; it would later become an imperial property. These island confiscations are of a piece with the seizure of the triremes, for Neapolis must have resumed her old strategic naval deployments at both islands to guard and police the Bay. Possibly Sulla also was eyeing the private villas and farms belonging to his political enemies, who like many prominent Romans were investing heavily in real estate on the Bay. The formal proscriptions of these men, initiated the following year, resulted in significant confiscations in coastal Campania.

Ettore Pais attractively suggests that Sulla's confidante Lucius Licinius Lucullus managed to acquire for himself the entire neighborhood of Pizzofalcone, engulfing the old town of Parthenope–Palaepolis. He converted his acquisition into a notorious luxury villa which later came into the imperial domain.[40] This confiscation of the historically Campanian enclave of Parthenope, now probably nothing more than a garrisoned ghost town, may have been a symbolic measure to impugn the remnants of an ethnically Campanian faction in Neapolis. Sulla had no love of Osco-Samnite peoples, whom he had battled during the Social War and who continued to fight with fierce intensity in the remnants of Marius' forces in Italy. They gave him the perfect political excuse, perhaps, to invoke Palaepolis' anti-Roman stance in 327/6 BCE. By contrast, he seems to have promoted a strongly Hellenophile policy in the city proper. After his retirement to the Bay in 80 BCE, he is said to have frequented Neapolis, partaking of its Greek customs.[41] Described as "a densely crowded town" at this time, the city suffered fairly little damage from the seizure. But we can only imagine the payback visited on the city leaders and their patronage networks. It may have been at this time that fine Roman-style houses, often with mosaics, began to appear in the neighborhood of the forum and on or near the central east-west street, modern Via dei Tribunali.[42]

40. See pp. 144, 299, 308, 318–19; Commentary 8.2, pp. 334–35.
41. Cicero, *For Rabirius Postumus* 26–27.
42. See pp. 186, 209–10, 362.

CHAPTER 4 🏛 NEAPOLIS AND THE RISE OF ROME

Sulla's partisans forcibly colonized the nearby towns and territories of Pompeii, Nola, Urbana, Abella, and Suessula. With the proscriptions in 81 BCE they also seized many farms and villas in the Ager Campanus of Capua. Under the circumstances, they cannot have spared Neapolitan territory. I will make the case in chapter 5 for a widespread Sullan land grab and reapportionment in the *Neapolitanum* which, for uncertain reasons, was never called colonization. The subsequent proliferation of Roman names here (Antonii, Cornelii, Domitii, Iunii, Septimii, Valerii, etc.), so evident in inscriptions of the imperial era, may be due in large part to the permanent influx of Sullans, as at Pompeii and other colonies. But the Neapolitan inscriptions also reveal the persistence of old Campanian families such as the Annii, Fuficii, Marii, Opsii, Paccii, and Poppaei.

The Sullan occupation of the city undeniably precipitated broad social and political changes. But did it destroy Neapolis' commercial vitality along with the old merchant class that had contributed so much to the Greek city's rise? That is Ettore Lepore's hypothesis. The subsequent historical record, he argues, confirms "the absence of an economic bourgeoisie" — a condition of parasitism that plagued Neapolis, in his view, for centuries thereafter. It is mostly an argument from silence. Compared to the epigraphic record of Puteoli, Capua, or Pompeii, Neapolis' surviving inscriptions — all of them from the post-Sullan era — reveal few individuals engaged in trade, banking, the merchant marine, and so forth.

Yet *culturally* the city was in the ascendant, as important Romans and their entourages increasingly peopled the villa landscape around the Bay, bringing with them a demand for the Greek arts, practical and aesthetic. "That city is now an abode of peace, a resting-place where the Muses dwell, and life there is free from pressing anxieties," wrote Silius Italicus in the late first century CE, when the migration was complete.[43] Lepore is right to observe that a transformation was taking place. His mistake is to presume that a Neapolis reinvented as a cultural capital and resort was inherently "decadent" and cannot possibly have matched the vitality of the old freewheeling port city. We will explore the salubrious cultural climate of Roman Neapolis in chapter 8.

43. *Punica* 12.31–32.

Commentary 4.1: Neapolis Remains Faithful to Rome

36. Winter [late 217 BCE] had already brought the fighting about Gereonium to a standstill, when envoys from Neapolis arrived in Rome. Bringing forty massive golden bowls into the senate-house, they delivered themselves to this effect: that they knew that the treasury of the Roman people was becoming exhausted by the war, and since it was being waged no less in behalf of the cities and lands of the allies than for the capital and citadel of Italy — the city of Rome — and for its empire, the Neapolitans had deemed it right to employ the gold which their ancestors had bequeathed them, whether for the adornment of their temples or as a subsidy in time of need, to assist the Roman People; had they thought themselves capable of helping with their persons, they would have offered these with the same heartiness; it would gratify them if the Roman senators and people would look on all the possessions of the Neapolitans as their own, and consider that their gift deserved a willing acceptance, as being greater and of more account in respect of the friendliness and goodwill of the givers than in actual value. The envoys received a vote of thanks for this generosity and thoughtfulness, and the bowl of least weight was accepted. [Livy, *History of Rome* 22.32.4–9]

Commentary 4.2: Hannibal's Attempts to Seize Neapolis

Though twice breached by treachery, Neapolis was virtually impossible to seize by force, as the Epirote army determined during the Pyrrhic War.[44] Hannibal is thought to have made two attempts on Neapolis at least; a third, though recorded by Livy, is dubious. The two reliable accounts, which Livy draws from the chronicle of Coelius Antipater, are set shortly before and after Hannibal's acquisition of Capua in 216.

37. [After the battle of Cannae, Hannibal] made his way through the Campanian region to the Lower Sea [the Tyrrhenian], intending to attack Neapolis, that he might have a seaport. On entering the territory of the Neapolitans, he stationed some of the Numidians in ambush, wherever he conveniently could (and most of the roads are deep-cut

---

44. Zonaras 8.4a.

CHAPTER 4 ▫ NEAPOLIS AND THE RISE OF ROME

and the turnings concealed). Other Numidians he ordered to ride up to the gates, making a display of the booty they were driving along before them from the farms. Against these men, because they seemed to be few in number and disorganized, a troop of cavalry made a sally, but being drawn into the ambush by the enemy's purposely retreating, it was overpowered. And not a man would have escaped if the proximity of the sea and the sight of vessels, chiefly of fishermen, not far from the shore had not given those who could swim a way of escape. However a number of young nobles were captured or slain in that battle, among them Hegeas, a cavalry commander, who fell as he rashly pursued the retreating. From besieging the city the Carthaginian was deterred by the sight of walls such as by no means invited an attacker. [Livy 23.1.5–10]

38. Upon arrival of the Roman praetor, the Carthaginian left the territory of Nola and came down to the sea near Neapolis, desiring to gain possession of a coast town to which ships might have a safe passage from Africa. But on learning that Neapolis was held by a Roman prefect — it was Marcus Junius Silanus, who had been called in by the Neapolitans themselves — he turned aside from Neapolis also, as he had from Nola, and made for Nuceria. [Livy 23.15.1–2]

Commentary 4.3: The Pottery Workshop of Corso Umberto

In the 1950s, excavations on the south side of the old city, under Corso Umberto near Piazza Nicola Amore, turned up an extraordinary amount of black-gloss pottery. What looked to untrained eyes like an extremely unpromising jumble of defective, miscellaneous castoffs has proven to be an important document of the city's economic history. Although the excavation was never published, one of the foremost archaeologists in Naples at the time, Werner Johannowsky, was quick to recognize the importance of this find. Only a few years earlier Nino Lamboglia had published his landmark study, *Per una classificazione preliminare della ceramica campana,* the first to identify and classify many of the forms of black-gloss pottery made from the distinctive clay quarried on Ischia. Lamboglia named this pottery "Campana A," to distinguish it from another prolific class of black-gloss pottery, his "Campana B," which he believed to have been produced at the inland centers of northern Campania. (More likely it comes from Latium, Etruria, or both.)

It quickly emerged that the debris was part of a discard heap from a nearby pottery. The constraints of urban archaeology rendered any search for adjoining buildings impossible; yet the heap of "clinkers" was windfall enough. In addition to the thousands of miscellaneous sherds of misfired pots, many terracotta spacers were found as well — sure evidence of a production facility. The spacers, used to isolate the pots from one another as they were stacked in the kiln, were of two kinds. Some were small, often pierced cylinders, resembling flattened spools; others were rings for supporting bowls and other vessels with convex undersides.

Every firing has its failed pots. Many of the pottery fragments from Corso Umberto are discolored, a sign of poor firing technique or bad positioning within the kiln. Others are fused together. In one case, the circular bases of five stacked vessels, their spacers intact between them, have been fused into a single, stratified mass. According to J. Paul Morel's exhaustive typology, the pottery forms discovered here date from the third century to the end of the second BCE. One of the oldest fragments belongs to a *skyphos*, a form that imitates a type of metal cup favored in the Hellenistic world.

CHAPTER 4 ⛩ NEAPOLIS AND THE RISE OF ROME

REFERENCES
Campania, Neapolis, and the Samnite Wars: Pugliese Carratelli 1952a: 257–62; Ciaceri 1966 [1924]: 3.18–21; Lepore 1967b; Frederiksen 1984: 148, 180–220; Beloch 1989 [1890]: 76–78; Lomas 1993: 41–43. **Neapolis and Rome in the third century BCE:** Lepore 1952: 310–12; 1967c: 241–76, 1985b; Frederiksen 1984: 221–37; Lomas 1993: 72, 77–78; Mele 2014: 201–10. **Neapolitan naval assistance to Rome:** Sgobbo 1926; Thiel 1954: 33–44; Frederiksen 1984: 225–26. **Romano-Campanian coinage:** Bahrfeldt 1899; Sambon 1903: 255–56, 421–45; Breglia 1952a; Thomsen 1957–1961: 1.49–54; Mitchell 1966; 1969; 1973; Burnett 1977; 1978; 1986; 1989; 1998; Caccamo Caltabiano 1981; Crawford 1985: 29–51; Burnett and Hook 1989; Holloway 1992; Pedroni 1996; Rutter 1997: 85–86, 91–92; Vitale 1998; 2001; Taliercio Mensitieri 1999; Cantilena 2014; Bernard 2018. **Hellenistic tombs:** De Petra 1898; Gabrici 1912; Napoli 1967e; Greco Pontrandolfo and Vecchio 1985; Greco Pontrandolfo 1986; Leiwo 1994: 69–87 et passim; Buchreiter 1999b; Valerio 2007; Nava 2008a; Colussi and Leggieri 2009; Esposito 2009. **Capua, the Second Punic War, and the sanctuary of Diana Tifatina:** Frederiksen 1984: 238–65; Beloch 1989 [1890]: 407–13; Carafa 2008: 121–24. **Neapolitans at Delos:** Hatzfeld 1912: 17, 46–47, 67, 73–74, 84, 98–99, et passim; Lepore 1952: 313–14; 1967c: 270; 1985a: 117; Deniaux 1981; Mancinetti Santamaria 1982: 83–84; Leiwo 1989; 1994: 23, 26, 72–73, 90–91, 96–97, 144; Lomas 1993: 97–99, 100. **Funerary stelae:** Rocco 1942–1946; Miranda 1985b; 1985c; Papadopoulos 1985b; Leiwo 1994: 69–87, 116–20; Antonelli et al. 2017; Emmerson 2017. **Greco-Italic amphoras and the Neapolitan wine trade:** Olcese 2010; 2011; 2017; Pugliese 2014; Giampaola et al. 2017. **"Campana A" pottery:** Lamboglia 1952; Lepore 1967c: 244–53; Morel 1981a; 1981b; 1985; 1986a; Febbraro and Giampaola 2012. **Corso Umberto workshop:** Accorona et al. 1985; LaForgia 1985a. **Neapolitan slipware:** Soricelli 1987; Soricelli et al. 1994; Faga 2010. **Ischia in Hellenistic and Roman times:** Pais 1908b; 1908c; Monti 1980: 127–281; Buchner and Gialanella 1994. **Sulla in Campania:** Pais 1900–1901; 1908a: 210–11; 1908b; Lepore 1952: 318; 1967c: 276–83; Pugliese Carratelli 1952: 266; Monti 1968: 89–90; 1980: 201–2; Franciosi 2002: 243–48; Minieri 2002:

254–56; D'Arms 2003 [1970]: 40–48; Savino 2009. **The question of Neapolitan decline after Sulla:** Lepore 1967d; 1985b; Leiwo 1994: 25–27; De Nardis 2015. **Ethnic mixing of names in Neapolitan families:** Leiwo 1994: passim; 1996. **Neapolis' status as a Roman colony:** Sartori 1953: 42–46; Taylor 2015a.

CHAPTER 5. FROM REPUBLIC TO EMPIRE

During the consular year of 51/50 BCE, Pompey the Great fell gravely ill. His recovery at Neapolis prompted elaborate local celebrations with garlands and torches. Gratifying as this must have seemed, it was an ominous turn in Pompey's relations with his fellow triumvir Caesar, who was furious at his rival's favorable treatment.[1] Cicero found the extravagant celebrations at Neapolis, Cumae, and Pozzuoli distasteful and excessively "Greekish," but nevertheless, from Pompey's perspective, "fortunate." The orator drew a hard lesson from this false fortune, for hindsight had revealed its dreadful result: Pompey's haughty resistance to Caesar, his flight and downfall, and the convulsions of civil war. Indeed, the convalescence at Neapolis became a kind of symbol of hubristic overreach: if only the great man had died at his peak, he would have safeguarded his enshrinement among the highest order of Romans — maybe even have spared Rome a devastating war. As it was, he walked headlong into ruin, dragging history with him. In effect, by propping him up, Neapolis enabled his fall.

Yet it is hard to ascribe to the city or the region any special motivation for favoring Pompey apart from its longstanding tradition of hospitality. If anything, the discreet, apolitical environment cultivated at Neapolis after Sulla's purge ensured that partisans of all stripes would come here to engage in dialogue, debate, and persuasion, off the record if necessary. During the ensuing civil war the city became, in Martti Leiwo's estimation, the center for Roman shuttle diplomacy. Naturally such intensive activity could shade into intrigue. Perhaps even the conspiracy that led to Caesar's assassination in 44 BCE was born here; certainly Neapolis loomed large in the aftermath. Deep into the summer following the Ides of March, Cassius and Brutus were still here, exploiting the territory's sanctuary status to temporize and strategize during Antony's advances.[2] From Neapolis and the suburban island retreat at Nesis (Nisida) — which probably belonged to his nephew M. Licinius Lucullus, son of the

1. Cicero, *Letters to Atticus* 10.13; *Tusculan Disputations* 1.86; Velleius Paterculus, *Compendium* 2.48.2; Plutarch, *Pompey* 57.
2. Cicero, *Letters to Atticus* 16.3–5, 7.

famous consul — Brutus planned the games that he was required to stage in Rome as urban praetor. He dared not venture to the capital himself, but he and his co-conspirators enjoyed complete mobility around Neapolis and its territory. The conspirators were great Hellenophiles (Brutus would soon be welcomed in Athens). They chose for the tutelary deity of their cause not a conventional Roman god, but rather Apollo, a god with far more presence around the Bay than in the *urbs* of Rome.[3] Indeed the god's manifestation in the *urbs* as "Medicus," the one who eliminates bodily pollution, may have sprung from the Cumaean cult. (Apollo later appeared in this guise in reliefs celebrating the nymphs of Roman Ischia.) This cultic identity, proposed by Fausto Zevi, makes sense if we perceive these men as self-appointed purifiers of a pestilential tyranny. Perhaps their affinity with the venerable Euboean cult encouraged them to linger too long as they hoped against hope for a change in the political winds at Rome.

On the strength of this evidence it is sometimes argued that Neapolitan opinion tended toward the anti-Caesarean, Pompeian faction. The argument is unsustainable. In the 30s BCE, because of its importance to the naval war with Sextus Pompey, the triumvir's son, who had taken over the islands of Ischia and Procida, the northwestern Bay became the center of Octavian's and Agrippa's operations against him. In 38 BCE, Octavian removed the entire population of the island of Lipara (modern Lipari, off the north coast of Sicily) to Neapolis for the duration of the war because they had sided with Pompey's heir.[4] Even in such a militarized environment, it would have been foolish to import potential Pompeian partisans into Neapolis if the city already had such proclivities. We may suppose that these islanders, perhaps alongside prisoners of war, were quartered at villas vacated by the co-conspirators in Caesar's murder (Nesis, maybe?), which must have been occupied by Octavian's allies or soldiers at this time — or even at Lucullus' property at Parthenope, which later probably quartered the praetorian guard.[5]

3. Plutarch, *Brutus* 24.6–7.
4. Dio Cassius, *Roman History* 48.48.6.
5. See pp. 144, 299, 308, 318–19; Commentary 8.2, pp. 334–35.

CHAPTER 5 ▥ REPUBLIC TO EMPIRE

Through all the turmoil, Neapolis welcomed a continuous influx of elite Roman sojourners and valetudinarians, consolidating its reputation as a peaceful haven of Hellenic refinement. Greek-style theater thrived here, and its practitioners were sought by Brutus for his games at Rome.[6] Yet traces of the old Greco-Campanian cultural hybridity persisted: from Neapolis and Velia alone the priestesses of Ceres (Greek Demeter) were chosen, for they alone preserved a sufficiently bicultural heritage.[7] Local families readily adopted Greek, Osco-Samnite, and other Italian names. During the final decades of the Republic and the reign of Augustus, the descendants of a certain Epilytos had names such as Aristole (Greek), Paccia, Vibius, and Trebius (Samnite), even Tarchius (Etruscan).[8] This multiethnic trend, with the additional injection of Roman names, continued at least through the second century CE. While the residents of other cities in Magna Graecia were systematically erasing their Greek names and heritage, Neapolis retained a more complex social identity, undoubtedly shot through with ideological and ethnic tensions.

One of the descendants of Epilytos, himself named Epilytos, was a priest of Augustus during the emperor's lifetime — that is, an *Augustalis,* charged with venerating the imperial *genius* (spirit) within the broader context of the cult of *lares,* local gods of the place. Under Augustus, many Italian cities were divided into *regiones* (districts) with subdivisions of *vici* (neighborhoods), in large part to create opportunities for priesthoods among freedmen. Neapolis, Pozzuoli, Nola, Pompeii, and other Campanian towns seem to have been reorganized accordingly at this time. Each neighborhood was given its own cult of *lares* overseen by *vicomagistri,* minor priests drawn from the class of freedmen. The most prominent freedmen of a given town, like Epilytos, were elected to priesthoods of the new imperial cult. The attendant responsibilities, such as sponsoring or maintaining a suitably majestic cult monument, were generally distributed across a college of six priests.

6. Plutarch, *Brutus* 21.5–6.
7. Cicero, *For Balbus* 55.
8. *SEG* 4 (1929): 96–101.

There was hardly a city in Italy that did not profit from the surge of local patronage under Augustus (27 BCE–14 CE), and Neapolis was no exception. The most prominent developments known to us from this period are the introduction of the Serino Aqueduct[9] and the establishment of the Isolympic Games of the Sebasta,[10] the latter supposedly after an earthquake and fire. Both events must have transformed the city physically. Like Pompeii or Pozzuoli, Neapolis would not have lacked for large public building programs in honor of the first emperor. The new water supply expanded the city's capacity for baths and fountains, and the augmentation of the games led to the development of an athletic district in the southern quarter of the city, where most of the Sebasta-related inscriptions, buildings, and artifacts have been found.[11] Yet due to the exceedingly fragmentary nature of archaeological discoveries in Naples, the character of the early imperial city remains elusive.

Neapolis was a favorite refuge of Claudius (emperor 41–54 CE), who frequented the city and enthusiastically participated in its games.[12] At this time the city gained a major private benefactor, Gaius Stertinius Xenophon, the emperor's personal physician. Pliny the Elder[13] records that Claudius gave him 500,000 sesterces, as he had to Stertinius' equally accomplished brother; "and the estates [of Xenophon], although exhausted by beautifying Neapolis with buildings, left to the heir thirty million." This was the second-largest bequest made by a private citizen in that time — an astounding level of wealth for a man of the professional class, but indicative of Claudius' meritocratic tendencies. Naturally, the famous doctor's domicile was in Rome. But evidently he spent much time in Neapolis, probably in attendance of the sickly emperor, for whom the local climate and therapeutic springs would have been an added attraction. Lacking any additional information about Xenophon's benefactions, we can say little more about the nature of his improvements to the city.

9. See chapter 7.
10. See chapter 8.
11. See pp. 212–18.
12. See p. 317.
13. *Natural History* 29.8.

Xenophon exemplifies an interesting phenomenon in Neapolis of the imperial era: the unusual prominence of major patrons from intellectual and artistic backgrounds. Compared to mercantile powerhouses like Pozzuoli and Nola, Neapolis seems to have produced relatively few pure politicians at the equestrian and senatorial ranks. Giuseppe Camodeca securely identifies only two Roman senatorial families from Neapolis, the Opsii under Tiberius (14–37 CE) and the Clodii Nummi under the Flavians and Trajan. (Lucius Acilius Strabo, consul suffect in 71 CE, possibly represents another.) From the second century BCE, Neapolis became aware of its unique value to Rome as a haven of Hellenism.[14] The city consciously took the lead in granting citizenship to men whose attainments were more suited to the academy, theater, or odeion than to the forum or law courts. After Neapolitan citizenship disappeared, it granted them specially adapted civic honors such as demarchates and memberships in phratries. Some were in the service of the emperor, and so a symbiosis developed between the city, which benefited from imperial patronage through the surrogacy of such men as Xenophon, and the imperial court, which especially in the first century CE spent much time on the Bay. Above all other emperors, Nero loved Neapolis for its *echt* Greekness; we will discuss his local patronage in chapter 8.

THE LANDSCAPE OF DISASTER

If we discount the unknown quake that purportedly led Augustus to refound the Sebasta Games,[15] it was again during Nero's principate, fatefully, that the city suffered its first serious earthquake. Under his Flavian successors seismic and volcanic events became so acute that they dominate the historical discourse about Neapolis in this period. The Bay of Naples has always been prone to tremors and small eruptions, but the 60s, 70s, and early 80s CE, capped by the eruption of Vesuvius in 79, were unusually traumatic. An earthquake in February 62 or 63, the first truly devastating natural event in local memory, badly damaged the towns in the southeast. Pompeii never completely recovered from it. It was less intense in the northwest, but far from negligible. According to Seneca,[16] Neapolis "lost many

14. See chapter 8.
15. Dio Cassius, *Roman History* 55.10.9.
16. *Natural Questions* 6.1.2.

private dwellings but no public buildings and was only mildly grazed by the disaster; but some villas collapsed, others here and there shook with the damage." This and subsequent tremors probably prompted Pliny the Elder's scientific observations about the strangely dichotomous physical effects of earthquakes at Neapolis [Commentary 5.1, p. 177]. The urban fabric here may have resembled that at Herculaneum and Pompeii, where one- and two-story townhouses were being expanded upward by enterprising landlords, sometimes with shoddy methods and materials. Other quakes followed: a severe tremor during Nero's performance debut there in 64 CE,[17] and in the 70s and early 80s, a penumbra of seismic events surrounded the eruption of Mt. Vesuvius.

The volcano erupted sometime in the fall of 79 CE — not August, as popularly believed. Yet so overshadowed was Neapolis' loss by the annihilation of the smaller towns to the south that the literary sources barely register the trauma she sustained. The city survived, even to the extent that fourteen years later Statius could remark, "not so utterly has Vesuvius' peak and the flaming tempest of the baleful mountain drained of their townsmen their terror-stricken cities; they stand yet and their people flourish."[18] The population surge within the cities was due in part to grim realities outside, for the eastern part of Neapolitan territory may have been rendered effectively sterile, at least for some decades.

The consequences of the eruption — its burial of the towns of Pompeii and Herculaneum, along with the areas to the east, south, and southwest of the volcano — are familiar. The prevailing winds were from the northwest that day, ensuring that the cities on that end of the Bay would survive. Yet Pliny the Younger's famous description of the phenomenon from his vantage point at Misenum, about sixteen miles due west of the volcano, vividly recollects the trauma of the event even on an area that experienced little damage:

> **39.** For several days past there had been earth tremors which were not particularly alarming because they are frequent in Campania: but that night the shocks were so

17. See pp. 340–41; Readings 92 and 93.
18. *Silvae* 3.5.72–74.

CHAPTER 5 ■ REPUBLIC TO EMPIRE

violent that everything felt as if it were not only shaken but overturned.... By now it was dawn, but the light was still dim and faint. The buildings round us were already tottering, and the open space we were in was too small for us not to be in real and imminent danger if the house collapsed. This finally decided us to leave town. We were followed by a panic-stricken mob of people.... Once beyond the buildings we stopped, and there we had some extraordinary experiences which thoroughly alarmed us. The carriages we had ordered to be brought out began to run in different directions though the ground was quite level, and would not remain stationary even when wedged with stones. We also saw the sea sucked away and apparently forced back by the earthquake: at any rate it receded from the shore so that quantities of sea creatures were left stranded on dry sand.... On the leeward side a fearful black cloud was rent by forked and quivering bursts of flame, and parted to reveal great tongues of fire, like flashes of lightning magnified in size.... Soon afterwards the cloud sank down to earth and covered the sea; it had already blotted out Capri and hidden the promontory of Misenum from sight.... Ashes were already falling, not as yet very thickly. I looked round: a dense black cloud was coming up behind us, spreading over the earth like a flood.... We had scarcely sat down to rest when darkness fell, not the dark of a moonless or cloudy night, but as if the lamp had been put out in a closed room.... A gleam of light returned, but we took this to be a warning of the approaching flames rather than daylight. However, the flames remained some distance off; then darkness came on once more and ashes began to fall again, this time in heavy showers. We rose from time to time and shook them off, otherwise we would have been buried and crushed beneath their weight.... At last the darkness thinned and dispersed into smoke or cloud; then there was genuine daylight, and the sun actually shone out, but yellowish as it is during an eclipse. We were terrified to see everything changed, buried deep in ashes like snowdrifts. We returned to Misenum where we attended to our physical needs as best we could, and then spent an anxious night alternating between hope and fear. Fear predominated, for the earthquakes went on. [*Epistles* 4.20]

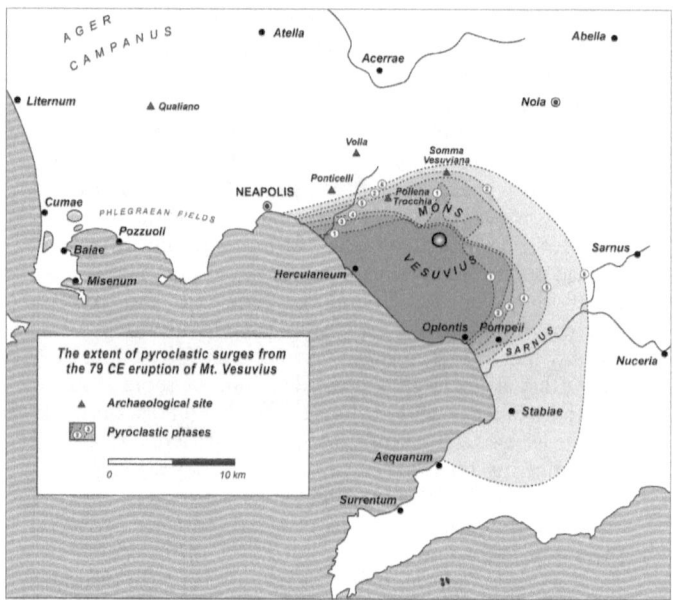

Fig. 5.1. Map indicating the extent of the six surges of the eruption of 79 CE. After Sigurdsson and Carey 2002.

The situation was bad enough at Misenum. It was worse around Neapolis, which lay halfway between Pliny's vantage point and the volcano. The stratigraphy of the region shows that pyroclastic surges rushing down the volcano's slopes in 79 repeatedly invaded the eastern Neapolitan territory; recent excavations at the villa of C. Olius Ampliatus at Ponticelli, some five kilometers east of the city walls, reveal evidence of surges comparable in destructive force to those at Herculaneum, flattening walls and toppling columns. The deadly sixth and final surge, which on the second day of the eruption killed Pliny the Elder on the beach of Stabiae at the opposite end of the Bay, reached the outskirts of Neapolis [Fig. 5.1]. In the arable plain east of the city, these surges and subsequent rain-washed mudslides of loose volcanic tephra would likely have erased the living landscape. Farther west, the effects were not so dire; Statius[19] praises the vineyards of Mt. Gaurus (Monte Barbaro), north of Pozzuoli, in the post-eruption landscape. The effect

19. *Silvae* 3.5.99.

CHAPTER 5 ☷ REPUBLIC TO EMPIRE

Fig. 5.2. Reconstructed cadastral grid of the territory of Neapolis. Background © 2020 Google. After Chouquer and Favory 1987.

may have resembled that suffered in central Luzon after the eruption of Mt. Pinatubo in 1991: outside a radius of about ten kilometers from the volcano little of permanence was obliterated, but the heavy accumulation of ash, granular lahar, and lapilli transformed a fertile plain into a desert. Hard-hit spots in the Neapolitan and Nolan landscape probably ceased production on a profitable scale for many years. Not once, in all his poems praising the delights of the Bay of Naples, does Statius specifically commend the inland territory of Neapolis herself. Rather, he is quite forthright about the blow the city incurred. In two apostrophes directed to Parthenope, he laments "the loss that mad Vesuvius caused you,"[20] and urges her to "lift up your head half-buried from the dust that suddenly whelmed you."[21] A few decades later, however, Dionysios Periegetes[22] was lauding "chaste Parthenope, heavy under the weight of grain-sheaves," and by the early third century CE, Dio Cassius[23] noted

20. *Silvae* 4.8.4–5.
21. 5.3.104–5.
22. *Description of the World* 358 Müller.
23. *Roman History* 66.21.3.

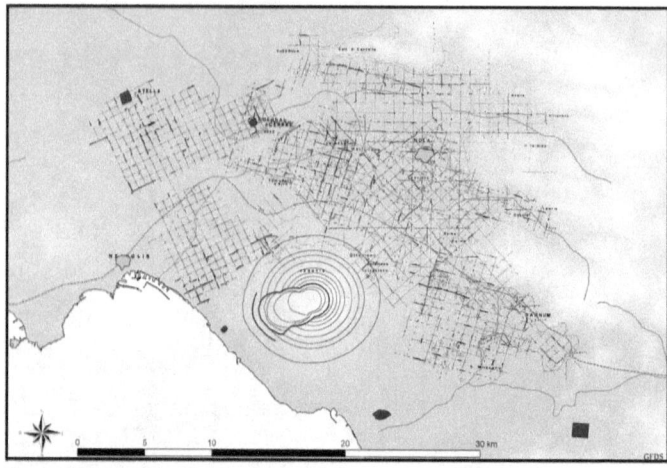

Fig. 5.3. Cadastral grids of the Vesuvian area. Illustration courtesy of G. F. De Simone.

that the volcano's "heights support both trees and vines in abundance." Yet Mario Pagano's research suggests that in many parts of the Vesuvian landscape, vine and olive production — let alone grain farming — remained greatly reduced until the fourth century CE.

Gérard Chouquer and François Favory identify a substantial cadastral grid in the agricultural area east and north of the city, extending from the lower slopes of Vesuvius north and west into the plain [Fig. 5.2]. In characteristic Roman fashion, it marks the partitioning of the land into squares of 16 × 16 *actus* (.322 km² per square) further divided into uniform rectangular farmsteads, often the size of a *iugerum* (=2 *actus*, 128 to a square). Unlike the Nolan territory to its east, with its confusing palimpsest of successive grids on different orientations, the *Neapolitanum* has only one. Girolamo F. De Simone has prepared a composite GIS map of the grids identified in the Nolan and Neapolitan territories [Fig. 5.3]. As he observes, the grid raises problems of interpretation. Where was the river that flowed here in antiquity, which had devolved into marshland by the Middle Ages? There seems to be no gap for it between Neapolis and Vesuvius. And when was this grid established? We will return to the issue of dating below. As for the river (the Sebethos?), it may simply have flowed right through the grid, creating no discontinuity in it. The territory

CHAPTER 5 ▥ REPUBLIC TO EMPIRE

of Capua, for example, had a grid laid without interruption over the meandering Volturno River. As drawn, most of the Neapolitan grid is extrapolated from a few surviving traces of property lines; the large gaps in the evidence could easily accommodate a riverbed. The river was probably filled in by lahar or pyroclastic tephra issuing from the volcano. Debris on the upper slopes continued to wash down into the floodplain with every rainfall, overwhelming it with ashy sediment. Such volcaniclastic erosion, well documented in the area, may have obliterated any remaining traces of the riverbanks' topography, leaving only a swamp.

Known architectural features of the Roman era seem to align with the grid, but these are few. Portions of post-79 villas have been identified on the lower north and west slopes of Vesuvius. Some features, such as a villa bath complex at Pollena Trocchia excavated by De Simone and two second-century-CE villas at Ponticelli east of Neapolis, survived as late as the sixth century, but only after a phase of total destruction in 79 followed by resettlement about a generation later. What became of the small farmsteads that dotted the pre-79 landscape? This area is mostly urban now, and extensive excavation and field survey are out of the question. But scattered evidence suggests that production farms were repurposed as leisure villas (e.g., at S. Gennarello) or abandoned altogether. The architecture of the recovery period, oriented toward sprawling luxury villas, has led De Simone to suggest that the Neapolitan territory was never returned to full productivity or diversity. Smallholders, unable to revive their vine stock or to replant in the ash, were simply wiped out. The seigneurial estates that replaced them certainly cultivated vine, but probably on a reduced scale.

Meticulous paleobotanical investigation, never undertaken within the borders of the ancient Neapolitan territory, could yet reveal much more about the agriculture of the post-79 landscape. At the Somma Vesuviana excavations [see Fig. 1.2], samples taken from the rich paleosol that developed on top of the massive eruption strata of 472 CE reveal the presence of numerous anthropogenic flora — grape, olive, chickpea, walnut, etc. — and an especially notable presence of chestnut. Chestnut (along with other human-introduced taxa, such as the plane tree) also emerges in the Roman phase of sediment cores taken from Lake Avernus. Still prominent in the area today, chestnut was a valued food crop in Neapolitan territory before the eruption of 79 [Commentary 5.2, p. 177]; but in the scientific samples, its presence is manifested mostly as timber. In Roman Italy chestnut may have been cultivated in conjunction with grapevines because the coppiced shoots made excellent and abundant vine poles.[24] Even if vines and annual crops suffered in 79, some trees would have survived. But these alone could not have revived the rural economy.

Traces of agricultural decline in the *Neapolitanum* are visible here and there — for example, in the farmstead at Qualiano, about twelve kilometers northwest of Neapolis [See Fig. 1.2]. It lies west of the known extent of the cadastral grid and certainly predates it; the structure is oriented to the points of the compass. Dedicated to olive-oil production, and altogether lacking refinements, this *villa rustica* flourished in two phases, the third to second centuries BCE and the Augustan period. No later improvements are evident, and although a few isolated finds are dated to the mid- or late Empire, the vast majority of them — including the pottery, well represented by "Campana A" and "B" and Arretine ware — correspond to the two building phases. It appears that the farm ceased operating in the first century CE and that the building was only fitfully inhabited thereafter. Certainly the eruption would not have destroyed such a westerly villa. Yet Vesuvius need not have damaged the olive trees in the region to effect this result; it had only to impede the harvesting or transporting them. Another villa, about eight kilometers east of Neapolis at San Sebastiano al Vesuvio, was buried under three meters of volcanic debris from the 79 eruption. At an unknown later date, one room was furnished with an olive press, a tiny testament to agriculture's revival against the odds. As we just noted, the sites at Ponticelli, only five to six kilometers east-northeast of the gates of Neapolis [See Fig. 1.2], were abandoned for a generation after the eruption. The complex that replaced one of these villas was on a far grander scale, complete with floor mosaics and what appears to be a slave cemetery. In general, the post-eruption landscape seems to have acquired a more

---

24. Columella, *On Agriculture* 4.30–33; Cassiodorus, *Variae* 11.14.3.

CHAPTER 5 ☒ REPUBLIC TO EMPIRE

open, less regimented form, punctuated by fewer buildings and larger estates. But the hegemony of the grid remained on the landscape.

After Vesuvius' eruption in the fall of 79, the official relief effort was forceful and swift. The emperor Titus himself was in Campania in 80 looking after the relief effort when news arrived of the outbreak of a great fire in Rome.[25] In happier times as crown prince, then as emperor, Titus had honored Neapolis with his presence. He had adjudicated the Sebasta Games several times before the eruption, and he had been granted the honorary title of demarch.[26] Suetonius and Dio Cassius shed some light on Titus' response to the eruption:

> 40. Immediately he chose commissioners by lot from among the ex-consuls for the relief of Campania; and the property of those who lost their lives by Vesuvius and had no heirs left alive he applied to the rebuilding of the afflicted cities. [Suetonius, *Titus* 8.4]

> 41. Titus accordingly sent two commissioners [*oikistai*] from among the ex-consuls to the Campanians to supervise the restoration of the region and bestowed upon the inhabitants not only general gifts of money, but also the property of such as had lost their lives and left no heirs. [Dio Cassius, *Roman History* 66.24.3]

With the assistance of Titus' commissioners, Neapolis took ownership of derelict properties in the Vesuvian region — of which there must have been many — to raise money for relief. An immediate task for the commissioners was to survey the region to reestablish obliterated property boundaries; only then could title claims be settled. The probable intent was to sell the derelict land as soon as possible — but how could this be achieved, if the farms were now devastated and unproductive?

The *Liber coloniarum,* a late-antique record of the colonial histories of Italian towns and territories, includes a list of Campanian towns, each with a brief historical summary of the land apportionment in its territory. Here is the entry for Neapolis:

25. Dio Cassius 66.24.1.
26. *IG* 14.729=*CIL* 10.1481.

42. Neapolis, enclosed within a wall. A right of way 80 feet wide is due to the public. But the land of its Siren, Parthenope, was apportioned in *iugera* by Greeks, and *limites intercisivi* were established, within which soldiers too received a parcel of land in *iugera* afterwards according to their merits, by a law of the emperor Titus. [*Gromatici veteres* 1.235 Lachmann, trans. Taylor]

Of seventy towns on the list, only Neapolis' territory is said to have been reapportioned by Titus. Setting aside the matter of whether the Neapolitan Greeks divided their territory into a uniform grid, as the text claims, we should evaluate the assertion that Titus settled his veterans on Neapolitan land. Such settlements had been common practice since the days of Marius and Sulla, and Titus' fellow commander in the Jewish War, his father Vespasian, had founded numerous *coloniae* for the veterans; so there is absolutely no reason to doubt the entry's veracity. But uniquely, it specifies that only a part of the territory, *Sirenae Parthenopae*, sometimes interpreted as "at Parthenope," was apportioned into *iugera*.[27] Does this mean the old town of Parthenope–Palaeopolis? If Lucullus had grabbed the whole promontory of Pizzofalcone, including Parthenope, during Sulla's reprisals,[28] then we can imagine that the resulting villa — now in imperial hands and known, perhaps, as the *castrum Lucullanum* (reminiscent of the similarly military-sounding *praetorium* at Baiae, an alternative name for the imperial palace there[29]) — was reapportioned by Titus for his soldiers. The difficulty is that a *iugerum* is a standard unit of agriculturally viable land; and the town of Parthenope, whether or not it had been reinhabited after 327/6 BCE, was on a rocky promontory with no agricultural advantages whatever.

The more likely interpretation is a genitive rather than a locative meaning of *"Sirenae Parthenopae,"* which would refer to Neapolis' lands "belonging to its Siren, Parthenope." In other words, estates belonging to the Siren Parthenope's *cult* (why else would the text have

27. On the troubled text of the words *Sirenae Parthenopae* in the MS tradition, see Taylor 2015.
28. See pp. 144, 299, 308, 318–19; Commentary 8.2, pp. 334–35.
29. *CIL* 5.5050.

CHAPTER 5 ▣ REPUBLIC TO EMPIRE

included the word *Sirenae?*) were put in reserve for Roman soldiers. Prominent cults in Campania, such as that of Diana Tifatina, could be quite land-rich. Thus we are glimpsing a quid pro quo, in which the city of Neapolis, perhaps out of gratitude to Titus for his relief efforts, offered up some of its landholdings to his soldiers. It was customary to ratify a land grant to veterans by passing a law, as we are told Titus did. But this reallotment of cult property would have been a small-scale venture, perhaps encompassing properties for a few hundred future veterans. What remains obscure, of course, is precisely what we want to know most: where were these properties, and how badly had the eruption compromised them? Were these soldiers, "according to their deserts," getting a raw deal? Perhaps not, if we consider first that the land was probably bought to be held in reserve, not for immediate redistribution; and second, that it was most likely in parts of Neapolitan territory remote enough from the devastation (the Glanis valley, perhaps?) to promise a full recovery in due time.

We now return to the origins of the Neapolitan cadastral grid. No source attributes it to Titus, and even if we doubt the claim by the *Liber coloniarum* that this feature was introduced by Greeks, we must take seriously the underlying supposition that it was already established in Titus' day. Roman intervention in Neapolitan territory may extend back to the 180s BCE, when Quintus Fabius Labeo reportedly arbitrated a territorial dispute between Neapolis and Nola;[30] but this incident surely did not involve the centuriation of the entire territory. Chouquer and Favory, reconstructing the grid solely on evidence visible in the modern landscape — none of which helps to date the grid itself — propose, without much conviction, an Augustan date. Yet in my opinion, historical circumstances favor the Sullan occupation. We have already seen that the city fell completely under Sulla's control in 82 BCE and that he issued harsh reprisals against the residents.[31] We also know from various sources that he had colonized the nearby territories of Nola and Pompeii; Sullans had also seized land in the fertile Capuan territory. By settling more veterans near Neapolis he was strengthening his own insurance policy. In his retirement near

30. Cicero, *On Duties* 1.33.
31. See pp. 142–46.

165

Pozzuoli he would have wanted plenty of clients nearby in a time of need. His veterans' loyalty was famous: "as they could not be secure in their own holdings unless all Sulla's system were on a firm foundation, they were his stoutest champions even after he died."[32] Even Publius Sulla — junior relative of the dictator, cofounder of the colony at Pompeii, and a participant in the dictator's bloodthirsty proscriptions — acquired a home in Neapolis, and by 64 BCE he had taken up residency there, retreating from politics.[33]

If Neapolis was colonized at this time, the *Liber coloniarum* makes no mention of its new status. This city's territory seems never to have been divided into *pagi* (rural districts), whereas the neighboring territory of Nola, a Sullan colony, preserves inscriptions of no fewer than seven *pagi*. Even if the Sullans did subject Neapolis to the customary fate of a conquered enemy city — forcible land redistribution — they may have had their reasons to refrain from colonizing it. The city and its territory had long enjoyed special relations with Rome that colonial status could not substantively improve. Even though it had accepted full Roman citizenship eight years earlier, and thus had relinquished its own laws, Neapolis retained certain prerogatives: on the one hand, Greek-style magistracies (if substantially redefined); on the other, safe haven for Roman capital criminals, an advantage that would have appealed to Sulla's notoriously ruthless and tainted partisans. Given the ferocious legal challenges to which their comrades in Capuan territory — and even a few in Neapolitan territory — were exposed later, in 63 BCE,[34] theirs was no idle worry. It is possible, at least, that Publius Sulla stuck close to Neapolis in these years because of the legal protection it offered.

Let me propose a further hypothesis: that in gratitude for gaining possession of Neapolis, the elder Sulla conveyed some of his confiscated lands to the cult of the city's patron goddess, Parthenope. He had done exactly the same thing on behalf of Diana Tifatina after seizing Capua's *ager Campanus* — another territory that he reapportioned without colonizing — donating extensive lands to the

32. Appian, *Civil Wars* 1.97.
33. Cicero, *Sulla* 17, 53; *Letters to His Friends* 9.15.5.
34. Cicero, *On the Agrarian Law* 2.86, 96.

CHAPTER 5 ☗ REPUBLIC TO EMPIRE

goddess' sanctuary.³⁵ If he did the same at Neapolis, then Titus, 162 years later, was likely obtaining some of the lots for assignment to his veterans from this very land reserve.

Did Titus, then, finally grant colonial status to Neapolis? The lack of a colonial designation in the *Liber coloniarum* is no guarantee that he did not, for this source is replete with errors and omissions. I conclude, tentatively, that Neapolis did become a *colonia* at this time on the basis of two textual references: first, the *Liber*'s observation that Titus' soldiers received apportionments "each according to his merits." The granting of lots of certain sizes according to a soldier's rank is a characterisitc practice of colonization, and is rarely seen in other contexts. Second, Dio Cassius' reference to the land commissioners as *oikistai*, "founders," best suits the circumstances of a colony as well. But at the moment this "refounding" was purely a paper transaction. Surely no soldiers were settled at this time. The allotments were bought in anticipation of future settlement, and likely concentrated in the west of the territory where the eruption had done the least damage.

A more substantial demographic change, and probably a crucial factor in the designation of Neapolis as a colony, was the migration of refugees of Vesuvius into the city itself. In the short term, Neapolis would have harbored refugees from the countryside and the lost towns; these may have been gainfully employed to shovel out the volcanic debris. In some cases, temporary refuge became permanent: one of the more interesting local documents of Neapolis is a late-antique inscription recording the existence of a "district of the Herculaneans," probably established with the money raised by Titus' commission [Commentary 5.3, pp. 177–78]. Another hint of a post-Vesuvian transplant comes, improbably, from Romania. Inscribed on the flanks of a commemorative altar just a stone's throw from the emperor Trajan's (98–117) famous victory monument at Adamclisi commemorating his two Dacian Wars were lists of Roman soldiers lost in battle, probably during a previous conflict with Dacians or Sarmatians under Domitian (81–96). Preserved among the fragments are details about the commanding officer in the battle. Though his

---

35. Velleius Paterculus, *Compendium* 2.25.4.

name is lost, we learn that he was a native of Pompeii but a resident of Neapolis at the time of his death.[36] Did the eruption prompt his migration? It would not be an unreasonable conjecture.

The urban core of Neapolis itself certainly suffered damage from Vesuvius, but how much damage, and of what kind, is hard to assess. It was spared the most destructive features of the eruption — huge volumes of ash and lapilli, falling embers that set roofs afire, and pyroclastic flows and surges. Harm probably came from two sources: falling ash resembling a heavy snowfall, perhaps accumulating to twice the thickness of Pliny's "snowdrifts" at Misenum; and earthquakes surrounding the eruption. The first was more an acute nuisance than a lethal scourge; the second was deadly. A Neapolitan inscription records that Titus promptly rededicated an earthquake-damaged structure in 80 or early 81 CE.[37] Another at Sorrento commemorates his restoration of a sundial, likewise toppled by an earthquake.[38] Terrifying as these events were, any systematic evacuations of the city were probably brief.

THE HIGH EMPIRE

Shaken by disaster, its population likely swollen from the influx of refugees, the city resumed operation shortly after the eruption. As a place of imperial resort, it barely missed a beat. The patronage from Rome was, if anything, stepped up in the wake of Titus' commission. The quinquennial games of the Sebasta went on as scheduled in 82, and Titus' brother and successor Domitian participated in them personally. He also built a new highway, the Via Domitiana, which diverged from the Via Appia at Sinuessa and connected to Cumae and Pozzuoli. A new theater was built north of the forum at about this time too.[39] After Domitian's death, Nerva began a restoration or improvement of a Neapolis–Pozzuoli road, which Trajan completed in 102.[40] The demarchate, once held by Titus, was conferred

36. *CIL* 3.14214.
37. *IG* 14.729 = *CIL* 10.1481 = Miranda 1990–1995 no. 20.
38. *NSc* 1901 363–64.
39. See pp. 191–96.
40. *CIL* 10.6926–28, 6931.

CHAPTER 5 ▥ REPUBLIC TO EMPIRE

to Trajan's successor, Hadrian (117–138 CE),[41] who is known to have made improvements at the imperial villa of Pausilypon (Posillipo) nearby[42] and may also have restored the coastal highway between Neapolis and Stabiae.[43] During the Antonine dynasty (138–193) we hear little about imperial intervention at Neapolis, though Antoninus Pius himself (138–161) was active in the region, founding new Greek games at Pozzuoli in honor of the deified Hadrian early in his reign, and much later refurbishing some of the architecture in the athletic quarter of Neapolis. Imperial protégés were achieving high status in the city, a fact intimating that the emperors too were spending abundant time in the vicinity. Around the mid-second century CE, Publius Aelius Antigenides, a professional musician and presumably an imperial freedman, achieved the demarchate.[44] Septimius Severus (193–211) also left his mark, restoring the Pausilypon–Pozzuoli branch road and refurbishing the harbor at Neapolis with a new mole.[45] Meanwhile, impressive luxury villas were going up in the eastern territory: at S. Gennarello (Hadrianic, replacing a pre-79 wine storage facility), Pollena Trocchia (second or third century CE, built on a pre-79 structure), Somma Vesuviana (Hadrianic or later; earlier phases unconfirmed, but its statuary may be Augustan), and elsewhere [See Fig. 1.2]. No return to the old agricultural regime is evident anywhere in the *Neapolitanum*.

Sometime in the late second or early third century, Neapolis acquired the official name of *Colonia Aurelia Augusta Antoniniana Felix Neapolis*.[46] By the second century, the conferral of colony status sometimes involved little more than applying a new imperial imprimatur to an existing *colonia*. The procedure bore little resemblance to republican or early imperial colonization, which settled veterans in an environment that assured them economic security and the full

41. *Historia Augusta, Hadrian* 1.19.1.
42. See pp. 282, 311–12.
43. *CIL* 10.6939–40.
44. *IG* 14.737: see p. 173; Commentary 8.9, pp. 342–43; *NSc* 1892: 479–81.
45. See pp. 218–25, 230.
46. *ILS* 6458; *NSc* 1890 220.

privileges of Roman citizenship. We don't know what motivated this change of status, or what advantages or disadvantages came with it. It may have been little more than an honorific gesture, possibly by Marcus Aurelius (161–180), but more probably Caracalla (211–217).[47] The inscription, dating to 222, gives no indication of when the city had acquired this honorific status. Much later inscriptions, probably of the fourth century, honor "patrons of the colony." As a young man, Marcus Aurelius himself had once expressed a low opinion of the city and its intelligentsia, but his disdain may have been little more than a callow affectation to impress his teacher and correspondent Fronto [Commentary 5.4, pp. 178–79]. I will discuss my reasons for a possible attribution of the new colonial status to Caracalla in chapter 6.

To the historian Ettore Lepore, all this imperial intervention bespeaks a decadent, enfeebled community, its mercantile and ruling classes too exhausted to take the initiative in restoring Neapolis' old vitality, which had been sapped ever since Sulla's seizure of the city centuries earlier. Even the retention of ornamental Greek magistracies such as demarch and laukelarch bespoke a "decline in the public civic spirit." As a character type embodying the decline, he adduces Trimalchio, the clownish parvenu in Petronius' picaresque novel *The Satyricon*, who inhabits a south-Italian port city modeled partly on Neapolis in the mid-first century CE [Commentary 5.5, pp. 179–81]. Vesuvius plays a negligible role in Lepore's paradigm; it only hastened the inevitable. This notion of Neapolis as a kind of proto-Antwerp, a once vibrant port city decimated by geopolitical contingency, has gained some favor in academic discourse. Yet evidence to support it remains utterly chimerical. I find nothing whatever to recommend the view that Neapolis in the high Empire was afflicted by political or economic paralysis. The imperial attention accorded to it, both before and after the eruption, signals nothing particularly momentous — neither a prolonged bailout of a zombie city deemed too big to fail, nor a resurgence of a fabled vitality, mercantile or otherwise. The literary sources' general silence about Neapolis' fortunes in this period is more apt to signal stability and even strength than the opposite. True, the city had relinquished its primacy in high commerce;

47. See pp. 234–35.

CHAPTER 5 ☖ REPUBLIC TO EMPIRE

from the time of Sulla, Pozzuoli had been the busiest port on the Bay. But Pozzuoli's gain — and later, Ostia's — was not necessarily Neapolis' loss, as I will suggest in the next chapter. Nor was the shock to the city's productive territory in 79 CE the unmitigated disaster it would have been for, say, Capua, which relied heavily on its agrarian economy. Not only did Neapolis maintain an important presence as a port city throughout the imperial era; it had already reinvented itself as the center of a service economy. The service provided was corporeal and cultural, its clients the mass of Romans seeking a pleasant and stimulating refuge, high culture, therapy at the baths, or the periodic diversion of Greek games. The Italian aristocracy continued to flock to the Bay, and it is no accident that they acquired available land in the post-Vesuvian countryside around Neapolis despite its diminished beauty and productivity. Proximity to the grand old Greek city beckoned withal. Location was everything.

POPULATION AND DEMOGRAPHICS

One index of Neapolis' continuing health is the robust presence of archaeological remains from the Roman imperial period just outside the city walls, especially to the west and south, around the harbor. A number of these have been associated with bathing establishments. As a resort center catering not only to the rich, but also to ordinary Romans taking the cure at the mineral springs in the city's western territory and on Ischia, Neapolis seems to have competed successfully with Baiae.[48] At no period can the ancient city's permanent population be estimated, but it comfortably exceeded that of Pompeii, estimated at somewhere between 8,000 and 12,000. Intramural Pompeii was about a third smaller than Neapolis, and its urban area probably extended only modestly beyond the walls. If we posit a similar density of occupation strictly within the walls, we might place Roman Neapolis at 12,000 to 18,000 (Emanuele Greco's estimate of 7,000 to 8,000 is too low). But this does not account for the unknown extent of urban extramural development. A zone of high density surely extended along the coast to the port. It also surged eastward with the neighborhood of the Herculaneans; quite possibly, another suburb for refugees from Pompeii remains to be found. In a recent epigraphic

48. See chapter 7.

analysis of regional cities in the wake of the 79-CE eruption, Steven Tuck finds that Neapolis, not unexpectedly, was among the cities demonstrating the strongest prosopographical evidence of absorbing the Pompeian diaspora. (Others were Cumae, Pozzuoli, and Ostia.)

Additionally, we must consider the sizable population of temporary residents, whether ordinary travelers, vacationers, or visitors to festivals and games. Cicero's characterization of Neapolis as "a densely crowded town" in Sulla's time[49] was corroborated by Statius a century and a half later, but with a caveat: few of the hordes were local citizens.[50] Leiwo observes that native Neapolitans are well represented in inscriptions of the praetorian guard, urban cohorts (police), and fire brigades at Rome, indicating that Neapolis had plenty of young males to export. But whether this signals a liability for Neapolis, or an asset, or neither, is impossible to say.

Regarding the city's demographics, again we cannot advance beyond mundane and fairly uninformative lists of names, and occasionally occupations, appearing on inscriptions. Few of the names fall outside the ethnicities of Latin, Osco-Samnite, or Greek. While the former two groups in particular may allow us some insight into the extent and mobility of families in the region (especially in relation to Capua, Pozzuoli, and Pompeii), they do not convey the full measure of a cosmopolitan harbor town. Pozzuoli and Pompeii have yielded a richer epigraphic record than Neapolis, with more information about trades, ethnic and religious communities, business and marriage connections, and so forth. But almost every hypothesis advanced about self-identifying communities in Neapolis — for example, Levantines and Jews — simply cannot be corroborated. Hard evidence for the early Neapolitan Christian church too is elusive before the fourth century. Later lists record nine bishops of Neapolis before the year 300, and first-century Neapolitan saints loom large in local tradition — for example, Candida and her brother Asprenus, first bishop of Neapolis, each supposedly baptized by St. Peter as he journeyed to Rome. But most evidence of the local early Christian community is anecdotal.[51]

49. For *Rabirius Postumus* 26.
50. *Silvae* 3.5.72–80.
51. See Bruzelius and Tronzo 2011: 12–32.

CHAPTER 5 ⛫ REPUBLIC TO EMPIRE

CITY GOVERNMENT

An inscription of 242 BCE from the island of Kos refers to a resolution of "the archons, the council, and the people" (*archontes, synkletos, demos*) of Neapolis, indicating that by the mid-third century BCE the (two?) archons were the principal magistrates of the city.[52] Another, post-Sullan inscription mentions a certain Seleukos, "ex-archon of the Four" (*arxas tessaron andron*).[53] The Four, or *quattuorviri*, were a fixture of Roman municipalities, equivalent to aediles. Here the participle *arxas*, although the aorist equivalent of *archon*, should simply be understood as "chief" or "foremost" of the aediles, and not as the archon of the city. The Four's appearance on the Neapolitan scene can be attributed, with all probability, to the Sullan reforms, which sought to Romanize local institutions. At this time, too, with the redistribution and redefinition of the Neapolitan territory, the demarchate would have been completely reorganized. No longer a council of mayors, it was reduced to a single office of purely honorific status. It was granted to emperors on occasion, and also to such unlikely candidates as a professional musician, Publius Aelius Antigenides, in the early Antonine period.[54] It does not seem to have figured in the careers of most serious politicians at Neapolis, i.e., those who aimed for the archonship. In the 70s CE, a series of inscriptions in both Greek and Latin indicate several individuals occupying a triad of magistracies: demarch, archon, and antarchon.[55] Franco Sartori believed the latter two may be taken as unequal colleagues: a chief and his deputy, sometimes referenced together simply as archons.[56] This formula, probably already apparent in the Kos inscription of 242 BCE, may have followed a Samnite model consisting of pairs of *meddices*, high municipal magistrates; but it is unclear whether the pairs recorded in Oscan inscriptions were truly unequal or were simply following the model of the Roman *duoviri*.

52. *SEG* 12.378.
53. *IG* 14.745.
54. *IG* 14.737; see Commentary 8.9, pp. 342–43.
55. *IG* 14.760, 757 = *CIL* 10.1489.
56. E.g., Paccius Caledus and Vibius Pollio in an inscription of 71 CE, *IG* 14.758.

The magistracy of *laukelarchos*, probably charged with convoking or presiding over the city council or assembly (*laon kelesthai*), was another prominent rung on the political career ladder.[57] Lesser conventional magistracies, such as *agoranomos* (aedile), are attested in inscriptions too, both Greek and Latin. One Neapolitan included among his career titles *duovir alimentorum quaestor*, which is specifically associated with the Trajanic program of supporting indigent children in Italy, and *curator frumenti comparandi*, charged with procuring or disbursing grain for the city.[58] Posts of this kind were not particularly distinctive, appearing in cities throughout Roman Italy.

The particulars of public life in Neapolis continue to elude us, but some measure of hybridity with Roman norms was inevitable. It is enough to recognize, on the one hand, an impulse toward Romanizing city government, probably attributable to the Sullans; and a continuing trend of countervailing conservatism to which we may attribute the persistence of Greek titles for magistrates. This general structure prevailed at least to the end of the third century CE, and perhaps beyond.

THE PHRATRIES IN THE ROMAN PERIOD

Obscure of origin and purpose, but probably quite ancient and certainly Greek, phratries became the most distinctive vehicles of aristocratic identity at Neapolis in the Roman imperial period. They are first mentioned by Varro, writing in the late Republic.[59] Strabo[60] observes that they were part of what made Neapolis so Hellenic in its customs. But only in the first century CE did phratry inscriptions first appear; they proliferated in the second and third. The most significant document either benefactions from wealthy individuals or the granting of honors to them — or both in succession [Commentary 5.3, pp. 177–78]. Probably formed as fraternities organized around various origin myths attached to strands of early Neapolitan society,[61] they

57. *IG* 14.716, 717, 741, 745 = Miranda 1990–1995 no. 3, 4, 30, 33.
58. *CIL* 10.1491.
59. *Latin Language* 5.8a.
60. *Geography* 5.4.7. See Readings 66, p. 291; 80, p. 325.
61. See pp. 65–66; Commentary 2.4, pp. 79–81.

CHAPTER 5 ⛫ REPUBLIC TO EMPIRE

seem to have evolved into aristocratic clubs of strictly ceremonial significance. The great majority of names in their inscriptions are Greek or conventionally Roman: either those of Campanian ancestry were excluded altogether, or their heritage was suppressed. This trend represents an extraordinary departure from the onomastic diversity evident in other Neapolitan inscriptions, and it cannot be accidental. It suggests that phratries preserved the now harmless political remnants of the pro-Roman, anti-Campanian collaborationists of 327/6 BCE. The preferred language of the phratry inscriptions is Greek, but there is abundant evidence that they were bilingual institutions — hardly a surprise, given the sheer abundance of Latin names among the members and benefactors. To enhance their membership rolls the phratries sought out senators and equestrians, some of whom were not Neapolitan natives or residents. Prominent women, such as the wealthy Latian vintner Caedicia Victrix, also were admitted.[62]

Qualitatively, the Roman-era phratries seem to have been fairly uniform. In function they resembled *collegia,* or trade associations, though their membership was confined to elites, many from the governing class.[63] Their principal raison d'être was social and honorific. Each evidently had a headquarters for meetings, speechifying, and banquets, and all were attached to specific religious cults, the shrines of which were maintained by members. Much effort has been wasted trying to identify phratry headquarters on the basis of the locations of inscriptions, yet not a single site can be securely established by these means. Most official business seems to have been accompanied by sacrificial rites to the *theoi phratrioi,* the in-house gods; and it would seem that members often chose to be buried with their brethren in tombs owned by the phratry, much like tradesmen in *collegia.* An inscription of the Aristaioi phratry enumerates the roster of officers: president, treasurer, curator, various administrators[64] — a lineup worthy of the local Elks lodge. Phratries were in competition, and some found their own ways to enhance their prestige. The Theotadai, for example, performed rites not just for their

62. *IG* 14.722 = Miranda 1990–1995 no. 10.
63. See pp. 294–95.
64. *IG* 14.759 = Miranda 1990–1995 no. 43.

175

theoi phratrioi, but for the emperor cult too.[65] The Eunostidai seem to have established a collateral branch, the Antinoïdai, to ingratiate themselves to the emperor Hadrian, who had founded an empire-wide cult to his deceased paramour Antinoös in the early 130s CE.[66] Phratries vied to enroll the most distinguished benefactors — in the case of the Artemisioi and the Kretondai, one consul each.[67]

CONCLUSION

Whatever its shortcomings in the Roman imperial period, Neapolis was not the exhausted Potemkin village portrayed by Lepore. If anything, the city managed to develop a relationship with Rome resembling the vibrant symbiosis of early modern Bath and London. Nobody denies that the history of Bath in Georgian and Regency England, the genteel concourse of aristocracy at leisure, was deeply intertwined with that of the capital. Nor would anyone claim that it lacked political, social, or cultural importance simply because it thrived on a service economy catering to influential sojourners. To be sure, Bath maintained an industrial base (ironworks in particular) to which Roman Neapolis offers no sure analog. But thanks to its serviceable harbor, the ancient city on the Bay also preserved a degree of commercial relevance even through late antiquity, as the sheer numbers of Roman transport wares found in the harbor excavations now attest.[68] Occasionally history was made within its walls, but next to the bustle of Pozzuoli or Capua, the place was a picture of quietude. So it remained, it seems, through the third century and into late antiquity.

Commentary 5.1: Neapolis' Anomalous Earthquake Dynamics

Pliny's striking description of the behavior of earthquakes at Neapolis would seem to be grounded in scientific fact. Recent research in earthquake dynamics reveals that solid materials pierced by voids — such as the heavily tunneled tuff under the city — tend to dissipate seismic waves as they

65. *IG* 14.723 = Miranda 1990–1995 no. 11.
66. *CIL* 6.1851.
67. *IG* 14.743, 744 = Miranda 1990–1995 no. 31, 32.
68. See pp. 218–25.

CHAPTER 5 ≡ REPUBLIC TO EMPIRE

are reflected and refracted by the cavities. This effect is best demonstrated in environments where continuous bedrock lies near the surface, like ancient Neapolis.

43. ...there is also a remedy for earthquake such as frequently caves too afford, as they supply an outlet for confined breath. This is noticed in whole towns: buildings pierced by frequent conduits for drainage are less shaken, and also among these the ones erected over vaults are much safer — as is noticed in Italy at Neapolis, the solidly built portion of the city being specially liable to collapses of this nature. [Pliny the Elder, *Natural History* 2.197]

Commentary 5.2: Neapolitan Chestnut Production

44. The most highly commended chestnuts come from Tarentum, and in Campania from Neapolis. [Pliny the Elder, *Natural History* 15.94]

45. In the territory of Neapolis an equestrian of Rome named Corellius, a native of Este, grafted a chestnut with a slip cut from the tree itself, and this is how the celebrated variety of chestnut tree named after him was produced. Subsequently his freedman Tereus grafted a Corellius chestnut again. The difference between the two varieties is this: the former is more prolific but the latter, the Tereus chestnut, of better quality. [17.122]

Commentary 5.3: The Herculanean District

Discovered in 1535, a late-Roman inscription records that the "foremost, resplendent district of the Herculaneans"[69] dedicated a statue to a "patron of the colony," Lucius Munatius Concessianus. Only two Neapolitan city districts are known from antiquity. The other is the *Regio Thermensium*.[70] Doubtless the entire city was divided into such districts on the model of Rome itself, which Augustus had organized into fourteen *regiones*. Each of these encompassed multiple *vici*, or neighborhoods. In one of

---

69. *regio primaria splendidissima Herculanensium*, CIL 10.1492.

70. See p. 273.

his papal letters[71] Gregory the Great, writing in the sixth century CE, decrees the consecration of a monastery built by a certain Rustica, "at Neapolis, at her own home, in the Herculean district (*regione Herculensi*) in the so-called Street [or Neighborhood] of the Torch" (*in vico qui appellatur Lampadi*). We cannot confirm that the *regio Herculensis* is the same as the *regio Herculanensium* (one references Hercules, the other the people of Herculaneum), but the match seems plausible, especially if the stricken town had been lost to memory. We see a similar medieval semantic slippage of the *Regio Thermensium* (Bathmen's District) into *Regio Thermensis* (Bathing District).

In light of the grim discovery in 1980–1981 of piles of corpses at Herculaneum, a mere seven miles southeast of Neapolis, the inscription is a precious document. Vesuvian pyroclastic flow annihilated Herculaneum swiftly and efficiently, asphyxiating or incinerating scores of inhabitants trapped on the beach. Yet the inscription suggests that many residents did escape westward and took up permanent residence in a new quarter of Neapolis. Rustica's aristocratic home there, along with the superlatives *primaria* and *splendidissima* describing the district, suggest that centuries later, this community of exiles rose to prosperity. Medieval nomenclature securely positions the *Regio Herculensis*, also known as *Furcillensis*, in the eastern part of the ancient city, corresponding to the eponymous modern neighborhood of Forcella.

Commentary 5.4: A Letter from Marcus Aurelius to Fronto

46. *Neapolis, 143 CE.* Since my last letter to you nothing has happened worth writing of, or the knowledge of which would be of the slightest interest. For we have passed whole days more or less in the same occupations: the same theater,[72] the same dislike of it....

We have been listening to panegyrists here, Greeks, of course, and wondrous creatures, so much so that I, who am as far

---

71. *Registrum epistularum* 3.58.

72. Since this theater was the venue of orations, it was probably the odeion north of the forum. See pp. 186, 191–96.

CHAPTER 5 ▣ REPUBLIC TO EMPIRE

removed from Greek literature as is my native Caelian Hill from the land of Greece, could nevertheless hope, matched with them, to be able to rival even Theopompus, the most eloquent, as I hear, of all the Greeks. So I, who am all but a breathing barbarian, have been impelled to write in Greek by men, as Caecilius says, of *unimpaired ignorance.*

The climate of Neapolis is decidedly pleasant, but violently variable. Every two minutes it gets colder or warmer or rawer. [Fronto, *Correspondence* 2.6 = LCL 1.143]

Commentary 5.5: The Site of Trimalchio's Feast

Scholars have long debated the identity of the "Greek city" in Italy that served as the venue for the most famous episode[73] in Petronius' comic novel, the *Satyricon:* a dinner party hosted by the wealthy freedman Trimalchio. This long, virtually unbroken narrative in an otherwise very fragmentary manuscript is full of geographic hints, but never openly professes its physical setting. The author's coyness itself is rather odd because the urban venues of other episodes in the novel, such as Massilia (Marseilles), Pergamon, and Kroton, are identified forthrightly. Possibly the crucial geographic marker has simply fallen from the text, which even in its more intact sections leaves much to be desired. But a few scholars have argued that Petronius intended the city to be an imaginary composite of two or more cities in the vicinity of the Bay of Naples.

Most, however, have sought to identify a particular city. Neapolis itself was once a favored identification, largely because it was the most obviously "Greek" city in all of Italy. In 1893 Enrico Cocchia argued at length for this identification. Ettore Lepore thought the same, if more in the spirit than in the letter. Other cities — Ancona, Capua, Cumae, Pompeii, Pozzuoli, Taranto — have been suggested too. In recent decades, however, a general preference has developed for Pozzuoli. From the text we may ascertain, with various degrees of certitude, that the city is a Roman colony (until after 79 CE, Neapolis was not); that it has an amphitheater (Neapolis did not); that it is big and disorderly

---

73. Petronius, *Satyricon* 26–78.

enough to get the protagonists hopelessly lost in its streets (Neapolis had an orderly grid, at least inside the walls); that it has a substantial stake in regional agriculture, which is suffering from a drought; that the city consequently is enduring a grain shortage; and that the shortage is exacerbated by a collusion between the bakers and the aediles, Roman-style magistrates who oversee grain distribution. A fragment of the *Satyricon's* text, without context, indicates that the protagonists of the tale traversed the Crypta Neapolitana between Neapolis and Pozzuoli.[74] Most famously, we are told that Trimalchio's city is a *Graeca urbs*. In the end, among all the candidates Pozzuoli alone is left standing, but only if we can accept that this heavily Romanized colony could still be called a Greek city in the time of Nero — even though it was run by Roman magistrates and featured that most un-Greek of amenities, an amphitheater. Perhaps it is best to imagine that Petronius' city was an unequal hybrid of Pozzuoli and Neapolis, but with the former dominating. One may find wisdom in the modern analogy from J.P. Sullivan, who favors a hybridized Pozzuoli: "a piece of fiction set in some locale named Oxbridge or Bradpool may often be tied down by significant descriptions to the specific town in the author's mind."

47. I was listening to him [Agamemnon, an elderly orator] so carefully that I did not notice Ascyltos slipping away. I was pacing the gardens in the heat of our conversation, when a great crowd of students came out into the porch, apparently from some master whose extemporary harangue had followed Agamemnon's discourse.... So while the young men were laughing at his epigrams, and denouncing the tendency of his style as a whole, I took occasion to steal away and began hurriedly to look for Ascyltos. But I did not remember the road accurately, and I did not know where our lodgings were. So wherever I went, I kept coming back to the same spot, till I was tired out with walking, and dripping with sweat. At last I went up to an old woman who was selling country vegetables and said, "Please, mother, do you happen to know where I live?" She

---

74. See pp. 266–68.

was charmed with such a polite fool. "Of course I do," she said, and got up and began to lead the way. I thought her a prophetess..., and when we had got into an obscure quarter the obliging old lady pushed back a patchwork curtain and said, "This should be your house." I was saying that I did not remember it, when I noticed some men and naked women walking cautiously about among placards of price. Too late, too late I realized that I had been taken into a bawdy-house. [Petronius, *Satyricon* 6–7]

Commentary 5.6: The Phratry Inscription of the Artemisioi

Dating to 194 CE, this is the longest and best-known of the phratry inscriptions. It follows the formula established in decrees of the city council. The main part, in Greek, describes how Lucius Munatius Hilarianus — member, patron, and *philopatris* (lover of his fatherland, by which we may suppose him a native-born Neapolitan) sponsored the adornment of the phratry headquarters and banquet hall and the construction of a shrine to Artemis. There follows a description of the honors voted to Hilarianus and his son Marius Verus. Two statues of each and two "images" of each, probably in the form of relief busts on shields (*imagines clipeatae*),[75] all to be displayed in the phratry headquarters, and fifty *chorai holokleroi*. Long interpreted as "complete parcels of land," this odd expression might refer to individual *iugera* owned by the phratry within Neapolitan territory. But Alain Bresson contends that the term refers to niches in a columbarium tomb, each designed to accommodate the cinerary urn of a deceased person. 197 CE seems far too late a date for the use of columbaria, which fell out of fashion in the first century CE; but some kind of burial plots may still be meant. A dues-paying member would be entitled to a plot, and he or she could buy additional ones for *familia* (family, slaves, and freedpersons). In this respect, the phratry operated just like a Roman *collegium*—i.e., as a funeral club. The inscription concludes with Hilarianus' letter of response

---

75. Distinguished members of the college of *Augustales* had garnered similar busts at their headquarters in nearby Misenum.

— first in Greek translation, and then in the original Latin. I reproduce this portion of the text.

48. L. Munatius Hilarianus to the Phrateres Artemisioi, greetings. I have gratefully accepted the honors you decreed to me, as well as the gifts for repaying my goodwill and favorable disposition — not just because of the magnitude of the things that you displayed when honoring me and my son, your hero [i.e., deceased] — but especially because of the resolution that you passed; for I can see that you are both good and just by the repayment that you offer. Thus I decline the fifty *chorai* you have offered me, being satisfied with fifteen; likewise, concerning the four images and four statues, one bronze statue and one painted image suffice for me, and just one statue in honor of my son; it is enough that, in your hearts, you have already set up many images and statues of us. But you, the best of men, my fellow phrateres, ought not to have before your eyes only such things as the splendor and beauty of the phratry; you should also look forward to other things from me: ever more does the disposition of my soul urge my will into your honor and grace. Farewell. [*SEG* 39.1055 = Miranda 1990–1995 no. 44, trans. Taylor]

CHAPTER 5 ☖ REPUBLIC TO EMPIRE

REFERENCES

Neapolis in the late Republic: Lepore 1967c: 280–88; Leiwo 1994: 27–30. **Brutus, Lucullus, and Nisida:** D'Arms 2003 [1970]: 176–79; Cardone 1992: 13–21; Keenan-Jones 2010: section 3.9.8. **Roman Neapolis' political and economic standing:** Lepore 1952; 1967c; 1967d; Leiwo 1994: 25–30; D'Arms 2003 [1970]: passim. **Forms of Roman citizenship:** Sherwin-White 1973. **Retention of Greek and Oscan names:** Lomas 1993: 170–72; Leiwo 1994: passim. **Senators from Neapolis:** Camodeca 1982: 106–8, 122–23. **Earthquakes:** Sogliano 1901; Lepore 1967d: 295; Andreau 1973; Bragantini and Gastaldi 1985: 40–46; Adam 1986; Arthur 1989a; Guidoboni 1989a: 140–44; 1989b; Guidoboni et al. 1994: 196–211, 214–27; Allison 1995; A. De Simone 1995; Guadagno 1995; Marturano and Rinaldis 1995; Pappalardo 1995; Gelis et al. 2005; Nasseri-Moghaddam et al. 2007; Taylor 2015a; Miranda de Martino 2017a. **Neapolitan agriculture, viticulture, and arboriculture:** Lepore 1967d: 304–9. **Effects of the eruption of Vesuvius:** Alagi 1971; Pisapia 1981; Sigurdsson et al. 1982; Sigurdsson et al. 1985; Widemann 1986; 1990; Pappalardo 1990; 2001; Pescatore and Sigurdsson 1993; Pagano 1995–1996; De Carolis 1997; Soricelli 1997; 2001; Allison 2002; Foss et al. 2002; Sigurdsson and Carey 2002; Perrotta et al. 2006; G.F. De Simone 2008; 2009; Perrotta and Scarpati 2009; Scarpati et al. 2009; A. De Simone 2009: 157–61; Taylor 2015a. **Date of the eruption of Vesuvius:** Pappalardo 1990; Renna 1992: 107–12; Savino 2004a; 2004b; Stefani 2001–2002; 2006; Rolandi et al. 2007. *Regio Herculanensium:* Lepore 1967d: 326; Napoli 1967d: 450–52; Capasso 1978 [1905]: 44–45; Beloch 1989 [1890]: 60; Leiwo 1994: 156; Taylor 2015a: 298–99; Tuck 2019. **Paleobotany:** Grüger et al. 2002; Allevato and Di Pasquale 2009; Allevato et al. 2010. **Chestnut cultivation:** Conedera et al. 2004. **Territory of Nola:** Camodeca 2001; Tarpin 2002: 40–43; Parma 2009. **Apportionment of Neapolitan territory:** De Petra 1891; Pais 1922: 60, 238; De Martino 1952: 342–43; Lepore 1967d: 290–92; Soraci 1982; Chouquer and Favory 1987: 207–12, 226–28; Carlsen 1994; Savino 2007; Taylor 2015a. **Neapolis–Pozzuoli highway:** Johannowsky 1952: 83–87; Flower 2001. **Villa at Qualiano:** D'Ambrosio 1972; G.F. De Simone 2009. **Villa at San Sebastiano al Vesuvio:** Cerulli

Irelli 1965; Pagano 1995–1996: 39 no. 6. **Villas at Ponticelli:** De Stefano and Carsana 1987; Pagano 1995–1996: 41 no. 52; Arthur 2002: 158; Cascella and Vecchio 2014. **Villa at Pollena Trocchia:** G.F. De Simone 2008; 2009; De Simone et al. 2009. **Villa at Somma Vesuviana:** Aoyagi et al. 2018. **The site of the Trimalchio episode in Petronius' Satyricon:** Cocchia 1893; Rose 1962: 403–7; Lepore 1967d: 294–95; Sullivan 1968: 46–47. **Antoninus Pius and local games:** Camodeca 2000–2001; Cavalieri Manasse et al. 2017. **Population of Neapolis:** Greco 1986: 215–16. **Refugees of Vesuvius:** Tuck 2019. **Neapolitan commander in the Dacian Wars:** Turner 2013. **City government and magistracies:** De Martino 1952; Sartori 1953: 42–60; Salmon 1967: 84–88; Pinsent 1969; Lomas 1993: 147–50; Girone 1994. **Kos inscription:** Lepore 1967c: 241–44. **Phratries of the Roman period:** De Marchi 1913; Mallardo 1913; De Sanctis 1914; Peterson 1919: 170–73; Guarducci 1938; Latte 1941; Napoli 1960; 1997 [1959]: 167–81; Roussel 1976: 91–157; Ferone 1988; Miranda 1988a; 1990–1995: 1.61–74; Fishwick 1989; Lomas 1993: 164–65; Leiwo 1994: 150–55; Buchreiter 1999a; Bresson 2013. **Religious cults:** Peterson 1919: 165–221; Ghinatti 1967; Lepore 1967d: 314–20; Papadopoulos 1985a; Miranda 1998; Taylor 2015b.

CHAPTER 6. A GLIMPSE OF ROMAN NEAPOLIS

INTRODUCTION

This chapter provides a brief portrait of the city of Neapolis in the first two and a half centuries of the Roman imperial era, roughly 30 BCE–220 CE. Like any portrait, it is selective and interpretive. In no sense does it aim to be a survey in either a geographically or a chronographically inclusive sense. If anything, it is thematic, building arguments around a few scattered but important nodes of the ancient city where archaeologists have concentrated their attention over the last forty years. In physical terms, ancient Neapolis remains mostly undiscovered. Its urban fabric, overspread by the medieval and modern city, can only be elucidated by tiny pinprick probes made in basements, courtyards, and streets, usually under dire constraints of time. Occasionally a disaster like the earthquake of 1980, or the introduction of a major utility like the new railway and Metropolitana (subway) lines of the 2000s, allows salvage excavations on a more ample scope; but even they are minuscule when compared to the opportunities available at physically unencumbered sites like Paestum or Cumae.

Yet enough pixels in the overall picture, by way of random discoveries and small excavations, have lit up over the last century and a half to allow a few general observations. To begin with something that may surprise. On the surface, Neapolis in the Roman era looked every bit as Roman as any other Italian city, at least inside the walls — this despite the fact that the city cultivated a self-image of hyper-Hellenicity. Just outside the defensive circuit, it carried forward the material legacy of its Greek roots with classical and Hellenistic tomb architecture, some adorned with Delian-style funerary reliefs.[1] The suburban districts associated with the Sebasta Games, to which we will return, presumably followed architectural principles drawn from the old country. But within the walled city, and along the waterfront too, we encounter hardly any traces of characteristically Hellenic urban features, such as the colonnaded *stoa*, the *prostas* or *pastas* house design, or the square *andron* for sympotic dining. Even Roman Pompeii preserved (in a ruined state) an exquisite Greek temple from its distant past, with a surrounding *crepis* and heavy Doric columns. Nothing

---

1. See pp. 136–38.

of the sort has turned up at Neapolis, whose two known temples, in fact, were built in the Roman Corinthian style, each set on a high podium. The Greek theater, which surely existed, seems to have been entirely supplanted by one in a canonical Roman form. Not enough is known about the adjoining odeion to judge its character, but just such roofed auditoria on a similar scale, or larger, were built in many cities under Roman rule. Athens acquired two enormous odeia, both sponsored by Roman-era luminaries, Agrippa and Herodes Atticus. Even Pompeii's smaller odeion was built under Roman control.[2]

We now know Neapolis had a freestanding imperial honorific arch down by the harbor: nothing could be more Roman than that. The one known marketplace was a Roman-style *macellum* on a terrace encased with Roman brick-faced vaulted and arched chambers. Many houses of the republican and imperial periods have offered up bits and pieces of their architectural schemes to archaeology, and with few exceptions, they seem indistinguishable from the Italian-vernacular residences that grace Pompeii and Herculaneum, with their *atria, tablina, cubicula, triclinia,* and peristyle gardens. As in any other Roman town, light industry and commerce coexisted with residential clusters, rich and poor lived in close proximity, and fresh, potable water was available to everyone at streetside fountains but was also piped into the houses of the wealthy. Bathing establishments were around almost every corner.

To acknowledge all of this is not in any sense to claim that Neapolis had traded in its Hellenic birthright for a mess of imperial pottage. The city probably never had an amphitheater, despite surrounding Campania's mania for blood sport. Not a single ancient graffito or inscription in Campania refers to gladiatorial games or other Roman-style entertainments here. What Neapolis did have instead is what every other western city lacked, except perhaps Cumae: a stadium and a gymnasium for hosting Panhellenic-style games.[3] Under the new name Sebasta (we might envision the neuter plural in English as "Augustana"), they were refounded during Augustus' lifetime according to the Isolympic model, retaining a rigorously

2. On the odeion and Roman theater, see pp. 191–96.
3. See pp. 211–18.

CHAPTER 6 ▥ ROMAN NEAPOLIS

Greek character and hosting contestants who mostly came from the Greek East. Their primary dedicatee was no god of the Olympian pantheon, of course, but the Roman emperor himself. In chapter 8 we will explore the many ways in which Neapolis kept the Hellenic ghost dancing within a brick-and-concrete machine that operated to please emperors, their entourages, and an aristocratic elite hungry for something different from the Latinate rhythms of Rome.

The outward Romanizing trend probably began under Sulla's occupation. Neapolis' formidable defenses were strong when the avenging conqueror, rampaging through Campania after his return from the East, resorted to treachery to seize the city in 82 BCE.[4] Subsequent regional threats, whether slave revolts or civil wars, would have warranted continued maintenance of the city walls. But with the ascent of Augustus, an unaccustomed peace settled on the Italian peninsula. During the ensuing two centuries of quietude — broken only by brief wars of succession — urban defensive circuits in Italy were reduced to mere symbols or tax boundaries. Ring roads sometimes developed around the walls to allow travelers, especially those with animals or vehicles banned from the urban center, to bypass it altogether or find quarters in the suburbs. At many cities, including Pompeii and Herculaneum, the centuries-old defenses seem to have been left mostly in place, but they were not immune to overbuilding or selective dismantling. This probably required some kind of an ordinance as Roman law recognized defensive walls to be *loca sancta,* inviolable places protected by sanction.[5] What exactly is meant by this, however, is in doubt: walls were in practice often violated during peacetime. Thus, for example, the western sector of Pompeii known to archaeologists as the Insula Occidentalis overran the wall entirely with a long block of luxury residences cascading down the hillside. Something similar may have happened on Neapolis' western side, where the walls are very poorly preserved. In other sectors—and here again Pompeii is analogous—the wall may have presented a convenient barrier beyond which to dump mountains of trash and debris which later could be quarried for landfill.

---

4. See pp. 142–46.
5. *Digest* 1.8.8–9.

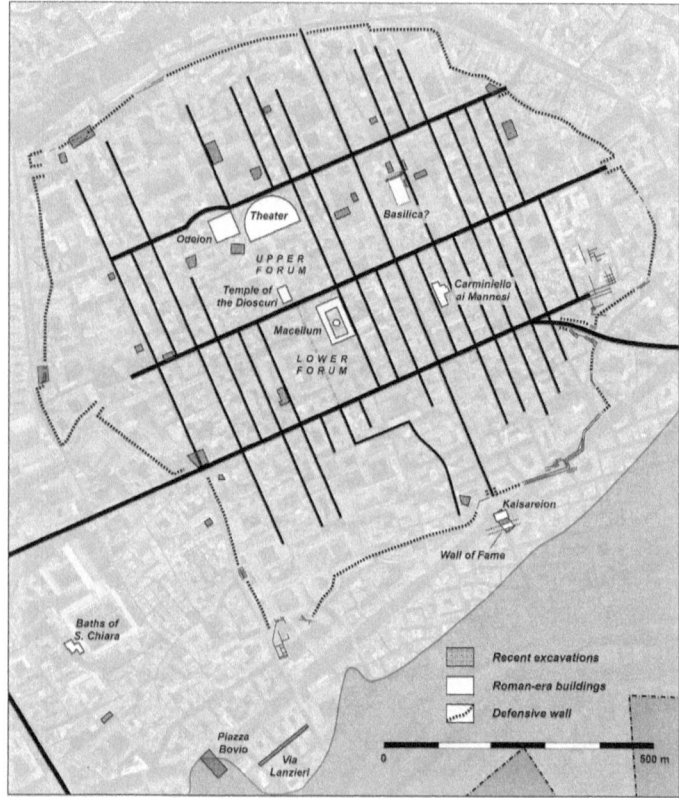

Fig. 6.1. Map of Roman Neapolis featuring the major known monuments and excavated areas.

FORUM DUPLEX

The topographical study of Neapolis' Roman forum, let alone the Greek *agora* that must have preceded it, remains an exercise in educated guesswork. Densely encumbered by the overburden of medieval and modern Naples, the ancient walled city lies mostly out of sight and mind. Archaeological anchor-points are few [Fig. 6.1]. The Renaissance antiquarian Fabio Giordano first postulated that Naples had an unusual *forum duplex*, a zone in two contiguous tiers extending southward from Via Pisanelli–Anticaglia. Other luminaries of

CHAPTER 6 ☖ ROMAN NEAPOLIS

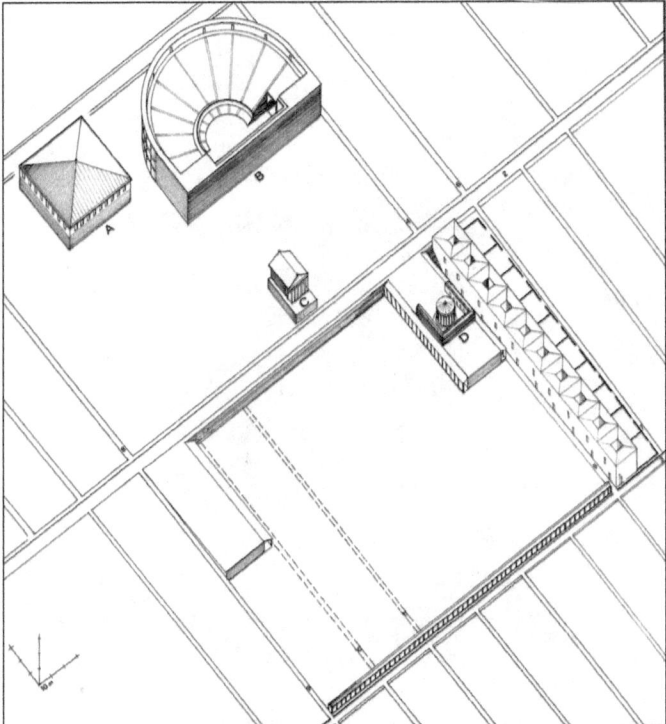

Fig. 6.2. Axonometric reconstruction of the forum area with the theater and odeion. Greco 1985a, 1986.

Neapolitan history and archaeology such as Bartolommeo Capasso, Roberto Pane, Mario Napoli, and Werner Johannowsky all offered refinements on this basic schema. Emanuele Greco's more recent recension of Giordano's idea, developed during the great reevaluation of Neapolitan archaeology in the early 1980s, remains the touchstone for current scholarship [Fig. 6.2]. According to his reconstruction, both tiers together formed a rectangle encompassing six short east-west blocks in width. The hypothetical western border of Greco's forum has recently been partially confirmed by excavations at the abandoned Istituto Filangieri adjoining the ecclesiastical complex of S. Gregorio Armeno [see Fig. 6.1]. These have revealed a high density of

Fig. 6.3. Anonymous sketch of the façade of S. Paolo Maggiore. Cabinet des Estampes. Courtesy of Bibliothèque Nationale de France.

underlying ancient walls and pavements, signaling a return to the urban fabric just west of the ancient north-south street that underlies the boundary between these two ecclesiastical structures. (The southern part of that street is preserved as the southern leg of Vico Sta. Luciella.)

The upper forum, extending one long block length down to Via dei Tribunali, accommodated the Roman theater and the adjacent odeion on its north side. Much of this area in its Roman phases remains terra incognita, but the scheme seems to have lacked the characteristic centripetal properties of a forum, wherein buildings and streets front onto the plaza from all sides. The temple south of the theaters, which in Roman fashion is unidirectional, was compelled by its isolation to turn its back on them, and on the intervening plaza, in order to preside over the southern forum.

CHAPTER 6 ▥ ROMAN NEAPOLIS

Thus the upper plaza seems to have functioned as a kind of belvedere with an open view southward across the lower forum, which progressed another city block to the avenue corresponding to Via S. Biagio dei Librai (Spaccanapoli). Perched for maximum effect on the south edge of the northern plaza, the hexastyle Corinthian temple rose on a high podium. This was the famous Roman imperial temple of the Dioscuri, which remained astoundingly intact until an earthquake in the seventeenth century, despite (or perhaps because of) its conversion into a church [Fig. 6.3]. The eastern wing of the lower forum was a lateral terrace, roughly level with the upper terrace, which jutted out horizontally over the descending terrain. This zone has seen some of the most thorough archaeological investigation in the city. Greco postulates another terrace mirroring it to the west, but that remains hypothetical.

THE ODEION AND THEATER

In the systematic reassessment of ancient Naples undertaken in the 1980s, Werner Johannowsky identified the oldest identifiable phases of both the odeion and the theater as Augustan (27 BCE–14 CE), or at least Julio-Claudian (27 BCE – 68 CE). At the time he recognized a Flavian phase (69–96 CE) for each building as well. The recent systematization and reassessment of the open-air theater, however, has clarified many aspects of this structure, whose ruins remain deeply encumbered by later buildings. While Johannowsky's dating of the odeion has not been challenged, it appears now that the open theater's earliest building phase is late Flavian, corresponding to the 80s or 90s CE. There is no evidence of an earlier theater on the site.

In many venerable Greek cities within the Roman world, the "Roman" theater was simply an adaptation of the original one, updating and reconfiguring a structure that was invariably set into a concave hillside or a hollow. Neapolis was built on a gentle slope, but within its walls there seems to be no swooping or scooping landform suited to hosting a full-scale hillside theater. The original Greek theater of Neapolis — and there surely was one — could not have occupied the Flavian theater's site. Only a freestanding Roman-style structure, built from the ground up with concrete piers and vaulting, could have risen here [see Fig. 6.2]. Neapolis' original theater, then,

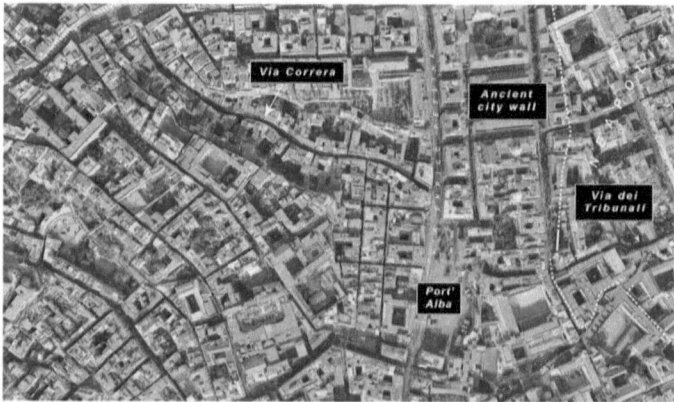

Fig. 6.4. Ravine and escarpments west of the ancient walled city. Satellite image © 2020 Google.

must have been outside the walls, probably in the western suburbs where the topography was much more suitable. One neighborhood deserving strong consideration as the old theater district is just west of Via Enrico Pessina, where a tuff outcrop is split by a canyon down the center of which runs Via Correra [Fig. 6.4]. This area is only a two-minute walk from the Port'Alba, the approximate site of the westernmost ancient city gate, and another minute from the city's central east-west avenue, modern Via dei Tribunali.

The western inner suburbs would therefore have been the fulcrum of activity when Brutus, taking refuge at Neapolis after the murder of Caesar in 44 BCE, recruited "a very large number of actors," including a particularly famous one, Canutius, for the games he sponsored in absentia at Rome.[6] Nero, a competent citharode, held his stage debut at Naples in 64. We are told that, astonishingly, the theater in which he performed shook with an earthquake while he performed and collapsed shortly after his performance, harming nobody.[7] For a Greek-style theater to collapse altogether, as Tacitus reports, seems impossible, given its ground-hugging design. Was Nero performing, then, in an odeion, which would have been roofed? Or was his venue

6. Plutarch, *Brutus* 21.

7. Suetonius, *Nero* 20; Tacitus, *Annals* 15.34. See Commentary 8.7, pp. 340–42 for readings and discussion.

a freestanding Roman predecessor of the Flavian theater? No sure answer is possible; the two reports of the event, as we shall see in chapter 8, are sketchy and hard to reconcile. I would even argue that nothing more than the stage scenery took a tumble, in which case a Greek-style theater, with its *episkenion* rising up behind the stage, was just as vulnerable as a Roman one. In any event, one thing about Nero urges the conclusion that he performed in a venue larger than an odeion: his huge entourage of stage groupies during his sojourns at Neapolis numbered some five thousand, not counting the regular audience.[8]

We get another glimpse of the pre-Flavian theater from a letter of Seneca, probably written shortly before the collapse:

> **49.** I have been hearing the lectures of a philosopher; four days have already passed since I have been attending his school and listening to the harangue, which begins at two o'clock.... But I am ashamed of mankind, as often as I enter the lecture-hall. On my way to the house of Metronax I am compelled to go, as you know, right past the Neapolitan Theater. The building is jammed; men are deciding, with tremendous zeal, who is entitled to be called a good flute-player; even the Greek piper and the herald draw their crowds. But in the other place, where the question discussed is: "What is a good man?" and the lesson which we learn is "How to be a good man," very few are in attendance, and the majority think that even these few are engaged in no good business; they have the name of being empty-headed idlers. [*Moral Epistles* 76.3–4]

The literal translation of *praeter ipsum theatrum Neapolitanum* is "past the Neapolitan theater *itself.*" The emphatic word *ipsum* emphasizes the theater's singularity. The type of music Seneca emphasizes — the flute and the Greek pipes — is associated with outdoor performances like the choral dance that accompanied plays and entertainments; and his emphasis on the herald *(praeco)* and the large crowds reinforces the notion that this was indeed the open theater and not the odeion. Were these competitions part of the Sebasta Games? Was the herald involved in its daily opening and closing ceremonies? If so, then we can probably pinpoint the event to August of 62 CE, the last games before

---

8. Suetonius, *Nero* 20.

Seneca's death.⁹ If in fact these competitions were unfolding in the open theater, and the odeion stood right next to it, it seems odd that Seneca would emphasize one entirely at the expense of the other, which was in fact the proper venue for lectures and declamation of the very sort that he was seeking out at the house of Metronax. We may conclude, tentatively, that Seneca was *not* walking along the north edge of the upper forum, or past the odeion that may or may not have been there already. Instead, he was passing the theater outside the city walls where Nero would soon perform his debut (in 64 CE). As we have seen, the replacement was built next to the (probably) preexisting odeion on the upper forum, but only in the late 80s or 90s, after a harrowing two decades of episodic earthquakes (in 62, 64, and on through the early 80s) punctuated by the fateful eruption of Vesuvius in 79.¹⁰

That Neapolis' early theater eludes discovery is no surprise. Apart from the possibility that it was dismantled, or quarried away from one of those tuff escarpments on the west side of town, there is a very real possibility that significant traces of the theater are still there, but impossible to see. Even the existing Roman theater, whose ruins were encased in later buildings, remained unidentified until the mid-nineteenth century. No theater of any kind has yet been found at Cumae or Pozzuoli, either, despite the certainty that they existed. As further illustration of the problem, those cities' respective stadia — Cumae's Hellenistic, Pozzuoli's high-imperial — long escaped discovery too and have only been excavated and published in the 2000s. What about Neapolis' stadium, and its hippodrome for equestrian events? Locations unknown.

Returning to what we *do* know, two freestanding theaters, one semicircular, the other smaller and box-shaped, once loomed side-by-side on the north edge of the upper forum but are now encased within later buildings. The theater, at least, has been partially cleared and parts of it are on view. Its impeccable concrete style, with crisp reticulate-and-brick facing, is visible throughout, though later repairs and alterations are many [Fig. 6.5]. The siting of both reflects

9. This epistle is a reflection on Seneca's old age (he would have been about sixty-six at the time), and Nero had him assassinated only three years later.

10. On these events see pp. 155–68.

CHAPTER 6 ☫ ROMAN NEAPOLIS

Fig. 6.5 (above). Barrel-vaulted corridor of the Roman theater. Photo: R. Taylor.
Fig. 6.6. (below). Theater and odeion of Pompeii. Photo: ElfQrin. Wikimedia Commons CC SA-4.0. Modified.

the confidence in the self-sustaining capacities of Roman concrete. This dual configuration was in place by about 93–95 CE, when the hometown poet Statius referred to the two theaters as "open and covered, a double mass."[11]

Setting a theater and an odeion side-by-side is unusual. Yet the arrangement is logical and has a precedent at nearby Pompeii [Fig. 6.6],

11. *Silvae* 3.5.91.

where by the 70s BCE the Sullan colonists had built their odeion into the city's south slope beside the existing Greco-Samnite theater. But at Neapolis, unlike Pompeii, the Roman theaters were set meaningfully into the forum at the heart of the city. This gave concentrated expression to the political character of the upper plaza, which is consequently sometimes called the civic *agora* to distinguish it from the commercial *agora* directly below it. Such a dichotomy between two specialized plazas was a commonplace in the Greek East, though (like the two theater types) the two *agorai* were rarely adjacent. As Johannowsky pointed out, Greek theaters were not just spaces for entertainment. They were often the main venues for deliberations of the city council, which could fit comfortably into the odeion, and the citizen assembly, which typically gathered in the open-air theater.[12] The upper forum, then, was not just an entertainment zone but also, critically, the city's political center.

THE TEMPLE OF THE DIOSCURI

Across the plaza from the main theater, and more or less aligned with its west side, stood the single ancient Neapolitan monument to have survived relatively intact into modern times, the temple of the Dioscuri [see Figs. 6.2; 6.3]. Like the theaters, this structure too faced south, signaling that the space it occupied was not a typical, centripetal Roman-style forum but instead a gently terraced overlook, rather like a grand Hellenistic sanctuary. From the temple's lofty podium, set back slightly from the street, one could probably get a fine view of the sea over the descending southerly neighborhoods of mostly two-story shops, baths, and dwellings. The lower forum remains largely undefined except for one outstanding feature on its east side, the city's *macellum* or central market, its lower tier occupied by shops, workshops, even a possible guildhall. It is on this evidence that the lower plaza has been called the commercial *agora*. I will return to it below.

The ancient temple of the Dioscuri and the Polis, once abandoned, seems to have served no steady purpose until the late eighth century. From that time until today the ancient podium and superstructure have been embedded in a sequence of church buildings

12. For a glimpse of how the council and assembly worked in Naples in the fourth century BCE, see pp. 64–65, 114–19.

CHAPTER 6 ⛫ ROMAN NEAPOLIS

Fig. 6.7. Façade of the church of S. Paolo Maggiore with remaining Roman columns and column bases in situ. Photo: R. Taylor.

dedicated to St. Paul. Except for a large gap in the center of the pediment, almost the whole marble façade of the Roman temple, including its sculpture, survived in place with only minor losses until a series of earthquakes in the 1680s toppled the pediment and most of the columns. Figure 6.3, an anonymous drawing in the Bibliothèque Nationale in Paris, shows the state of the building not long before the collapse. Today the meager remains are integrated into the façade of the church of S. Paolo Maggiore [Fig. 6.7]. Only the two outer porch columns that stood directly behind the hexastyle façade remain in place, along with two bases from the façade and a broken pediment over the central doorway. It is believed, however, that the walls of the temple's main chamber are still encased in the baroque church —

though, without a doubt, badly disfigured. A splendid Augustan-era marble temple on the citadel at Pozzuoli suffered the same fate in the seventeenth century, sacrificing huge arcs in its walls to side chapels.

The Neapolitan temple stood on a high podium faced in Roman imperial *opus reticulatum*, two sections of which are visible at street level. Many of the fallen elements remained on display in the plaza below for decades after the collapse, but inexplicably and tragically, except for a small fragment of the inscription, they are lost today. Fortunately the French drawing and others before it faithfully documented the architecture, the pedimental sculpture, and the Greek dedicatory inscription. This read:

> 50. TIBERIUS JULIUS TARSOS [DEDICATED] THIS TEMPLE AND EVERYTHING IN IT TO THE DIOSCURI AND THE CITY [POLIS]. PELAGON, FREEDMAN AND PROCURATOR OF THE EMPEROR, COMPLETED IT WITH HIS OWN MONEY AND CONSECRATED IT.
> [*IG* 14.714]

Widely worshiped around the hellenized Mediterranean, the deified twin horsemen known as Kastor and Polydeukes (Castor and Pollux to the Romans) were commonly called the Dioskouroi (literally "Sons of Zeus"), which we Latinize into Dioscuri. In port cities they were often hailed as protectors of sailors and seaborne merchants. The two sponsors of the Neapolitan temple have been identified as wealthy Asian-born freedmen of Tiberius (emperor 14–38 CE) who may have had commercial or official connections to Neapolis. At Rome, this emperor's devotion to the twin gods was famously expressed in his complete redesign and reconstruction of a venerable temple on the forum dedicated to them, which had already been in place (in one iteration or another) for nearly 500 years. In Naples, however, the lack of any significant archaeological work at the temple leaves us in the dark about its site history. At the moment we have no way of confirming whether the Tiberian building represents a comparable renewal of an older cult site dedicated to the same gods. But the cult itself, celebrated on Neapolitan coinage of an earlier era,[13] was probably as old as that of Parthenope.

Fortunately the Tiberian building is fairly well documented, especially in the French drawing but also in a remarkably precise ink and

---

13. See pp. 133–34.

CHAPTER 6 ⛫ ROMAN NEAPOLIS

Fig. 6.8. Ink drawing of the pediment at S. Paolo Maggiore. Fol. 45 v from the manuscript of Os desenhos das antiqualhas *by Francisco de Holanda,* Real Biblioteca del Monasterio de El Escorial. © Patrimonio Nacional (Spain).

chalk elevation drawing of the façade from 1540 by the Portuguese artist Francisco de Holanda [Fig. 6.8]. De Holanda's presentation is somewhat more stylized. It imagines away the church behind the

Fig. 6.9. Details of Fig. 6.8.

classical façade altogether, presenting it against the open sky. But he presents the architectural ornament, the pedimental sculpture, and the inscription in meticulous and faithful detail.

Even with the help of these drawings, we face a serious challenge in interpreting the sculptural program. Following a practice characteristic of the Roman imperial era, the figures were carved in high relief against a solid background. They were not freestanding as in the famous Greek temples of earlier times. At some point in the Middle Ages the central figures and their backing had fallen away. The Paris drawing suggests that the damage continued up to the acroterial statue pedestal crowning the center of the pediment; the pedestal seems to have lost its front half [see Fig. 6.3]. When the central slabs of the pediment relief fell off, the chevron-shaped central sima block slipped downward, necessitating some kind of shoring masonry to plug the

CHAPTER 6 ⛫ ROMAN NEAPOLIS

gap. (The open gap in de Holanda's drawing is part of his fanciful excision of all postclassical features.)

Apart from the missing central figures, the pediment was in excellent condition when de Holanda saw it. Each corner framed a reclining figure being attended to by a triton (half human with bare torso, half sea serpent) whose sinuous tail tapered into the angle [Fig. 6.9]. The left-hand reclining figure is a conventional female allegory of earthly abundance. Her left elbow rested on a grain bushel, symbolizing the harvest; in her right arm nestled a cornucopia. A billow of drapery swelled behind her head and shoulders. Her equivalent on the right side was a mature, bearded male, his elbow propped on an overturned urn. These figures have been variously interpreted; but there is little doubt that the male, who conforms to Roman iconographic conventions, is a river god — perhaps Neapolis' own Sebethos, or simply a more general representation of the regional rivers, especially the navigable ones that had a bearing on regional commerce. The representation of river gods as bull-men had dissipated along with Greek coinage. Now rivers were popularly represented as reclining deities (mostly male), often amid marsh reeds, their waters flowing from a supporting urn.

The attending tritons, in contrast, are creatures of the sea. So what are they doing attending to these landlocked allegories? The one on the left seems to be reaching into the cornucopia to pluck its fruits. Such impudence might seem jarring, but actually it chimes well with the times. A playful, even ironic tone characteristic of late Hellenistic taste sometimes enlivened Roman imperial public art in this era. The scene seems to send a salutary message: the land offers some of its fruits to the sea, the medium by which the fruits themselves might have been transported. On the right side, the triton is pouring a libation from a bowl (?) onto the river god's shoulder, as one might pour a sacrificial offering into the river itself. The two pendent scenes thus seem to represent a trilateral alliance of mutual benefit among arable land, navigable rivers, and the sea, a reciprocity of giving and receiving, of exploitation and tribute. But the landbound figures clearly dominate; the sea creatures are in their service.

We now turn to the standing figures between these extremes. The two males on the left are on different scales, and may thus represent a human and a god. Both seem to react with upraised arm to some event in the lost center. The smaller figure wears a voluminous garment reminiscent of a human sacrificant, as we see in other contexts. The larger, probably Apollo, one of the founding gods (*dii patres*) of Neapolis,[14] is draped in a heroic, mythic mode, his torso bare and his chiton loose about his hips. An eyewitness report mentioned a tripod between the two figures, but that was a misunderstanding; it is a low, three-legged table of a sort often used in sacrifices. Just as striking, and evidently noticed by nobody, is the horned head of the sacrificial bull directly above it, wedged between the god and the sacrificant. On the right, the intermediate standing figure, beside the river god, is Artemis-Diana in her hunting guise, her tunic drawn up to its characteristic knee length and a bow in her left hand. Her presence may be explained simply by that of her brother Apollo. But this goddess' significance to Neapolitan historical identity has been explored elsewhere in this book.[15] Beside her would originally have stood a larger figure, on Apollo's scale, now entirely lost. This, I have conjectured, was another of the city's founding gods, Demeter, whose sanctuary lay on the north edge of the walled city at Caponapoli.[16] We are left, then, with room for one dominant, central figure. Certainly there was no room for both Dioscuri, who typically appeared together, and often with their horses. If not them, who?

The temple, it must be emphasized, was dedicated to the Dioscuri *and the City*. Cities in the Greek East were often represented by an allegorical figure of Tyche, their "Good Fortune." In the West such allegories were less common, but the city of Rome itself sometimes pressed the goddess Roma into this service, though she typically represented Roman power in a more global sense. Such a thoroughly Hellenized city as Neapolis was perhaps the most likely of all western cities to follow this lead in the imperial era, and indeed a first-century-CE dedication inscription to "Tyche of Neapolis" survives.[17] In the center between Apollo and Demeter, then, we may expect to have seen an allegorical figure representing Neapolis in the form of a conventional Greek tutelary goddess

14. Statius, *Silvae* 4.8.45–54.
15. See pp. 133–35, 167.
16. See pp. 51–52.
17. *IG* 14.720.

CHAPTER 6 ⛫ ROMAN NEAPOLIS

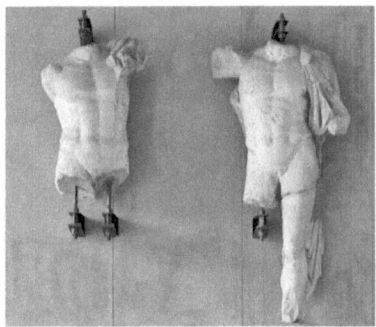

Fig. 6.10. Fragmentary remains of the statues of the Dioscuri from S. Paolo Maggiore. Naples, Museo Archeologico Nazionale. Photo: R. Taylor.

of a city. Probably she was understood to be the Siren Parthenope herself, reborn as the city's patron goddess.[18] Her dramatic appearance in the center would merit the attentive or even startled reactions of the subsidiary figures. Her presence might even historicize the sacrifice scene. Could the sacrificant beside Apollo, heavily wrapped in a Greek *himation*, be the Athenian Diotimos, who upon his arrival at Neapolis in the mid-fifth century BCE sacrificed to Parthenope, revived her cult, and instituted torch races in her honor?[19] This dedication, combined with that to the Dioscuri, would have blended Tiberius' patronage with local Neapolitan identity.

Where, then, were the Dioscuri themselves, who shared the dedication with the *polis*? As the third component of the triad (or tetrad, accounting for the duality of the Dioscuri) of ancestor gods of Neapolis mentioned by Statius, they certainly deserved prominent representation. Here again, Rome can serve as a precedent. Two colossal freestanding pairs of the twins with their horses have been excavated there, and are prominently displayed in the city today. One of those pairs, flanking the top of the broad access ramp rising to the Piazza del Campidoglio, was recovered from a second temple of the twins nearby on the east bank of the Tiber. Too bulky to have adorned the temple's roof, originally that pair probably stood sentinel on either side of its broad central stairway.

Neapolis seems to present a parallel. For centuries two fragmentary nude male statues in white marble were preserved in wall niches at the church of S. Paolo built into the temple's ruins. Now they are in the Museo Archeologico di Napoli [Fig. 6.10]. Rendered in the

18. See pp. 38–46.
19. See pp. 55–59.

Fig. 6.11. Model of the Temple of the Dioscuri in its forum context on display at the church of S. Lorenzo Maggiore. Photo: R. Taylor.

heroic style of the classical sculptor Polykleitos, with mirror-image stances and *chlamydes* draped over their left shoulders, they unmistakably represent the Dioscuri. Carved fully in the round, they cannot have belonged to the temple pediment and they are too small to have served as cult statues inside the temple. Each has an arm extended to control the reins of a horse, but the horses themselves are entirely lost. Conceivably they were set on the acroterial pedestals visible (vestigially) on the rooftop in the French drawing [see Fig. 6.3], either symmetrically at the far corners, or together on the central pedestal. But roof sculpture, with its demand for lightness and high tensile strength to resist wind, was usually made of hollow bronze.

CHAPTER 6 ⛩ ROMAN NEAPOLIS

These gods were probably set up as pendent statues down below in front of the temple façade. Pedestals on either side of the stair, such as those reimagined in a scale model on display at S. Lorenzo Maggiore nearby [Fig. 6.11], again suggest themselves.

If this was the most important temple of Roman Neapolis, as seems probable, then we should pause for a moment and think about it in context. Roman-style temples like this one are unidirectional: they have an obvious front and back. The architects had a choice: they could turn the temple northward to face the theaters and create a properly bounded, inward-looking forum space. But instead they followed the precedent of Hellenistic sanctuaries and oriented the temple out toward the sea. To be sure, it was not sited on an impressive promontory like the Augustan temple at Pozzuoli or the two great hill temples of Cumae. But the declivity southward is quite noticeable, and it was even more pronounced in antiquity. Clearance across the lower forum was a full 185 meters, over which the terrain dropped by as much as 10 meters or more. Surely the temple's connection to the sea was intentional, and in a multivalent way. The Dioscuri were patrons of the seafaring life, and Parthenope herself was reclaimed and reborn from the waves.[20] The temple mediated symbolically between the civic and commercial fora by engaging the city's terrestrial identity, which had developed out of a quasi-republican demarchate of satellite communities that had once controlled the civic assembly, in conversation with its maritime identity as the port city that had betimes dominated the Tyrrhenian.[21] We should probably think of this upper forum as the material expression of a heavily Romanized version of the city's Greek identity, which in its own way had already suppressed Neapolis' mixed Greco-Samnite parentage.

THE COMPLEX AT S. LORENZO MAGGIORE

On to the lower forum. One day in the late 1950s, near the cloister of the great church of S. Lorenzo Maggiore, some forty meters to the southeast of S. Paolo Maggiore, a piece of heavy construction equipment crashed through the earth into a void below. A look inside the void revealed that the great church and its satellite buildings had been

20. See pp. 42–46.
21. See chapters 2–4.

Fig. 6.12. Eastern sector of the excavations at S. Lorenzo Maggiore, looking south. Photo: R. Taylor.

built directly over one of the ancient streets forming the original city grid [Fig. 6.12]. Fronting the street on the west, the sanctuary and cloister rested on a large rectangular terrace formed by a mighty retaining wall of tuff blocks elegantly battered to create a gently splayed wall face and lined on two sides with later vaulted chambers [Fig. 6.13; see Fig. 6.2]. On the basis of its masonry style, archaeologists long dated the terrace to the fifth or fourth century BCE. But recent ceramic analysis at the southwest corner suggest that at the very least it was completely refurbished in the mid-second century BCE, during the height of Neapolis' commercial success with Greco-Italic amphora production and "Campana A" export tablewares,[22] fragments of which have been found in the fill of the retaining wall.

In the Roman imperial period the terrace underwent substantial changes [Fig. 6.14a]. Around the top was built a portico of shop entrances. At its center stood a distinctive circular pavilion identifying the space as a *macellum*, or market plaza. Its floor was paved with slabs of colored marble, and a hydraulic system featured some kind of waterplay. Similar *macella* are known at both Pompeii and Pozzuoli [see Fig. 1.4] as well as many other Roman cities. Decked out in the

22. See pp. 139–43; Commentary 4.3, pp. 147–48.

CHAPTER 6 ⚱ ROMAN NEAPOLIS

Fig. 6.13. Remains of the Roman macellum under the structures of the church and cloister of S. Lorenzo Maggiore in Naples. Illustration by Francesco Corni.

distinctive international colored marbles quarried at the emperor's pleasure, this was another marker of imperial *Romanitas* in the Greek city.

Below, following the sloping topography of the ground, a row of shops and workspaces wrapped around the terrace's east and south sides, many of them fitted with light shafts angling up through the terrace floor [Fig. 6.14b]. Built in brick and reticulate of the late first century CE, with an unbroken brick facade sometimes finely detailed in relief [see Fig. 6.12], the eastern shops are reminiscent

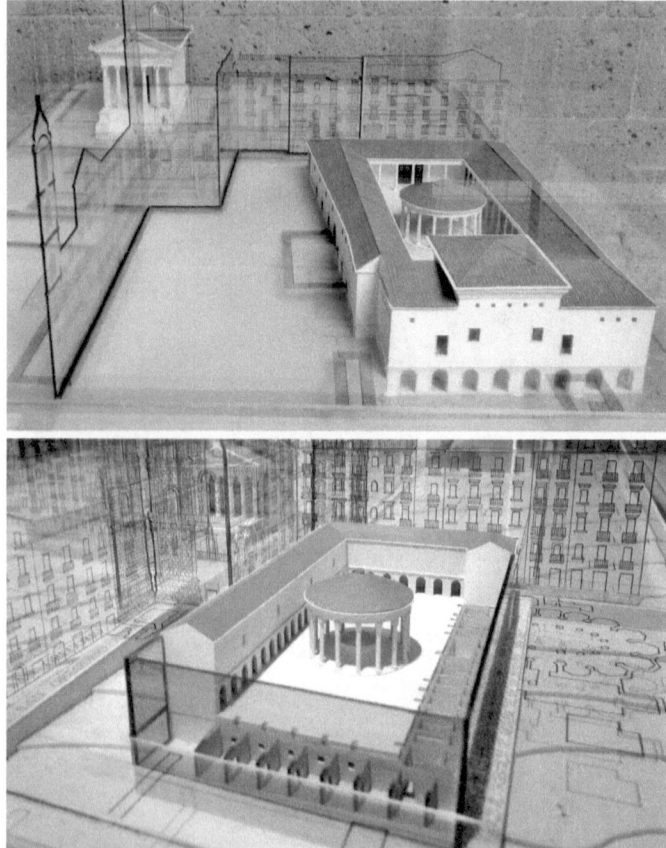

Fig. 6.14a (above), Fig. 6.14b (below). Complete and cutaway models at the church of S. Lorenzo Maggiore representing the Roman macellum *and commercial precinct excavated under the church.*

of commercial architecture of Ostia. Some have been identified by function: a laundry, a fullery, even a treasury, its streetside window once fitted with metal bars. On the south side, the architecture changes substantively [Fig. 6.15]. In lieu of an east–west street here a spacious walkway was created by opening up the dividing walls of the shops themselves with broad arches.

CHAPTER 6 ▥ ROMAN NEAPOLIS

Fig. 6.15. Southern sector of the excavations under S. Lorenzo Maggiore, looking west. Photo: R. Taylor.

A new sector of the southwest corner of the terrace, opened to the public in 2009, reveals a less regular scheme. At this corner the floor level rose to rest upon the massive stone barrel vault of a dropshaft for a Hellenistic storm drain. The shaft is lined with the same battered ashlar masonry as the retaining wall. Built over and around it, however, is a Roman-era chamber with a reticulate wall and a concrete barrel vault aligned with the stone vault below — essentially the same arrangement as the shops to the east but on a somewhat higher level. Even a light shaft was included. This system drained the entire terrace.

Along the western retaining wall of the terrace a large, multi-room structure in the Roman style — I will call it the western annex — was built directly against the older Greek retaining wall. In contrast to the commercial and quasi-public spaces on the east and south sides, its rooms carried timber roofs, not vaults, and were not as integrated into the platform structure. An atrium-like hall, complete with an *impluvium,* stands at the southwest corner of the terrace west of the dropshaft. A row of interconnected rooms extends northward from it built in quasi-reticulate punctuated by widely spaced horizontal bands of brick and finished with a fresco of the fourth Pompeian style (mid- to late first century CE). Traces of brick columns toward

Fig. 6.16. *Western sector of the excavations under S. Lorenzo Maggiore, looking north northeast.* Photo: R. Taylor.

the still unexcavated west side of the annex may indicate the presence there of a colonnaded courtyard in the manner of houses at Pompeii or Herculaneum — not quite like the uniform portico façade envisioned on the models [see Fig. 6.14]. The complex culminates at the north in a large rectangular room paved with a finely tessellated white mosaic bordered by a double black band. Here the quasi-reticulate of its east wall is laid so thinly against the Greek retaining wall that it is barely thicker than the plaster on its surface [Fig. 6.16]. The ample proportions of these rooms have suggested to some that the whole western annex was a *schola*, or meeting-place for a guild or phratry.[23] Decidedly earlier than the Roman shops on the east side, its construction has been provisionally dated to the late first century BCE or the early first century CE.

The fourth-style frescos, though considerably later than the construction phase of the walls, were never replaced by later fashions, remaining in place until the complex became a burial ground in the sixth or seventh century CE. South of the large hall, probably after the fresco phase, the mosaic floor in one of the smaller rooms

23. On phratries, see pp. 65–66, 174–76, 294–95; and Commentary 2.4, pp. 79–81.

was covered with a layer of *opus signinum,* a pink hydraulic cement. Later still, probably in the second or third century CE, this room, the *impluvium* in the atrium-like room, and a room adjoining the atrium on the west were lined with colored marbles. Whatever the precise function of this complex through the Roman imperial period, it was treated with all the care due to a high-status building in a premier location.

What exactly lay to the west of this terrace we don't know; but Greco conjectures that it was originally Neapolis' commons, used for military drilling in the manner of the cities of Miletos or Olynthos. Later it may have been adapted to an open space for temporary market stalls, like modern Italian markets.

THE SEBASTA GAMES AND THE KAISAREION

For nearly six decades after 2 CE Neapolis was the exclusive venue of international Greek-style games in Italy.[24] Though Rome and Pozzuoli acquired such games later on, it cannot be said that either of those cities invested so deeply in their symbolic and social capital. Bringing in hordes of visitors in August once every four years, the games served both sides of Neapolis' dual identity as an important harbor town and a cultural refuge that nourished artistry and leisure of all kinds.[25] As far as we know, the games were held regularly throughout the first and second centuries CE and on into the third, bringing together perhaps well over 100,000 outsiders and locals. How the city and its suburbs absorbed them is unknown, but the East offered plenty of models to follow, including some in urban areas. As with the modern Olympics we may presume that attendance and participation were distributed around several discrete venues in the greater metropolitan area.

Greek games of the Roman era encompassed two principal categories of competition: performance, and athletic and equestrian

24. On the games see pp. 313–22. Eventually there would be two more: the *Capitolina* in Rome, and the *Eusebeia* in neighboring Pozzuoli. The short-lived Neronia were held only twice. Cumae had a Hellenistic-era stadium, but its games seem to have remained on a small, regional scale.

25. See chapter 8.

Fig. 6.17. Roman imperial statue of Nike. Naples, Museo Archeologico Nazionale. Photo: R. Taylor.

events. The Sebasta at Neapolis offered a considerable range of categories, as its many surviving inscriptions attest.[26] I have already emphasized that many of the performance events would have taken place at the city's theaters, either the open theater or the smaller, roofed odeion. Athletic events took place elsewhere: a gymnasium and practice track for training and possibly boxing and wrestling events (which could also be held in the stadium), the stadium for the footraces, the hippodrome for the chariot and horse racing. These latter venues were necessarily enormous. The second-century-CE stadium at Pozzuoli was some 260 x 70 meters, and any hippodrome would have exceeded that size considerably. No trace of either has been found at Neapolis. There seems to be no accommodation for them inside the walls, and so they must be sought in the suburbs.

What we know about the topographic disposition of the games has little directly to do with the athletic or performance venues. The ceremonial center, it would seem, was itself just outside the walls to the south. The recent discoveries at Piazza Nicola Amore may confirm a longstanding hypothesis that the main gymnasium was in that district just outside the Greek walls on the south side of the city. Many other inscriptions related to the Sebasta had been found in the vicinity, as well as a lifesize marble Nike in the manner of Paionios'

26. See pp. 317–22.

CHAPTER 6 ⛫ ROMAN NEAPOLIS

famous prototype at Olympia [Fig. 6.17]. The excavations have revealed not only a temple and a portico clearly associated with the games but a paved area between the two monuments. This straight segment of pavement, according to Elena Miranda De Martino, conforms neatly to a racetrack described by Dio Chrysostom:

> 51. After coming up from the harbor, we strolled over at once to have a look at the athletes, just as if the sole purpose of our trip had been to view the contests. When we got near the gymnasium we saw a number running on the track outside of it, and there was a roar as the crowd cheered them on; and we also saw the athletes who were exercising in other ways. [*Discourse* 28.1]

Miranda's hypothesis may presume more than the evidence will support, though it is certainly possible: many gymnasia had parallel covered and uncovered racing tracks. The excavators, in contrast, believe that this segment of portico may have been part of an enclosure surrounding the temple, not a discrete building separated from it by a track.

The temple was among the discoveries made at the Stazione Duomo Metropolitana site in 2003–2004. A small Corinthian structure in white marble, dating to the early first century CE, it lay about fifteen meters south of, and parallel to, a gate in the Greek walls — and very close to the waterfront [see Fig. 6.1; Commentary 6.1, p. 244]. Viewed from its side, the temple was directly aligned with the major north-south street corresponding to the modern Via Duomo. Assuming there was no wall between it and the gate, then it could have been seen from a great distance down the arrow-straight street. A wall of reticulate and brick facing ran parallel to the temple on its south side, fronted by a portico — a striking backdrop for those approaching the temple from the north. Fallen from the wall, hundreds of fragmentary inscribed marble slabs were recovered there, consisting of lists of victors in events at the Sebasta spanning from Domitian's reign [81–98 CE] up to the third century.[27] The wall may have extended for some distance in both directions (the excavated station footprint is tiny), documenting games both earlier and later

27. See Commentary 8.6, pp. 339–40.

Fig. 6.18. Fragments of the columns and roof of the Kaisareion. Naples, Museo Archeologico Nazionale. Photo: R. Taylor.

than these. Potentially, thousands more inscription fragments lie just out of reach of archaeologists.

A well-known inscription of the Roman imperial era found at Olympia, unfortunately too fragmentary to extract here,[28] indicates that at some point in the proceedings of the Sebasta at Neapolis contestants and city officials made a procession to a *Kaisareion* to sacrifice to the gods and the deified Augustus. Two tenth-century Latin documents situate a *Caesareum* in the *Regio Thermensis*,[29] an ancient and medieval neighborhood in the southeastern part of town. The term, whether transliterated or not, can have a range of meanings, but it is naturally understood to be a temple or shrine of the imperial cult. Scholars are therefore comfortable identifying this very temple as the Kaisareion, though its battered remains offer no clue about its dedication [Fig. 6.18]. The marble head of a Julio-Claudian prince, found nearby, might at least suggest that Augustus and his family were worshiped here. The winged Nike statue may have adorned the temple,

28. *Inschriften von Olympia* 56.
29. On this neighborhood, see p. 273; Commentary 5.3, pp. 177–78.

CHAPTER 6 ☖ ROMAN NEAPOLIS

but a direct association between the two is shaky, especially in light of the crude character of the temple's carving, so different from the statue's [see Commentary 6.1, p. 244]. The structure was dismantled and restored shortly after 157 CE (a coin of that date was found in the refurbished podium). The podium was raised, and the early Julio-Claudian carved components were restored to their place but on a somewhat different plan. The temple collapsed in the fourth century, long before the portico, and its fallen ruins were simply left to lie. Much of the marble was ransacked but some obviously remained, never to be recovered.

This unusually early demise and untidy aftermath may betoken a natural disaster like an earthquake accompanied, perhaps, by a more definitive stroke of doom: I would suggest a long period of bradyseismic descent, bringing down the ground level at the shore and flooding the area. The curious phenomenon known as bradyseism is the uplift or descent of the ground level on account of the movement of magma or geothermal activity far below the surface. On first examination, such a scenario has its problems. For example, if the marble had been exposed to seawater over time, it would have been encrusted with shells or barnacles and pockmarked by lithophaga. It is not. But the general scenario, even if it doesn't come into perfect focus, is not just plausible in light of what I will describe below concerning the harbor. It also finds confirmation in the site history itself. Fierce storm surges, rather than perpetual inundation, may have been what this intervention was protecting against. The first hint comes with the raising of the podium and the entire superstructure by half a meter to 2.2 meters in the late 150s or the 160s CE. "It is astonishing," remarks Irene Bragantini, "that in the second half of the second century CE a sacred building, and a famous and important one at that, was rebuilt with the same architectural materials, dating back more than a century." This was no stem-to-stern remodeling of the normal Roman kind. Was it instead an attempt to jack up a venerable temple on the cheap to protect its contents from ever more damaging storm surges? The second hint comes with successive attempts to adapt the Wall of Fame to circumstances: first, a parapet was added just inside the colonnade in the late second century CE (again, maybe a surge protector?) and then the portico floor, and presumably the ground

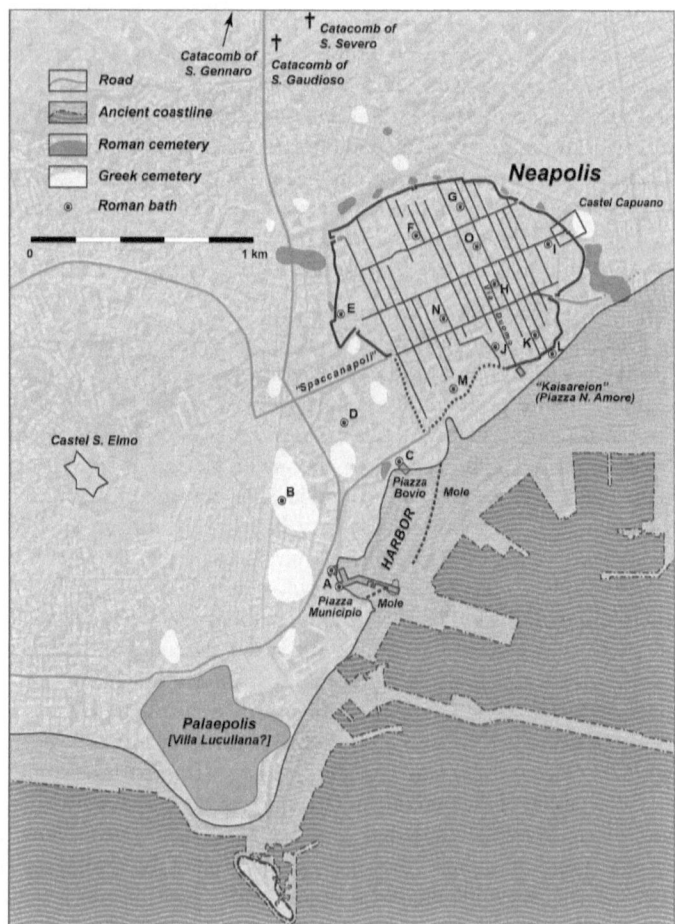

Fig. 6.19. Map of Roman Neapolis highlighting known cemetery zones and bathing establishments.

level of the entire precinct, was raised by half a meter in the first half of the third century. At this time the parapet in the portico was raised *again*.

Unforeseen misfortunes aside, this small temple was undeniably in a prime location, serving as the focal point along two lines of sight: from

CHAPTER 6 ▥ ROMAN NEAPOLIS

the north, as already described, and from the west, on axis with its façade. The inscribed portico to the south, only a small sector of which was excavated, added clarity and monumentality to the ensemble, but in its earliest, second-century-BCE phase, predates the temple. The lower strata in this area are very different but indicate that some kind of cult activity took place here in the fourth century BCE. Ritual pits containing the bones of sacrificed animals and ceramic libation bowls were found, and just above them cremation burials of infants. In a slightly later phase, around 300 BCE, two structures emerged, separated by a street. In the corresponding strata were found fragments of locally manufactured Greco-Italic amphoras, some bearing the crown motif that Gloria Olcese associates with the pre-Roman games at Neapolis. So we now have good reason to believe that the area had been associated with the torch races of Parthenope long before the foundation of the Sebasta. In this phase the site was more enclosed, lacking the later monumentality or concern for sightlines, but the relative fixity of purpose here does suggest that we are at least close to some of the action — perhaps, as suggested above, the gymnasium. Presumably the gymnasium proper lay just out of the picture, either to east or west, or just inside the gate. And since this area was called the Region of the Bathmen, and later Region of the Baths (*Regio Thermensium* or *Thermensis*),[30] the intimations of a high concentration of bathing establishments chime well with a district that served a steady clientele of athletes: the Greco-Roman association of bathing with sport was close and widespread. Known Roman baths in this region are marked J, K, and L on Fig. 6.19 and will be revisited in the next chapter.

Everything here is very close to the ancient shoreline, and by the late second century CE that proved to be a problem. But what *supporting* roles, if any, did the sea play in the Sebasta experience? If this temple is where the customary hecatomb sacrifice was made at the start of the games, then it was surely meant to be part of a processional way starting somewhere to the southwest along the shore. And as I will argue in chapter 8, the shore may have had another function. The opening or closing ceremonies seem to have featured aquatic displays, a genre of entertainment of which people around the Bay were exceedingly fond. These, I contend, consisted of whimsical

30. See p. 273; Commentary 5.3, pp. 177–78.

reenactments of Augustus' famous naval victories over Sextus Pompey, Mark Antony, and Cleopatra.[31] Unencumbered by cluttered harbor frontage like that to the southwest, this length of shoreline right outside the city walls may have been the ideal spot from which the gathered masses could stand or sit to watch the spectacle out on the water, perhaps even while they dined on the sacrificial meat butchered and roasted near the altar of the Kaisareion.

One last point about the athletic district needs emphasis. It is absurd to think that a *quinquennial* event, which unfolded over one or two weeks out of every two hundred (208.7 weeks, to be exact), could somehow lay exclusive claim to these places. Neapolis was, emphatically, a city that celebrated all of the Greek arts, athletics among them. Just as the Artists of Dionysos had a permanent presence of professional actors here, and just as famous and emerging musicians, orators, and dancers either resided in Neapolis or kept it on their busy travel agendas, we can also expect that athletes lived, trained, or competed here continually. To judge from the victor lists preserved on the Wall of Fame, some cities (especially in Greece and Asia Minor) sent entire teams to the games circuit, rather as modern nations do — not just to the Olympics, but to the annual world championships, regional competitions, and so forth. Neapolis probably cultivated its own teams of specialists and hosted smaller-scale events regularly.

THE HARBOR

All harbors change over time, many drastically. Sailors seeking an anchorage or a mooring-place love calm, protected places; but so does sediment, which is prone to settle and accumulate in areas that are not constantly pounded by surf. In consequence one defining advantage of a harbor, quietude, undermines the other, depth. Maintaining both simultaneously is a perpetual challenge requiring remedies that have not changed much over time: extending the natural cove of a harbor with a mole (both to calm the water and minimize the inflow of sediment), and dredging the sea floor to improve depth. Neapolis tried both expedients, but after the third century BCE the city seems to have given up on dredging. Thereafter, the port relied on a mole alone, probably consisting of two enclosing arms [see Fig. 6.19]. Over the centuries it

31. See Commentary 8.5, pp. 337–39.

CHAPTER 6 ⛪ ROMAN NEAPOLIS

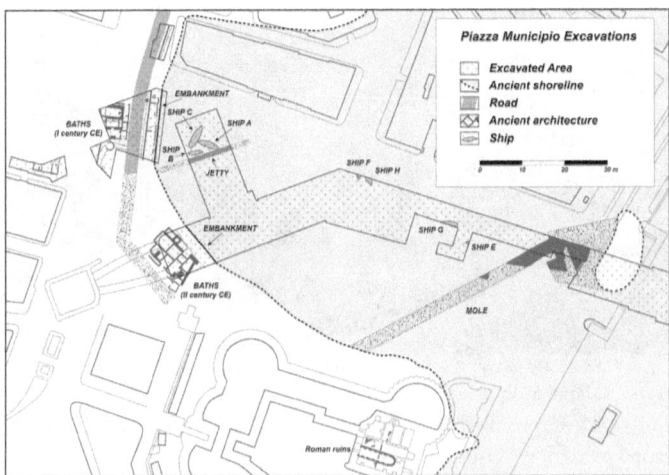

Fig. 6.20. Map of the harbor excavations at Piazza Municipio with remains of Roman architecture and ships. After Boetto 2019.

alternately benefited and suffered from bradyseism, which can raise or lower ground and seafloor levels by as much as several meters.

Throughout antiquity the harbor remained fixed in place between Parthenope and the New City. Until the Metropolitana project, however, its location and physical disposition were unknown, though everyone agreed that the shoreline has advanced since antiquity, leaving the old harbor(s) landlocked and buried. For centuries, antiquarians and scholars speculated about these matters, and some ventured educated guesses about the harbor's position and size. But they could not test their hypothesis, let alone sketch out a history of the seashore's changes over time. Definitive evidence finally arrived with the systematic geomorphological study made for the subway project along with the dramatic discovery during the Municipio station excavations in 2003 of three ships and sections of embankment and jetties some 270 meters inland from the modern waterfront. By a lucky stroke, the next station north, at Piazza Bovio, came down on the northern edge of the harbor [see Fig. 6.19]. Subsequent publications continue to fill in the initial outlines of discovery. The coring campaign revealed the long-term morphology of the coastline, but

Fig. 6.21. Selection of pottery recovered from the harbor excavations. Naples, Museo Archeologico Nazionale. Photo: R. Taylor.

only excavations at the station sites provided concentrated and detailed evidence of human activity.

The harbor was a shallow inlet extending roughly 650 meters from south southwest to north northeast. Spurs of tuff and sand defined it at either extremity, and from them were extended the arms of a concrete mole. The three well-preserved Roman ships at Piazza Municipio were discovered in a cluster along with thousands of other artifacts. Four more ships have since been unearthed [Commentary

Fig. 6.22. Model of the ships A, B, and C from the harbor excavations at Piazza Municipio. Naples, Museo Archeologico Nazionale. The pilings and rubble to the left formed a jetty; just to its left are the scooped recesses in the tuff bedrock formed by a rotary dredge. Photo: R. Taylor.

6.2, p. 244; Figs. 6.20; 6.21]. Stratigraphic excavation of the site turned up layer upon layer of sandy sedimentation stacked from three meters to seven meters below modern sea level, many of the strata dense with ceramics, coins, tools, marine equipment (including coils of rope, fish hooks, and anchors), and botanical and faunal remains.

CHAPTER 6 ⚱ ROMAN NEAPOLIS

Consistent with excavations in other parts of Naples, residual ceramic finds indicated a Greek presence from the late eighth or early seventh century BCE onward. No stratigraphy was preserved for the early centuries, however. The excavators found clear evidence of wheel dredging in the Hellenistic period (see Fig. 6.22, far left), which would have churned up and displaced all earlier material. Despite the fact that the practice continued for another three centuries, some areas preserve a fairly continuous stratigraphy from the fourth century BCE onward into the early medieval period. Daniela Giampaola and Vittoria Carsana observe that the dredging — which was so intensive that it cut big arcs into the solid rock — was undertaken during Neapolis' greatest years as a maritime power, extending from the time of its treaty with Rome in the fourth century BCE through the height of the city's production and export of "Campana A" pottery. Why the dredging stopped is unclear. It does not signal a discernible decline in the harbor's functionality, though alluviation did eventually doom the harbor in late antiquity. As we saw with the Kaisareion precinct, though, this is a coastal region with very weird geological habits; that fact alone may provide an explanation.

In the early 1890s, a large marble inscription in Latin was discovered intact during utility work on Via Lanzieri, just east of Piazza Bovio [see Fig. 6.1].[32] Dating to the Severan dynasty, it had probably been affixed to a seawall made of mortared rubble, remains of which were found during the excavation. In the text below I omit most of the formulaic nomenclature that characterizes official imperial inscriptions of this era. In abbreviated form, it declares:

> **52.** IMPERATOR CAESAR ... LUCIUS SEPTIMIUS SEVERUS..., PONTIFEX MAXIMUS, IN THE TENTH YEAR OF HIS TRIBUNICIAN POWER, IMPERATOR FOR THE ELEVENTH TIME, CONSUL FOR THE THIRD TIME [=202 CE], FATHER OF THE FATHERLAND AND PROCONSUL, AND HIS SON ... MARCUS AURELIUS ANTONINUS PIUS FELIX AUGUSTUS, IN THE FIFTH YEAR OF HIS TRIBUNICIAN POWER, CONSUL AND PROCONSUL, MADE A NEW MOLE TO PROTECT PASSAGE [*VIA*], WHICH HAD BEEN DAMAGED BY THE INFLUX OF THE SEA. [trans. Taylor]

32. *NSc* 1892 479–81.

The word *via,* offered with no explanatory adjective or genitives, is often mistranslated as "the street," presumed to be a harborside route along which the inscription was affixed. But here, as in other Roman inscriptions, it more probably carries the legal meaning "passage," referring to the right of mariners to a clear channel of access. The final phrase *adluvione maris* neatly captures the mole's dual function: it can mean either "by the surge of the sea" or "by the sedimentation of the sea."

Was the constant sedimentation of the harbor floor coming from the mouth of a nearby river? In the mid-twentieth century, Mario Napoli conjectured that the ancient Sebethos River — following the southward course of Via Toledo, then Via Monteoliveto and Via Medina — had emptied directly into the harbor, which he had situated in this general area. Surely it was not so. If it had been, the harbor mole would have trapped the alluvium inside the harbor, not kept it out. Geomorphological survey shows no conclusive evidence of a river here, but masses of sediment did wash down by some means from the heavily eroded hills. Still, the mole of Neapolis had an effect similar to one found recently at an ancient harbor of Constantinople: intended to keep sediment out, it may eventually have been defeated by sedimentation from within.

An equally significant, and much less predictable, factor was also at work, however: the rising and falling of ground level, and thus the harbor floor, from bradyseism. On the shore of the harbor's southwestern bight, a Hellenistic boat ramp underlying a second-century bath building [A on Fig. 6.19; see Fig. 6.20] preserved an oyster reef at a level that is currently 2.1 meters below modern sea level. Since oysters cluster at sea level, and the sea has not risen by such a distance in the interval, it must be concluded that this sector once sat higher than it does today — by my own reckoning, about three quarters of a meter [see Commentary 6.3, pp. 245–46]. Similar encrustations on the embankments nearby, in contexts dated to the first century CE, lie about 1.6 meters below sea level, a difference of half a meter. To return momentarily to the Severan inscription: reports unfortunately vary as to whether it was found 20 centimeters above modern sea level or 2 meters below, but the bottom eight of its twenty-eight

CHAPTER 6 ☗ ROMAN NEAPOLIS

lines were covered with a calcareous encrustation from the sea. This could only have happened while the inscription was affixed to an exposed wall. At some time after its installation, the inscription sat partially inundated. The slab is 2.27 meters high, and about 60 centimeters of it was immersed long enough for bivalves and barnacles to attach to it. Since the slab would not have been installed at ground level, and ground level itself would normally have been well above the water, it is hard to avoid envisioning a subsidence here on the order of several meters. The geomorphological survey confirms these conditions spectacularly: it found that the north end of the harbor was entirely submerged from the late second up to the fourth century CE. The inscription, erected in 202, may have dipped into the sea within decades and remained partly underwater for centuries.

Certainly the beginnings of this episode, which continued on for many years, as the evidence of the Kaisareion suggests, could have prompted the Severan intervention. A sharp descent of the sea floor would have taken the old mole down with it, making the harbor vulnerable to wave action and sedimentation from without. The inscription's reference to a "new mole" clearly implies a failed predecessor. The fragmentary ruins, supposedly Augustan in date, of a concrete breakwater discovered between 2013 and 2015 at the harbor's south end [see Figs. 6.19; 6.20] must be a relic of it. Whether this exclusively Augustan attribution is justified, I do not know; to my knowledge, no evidence of a later restoration phase has been reported. The more severe subsidence seems to have trended northward, probably requiring repairs to the longer northern arm of the mole. This sector lies unexcavated, but would have reached land near the spot where the inscription was found [see Figs. 6.1; 6.19].

The harbor stratigraphy may bear out the broader scenario I am suggesting: two or more episodes of descent in the first and second centuries CE that were not entirely reversed by subsequent uplift. Over the course of the first century CE, a full 1.3 meters of sandy sedimentation accumulated in the excavated area. A jetty was built at the end of this period [see Figs. 6.20; 6.22]; wooden piers projecting from it were added in the second century. The sheer abundance of

Fig. 6.23. First-century-CE bath building beside the harbor, before demolition. Photo: R. Taylor.

finds, many of them consumer wares that dropped overboard [see Fig. 6.21], demonstrates that the jetty was a loading and offloading zone. Giampaola and Carsana hypothesize that this phase of unusually rapid accumulation was associated with a bradyseismic subsidence of the sea floor in the first century — an event that has been dramatically confirmed at nearby Herculaneum, where the waterfront suffered a significant drop shortly before the eruption of 79. At Neapolis such a fortuitous descent would have bought some time for the ailing harbor by improving the depth of its waters temporarily. What was good for the harbor itself, however, was bad for the harborside infrastructure. One Roman bath complex on the shore was renovated in a most unusual and telling way: a second hypocaust was thrown up on top of the first. The whole floor and subfloor system was jacked up by a meter or more, probably because the older drainage system was inundated as the waterfront sank into the sea [Fig. 6.23].

Running perpendicularly out from the western embankment, the jetty may indicate that sedimentation had canceled out the temporary advantage of subsidence by the end of the first century. One way to prolong a shallow port's usefulness was simply to build

CHAPTER 6 ⛫ ROMAN NEAPOLIS

longer piers out into deeper water, as the jetty was evidently designed to do. In effect, it was a kind of prosthesis to compensate for a gradual amputation. Although the angles of the wooden piers extending from it are rather baffling, it would seem that the jetty was intended to add new berths for heavily loaded craft at some distance from the shallows of the waterfront. Other similar structures may lie undiscovered nearby. Interestingly, the jetty and its piers were abandoned around 200 CE, at about the same time as the Severan co-emperors replaced the old harbor mole. The cause of both measures, we may conjecture, was a second bradyseismic event. By this time, the harbor's southwestern bight was a graveyard for derelict ships, which lie scattered randomly on its floor. That in itself does not signal abandonment; in harbors around the ancient world, old ships sometimes sank suddenly or were even scuttled in place, after which removing the hulk was deemed not worth the effort, though the upper parts might have required dismantling as a precaution to other ships. More telling is the fact that the lower parts of the ships are preserved at all: exposed wood does not survive Mediterranean waters for more than a few decades. The only possible preservative is the rapid accumulation of new layers of sediment, whose anoxic environment excludes the many wood-eating sea creatures and microbes that thrive in the water.

Whatever reprieves the harbor of Roman Neapolis enjoyed by subsidence, over the long run the waters in this zone grew ever shallower as those four meters of sediment accumulated. To be sure, the harbor may have ceded its primacy to the one of Puteoli as early as the Sullan occupation. Yet the city remained an important port of call, and some of its wharves continued to function vigorously, as the rich array of artifacts on the sea floor indicates. Yet those artifacts also tell a tale of decline. The number of ceramic fragments corresponding roughly to the Julio-Claudian period found at the Municipio dig (nearly 200,000) marks the high point of the imperial age. The second half of the first century CE (43,232) signals a sharp decline that continued over the entire second century (61,491) and accelerated in the third (10,300).

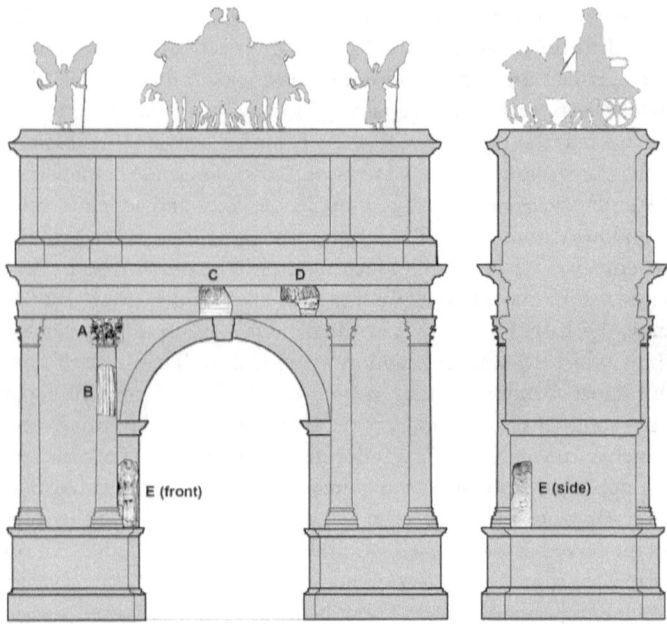

Fig. 6.24. Reconstruction of a dismantled Severan honorific arch with hypothetical placement of several key components. After Cavalieri and Hesberg 2010, with modifications.

THE HONORIFIC ARCH AT PIAZZA BOVIO

We turn now to the Piazza Bovio excavations, and some discoveries that will bring us back to the question of the harbor's vigor and viability in the imperial age. Here were discovered a group of carved marble fragments that have been identified as parts of a single public monument, probably an honorific or commemorative arch of the Severan period [Fig. 6.24]. All were recovered from the ruins of a medieval tower. (The reader hardly needs reminding that everything found in the subway excavations had to be dismantled and removed.) The most distinctive fragments recovered were a Corinthian capital [A], part of a fluted column shaft (B), two sections of a frieze showing a disembarkation and gathering of togate men in relief (C and D), as well as a curious corner pilaster [E; Fig. 6.25] representing on its front side a military trophy and on its adjacent face the

CHAPTER 6 ROMAN NEAPOLIS

Fig. 6.25. The two finished sides of a corner fragment from the Severan arch. Naples, Museo Archeologico Nazionale. Photo: R. Taylor.

stern of a transport ship culminating in a swan's head. These, along with several other fragments, were enough to allow a hypothetical reconstruction of the monument on the basis of loosely comparable imperial arches elsewhere. The style of the trophy, which includes a military standard, evokes the symbolism of the praetorian guard, and thus of the emperor(s) of Rome. The emperor himself would have appeared repeatedly in the frieze, as elsewhere on the arch.

Fig. 6.26. Frieze fragment of the Severan arch representing a scene of imperial disembarkment and sacrifice. Naples, Museo Archeologico Nazionale. Photo: R. Taylor.

The battered surviving fragments of this continuous band seem to represent two phases of a single event:

- A fragmentary landing scene in which soldiers and togate civilians descend a gangplank on the left; on shore, the emperor in a heavy priestly toga sacrifices at a portable altar amid a cluster of men, one a lictor bearing the *fasces*, the bundled staff of magisterial power, another a bearded man wearing the short toga of the equestrian order. Two other togate men and two diminutive servants attend; other figures probably stood off to the right. [Fig. 6.26]
- A formal scene of address [Fig. 6.27] with togate figures standing on and beside a low dais while armed soldiers stand at one side. The dais extended to the right, beyond the break in the stone, and thus also probably accommodated additional figures.

Stylistic considerations, such as the stocky figural style and the heavy use of the running drill in the drapery, have led Giuliana Cavalieri Manasse and Henner von Hesberg to propose that the monument dates to the Severan dynasty, though it may have appropriated some architectural elements, such as the capital, from a Flavian monument. Specifically they attribute the arch to the same co-emperors who dedicated the inscription found nearby, Septimius

CHAPTER 6 ☗ ROMAN NEAPOLIS

Fig. 6.27. Frieze fragment of the Severan arch representing a scene of imperial address. Naples, Museo Archeologico Nazionale. Photo: R. Taylor.

Severus (emperor 193–211 CE) and his son Caracalla (co-emperor and then sole emperor 198–217).

The arch's fragments probably did not stray too far from their point of origin — perhaps not the sinking northern rim of the harbor, but somewhere on slightly higher ground along its western edge where the monument, raised to a safe height, was visible from approaching ships. We know that imperial arches of this kind were already on display at other cities in central and southern Italy. Drawing on provocative evidence from just two known fragments, Harriet Flower demonstrates that Trajan (98–117) built a similar monument at Pozzuoli with material ransacked from a statue base honoring his deposed and maligned predecessor, Domitian (81–96). Indeed Trajan's arch may have celebrated, in time-honored imperial fashion, the completion and appropriation of Domitian's project: the Via Domitiana, a highly engineered, fast, and direct route between Rome and Pozzuoli, which Nerva and then Trajan extended to Neapolis.[33] Trajan erected

33. *CIL* 10.6926, 6927, 6931.

a similar monument at the terminus of his new road, the Via Traiana, at Beneventum; another adorned his port of departure to the Dacian Wars on the Adriatic, Ancona.

On the Beneventan arch Trajan devoted more space to his civil achievements than to his military triumphs, including the construction of the road itself and his extension of Rome's harbor at Portus. The Neapolitan arch seems cut from the same cloth. Though a martial message is to be expected on any imperial monument of its probable size and complexity, the meager surviving fragments reveal no overt imagery of a military campaign or triumph, only an emperor's travels with his praetorian cohorts. Further, the fragments juxtapose generic military symbolism, the trophy and insignia, with a more salient signifier of civilian activity: the merchant ship. Cavalieri Manasse and von Hesberg thus tentatively associate the arch with Septimius and Caracalla's harbor reclamation project in 202 CE discussed above. My own opinion is that this was a consequence of what seemed a temporary stroke of good luck, the deepening of the harbor by way of a natural phenomenon. Thus the whole enterprise of repairing its mole and surrounding infrastructure may have seemed particularly celebratory because of the port's unanticipated new capacity to accommodate larger craft with deeper drafts and heavier cargoes. Soon enough, the relentless forces already in motion may have clouded this optimism, but they were hardly fatal to the city's fortunes.

NEAPOLIS AND THE FOOD SUPPLY FOR ITALY

Let us now return to the broader question of the port's importance in the high Empire. This is not the place to rehearse the intricacies of the *annona,* the imperially coordinated influx of massive stores of grain to Italy from the provinces, particularly Egypt and Africa Proconsularis. But as J. Rasmus Brandt has demonstrated, the annual grain flotilla to Italy put a significant strain on her principal imperial ports, those at Portus and Pozzuoli, at particular times of year. Brandt's study considers additionally, as it must, the comparably titanic influx of wine and olive oil as well as other staples, such as *garum,* the popular Roman fish sauce. The 200 kilometers of coastal sea lane between the Bay and the Tiber River would have churned with cabotage vessels in transit. The Tiber in turn teemed with barges hauled up both

CHAPTER 6 ⚲ ROMAN NEAPOLIS

banks while returning boats streamed down the middle. Many originated from Portus, just north of the river's mouth, which communicated with the river by means of two short canals; many more carried goods transshipped from the Bay by the coastal fleet. These probably never reached Portus but turned up the river's mouth at Ostia, where they paused only long enough to requisition draft teams and refit their rigging as river barges; then they proceeded up the river, where they would merge into the barge traffic from Portus.

For all their brilliance, Brandt's calculations hold to a peculiarly conservative perspective. They consider only foodstuffs destined for imperial Rome itself, a city of roughly a million people and perhaps a few tens of thousands of large animals. (Animals may not have consumed the *annona* directly, but they certainly displaced human demand further in its direction.) No accounting is attempted for the millions of Italians living outside Rome who must also have relied, at least in part, on food imports arriving at Tyrrhenian ports. The threat of snarled traffic and boat queues on the Tiber, in turn, throws the Via Domitiana back into the limelight. This highway, joining up with the Via Appia at Sinuessa, was now the principal land route between Neapolis, Pozzuoli, and Rome, and it surely rumbled with hundreds of oxcarts on any given day during the shipping season, and even more in the winter. The truism that imported goods traveled by water because water transport is far cheaper than land transport is valid, up to a point; but it is often invoked without reflection. On the one hand, Campania had few navigable rivers, leaving the task of serving many inland markets to oxen, donkeys, mules, and drovers. On the other hand, the Sarno, Volturno, and Tiber rivers all presented problems for boat transport. For the busy Tiber, Brandt sets the saturation point at about 10,000 boats per year; yet his figures are calculated entirely on the basis of Rome's requirements alone. At least for shallow-draft barges, the Tiber was navigable for about 170 kilometers from its mouth, and several river ports above the capital would also have relied on goods transshipped from Portus and the Bay. They in turn distributed them among their own road networks. Add to this bustle the thousands of other commodities shipped up and down the river, along with boats on other business (fishing, for example), and the specter of congestion grows ever larger.

This book is not in the numbers business. It is enough to conclude, as Brandt himself does, that imperial Italy's reliance on imported food staples, combined with the movement of other goods, demanded recourse to every avenue of transport and every port of entry, if only to ensure adequate stockpiles in strategic points of distribution as a hedge against major disruptions such as drought, flooding, pests, spoilage, and shipwreck, all of them common misfortunes in Roman antiquity. When we envision all the pieces of the puzzle together, even if some are missing and therefore hypothetical, the distinct impression emerges that the Bay, its ports, and its roads retained a greater importance in the *annona* and other crucial imports than even John D'Arms imagined when he defended Pozzuoli's honor against a stubborn consensus (now roundly demolished) that Portus had stolen it all away by the early second century CE. Recent archaeological investigations suggest that the commercial waterfront of imperial Pozzuoli extended well beyond the Portus Julius, Agrippa's inland harbor connecting Lakes Avernus and Lucrinus to the Bay by a canal. Interspersed with maritime villas, bathing establishments, and fish and oyster farms, the mercantile zone probably reached southward to Baiae — which had its own recessed port with a canal entrance — and east all the way to Rione Terra, the historic town center of Pozzuoli where the famous arched harbor mole began.[34] More important than the dockage for ships, which is generally not detectable at Pozzuoli (it was probably confined mostly to Lake Avernus, Lake Lucrinus, and, in the overflow season, probably Baiae), was the need for warehouses along the frontage to store the goods temporarily. On this second class of evidence, underwater archaeology campaigns at Pozzuoli continue to yield new information sporadically.

Our understanding of the port of Neapolis is more constrained, but at least its general dimensions are now understood [see Fig. 6.19]. We may safely submit, despite the limitations of the evidence, that throughout the Roman imperial era the city played a vital if gradually diminishing supporting role in the *annona*. Even Trajan — the very emperor who expanded Portus and thereby (so the narrative went) supposedly put the Bay's harbors out of business — felt compelled

34. On pisciculture, see pp. 16, 245, 255, 298–99, 307, 334–35.

CHAPTER 6 ⛩ ROMAN NEAPOLIS

not only to develop *two additional* harbors along the Tyrrhenian coast (Terracina and Civitavecchia) but also to complete the Via Domitiana's extension to Neapolis, a city that previously may have had difficulty dispatching laden carts on the old Greek dirt road across the tufaceous badlands of the Campi Phlegraei. The ancient name of the extension is unknown, but it is conventionally called the Via Antiniana. A sector of this road at Pozzuoli unearthed in the 1990s demonstrates just how crucial, and how vulnerable, this track was. Excavations revealed that this stretch of the road accumulated ten thick colluvial strata in antiquity, some with wheel marks. The earliest dates back to around 600 BCE. Clearly the road had experienced hard use across the centuries, and required interventions after each serious flood or mudslide. So it seems that the engineers of the Via Domitiana–Antiniana, at least in places, followed this ancient Greek dirt road, which would have linked Cumae to Parthenope by way of Pozzuoli. Their great contribution was to grade and pave this track with the trademark Roman basalt slabs. But even the paving at Pozzuoli predates Trajan, Nerva, and even Domitian. This sector, at least, had already been paved earlier in the first century CE. Clearly Trajan's men did not produce the Via Antiniana out of whole cloth. At most, they improved it.

Now we fast-forward nearly a century to Septimius Severus. Like Trajan, this emperor burnished his impressive military credentials with major civil reforms. At Rome he instituted anti-fraud measures to convert grain, which can be stored for as long as two annual harvest cycles, to flour — which, because of its limited shelf life, could not be stockpiled secretly by corrupt officials for future profit. In an evident expansion of the *annona,* his ancient biographer reports, Septimius added an olive oil ration to supplement the free flour dole distributed monthly to several hundred thousand qualifying recipients in Rome. The same source reports:

> 53. At his death, he left a surplus of grain to the amount of seven years' tribute, or enough to distribute seventy-five thousand pecks [*modii*] a day, and so much oil, indeed, that for five years there was plenty for the uses, not only of the city, but also for as much of Italy as was in need of it. [*Historia Augusta, Septimius Severus* 18.3; 23.2]

This testimony, coming from an unreliable source, has been often questioned, but recent scholarship sensibly accepts the gist of the claims even if the numbers strain credulity. All the Tyrrhenian ports were busy enough through the second century CE. But the Severan reforms probably occasioned an overall expansion of imports — especially of oil from Septimius' native province of Africa — and a concomitant expansion of imperially controlled, publicly visible storage space. In his bid to install a stable new dynasty through the turbulent civil war of the early 190s, he strove to ingratiate himself to the people and banish the notorious corruption that had festered under his predecessor Commodus. Evidently the Via Antiniana was repaired under Septimius and Caracalla in 210/211 CE as well: a boundary marker found just outside the Crypta Neapolitana documents their sponsorship of repairs.[35] Thus by reengineering the beleaguered port of Neapolis, by erecting inscriptions and an arch to commemorate his facilitation of the city's seaborne transport and trade, and perhaps by restoring a key land transport route connecting it to Pozzuoli and Rome, Septimius was building on a broad and comprehensive plan.

What we don't see on the surface, but was at work behind the scenes, was a sweeping consolidation of imperial power into a more centralized system that maximized the emperor's control and ownership of assets. If the hypothesis about the harbor's second natural subsidence in the late second century is right (and the evidence seems decisive), then Septimius, rightly or wrongly, saw an opportunity here at Neapolis. The unlooked-for improvement in the harbor's depth allowed larger ships to moor along its berths; this efficiency in turn brought more tonnage to port. What the Severan propagandists didn't anticipate was the sobering principle that every dredging foreman must have understood to his own profit: deepening accelerates sedimentation.

Although it is impossible to confirm, it seems a strong possibility that these developments led to Neapolis' adornment, probably early in Caracalla's sole reign after his father's death, with the ceremonial title *Colonia Aurelia Augusta Antoniniana Felix Neapolis*.[36]

35. *CIL* 10.6929.
36. *ILS* 6458; *NSc* 1890 220. See p. 170. The inscription dates to 222 CE, during the reign of Alexander Severus.

CHAPTER 6 ✦ ROMAN NEAPOLIS

The distinction may have brought no new political privileges, but it was nonetheless significant and must have marked a special relationship between the town and the imperial house. The nomenclature *Aurelius Antoninianus* (the interposed *Aug.* on this inscription is a bit out of place in the normal sequence) best fits the habits of Caracalla. He freely adopted the epigraphic titulature of his Antonine predecessors while completely eliding his biological family name, Severus, and used it frequently both during and after the co-emperorship with his father Septimius.

What all this means for the urban fabric of Neapolis is hard to say specifically. But in general terms we can expect to have seen across its waterfront patterns not so different from those at imperial Pozzuoli, Ostia, Portus, and Rome itself, if on a smaller scale. The following description of the urban waterfront is hypothetical, but reflects the architecture along the nearby shoreline at Pozzuoli and Portus Julius. Near the docks, and extending northeast for some distance, but not so far as the ceremonial district of the Kaisareion, rows or clusters of two-story warehouses would have risen in crisp brick-faced concrete, many with raised, ventilated floors. Some were undoubtedly vaulted, others had timber-and-tile roofs; some were linear, their storage cells opening onto a frontal covered portico; others enveloped a porticated courtyard. In line with Septimius' crackdown on the old, less centrally controlled system, we can presume that warehouses stocking imperial grain and oil were now under his direct ownership and control.

The southwest end of the harbor, however, where some waterfront architecture has actually been uncovered, is quite different. Here two bath buildings,[37] one of the first, another of the second century CE, fronted on the harbor road to cater to the dockside clientele [see Figs. 6.20; 6.23]. No doubt boarding houses, bars, eateries, and brothels stood nearby. Since the second-century-CE bath was built directly over an abandoned Hellenistic boat ramp, we might conjecture that this area had once been a dockyard dedicated to repairs and perhaps even shipbuilding. But with the post-Vesuvius improvements in the

37. See pp. 224, 275.

city's water supply,[38] and significant urban expansion in the area, it had evidently evolved into more of a hospitality zone for sailors and dockmen not unlike the waterfront district outside the Marine Gate at Ostia, which accommodated shops, eateries, and at least three bathhouses.

OUTSIDE THE WALLS. CEMETERIES

The reengineering, metaling, and paving of roads was of course a key manifestation of Roman *habitus*. What we sometimes fail to appreciate is the extent to which this stabilization of land routes was a prerequisite for their monumentalization with another commonplace of the Roman landscape, streets of the dead. Although the "Tomb of Virgil" stands in splendid isolation today at the eastern entrance to the Crypta Neapolitana,[39] we must envision the suburban roads of Roman imperial Neapolis densely crowded with tombs — a few Hellenistic- and republican-era burials, the *columbaria* of the early Empire, inhumation tombs of the second and third centuries CE, more modest inhumation burials sprinkled about among them — and eventually, north of town, catacombs. We saw how phratries may have operated like Roman *collegia* in reserving burial plots for their members.[40] Self-respecting persons of the Roman imperial period sought an honorable burial, though few could afford to build full-scale tombs. Those with connections, through occupation, phratry, patronage, or family, generally held a share in a tomb by securing a burial inside it. Those without connections but with modest financial means would be laid to rest in graves not so different from American cemetery plots, but with a few architectural touches.

Numerous cemeteries and isolated tombs of the Roman era have been discovered at Naples, most of them just outside the city walls [see Fig. 6.19]. They have received little attention by comparison with the Greek cemeteries, and in consequence a synthetic analysis of Neapolitan Roman-era burials is impossible. The excavated areas, several concentrated along the city walls, reflect a characteristic distribution of extramural burials. What they do not capture is the more

38. See pp. 274, 364–65.
39. See pp. 303–6.
40. See pp. 175–76; Commentary 5.6, pp. 181–82.

CHAPTER 6 ☥ ROMAN NEAPOLIS

Fig. 6.28. Satellite view of the Via Celle necropolis at Pozzuoli. © Google, Maxar Technologies.

distinctly Roman phenomenon of streets of the dead, which followed the highways out of town like rays of a star. But at Neapolis the roads themselves have not been excavated, leaving us to rely on the evidence of other towns. Rows of tombs characteristically ran a few hundred meters up both sides of the roads outside the city gates but often extended in sparser concentrations for considerable distances. We might envision them running southwest along Spaccanopoli and the coastal road [see Fig. 6.19], with clusters of tombs cropping up intermittently all the way to Virgil's Tomb and the Crypta Neapolitana two to three Roman miles out on the Via Antiniana [see Fig. 1.1]. The Nola, Herculaneum, and Capua roads probably were no different, especially when we consider that the later catacombs, starting nearly one kilometer north of the wall, were at least partially a remedy for the depletion of real estate above ground.

Pompeii provides a limited picture of how clusters of tombs would have appeared outside every gate of the city walls. But in some ways the density and variety of Roman roadside burial culture are better captured by cemeteries unearthed elsewhere, such as the Isola Sacra at Portus and the excavated portions of Via Celle [Fig. 6.28] and the Via Antiniana at Pozzuoli, the latter exposed for a distance of some 400 meters. Many of the tombs at Pozzuoli were of the *columbarium* type, with small serried niches for cinerary urns filling the walls. When burial habits among the mercantile and moneyed classes shifted from cremation to inhumation in the early second century CE, these tombs, their niches already dense with urns, began accommodating "cassette" burials, basically simple, stackable sarcophagi that through the course of that century could pack the central chamber up to the springing of the vaults. The more monumental tombs, typically built of concrete faced with brick and reticulate (or brick exclusively later in the second century), lined the roads with facades enlivened by architectural detail, relief sculpture, and inscriptions. Intermixed with the controlled chaos, much humbler cassette burials were scattered about at ground level, their tiny pitched roofs projecting from the earth, or perhaps just the top half of an amphora to accommodate poured libations for the dead. These last were the humble plots of the poor and unconnected.

SUBURBS

Neapolis' ancient *suburbium*, much of it underlying the dense megalopolis of the modern Bay, is hard to assess. The rugged hills to the west and southwest of the ancient city, so resistant to transport and travel, offered plenty of slopes and overlooks on which to perch picturesque luxury villas. Actual physical evidence of villa architecture is hard to come by, however, with one grand exception. Southwest of the conurbation of Neapolis and erstwhile Parthenope, and beyond the modern district of Chiaia, lies a peninsula known as Capo di Posillipo or Pausilypon [see Fig. 1.1].[41] Its character is divided. The eastern flank, with its dramatic ravines, gorgeous cliffside views, and winding hairpin lanes remains a rather exclusive neighborhood today, and it was here that many of the grandest Neapolitan villas of the Roman era were concentrated. This vertiginous terrain continues down to the headland's southern extreme, culminating in the grand imperial villa for which it is named, Pausilypon. Just to the west, the wrinkled ridge abruptly ends in a steep escarpment. A plain opens out below. Two Roman tunnels decant into it: the Crypta Neapolitana at Fuorigrotta, and the "Grotta di Seiano" connecting Pausilypon to the plain of Coriglio and Bagnoli.

Here we must imagine away the moldering industrial sprawl of modernity and replace it with a pleasant, low-density neighborhood

41. See pp. 281–82, 304–13.

CHAPTER 6 ☗ ROMAN NEAPOLIS

of thermal bathing establishments interspersed with small farms, villas, inns, and rental residences in the manner of Baiae on the western rim of the Bay, though quieter, flatter, and less crowded.[42] The character of the local bathing culture was rather different from that in the city. These were resorts catering to paying vacationers or convalescents who, like countless Europeans today, vacation at spas to improve their health and wellbeing.[43] The archaeology here doesn't come into focus, nor does the district receive much attention in the literary or epigraphic record. But we might catch a glimpse of what this relaxed suburban neighborhood was like by comparing it to Aidepsos (Latin Aedepsus, modern Edipsos) in Euboea, Greece.[44] Plutarch, who grew up in nearby Boeotia, knew the place well, and refers to it several times in his voluminous writings:

> **54.** Aedepsus in Euboea has become a popular resort for people from all over Greece, particularly because of the place called Hot Springs [*ta therma*], which possesses many natural resources for the worthy enjoyment of leisure, and is further embellished by villas and elegant apartment houses [*diaitai*]. Game and fowl are caught there in abundance, and the sea no less lavishly supplies the market with provisions for the table, producing many a fine, noble fish in the deep, clear waters close to shore. This resort flourishes especially when spring is at its height, for many continue to come there all that season. They gather together, exempt from every want, and, having the leisure, engage endlessly in conversation. [*Table Talk* 4.4.1 (667c)]
>
> **55.** While Sulla was tarrying at Athens, his feet were attacked by numbness and a feeling of heaviness, which Strabo says is premonitory gout. He therefore crossed the straits to Aedepsus and used the hot waters there, taking a holiday at the same time, and passing his time pleasantly with the theatrical artists. [*Sulla* 26.3]

---

42. Strabo, *Geography* 5.4.7. See Reading 58, p. 257.
43. See pp. 253–62.
44. Strabo 9.4.2; Ptolemy 3.15.23.

Fig. 6.29. Western entrance of the "Grotta di Seiano" at the villa of Pausilypon. Photo: R. Taylor.

CHAPTER 6 ⚱ ROMAN NEAPOLIS

Aidepsos, like Neapolis' western suburbs and Baiae, was a profitable rarity: a seaside hydrothermal resort. Like both the Italian venues, it was close enough to several large urban centers to be accessible by land or sea within a few days' travel. It was also peppered with aristocratic villas (*oikeseis*) of the aristocracy, which would probably have been the exclusive recourse of men like Plutarch and Sulla. We can presume that Sulla, some two centuries before Plutarch was writing, sojourned among the local Hellenistic elite. But it is a telling detail that already in the 80s BCE the town hosted a theater troupe of stature befitting the attentions of a Roman conqueror. Further, the place also had *diaitai,* houses or rooms for rent that catered to visitors without connections to the landed elite. Clement's translation presumes that such places are "elegant" and thus includes the adjective where none exists in the original Greek. If an adjective is needed, "pleasant" might be more appropriate. There is nothing in the term *diaita* to exclude the sub-elite, the mass of tourists who could afford a few weeks at a middling-class rental on the order of a beach house today.

Now let us compare this Euboean resort to the plain of Coriglio and Bagnoli, along with the low hills and crater lakes just to its north, which also hosted thermal spas in antiquity.[45] We know little about this region's archaeology, apart from the remains of a couple of the baths themselves, one hydrothermal and the other conventional. These will be revisited in the next chapter. Certainly the region accommodated enough resorts to cater to a variety of clienteles, just as at Baiae. The neighborhood may have been quiet and relaxed, but high culture was within reach. No great distance to the east loomed, from the Augustan era onward, the great western portal of the "Grotta di Seiano" [Fig. 6.29].[46] On the tunnel's far end awaited the villa of Pausilypon with a theater seating fifteen hundred, an odeion, baths, and other entertainments [Fig. 6.30]. The tunnel itself, probably cut as part of Agrippa's land communication network during the war against Sextus Pompey in the 30s BCE,[47] may have reverted to a public or quasi-public road thereafter. The road it served led to

45. See pp. 15, 259–60.
46. See pp. 309–10.
47. See p. 16; Commentary 8.5, pp. 337–39.

Fig. 6.30. Aerial view of the Pausilypon villa. Photo: S. Capuano / Wikimedia Commons CC BY-SA 2.0.

a chain of coastal bathing establishments to its west. By way of this convenient connector, the villa may have offered entertainments to the bathing clientele [Fig. 1.1]. Other notable villas occupied the corrugated wonderland to the northeast. One among them, the villa of Limon of Epilimones, was immortalized by Statius.[48] Belonging to the aristocracy, and not the emperor, these were more exclusive places devoted to narrower patronage networks, like the ones Plutarch knew at Aidepsos.

But Pausilypon was different. Augustus, who upon inheriting the villa from a notoriously self-indulgent plutocrat, sought to make an example of him.[49] Thus he would likely have improved the villa's cultural amenities and made them available to the public, as he did many properties in Rome after their owners bequeathed them to his patrimony. I will argue in chapter 8 that the magnificent Neapolitan art gallery described by Philostratos in his *Images* was grounded in

48. *Silvae* 2.2, 3.1.
49. Dio Cassius, *Roman History* 54.23. See pp. 301, 307–8.

fact, and that its prototype was at Pausilypon. Like other grand imperial villas with large entertainment spaces, this one may have admitted the public in controlled groups as a gesture of noblesse oblige and a way to strengthen the emperor's vast patronage network, which included the mercantile class of freedmen and the freeborn public at large.

HEDGING HER BETS

Neapolis' stature as a cultural destination grew steadily from the late Republic into the third century CE. Later chapters will address this phenomenon at greater length, but it bears mentioning now as a hedge against relying too heavily on the usual econometric indicators of urban health such as manufacturing, transport, finance, and retail activity. Over time, Neapolis relied more on cultural capital as its role in Mediterranean commerce diminished. Additionally, as I have tried to argue above, the city developed and maintained an important logistical role in the provisioning of Italy with imported goods, a sizable portion of which, because it was entirely under imperial control and was not market-driven, had no *commercial* significance at all, except in the modest sense that the imperial bureaucracy that managed it augmented the local population and thus contributed to the local and regional economy. The importance of this role was strategic above all. It certainly did not hurt that the Bay enjoyed great cultural favor among emperors from Augustus until at least Alexander Severus (emperor 222–235 CE), who undertook major building projects at Baiae.[50] By doing the emperors good, the city continued to do well.

---

50. *Historia Augusta, Severus Alexander* 26.9–10.

Commentary 6.1: The Kaisareion's Decoration

The temple architecture and iconography of the Kaisareion are unusual [Fig. 6.18]. Typically the sima, or eaves blocks, of marble temples are modestly proportioned, overhanging molded elements adorned with lion-head drain spouts. But here the spouts appear on a bold register with a vertical face in the style of old-fashioned terracotta revetments. The front surface carries a repeating relief pattern of frontal bulls carved in the round, the spout emerging between the legs. A winged Eros in low relief rides on every bull's back. He grasps the manes of heraldically positioned lions on either side. Beneath each lion lies an angled ox skull. The bulls and skulls are generic images of sacrifice, and indicate that this is a sacred building. The carving has an unfinished quality that gives it a slightly rustic look.

Commentary 6.2: The Ships of Neapolis

The three vessels recovered in the 2004 Piazza Municipio excavations were concentrated in a tight cluster on the north flank of the jetty [Figs. 6.20; 6.22]. All were in good condition, in some cases still equipped with coiled ropes, blocks, and tackle. Vessels A and C are of similar size and date but different design. Both had been cleared of their contents and intentionally scuttled; A had a light ballast of stones. They rested on the same stratum as the jetty, and so their scuttling belongs to roughly the same phase of the harbor's history, the late first century CE. A few decades later, a piling of one of the oblique wooden piers was driven right through the hull of vessel A. In the third century another vessel, B, sank here — accidentally, for its cargo of lime was still partly intact and its stone anchor still in place. Vessels A and B are medium-tonnage cargo transports. C is more unusual, having a vertical prow. It is believed to be a *horeia*, a multipurpose vessel used for fishing, transport, or harbor duty.

Between 2013 and 2015 four more ships were discovered randomly scattered about just a little farther out in the harbor, probably all of the early Roman imperial period or somewhat earlier. One is a *horeia*, one a standard sail-bearing transport. The other two are too fragmentary to identify.

CHAPTER 6 ⛫ ROMAN NEAPOLIS

Commentary 6.3: Sea-Level Change in the Tyrrhenian

The Tyrrhenian coast of Italy provides an excellent laboratory to measure the change in sea level since Roman times, for several reasons. First, the Romans produced fixed features on the coast that allow for easy and accurate measurement of sea level some 2000+ years ago: *piscinae*, artificial fishponds, often carved into the coastal bedrock, for the raising and hatching of popular food fish. Second, this region has only modest tides of 40–45 cm. Any fixed features indicating precise sea level in antiquity, such as a line of oysters on a concrete pier, or the floor level of a seaside fish hatchery, do not have to be interpreted in relation to a wide daily fluctuation in water level. And third, parts of central Italy where good evidence of this sort can be found are geologically very stable, unlike the Bay of Naples. Roman *piscinae* featured sluice channels whose side walls extended just slightly above high tide level so that the channels could introduce salt water, without any overflow, into the hatcheries as the tide rose to its maximum.

Estimating that the tops of the sluice gates were about 20 centimeters above high tide level, a team of Italian and Australian geologists took measurements at ten *piscina* sites. The results show that sea levels were between 1.1 and 1.8 meters lower than today, with a weighted mean of -1.35 ± 0.07 meters. This is the figure against which the line of oyster shells on the Hellenistic ramp of Neapolis' harbor should be compared. Assuming little change between the Hellenistic and the early Roman imperial period, we can subtract Lambeck *et alii*'s mean from the 2.1-meter differential at Naples and arrive at the conclusion that bradyseism accounts for roughly three quarters of a meter of the total difference. This does not in any sense tell the whole story, of course, because bradyseism is apt to reverse itself. Most likely the harbor sank by several meters between the first and third centuries, and perhaps rebounded in the early Middle Ages when the harbor went out of use.

One more important caveat is due. The sea level change based on actual water volume over the last 2000 years is nowhere near this simple arithmetic differential of 1.35

meters. The reason is that eustatic change of sea level — a function of the actual volume of water in the sea, measured from the earth's center — is accompanied by isostatic change, the rise or fall of the level of the land due to its compression or decompression from accumulated ice. When land is compressed downward, it spreads outward slightly, or the seabed rises slightly in compensation, diminishing the size of the basin overall and raising the water level accordingly. Isostatic changes vary by location and sometimes require complex calculations to account for multiple variables. When corrected for regional isostatic adjustment of deglaciation in the Tyrrhenian area, the resulting change of sea level over the past 2000 years is much more modest: 0.13 ± 0.09 m. In lay terms, you can measure the notional rise in sea level during that interval — that is, the rise you would expect in a perfectly rigid basin that does not change shape — between your thumb and forefinger. By either measure, the annual ascent of sea level has been accelerating greatly in recent decades due to global warming.

🏛

REFERENCES

Walls, suburbs, and disposal of debris in Roman cities: Emmerson 2020: 92–124. **Forum:** Capasso 1978 [1905]: 82–90; Gabrici 1951; Napoli 1959: 68–79, 88; 1967c: 444–46; Johannowsky 1961a; Greco 1985a; 1986: 208–13; 1994; Giampaola 2013. **Theaters:** De Petra 1884; 1895; Castaldo 1910; Magaldi 1932; Johannowsky 1985b; Sampaolo 2005: 695–96; Nava 2006b; 2007c; 2008b; Guzzo 2009: 1012–13; Baldassare 2010b. **Temple of the Dioscuri:** Correra 1905; Duhn 1910; Trendelenburg 1911; Bernabò Brea 1936; Hommel 1954: 52–54; Strandberg 1961; Lattimore 1974; Adamo Muscettola 1985c; Carafa 2008 44–48; Cristilli 2012: 69–80; Taylor 2015b. **Temple of the Dioscuri in the medieval and modern eras:** Bruzelius and Tronzo 2011: 6–8; Lenzo 2011; 2015; Nichols and McGregor 2019: 46–47, 384–88, 464. **Marble temple at Pozzuoli and its forum:** Zevi and Cavalierie Manasse 2005; Zevi and Valeri 2008; Cavalieri Manasse and Gialanella 2016. **S. Lorenzo Maggiore complex:** Johannowsky 1961a; De Simone 1985;

CHAPTER 6 🏛 ROMAN NEAPOLIS

1986; 1987; Febbraro 2005; Giampaola 2005; Pugliese 2005; Faga 2006; Nava 2007a. **Stadia of Cumae and Pozzuoli:** Camodeca 2000–2001; Giglio and Camodeca 2009. **Stazione Duomo excavations and the Kaisareion:** Nava 2007c, 2008c; Di Nanni Durante 2007–2008; Bragantini et al. 2010; Cavalieri Manasse et al. 2017. **Nike statue:** Adamo Muscettola 1985b: 413–14; Cristilli 2007; 2012: 114–17. **Bathing culture:** Dunbabin 1989; Marasco 2001; Yegül 1991; 1996; 2010; Fagan 1999. **Harbor of Neapolis:** Cozzolino 1960; Napoli 1997 [1959]: 121–35; Boetto 2005; Boetto et al. 2010; 2019; Giampaola 2004; Giampaola et al. 2004; 2005; Sampaolo 2005: 696–700; Giampaola and Carsana 2007; Amato et al. 2009; Carsana et al. 2009; Allevato et al. 2010; Boetto 2019. **Harbor of Constantinople:** Rose and Aydingün 2007. **Severan harbor inscription:** Sogliano 1892; Colonna 1898: 449–52; Cozzolino 1960: 157–59; *Napoli antica:* 484 no. 173. **Cemeteries:** Amodio 2014. **Bradyseism at Herculaneum:** Wallace-Hadrill 2011: 18–25, 249. **Honorific arch at Piazza Bovio:** Cavalieri Manasse and Hesberg 2010. **Honorific arch at Pozzuoli:** Johannowsky 1952: 143–46; Flower 2001. ***Annona* and its transport:** Rickman 1980; Zevi 2004; Brandt 2006; Taylor 2010. **The harbors and waterfront at Pozzuoli and Baiae:** D'Arms 1974; Ostrow 1977; 1979; Pagano 1982; 1983–1984; Frederiksen 1984: 324–37; Di Fraia 1993; Gianfrotta 1993; 1998; 2010; 2011; 2012a; 2012b; Camodeca 1994; Zevi 2004: 214–15; Scognamilio 2009a; 2009b; Rossi 2014; 2016; Popkin 2018. **Road system outside the walls:** Johannowsky 1952; 1985a; Gialanella 2000: 64–65; Gialanella and Di Giovanni 2001: 160. **Via Domitiana and Via Antiniana:** Johannowsky 1952; 1985a; Ostrow 1977 (diss.) 28–36; Flower 2001; Longobardo 2004. **Cemeteries of Puteoli:** Gialanella 2000; Gialanella and Di Giovanni 2001. **Carminiello ai Mannesi complex:** Arthur 1994; Arthur and Vecchio 1995.

Fig. 7.1. Relief from Ischia representing Apollo and two of the Nitrodes nymphs. One nymph delivers spring water from a basin with which the nude dedicant, Capellina, washes her hair. Naples, Museo Archeologico Nazionale.

CHAPTER 7. THE CULTURE OF WATER

56. Everywhere in many lands gush forth beneficent waters, here cold, there hot, there both....Water adds to the number of gods by its various names, and founds cities, such as Puteoli [Pozzuoli] in Campania, Statiellae [Acqui Terme] in Liguria, and Sextiae [Aix-en-Provence] in the province of Narbonensis. [Pliny the Elder, *Natural History* 31.4]

57. Let the Euboean land rise to the bright sky and Sebethos swell with pride in his fair nursling [Neapolis]. Nor let the Lucrine Naiads [water nymphs of Baiae] more plume themselves in their sulfur caverns nor the quiet waters of Pompeian Sarnus. [Statius, *Silvae* 1.2.262–65]

The notion that a city could be "founded" or "nursed" by its own waters may seem strange to us, but to ancient Romans it needed no explanation. Pliny and Statius are referring not to the historical, Roman (re)foundations of water-rich cities, but to mythologies and religious cults that had grown up around their local water features much earlier. Their local traditions would have included older and more venerable foundation myths in which the waters themselves, as anthropomorphic personalities, took part. This pattern of folk belief was common in ancient Mediterranean societies, particularly in regions like Magna Graecia where colonization required an ideological justification. Apart from a few paltry hints, the foundation myths of Neapolis and its predecessor(s) are lost.[1] But we may glean something of them from the city's coinage.

Neapolis was almost unique in its ability to capitalize on water both for transport and for consumption, and in its Roman phase only Pozzuoli, with its suburb Baiae, outstripped it. On the one hand, Greek Neapolis was a maritime power favored with a magnificent natural harbor; and on the other, it was the home of many useful and therapeutic sources of water on land (Statius' "sulfur caves"). In the Greek period the city's very existence depended on a functioning harbor, a formidable navy, and a robust merchant marine. The appeal of the thermo-mineral baths accumulated more gradually but built to a steady crescendo that continued to resonate deep into the Middle Ages.

1. See pp. 42–46, 55–56, 101–2.

GODS OF THE WATER

As we have already seen, the coins of Greek Neapolis portrayed a bust of the Siren Parthenope on one side and the striding or kneeling bull-man representing the Sebethos River on the other.[2] Both of these water gods enjoyed local cults, but information about them is sparse. A Latin inscription of the Roman imperial period[3] records that a certain Publius Mevius Eutychus restored a shrine (*aedicula*) to Sebethos. Virgil even speaks of a local nymph Sebethis, wife of Telos and mother of Oibalos.[4] Similar river cults are known in the region and elsewhere in south Italy. For example, a terracotta horned head in the museum of Nocera Inferiore is probably an effigy of the local Sarno River. At least one bull–man of the Sarno is known to us: a certain C. Epidius, who according to legend fell into the river and was reborn as a god, with the gilded horns of a sacrificial bull.[5]

The cult of the Sirens was an exclusive phenomenon of communities along the Tyrrhenian coast. It seems to have been driven, at least in part, by a competition among cities of the region to attach their own histories to the travels of Odysseus or Aeneas. Toponyms bear this out: for example, Misenum, named for Aeneas' trumpeter Misenos, and Baiae, for Odysseus' helmsman Baios. According to Dionysios, the cities of Antium [Anzio], Ardea, and even Rome were each named for homophonous sons of Odysseus and Circe.[6] Circe herself had a monument, at Monte Circeo — a dramatic promontory near the ancient boundary of Latium and Campania, where tradition held that she had resided. Nearby was the tomb of Elpenor, a companion of Odysseus who had died during their imprisonment at Circe's home. Cumae and Lake Avernus, of course, came to be indelibly associated with Aeneas' trip to the underworld. Farther south, in Lucania, a Siren named Molpe was worshiped at a site near Palinurus, named for the helmsman of Aeneas.

2. See chapter 3.

3. *CIL* 10.1480.

4. *Aeneid* 7.733–35.

5. Suetonius, *Rhetoricians* 28. On the sacrificial nature of the *kneeling* bull-man, see pp. 90–91.

6. *Roman Antiquities* 1.72.

CHAPTER 7 🏛 THE CULTURE OF WATER

The number, names, and homeland of the Sirens were all in great dispute in antiquity. The tradition taken up by Neapolis, it seems, was the one retailed by Lykophron in the *Alexandra*.[7] His likely source, Timaios of Tauromenion, set the famous Siren episode of the *Odyssey* at the southern extreme of the Bay of Naples, the Sorrentine Peninsula. On this promontory, called the Seirenoussai or Mons Sirenianus, was situated a venerable sanctuary of the Sirens, while directly to the south were three islands known collectively as the Sirens.[8] Today they are called Li Galli [see Fig. 1.2]. The true origins and precise location of the sanctuary are uncertain. Emmanuele Greco proposes that the main cult center was east of Sorrento at Località Trinità, where remains of a very ancient sanctuary have been found.

Little is known about the Sirens as objects of religious devotion. They share certain properties with other female mythological creatures that operate in groups, such as the Muses, the Fates, and the Furies.[9] But like Virgil's Harpies, the Sirens — at least in their earlier manifestations, before they became associated with Persephone and the underworld — were geographically fixed. In the Tyrrhenian realm, in fact, they were defined by their places of abode and deification. To Homer, they were little more than malicious guardian spirits of the place. Like shore birds, they haunted a particular patch of coast, never venturing inland or out to sea. They fed on mariners ensnared by their irresistible song. From the Classical period onward they were usually represented as birds with a human head or protome [see Figs. 2.3; 3.8], or as winged women.

The Sirens were mortals, and local tradition held that their failure to foil Odysseus doomed them to death. According to Lykophron, the local cults of this threesome — Parthenope, Leukosia, and Ligeia — were established in each of the places to which their bodies washed ashore: the future Neapolis, Capo Licosa in the gulf of Paestum, and Tereina to the south.[10] Their second lives as goddesses must be understood within the context of Greek hero worship. Only

7. See chapter 2.
8. Strabo, *Geography* 5.4.8.
9. See pp. 97–98.
10. See pp. 42–43, 96–99.

after death and deification could they be reappropriated as local deities. The more typical pattern of Greek colonies in the Archaic period was to worship a founder-hero — often a wandering outcast who, having consulted an oracle of Apollo, established a new city in expiation for some personal sin or taint of pollution. We have little information about how the Sirens' cult sites were established or what they meant to the local peoples. But Maurizio Giangiulio's insight, discussed in chapter 2, that the Sirens belong to a type of local deity that guards narrow passages is plausible. One of their defining characteristics is an apotheosis after drowning in the sea. In the case of the settlement of Parthenope and the appropriation of its earliest cult, an oracle was doubtless consulted. Such was the standard procedure both for colonies and their local cults. Whether or not Cumae housed an oracle at this time (the local Sibyl later grew world-famous), the ways of the divinatory god ran strong through her people, who came from Apollo-worshiping territory on the island of Euboea. This is certainly Statius' understanding when he invokes "the dwellings of Dicaearchus [perhaps a mythical hero-founder of Dikaiarcheia–Pozzuoli] founded under Phoebus' auspices" — or allows that Apollo guided Parthenope's body to the site of Neapolis.[11] Even Statius' patron Pollius Felix sought an oracle of this god to find springs on his property near Sorrento.[12]

There were many ways to attach a local cult to a mythical figure. The Sirens were a rational choice, for like archetypal founding heroes they were seen as despised outcasts, damned souls in need of expiation. (The nature of their sin was a matter of speculation.) Moreover, they were creatures of water, and water had a special place in the symbolism of colonization. They lived by water, died in it, and were reborn as gods. Water is the realm of special knowledge, and thus of oracles. It cleanses, and is thereby a powerful symbol of atonement. It is an agent of generation and regeneration. And, like the landscape itself, it is subject to conquest, reclamation, and beneficial manipulation. Taken together, these properties presented a suitable symbolism for new colonies. The colonists themselves were often outcasts in

11. *Silvae* 3.5.74–75, 78–80.
12. *Silvae* 2.2.39–40.

CHAPTER 7 ☱ THE CULTURE OF WATER

need of purification and a fresh start. They also were aware of the dangers of appropriating new territory, and so they cast the local waters as sacrificial hero–victims to appease the gods of the place.

This is the meaning of the ubiquitous bull-man. He was characteristically presented as a wandering human hero who became a surrogate for a local river by drowning in its waters and achieving a miraculous rebirth as a sacrificial scapegoat for the colonists' trespass upon the land: the bull, after all, was the quintessential sacrificial animal. Because of this, I believe, the early Acheloös-type coinage in Italy and Sicily represented the bull-man *kneeling*, not swimming or running, as is often mistakenly claimed: this proleptically connoted the willingness to be sacrificed [see Figs. 3.1; 3.5].[13] We don't know the mythology of the Sebethos River. But as Lykophron indicates, at the companion site of Tereina, the Okinaros River too was presented as a bull–man whose waters washed the shores of the tomb of the Siren Ligeia.[14] At Tereina, the river god and the Siren had become partners: one representing the burdens and opportunities faced by the colonists, the other a surrogate for a founder-hero; one signaling human conquest of the landscape, the other mastery of the sea; and both establishing cultic and mythic credentials for a place that had few claims to a local mythology. There is no reason to believe that Parthenope's town was any different in this respect.

THE THERMO-MINERAL BATHS

The early settlers chose to represent their city with the symbol of their tauriform river god and a mythic creature of the seashore, both symbols of death and renewal. But the region of ancient Neapolis was also abundantly blessed with beneficial waters of many kinds, and for this it became famous. The area extending from the western suburbs all the way to the Capo Miseno was known in Roman times as the Phlegraean Fields (modern Campi Flegrei), "Fields of Fire," derived from the region's volcanism, its many hot mineral springs, its bubbling and steaming badlands, and collapsed craters. The early Greek residents surely took advantage of the teeming abundance of therapeutic

13. See pp. 90–91.
14. See pp. 42–43, 98–99.

Fig. 7.2. The Roman thermo-mineral baths at Baiae. Photo: R. Taylor.

springs in this area, but of these matters we know nothing. We may imagine that cults and sanctuaries emerged to honor the nymphs and chthonic gods that Greeks habitually associated with springs of every kind. Fifty miles east of Neapolis, in the Valle d'Ansanto in Irpinia, lies a major sanctuary of Mephitis, a god with special ties to sulfurous thermal springs. The sanctuary preserves a rich deposit of ex votos and coins — some of these from the Neapolitan region — dating from the sixth century BCE onwards. Nothing comparable has yet been found in the Campi Phlegraei, nor are cultic practices of the pre-Roman era in the area known from the literary record. The history of the culture of water in ancient Neapolis is perforce founded on the Roman evidence, and that alone. The underlying Greek text on this dense palimpsest is faint beyond recovery.

When the Romans recolonized Dikaiarcheia in 194 BCE they chose to name it Puteoli, "little wells," in reference to the pores and fumaroles in the earth from which hot water, steam, or sulfurous gases issued.[15] The modern name has evolved with the language so that today Pozzuoli still reminds Italians of *pozzi*, wells. Less than two decades after the Roman colonization, the consul Cnaeus Cornelius

---

15. Strabo, *Geography* 5.4.6.

CHAPTER 7 ⛲ THE CULTURE OF WATER

was seeking relief for an injury at these *aquae Cumanae*.[16] Quite possibly Pozzuoli had its own nymphs, which seem to be invoked by a local resident, Aulus Avianius Cilo, on a dedicatory inscription.[17] A carved votive relief long grouped among a series of similar reliefs depicts the Nitrodes, water nymphs of Ischia [Commentary 7.1, pp. 283–84]. This has been recently provenanced to Pozzuoli and may therefore represent a distinct cult of nymphs bearing the same name. Thermal baths were among the amenities that Sulla confiscated from his slain enemies along with their houses and pleasure gardens.[18] Doubtless many of these were along the western Bay of Naples, where Sulla himself lived in retirement. By the first century BCE a booming and notorious resort town had developed at Baiae on the west shore of the Bay of Pozzuoli. Baiae eclipsed all other ancient thermo-mineral spas, and among therapeutic hot springs it indisputably reigned supreme [Fig. 7.2]. It was a laboratory for the Roman hypocaust bath, soon to become the standard around the empire. Here a villa owner and entrepreneur named Sergius Orata, active sometime between 120 and 91 BCE, developed artificial oyster farms in the Lucrine Lake for the wealthy seaside set. They soon became wildly popular adjuncts to maritime villas alongside *piscinae* for any number of exotic fish varieties. But more importantly, Orata reportedly invented *pensiles balineae* — literally, "hanging baths."[19]

The meaning of this term (and similar terms ancient authors applied to Orata's invention) has been disputed, but the traditional interpretation may be the best: Roman-style hypocaust baths. The Greeks had developed a limited kind of underfloor system for the convection of heated air, but it was Romans and other central Italians who first experimented with heating systems comprising entirely hollow floors and walls. The floors consisted of large square tiles "suspended" at the corners upon thin pillars. The earliest known example of a complete underfloor hypocaust, a tiny

16. Livy, *History of Rome* 41.16.
17. *CIL* 10.6791; 10.2133.
18. Plutarch, *Sulla* 31.5
19. Valerius Maximus 9.1.1; Pliny, *Natural History* 9.168.

Fig. 7.3. The Roman bath of Tritoli. Illustration by G. B. Natali, in Paoli 1768.

room in the baths at Fregellae in Lazio, predates Orata's heyday by a century. Orata may thus simply have taken credit for perfecting and mass marketing the technology. It is only natural that such a system should have been ascribed to Baiae, where enterprising designers and engineers harnessed the abundant thermal steams and gases for their fabled *sudatoria* and *laconica,* the ubiquitous local sweat-baths. For example, geothermal sweat-baths were central to the great Roman establishment at Tritoli between Baiae and the Lucrine Lake, still accessible in the eighteenth century [Fig. 7.3]. Orata may in

CHAPTER 7 ▪ THE CULTURE OF WATER

fact have known the physician Asklepiades of Bithynia, who popularized heat treatments, both wet and dry, as a curative for a variety of ailments. Therapeutic heat, Celsus writes, was the product of "natural sweating places, where hot vapor rising from the ground is confined within a building, as we have it in the myrtle groves above Baiae."[20] These he distinguishes from "ovens" and places heated by hot sand, whose drier heat more closely resembled that of the modern sauna.

While Baiae and Pozzuoli dominated the resorts of the western Phlegraean Fields, Neapolis was a formidable competitor to the east. According to Strabo,

> **58.** Neapolis has springs of hot water and bathing-establishments that are not inferior to those at Baiae, although it is far short of Baiae in the number of people, for at Baiae, where palace on palace has been built, one after another, a new city has arisen, not inferior to Dikaiarcheia [Pozzuoli]." [*Geography* 5.4.7]

In Strabo's assessment, Neapolis' baths were inseparable from her fame as a cultural mecca. Baiae was a purpose-built luxury resort with no urban core or administration, few permanent residents, and a reputation for scandal. Horace imagines its resorts utterly deserted, should the fickle public embrace colder cures.[21] Neapolis was a mature city, able to satisfy a more discerning clientele with broader cultural interests. Like some other urban spas in history (most notably Bath in Georgian England), the place developed a reputation for not only healing the body but also enlivening the mind, delighting the senses, and attracting a sophisticated clientele who demanded a steady diet of high culture as they took the waters. And, as one might expect, among the city's cultural assets was a community of prominent physicians;[22] among them was Claudius' famous personal doctor, Gaius Stertinius Xenophon, who spent millions to adorn the city.[23] Apollo, already a prominent god in the local

---

20. *On Medicine* 2.17.1.
21. *Epistles* 1.15.
22. *CIL* 10.1497, 1545; *IG* 14.809.
23. Pliny, *Natural History* 29.8. See pp. 154–55.

Fig. 7.4. "I Pisciarelli." Illustration by P. Fabris, in W. Hamilton, Campi Phlegraei *(Naples 1776).*

pantheon, was worshiped in his healing guise (Medicus) around the northern Bay, along with Asklepios and Hygieia.[24]

Roman Neapolis controlled two regions of thermal spas: one on the island of Ischia [see Commentary 7.1, pp. 283–84], the other in its own western suburbs. The latter, like Baiae, were full of thermal springs and steam baths with mineral properties believed to alleviate specific maladies [Commentary 7.2, pp. 284–85]. Pliny the Elder[25] observes that the sulfurous spring of Araxus at the chalk quarries on Collis Leucogaeus ("White-Earth Hill") between Pozzuoli and Neapolis was beneficial for eye complaints, wounds, and weak teeth [Fig. 7.4]. This hill, called I Pisciarelli today, lies just northeast of La Solfatara, the burping, steaming, sulfurous crater that today epitomizes the Campi Phlegraei [see Fig. 1.7]. From the time of Octavian's establishment of a colony at Capua in 36 BCE,[26] he and subsequent emperors leased the property from Neapolis for the extraordinary sum of 200,000 sesterces a year. The stated reason was for the valuable chalk, which was mixed with *alica,* a grain meal, to create a noted ancient Campanian delicacy. But it may be suspected that the spa on the same hill turned a tidy profit too.

24. *IG* 14.809; *CIL* 10.1544–47.
25. *Natural History* 18.114, 31.12.
26. Dio Cassius, *Roman History* 49.14.5; Velleius Paterculus, *Compendium* 2.81.

CHAPTER 7 ☐ THE CULTURE OF WATER

Fig. 7.5. Illumination from Peter of Eboli's De balneis Puteolanis. *Biblioteca Angelica, Rome. Denghiù / Wikimedia Commons.*

A unique document of the early thirteenth century, the *De balneis Puteolanis* by Peter of Eboli, celebrates dozens of bathing establishments throughout the Phlegraean Fields still operating in his time, including twelve between Naples and Pozzuoli [Fig. 7.5]. Several of these were

Fig. 7.6. Baths of Agnano in the early twentieth century. Anonymous photo. CC BY-SA.

on the littoral of modern Bagnoli, which is named for one of them, Balneoli. Others were in the rugged hills to the north, including Pliny the Elder's baths of Collis Leucogaeus, which Peter called Balneum Bullae ("boiling bath"). Many of the ancient baths in this area are long defunct; but one, at Agnano, was a popular resort in the nineteenth and twentieth centuries and still operates today [Fig. 7.6]. The Roman complex (sometimes mistakenly called the Thermae Alinarum) was vast, extending at least 300 meters along the slopes of Monte Spina on terraces of Roman brick and stone reticulate [Fig. 1.1, J]. From the high Middle Ages until the 1860s it stood on the shores of a shallow crater lake to its north, Lago d'Agnano (Lacus Anianus), fully as large as the famed Lake Avernus to the west. The lake's therapeutic waters figure prominently in Peter's encomium of the baths and the accompanying illustrations [see Fig. 7.5]. But it was drained and today accommodates a Fascist-era hippodrome. Although ordinary bathing facilities were in good supply, Agnano's specialty was the dry sweat treatment — hence the name Balneum Siccum ("Dry Bath") in Peter's text. Included in the ancient complex, and adapted for modern use, are the so-called Stufe di S. Germano: the sweat-chambers in which, according to a legend known to Peter, Germanus, bishop of Capua (*floruit* c. 500 CE), took the cure. During his regimen he encountered the tormented apparition of a deceased deacon, Paschasius; the ghost was imprisoned in the bath for

CHAPTER 7 ⌂ THE CULTURE OF WATER

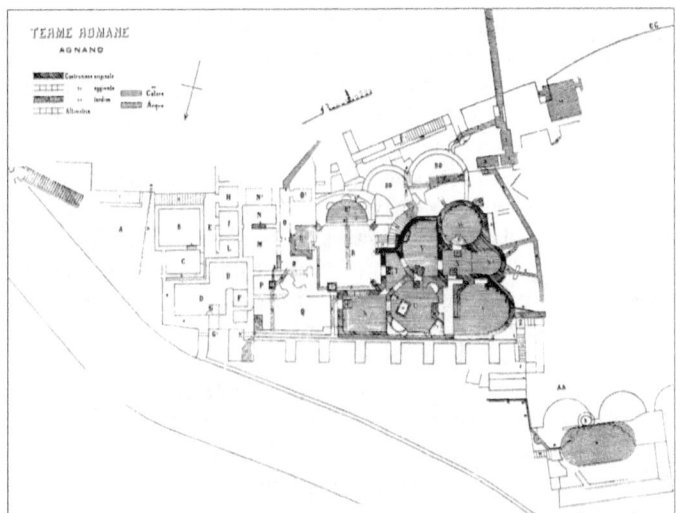

Fig. 7.7. Plan of the Roman baths at Agnano. Macchioro 1912.

having supported, in life, the antipope Laurentius (elected pope on the same day as Symmachus in 498 AD):

> **59.** Germanus was shocked and asked what a man of his dignity was doing in such a place. "The only reason I am serving here," the deacon answered, "is that I endorsed the party of Lawrence against Symmachus. But I beg you, pray for me to the Lord. When you come back and no longer find me here, you will know that your prayers have been heard." Germanus, therefore, gave himself to fervent prayer, and, when he returned a few days later, Paschasius no longer appeared. This purification from sin after death was possible because the deacon had sinned through ignorance and not through malice. [Gregory I, *Dialogue* 4.40, trans. Zimmerman]

Why a place of healing should be regarded as an apt venue for a heterodox deacon's purgatory is not explained, probably because no explanation was necessary. Christian writers could be deeply ambivalent about the moral value of bathing. Especially at natural hydrothermal baths, the sulfurous vapors offered irresistible associations with the infernal realms below.

The best-preserved Roman baths at Agnano are south of the modern spa. This complex developed in at least four phases. The aqueduct branch was introduced in the Augustan period, when the first traces of a bath structure were built. The dominant phase, in the first half of the second century CE, gave rise to the structure as we know it: an asymmetrical cluster of vaulted spaces arranged in a classic ring design [Fig. 7.7]. Two minor restoration phases followed in the third and late fourth centuries. This was a full-service establishment, its hybrid infrastructure relying partly on the geothermal spring, partly on aqueduct water and furnaces. Water from the Serino Aqueduct reached the baths by a tunnel running 70 meters through Monte Spina. When the Agnano complex was excavated around the turn of the twentieth century, several statues on mythological themes were found in situ. Recent excavations have turned up fragments of inscribed votive vessels and evidence of a large lustral pool suggesting that in the fourth century BCE, the spring was dedicated to the oft-encountered duo of healing gods, Asklepios and Hygieia.

THE ROMAN HYDRAULIC INFRASTRUCTURE
THE SERINO AQUEDUCT

Roman cities, with their ubiquitous baths and perpetually flowing fountains, consumed water liberally. For all its many natural advantages the rich and complex hydrology of Neapolis could not easily support the mature city on a truly Roman scale. At least from the time of Augustus, the city was supplied by an aqueduct that was extraordinary in two respects. First, it was very long; second, it ramified into branches that eventually served at least eight cities. The principal point of origin, some ninety-six kilometers from its terminal points at Misenum and Cumae, was the Acquaro–Pelosi spring in the village of Serino, which again today delivers a healthy volume of pure water to Naples from its karst aquifer in the rugged hills of Avellino. Though poorly preserved today, the Roman aqueduct has been surveyed three times. The last occasion for a close investigation came about during excavations in the 1930s for a modern expansion of a nineteenth-century aqueduct system. Near the source, a complete inscription on a slab of green *cipollino* marble was unearthed celebrating a restoration of the aqueduct by the emperor Constantine in 324 CE [Commentary 7.3, p. 286].

CHAPTER 7 ☗ THE CULTURE OF WATER

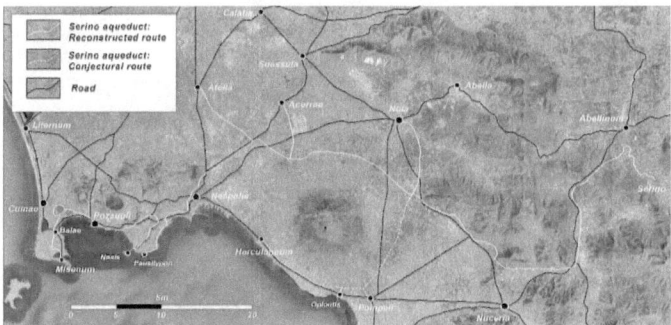

Fig. 7.8. Map of the course of the Serino Aqueduct. Background © 2020 Google.

The inscription revealed that the aqueduct served all the most important towns around the Bay of Naples except Sorrento (poignantly, Pompeii and Herculaneum are missing from the list, for they had ceased to exist in 79 CE), and that its source was named Fons Augusteus. The aqueduct's construction style, with its avoidance of brick and heavy dependence on isodomic tuff blocks and *opus reticulatum,* is distinctly Augustan. A fragmentary inscription from Pozzuoli refers to a "commissioner of the Augustan Aqueduct" (*curatori aquae Augustae*).[27] The aqueduct was probably to be associated with Augustus' sustained program of benefaction toward the Bay's western cities, where his adjutant Agrippa had established his naval base during the power struggles of the 30s BCE. Especially after the publication of Virgil's *Aeneid* around 19 BCE, how could that celebrated region, now thoroughly woven into the mythology of Roman identity, have been allowed to remain so un-Roman as to lack an aqueduct?

The extant ruins of the aqueduct's channels documented by Pietrantonio Lettieri in the 1560s and by Felice Abate in the mid-nineteenth century, combined with more recent observations, allow for a schematic reconstruction of the entire Serino network [Fig. 7.8]. With its branches, it comprised at least 145 kilometers of conduit, making it the longest known aqueduct system of the Roman world.

The trunk line approached Neapolis from the northeast. Tunneling underground, it roughly followed the Ramo Capodichino of the A1

27. *CIL* 10² *auct.*, p. 1009.

Fig. 7.9. Remains of the Serino Aqueduct known as the Ponti Rossi. Photo: R. Taylor.

highway immediately south of, and roughly parallel to, the modern airport runway. It emerged on a double arcade to cross the valley occupied today by Via Nicola Nicolini. Two nearly parallel segments of this arcade, known together as the Ponti Rossi ("Red Bridges"), are the only significant surface remains of the ancient aqueduct visible in Naples today [A on Fig. 1.1; Fig. 7.9]. The purpose and extent of the doubling are not known, but elsewhere in the system doubling has been associated with a need to reconfigure a segment of channel after geological uplift or subsidence disrupted the level of the original channel. The south segment (visible in the background of Fig. 7.9) consists of an eclectic mix of masonry, with facing elements in brick, squared tuff, and reticulate; the brickwork, for the most part, is from later phases. The truncated northern segment has undergone much more modification, but as Duncan Keenan-Jones observes, its piers originally seem to have had the same squared tuff construction as those of the companion arcade. The two channels penetrated the hill of Capodimonte (B) and then turned south to Piazza Cavour (C). From there one branch evidently entered the walled city at the north end of Via Costantinopoli and progressed south to the vicinity of Port'Alba (D). Here, perhaps, was a *castellum*, or distribution tank, from which the old city was provisioned by means of lead

CHAPTER 7 ⛪ THE CULTURE OF WATER

Fig. 7.10. View of the eastern end of the Crypta Neapolitana. Photo: R. Taylor.

pipes. Meanwhile, the trunk line continued south-southwest, skirting the eastern flanks of Colle S. Elmo on a brick arcade still visible in the early sixteenth century, straight into the Spanish Quarter. Near Piazzetta Trinità degli Spagnoli the channel encountered a large, circular *castellum* made of early-imperial reticulate (E), probably to service the harbor district and the neighborhoods to its west. From here it continued south to the beach of Chiaia. Turning west, it paralleled the shoreline to Mergellina (F), where the line again divided (G); but first it plunged into the precipitous slope of the promontory. In 1882, tunnel excavations for a tram line in the zone just before the split led to some interesting discoveries [Commentary 7.4, pp. 286–87]. The south branch supplied the seaside villas along the eastern side of Capo di Posillipo, while the trunk line joined the great Neapolis–Pozzuoli

265

Fig. 7.11. View of the western end of the Crypta Neapolitana. Photo: R. Taylor.

highway tunnel called the Crypta Neapolitana or, in modern times, the Grotta vecchia di Pozzuoli or Grotta di Posillipo [Fig. 7.10].

The tunnel, Mario Napoli believed, was part of a grand military communication system initiated by Octavian and Agrippa in the 30s BCE. This would have included, to the west, the "Grotta di Seiano"; a tunnel on the peninsula (now an islet) leading to the island of Nesis (Nisida); a recently discovered tunnel between the Lucrine Lake and Baiae; and the "Grotta di Cocceio" connecting Lake Avernus to Cumae. The latter, Strabo tells us, was designed by the same architect as the Crypta: Cocceius.[28] Running 700 meters southwest through

28. 5.4.5.

CHAPTER 7 ⛫ THE CULTURE OF WATER

Fig. 7.12. The Grotto of Posillipo at Naples, *oil painting by A.S. Pitloo, 1826. Rijksmuseum.*

a tufaceous ridge, the Crypta emerges at the head of Via della Grotta Vecchia [Fig. 7.11]. Though the entrances are monumental today, the tunnel's initial average height was about 5 meters, its width 4.5 meters — enough to allow two carts to pass,[29] but an oppressively confining

---

29. Strabo, *Geography* 5.4.7.

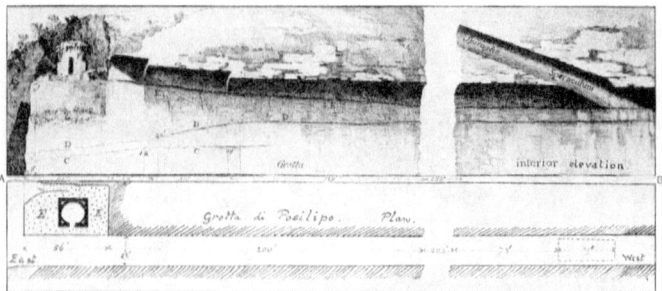

Fig. 7.13. Cross-section of the Crypta Neapolitana, eastern end. Günther 1913, after Paoli 1768.

space.[30] It was widened and the floor cut down markedly during the Renaissance, creating a level floor that allowed a view to the far end [Fig. 7.12]. Two intermediate floor levels of unknown date are clearly visible in Paolo Antonio Paoli's section drawing of the east end [C and D on Fig. 7.13]. The floor was again raised thereafter in attempts to shore up the tunnel's wall [compare Figs. 7.10 and 7.12], but further collapses have forced permanent closure.

As the aqueduct approaches the Crypta three short lengths of the main channel, segmented by later quarrying, trace an S-shaped path in the bluffs, far above ground today but slightly below the ancient floor level of the tunnel. At a small medieval chapel, the sinuous turns cease, resolving into a path that parallels the tunnel in a straight line on the north side. At this very point, Keenan-Jones has recently determined, the Pausilypon branch veered off to the south [G on Fig. 1.1]. Steepening its gradient momentarily, the branch dipped under the original floor level of the Crypta, now excavated away.

Upon exiting to the west (H), the main channel divided yet again. A subsurface branch wended southward, hugging the precipitous western scarp of the promontory that divides the heights of Posillipo from the plain of Bagnoli (I), and finally crossing the water, presumably on arches, to the tiny island of Nesis, the erstwhile villa refuge of Lucullus *fils* and Brutus that Augustus undoubtedly later confiscated. The trunk line, as we have already seen, made for the baths of Agnano,

30. See p. 13.

CHAPTER 7 ☗ THE CULTURE OF WATER

Fig. 7.14. Satellite view of Pizzofalcone highlighting the ancient rock-cut nymphaeum at Palazzo Carafa di S. Severino. Satellite imagery: © 2020 Google, CNES / Airbus, Maxar Technologies. Inset photo: R. Taylor.

tunneling through Monte Spina and onward to northern Bagnoli where Sgobbo discovered a stretch of the channel set into the *pozzolana* slope above the Metropolitana train station (J). From there, it drove through the tuff and basalt ridge of Monte Olibano to Pozzuoli. The same system served Cumae, Baiae, Bauli (Bacoli), and Misenum.

In Roman times, the city's excellent but finite water supply served a number of priorities: baths, cisterns, private concessions, public street fountains, and larger display fountains. Of the latter category none are known today. However, at the crest of the promontory of Pizzofalcone, carved from the living tuff that forms the foundation for the Palazzo Carafa di Sta. Severina behind it, stand the weathered remains of a nymphaeum, or monumental fountain [Fig. 7.14]. Without further investigation little can be said for certain about it. But the concept itself — a row of five display niches on the front, and a water supply channel lined with hydraulic cement cutting across the top — is distinctly Roman. This monument, which potentially released water from several sides of its faceted façade, commanded a panoramic view of the sea. At roughly 60 meters above sea level, the elevation of its top channels well exceeds the Serino Aqueduct (41.2 meters above sea level upstream at Ponti Rossi). Thus the fountain was fed from a cistern; both perhaps belonged to the Lucullan estate that fell into

Fig. 7.15. Rear slab of a marble fountain basin from Via del Cerriglio. Naples, Museo Archeologico Nazionale. Photo: R. Taylor.

imperial hands.[31] Symbolically it functioned almost like a figurehead affixed to the great prow of Parthenope. One can imagine that it was in Strabo's sights when he described the Bay as a mighty megalopolis; or that Statius had it in mind when he sought to persuade his wife of the visual pleasures on the Bay of Naples.[32]

31. See pp. 127, 144, 164, 299, 308, 318–19; Commentary 8.2, pp. 334–35.
32. *Silvae* 3.5; see pp. 315–16.

CHAPTER 7 ⛫ THE CULTURE OF WATER

In customary Roman fashion, the streets of lower Neapolis were equipped with small public fountains in the manner of Pompeii or Herculaneum: simple, squared basins of stone facing the street, the rear panel raised higher than the others to accommodate a metal standpipe from which the water issued in a steady flow into the basin. Often the raised area was adorned with a relief. A good specimen was found on Via del Cerriglio, in the Roman harbor district just west of Piazza Bovio [Fig. 7.15]. Its relief depicts a seated Hercules overseeing a boxing match. This may be a reference to the Sebasta Games. Dio Chrysostom situates agonistic boxing matches at an "Exedra of Herakles," thought to be at Neapolis.[33] But it also suits the harbor district where it was found, given the god's immense popularity among traders and merchants. One shoulder of the slab is worn slightly concave by the countless jars dragged over its surface.

Based on the cross-section and gradient of its main channel, the mean volume of the Serino Aqueduct has been estimated at 86,400 cubic meters per day — which squares well with the mean flow rate of the same sources today (34,500 to 121,000 varying seasonally). This is on the same order of magnitude as one of the larger of eleven aqueducts serving imperial Rome. For a single city the size of Pozzuoli or Neapolis, with their local sources of supplementary water, it would have more than sufficed. But shared among so many other destinations, the aqueduct must have been sorely strained, especially in the dry summer months. Whether it was supplemented by other springs, such as those at Avella or Somma, remains an open question. Either way, Neapolis and other cities in the network employed abundant wells and cisterns, either attached to the aqueduct system or independent of it. One modest example is a two-chambered, cross-vaulted cistern of the Flavian period found in 1957 under the Palazzo Sansevero in the heart of walled Neapolis. Remains of larger cisterns too have been found, as in Piazza Amedeo. Like the great cisterns found at Pozzuoli — and most famously, the massive Piscina Mirabile at Misenum — many of them collected water reserves during off-peak hours.

33. *Discourse* 28.2.

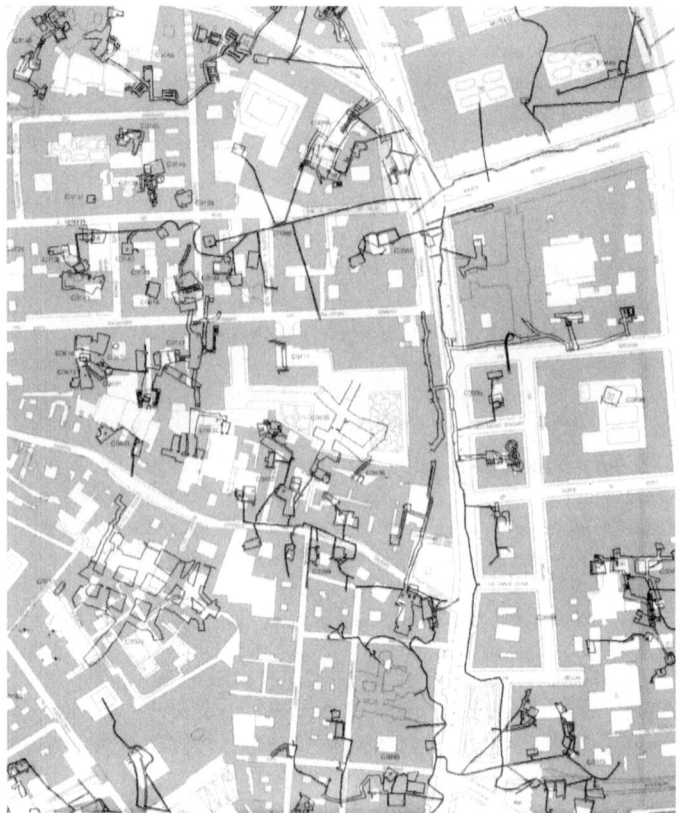

Fig. 7.16. Plan of known rock-cut underground features in the area northwest of Piazza Dante. Esposito 2018.

THE BOLLA AQUEDUCT

Deep below the Centro Storico, in the tangle of tunnels cut through the tuff, lies abundant evidence of a mysterious secondary system whose beginnings may reach back beyond the Serino Aqueduct. The origins of this aqueduct, known as the Bolla, cannot be securely established, but parts of it are ancient; sections in Roman reticulate masonry still exist. Its main source, investigated by Luigi Cangiano in the nineteenth century, was eight kilometers to the northeast at Volla [see Fig. 1.2] in the alluvial plain west of Vesuvius. Whereas the Serino Aqueduct served

CHAPTER 7 🏛 THE CULTURE OF WATER

the northern and western parts of greater Neapolis, the Bolla was concentrated in the central and eastern parts of the walled city. The aqueduct itself entered from the east, at the "Porta dell'acquedotto" near the church of Sta. Sofia. Here it was only 13 meters above sea level, far too low to serve the surface of the walled city, which sloped from about 53 to 24 meters above sea level. Thus it evolved into the bewildering web of rock-cut conduits, drains, cisterns, and well shafts that make underground Naples an explorer's wonderland [Fig. 7.16]. For nearly two millennia its excellent potable water was raised to the surface with bucket chains or other lifting devices. In 2007 a well with a pre-Augustan water-lifting device was found at S. Andrea delle Dame, near the walled city's acropolis. If the reports are correct, then the device predates the Serino Aqueduct and must therefore have descended an impressive 35 meters or more below grade to reach the Bolla's waters.

A lost inscription of the late third or fourth century CE mentions a Neapolitan district called the *Regio Thermensium*.[34] The unusual genitive plural refers to a district of bathing establishments — literally, "of the bathmen." Modified in medieval times to *Regio Thermensis* ("bath district"), this name was identified as the eastern part of the old city, roughly between Via Duomo and Castel Capuano [see Fig. 6.19]; in short, the area first served by the Bolla. It seems odd that a neighborhood primarily provisioned by a subterranean aqueduct should have become noted for its Roman baths, given the proclivity of baths to rely on abundant aboveground or pressurized water. The nomenclature suggests to me that this district acquired its name by virtue of having the *first* Roman-style baths in the city, which like the pre-aqueduct Stabian and Republican baths in Pompeii relied on water-lifting devices. The Pompeian baths probably adopted Sergius Orata's advancements in bathing technology around 100 BCE, but these still relied on a bucket chain to tap an aquifer until the first aqueduct was introduced under Augustus. Cosmopolitan Neapolis surely would have kept pace with fashion. The original Bolla Aqueduct, then, could be of similar vintage, i.e., the first half of the first century BCE or even earlier. The Stabian Baths at Pompeii are now dated in their earliest phase to about 125 BCE.

34. *CIL* 10.1680. See Commentary 5.3, pp. 177–78.

Many of the idiosyncrasies of the Serino line, including parallel channels (as at the Ponti Rossi), are probably due to repairs after the earthquakes of the 60s CE or the eruption of 79. Ground deformations too may have taken their toll and required some rerouting of the original channel. A recent isotopic analysis of lead in the harbor strata reveals that the urban water distribution system before the 79-CE eruption of Vesuvius consisted of lead pipes bearing a chemical signature characteristic of the mines in southern Spain. After the eruption the aqueduct may have suffered a hiatus of a decade or two; but then the ratio of imported lead only increased, marking a significant expansion of the pre-79 network. This augmentation may reflect a zero-sum gain against the system's loss of Pompeii and Herculaneum, or simply an expansion of the Bolla system, or both. But the Bolla option is unlikely: lead pipes were used for high-volume, pressurized water systems, not the lift-and-pour variety.

We know the Serino Aqueduct was repaired by Constantine and again in the late fourth century [see Commentary 7.3, p. 286]. Its duration thereafter is a matter of contention. The Bolla system, its sources much modified, was still flowing in the nineteenth century, but with diminished quality and capacity. Contaminated by an encroaching web of sewers, its waters instigated the great cholera epidemic of 1884; this in turn precipitated the Risanamento, the great reclamation project that transformed late-nineteenth-century Naples. One or both of these aqueducts played a role in the dramatic siege by the Byzantine general Belisarius in 536, at which time the reduced city population had no difficulty surviving on groundwater and cisterns when the supply was shut off.[35] While Procopius makes no attempt to distinguish the two aqueducts, he implies the existence of both a functioning and an abandoned line. We just noted that one, "which brought in water," was shut off. Yet Belisarius' soldiers were able to invade the city by way of a collapsed section of channel and a derelict "building" (*oikema*: settling or distribution tank?) directly adjoining it.[36] Keenan-Jones reasonably suspects that it was the Bolla that was shut off, and the Serino Aqueduct that was out of use. The former was probably too far underground and too cramped

35. Procopius, *Gothic War* 1.8.45.
36. 1.10.14.

CHAPTER 7 ☩ THE CULTURE OF WATER

to accommodate an invading army, even single file, whereas the latter (witness the Ponti Rossi) entered the city at or just above ground level, thus presenting a vulnerable point of enemy infiltration.

CONVENTIONAL BATHS

To judge by many conventional, aqueduct-fed bathing establishments (quite apart from thermo-mineral ones) randomly discovered around the city [see Fig. 6.19], Neapolis of the imperial era was as well bathed as any Roman city. Public baths stood open to all, and more intimate private establishments served homes and neighborhoods. A bath patronized by Nero during one visit to the city must have been among the finest available, but it was not monumental. When bathing there privately he craved an audience and so betook himself to the theater.[37] Indeed none of the baths found to date in Naples is large; what surprises is their frequency, at least relative to the limited opportunities for excavation in the city. This bespeaks a dense scattering of neighborhood baths throughout the city and its suburbs. Here is a partial list, enumerating only the more significant finds:

- Piazza Municipio [A on Fig. 6.19; Figs. 6.20; 6.23]. Two Roman bathing establishments, one of the first century CE and another of the second, were discovered in the Metropolitana excavations, each fronting directly on the harbor's western edge.[38] Daniela Giampaola, the chief project archaeologist, hypothesizes the existence of an extensive network of baths and waterworks on this side of town, all fed by the trunk line of the Serino Aqueduct, whose known distribution tank in the Spanish Quarter was no more than 700 meters due west.

- Via Armando Díaz (B). Dating to the first half of the second century CE, remains of baths have been found on this street near Via Toledo. These were due west of the port in a commercial and residential neighborhood.

- Piazza Bovio (C). In 1894, a bath complex was discovered here. It is not visible today. Reportedly the remains of a Roman bath underlie the Cappella di S. Aspreno, now enclosed within the Palazzo della

37. Suetonius, *Nero* 20.2.
38. See pp. 222, 224, 235–36.

Fig. 7.17. Roman bath under the church of Sta. Chiara. Photo: R. Taylor.

Borsa. This area was known in the Middle Ages as the Acquari because of the abundance of water (probably from the derelict Serino Aqueduct) and many visible remains of Roman baths.

- Sta. Chiara (D). When Allied bombing in August 1943 destroyed large parts of this Franciscan church and monastery, it laid bare parts of an ancient and medieval bath complex on the south and west sides of the cloister. The late-first- or early-second-century-CE building, refurbished in late antiquity, features a prominent rectangular *natatio* (wading pool) and a circular *laconicum* (sweat bath) with a hypocaust and four deep niches [Fig. 7.17] as well as a large cistern of later date. Framing the northwest border of the cistern is a brick arcade of the original building. Among the finds was a fragmentary marble table with a splendid bull's-head protome.

- Piazza Bellini (E). Ferdinando Colonna reports briefly on the discovery of a bath complex here, almost directly along the urban line of the aqueduct. Nothing can be seen of it now.

- Vicolo Limoncello (F). Just north of the theater, this group of parallel vaulted chambers is thought by Mario Napoli to have been the venue of Nero's bath. But even if it is a bath, Suetonius' narrative gives no cause to presume a close proximity between bath and theater. What's more, the theater is now dated to after Nero's death.

CHAPTER 7 🏛 THE CULTURE OF WATER

Fig. 7.18 (above). Multi-use Roman complex at Via Carminiello ai Mannesi. Photo: R. Taylor.

Fig. 7.19 (below). Isometric cutaway reconstruction by Sheila Gibson of the complex of Carminiello ai Mannesi in the second century CE. Arthur, ed. 1994. Courtesy of Paul Arthur.

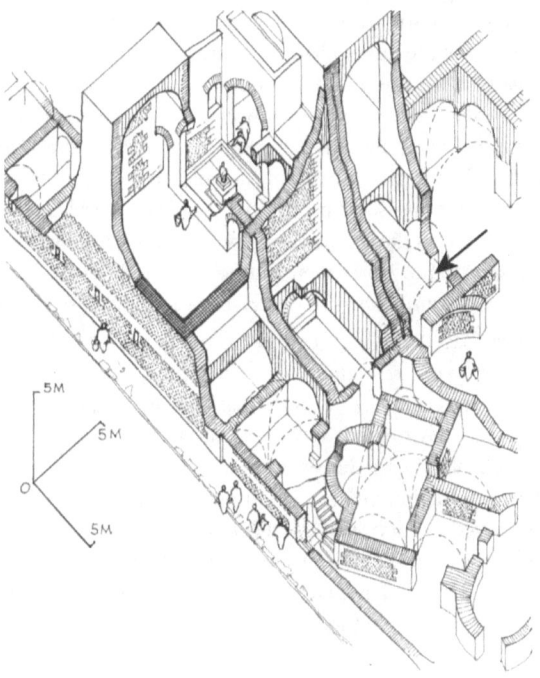

- Donnaregina Vecchia (G). A room of the second or third century CE with a hypocaust and a colored floor mosaic was excavated in 1988 at the site of this church north of the Duomo.
- Vico Carminiello ai Mannesi (H). This large bathing and storage complex [Fig. 7.18; 7.19] lay hidden within the church of Sta. Maria del Carmine ai Mannesi until the 1943 bombardment. Excavations led by Paul Arthur revealed a structure of several phases built around an apsidal republican-era room with a mosaic floor and remains of simple frescos on the walls. Most of the present complex was built in *opus mixtum* or brickwork of the first century CE. Oriented along a narrow street paralleling Via Duomo to the east, it comprised at least two stories. The lower vaulted chambers were mostly used for storage. One was later converted into a Mithraeum, and it still shows traces in stucco relief of the god's effigy.[39] The upper level, with its handsome stuccoed cornice still partly intact, was clearly a presentation space. At least two of the upper chambers, fitted variously with hypocausts, *tubuli* (parallel wall flues) and floors of the pinkish hydraulic cement called *cocciopesto* or *opus signinum* constitute part of a small bathing establishment. The most striking room at this level is also the smallest: at its center is a rectangular stepped fountain with its marble cladding still intact [Fig. 7.20]. Two marble statue heads were found in the excavations, one from a Hermes in the style of Polykleitos, the other representing an unidentified idealized female. Also found here was the fragmentary marble statue of a satyr.
- Castel Capuano (I). A record from the year 1024 mentions a *balneum vetus destructum* ("an ancient ruined bath") on Via Capuana. Recent work in the southeastern sector of the Castel Capuano has turned up architectural fragments and sculpture of high quality. To the west, under the Archivio Storico of the Banco di Napoli on Via dei Tribunali, bathing rooms and a mosaic-paved portico (perhaps a *palaestra,* the exercise grounds of a bathing establishment) have been found. Fragmentary statues of athletes, including a *Diadoumenos* of Polykleitos, chime with the bathing or *palaestra* theme.

39. See p. 355.

CHAPTER 7 ☗ THE CULTURE OF WATER

Fig. 7.20. Fountain in the complex at Via Carminiello ai Mannesi. Photo: R. Taylor.

- Vicinity of Piazza Nicola Amore (J, K, L). Several bath buildings are attested in the neighborhood. One, discovered in 1164 on Via Ferri Vecchi, is described as *balneum vetere cum spoliatorio et... fornace suis* ("a bath with an ancient dressing room and its own furnace"). Another, "newer" bath, was believed by Bartolommeo Capasso to lie to its east, "toward S. Agostino alla Zecca," in a district known as Balnei Novi ("New Baths") in the Middle Ages. In the early 1890s a cross-vaulted porticated structure with elaborate frescos was unearthed about two modern city blocks south of the church, at Via Duca di S. Donato. Adjoining it was a round plunge pool belonging to a bath. The building had two phases: one

Fig. 7.21. Baths of the Via Terracina. Photo: R. Taylor.

more or less contemporary with the Pompeian fourth style (c.62–79 CE), the second undated.

- Monastery of S. Marcellino e Festo (M). A medieval document recording the monastery's construction refers to an ancient structure on the site with a well, dressing room, "towel room" (*lenarium*), furnaces, and *stationes* (waiting rooms?). The complex was still known in the fourteenth century, by which time it was called, unaccountably, the "Bath of Plato."

- Via S. Gregorio Armeno (N). A bath was reportedly built here by St. Nostrianus, a fourth-century bishop of Neapolis. Its memory was preserved in the name of a sixteenth-century church, Sta. Maria ad Balneum, now deconsecrated.

- Via Terracina [Figs. 1.1; 7.21]. Unearthed during massive excavations for the Mostra d'Oltremare in the 1930s and published by Elena LaForgia in 1981, this is the only approximately complete bath complex to be investigated in Naples. It lies west of the Crypta Neapolitana along the ancient Neapolis–Pozzuoli highway, where, as Werner Johannowsky has proposed, it probably was part of a hospitality district serving intercity travelers. In the 1930s project a segment of the Serino Aqueduct was found nearby.[40] Almost certainly the aqueduct, and not thermal springs,

40. See p. 269.

CHAPTER 7 ⚱ THE CULTURE OF WATER

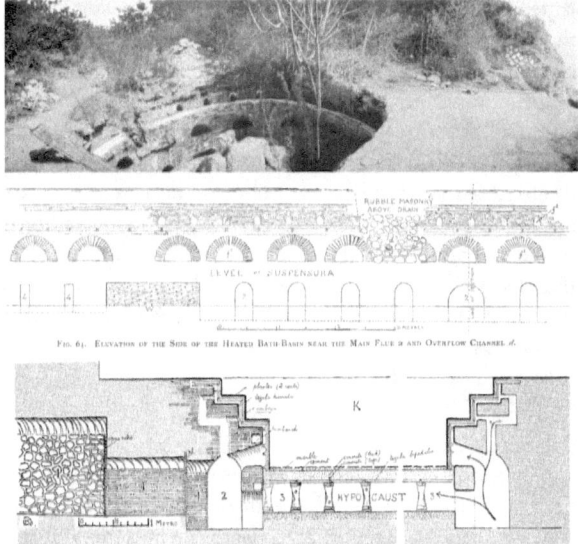

Fig. 7.22. View and elevations of the circular bathing pool at Pausilypon. Günther 1913.

supplied water to this bath. Characteristically, the hot and warm rooms are arranged to the south and west. The largest and most elegantly decorated rooms are the *apodyterium*, or changing room, at the north corner, and the *frigidarium*, which serves as the core from which rooms or plunge pools open in all directions. In the former, a black-and-white mosaic floor panel depicts a Nereid riding on the tail of a Triton, with erotes hovering above. On axis with this room, and once screened from it by a pair of columns, the *frigidarium* carries a splendid full-floor black-and-white mosaic representing Poseidon with his entourage of mythic marine creatures. Wall construction, of *opus listatum* (several courses of brick alternating with bands of small tuff blocks laid horizontally), suggests a date in the early second century CE. Off the *apodyterium*, a semicircular latrine featured a charming dolphin mosaic.

- Pausilypon. This great imperial pleasure villa, discussed further in chapters 6 and 8, had its own branch of the Serino Aqueduct, as we just saw. It fed the known cisterns on the premises (surely there were others), totaling about 380,000 liters. Reportedly large quantities of Roman lead pipe were extracted by one of the property's former owners; a surviving inscribed segment records the patronage of the emperor Hadrian. A century ago R.T. Günther described the two extant bath complexes (and a possible nymphaeum) there in detail. The better-preserved Upper Baths are of Hadrian's era, much modified thereafter. Günther carefully analyzed the unusual circular *caldarium* with its complicated hypocaust system that heated not only the floor under the central pool but also the stepped seating areas surrounding it [Fig. 7.22]. Runoff from the baths may have been used to supply the monumental nymphaeum known as the "School of Virgil" at water's edge. An unusual oblong pool has been excavated at orchestra level in the theater.[41]

- Marechiaro. Just east of Pausilypon, in the vicinity of the "Tempio degli Spiriti," Günther describes a small terraced complex of rooms — two rectangular, one circular in plan — similar to those at the "Temple of Mercury" at Baiae. These were probably supplied by a large cistern nearby with a capacity of some 660,000 liters.
- Agnano. Discussed above.[42]

The love of social and therapeutic bathing, of course, is a universally acknowledged feature of the Roman character. All of the structures just enumerated were indisputably of the Roman era, and whether evaluated by type or by numbers they could be regarded as typical of any Roman urban area that enjoyed both natural thermal springs and artificially supplied water. What makes Neapolis unusual, perhaps, is the extent to which this aggressively Roman practice was blended, partly by nature and partly by artifice, with the area's Greek cultural heritage. To be sure, the Hellenization of bathing, taken in the abstract, can be regarded as a distinctly Roman cultural construct — the merging of Greek gymnastics and the *palaestra,* for example, into the Roman bathing experience, or the blending of Greek healing gods, such as Apollo, Asklepios and Hygieia, into the sculptural

41. See pp. 311–12.
42. See pp. 260–62.

CHAPTER 7 ⛩ THE CULTURE OF WATER

programs of baths. But Neapolis cherished its reputation as a hothouse of Hellenism in a region that was withdrawing many cultural ties to its Greek past. The city's carefully curated associations with an ancient maritime identity on the one hand, and with the cults of watery gods on the other (most notably Parthenope), promised a particular and unique experience underscored by the Greek chthonic mythologies delivered by way of the region's crater lakes, fumarole fields, and hydrothermal springs. Dense with meaning, sensory pleasure, and nostalgia, the heavily Hellenized Neapolitan way of living only grew in popularity as it withdrew from the rest of Italy.

⛩

Commentary 7.1: The Spas of Ischia

In antiquity as today, Ischia (Pithekoussai to the Greeks, Aenaria to the Romans, the "island burning with flame" in Lykophron's words) was renowned for its thermal springs. According to Pliny the Elder,[43] Strabo,[44] and the physician Soranos,[45] its abundant waters were renowned for curing urological complaints such as stones in the bladder. Knowing this, one cannot fail to be struck by the discovery on the island of a terracotta ex voto representing male genitals. It was found in the 1950s at the site of one of the thermal springs on the island, today the Terme Regina Isabella in the town of Lacco Ameno. Effigies of this kind, dedicated by ailing or cured supplicants to a sympathetic god, are a sure mark of the presence of a healing cult. Undoubtedly sanctuaries enclosed the springs to house and treat the visitors who sought relief from their complaints.

One of the island's best-known ancient springs is still active today: Nitroli, named for the local water nymphs of antiquity, the Nitrodes or Nitrodiae (derived from the Greek *nitron*, "soda"). In 1757, ten or eleven Roman votive reliefs dating from the first to the third centuries CE were unearthed in the vicinity of the spring. Inscribed with dedications to Apollo

43. *Natural History* 31.9.
44. *Geography* 5.9.
45. Caelius Aurelianus, *On Acute Diseases* 5.77.

and the Nitrodes, a number of them represent the god — a habitual resident of healing cults and one of the "parent gods" of Neapolis[46] — alongside the attendant nymphs, who carry pitchers or cockle-shaped basins to represent their healing waters. In one case, a protagonist, presumably the dedicant Capellina, is shown taking the cure. As the naked woman washes her hair, a beneficent Apollo and two nymphs stand in attendance. One nymph holds a washbasin, the other a decanting vessel [Fig. 7.1]. Another relief shows a dedicant evidently in the act of drinking the salubrious waters as she bathes. On yet another example, "Menippus, doctor from the Cisalpine region" explicitly stated his calling.

The reliefs of Nitroli, today in the Museo Archeologico at Naples (another at the Hermitage in St. Petersburg is of uncertain origin), are among the best visual documents of a healing cult in south Italy, where objects of this kind are rarely found. Yet two fragmentary inscribed reliefs from the vicinity of Rome — one in the Carpi collection, the other recorded only in an illustration by Pirro Ligorio — also were dedicated to *Nymphae Nitrodes*. In both cases they depicted seminude seated female figures with capsized urns gushing forth at their sides. There is no obvious connection between them and the island nymphs other than the alkaline, diuretic quality for which their waters were celebrated.

Commentary 7.2: Ancient Authors on the Phlegraean Fields

60. Nowhere... is water more bountiful than in the Bay of Baiae, or with more variety of relief: some has the virtue of sulfur, some of alum, some of salt, some of soda, some of bitumen, some are even acid and salt in combination; of some the mere steam is beneficial, of which the power is so great that it heats baths and even makes cold water boil in the tubs. The water called Posidian in the region of Baiae, getting its name from a freedman of Claudius Caesar, cooks thoroughly even meat. In the sea itself too, steam rises from the water that belonged to Licinius Crassus, and there comes something valuable to health in the very midst of the billows. [Pliny the Elder, *Natural History* 31.4–5]

46. Statius, *Silvae* 4.8.45-49.

CHAPTER 7 ⛫ THE CULTURE OF WATER

61. In front of Dikaiarcheia [Pozzuoli] also, in the land of the Etruscans, there is water boiling in the sea, and an artificial island has been made through it, so that this water is not "untilled," but serves for hot baths. [Pausanias, *Description of Greece* 8.7.3]

62. There is also a kind of powder which, by nature, produces wonderful results. It is found in the neighborhood of Baiae and in the lands of the municipalities round Mount Vesuvius. This being mixed with lime and rubble, not only furnishes strength to other buildings, but also, when piers are built in the sea, they set under water. Now this seems to happen for this reason: that under these mountainous regions there are both hot earth and many springs. And these would not be unless deep down they had huge blazing fires of sulfur, alum or pitch. Therefore the fire and vapor of flame within, flowing through the cracks, makes the earth light.... But that there are fervent heats in these districts may be proved by this circumstance. In the hills of Baiae which belong to Cumae sites are excavated for sweating-rooms. In these hot vapor rising deep down perforates the soil by the violence of its heat, and passing through it rises in these places, and so produces striking advantages in sweating-rooms.... If, therefore, in these places there are found hot springs, and in all excavations, warm vapors, and if these very places are related by the ancients to have had fires ranging over the fields, it seems to be certain that by the violence of fire, moisture has been removed from the tuff and earth just as from lime in kilns. Therefore, when unlike and unequal substances are caught together and brought into one nature, the hot desiccation, suddenly saturated with water, seethes together with the latent heat in the bodies affected, and causes them to combine vehemently and to gain rapidly one strong solidity. [Vitruvius, *Ten Books on Architecture* 2.6.1–4]

Commentary 7.3: Serino Aqueduct Documents

63. Our lords Flavius Constantinus Maximus Pius Felix Victor Augustus [306–337] and the most noble Caesars, Flavius Julius Crispus and Flavius Claudius Constantinus, instructed that the aqueduct of the Augustan Spring, crippled by long neglect and age, be restored at their expense to magnify their accustomed generosity; and they returned it to the service of the cities listed below. Dedicated by Ceionius Julianus, *vir clarissimus,* Consular of Campania, and overseen by Pontianus, *vir perfectissimus,* in charge of the same aqueduct. Names of the cities: Puteoli [Pozzuoli]; Neapolis; Nola; Atella; Cumae; Acerra; Baiae; Misenum. [*CIL* 10.1805, trans. Taylor]

64. [Co-emperors Arcadius (377–408) and Honorius (395–423)] to Messala, Praetorian Prefect. No person shall presume to appropriate for private use any water out of the aqueduct named Augusta, which has been repaired at public expense in Campania, and to no person hereafter shall the right be granted to divert water therefrom. If, moreover, any person should dare to divert the channel of water, he shall be compelled to pay five pounds of gold to Our treasury. Also if anything for the sake of such a fraud should be elicited by rescript or attempted by any trickery, it shall be held void. *Given on the fifth day before the calends of January at Milan in the year of the consulship of the Most Noble Theodorus.* — December 28, 399. [*Theodosian Code* 15.2.8, trans. Pharr]

Commentary 7.4: The Aqueduct Tunnel Inscriptions

During tunnel excavations for a Naples–Pozzuoli tram line in 1882, workers came upon a previously unknown segment of the Serino Aqueduct. Piercing the walls obliquely 4.4 meters above track level, its channel was investigated in both directions. To the surprise of everyone, deep inside the channel several hundred meters from the western point of exit, three inscriptions, repeated with slight variations, were found etched onto the mortar lining on either wall above the waterline.[47] The longest version, a single line 14.35 meters long with letters 25 centimeters high, reads:

65. MACRINUS, AGENT OF DIADUMENUS ANTONIANUS, FREEDMAN AND PROCURATOR OF THE EMPEROR, WALKED HERE FROM THE VILLA OF POLLIUS FELIX CALLED EPILIMONES ["AMONG THE MEADOWS"] TO THE PACONIAN OUTLET. IN THE YEAR OF THE CONSULSHIP OF NERVA AND VESTINUS [65 CE].

47. *ILS* 5798.

CHAPTER 7 🏛 THE CULTURE OF WATER

Macrinus, it would seem, had been charged with overseeing the mortaring or remortaring of a segment of channel, probably the eastern branch of Capo di Posillipo, which served the villa of Limon or Epilimones along the way. This villa belonged to none other than Pollius Felix, future patron of the poet Statius,[48] who mentions that it had a view across the bay to the Sorrentine Peninsula. Thus it must have been on the east side of the ridge of Posillipo. Duncan Keenan-Jones submits that the term "Paconian outlet" refers to an early commissioner of the Serino Aqueduct whose name he reconstructs from a weathered inscription of 10 CE[49] as Decimus Satrius Paconianus. If this is right, we may conjecture that Paconianus' branch was part of a second phase of the aqueduct completed during Augustus' lifetime. Its target was Pausilypon, which Vedius Pollio bequeathed to the emperor in 15 BCE. But it clearly served other villas along the way.

The workers also found a number of inscriptions marking distance measurements. Most were marked on the upper parts of the mortar: on one side, C, CC, CCC, CCCC, D; on the other, M, CM, DCCC [DCC DC]. Each numeral was 100 Roman feet distant from the next. They seem to be progress marks made by the mortarers, who worked 500 feet in one direction, then mortared the other side in the opposite direction. The reference points for these marks were a differently numbered set of measurements incised in the stone under the mortar. They probably related to the initial surveying of the channel.

---

48. *Silvae* 2.2, 3.1.
49. Published in Camodeca 1997, who reads the *cognomen as* Ragonianus.

REFERENCES

Sirens: De Petra 1908; Pugliese Carratelli 1952b; 1967: 122; Sbordone 1967a; Breglia Pulci Doria 1987; Greco 1992; Napoli 1997 [1959]: 159–65; Taylor 2014. **Foundation myths and colonization:** Dougherty 1993, 1998; Taylor 2009. **Thermo-mineral baths in the region of Neapolis:** Macchioro 1912; Sgobbo 1929; LaForgia 1981, 1985b; Amalfitano et al. 1990: 19–73; Yegül 1991: 92–110; 1996; Di Bonito and Giamminelli 1992; Zampino 1995; Clark 1999; Marasco 2001; Gianfrotta 2010; Giglio 2014–2015; 2016. **Geology, hydrology, and geography of Ischia:** Pais 1908b; Buchner Niola 1965; Monti 1980: 9–25; Rittmann and Gottini 1981; Buchner 1986; Luongo et al. 1987; Vezzoli 1988. **Relief of Nymphs attributed to Pozzuoli:** Adamo Muscettola 2001. **Reliefs of Nitroli, Ischia and their inscriptions:** Forti 1951; Monti 1968: 96–105; Schraudolph 1993: 149–59; Buchner and Gialanella 1994: 95–98; Adamo Muscettola 2002; Castagna 2003: 322–38; Iapino 2003; Scatozza Höricht 2007: 85–86. **Relief of the Nitrodes found near Rome:** Luschi 1999. **Sergius Orata and his "inventions":** Pagano 1983–1984: 122–25; Yegül 1991: 379–80; 2010: 80–86; 2013; Nielsen 1993: 21–22; Fagan 1996; Wikander 1996; D'Arms 2003 [1970]: 31–37; Bannon 2014; Marzano 2015. **Hydrothermal bathing on the Bay in late antiquity and the Middle Ages:** Kaufmann 1959; Zampino 1995; Yegül 1996; Clark 1999; Maddalo 2003; Gialanella 2012; Musto 2013: 117–19; Taylor 2017. **Regio Thermensium:** Capasso 1978 [1905]: 44–45, 77; Napoli 1967c: 441–42; 1997 [1959]: 196–97; Camodeca 1977: 74–75; Beloch 1989 [1890]: 85. **New date of the Stabian Baths at Pompeii:** Trümper et al. 2019. **Serino and Bolla aqueducts:** Cangiano 1843; Abate 1864; Melisurgo 1889; Elia 1938; Sgobbo 1938; Johannowsky 1952: 104–5; 1985a: 338–39; Bellucci 1961; Mariniello 1981; Esposito 1992; Miccio and Potenza 1994: 21–52; Potenza 1996; Camodeca 1997; Ohlig 2001, esp. 49–84; Montuono 2002; 2010; Rasulo 2002; Riccio 2002; De Feo and Napoli 2007; Döring 2007; Giampaola 2009: 53–54; Rasulo and Rasulo 2009; Keenan-Jones 2010; 2015; Delile et al. 2016; Ferrari and Lamagna 2016; Libertini et al. 2017; Esposito 2018; Nichols and McGregor 2019: 99–101, 219–20. **Underground Naples:** Melisurgo 1997 [1889]; Liccardo 2004; Esposito 2018. **Crypta Neapolitana:** Paoli 1768; Cocchia 1889:

CHAPTER 7 🏛 THE CULTURE OF WATER

47–61; Günther 1913: 15–20; Napoli 1967d: 455–58, 467; 1997 [1959]: 117–18; Amalfitano et al. 1990: 38–41; Amato et al. 2001. **Aqueduct tunnel inscriptions of Macrinus:** Ruggiero 1883; Cocchia 1889: 45–47; Colonna 1898: 67–79; D'Arms 2003 [1970]: 112, 210; Keenan-Jones 2010: section 5.4.3. **Nymphaea of Neapolis:** Pane 1964; Neuerburg 1965: 28, 47, 86, 137; Napoli 1967d: 454; Letzner 1990: 340, no. 126; 457, no. 334. **Cistern of Palazzo Sansevero:** Johannowsky 1961b; *Napoli antica:* 474, no. 62; Montuono 2010: 1035. **Cistern of Piazza Amedeo:** Johannowsky 1952: 142. **Fountain basin with relief of Hercules:** Colonna 1898: 448–49. **Conventional Roman baths of Neapolis:** Capasso 1893: 119–21; Spinazzola 1893; Viola 1894: 171–74; Colonna 1898: 253–55; De Franciscis 1954; Arthur and Vecchio 1985; Vecchio 1985a; *Napoli antica:* 468, no. 43; LaForgia 1985b; Amalfitano et al. 1990: 46–55, 62–67; Arthur 1994; 1999; 2002: 44–45, 156–57; Marrone 1996: 44–45; Napoli 1997 [1959]: 196–97; Zevi, *Neapolis*: 71–77; Giglio 2014–2015; 2016; Cinquantaquattro 2015: 871–73. **Water supply of Pausilypon:** Günther 1913: 126–33; Diana 1999: 30–48; Berlan-Bajard 2006: 229–31, 258, 298–300, 444–46; Varriale 2007. **Baths of Pausilypon and Marechiaro:** Günther 1913: 92–117, 177–78; Varriale 2007.

CHAPTER 8. HAVEN OF HELLENISM: GREEK CULTURE IN ROMAN NEAPOLIS

66. Greater vogue is given to the Greek mode of life at Neapolis by the people who withdraw thither from Rome for the sake of rest — I mean the class who have made their livelihood by training the young, or still others who, because of old age or infirmity, long to live in relaxation; and some Romans, too, taking delight in this way of living and observing the great number of men of the same culture as themselves sojourning there, gladly fall in love with the place and make it their permanent abode. [Strabo, *Geography* 5.4.7]

67. That city is now an abode of peace, a resting-place where the Muses dwell, and life there is free from pressing anxieties. [Silius Italicus, *Punica* 12.31–32]

As Greek identity gradually ebbed from south Italy under Roman control in the second and first centuries BCE, those few cities that were willing and able to maintain their Hellenic traditions, like Rhegion (Reggio Calabria), Taras (Tarentum, Taranto) and Elea (Velia), came to be valued for their old-world cultural roots. First among them was Neapolis, by virtue of its political and economic advantages and especially its geography. It was closer to Rome and enjoyed a ravishingly beautiful setting overlooking the dreamy blue Bay. The city remained vibrant and prosperous, but it had long ceased to exercise significant political power or influence — apart from the rare compulsion (shared by every other Italian city) to choose sides during civil wars. And it had a ready-made, if somewhat irregular, population of vacationing culture vultures: Rome's ruling class.

Neapolis traded not just in goods, but in the good life. No longer the dominant mercantile power on the Tyrrhenian sea, it nonetheless continued playing an important supporting role for Pozzuoli and Rome. Its navy had long ago given way to the Roman fleet, now at Misenum. Eradicating any vestiges of military or political relevance, it reinvented itself as a timeless Elysium where Romans of culture and discernment came to rest, to recharge, and to retire — and where gifted Greeks came to do what Greeks did best, by their own admission: exalt and cherish the mind, voice, and body. The peak of

Neapolis' influence on Rome fell within the first century CE, when emperors actively participated in her affairs. But the Hellenophile intellectualism of the Second Sophistic, arising under Hadrian, again filled the sails of traditional Greek arts, propelling them, and thus Neapolis' relevance, well into the third century CE.

Over the centuries of Roman control, a studied neutrality was sought and granted — perhaps along with the legal right of *asylia*, safe harbor for political fugitives.[1] Hospitality was the city's hallmark, and it strove to please without judgment. As Alex Hardie observes, when Neapolis sacrificed to restore Pompey's health during his serious illness there in 51/50 BCE, and held festivities upon his recovery,[2] the gesture was not an act of partisanship, though it was perceived that way. It was *soteria*, a Greek city's religious obligation to do everything in its power to relieve a crisis.[3]

When at Neapolis, even hard-bitten politicians like Sulla, who retired to a villa nearby, shed the toga and donned the Greek chlamys.[4] In 14 CE, when Augustus was on Capri, which had long been a possession of Neapolis, he distributed the *pallium* (Greek *himation*) to his Latin-speaking companions and togas to the Greeks, "stipulating that the Romans should use the Greek dress and language and the Greeks the Roman."[5] This game of dual identity was perfectly in keeping with the place. In Cicero's time only Neapolis and Velia were deemed sufficiently bicultural in Greek and "domestic" practices to provide priestesses for the syncretistic cult of Ceres–Demeter in Rome.[6] Neapolitans spoke Latin and Greek in equal measure for three centuries at least. Martti Leiwo's study of bilingualism in the city has revealed an extraordinary number of expressions, loan words, formulas, and styles in the inscriptions of one language borrowed from the other. Such was the

1. Polybios, *Histories* 6.14.8.
2. See pp. 151–52.
3. Cicero, *Tusculan Disputations* 1.86; Velleius Paterculus, *Compendium* 2.48.2; Plutarch, *Pompey* 57; Appian, *Civil Wars* 2.28.
4. Cicero, *For Rabirius Postumus* 26–27.
5. Suetonius, *Augustus* 98.3.
6. *For Balbus* 55.

CHAPTER 8 ⚱ HAVEN OF HELLENISM

epigraphic norm by the early imperial period, and it continued well into the third century CE. Many inscriptions were recorded in both languages. This was fertile soil for someone like Statius' father, who came to Neapolis from Velia to make a brilliant career as a Greek poet and rhetorician but who also wore the *toga virilis* of the Roman citizen. In the second century CE, young men of high birth and ambition were still coming to Neapolis to study declamation in both languages.[7]

Except for occasional names and linguistic oddities on inscriptions, the Campanian culture that had been so prominent in earlier centuries disappeared from the record. Long gone were the distinctions visible in tomb assemblages of earlier generations. Osco-Samnite names survived (including the *cognomen* of Statius), but the old language and institutions are absent from inscriptions of Roman Neapolis. A soft kind of ethnic cleansing was taking place, similar to the eradication of Etruscan language and institutions elsewhere. Whether to ingratiate the Romans, to compete with great cities of the east, or for some other reason, Neapolis progressively purified and distilled its Greek heritage at the expense of the Campanian. This revisionism is evident in an oration on Fortuna spuriously attributed to Dio Chrysostom (*Discourse* 64) but more likely composed by Favorinus of Arles, a noted orator of the Hadrianic period, and probably delivered to the Neapolitans. H. Lamar Crosby and Adelmo Barigazzi have noted that the speech's preoccupation with the early history of Attica and Euboea and its claim that the Euboeans sprang from the race of Athens[8] are uniquely calibrated to appeal to Neapolis' traditional connections to those two peoples. Hundreds of years of Neapolitan history in which the Campani played a critical role are swept under the rug:

> **68.** *Thus do thou wander now upon the deep,*
> *With many an evil mischance, till the day*
> *When thou dost meet with men beloved of Zeus.*
> [Homer, *Odyssey* 5.377–78]

---

7. Aulus Gellius, *Attic Nights* 9.15.
8. Cf. Velleius Paterculus, *Compendium* 1.4.1.

69. What is more, the ancient stock of your ancestors, those autochthonous and earliest Athenians who boasted the soil as mother, Demeter as nurse, and Athena as namesake and ally, Fortune first led forth from Athens to Euboea; but since if they remained there the sea could not please them nor the land support, and since also they could not endure the disgrace of what had happened, their having turned islanders instead of occupants of the mainland, Fortune made a second and better plan. For though Euboea is truly a venerable island, still who among you ever was able to endure dwelling in a rugged land, or being neighbor to narrow waters and subjected to many shifts of condition, more numerous than the shifts of current in the strait? At one moment you must needs endure the Boeotians and the stupidity of the Thebans, and the next it was the Athenians, who treated you no longer as sons, but rather as slaves. So it came to pass that the goddess took and established you here, with one of her hands contriving and directing the voyage, and with the other abundantly providing and bestowing her fruits. [*Discourse* 64.11–13]

A service sector grew up to satisfy the cultural nostalgia among the elite sojourning in the region. Teachers of high standing, like the elder Statius, prospered. Conservative Greek institutions were carefully cultivated like exotic plants in a hothouse. Magistracies with titles such as *archon, demarchos,* and the mysterious *laukelarchos* persisted, whereas other western cities had long ago resorted to Roman-style titulature such as *duumvir* and *aedilis*. The phratries of the city,[9] a holdover of a pre-Roman urban kinship structure, survived as institutions of aristocratic pretension adorning the fairly mundane Roman structure of the *collegium,* but lacking the guild-like associations with a trade. Their concern barely extended beyond matters of euergetism and patronage. They burnished their membership rolls with the names of distinguished outsiders, such as the emperor Claudius. Neapolitans developed an eccentric habit of delivering and recording public "consolation decrees," elaborate eulogies in Greek offered by the city council to mourners of deceased worthies. Attested in Asia Minor and Athens, this epigraphic tradition was barely known elsewhere

9. See pp. 65–66, 174–76, 294–95; Commentary 2.4, pp. 79–81.

CHAPTER 8 ☗ HAVEN OF HELLENISM

(Pozzuoli only, and only in Latin). Such decrees were more a result of Hellenophilia than Hellenism per se. In Kathryn Lomas' words, the dichotomy between Greek language and the Latin names that appear on most of these inscriptions "underlines the fact that this Hellenism is a cultural construct, not something which is consequent on ethnicity."

Another Neapolitan speech attributed to Dio Chrysostom honoring the boxer Melankomas fits this model — though it is a personalized funeral oration, rather than a city decree, and thus belongs to a much broader literary tradition. Delivered during the reign of Vespasian (69–79 CE) by an unknown friend of the deceased, it is soaked in familiar Greek homoerotic traditions that made a public virtue of the aestheticized male body:

> 70. When it is a question of perfect and true beauty, it would be surprising if anyone ever possessed it as this man did. For he had it in his whole body and always to the same degree, both before he reached years of manhood and afterward; and he would never have lived long enough, even if he had reached an extreme old age, to have dimmed his beauty.... And he was seen by practically all mankind. For there was no city of repute, and no nation, which he did not visit; and among all alike the same opinion of him prevailed — that they had seen no one more beautiful. [*Discourse* 29.5–6]

Dio's speech stood no chance of a hearing in the forum of Flavian Rome, but nobody would have wished it denied to Neapolis. An audience of Romans here would have found it not only appropriately Greek, but perfectly in keeping with their own, privately expressed norms. Indeed Melankomas had purportedly enjoyed the sexual patronage of no less a personage than Titus, the emperor's son and future emperor.[10] If there is a pattern to the Hellenizing institutions of Roman Neapolis, it is that they show abundant evidence of active support and participation from the highest levels of the Roman elite. With the blessing of a compliant city administration, powerful Romans enjoyed an easygoing, laissez-faire environment that public life at Rome denied them.

---

10. Themistios, *Oration* 10 139a.

THE LANDSCAPE OF THE MIND

It is perhaps no exaggeration to say that Neapolis was an ongoing project to reinvent the Greeks as Romans wished them to be. But the city was no mere theme park. In spite of everything, it retained enough autonomy, integrity, and authenticity to compete with the great Hellenic cultural centers of the East, particularly on intellectual terms. Throughout the Roman period philosophy retained an important role in the education of the aristocracy — and a distinctly Greek demeanor. Its pursuit was consciously isolated from the forum, the marketplace, and the demands of everyday life. Elevated, philosophic discourse was rarely conducted in public. It was the province of private dinner parties and strolls under shaded pergolas — in short, of upper-class male camaraderie. Its venue was traditionally the rural or suburban villa. The Greek word *schole*, from which we derive our word "school," denoted leisure — particularly of a high-minded, aristocratic kind that came to be cultivated hand-in-hand with the Roman traditions of friendship, patronage, and hospitality. Young Roman males of adequate means and promise were often packed off to Greece for their formal education or, increasingly over time, entrusted to the services of bilingual tutors closer to home. The best of these teachers, men like Musonius Rufus, Herodes Atticus, and Fronto (who once lamented that all those he loved most were in Neapolis, while he was far from it), were among the leading intellectuals of their day. Aulus Gellius[11] vividly invokes an episode in a rhetorical school in Neapolis to which he had brought the distinguished orator Antonius Julianus as a guest. (Their pleasure was wrecked by an insufferable young Turk who bungled his way through a Greek-style rhetorical problem on sheer bravado.) From the classroom there developed lifelong bonds of friendship among students and mentor, intensified by long villa sojourns full of edifying philosophical discourse — sometimes even full-blown intellectual salons.

Oratory required one kind of setting; philosophy called for quite another. The importance of the *locus amoenus*, the delightful retreat, in Roman letters cannot be overemphasized. Cicero wrote many of his philosophical treatises with astounding fluidity and speed during his

11. *Attic Nights* 11.9.15.

CHAPTER 8 ✤ HAVEN OF HELLENISM

sojourns at one or another of his country villas. Naturally enough, he often framed them as dialogues set in the villas of his fellow Roman aristocrats. Other writers of comparable prominence, like Varro and Pliny the Younger, celebrated the villa life in their writings.

It is no surprise, really, that Neapolis was the consummate *locus amoenus* for intellectual discourse in Roman Italy, for its history and geography uniquely suited its role as a conservatory of Hellenism in the West. As Carmine Pisano argues, Neapolis had an unusual degree of autonomy in cultivating this hothouse Hellenism that Romans so admired. Whereas it is now often argued that Romans artificially resuscitated and manipulated Greek culture in the East to habituate regional aristocracies to imperial control, Naples maintained an unusual degree of continuity with its past while adapting seamlessly to Roman priorities. The maritime villas of Italy's power brokers and landed elite occupied the surrounding coastline. The city was the custodian of bathing resorts, lecture halls, and art galleries. From Augustan times it hosted important pan-Mediterranean games; and, since the fall of Tarentum to Rome, it had brooked no rivals as the most significant center of Greek culture in Italy.

Everybody of consequence had acquired villas in the vicinity: Scipio the Younger, the orators Marcus Antonius and Lucius Licinius Crassus, Marius, Sulla, Hortensius, Lucullus, Marcus Crassus, Caesar, Cicero, and hundreds of others. Geologically, the region extending from Neapolis to the western end of the Bay suited maritime pleasure villas like no other. In R. T. Günther's estimation, "no spot on the Italian littoral, extensive as that littoral is, lends itself to the development of the peculiar [Roman] style of marine architecture... so well as this short strip of Campania that lies between Misenum and Pausilypon [Posillipo]." Other advantages beckoned just as insistently: quick and easy access from Rome, a gentle climate, and the superior agricultural properties of the volcanic soil. Scattered along the Bay were thermal spas catering to every class of society and easily reached by sea. This was both a vacationland for the less privileged and a private refuge for the rich.

Otium, the Romans' approximate equivalent of *schole,* hand-in-hand with learning for its own sake, became conventional occupations at the city on the Bay. Virgil, in concluding his *Georgics,* refers to his poem as *ignobile otium,* "inglorious ease," written while he lingered in "sweet Parthenope" [Commentary 8.1, pp. 333–34]. Ovid too lauds "Parthenope, born to *otium*";[12] and the phrase *docta* ("learned") *Neapolis* had resonance among later writers.[13] The great classical archaeologist Ernst Curtius characterized Roman *otium* not as simple leisure but as a sense of one's own destiny, enabled by the release from care and labor. Virgil in particular, according to Marcello Gigante, felt the benefits of *otium* most intensely in south Italy, "a human landscape where man's destiny was realized in the rediscovery of nature and the resources of the earth." Whether or not this is true, it cannot be denied that the Bay of Naples came to be known as a place of leisure by the sheer power of association.

THE VILLA CULTURE UNDER THE REPUBLIC

In the turbulent final century of the Roman Republic, alongside the positive image of the Hellenized Roman villa as a restorative pleasance, there emerged a darker paradigm of wretched excess and decadent self-indulgence. Cicero's famous nickname for the Bay of Naples, *crater ille delicatus,*[14] calls to mind a mixing bowl replete with human delights. But the adjective is slightly accusatory, tinged with intimations of frivolity, effeminacy, and decadence — while the noun connotes cultural dilution, the watering down of the strong wine of Roman values. He probably had in mind the extravagant maritime villas of plutocrats like Lucullus, and certainly the bathing establishments of Baiae, which in his day were notorious venues of sexual adventure and ostentatious vice. Neapolis itself stood somewhat apart, autonomous, subject to its own Greek laws and mores, but still tainted by association.

Lucullus, the richest Roman of his age, reportedly spent more money at his Neapolitan villa excavating a tunnel from his fishponds to the sea than on the dwelling itself [Commentary 8.2, pp. 334–35]. Varro

12. *Metamorphoses* 15.709–12.
13. Columella, *On Agriculture* 10.134; Martial, *Epigrams* 5.78.14–15.
14. *Letters to Atticus* 2.8.6.

CHAPTER 8 ☖ HAVEN OF HELLENISM

and Pliny the Elder report that some villa owners in the vicinity, like Hortensius, were consumed by their love of exotic pet fish, which they cultivated in exclusive seaside *piscinae*.[15] *Otium,* in the mind of moralists like Cicero, could easily degenerate into *luxuria*. A man too long at leisure or study was a *graeculus,* an excessively cultured "Greekling," forever preening and parsing, forever self-absorbed and self-indulgent. Like the villas, Greekness itself — even in the visitor-friendly guise cultivated by Neapolis — excited impulses among the arbiters of Roman morals that oscillated irrationally between delight and contempt.

But Neapolis banked on the correct intuition that this dichotomy of the Greek soul was largely a rhetorical fiction. Posing no risk to Rome, the city on the Bay exploited its privileged status as a Hellenistic center of learning and *amoenitas,* and the Roman aristocracy endorsed it with enthusiasm. Neapolis eagerly granted citizenship to Greek public intellectuals, such as the precocious poet Archias, who as a teenage sensation evidently received citizenship here toward the end of the second century BCE — and at several other South Italian cities:

> **71.** Italy was at that time full of Greek science and of Greek systems, and these studies were at that time cultivated in Latium with greater zeal than they now are in the same towns; and here too at Rome, on account of the tranquil state of the Republic at that time, they were far from neglected. Therefore, the people of Tarentum, and Rhegium, and Neapolis, presented him with the freedom of the city and with other gifts; and all men who were capable of judging of genius thought him deserving of their acquaintance and hospitality....
>
> In truth, as men in Greece were in the habit of giving rights of citizenship to many men of very ordinary qualifications, and endowed with no talents at all, or with very moderate ones, without any payment, it is likely, I suppose, that the Rhegians, and Locrians, and Neapolitans, and Tarentines should have been unwilling to give to this man, enjoying the highest possible reputation for genius, what they were in the habit of giving even to theatrical artists. [Cicero, *For Archias* 5, 10]

15. *On Agriculture* 3.17.5; *Natural History* 9.172.

Aristocrats who shunned public life, like Cicero's friend and correspondent L. Papirius Paetus, lived honorable lives of contemplation at Neapolis without reproof. Traveling grammarians and philosophers made sure to put the city on their itineraries and sometimes took up residence there or in nearby Cumae. All the major philosophical schools were represented. In the mid-first century BCE we see a pattern developing here: the symbiotic residency of a noted intellectual and his aristocratic host. At the pleasure of his patron, M. Pupius Piso Frugi Calpurnianus, the Peripatetic philosopher Staseas lived and taught at Neapolis.[16] Dion, an adherent of the Academy, also spent time here, probably with the assistance of a patron.[17] The influential Stoic philosopher and scholar Poseidonios of Apamea knew Neapolis.[18] But it was Epicureanism that seems to have predominated around the Bay, especially among Roman men of affairs who indulged their philosophic predilection as their busy schedules allowed. This was perhaps because the ideals of the school conformed so splendidly to the life of contemplative seclusion [Commentaries 8.1, p. 333; 8.3, pp. 335–36.] As John D'Arms says in his magisterial study of Romans on the Bay:

> The essence of the attraction lay in the ancient Greek institutions in cities such as Cumae and especially Neapolis, where *otium* carried none of the opprobrium attached to it at Rome, but was instead woven deep into the way of daily life.... [The] pace and spirit of Neapolitan life in this period are best captured by Cicero, who states that P. Sulla fled Rome in Neapolis, a city suited more for soothing men's passions than for rekindling the animosities of men in trouble. The busy pursuits at Neapolis — philosophy, poetry — were the pursuits of leisure; the quiet doctrines of Epikouros were thus here thoroughly at home.

The name *Pausilypon* ("Release of Cares," modern Posillipo), given by the wealthy equestrian Publius Vedius Pollio to his Neapolitan villa around this time,[19] has echoes of a metaphor beloved of Epicurean

16. Cicero, *On the Ends of Good and Evil* 5.8, 5.75.
17. Cicero, *Letters to His Friends* 9.26.1.
18. Athenaeus, *Deipnosophists* 9.401.1.
19. See pp. 241–43, 282, 304–5, 306–13.

CHAPTER 8 ☫ HAVEN OF HELLENISM

Fig. 8.1. Analytical reconstruction of the Villa of the Papyri at Herculaneum. Illustration by Rocío Espín Piñar.

philosophers and often applied to Neapolis itself: the calm haven of philosophy. The metaphor was employed by Philodemos of Gadara, the head of a philosophical circle based in Herculaneum just a few miles to the southeast. The works of Philodemos appear prominently among the papyrus rolls recovered from the Villa of the Papyri at Herculaneum [Fig. 8.1]. It is generally believed that Cicero's contemporary and rival L. Calpurnius Piso Caesoninus, the master of this splendid villa and a devoted Epicurean, was himself Philodemos' patron. What little we know of the philosopher's life suggests that he left his homeland in Syria to direct the school of Epicurus at Athens. After the First Mithridatic War (88–84 BCE) he went to Rome and met Piso. The latter, like many of his contemporaries, lived the schizophrenic life so splendidly captured by the Epicurean dichotomy: the world of public cares, characterized by rhetoric; and the world of private retreat attached to philosophy. Piso, it seems, provided permanent harborage for Philodemos in Herculaneum. Around the philosopher there grew up a famous salon.

Somewhere in the western suburbs of Neapolis lay the villa headquarters of another circle of Epicurean intellectuals. This venue was less opulent than Piso's, but it would resonate through the ages, for it attracted the poet Virgil and eventually became his property. References to the place appear in the *Appendix Virgiliana,* a collection of poems of miscellaneous origin and composition, most of them without any authentic connection to Virgil. Claims for the poet's authorship might best be made for two famous poems from this source that celebrate, respectively, his anticipation at coming to Neapolis to study with Siro, a Roman philosopher-gentleman whom he presents as a herald of truth in an age of charlatans; and later, his inheritance of Siro's villa, where the poet's father is destined to spend his final years [see Commentary 8.1, pp. 333–34]. Another poem from the *Appendix,* the *Ciris,* begins with a tribute to the place of its composition: a "little Athenian garden (*Cecropius hortulus*), soft-breathing, embraces me in verdant shade of flowering Wisdom." This refers obliquely to the origins of Epikouros' school in the garden of his house in Athens, now replicated (as it were) by Siro's little villa at Naples.

Siro was well known among the elite in Rome. Cicero calls him a friend.[20] Both Siro and Philodemos, Cicero says elsewhere, were "the best of men, and persons of immense learning."[21] A fragment of Philodemos from one of the Herculaneum papyri reads,

> **72.** We decided to return to Neapolis with our party to our most beloved Siro and his retreat there, and engage the philosophical [homilies]; then, on to Herculaneum to seek it with others. [*PHerc* 312]

The badly damaged fragments of another papyrus roll recovered from the Villa of the Papyri in the 1750s have been partially deciphered using multispectral scanning. One early result of this process, published in 1989, demonstrates that a tight-knit salon dominated by four names had gathered around Siro. A fragment of its concluding section addresses these four as dedicatees:

> **73.** So this is what it pleases us to say about these people, and about these calumniators in general, O Plotius and Varius, Virgil and Quintilius.[22]

20. *Letters to His Friends* 6.11.2.
21. *On the Ends of Good and Evil* 2.119.
22. *PHerc Paris* 2.21–23. Cf. *PHerc* 253 fr. 12.

CHAPTER 8 ※ HAVEN OF HELLENISM

Interpreted as a treatise on calumny by Philodemos, the document was addressed specifically to Virgil and his close literary circle: Plotius Tucca and Varius Rufus, who served as the poet's literary executors and edited the *Aeneid* for publication after his death; and Quintilius Varus, a distinguished literary critic. The poet Horace, too, although hardly a doctrinaire adherent of any philosophical school, counted all of these men among his friends and literary peers; Philodemos he revered as much as Cicero did. Especially in his *Epistles* and *Satires,* Horace colored his verse with Epicurean thinking. We may conjecture, with David Armstrong, that he was welcome at Siro's and Philodemos' salons during his occasional visits to the area.

THE CULT AND TOMB OF VIRGIL

But to posterity, all intellectual rivals and peers paled before the great Virgil. It seems that the author of the *Aeneid* made Neapolis his permanent home. The locals had their own nickname for him derived from his chastity: Parthenias ("Virgin");[23] and he may have owned additional property near Vesuvius.[24] Naples never lost sight of him or his legacy, and legends of his memory hover over the city to this very day. Inspired by his messianic Fourth Eclogue, medieval legend accorded him the powers not just of a sage, but of a mage: his poem was interpreted as a prediction of the birth of Christ. Virgil became an unofficial patron saint of medieval Naples, and to him were attributed all sorts of beneficent and apotropaic acts, both in life and in death. He was said to have enclosed a model of the city inside a glass bottle, thereby protecting the real city from harm (until the glass cracked during the invasion of Henry VI in 1194: there is always an escape clause). By affixing a bronze effigy of a fly over a city gate, he kept flies and their diseases away, and miraculously preserved meat in the markets for six weeks. He drew a fish on a stone, rendering the fisheries of Naples among the richest in the world. And like a Mediterranean St. Patrick, he banished all serpents from the city.

23. Suetonius, *Life of Virgil* 36.
24. Aulus Gellius, *Attic Nights* 6.20; Servius, *Georgics* 2.224; Servius, *Aeneid* 7.740.

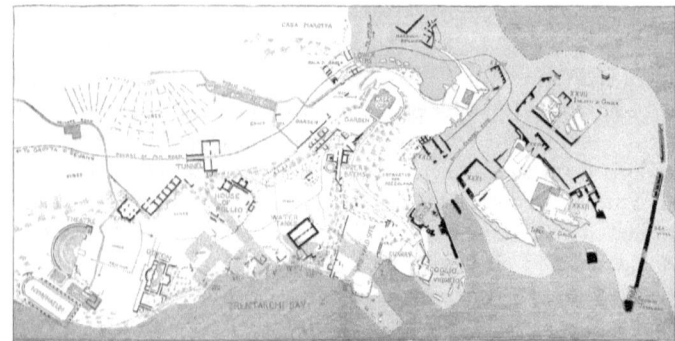

Fig. 8.2 (above). Plan of the ruins in the vicinity of Pausilypon. Günther 1913.
Fig. 8.3 (below, L). The "Scuola di Virgilio." Illustration by G. B. Natali, in Paoli 1768.
Fig. 8.4 (below, R). Interior of the so-called Tomb of Virgil. Illustration by G. B. Natali, in Paoli 1768.

The poet's association with Siro's "Little Athenian garden" led the local medieval tradition to include the entire Capo di Posillipo[25] within Virgil's haunts. At the southern point of the cape stand terraced ruins on the "Rock of Virgil" (Scoglio di Virgilio); and embedded in it at sea level, the "School of Virgil" (Scuola di Virgilio), actually a large vaulted nymphaeum and dining or reception hall that belonged to the villa of Pausilypon [Figs. 8.2, 8.3]. The rock is supposedly where the poet issued his prophecies, and his "school" where he taught the magical arts to aristocratic youth. These shores have been believed

25. See pp. 15, 16, 265–66, 307.

CHAPTER 8 ⛫ HAVEN OF HELLENISM

haunted by the ghosts of Virgil and his companions — especially the islet of Gaiola and the "Palazzo degli Spiriti," an evocative waterfront ruin just east of Pausilypon. But the foremost monument attached to the local Virgilian folklore is the Tomba di Virgilio, a vaulted, cylindrical tomb perched on a man-made precipice cut from the living tuff at the eastern entrance to the Crypta Neapolitana [Fig. 8.4; see Figs. 7.10, 7.13]. At the time of its construction, it would have been at street level.[26]

Was this really Virgil's final resting place? As the only surviving aboveground tomb in the vicinity of Naples, it may have won the distinction by default: hundreds of similar tombs would have dotted the countryside around Neapolis in antiquity. But undeniably this *could* be the tomb of Virgil, and many antiquarians, authors, and scholars, from Boccaccio to Bartolommeo Capasso, have favored the attribution. Others, like Mario Napoli and Werner Johannowsky, just as vehemently disagree.

The poet died in 19 BCE at Brindisi, on the east coast of Italy, after a trip to Greece with Augustus. According to chapter 36 of *The Life of Virgil* attributed to Suetonius, his remains were transferred to Neapolis and "enclosed in a tumulus on the Pozzuoli Road inside the second milestone." St. Jerome, following Eusebius, put the tomb "at the second milestone."[27] A two-line epitaph circulated almost immediately after Virgil's death, and may in fact have been his own: "Mantua bore me, Calabria [i.e., Brindisi] took my life, Parthenope is now my keeper. I sang of pastures, fields, and princes."[28] Thus, with admirable economy, are presented Virgil's birth, death, and three great poetic works: the *Eclogues* (pastoral), the *Georgics* (agricultural), and the *Aeneid* (epic). His tomb soon became one of the most famous monuments of Neapolis but evidently because Virgil had little or no family in the area to see to its maintenance, it fell into disrepair. A century after his death the poet Silius Italicus, whose devotion to his predecessor approached that of a cultist, gained custody of the monument. He spent his later years in Neapolis looking after it "as if it were a temple,"

---

26. On the tunnel road's changes in elevation, see pp. 266–68.
27. *Chronicle*, year 1999.
28. Suetonius, *Life of Virgil* 36.

even celebrating Virgil's birthday there.²⁹ His contemporary Statius too gained inspiration while sitting beside the monument.³⁰

In keeping with the ancient sources (more or less), the tomb lies somewhat less than two Roman miles from the western gates of Neapolis — depending on the course of the road, a matter of dispute. The structure is typical of Roman design: a cylinder rising from a half-cube, enclosing a barrel-vaulted chamber on a rectangular plan. (A similar tomb, called "The Distaff" by modern Neapolitans, once stood in the gardens of Capodimonte.) The facing of the tomb's exterior has been stripped, exposing the rough rubble-laden concrete core; but the original reticulate with small tuff-block quoins and voussoirs, characteristic of early Augustan construction in Neapolis, can still be seen inside, along with remains of plaster. It is a family columbarium, with light shafts in the concrete vault and ten (originally eleven) arched niches in the walls to accommodate cinerary urns. (The eighteenth-century etching in Figure 8.4 accurately conveys the workmanship but exaggerates the scale.) Were all these additional niches for Virgil's father and his slaves and freedmen? Sadly, no traces of the tomb's contents, decoration, or inscriptions survive. But one thing is for certain: the monument is in an extremely prominent spot, positioned beside the Crypta almost as if it were at the gates of Aeneas' underworld, and enjoying a commanding view over the city to the east. In the end, it hardly matters whether this tomb belonged to Virgil or not. Popular opinion has definitively selected it for this distinction, just as it chose a particular tomb in the Vatican to be that of St. Peter. Memory thrives on a fetish, and Virgil would surely have been satisfied with any suitable monument on which to hang his legend.

PAUSILYPON AND OTHER IMPERIAL VILLAS

Prestige, natural beauty, and proximity to Rome ensured that when the Roman Republic gave way to the Empire, some choice villas around the Bay would be absorbed into the property of the emperor and his family. Lucullus' villa at Neapolis, with its artificial tunnel and lucrative seaside fishponds, was among them. His property at Misenum, perhaps,

---

29. Pliny, *Letters* 3.7.8; Martial, *Epigrams* 11.48, 12.67.
30. *Silvae* 4.4.44–45.

CHAPTER 8 ⛫ HAVEN OF HELLENISM

was another.[31] When Augustus appropriated Capri from Neapolis, he built upon it at will; the island became the exclusive domain of the imperial family.[32] The foremost retreat on Capri, the Villa Jovis, perched atop the formidable cliffs of the island's eastern extremity, was domicile to the aged Tiberius during his self-imposed exile from Rome; but there were many others. At Baiae, an attested imperial *palatium* or *praetorium* remains unidentified, despite its sporadic identification with the modern archaeological park [See Fig. 7.2]. In the particulars, only these properties on the Bay can be assigned to the emperor with assurance. But literature and inscriptions leave no doubt that imperial holdings in the region were vast and ever-growing. As Aniello Parma has shown, the local commemoration of managers of property belonging to emperors or empresses — even a master gardener (*topiarius*) of Marcus Aurelius [emperor 161–180 CE] and the empress Faustina — hint at the inexorable expansion of imperial acquisitions around the Bay.

Also destined for imperial ownership was one of the grandest maritime villas in the vicinity: Pausilypon. This complex occupied much of the southern part of the eponymous Capo di Posillipo, today an exclusive suburb of Naples. It belonged to the notorious bon vivant Vedius Pollio, whose career spanned the age of Caesar and the first decade and a half of Augustus' rule. He died in 15 BCE. It may have been at Pausilypon that Vedius saw fit to throw errant slaves into a fishpond stocked with man-eating morays.[33] Pressed by obligations of patronage, or pure duress, Vedius bequeathed the villa and his palatial house in Rome to Augustus. Although a mere equestrian, he had received the extraordinary privilege of the governorship of Asia in 30 BCE, the year after Augustus — then still known as Octavian — had asserted his supremacy at the Battle of Aktion. At Ephesos, he established an endowment for quinquennial[34] games in honor of Augustus,

31. Tacitus, *Annals* 6.50.

32. Strabo, *Geography* 5.4.9.

33. See Commentary 8.4, pp. 336–37; Pliny, *Natural History* 9.39; Seneca, *On Clemency* 1.18.2; *On Anger* 3.40.

34. Meaning "every five years," this is the standard classical term applied to games held, in fact, *quadrennially* (every four years), because the Romans counted the years on either end of the interval.

an idea that would soon take hold in Neapolis; and he built a temple to Augustus at his hometown, Beneventum. But the souring relationship between the emperor and his subject is captured in the famous story about Vedius and his moray eels. After his death, writes Ovid, Vedius' house in Rome was "leveled to the ground, not on a charge of treason, but because its *luxuria* was deemed harmful."[35]

The maritime villa was spared, however, and absorbed into the growing network of imperial properties around Italy. As I have indicated, Pausilypon and the "imperial palace" or *praetorium* at Baiae are widely attributed to the imperial patrimony. A third likely candidate, the old villa of Lucullus at Pizzofalcone, was converted at some point into the *Castrum Lucullanum,* probably to serve as quarters for the praetorian guard during imperial visits to Neapolis [see Commentary 8.2, pp. 334–35]. All were on the northwest half of the bay and were chosen in part because of their proximity to two of the most important strategic assets in all Italy: Pozzuoli, the principal port of Rome until the late first century CE, and the single naval base on the west coast of Italy, first established by Agrippa at the Lucrine Lake north of Baiae, then moved to Misenum. We do not know if Augustus favored Pausilypon with frequent visits, but its evocative name ("End of Cares") may have inspired him to give a villa retreat on a satellite island of Capri (perhaps the islet of Monacone) the name of Apragopolis: "City without labor" or "Idletown."[36]

It has been argued with some justification that the patterns of public and private life changed profoundly and permanently during the long reign of Augustus. As power was consolidated in the hands of Caesar's heir, and as public factionalism was purged through an interfering wave pattern of stern reprisal and unforeseen clemency, the house and the villa replaced the forum as the only places where Romans of high birth, ambition, or accomplishment could safely express themselves in subversive or unconventional ways. Yet even private misbehavior had its limits under Augustus, who was seeking to transform not only the political landscape of Rome but the morals of its aristocracy. Stefano De Caro and Giuseppe Vecchio see Vedius' career trajectory

35. *Fasti* 6.641–44.
36. Suetonius, *Augustus* 98.4.

CHAPTER 8 ⚜ HAVEN OF HELLENISM

Fig. 8.5. Villa of Pausilypon, seen from the west. Photo: R. Taylor.

as a gradual loss of relevance: the man was a relic of a bygone era, when a provincial proconsulship was still an opportunity for exploitation and self-enrichment on a staggering scale, when wealth could be commuted into indulgences like pampered eels raised in extravagant seaside *piscinae*. Whether or not Augustus genuinely disapproved of Vedius' casual cruelty, he perfectly understood the species of cynical opportunists to which the man belonged, hardened and enriched by perpetual war. Augustus had been one himself.

If the vitality of public life in republican Rome withdrew to the villa in the imperial period, its retreat came with an upside: the selective urbanization of Roman villas. There is no better exemplar of this than Pausilypon [Fig. 8.5; see Figs. 6.30, 8.2]. Within its roughly nine hectares there grew up a miniature city, complete with a basilical temple or reception hall; a theater seating about fifteen hundred; an odeion for music, recitation, and lectures; a garden-stadium or monumental nymphaeum; two or more baths; and the "School of Virgil," discussed above [see Figs. 8.2, 8.3]. Even the Lucullan precedent of a rock-cut shoreside passageway was super-sized into an 800-meter tunnel, called today the "Grotta di Seiano," driven through the towering headland of the modern Parco Virgiliano to the plain of Bagnoli [Fig. 8.6; see Fig. 6.29], where its road ran north to join the Neapolis–Pozzuoli highway and probably forked west to provide

309

Fig. 8.6. Eastern end of the "Grotta di Seiano." Photo: R. Taylor.

easy access to the nearby thermal baths.[37] The compact residence block itself, or what remains of it, seems almost an afterthought to the monumental pleasure pavilions, which are scattered about on the

37. See pp. 15, 238–43.

CHAPTER 8 ⛫ HAVEN OF HELLENISM

slopes and shoreline to take full advantage of the dramatic topography and sightlines.

The theater, of tuff reticulate, possibly existed even in the later years of Vedius' life. In one respect it is truly extraordinary. Splitting the orchestra, and running axially under the missing stage building — which, being made of timber, must have minimized any obstruction to the view — is a long, narrow pool, roughly 15 x 100 Roman feet, contemporary with the seating area [see Fig. 6.30].[38] In the bottom of the pool, in parallel rows down either side, are two parallel rows of vertical sockets, supposedly for beams to support temporary wooden flooring over the water. A transverse row of mysterious rectangular pits takes the place of the stage proscenium. It is commonly believed that this pool served as an early venue for Roman water spectacle. Yet it is completely unsuited to small-scale *naumachiae*, or mock naval battles [Commentary 8.5, pp. 337–39], which required far more breadth for maneuvering boats. Most probably, the pool accommodated dramatized scenes of Nilotic pageantry. If Vedius built it, then the theater complex would have coincided with the height of Augustan Egyptomania. *Aegyptus Capta*, Captive Egypt, a common motif after Octavian's victory over Antony and Cleopatra in 31 BCE, could successfully have been advertised by a miniaturized Nile upon which to stage fanciful triumphal processions complete with approving sea gods and naked nymphs. A century and a half later, this kind of arrangement may even have inspired various examples of water spectacle architecture attributed to Hadrian, such as the aqueduct displays at Antioch known as the "theater" and "little theater,"[39] or the famous Canopus at his villa at Tivoli, a long, narrow reflecting pool on a Nilotic theme terminated by a semicircular dining and viewing pavilion. Hadrian made documented improvements at Pausilypon,[40] and surely he knew the villa well. Baiae (where Hadrian convalesced and died in 138) and Bauli, very close by, also feature semicircular water theaters, but (it seems) with fish or eel ponds as the focus of

38. See p. 241.
39. Malalas, *Chronographia*, Bonn 277–78.
40. See p. 282.

Fig. 8.7. Early-imperial marble statue of a Nereid and pistrix. *Naples, Museo Archeologico Nazionale. Photo: R. Taylor.*

attention. Were Vedius' morays as instruments of mortal spectacle less anomalous than we think?

Garden areas to either side of the pool at Pausilypon remain largely unexplored. De Caro and Vecchio speculate that a well-known statue found at the villa in 1840 featuring a Nereid riding a sea monster [Fig. 8.7] came from here. Other substantial sculptural finds from the villa may also have adorned the theater area. A magnificent classicizing bearded Dionysos was found near the "Grotta di Seiano," not far away. Unfortunately the villa has been plundered since the seventeenth century for statuary, much of which has been lost or dispersed. Enticing reports, such as the "many fine statues" extracted for the duke of Medina's villa at Mergellina, remain entirely in limbo. Of the remaining statues from the villa today in the Museo Archeologico Nazionale, the most striking are a standing African of the Antonine

CHAPTER 8 ☗ HAVEN OF HELLENISM

Fig. 8.8. Marble statues of an African fisherman (second century CE, L) and a Muse (uncertain date, R). Naples, Museo Archeologico Nazionale. Photos: R. Taylor.

period, found on the islet of Gaiola at the villa's southern extremity, and a fragmentary seated Urania that clearly was taken from one of the regions of the villa now submerged by bradyseism, for it is badly pitted by stone-boring date mussels and still has seashells cemented to its surface [Fig. 8.8].

STATIUS

Publius Papinius Statius was born at Neapolis between 45 and 50 CE and spent his childhood there before moving to Rome with his father. Though he came of age in Neronian Rome and wrote in Latin, he was raised on Greek poetry and declamation. Many of his poems embody the popular Greek genre known as *epideixis:* encomiastic poetry delivered in an elaborate and learned rhetorical style. He and his father fit the Helleno-Roman model of the traveling professional poet and rhetorician, garnering crowns and cash prizes in competitions around the Greek world. Both father and son did very well in the Sebasta, the international games hosted by Neapolis,[41] whose prizes were generous but not extravagant: 3,000 to 4,000 drachms. The father supplemented his income as a distinguished teacher of *generosa pubes* (aristocratic youth),[42] including perhaps the future emperor Domitian (81–96 CE), and was probably affiliated with gymnasia in both Rome and Neapolis. The son had the good fortune to acquire the sustained patronage of the Hellenophile Pollius Felix,[43] whose generosity relieved him of the need to teach. He also had the sporadic but uncertain support of Domitian himself.

Pollius, a wealthy benefactor of both Pozzuoli and Neapolis, had a profound financial and political stake in his native Campania. Statius proved a loyal client, praising his patron profusely and even supporting his relatives in their political careers at Neapolis. One poem of his cycle known collectively as the *Silvae*[44] applauds Julius Menecrates, Pollius' son-in-law, a man of *opes et origo:* wealth and good family. Delivered on the occasion of the birth of one of Menecrates' sons, the poem anticipates an illustrious future career for the offspring of so distinguished a man. Written in the highly wrought, obsequious style of the epideictic tradition, it is equally well suited to be delivered in the city's chambers of government or in the public odeion; in reality, this and other poems of its kind were delivered privately and published only after the fact.

Alex Hardie's study of Statius and the *Silvae* has revealed just how profoundly rooted in his hometown culture was Neapolis' most famous native son — and how thoroughly poets of his kind relied on advancing their careers at games and competitions, among which the Sebasta loomed large. Like his father, Statius established his career by aggressively pursuing the "pro circuit" of contests in

41. See pp. 211–18.
42. *Silvae* 5.3.146.
43. See pp. 9, 252; Commentary 7.4, pp. 286–87.
44. 4.8.59.

CHAPTER 8 ☗ HAVEN OF HELLENISM

performance around the eastern Mediterranean and Italy. In one of his poems, he says that his participation in the Neapolitan games has left him eager for the repose of his patron's favorite villa on the Sorrentine Peninsula:

> 74. Between the walls well-known by the Sirens' name and the cliffs burdened with Tyrrhene Minerva's temple there is a lofty villa looking out upon the Dicarchean deep, where the land is dear to Bromius and the grapes ripen on the high hills nor envy Falernian presses. Hither I came gladly across my native bay after the quinquennial festival of my home, when a lazy lull had settled on the stadium and the dust lay white as the athletes turned to Ambracian laurels [i.e., the Aktia games]. I was drawn by the eloquence of gentle Pollius and elegant Polla's youthful grace, though already eager to bend my steps where Appia, queen of long highways, takes the traveler along her familiar track. [Statius, *Silvae* 2.2.1–13]

This poem refers to the summer of 90 CE, at a time when Statius was living in Rome and actively struggling for imperial patronage. He had already competed in the Alban and Capitoline games that year, enduring a psychological roller-coaster ride: a victory in Alba Longa but a bitter loss in Rome. We do not know of any outcome at Neapolis, or even if he competed. He did not accompany the competitors to their next stop on the circuit, the Aktia Games on the Illyrian coast, but retreated, evidently with some relief, to the villa of Pollius Felix.

Around 93, after a period of illness and imperial disfavor, Statius moved back to his beloved Neapolis. His wife Claudia, whom he had met and married in Rome, still needed some persuasion to leave behind the metropolis and accompany him. In a poem addressed to Claudia, he urges her to open her heart to the place's quiet gentility and evocative grandeur. Though couched (as always) in high artifice, betraying not the slightest hint of genuine emotion, the celebration of the delights of his hometown and its incomparable setting was surely heartfelt. It is also the most sustained description of Neapolis in any ancient source.

75. Not so entirely has Vesuvius' summit and the flaming tempest of the dire mountain drained the terrified cities of their population; they stand and flourish with folk. On one side are the dwellings of Dicaearchus [Pozzuoli] founded under Phoebus' auspices and the harbor and world-welcoming strand, on the other the walls that Capys filled with Teucrian migrants, mimicking the expanses of great Rome. There also is our Parthenope, neither meager in her own folk nor lacking in settlers; to her, a traveler from overseas, Apollo himself showed a gentle soil with Dione's [Aphrodite's] dove.

This is the dwelling-place (for I was not born in barbarous Thrace or Libya) to which I am trying to bring you, tempered by mild winter and cool summer, washed by the lazy waves of an unwarlike sea. Peace secure is there, the leisure of a quiet life, tranquility undisturbed, sleep that runs its course. No madness in the Forum, no laws unsheathed for brawling. Our men are ruled only by manners and right that needs no rods.

Why should I now praise the splendid sights and adornments of the place, the temples, the spaces marked out with countless columns, the theaters, open and covered, a double mass, the quinquennial contests ranking next to the lusters of the Capitol? Why the shows, the freedom of jest, a mingling of Roman dignity and Greek license? Nor lack surrounding entertainments to give life variety. You may please to visit the seductive beach of steaming Baiae or the prophetic Sibyl's numinous abode or the hills made memorable by the Ilian oar; or shall it be the flowing vineyards of Bacchic Gaurus and the dwellings of the Teleboi, where the Pharos raises a light like the night-wandering moon, sweet to frightened sailors, where are the Surrentine hills dear to Lyaeus in no gentle mood, hills that my Pollius above all others enhnaces with his residence, and the healing pools of the Veins, and renascent Stabiae? [*Silvae* 3.5.72–105]

THE GAMES AT NEAPOLIS

Roman Neapolis made the most of its prominent role in the sisterhood of Greek cities (and, under the emperors, a handful of non-Greek cities

CHAPTER 8 ▥ HAVEN OF HELLENISM

too) that hosted games. Within that redoubtable network of institutions devoted to preserving cultural uniformity and Hellenic identity, an able and mobile athlete, author, orator, or performer could live comfortably. The support came from many sources, from private and municipal endowments to imperial patronage. In 44 BCE, the city had a chapter of the powerful guild of the Artists of Dionysos, whose stable of performers (*technitai*) Brutus sought to employ at games he was planning for Rome.[45] Augustus and Titus are known to have presided over competitions in the games. The emperor Claudius (41–54 CE) participated in them as a producer of a Greek drama in memory of his brother Germanicus.[46] A new class of competitors, the "Claudian youths," were added in his honor. He seems to have loved both the games and the carefree lifestyle at Neapolis. Here, reportedly, he "lived altogether like an ordinary citizen; for both he and his associates adopted the Greek manner of life in all respects, wearing a himation and high boots, for example, at the musical exhibitions, and a purple mantle and golden crown at the gymnastic contest."[47] And now we have new inscriptional evidence that Domitian performed in the games too, as an encomiast celebrating the life of his brother Titus [Commentary 8.6, pp. 339–40].

Claudius' successor Nero (54–68 CE), an accomplished poet, rhetorician, and musician, adored Neapolis, whose cosmopolitan residents, he felt, understood his artistic temperament and appreciated his art. And while there is no evidence that he competed in the games, he clearly viewed his debut performance at Neapolis in 64 [Commentary 8.7, pp. 340–42] as a rehearsal for his competition the following year at the games he had founded in Rome. Nero often took refuge here in his later years — certainly out of fondness for the place, but perhaps also because of the city's reputation as a political safe haven.[48] When in 67 he returned victorious from all four Panhellenic games — they had been specially scheduled to

45. Plutarch, *Brutus* 21.5–6.
46. Suetonius, *Claudius* 11.2.
47. Dio Cassius, *Roman History* 60.6.1–2.
48. See pp. 129–30, 166–67, 292.

coordinate with his visit to Greece — he chose this city as his port of reentry. Here, and also at his birthplace Antium (modern Anzio), and Rome's "birthplace," Alba Longa (each of which happened to house favorite imperial residences), and finally at Rome, he celebrated the *eiselasis*.[49] According to this ancient Greek tradition, a triumphant victor in especially prestigious ("iselastic") games was granted the honor of riding on a white horse through a fresh breach in the defensive walls of his native town. By choosing Neapolis first, was he telling the world that it was his adopted hometown? Hard to say; but soon thereafter, as trouble mounted in Rome and around the empire, Nero again took refuge here, nursing his growing delusions in the pursuit of Greek sporting events while an uprising in Gaul, led by its governor Vindex, developed relentlessly into his downfall:

> **76.** He was at Neapolis when he learned of the uprising of the Gallic provinces, on the anniversary of his mother's murder, and received the news with such calmness and indifference that he incurred the suspicion of actually rejoicing in it, because it gave him an excuse for pillaging those wealthy provinces according to the laws of war. And he at once proceeded to the gymnasium, where he watched the contests of the athletes with rapt interest. At dinner, too, when interrupted by more disturbing letters, he flared up only so far as to threaten vengeance on the rebels. In short, for eight whole days making no attempt to write a reply to anyone, none to give any commission or command, he blotted out the affair with silence. At last he was driven by numerous insulting edicts of Vindex to urge the Senate in a letter to avenge him and the state, alleging a throat trouble as his excuse for not appearing in person. Yet there was nothing which he so much resented as the taunt that he was a wretched lyre-player and that he was addressed as Ahenobarbus ["red beard," his family name] instead of Nero. [Suetonius, *Nero* 40.4–41.1]

The name Ahenobarbus may have been not only a direct repudiation of Nero's imperial titulature, but also a dig at his ancestor, L. Domitius Ahenobarbus, consul of 54 BCE. The elder Ahenobarbus' family sought asylum at Neapolis from the Caesarean party in 49

---

49. Suetonius, *Nero* 25.1.

CHAPTER 8 ⚏ HAVEN OF HELLENISM

BCE, probably (as D'Arms suggests) at the villa of the recently deceased Lucullus. Nero himself, I conjecture, would have been sojourning with his claque at the very same villa more than a century later, the *Castrum Lucullanum* attested in various documents of late antiquity [see Commentary 8.2, pp. 334–35]. "Wretched lyre players," of course, along with every other kind of skilled performer favored in Greek-style competitions, were always welcome in Neapolis. In a city that had hosted a public funeral for the poet Lucilius as early as 103 BCE[50] and had remained faithful to its performative character ever since, athletes, musicians, and dramatists erected statues and inscriptions all over the city and its suburbs celebrating their agonistic achievements [Commentaries 8.8, p. 342; 8.9, pp. 342–43].

Prominently missing from the record of Neapolis is evidence of enthusiasm for some of the sports that were most popular elsewhere in Roman Italy, those of the amphitheater. The local distaste for aestheticized killing stands in sharp contrast to the enthusiasm shown for it in neighboring urban centers such as Nola, Capua, Pompeii, and Pozzuoli (which also acquired Greek games in 138 CE, but which retained its ravenous appetite for blood sports) — even Cumae. This striking anomaly remains one of the best indicators of Neapolis' self-conscious avoidance of a purely Roman identity. Neapolitans sought out a more controlled and more genteel kind of conflict to set before the public eye — though the thoroughly Greek sports of boxing, *pankration,* and chariot racing rivaled gladiatorial combat in their claims on blood and adrenaline. A bloodless version of the Roman *naumachia* may have been introduced to the Neapolitan games too [see Commentary 8.5, pp. 337–39]. And at least once a local magistrate had tried to introduce a *venatio,* or animal-hunting spectacle, but without success.[51] Even a Roman senator or emperor would feel no compunction mingling with athletes of the Greek kind, or celebrating their beauty of mind, character, and body. Consider the oration of Dio Chrysostom honoring Melankomas, the boxer who died at

---

50. Jerome, *Chronicle,* year 1914.
51. *CIL* 10.1491.

Neapolis during the games.[52] Nobody would have accorded similar honors to gladiators or *venatores* — polluted men, men of low birth and limited expectations — however rich and popular they became. Something of the old aristocratic *erastes–eromenos* (lover–beloved) patronage structure hovered in the air of this strangely artificial, and still deeply attractive, world.

Dio Cassius informs us that the Neapolitans founded the games to honor Augustus ostensibly in gratitude for his assistance after fires and earthquakes, of which we have no other information. But the real reason, Dio says,[53] was the Neapolitan love of Greek traditions. The games' official title was *Italika Rhomaia Sebasta Isolympia:* "Italian Roman Augustan Isolympics." Until Domitian established his Capitoline Games in Rome in 86 CE, they were the most important and prestigious games in the West. Yet despite the "Roman" epithet, their structure and inspiration were entirely Hellenic. The contestants were mostly from Greek cities, and the language of record was a correct and canonical Attic Greek. In the East, only the four major Panhellenic games (Olympic, Isthmian, Nemean, Pythian) ranked incontestably higher. The term *Isolympia,* "equal to the Olympics," reflects no special pleading for status. It is a technical term guaranteeing that the rules, eligibility, and prizes corresponded to those of the most venerable games in the Greek world — but only insofar as athletic and equestrian events are concerned. The Olympic and Nemean games excluded competitions in performance — drama, music, composition, and recitation of poetry — all of which were important events in the Sebasta. The other Panhellenic games were more inclusive, and probably served as models for the Neapolitan performance events.

The most important surviving document relating to the Sebasta was found not at Naples, but at Olympia, and published in 1896: a fragmentary inscription probably set up by the city council of Neapolis.[54] Much of what we know of the games is derived from

52. See pp. 295–96, 322, 329.
53. *Roman History* 55.10.9.
54. *SEG* 14.349 = 22.344 = 37.356 = 48.543.

CHAPTER 8 🏛 HAVEN OF HELLENISM

Fig. 8.9. Marble agonistic inscription of Hermagoras. Naples, Museo Archeologico Nazionale. Photo: R. Taylor.

it: divisions of competitors (teenagers and adults); rules and cost-of-living stipends for participants; the functions of overseeing officials. Prizes in the athletic and equestrian events were rigidly traditional: crowns of wheat, nothing more. The performance events, on the other hand, offered cash prizes. Cash was less prestigious than crowns, but obviously it provided the means for athletes and performers to earn a living. The monument of the wrestler Hermagoras in [Fig. 8.9, see Commentary 8.8, p. 342] informs us that he won 127 cash prizes during his career, as compared to 29 crowns. He chose to emphasize the crowns. Certain events for adolescents had special classes open exclusively to citizens of the host city.

Over the centuries, many inscriptions relating to the Sebasta have been found in Naples, mostly catalogs listing victors and their events. The majority of these were found in the vicinity of Piazza Nicola Amore, now the site of the Duomo Metropolitana station. As will be discussed below, here a vast new trove of Sebasta inscriptions was found in 2004. From all this evidence we can compile a roster of athletic events that was thoroughly Olympian in character: wrestling, boxing, *pankration* (a combination of wrestling and boxing), *stadion* footrace, *diaulos* (double-length footrace), pentathlon, a race in armor, torch race, and a contest for armed charioteers. Equestrian events included two- and four-horse chariot races and races on horseback. The numerous performance events mostly fell within the categories of drama, instrumental music, poetry sung with instrumental accompaniment, and poetic composition or recitation. Choral dance and pantomime were introduced at some point too, probably in the late first or early second century CE.[55] The presiding officer at the games was known as the agonothete. The emperor Domitian held the title five times; his older brother Titus, three. Titus had a personal motive, perhaps, for frequenting the Neapolitan games: his erotic attachment to Melankomas, the divinely handsome pugilist.

The Neapolitan games admitted female competitors both in athletics and in performance. As victors, they are much more sparsely attested than the males — a clear indicator that both sexes competed together, even in athletic events. (The evident exception is the special class of contests reserved for daughters of magistrates of the city.) Of the roughly 170 competitors identified in the newly discovered inscriptions, two females stand out: Flavia Thalassia of Ephesos, and Aemilia Rectina (hometown unknown). Both won crowns in footraces, events in which able females — particularly in the category for youths — would have been competitive. Whether the Neapolitans were so traditional as to insist on nudity among the competitors remains an interesting but open question.

ROOTS OF THE GAMES

The Sebasta were not the first cyclical competition to be held in Neapolis.[56] The Hellenistic poet Lykophron, writing in the manner of a prophecy foretelling the greatness of Italy and her colonies on the Tyrrhenian coast, writes,

> **77.** The residents there [at Neapolis] shall build a monument to the girl, wailing for Parthenope with libations and *thysthla;* and each year they shall glorify the bird-goddess. [*Alexandra* 220–22, trans. Taylor]

> **78.** And there [at Neapolis] one day in honor of the first goddess of the sisterhood shall the ruler of all the navy of Mopsops [i.e., of Athens] array for his mariners a torch race, in obedience to an oracle, which one day the people of the Neapolitans shall celebrate. [733–36]

---

55. Lucian, *The Dance* 32; *CIL* 6.10114.
56. See pp. 44–45, 57, 96, 101, 129, 186–87, 211–12, 217.

CHAPTER 8 ⛫ HAVEN OF HELLENISM

The obscure Homeric word *thysthla* refers to the gear of ecstatic cults, perhaps in a funerary context; certainly torches can be understood here. One of Tzetzes' scholia of Lykophron clarifies the matter by citing the historian Timaios:

> 79. When Diotimos, the Athenian navarch, was approaching Neapolis, he sacrificed to Parthenope to fulfill an oracle. Having established a torch race — the Neapolitans put on this torch contest and race every year — Diotimos entered Neapolis, at the time when as an Athenian admiral he was at war with the Sikels. [Scholium of verse 733, trans. Taylor]

We may reasonably follow Julius Beloch and most subsequent interpreters in concluding that the race was dedicated to Parthenope. Strabo,[57] writing after Augustus' death, seems to associate the Sebasta with the oracle that spurred Diotimos to found the games. However, some connection to Demeter, one of the city's "parent gods,"[58] is also possible. The victors' crowns were made of midsummer wheat — the symbol *par excellence* of the goddess of the harvest. In the late Republic, as we have already seen in this chapter, daughters of Neapolis were habitually chosen as her priestesses in Rome. The games honored other gods too. In fact, in the high Empire, one lost inscription seems to have cited the master of ceremonies *(archon)* of "the quinquennial honorary event [---] of Aphrodite,"[59] an ambiguous phrase that may encompass the entire games[60] or (more likely) simply one aspect of it. Under the second scenario, we may envision the games partitioned into divisions, each dominated by a cult and overseen by an honorific archon.

But the cultic roots of the games went back to Parthenope. Like most torch ceremonies, and many games, these were funerary and expiatory in origin.[61] Torch events may even enact, distantly, a tradition of human

57. *Geography* 5.4.7. See Reading 14, p. 39.
58. See p. 202.
59. *IG* 14.745 = Miranda 1990–1995 no. 33.
60. For another broad connection of the Sebasta to Aphrodite–Venus, see Commentary 8.5, pp. 337–39.
61. See pp. 44–45, 57.

Fig. 8.10. Impression from a gem once in the British Museum; now presumed lost. From F. Imhoof-Blumer, Tier- und Pflanzenbilder auf Münzen und Gemmen des klassischen Altertums. Leipzig 1889.

sacrifice to gods of the dead.[62] Those at Neapolis were formerly held yearly, presumably to commemorate the dead Siren's blessed arrival on the shores of the future city. A Hellenistic gem, once in the British Museum but now presumed lost, seems to cement the deity's relationship to the event [Fig. 8.10]. A winged, bird-legged siren is shown carrying a wreath and torch in her right hand — surely representing the torch races in her honor, as Roy Merle Peterson recognized long ago — and holding aloft a wine amphora. The vessel's Rhodian morphology — long neck and flared, angular handles — dates the gem to sometime from the third to the first century BCE, when Rhodian wine was sought around the Mediterranean. Peterson may be right to suggest that an amphora of wine served for a prize, as in the famous Panathenaic games at Athens. It is also feasible, as Lydia Pugliese argues,[63] that a distinctive subset of the wine amphoras produced at Neapolis in the late fourth and third centuries BCE, stamped with the symbol of a victor's crown, were connected to this signature event and perhaps sanctioned by its cult.

The torch race would have taken place mostly outside the walls of Neapolis and probably began or ended at the tomb of Parthenope. Beloch suggests that in every fourth year the contest was expanded, like the Greater Panathenaic Festival, into more comprehensive games, which under Augustus were reformulated into the Sebasta. Significantly, Timaios' passage above mentions both a torch "contest" and a torch "race." It would seem that even in his day (the late fourth and early

62. Macrobius, Saturnalia 1.7.31.
63. See pp. 129–30, 217.

CHAPTER 8 ⛫ HAVEN OF HELLENISM

third centuries BCE, when the crown amphoras may already have been in production) a somewhat diversified program existed, though nothing can be said about the distinction between the two. Variability was certainly possible in torch events, which typically involved transmitting a flame between altars, or between a shrine or tomb and an altar, in the dark of night. Some were relay races, some not; one of the five known torch races at Athens, that of Artemis Bendaia, was run on horseback.

Apart from Athens, other models were at hand: Isthmia, for example, whose funeral games reputedly were founded by Sisyphos, legendary king of Corinth, to honor the dead Melikertes–Palaimon.[64] This youth had drowned tragically, and his body had been carried to Isthmian shores by a dolphin: echoes of Parthenope, who washed ashore at the future site of Neapolis. Theseus, the Athenian king, was credited with developing the Isthmian Games into one of the four great Panhellenic contests.[65] These would eventually include — like Neapolis, but unlike Olympia — competitions in performing arts. In the Roman period, nighttime sacrificial rituals in a subterranean chamber at Palaimon's temple (which may have been near his still unidentified tomb) occurred during the games; hundreds of lamps have been found at the site. Similar rituals surely were taking place, perhaps at Palaimon's tomb, in preceding centuries too. Were torches also involved? They would not have left any identifiable traces, unfortunately.

Writing shortly before or after Augustus' death, but certainly after the founding of the Sebasta, Strabo adds a few additional details:

> 80. A monument of Parthenope, one of the Sirens, is pointed out in Neapolis, and in accordance with an oracle an athletic contest is celebrated there.... And very many traces of Greek culture are preserved there — gymnasia, ephebeia, phratries, and Greek names of things, although the people are Romans. And at the present time a sacred contest is celebrated among them every four years, in performing arts as well as athletics; it lasts for several days, and vies with the most famous of those celebrated in Greece. [*Geography* 5.4.7]

64. See pp. 44–46.
65. Apollodoros, *Voyage of the Argo* 3.4.3; Pausanias, *Description of Greece* 2.1.3, 2.2.1; Plutarch, *Theseus* 25.4–5.

Strabo's language is vague in the extreme. He does not definitively associate any games with Parthenope; we rely on Lykophron, cited above, for that information. We do not know whether the first "athletic contest" he mentions was distinct from the second "sacred contest" or whether the latter, inclusive of both athletics and performance, encompassed the former. Conceivably the literary, dramatic, and musical component of the Neapolitan games arrived from Athens long before, with Diotimos. Certainly Athens was the first major Greek city to gain fame for its competitions in performance, especially drama. We should note, additionally, that according to the technical language of Greek games, these were the component that was *not* "sacred" *(hiera)*, because the participants competed for cash prizes *(thematika)*.

With good reason, it has long been conjectured that the games honoring Augustus were a continuation or resuscitation of the old Athenian-style torch races. Such an evolution would hardly have been unique. The Aktia Games, for example, instituted at Nikopolis for Augustus in commemoration of his Illyrian victory over Antony and Cleopatra, reconstituted an older local festival. Until recently the idea of continuity in the Neapolitan games was founded entirely on the circumstantial evidence we have already reviewed. In 2004, however, over a thousand marble fragments of Greek inscriptions pertaining to the Sebasta were discovered fallen from the wall of the "gymnasium" portico — what I call the Wall of Fame[66] — which lies parallel to the Kaisareion. Dating mostly to the late 90s, the inscriptions catalogue the names of victors in the games and their events. (Alas, Statius makes no appearance.)

One of the events listed is "*lampas* [torch] for Augustus." It is our first direct confirmation that the Sebasta included a torch race. The fact that *lampas* has a qualifier, "for Augustus," may suggest that there were others too, including perhaps one for Parthenope and other heroes or gods. This discovery, in turn, could confirm an idea introduced more than a century ago by Bartolommeo Capasso. A letter of Gregory the Great refers to a "Street [or Neighborhood] of the

---

66. See pp. 211–18; Commentaries 8.8 and 8.9, pp. 342–43.

CHAPTER 8 ☗ HAVEN OF HELLENISM

Torch" in the *regio Herculensis*.[67] Was this street the Roman venue of the torch races introduced centuries earlier by the Athenians? The street known today as Via [Egiziaca a] Forcella, whose name is linked in medieval sources to the *regio Herculensis*,[68] lies only 400 meters northeast of the newly discovered inscriptions. The ancient Street of the Torch, then, was probably in the vicinity and may have derived its name from the route of a torch race originating or culminating in the athletic district.

Obviously the Sebasta were a much larger enterprise than anything that preceded them at Neapolis, and the new priorities of imperial patronage inevitably overwhelmed the old ones of the Greek city-state. For the purpose of continuity, it sufficed simply to absorb the torch event(s) into these games and to accord them a special commemorative status that matched the solemnity of the original. Funeral games often honored the cults of founding heroes, whose tombs or memorials would have served as important venues in the events. Parthenope was a "founder" of the city de facto, if only in death. Her tomb was still a famous monument in Augustus' time, as Strabo indicates. But other founders, mythic or genuine, who have fallen from the record would also have been given their due. As I have already suggested,[69] there was probably a "finder" of her body (Phaleros, perhaps?) to fit the founding mytheme, just as the drowned Palaimon had Sisyphos, his "finder" at Isthmia. We forget at our peril that the entire foundation myth of Parthenope, with its eponymous heroes, leaders, and ancestors, is lost. It was vividly present to the residents of the Roman city. Indeed three of the city's known phratries, still active in Roman times, were named for heroes who mean nothing to us.[70]

Let us return to an episode on Capri in the final chapter of Augustus' life. We have already referred to this event, recorded by Suetonius. In the summer of 14 CE, the aged Augustus made his final sojourn on the island. Here he attended the exercises of local

---

67. *Registrum epistularum* 3.58.
68. See Commentarty 5.3, pp. 177–78.
69. See pp. 44–45.
70. See Commentary 2.4, pp. 79–81.

ephebes, inviting them to a dinner party to participate in a generally celebratory and light-hearted spirit:

> **81.** An island [Monacone?] near Capri he called Apragopolis ["Idletown"],... from the idleness of those who used to withdraw to it from his retinue. But one of his favorites, named Masgaba, he was in the habit of calling Ktistes ["Founder"], as if he were the first to found a settlement on the island. When he had noticed from his dining room that the tomb of this Masgaba, who had died the year before, was visited by a large crowd with many torches, he recited aloud a verse he had extemporized [in Greek]: "I am looking on a founder's tomb aglow with fire." Then, turning to Thrasyllus,... who was reclining opposite him and knew nothing about the matter, he asked of what poet he thought the line to be. As he hesitated to reply, Augustus added another verse: "Do you see the honor paid to Masgaba with torches?" and asked his opinion of this one also. When Thrasyllus could only reply that the lines were very good, whoever the author of them might be, he set up a laugh and fell to cracking jokes. [Suetonius, *Augustus* 98.4, trans. McDaniel]

Immediately after this event, Augustus sailed over to Neapolis to attend the Sebasta. Days later, on August 19, he died.

The significance for us of this curious episode is the likelihood that it unfolded during the games, or their preliminary ceremonies. The Sebasta were held in early August, the month named after their dedicatee. Capri, recently appropriated by the emperor, had been a possession of Neapolis for centuries, and its permanent residents would have absorbed the city's traditions and belonged to its citizenry. Yet the entire episode has an element of satire about it: the African freedman who is named "founder" of "Idletown"; the jesting verses, uttered at a banquet from which Augustus has banished pretension and seriousness. Perhaps, as Walton McDaniel suggests, even the torchbearers at the tomb acted in jest. More likely, they were carrying out a longstanding tradition while also hoping to please the emperor, who had favored Masgaba. Whatever the motivation of the principals in this little drama, they are following a cultural pattern; a satire too must have a model. That model was probably the Sebasta themselves or their predecessor.

CHAPTER 8 ⛫ HAVEN OF HELLENISM

I therefore conjecture that at the outset, citizens of Neapolis and its territory gathered with torches at the tombs of the local founding heroes, including (of course) Parthenope. Perhaps a torch representing each heroön was featured in the original race. In later years the Sebasta encompassed various categories of literary recitation, including encomia praising Augustus and other deified emperors [see Commentary 8.8, p. 342]. But during Augustus' lifetime and earlier, encomium competitions would also have been directed at Neapolis' founding heroes, genuine and mythic. We might even take as an example of the genre Dio's Neapolitan encomium of the dead Melankomas, though the boxer had no special ties to Neapolis. The point of Augustus' puzzling versification, it seems, is that it is imitating — in a light-hearted way — the verses of encomiasts competing at the games, singing the praises of bygone heroes.

The military or athletic exercises of ephebes on Capri, which Augustus attended just before the Sebasta, may have been part of the run-up to the games, just like the torch ceremonies. Ephebic training was an old Greek tradition that had become quaint enough in Italy to require explanation from Suetonius: "there was still a goodly number [of ephebes] at Capri according to the ancient usage."[71] If these local youths had retained their political affiliation with Neapolis, they may have been training for competition in the special categories of the Sebasta confined to the citizenry of the city, which are known to have existed later. This feature is more characteristic of Attic than of Panhellenic games. The Athenian torch races were local affairs, open only to the tribes of Attica and specifically the ephebes of that district.[72] I will suggest that ephebes also contested in open-water *naumachiae*, perhaps at the opening or closing ceremonies [see Commentary 8.5, pp. 337–39]. But the fact remains that there is almost no hard information about the Neapolitan games either before they were transformed under Augustus, or during his lifetime. Most of our evidence for the games comes from later inscriptions.

The Sebasta continued into the late third century CE, perhaps even the early fourth. With the ascendancy of Christianity under

---

71. *Augustus* 98.3.
72. *IG* 2^2 1006 l. 54; 2^2 2130 (relief image); 2^2 2998.

Constantine and his successors emperor worship died, and the enthusiasm for athletics and the focus on the human body in general waned. Chariot racing and epideictic poetry would continue to command fervent interest in great cities of the Byzantine realm, but the old Greek gymnastic events faded from the scene.

VISUAL ARTS

The games — especially in a cosmopolitan city like Neapolis — were bound to stimulate other cultural categories. One may imagine that the kinds of convergences at the Sebasta, occasioned by an urbane local population encountering an influx of visiting worthies, would satisfy every poet, philosopher, rhetorician, physician, grammarian, and connoisseur more than anything to be found at the small-town Panhellenic sites, for all their undeniable prestige. It was on the occasion of the Sebasta that the first-person protagonist of Philostratos' *Images* was drawn to the city and encountered a spectacular picture gallery in one of its suburban villas. The gallery would serve as the setting for his *ekphrasis* of paintings on mythological themes. We may take it to have existed at Neapolis during Philostratos' own career, centered in the early third century CE:

> 82. It was the time of the public games at Neapolis, a city in Italy settled by men of the Greek race and people of culture, and therefore Greek in their enthusiasm for discussion. And as I did not wish to deliver my addresses in public, the young men kept coming to the house of my host and importuning me. I was lodging outside the walls in a suburb facing the sea, where there was a portico built on four, I think, or possibly five terraces, open to the west wind and looking out on the Tyrrhenian Sea. It was resplendent with all the marbles favored by luxury, but it was particularly splendid by reason of the panel-paintings set in the walls, paintings which I thought had been collected with real judgment, for they exhibited the skill of very many painters. [*Images* 1.pr.]

Such a sloping, westward exposure on the suburban waterfront conforms to only two locales in reality: Parthenope (i.e., the quondam villa of Lucullus) and Pausilypon. Since the former was probably an imperial *praetorium*, the latter is the likeliest location. I have already

CHAPTER 8 ⛪ HAVEN OF HELLENISM

Fig. 8.11 (above). Room 14 at the Villa of Oplontis near Pompeii, featuring elaborate Second-Style architectural frescos. Photo: R. Taylor.
Fig. 8.12 (below). Room 15 at the Villa of Oplontis. Photo: R. Taylor.

suggested that this grand villa served as a quasi-public performing arts center catering to the lively thermal bathing scene in the far western suburbs. A multiroom gallery of the sort Philostratus describes could

331

have perched along the now-eroded slopes west or south of the theater [see Fig. 6.30, 8.2].[73]

There can be little doubt, given the wealth and education of the Romans who vacationed on the Bay, that fine art immigrated in quantity. One famous painting, at least, is attested at Neapolis: a portrait of an old woman by Iaia of Kyzikos, a female artist who worked in Rome in the late Republic.[74] While Neapolis was bound to be full of collectors and connoisseurs, there is little evidence in the literary sources of major production centers or schools. However, the city is often mentioned as the likely home of Pasiteles, a famous neo-Attic sculptor active at the end of the Republic; yet Pliny says only that he was born "on Italy's Greek coast."[75] The random nature of salvage archaeology in the city can tell us little about such matters, especially with regard to master paintings on wooden panels, now invariably lost. Only the walls and mosaics of Pompeii, Herculaneum, and the Vesuvian villas can give us some approximation of what must have been encountered at Neapolis on a grand scale [Figs. 8.11; 8.12].

Much sculpture in the Roman era was mass-produced, and the games — which generated an insatiable appetite for commemorative statues and reliefs — would have ensured a healthy trade in bronze and marble portraits. Jean-Paul Morel has remarked on the extraordinary number of copies around the Bay of famous Greek originals by Polykleitos, Myron, Pheidias, and others. It reflects a typically eclectic taste, demonstrating "plus de savoir-faire que de créativité." A sculpture workshop specializing in mass-production of such copies has been found at Baiae, and a district of *marmorarii*, sculptors in marble, is known at Pozzuoli, as is the name of one local sculptor of the Augustan period, Karos. But so far, nothing of the kind has surfaced at Neapolis.

---

73. See pp. 312–13.
74. Pliny, *Natural History* 35.147.
75. *Natural History* 36.40.

CHAPTER 8 ☥ HAVEN OF HELLENISM

Commentary 8.1: Virgil's Epicurean Awakening

With the publication around 55 BCE of Lucretius' brilliant philosophical poem *On the Nature of Things*, the allure of Epicurean philosophy washed like a wave over the intelligentsia of the late Roman Republic. Sickened by the endless strife of civil war, men of acute sensibility found much to love in this Greek rationalism, which despised politics, rejected religiosity, and idealized the life of secluded contemplation. Virgil discovered the intoxicating Epicurean philosophy of Siro and Philodemos sometime in his late twenties or early thirties, probably after completing his famous collection of poems known as the *Eclogues* or *Bucolics* in 39 BCE. From this time onward their hometown, Neapolis, would be his own. In his next great project, the *Georgics*, he concluded with the famous lines:

83. Thus I sang of the care of fields, of cattle, and of trees, while great Caesar thundered in war by deep Euphrates and gave a victor's laws unto willing nations, and essayed the path to heaven. In those days I, Virgil, was nursed of sweet Parthenope, and rejoiced in the arts of inglorious ease [*ignobile otium*] — I who dallied with shepherds' songs, and, in youth's boldness, sang, Tityrus, of you under your spreading beech's covert. [4.559-66]

A compendium of pseudo-Virgilian epigrams known as the *Catalepton* includes two references to Virgil's happy role as a participant, if not a disciple, in the philosophical circle sometimes known as the Garden of Naples. Even if we can no longer ascribe these poems directly to the master, his biography was certainly foremost in the mind of his pseudepigrapher. Here the bliss that Virgil seeks is tinged with regret: he evidently feels that pure philosophy does not comport well with poetry, despite his teacher's skill in both genres. Poetry is a divine madness, and madness has no place in rational thought. Therefore he professes, if only temporarily, and probably insincerely, to banish the Muses from his presence:

84. Away with you, begone, you empty paint-pots of rhetoricians, verbiage inflated with an un-Attic screeching!

333

And you, too, Selius, and Tarquitius, and Varro, a tribe of pedants dripping with fat, begone, you empty cymbals of our youth! Even you, Sextus Sabinus, heart of my heart, farewell! Now fare ye well, my lovely chums!

We are spreading sail for blissful havens, in quest of noble Siro's learned lore, and will free our life from all worries. Away with you, ye Muses! Yes, away even with you, sweet Muses! For let us confess the truth — you have been sweet. Yet even so, revisit my pages, but come modestly and not too often! [*Appendix Virgiliana, Catalepton* 5]

85. O little villa, once Siro's, and you, poor little farm — yet to such an owner you were wealth — to you, should I hear anything ill of my homeland, I entrust myself and with me these folk, whom I have always loved, my father foremost. You must now be to him what Mantua had been and before that Cremona [i.e., his home]." [*Appendix Virgiliana, Catalepton* 8]

Commentary 8.2: *Lucullus' Neapolitan Villa*

Lucullus' villa has not been positively identified, but it was probably on the promontory of Pizzofalcone, which retained the name Luculliano at least until the seventeenth century. The villa seems to have passed from Lucullus' family into imperial hands. Part of it became a military base, presumably for the praetorian guard, known as the *Castrum Lucullanum*. One can imagine Nero's entourage of praetorians who attended his performance in 64 being quartered here. It was here, too, that the last Roman emperor of the West, Romulus Augustulus, was confined, "in the Lucullan fortress *(castellum)* of Campania," in 476 CE.[76] In the 490s the *castrum* became a monastery, which in the time of Boethius was one of the most important centers for preserving and disseminating Greek texts in the West. This may have been where the antipope Laurentius spent his retirement in the first years of the sixth century.

During Lucullus' lifetime, his villa was most notorious for its seaside fishponds, which required some extravagant

---

76. Marcellinus Comes, *Chronicle*, year 476.

CHAPTER 8 ⛫ HAVEN OF HELLENISM

engineering to mix sweet water from the shore, probably delivered by aqueduct, with salty water introduced from the sea. Nothing remains of these works today.

86. As for Lucullus, who was otherwise a great man, he was the first to set the example for our present lavish extravagance in building, in banquets, and in furnishings. Because of the massive piles which he built in the sea, and of his letting the sea in upon the land by digging through mountains, Pompey used to call him, and not without point, Xerxes in a toga. [Velleius Paterculus, *Compendium* 2.33.4]

87. In the same period [as Sergius Orata's invention of oyster farms] the elder Licinius Murena invented fishponds for all the other sorts of fish, and his example was subsequently followed by the celebrated record of Philippus and Hortensius. Lucullus had built a channel that cost more than a country house, by actually cutting through a mountain near Neapolis and letting in the sea....After his decease the fish from this pond sold for 4,000,000 sesterces. [Pliny the Elder, *Natural History* 9.170]

Commentary 8.3: An Epicurean Funerary Epigram

Epigrams inscribed on tombs of the Roman period usually convey well-worn, conventional sentiments, and in Neapolis they tend to be written in Greek. But one, discovered in 1685 near the Chiesa della Sanità, is quite different. Composed in the first century BCE, it is written in Latin, though influenced by Greek, and — quite unusually — it celebrates the deceased man's Epicurean philosophy.

88. STALLIUS GAIUS HAURANUS KEEPS WATCH OVER THIS PLACE, THANKS TO THE EPICUREAN CHORUS, ALIVE WITH JOY [*GAUDIVIGENS*]. [*CIL* 10.2971]

One wonders what the "chorus" was (a *collegium* or club, which paid for the monument?), and why it is described using an adjective that appears nowhere else in extant Latin. It would seem to suggest that the Epicurean craze of the late Republic trickled down from the aristocracy to ordinary Neapolitans, some of whom formed their own intellectual or even devotional circles. Just possibly, there is more than meets the eye here. Stallius, as his full name indicates, came from the Hauran in Coele Syria. Is it mere coincidence that Philodemos himself, the leading light of the Epicurean school in the region of Neapolis, came from Gadara, in the same region? Conceivably, the great philosopher attracted to Italy an entourage of followers from his native region, perhaps by way of Athens, where Philodemos learned his craft — and where two Stallii are attested as architects in the mid-first century BCE.[77]

Commentary 8.4: *Vedius Pollio*

89. This same year Vedius Pollio died, a man who in general had done nothing deserving of remembrance, as he was sprung from freedmen, belonged to the knights, and performed no brilliant deeds; but he had become very famous for his wealth and for his cruelty, so that he has even gained a place in history. Most of the things he did it would be wearisome to relate, but I may mention that he kept in reservoirs huge eels that had been trained to eat men, and he was accustomed to throw to them such of his slaves as he desired to put to death. Once, when he was entertaining Augustus, his cup-bearer broke a crystal goblet, and without regard for his guest, Pollio ordered the fellow to be thrown to the eels. Hereupon the slave fell on his knees before Augustus and supplicated to him, and Augustus at first tried to persuade Pollio not to commit so monstrous a deed. Then, when Pollio paid no heed to him, the emperor said, 'Bring all the rest of the drinking vessels which are of like sort or any others of value that you possess, in order that I may use them,' and when they were brought, he ordered them to be broken. When Pollio saw this, he was vexed, of course; but since he was no longer angry over the one goblet, considering the great number of the others that were ruined, and, on the other hand, could not punish his servant for what Augustus also had done, he held his peace, though much against his will. This is the sort of person Pollio was, who died at this time. Among his many bequests to many persons he left to Augustus a good share of his estate

77. *IG* 2/3² 3426.

together with Pausilypon, the place between Neapolis and Puteoli [Pozzuoli], with instructions that some public work of great beauty should be erected there. Augustus razed Pollio's house to the ground, on the pretext of preparing for the erection of the other structure, but really with the purpose that Pollio should have no monument in the city; and he built a colonnade, inscribing on it the name, not of Pollio, but of Livia. [Dio Cassius, *Roman History* 54.23.1–6]

Commentary 8.5: A View of the Sebasta from Late Antiquity

In the late fourth century CE, the distinguished intellectual Ausonius wrote the *Moselle*, a paean to the Moselle River on the German frontier. In one particularly elaborate conceit he compares the good-natured jostling of youthful boatmen on the river to a rather more spectacular event that had once unfolded on the Bay of Naples. The setting would have been immediately apparent to the educated reader: Liber (Dionysos) was worshiped all around the region of Mt. Vesuvius, thanks to the fine vintages produced on its slopes. Gaurus (Monte Barbaro, near Cumae) stands in for the entire Campi Phlegraei west of Neapolis:

90. Liber peers down at games such as this on the Cumaean swell when he walks along the cultivated ridges of sulfurous Gaurus and the vineyards of steaming Vesuvius; and when Venus, glad at Augustus' Actian triumph, orders lascivious Cupids to enact the kind of savage battles the fleets of the Nile and Latian triremes fought beneath the citadels of Apollonian Leukas; or when Euboean skiffs reenact the dangers of Mylae in the war with Pompey across resounding Avernus; or when the sky-blue sea under a verdant sheen reflects the harmless collisions of prows and the jesting battles of a *naumachia* such as was seen at Sicilian Peloros. [208–19, trans. Taylor]

This passage is rarely cited with reference to the Sebasta, yet it expressly refers to *ludi* (games) in the Bay of Naples, which, Ausonius adds, were held in honor of Augustus and his naval triumph at Aktion, a site that had its own games and naval contest.[78] The *naumachia* (mock naval battle) was a

78. Stephen of Byzantion, *On Cities*, s.v. *"Aktion."*

distinctly Roman spectacle initiated by Julius Caesar and his adopted son Augustus. In Rome, *naumachiae* were genuinely violent affairs in which convicts or captives were teamed off in life-or-death struggles staged in enormous artificial pools. Neapolis had its own natural pool, the bay — complete with spectator seating on the shore and hillsides.

Ausonius, far removed from the events in time and space, seems to believe the *naumachiae* of Neapolis were nothing more than "harmless collisions." We cannot confirm that for a fact. Nor should we presume the "lascivious Cupids" manning the boats were mere children. Like their kind in Rome, the combatants may have been desperate men in costume, playing their game in dead earnest. But Neapolis' purely Greek-style games would not have countenanced blood sport. These were surely like the coastal *naumachiai* of Attica attested in second-century-CE inscriptions, bloodless tactical maneuverings in which teams of local ephebes contended for prizes. These too reenacted a famous naval victory: the Battle of Salamis, when Athenians and their allies defeated the Persians at the nearby island of that name.

Why would the Neapolitan youths have been identified as Cupids in particular? Just to add a whimsical touch inspired by Roman art, which often sentimentalized violent pursuits like hunting, chariot racing, and *naumachiae* by transmuting the participants into winged tots, charming misfits in the arts of war and sport? Horace playfully invokes reenactments of Aktion in skiffs on a pond: here boys (or slaves: *pueri*) take the part of combatants.[79] But the choice of Cupids in a public spectacle may have been more deliberate. Augustus claimed Venus, the mother of Cupid, for an ancestor and exalted her cult throughout his rule. The cult of Venus–Aphrodite was already well established in the Neapolitan region. As we have seen, one inscription ties her directly to the games.[80] Aphrodite Euploia was worshiped at Neapolis, and according to tradition, her dove led the way

---

79. *Epistle* 1.18.61–64.

80. *IG* 14.745.

CHAPTER 8 🏛 HAVEN OF HELLENISM

to the Bay of Naples for the city's Euboean ancestors.[81] We may reasonably presume that she was one of the principal gods — perhaps alongside Parthenope, Apollo, Demeter, and Augustus himself — honored in the games. Hence Ausonius' conceit that Venus, "glad at Augustus' Actian triumph," was responsible for the *naumachia* itself.

This particular event was probably part of the opening or closing ceremonies for the Sebasta. Ausonius' "Cupids" reenact three of Augustus' famous naval battles: 1) Mylai, an engagement between Agrippa and Sextus Pompey's admiral Papias near the straits of Messina in 36 BCE; 2) the decisive naval defeat of Pompey at Naulochos shortly thereafter (near "Sicilian Peloros"); and 3) the triumph over Antony and Cleopatra's fleet in 31, near Aktion ("Apollonian Leukas"). There was good reason for Neapolitans to commemorate Augustus' famous naval battles. Many of the warships involved in these battles — some probably built and commissioned at Neapolis itself — had been stationed nearby at Agrippa's Lucrine harbor in 37 BCE expressly to counteract Sextus Pompey's piracy.

Commentary 8.6: *An Inscription from the Games*

One of the best-preserved slabs from the Stazione Duomo excavations provides new information about the types of contests included in the Sebasta Games. The following inscription, recently on display at the Museo Archeologico Nazionale, covers certain classes of drama and oral performance. Most of the victors come from Asia Minor. Some have Roman (or Romanized) names, which are characteristically in three parts. Others have Greek names, which are single and come with a patronymic. There are also several freedmen of the Flavian emperors, whose names begin with Titus Flavius (the official first and family name of all three Flavian emperors), and end with a personal Greek name. Startlingly, amid the names of the victors appears Imperator Caesar Augustus — part of the nomenclature of an emperor. However, his personal name has been left blank. The emperor in question must therefore

---

81. Statius, *Silvae* 3.5.78-80; Velleius Paterculus, *Compendium* 1.4.2.

be Domitian, the third and last Flavian emperor, who alone among the emperors of this period suffered *damnatio memoriae*, an official erasure of his official memory after his death. Here the erasure was part of the inscription's design, indicating that the stone was first engraved after Domitian's death. Evidently it would not do to omit the name of an official winner at the games altogether. It seems, then, that the emperor himself had entered and won a contest of encomia honoring his deceased brother and predecessor as emperor, Titus, who had died in 81 CE.

91. TITUS FLAVIUS [—]
TITUS FLAVIUS [--].
AMONG THE ACTORS, GAIUS ANICIUS [--].
AMONG THE TRAGIC ACTORS, A DRAW [*HIERA*].
AMONG THE CITHARA PLAYERS, LUCIUS POSTUMULENUS POLLIO OF MAGNESIA.
AMONG THE COMIC ACTORS *EN PLASMATI*, QUINTUS GRANIUS MELPON OF NIKOMEDEIA.
AMONG THE ENCOMIASTS OF DEIFIED AUGUSTUS, HERMOGENES SON OF APOLLONIOS OF SMYRNA.
AMONG THE EPIC POETS HONORING THE SAME, TITUS FLAVIUS DIONYSIOS OF SMYRNA.
AMONG THE ENCOMIASTS OF DEIFIED AUGUSTA [I.E., LIVIA], LUCIUS TITELLIUS RUFUS OF SMYRNA.
AMONG THE EPIC POETS HONORING THE SAME, TITUS FLAVIUS DIONYSIOS OF SMYRNA.
AMONG THE ENCOMIASTS OF DEIFIED CLAUDIUS, GAIUS JULIUS VALERIANUS OF NEAPOLIS.
AMONG THE EPIC POETS HONORING THE SAME, TITUS FLAVIUS DIONYSIOS OF SMYRNA.
AMONG THE ENCOMIASTS OF DEIFIED VESPASIAN, MARCUS ANTONIUS THEOPHILUS OF PERINTHOS.
AMONG THE EPIC POETS HONORING THE SAME, ATHENAGORAS SON OF SAMIOS OF PERGAMON.
AMONG THE ENCOMIASTS OF DEIFIED TITUS, IMPERATOR CAESAR AUGUSTUS ---------- [DOMITIANUS].
AMONG THE EPIC POETS HONORING THE SAME, TITUS JULIUS LONGINUS OF PER[--].
AMONG THE ENCOMIASTS OF [-- DOMITIA?], HERMOGENES SON OF APOLLONIOS OF SMYRNA.

CHAPTER 8 ☖ HAVEN OF HELLENISM

AMONG THE EPIC POETS HONORING [THE SAME], GAIUS VETUTIUS FLACCUS OF L[AODIKEIA]....[Miranda de Martino 2014]

Commentary 8.7: Nero's Stage Debut

Nero's performance debut took place at Neapolis, and it could hardly have been more dramatic. It was the early summer of 64 CE, during a period of some months that the emperor spent in Campania before his return to Rome and Antium — and to a fateful conflagration. Nero adopted Greek language and manners during his stay, and performed in a traditional Greek agonistic category: that of the citharode, singing lyric or epic poetry while accompanying himself on the *kithara*. This was no contest, though: it was neither the month nor the year of the Sebasta, and no mention is made of special games.

92. And he made his debut at Neapolis, where he did not cease singing until he had finished the number which he had begun, even though the theater was shaken by a sudden earthquake shock. In the same city he sang frequently and for several successive days. Even when he took a short time to rest his voice, he could not keep out of sight, but went to the theater after bathing, and dined in the orchestra with the people all about him, promising them in Greek that when he had wet his whistle a bit, he would ring out something good and loud. He was greatly taken, too, with the rhythmic applause of some Alexandrians, who had flocked to Neapolis from a fleet that had lately arrived, and summoned more men from Alexandria. Not content with that, he selected some young men of the order of equestrians and more than five thousand sturdy young plebeians, to be divided into groups and learn the Alexandrian styles of applause..., and to ply them vigorously whenever he sang. These men were noticeable for their thick hair and fine apparel; their left hands were bare and without rings, and the leaders were paid four hundred thousand sesterces each. [Suetonius, *Nero* 20]

The "sudden earthquake shock" was more serious than Suetonius suggests. Tacitus elaborates:

93. There an incident took place, sinister in the eyes of many, providential and a mark of divine favor in those of the sovereign; for, after the audience had left, the theater, now empty, collapsed without injury to anyone. Therefore, celebrating in a set of verses his gratitude to Heaven, together with the happy course of the late accident, Nero... came to rest for the moment at Beneventum.... [Tacitus, *Annals* 15.34]

Due to the size of the audience, the event must have taken place in the theater rather than the odeion, the expected venue for a poetry recital.[82] Five thousand would have constituted well over half the capacity of a large urban theater. If, as Suetonius says, the first shock of the earthquake took place during the performance, the outcome might have been very different within the odeion, whose heavy roof, even if never genuinely threatened by the tremor, would likely have incited panic.

Commentary 8.8: A Personal Agonistic Inscription

A fine agonistic inscription[83] carved with reliefs, discovered in the 1860s in Via Sta. Anna alle Paludi and now in the Museo Archeologico Nazionale, dates to the second half of the second century CE [Fig. 8.9]. A freedman of the emperor Marcus Aurelius, M. Aurelius Hermagoras of Magnesia on the Sipylos, recorded on this stone his victories (and some draws as well) achieved in wrestling contests all around Greece and Asia Minor. Each venue at which he won at least one crown is represented by the crown itself carved in relief, the title of the games and number of victories inscribed within it:

94. AKTIA: TWO; NEMEA: THREE; ASPIDA: TWO,...

Ironically, there is no record that he won anything at Neapolis or was accorded there the same honorific posts as he received elsewhere. But clearly he was in his element here, where it was customary for accomplished residents to mark their achievements in Greek games with statues on

---

82. On the likely location of this theater, see pp. 191–96.

83. *IG* 14.739 = Miranda 1990–1995 no. 49.

CHAPTER 8 ▥ HAVEN OF HELLENISM

inscribed bases. The inscription itself was probably intended to accompany a statue of Hermagoras, though its precise context is unknown.

Commentary 8.9: A Public Inscription Honoring a Prominent Musician

The city's pride in its own citizens' success in Greek competitions is exemplified by this fragmentary inscription of the mid-second century CE, on a large marble base found near the Roman theater.[84] The upper part, now lost, enumerated his victories. The family name Aelius suggests that the honoree was either a freedman of the emperor, possibly Hadrian (117–138 CE), but more likely Antoninus Pius (138–161 CE), or a descendant of such a freedman. Neapolis, where he received his second citizenship, saw fit to confer upon him the demarchate, an honorary magistracy granted to distinguished men (including the occasional emperor) with special ties to the city.

95. [...] BY DECREE OF THE COUNCIL, THE CITY OF NEAPOLIS HONORS PUBLIUS AELIUS ANTIGENIDES, CITIZEN OF NEAPOLIS AND NIKOMEDEIA — DEMARCH, [...], HIGH PRIEST OF THE SACRED TIMELIC SYNOD OF THE BACCHIC ARTISTS; THE FIRST AND ONLY EVER TO HAVE WON SUCCESSIVELY ALL THE AFOREMENTIONED CONTESTS, WITHOUT A LOSS, IN THE FOLLOWING GAMES: ROME, TWICE; NEAPOLIS, THREE TIMES, INCLUDING THE OVERALL CONTEST; POZZUOLI, IN THE FIRST MEETING OF THE GAMES FOUNDED [IN 138 CE] BY OUR LORD EMPEROR ANTONINUS PIUS, AND AGAIN IN THEIR NEXT MEETING; AND IN HIS HOMETOWN NIKOMEDEIA, IN THE GAMES NAMED FOR ASKLEPIOS, WINNING IN THE SAME MEETING BOTH THE SOLO PIPES AND THOSE ACCOMPANIED BY CHORUS. HE DIED IN HIS THIRTY-FIFTH YEAR, AFTER HAVING PLAYED THE PIPES FOR TWENTY YEARS FOR THE ROMAN PEOPLE [*DEMOI RHOMAION*, i.e., professionally in Rome? Trans. Taylor].

---

84. *IG* 14.737 = Miranda 1990–1995 no. 47.

REFERENCES

Roman Neapolis and Hellenic culture: Sbordone 1967a–d; Hardie 1983: 2–14, 58–59, 67–68; Lomas 1993: 103–6, 172–82; 1995: 111–12; 2015; Leiwo 1994: passim; D'Arms 2003 [1970]: 140–49, 151–52, 157–58; Landi 2004; Taylor 2015b; Pisano 2017. **Speech of Favorinus:** Barigazzi 1951; Raviola 1995: 80–83. **Consolation decrees:** Miranda 1990–1995: 1.115–30; Lomas 1993: 174–79; Leiwo 1994: 133–42; Strubbe 1998. **Villa culture around the Bay of Naples:** D'Arms 1981: 72–96; 2003 [1970]. **Fish and shellfish farming at Roman villas:** Di Fraia 1993: 40–48; Higginbotham 1997; Marzano 2015. **Epicurean epigram of Stallius:** Leiwo 1994: 130–31. **Virgil, Siro, Philodemos, and Neapolis:** De Witt 1922; Rostagni 1952; Sbordone 1967b–c; Fernández Murga 1982; Gigante 1984; 1992; 1995; 2004; Gigante and Capasso 1989; Sider 1997: passim; Armstrong 2004b; Chambert 2004; Gigante 2004; Longo Auricchio 2004; Oosterhuis 2007: 124–64; Rigsby 2008; Vesperini 2009. **L. Papirius Paetus:** Hanslik 1949. **Horace and the school of Neapolis:** Armstrong 2004a. **Cult and tomb of Virgil:** Cocchia 1889: 68–150; Capasso 1893: esp. 115–20; Günther 1913: 201–4; Johannowsky 1952: 118, 139–42; Napoli 1967d: 466–67, 483; Gigante 1984: 36–39; Trapp 1984; 1986: 1–10; Comparetti 1997 [1872]; Diana 1999: 25–30, 44–48; Ziolkowski and Putnam 2008: passim; Musto 2013: 96–98, 121–22, et passim. **Vedius Pollio:** Syme 1961; Atkinson 1962; Scherrer 1990; De Caro and Vecchio 1994; Taylor 2014b; Berdowsky 2017–2018. **Pausilypon:** Ruggiero 1888: 33–39; Günther 1913; Della Valle 1938; Traversari 1960: 65–68; Napoli 1967d: 466–68; Pagano 1980–1981; Vecchio 1985c; Gallottini 1992; De Caro and Vecchio 1994; Diana 1999; Castronuovo 2000; Berlan-Bajard 2006: 229–31, 258, 298–300, 444–46; Sear 2006: 46–47, 129–30; Varriale 2007; 2015. **Apragopolis:** McDaniel 1914; Della Corte 2009. *Castrum Lucullanum:* Cocchia 1889: 56; Ceci 1892; Pais 1908a: 208, 211; Ambrasi 1967: 717–24; Napoli 1967d: 466; Beloch 1989 [1890]: 98–100; D'Arms 2003 [1970]: 178; Musto 2013: 1–5. **Water theater of Antioch:** Chowen 1956; Berlan-Bajard 2006: 120–22, 127–28, 385–86, 457–66. **Water spectacle:** Coleman 1993; Newby 2005: 179–92; Berlan-Bajard 2006; Viscardi 2013; Taylor forthcoming. **Sculpture from Pausilypon and the "Grotta di**

CHAPTER 8 📖 HAVEN OF HELLENISM

Seiano": Günther 1913: 257–72; Facenna 1949; Adamo Muscettola 1985; Cristilli 2003: 19–23; 2012: 126–50. **Statius and Neapolis:** Sbordone 1967d; Hardie 1983; Newlands 2012. **Games:** Civitelli 1893; Peterson 1919: 176–78, 210–11; Geer 1935; Robert 1939: 241–44; Moretti 1953; Sbordone 1967e; Merkelbach 1974; Miranda 1982; 1985a; 1990–1995: 1.75–114; Beloch 1989 [1890]: 73–76; Caldelli 1993: 28–37; Napoli 1997 [1959]: 193–96; Newby 2005; Miranda de Martino 2007; 2013; 2014; 2016; 2017a; 2017b; 2018; Mele 2014: 151–60, 180–87; Pugliese 2014: esp. 131–37; De Nardis 2015; Lomas 2015; Di Nanni Durante 2007–2008; 2016; 2017a; 2017b; Giampaola 2017; La Foresta and Miele 2017. **Antigenides inscription:** Lepore 1967d: 300–2; Sbordone 1967e: 562–63; Miranda 1985a: 390–91; 1990–1995: 1.75–77; Landi 2004: 211. **Titus at the games:** Miranda 1988b; 1990–1995: 1.35–39; Miranda de Martino 2007: 211–12; 2016. **Nero's debut in the theater of Neapolis:** Napoli 1997 [1959]: 184, 188–89. **Hermagoras inscription:** Moretti 1953: 224–26; Miranda 1985a: 391–92; 1990–1995: 1.79–83. **Torch races:** Smith 1899; Liddell and Marindin 1890; Capasso 1978 [1905]: 45–46. **Olympia inscription:** Dittenberger and Purgold 1896: 117–26 (no. 56); Buchner et al. 1952: 406–7; Moretti 1953: 29–35; Merkelbach 1975; Crowther 1989; Weiler 2018. **Isthmia:** Broneer 1973: 99–112; Gebhard and Dickie 1999. **Art in Hellenistic and Roman Neapolis:** Napoli 1967a: 604–22; Morel 1986b: 311–17; Baldassare 1998; Cristilli 2003; 2007; 2008; 2012; Taylor 2015b. **Philostratos' Neapolitan art gallery:** Lehmann-Hartleben 1941; Sbordone 1967f.

📖

CHAPTER 9. THE THIRD CENTURY AND CONSTANTINE

THE THIRD CENTURY

The Severan period witnessed the last great wave of urban development on the Bay before the rise of imperially sanctioned Christianity under Constantine I [312–337]. A long, dark century slid by in the interim, a period known to posterity mostly by the broadly drawn, but narrowly conceived, political lineaments recounted by such second-drawer biographical compilations as the *Historia Augusta* and the *Epitome de Caesaribus*. Archaeology and epigraphy have the potential to elucidate, complicate, or contest such narratives, but at Neapolis, as in other cities around Campania, the combined evidence for the third century remains frustratingly slim. The "mini-dark age" of the third century is usually conceived as roughly half a century, from the death of the final emperor of the Severan dynasty, Alexander Severus [222–235 CE], to the accession of Diocletian, architect of the Tetrarchy [284–305]. For Neapolis, however, the silence extends for more than a century, from the death of Caracalla [d. 217] to the 320s, when Constantine, fully committing himself to the expansion of Christianity, seeded several Italian cities with churches that adapted the old Roman secular form of the three- or five-aisled basilica to a new religious purpose.

Though he left no known traces at Neapolis of his ambitious building program in Italy, Alexander Severus is said to have undertaken several projects nearby, which he clearly envisioned as dynastic monuments. Unfortunately for him and his domineering mother, Julia Mamaea, the dynasty would reach a sanguinary end in 235. After this moment, the lights of history went off around the Bay. But Alexander was an avid builder both in Rome and on the Bay, as the *Historia Augusta* relates:

> 96. Toward his mother Mamaea he showed singular devotion, even to the extent of constructing in the palace at Rome certain apartments named after her (which the ignorant mob of today calls "ad Mammam") and also near Baiae a palace and a pool, still listed officially under the name of Mamaea. He also built in the district of Baiae other

magnificent public works in honour of his kinsmen, and huge pools, besides, formed by letting in the sea. [*Severus Alexander* 26.9–10]

If this account is reliable (it lacks archaeological confirmation), Alexander's projects mark the last known imperial intervention on the Bay for nearly a century. During that long lacuna, Baiae is mentioned only once in surviving literature, as the site of a villa of the emperor Tacitus [275–276].[1] Pozzuoli continued to operate more or less on its former scale — after all, Italy still needed feeding — but with no sign of its accustomed éclat. Misenum and Cumae retreated from view.

Relative to its size and importance, Neapolis is mutest of all. Archaeology might yet offer some relief against the scarcity of literary or epigraphic information, but so far the material record simply amplifies the silence of other media. While the world outside reeled from the so-called Crisis of the Third Century — a time of barbarian invasions in the provinces, pandemic, religious persecution, economic decline, monetary instability, and perpetual palace intrigue — Neapolis seems to have carried on more or less as it had before, but in reduced circumstances. The city ceased to develop or grow. The proxies for conspicuous wealth, political ambition, high social advancement, or imperial favor, so familiar from earlier times, make no appearance. The former indices of a vibrant cultural and commercial life such as phratry inscriptions, statue dedications, votive inscriptions, and honors associated with the Sebasta Games simply vanish. Though signs of construction from the third century (mostly repairs) are not entirely absent, even those few exceptions are often attributed to the Severan period, which marks the far bookend of the crisis. It remains fiendishly hard to attribute any work specifically to the century between Caracalla and Constantine.

Yet nothing emerges to indicate social unrest or destruction by violence, fire, or earthquake. Any changes in living conditions that might suggest financial exigency, precipitous depopulation, or broad social change are invisible too. In fact, the city largely ceased to acquire strata of any kind — an unusual archaeological phenomenon for any

1. *Historia Augusta, Tacitus* 7.6, 19.5.

CHAPTER 9 ⚱ THE 3RD CENTURY & CONSTANTINE

inhabited area in the notoriously untidy Roman world, where trash and debris, or fill made from it, normally accumulated like pages in an ever thickening book. We are consequently left with a great lacuna in the Neapolitan archaeological codex, as if a fat 64-page signature had been yanked clean out of the binding. This oddity may suggest material privation, a radical diminution of resources. But it may just as easily telegraph a change of habit wherein Neapolitans found new reasons to reduce their consumption footprint or purge their refuse from the city. Nearby Pompeii stands in stark contrast: it was veritably awash in everyday trash at the time of its sudden extinction. On the one hand, new excavations consistently show its streets were choked with debris—while on the other, the cartwheel ruts cutting right through it suggest that such disorder was the normal state of affairs.

In fact Neapolis' stratigraphic gap began well before the crisis, even before the Severan era. It seems to have commenced around 150 CE, a period of widespread peace, plenty, and prosperity. In Paul Arthur's words,

> The relative lack of archaeological contexts dating to the second century is more a sign of efficient urban management than of malaise. The abundant late Republican and early imperial contexts relate to the massive building programmes that were to give Neapolis its Roman imprint. The abundant late antique and early medieval contexts relate to abandonment of urban spaces and decline in social services. The absence of mid-imperial contexts is thus probably to be viewed not only as evidence for an absence of large building programmes, but also as an indication of functioning services that kept the town clean.

"Absence of evidence is not evidence of absence." The archaeologist's dictum never rang truer than in the case of Neapolis between c.150 and 320 CE. Her people were present and going about their lives. This we must infer from the continued maintenance of houses, public areas, and baths, as well as a lack of signs of widespread contraction, decay, or abandonment.

But just as certainly, all was not well. We need not dwell on the scholarly debates surrounding the Crisis of the Third Century or the nature of its social, economic, and political comorbidities. We can presume, even in our near-total ignorance about life on the Bay during this period, that the hardships attendant on those times were complex, inconstant, and textured, and that the locals handled them with resilience and flexibility. One factor, however, deserves special mention, if only because it reflects a particular vulnerability of port cities. Two of the greatest plagues of Mediterranean antiquity fell within a century of each other, one at the Empire's height and the other in the depths of the crisis years. The Antonine Plague first appeared in 165 CE during Marcus Aurelius' and Lucius Verus' joint reign and swept across the Mediterranean from port to port, then inland up the roads and rivers. Probably a close relative of smallpox, it arrived at Rome in the following year and ravaged it, laying low a significant proportion of the urban population. It wiped out the famous physician Galen's retinue of slaves, inducing him to flee to his native Pergamon. In Kyle Harper's words,

> the metropolis would have been a pathogen bomb, diffusing carriers of the disease across the western Mediterranean. The pandemic was raging among troops in Aquileia by AD 168, advancing from one node of population to the next, unevenly diffusing in fractal spirals across the west.

By 172, the army had been decimated, forcing Marcus Aurelius to conscript slaves and gladiators.[2] Silver mining collapsed and never recovered, precipitating a profound and enduring crisis in coinage and monetary value. During a relapse in 189 or 191, over 2,000 people were dying in Rome *daily*:[3] that represents one percent of the city's entire population every five days.

Harper plausibly estimates the mortality rate across the Roman population at 10 percent: "If the virus did carry off 7 to 8 of the empire's 75 million souls, it was, in absolute terms, the worst disease event in human history up to that time." He allows for double that rate in hard-hit places like Rome. It is entirely plausible, then, that the port cities on the Bay also took a population hit of 20 percent, along with the attendant assault on their collective psyche. Under such extreme duress we would expect to see evidence of contraction, especially in

2. Jerome, *Chronicle,* year 172; *Historia Augusta, Marcus Aurelius* 17.2; 21.6.
3. Dio Cassius, *Roman History* 72.14.3–4.

CHAPTER 9 🏛 THE 3RD CENTURY & CONSTANTINE

residential areas; but so far, it has not surfaced in any systemic way. Small excavations in 1983 at the northeast and southeast corners of the Policlinico complex along Via del Sole did show evidence of a once-prosperous residential quarter in the ancient city's western sector that had been abandoned by the third or fourth century (no more precise dating was possible), and remained abandoned for half a millennium thereafter. From these limited soundings Bruno D'Agostino postulated, cautiously, that "from that time up to the eighth century CE, this part of the city was depopulated and marginal." The scenario is entirely plausible, but remains to be tested.

In general, archaeology is helpless to register incorporeal disasters like plagues, which explode softly, like neutron bombs, and often leave the landscape relatively unscathed but for the bodies. Bodies, in fact, are our only hope of confirming or documenting such events when written evidence falls short and the debris of everyday life is lacking. Unfortunately the discovery of mass plague burials is so rare that no more than a handful have been plausibly identified across the Roman world. Though we are left to guess at the fallout on the Bay, our guess is highly educated, having the benefit of extremely productive scholarship on ancient plagues within the last two decades. Most of this work points in one direction. The three pandemics of Mediterranean antiquity (the Antonine Plague, the Plague of Cyprian, and the Justinianic Plague), long minimized by historians, are now accorded mortality rates on the same order of magnitude as the Black Death of the fourteenth and fifteenth centuries. Relentless and far-reaching, they infected a majority of people within their enormous geographic scope and carried away somewhere between a tenth and third of them.

It is probably no coincidence that late-Antonine Neapolis and Pozzuoli saw a significant lull in building, dedications, and literary references before the revival of the Severan era, by which time the danger had subsided. Both cities could well have lost a fifth of their inhabitants to disease and many more to flight without leaving any widespread archaeological traces of a crumbling urban dystopia. Public areas would have been maintained. Residential neighborhoods probably suffered abandonments, but these need not have been either extensive or permanent. Speculators could have bought abandoned properties at bargain prices, or squatted on them for free, and ridden out the worst of the calamity in hopes of a quick recovery. The shock to the workforce was undoubtedly dire, but as happened in many regions of medieval Europe during the Black Death, survivors — sorted out by herd immunity, quarantines, other civic regulations, and luck — would have prospered in a market boosted by a labor shortage that drew people from the countryside to cities. Plagues, Walter Scheidel has observed, destroy neither capital wealth nor productive land, and like more materially destructive disasters they tend to redistribute wealth downward. In economic terms, at least, the survivors of pandemic on the Bay were apt to face a less bleak landscape of recovery than would have confronted their ancestors after such extreme events of Campania's past as the Second Punic War or the eruption of Vesuvius — neither of which, I may note, is visible in Naples' urban archaeological record *either*. Death may have been in the air, but collapse was not in the cards.

The next great pandemic to befall the empire was the Plague of Cyprian between 249 and 270. Cyprian was the bishop of Carthage who documented the disease and undertook a mission of mercy to care for its victims in the stricken city. This plague seems to have assaulted cities on a comparable scale. Though its gruesome, bloody pathology is harder to diagnose than the smallpox symptoms of the previous century, Harper hypothesizes that it may have been a severe form of influenza or a viral hemorrhagic fever comparable to ebola, which has a case fatality rate of 50–70 percent. The plague's advance was obdurate and its toll again horrific. Alexandria's population, for example, may have plummeted by over 60 percent. The cities on the Bay leave no record of their own travails, but the same can be said for most urban centers in that reticent age. Again, it is inconceivable that they escaped the pandemic in full spate. Again, their mortality rate probably approached that of the Antonine Plague.

With such strains on local populations and on the collective psyche, we shouldn't wonder that the pandemics accelerated quiet cultural forces already at work. One discernible change at Neapolis in the third century is the demise of Greek inscriptions. Latin had gained a foothold in the city's epigraphy in the second century, and the few surviving epigraphs from the third show the Greek language in prolonged retreat

CHAPTER 9 🏛 THE 3RD CENTURY & CONSTANTINE

Fig. 9.1. *Catacomb of S. Gennaro. Photo: Peppe Guida / Wikimedia Commons CC BY-SA 4.0. Modified.*

until, by the reign of Diocletian, it had surrendered almost entirely to Latin. Neapolis was losing its cherished ethnic identity as the last bastion of authentic Hellenism in the West. The Sebasta Games petered out more or less hand-in-hand with this decline. The sister games at Pozzuoli lingered into the second half of the third century, and then they too expired. Perhaps within the span of Diocletian's Tetrarchy, or shortly thereafter, another Greek cultural relic disappeared from Neapolis, the demarchate, as did the other quaintly archaic honorific titles to which the city's institutions had clung.[4]

The few inscriptions datable to this period are reticent epitaphs from suburban cemeteries. Funerary inscriptions were mostly in Latin from this time onward, but some retained the Greek language into the fourth century. The most remarkable phenomenon surrounding funerary habits in this era is a shift, seen also at Rome, from burials in crowded above-ground cemeteries to a new kind of subterranean cemetery, the catacomb, tunneled into the ubiquitous soft tuff. At Neapolis, catacombs emerged exclusively in the northern suburbs. From the earliest sector of the largest of them, that of S. Gennaro at Capodimonte [Fig. 9.1], we begin to see evidence of a cohesive community of Christians. A few third-century Greek inscriptions in the *"zona Greca,"* one of the oldest sectors of

4. See pp. 63–65, 155, 169–70, 173–74.

353

the catacomb, commemorate them. These tend to be neutral in tone, lacking the more specialized language of rank and devotion that developed in the following century. Often they consist only of a name. A pair of more sophisticated Neapolitan Christian inscriptions, however, have recently been dated to roughly the same period, the third or fourth century. Both are in Greek and of unknown origin (thus not necessarily from the catacombs). One reads as follows:

> 97. HERE LIES PAULA, DAUGHTER OF PAUL THE SUBDEACON, WHO LIVED IN PEACE FOR FOUR YEARS AND TWO MONTHS. SHE WENT TO HER REST ON THE SEVENTH DAY BEFORE THE KALENDS OF JUNE. [*IG* 14.823, trans. Taylor]

Presenting more developed devotional language than those in the *zona Greca*, and even a churchly title (subdeacon), this inscription trends toward the fourth century, though not necessarily as late as the reign of Constantine. Roman Christians began to mark their epitaphs with the date of death in the mid-third century. This unique practice registered the moment at which the afterlife began. The conventional "lived in peace" and "went to her rest" *(anepausato)* are also formulaic expressions of the faith community.

The third century is when the Church catapulted into the world as a cultural force to conjure with. The Plague of Cyprian itself may have accelerated Christianity's rise by highlighting the unparalleled capacity of Christian networks to effect a rapid, coordinated, and compassionate response, as was Bishop Cyprian's in Carthage. Holding themselves as witnesses against the emperor Decius' brutal and ineffectual empire-wide persecution of Christians in 250, the international community of believers met the moment head-on, providing care and relief when local governments and the centralized imperial apparatus fell short. With a deadly disease besetting them from one side and real or threatened persecution and martyrdom from another, Christians were not just testing and professing their faith but also building their cults of saints. They developed etiological myths around their martyrs and spiritual heroes, old and new, and grounded those stories in geography. It would have to wait until Constantine to found churches and establish clerical bureaucracies devoted to them, but the business of competitive hagiography was already well under way.

CHAPTER 9 ⚱ THE 3RD CENTURY & CONSTANTINE

Neapolis also exhibits evidence of a powerful but ultimately unsuccessful rival to Christianity among its population: the cult of the mystical eastern god Mithras, disseminated mainly by the army and its veterans, which peaked in the third and early fourth centuries. Because the cultic assembly sites for this god were sheltered underground and concentrated in cities, many have survived in the archaeological record. Arthur and his team excavated a Mithraeum in a service area at the Carminiello ai Mannesi complex east of the Duomo [see Figs. 6.1, 7.18, 7.19].[5] A second site in the walled city's southeast corner, just south of the Herculaneum gate, produced a relief representing the formulaic cult image of Mithras slaying a bull. A similar relief was set into the Crypta Neapolitana in the western suburbs. These three pieces of evidence represent a cultic lifespan of some two centuries or more, from sometime after the mid-second century (the Carminiello complex) to the late fourth century (the Crypta). Given how little of Neapolis has been excavated, the recovered evidence of three independent Mithraea is remarkable. These random finds hint that comparable cult sites were distributed widely across the urban area. As a rough analog of their density, we might consider Ostia, where eighteen known Mithraea are spread over its excavated area and others surely remain to be uncovered in the town's unexcavated expanses. In this respect, Neapolis is simply demonstrating how conventionally Roman it had become, at least in its material manifestations, by late antiquity.

Meanwhile the commercial port's decline accelerated. The paucity of ceramic finds from the third century marks a collapse in the movement of goods through the harbor; their volume dwindled by sixfold from the previous century.[6] Certainly we shouldn't jump to drastic conclusions, as the finds were necessarily concentrated in the small excavated sectors of the harbor overall, and the city likely adapted to natural setbacks in ways we cannot see. Still, it is hard to escape the conclusion that Neapolis retreated almost entirely from its erstwhile role as a subsidiary Tyrrhenian entrepôt for trade and supply, sharing with Pozzuoli and Portus the critical task of managing the *annona*. It would probably have reserved its remaining dockage for supplying

5. See p. 278.
6. See p. 225.

itself and its suburbs, and — we may suppose — for maintaining its still considerable cultural assets.

More abrupt changes are also visible, but just barely. The city's long-standing bicameral structure of governance remained, now called by the Latin terms *ordo* (the senate or city council, the old *boule*) and *populus* (the assembly, i.e., the old *demos*).[7] Yet, despite this nominal continuity, the cities of Campania were losing their long-cherished autonomy. In the 280s Campania was converted into a province, losing the tax-exempt status that all of Italy had enjoyed for centuries. For a while, a new official emerged at its head: the *corrector Campaniae*, soon followed by a genuine magistracy, the *consularis Campaniae*. In effect, these were viceroys or governors imposed upon regions that had never had a centralized government of their own. We know little about their specific powers or responsibilities. The title *corrector* (usually associated with a geographic region; there was a *corrector Italiae* in 286) is sometimes translated, perhaps too informally, as "troubleshooter." It was an ad-hoc position, signaling that irregularities had arisen in a particular region that called for a response. In Campania of the 280s and 290s, such an official probably had a serious and unenviable charge: setting up and enforcing a system to collect taxes from local elites who had long enjoyed the privilege of tax exemption. As the elites in Campania included many of senatorial rank, the *corrector* also was drawn from their order. To seal their authority, *correctores* seem to have been granted the old magisterial prerogative of *imperium*, which gave them considerable police and punitive powers. Inevitably the reorganization of Italy's regions into provinces overseen by such officials precipitated a radical change in relations between Italian cities and the ever more centralized, if highly mobile, imperial court.

CONSTANTINE AND THE CITY

As has long been recognized, the Bay of Naples returned to a degree of civic prominence under Constantine I. The deep social value of this restoration remains uncertain. We have no indices of general prosperity or inequality in the region, nor can we estimate the size or flux of populations with any rigor. Most of the scholarship about Constantinian Neapolis is concerned with the growing role of the

7. See pp. 64–65, 114–19, 173–74.

CHAPTER 9 ⚖ THE 3RD CENTURY & CONSTANTINE

imperially sanctioned Church there, which may have been more symbolic than substantive. But in matters of imperial patronage substance often followed on symbolism, so the phenomenon is worth a closer look.

Constantine's impact on Neapolis is a matter of some debate. Archaeological and documentary evidence of his patronage here, or that of his family, is not robust, but various kinds of circumstantial evidence have led scholars in recent years to contend that the ties binding this city, as well as Pozzuoli, to the first Christian emperor were substantive and meaningful. First, the emperor elevated Campania to the rank of consular province, and this would have brought benefits to all the large cities in the region. One benefit became evident in 324, when the first known *consularis* of the region, Ceionius Julianus, restored the Aqua Augusta, the aqueduct originating at Serino that had been introduced by Augustus more than three hundred years earlier [see Figs. 7.8, 7.9].[8] A now-lost inscription found at the source of Acquaro in the 1930s documents the restoration:

> **98.** ON ACCOUNT OF THEIR MAGNIFICENT AND ACCUSTOMED GENEROSITY, OUR LORDS FLAVIUS CONSTANTINUS THE GREAT, PIOUS AND FORTUNATE VICTOR AUGUSTUS, FLAVIUS JULIUS CRISPUS, AND FLAVIUS CLAUDIUS CONSTANTINUS, MOST NOBLE CAESARS, HAVE ORDERED THE RESTORATION AT THEIR OWN EXPENSE OF THE AQUEDUCT OF THE AUGUSTAN SPRING, DILAPIDATED BY LONG NEGLECT AND OLD AGE, AND HAVE RETURNED IT TO THE BENEFIT OF THE CITIES NAMED BELOW. HIS EXCELLENCY [*VIR CLARISSIMUS,* OF THE SENATORIAL ORDER] CEIONIUS JULIANUS, CONSULAR OF CAMPANIA, WAS THE DEDICANT. HIS EMINENCE [*VIR EGREGIUS,* OF THE EQUESTRIAN ORDER] PONTIANUS OVERSAW SAID AQUEDUCT. THE NAMES OF THE CITIES ARE POZZUOLI, NEAPOLIS, NOLA, ATELLA, CUMAE, ACERRAE, BAIAE, AND MISENUM. [*CIL* 10.1805 = *AE* 1939, 131, trans. Taylor]

The cities are listed not in any intelligible geographic sequence, but evidently in order of their importance — demonstrated probably by the volume of water allotted to each. Neapolis unsurprisingly takes second place after Pozzuoli, whose busy harbor, in Giuseppe

---

8. See pp. 262–82; Commentaries 7.3 and 7.4, pp. 286–87.

Camodeca's words, was operating "at full efficiency" at this time. Like his predecessors Trajan and Septimius Severus, Constantine also seems to have repaired the Via Antiniana, the Neapolis–Pozzuoli road, as implied by an inscribed milestone found at Chiaia.[9] In gratitude for the emperor's munificence, the city dedicated statues in his honor and that of his mother Helena.[10] Furthermore, between 325 and 330, Neapolis and Pozzuoli together sponsored the construction of colonnaded porticoes at the emperor's new capital of Constantinople. These benefactions are recorded in a sixth-century source describing the structures destroyed by fire during the Nika riots at Constantinople in 532:

> **99.** When structures of such grandeur had been turned into flames, the colonnades which lined the city all the way up to the Forum of Constantine and shaded the broad street [the Mese, or Middle Way] with graceful contours by the beauty and size of their columns were inescapably caught up. Campanians are said to have constructed these by way of gratitude to Constantine; they had come to Byzantium [i.e., Constantinople] from Parthenope, the Neapolis of our day, and from the city formerly called Dicaearchia, but now Puteoli, to please the emperor. [John the Lydian, *On Powers* 3.70 Wuensch, trans. Bandy]

The Neapolitans' gift was doubtless a quid pro quo for Constantine's improvements in their city's infrastructure, but more fundamentally it responded to an even more significant act of local imperial benefaction: a Christian basilica. Built on the model Constantine and Helena were establishing in Rome, Constantinople, and the Holy Land [Commentary 9.1, pp. 369–70], this church must have been conceived more or less contemporaneously with the other improvements. Whether it leaves visible traces, or even whether it ever existed, are matters of debate. Many scholars, however, following an opinion expressed in the ninth-century *Gesta episcoporum neapolitanorum*,[11] identify it as the earliest incarnation of the church of Sta. Restituta. The same source, however, refers to the original cathedral

9. *CIL* 10.6930.
10. *CIL* 10.1482–1484.
11. P. 404.

CHAPTER 9 ☒ THE 3RD CENTURY & CONSTANTINE

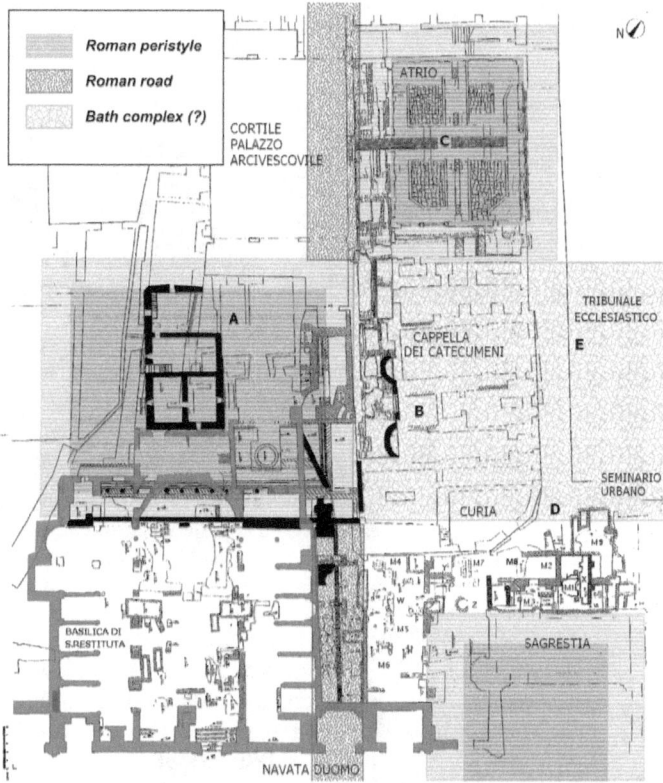

Fig. 9.2. Plan of the excavations under Sta. Restituta and dependencies of the cathedral. Base plan from Amodio 2015; overlay providing the approximate layout of the earlier Roman structures by R. Taylor.

as a different church altogether, dedicated to the Savior or to a certain Bishop Stephen. Sta. Restituta, which at its core probably dates to the fourth century, projects perpendicularly out of the nave of the city's much later cathedral (*Duomo*), Sta. Maria Assunta, popularly known as S. Gennaro [Fig. 9.2; see Fig. 6.1].

Today the entire ecclesiastical complex around the Duomo (the *"Insula episcopalis"*) occupies what was once a four-block sector of the ancient city's street grid extending north–south between Via dei Tribunali and Via Donnaregina and four short blocks eastward from Via

RABUN M. TAYLOR 🏛 ANCIENT NAPLES

Fig. 9.3 (above). Small vaulted chamber in the excavated area under S. Gennaro with a Roman opus reticulatum wall projecting from a Greek ashlar retaining wall. Photo: R. Taylor.
Fig. 9.4 (below). Roman gutter bounding the peristyle of area A in Fig. 9.3, running under the apse of Sta. Restituta. Photo: R. Taylor.

Duomo. That the city's principal church, and possibly its bishopric too, should have maintained a pied à terre here from the earliest days of state-sanctioned Christianity is plausible. Of the site's history of pre-Christian occupation, however, only a shadowy image emerges, and only from the Roman imperial period onward. The plot sloped markedly downward toward the southeast, requiring a system of terracing already in the Greek period. Excavations under Sta. Restituta, the archepiscopal palace to its north, and the ecclesiastical structures to their east have revealed

CHAPTER 9 🏛 THE 3RD CENTURY & CONSTANTINE

Fig. 9.5. General view of the excavated area under S. Gennaro and Sta. Restituta. Photo courtesy of M. Jodice.

traces of these terraces along with four peristyle structures of the imperial era, at least three of them probably belonging to ample residences of the Roman imperial era [Figs. 9.3; 9.4; 9.5]. Two apsidal halls with a hypocaust system have been identified as a private bathing suite [B on Fig. 9.2]. Recently Maria Amodio has proposed that by the time of its greatest elaboration in the late second or early third century the bath complex was public, and scaled accordingly. Thus, she argues, the large peristyle in zone A [see Fig. 9.2], extending north of Sta. Restituta and its splendid fifth-century baptistery, S. Giovanni in Fonte, was the baths' accompanying exercise ground *(palaestra)*. She associates this activity with an inscription long believed to have come from Pozzuoli but now shown to have been found right on the premises of this bath:

100. THE MOST SPLENDID CITY COUNCIL AND THE MOST HONORABLE POPULACE TO THEIR OUTSTANDING PATRON, HIS EXCELLENCY SEPTIMIUS RUSTICUS, CONSULAR OF CAMPANIA, OVERSEER OF THE CITY COUNCIL, RESTORER OF THE BATHS [*THERMAE*], ON ACCOUNT OF HIS EXTRAORDINARY AFFECTION. [*CIL* 10.1707, trans. Taylor]

Now reunified with its original context, the inscription seems to honor the otherwise unknown Rusticus, *consularis Campaniae,* specifically for "restoring" the baths that bore the inscription. Amodio's reading of the "restoration" calls for a considerable contraction of the baths themselves and a reappropriation of much of its grounds for the city's first basilica and possibly an adjoining episcopal complex. This all makes sense. The term *thermae* suggests a sizable public facility, not the smaller private baths normally called *balnea*. Nor was it unusual for the growing Church, hungry for land and increasingly deft at infiltrating city elites, to appropriate a large bath complex on which to implant an ecclesiastical compound. In this case parts of the bathing facilities themselves were probably retained for the clerics but curtailed and consolidated to suit Christian norms of modesty. The rest of their grounds, and probably several large private residences too, gave way to the church and its dependencies. For comparison Amodio references the West Baths at the Greek island city of Kos, where the bathing area was constricted into the old *caldarium* and the *palaestra* was overbuilt with churches and an episcopal residence. Analogous developments can be found elsewhere too; indeed urban baths often made their way into Church ownership to be adapted to ecclesiastical needs.

Roman baths were valuable urban assets even in reduced form, and many survived into the early Middle Ages. Yet they were also handy sources of ready-made columns and entablatures at a time when new churches (and the streets and fora of Rome and Constantinople too) demanded them, and when the imperial capacity to quarry, transport, and carve such elements was at a low ebb. The emperor needed widespread cooperation to satisfy his insatiable thirst for column shafts of granite, marble, or porphyry as well as delicate bases, capitals, and architraves of contrasting light-colored marble, most

CHAPTER 9 🏛 THE 3RD CENTURY & CONSTANTINE

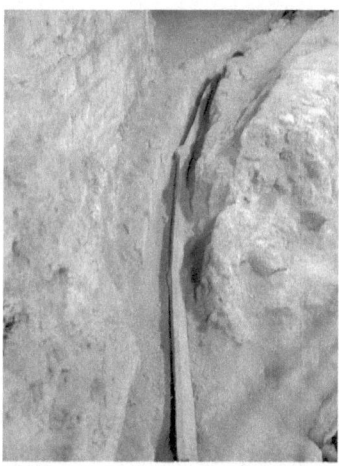

Fig. 9.6. *Late Roman lead pipe in the excavated area under S. Gennaro. Photo: R. Taylor.*

of which in this era had to be extracted from despoiled buildings of the high imperial era. To count as "restored," then, the much reduced baths must have acquired compensating assets of some kind, probably a redecoration to suit the subdivision and reconfiguration of the core. Much of the implicit glory of the restoration (and many columns!) must have migrated to the newly minted basilica on the premises. And lest we balk at the inscription's glaring omission of that basilica, which would naturally have been the central object of pride for the project, we need only recall that the glory of it — as chronicled in the *Liber pontificalis* [Commentary 9.1, pp. 369–70] — was Constantine's alone. No imperial functionary in his right mind, even such an "outstanding patron" as Rusticus, would have sought to steal credit for what was rightfully due to the highest *patronus* of all.

The subterranean archaeological zone at Sta. Restituta has been open sporadically to the public in recent decades [Fig. 9.5]. As one walks the low catwalk over the ancient remains just east of the baptistery, a Roman lead pipe comes into view, set into a groove that once passed under floors and an intervening paved street [Fig. 9.6, alongside the diagonal wall in the center of Fig. 9.2]. One of its segments is inscribed with the name *Aurelius Eutycianus* in the genitive case. Forging an ingenious chain of arguments that potentially link this man to the family of an Aurelia Eutychiana buried in the catacomb of S. Gennaro at Capodimonte, Amodio concludes that the pipe too is probably of Constantinian date and that Aurelius was the pipemaker. Thus emerges the barest possibility that the pipe is to be associated with a reconfiguration of the baths in conjunction with

363

the basilica project and perhaps the aqueduct's famous restoration and reallocation too.

Amodio's interlocked hypotheses are ingenious but circumstantial. Other scholars, like William Tronzo, question whether Constantine ever sponsored a Neapolitan basilica at all, given that most of the emperor's commissions, and those of his family, arose either at burial sites of revered martyrs or at Constantinople. Yet it bears suggesting that a few Italian cities may have been granted imperial basilicas to serve as ritual staging posts, or "welcome centers," for foreign pilgrims on their way to Rome. The same biography of Pope Sylvester that records Constantine's foundation of a basilica at Neapolis also mentions one at Ostia, dedicated to Peter, Paul, and John the Baptist[12] — the very three super-saints who awaited arriving visitors just up the river at Rome, and for whom the emperor had founded Rome's three most famous basilicas. That biographical detail has recently been vindicated by the discovery of a large, three-aisled basilica in Ostia's southeastern sector dating unambiguously to the early fourth century—and thus, almost by necessity, to Constantine.

The dedicatory inscription of the Constantinian aqueduct restoration refers to two officials.[13] With the increasing centralization of command and control mechanisms from the Severan period onward, public bath facilities would have fallen under the purview of Pontianus, presumably the regional water commissioner, who answered to the *consularis Campaniae*, Julianus, a close predecessor of Rusticus. Recall that the Neapolitan water-supply system had rebounded after the disaster of Vesuvius as the delivery network was refitted with new lead pipes from a different geographic source.[14] This refitting is a bit of a mystery. Why had Neapolis' urban water distribution system required new pipes as it was brought back online in the late first and early second centuries? One possibility is that the old pipes had been choked with accumulating lime, as sometimes happens with hard-water aqueducts originating in karst landscapes,

12. *Liber pontificalis* 34.28 Duchesne.
13. See Commentary 7.3, p. 286.
14. See p. 274.

CHAPTER 9 ★ THE 3RD CENTURY & CONSTANTINE

and had been switched out. But Pompeii's and Herculaneum's pipes, which supposedly were connected to the Serino system too, show no serious blockage. Furthermore, pipes with heavy lime accumulation tend not to leave strong isotopic signatures of their lead content because the lime insulates the water from the lead; yet Neapolis' system clearly had leached plenty of lead into the harbor by way of its wastewater both before and after the refitting. More likely, the new pipes of the post-79 era simply reflect an expansion of the old system. With Pompeii and Herculaneum permanently shut off by the eruption of Vesuvius, there had been more water to go around. New baths, such as those at Sta. Chiara and Via Terracina, had been added to the network in the city's salad days.[15]

But by the early fourth century Neapolis had probably suffered irrecoverable losses, if not of numbers then of revenue. With the demise of the Sebasta Games in the third century the southeastern bathing sector probably had fallen into steep decline as well. The network was delivering too much horsepower to a much lighter vehicle than before. Consequently the freshly restored aqueduct under Constantine may actually have *reduced* overall delivery volume to Neapolis, especially if some of the cities on the inscribed list, such as Acerrae, Atella and Nola, were being added to the network for the first time. Under these circumstances any potential distaste for consigning a public bath over to the Christian church would have been diminished both by not-so-subtle signals from Constantinople soliciting a gift of some fine marble columns and by the compensatory honor of hosting a grand imperial basilica on the bath site.

Of course no such basilica could have been justified solely on such transactional grounds. A need for it must have been felt from several directions, imperial, regional, and local, but also with an eye to Rome-bound pilgrims. One wonders why Neapolis acquired a basilica at this time while Pozzuoli, indisputably the dominant sister city, evidently did not. Both, after all, were contributing to the beautification of the emperor's new capital, presumably by scavenging columns from their own premises to adorn the sidewalks along Constantinople's main corridor. One possible explanation for this

15. See pp. 275–82.

asymmetric relationship is that the two cities in this era were less competitors than partners: each benefited from the other's complementary specializations, rather in the way that Ostia and Portus formed a cooperative symbiosis nourished on their differences. Neapolis, with its diminished port facilities and its longstanding distinction as a cultural capital and vacation destination, may have sought to attract religious tourists as a stopover on their way to Rome or back. Campania had not yet developed Christian destinations of its own, though later in the century Bishop Paulinus would establish a popular pilgrimage church complex at Cimitile near Nola. Whether coming or going, seaborne tourists may have been encouraged to stop at Neapolis to partake of the city's still formidable cultural assets. Constantine reportedly built a basilica at Capua too, dedicated to the apostles,[16] though nothing more is known of it. Thus we might see the outlines of a Christian itinerary developing: perhaps Ostia–Rome upon arrival, which at the capital could include the churches of S. Paolo fuori le Mura, St. Peter, S. Croce in Gerusalemme, and St. John Lateran; and Rome–Capua–Neapolis on the return, starting with the martyrium churches east and southeast of Rome: S. Lorenzo fuori le Mura, S. Agnese, S. Marcellino, and St. Peter's.

Tradition holds that the Church as an entity came to the Bay by way of the apostles Peter and Paul. Christians already inhabited its towns, but they had little structural organization apart from small and discrete assemblies. It dawned on Christian urban communities as they gained imperial sanction that they could use their martyrs to their own advantage, especially if those martyrs had local connections. Paul's association with Pozzuoli has a solid scriptural foundation: his arrival there, and his subsequent journey to Rome, are attested in *The Acts of the Apostles*:

> 101. The next day [at Rhegium, modern Reggio Calabria] the south wind came up, and on the following day we reached Puteoli. There we found some brothers and sisters who invited us to spend a week with them. And so we came to Rome. [*Acts* 28.13–14, New International Version]

16. *Liber pontificalis* 34.31 Duchesne.

CHAPTER 9 🏛 THE 3RD CENTURY & CONSTANTINE

The problem for Pozzuoli is that, in one authoritative stroke, this passage in *Acts* disqualifies Paul from playing a credible role in founding the Church on the Bay. The geographic authority of Christ and the saints rested on the locations either of their birth, of their good works, of their martyrdom, or of their posthumous remains. In consequence the brevity of Paul's visit and the town's obvious role as a mere springboard to Rome, a stopover where he accomplished nothing of note, presented a real problem for a city seeking Constantine's patronage. Was it going to be up to Peter, then, to do the heavy lifting for the Bay? The story of Peter's journey to Italy was not scripturally sanctioned, and so it was likely to emerge from a welter of contentious counter-narratives. The apocryphal *Acts of Peter*, composed probably in the second century, has the apostle arriving at Pozzuoli after Paul has departed Rome for Spain. Here Peter encounters a Christian from Rome, Theon, whose all-consuming desire is to return immediately to the metropolis with Peter to purge it of the spell cast by a wicked Jew, Simon Magus. Peter too is filled with zeal, and when his host relents long enough to offer him a chance to rest at Pozzuoli, "by no exhortation could Theon prevail to persuade him to tarry there even one day."[17] Again, Pozzuoli is left high and dry. Neapolis must have smelled an opportunity.

And indeed a Neapolitan tradition of Peter's local ministrations did arise. It appears only in much later documents beginning in the ninth century; thus its antiquity is in doubt. According to this narrative, Peter took a founding role at Naples. Upon his arrival he miraculously cured a paralyzed man named Aspren (or Asprenus), baptized him, and ordained him as the city's first bishop before proceeding to Rome.[18] Thus did the future first pope come to acquire agency in the early local church. This story may have been the hook that Neapolis needed to reel in the emperor's attention.

Vinni Lucherini ponders the various traditions associated with the early basilica at Neapolis and its potential affiliation with Peter through a succession of bishops going back to Aspren; but in the end, the strands of this legend simply prove untraceable, and she concludes

17. *Acts of Peter* 6; trans. James.
18. *Life of St. Asprenus*, BHL 725; *Life of Athanasius*, BHL 735, 737.

that the injection of Peter into the story of Aspren was an innovation of the ninth century coming after publication of the *Gesta episcoporum neapolitanorum*. Perhaps. But since the story of Peter's mission and martyrdom at Rome had been firmly established in Italy by the second century we should expect that rival traditions developed at that time around his travels. In the end we can only say that it is *feasible* to suppose that the tradition of Peter's Neapolitan ministry reaches back to the Roman imperial period, and to suggest that it developed either contemporaneously with the alternate story in the second century or in quick succession to it.

We might further conjecture that the Neapolitan tradition had already prevailed by the early fourth century and that it played a crucial part in winning the city a great prize, one that Pozzuoli could not hope to attain: Constantine's attention and the favor of an imperial church. Oddly, the *Liber Pontificalis* omits the name of the Neapolitan basilica's dedicatee saint. But if we look at the dedicatory pattern established at Capua (the Apostles) and Ostia (the Apostles Peter and Paul, and John the Baptist), then a dedication at Neapolis to the Apostle Peter would be appropriate. Unfortunately our documentary sources are poor. Lively and complex mythologies of local saints have probably been forgotten or muted, not unlike the founding myths of Parthenope. We should not doubt the plenitude and magnitude of things lost any more than we should wonder that churches of obvious early prominence, such as the Constantinian basilicas at Ostia and Capua, though remembered in the sole surviving chronicle of the early popes, were so completely effaced and forgotten — even in their own host cities — that the only hope of recovering their memory is by chance discovery or archaeology.

Neapolis under Constantine was no more a Christian city than Rome or Ostia. While the Church and its membership were growing exponentially, professed Christianity remained but one of a multitude of vibrant sectors of the city's diverse and cosmopolitan social landscape. It may seem excessively teleological to have focused so much of this chapter on a social and religious trend that would have seemed neither dominant nor inevitable at the time. But as I said above, substance follows symbolism; and eventually the physical,

CHAPTER 9 🏛 THE 3RD CENTURY & CONSTANTINE

documentary, and doctrinal trappings of the new order engulfed the older social landscape and overwrote the palimpsest. We would dearly love to know an order of magnitude more about the social texture and the inner world of this great port city in the third and fourth centuries, but the only hope of achieving that goal would be by way of a calamity on the scale of the cholera epidemic of 1884 or the 1980 earthquake, the two greatest catalysts of archaeological knowledge in the city's history so far. We should not wish to have knowledge revealed through fields of rubble, whether induced by overzealous development or by disaster. Let us then be grateful for the Naples we have, and take satisfaction in the occasional endoscopic glimpse into the astonishingly intense lost world that still lies under our feet.

Commentary 9.1: Constantine's Gifts to Neapolis

The following passage from the life of Pope Sylvester I (314–335) in the sixth-century compendium of papal biographies, the *Liber pontificalis*, is typical of the ledger-like entries characterizing this man's pontificate. His papacy was dominated by the emperor Constantine's foundation of basilical churches in Italy: seven at Rome and one each at Ostia, Alba, Capua, and Neapolis.

102. At the same time Constantine Augustus built a basilica in the city of Neapolis, to which he offered the following:
2 silver patens, weighing each 15 lbs.;
2 silver goblets, weighing each 10 lbs.;
15 chalices for service weighing each 2 lbs.;
20 silver lamps, weighing each 8 lbs.;
20 bronze lamps, weighing each 10 lbs.
He built likewise an aqueduct, 8 miles in length; he built also a forum in the same city and he offered the following gift:
the property of Macarus, yielding 150 *solidi*;
the Cimbrian property, yielding 105 *sol.*;
the property of Sclina, yielding 108 *sol.*;
the property of Afilae, yielding 140 *sol.*;
the property of Nymfulae, yielding 90 *sol.*;
the property of the island with the fortress, yielding 80 *sol.*
[*Liber pontificalis* 34.32 Duchesne, trans. Loomis]

The entry is as puzzling as it is interesting. Neither the aqueduct conduit nor the forum referenced here, both of which he "made" or "built" *(fecit)*, is known from any other source. Yet the endowment accompanying these improvements, presumably given to assist with their maintenance, closely resembles those from other entries and has the ring of truth. A portion of the property called Nymfulae is also cited in the endowment for the basilica at Ostia. What's more, "the island with the fortress" sounds like Megaris, the future Castel dell'Ovo, on the islet just off Parthenope. That was probably part of the fortified Castrum Lucullanum,[19] which would most assuredly have come down to Constantine in the imperial patrimony. Yet this very fact militates against the identification, for emperors did not blithely give away their patrimony, whose assets were considered part of the perpetual imperial fisc. And why was the island's name not transmitted here? No other island fortifications have been identified in the vicinity, leaving one to ponder whether the Latin word *insula* here should be understood by one of its other common meanings, such as "city block." As for the aqueduct, the Latin could more naturally be translated, "He also built the channel of an aqueduct across eight miles' length" (*Fecit autem formam aquaeductus per milia VIII*). This could easily refer to repairs or rerouting of the Aqua Augusta — a reading that I believe reflects a more natural understanding of the text, which references part of the whole. "Channel of an aqueduct" excludes important components of the hydraulic system, such as its settling and distribution tanks and its pipe network. A hydraulic project undertaken *de novo*, on the other hand, would most naturally be called simply "an aqueduct." Understood as part of the Serino system, Constantine's improvement cannot be taken to have benefited Neapolis solely. But as the only city within the system mentioned in the biography, Neapolis was specified as the beneficiary.

19. See pp. 144, 299, 308, 318–19; Commentary 8.2, pp. 334–35.

CHAPTER 9 ⚱ THE 3RD CENTURY & CONSTANTINE

REFERENCES

Neapolis in the third century: Ambrasi 1967a; Arthur 2002: 9; Amodio 2014: 53–61. **Antonine Plague and the Plague of Cyprian:** Harper 2015; 2017; Duncan-Jones 2018. **Plague and recovery through history:** Scheidel 2016. **Policlinico excavations:** D'Agostino 1984: 128–29; Arthur 2002: 157. **Mithraea:** Lacerenza and Morisco 1994; 1998. **Loss of Greek:** Leiwo 1994: 110–15; 149; 170–71. **Christian inscriptions:** Fasola 1975: 29–33; Liccardo 1992; Leiwo 1994: 108–9. **Catacombs:** Fasola 1975; Amodio 2014; Bruzelius and Tronzo 2011: 12–24. **Constantine I and Neapolis:** Ambrasi 1967b; Savino 2005: 21–26; Lucherini 2009: 63–89; Bruzelius and Tronzo 2011: 24–32; Amodio 2015. **Constantine I and Pozzuoli:** Camodeca 1980–1981: 62–77. **Tradition of St. Peter at Neapolis:** Lucherini 2009: 146–48, 154–56, 337–55. **Excavations at Sta. Restituta:** Di Stefano 1974; Ciavolino and Dovere 1991; Arthur 2002: 62–63: Ebanista 2009; Amodio 2015a, 2015b; Cristilli 2015. **Roman baths and the Church in late antiquity:** Maréchal 2020: 202–22. **Constantinian basilica at Ostia:** Martin and Heinzelmann 2000.

BIBLIOGRAPHY

Abate, F. 1864. *Studii sull'acquidotto Claudio e progetto per fornire d'acqua potabile la città di Napoli.* Naples: Stamperia del Giornale di Napoli.

Accame, S. 1980. "Pitagora e la fondazione di Dicearchia." In *Settima miscellanea greca e romana.* Rome: Istituto Italiano per la Storia Antica, 3–44.

Accorona, F., et al. 1985. "La fornace di Corso Umberto." In *Napoli antica*, 378–85.

Adam, J.-P. 1986. "Observations techniques sur les suites du séisme de 62 à Pompéi." In *Tremblements*, 67–87.

Adamo Muscettola, S. 1985a. "La statua di negro da Posillipo." In *Napoli antica*, 351.

Adamo Muscettola, S. 1985b. "I rinvenimenti archeolgici." In *Napoli antica*, 413–16.

Adamo Muscettola, S. 1985c. "Il tempio dei Dioscuri." In *Napoli antica*, 196–206.

Adamo Muscettola, S. 2002. "Gli ex-voto alle ninfe di Ischia: La parabola di una cultura marginale." *RIA* 57:37–61.

Adinolfi, R. 1977. "Ricerca sulla fondazione e sul periodo greco di Dicearchia." *Puteoli* 1:7–26.

Adinolfi, R. 1987. "La facies protostorica e precoloniale di Pozzuoli." *Puteoli* 11:93–106.

Alagi, G. 1971. "La zona vesuviana dal I al IV secolo." *Campania sacra* 2:3–13.

Albore Livadie, C. 1985a. "Cuma preelenica." In *Napoli antica*, 62–75.

Albore Livadie, C. 1985b. "Il territorio flegreo: Dall'eneolitico al preelenico di Cuma." In *Napoli antica*, 55–62.

Albore Livadie, C., ed. 1999. *L'eruzione vesuviana delle "Pomici di Avellino" e la facies di Palma Campania (Bronzo antico): Atti del Seminario Internazionale di Ravello, 15–17 luglio 1994.* Bari: Edipuglia.

Allevato, E., and G. Di Pasquale. 2009. "Archaeobotanical Data from Vesuvius Region in the Roman Period: State of the Art and Perspective." In *Apolline Project*, 298–314.

Allevato, E., et al. 2010. "Pollen-Wood Analysis at the Neapolis Harbour Site (1st–3rd Century AD, Southern Italy) and its Archaeobotanical Implications." *Journal of Archaeological Science* 37:2365–75.

Allison, P.M. 1995. "On-going Seismic Activity and Its Effects on the Living Conditions in Pompeii in the Last Decades." In *Archäologie und Seismologie*, 183–89.

Allison, P.M. 2002. "Recurring Tremors: The Continuing Impact of the AD 79 Eruption of Mt Vesuvius." In *Natural Disasters and Cultural Change*. R. Torrence and J. Grattan, ed. London and New York: Routledge, 107–25.

Amalfitano, P., et al., ed. 1990. *I Campi Flegrei: Un itinerario archeologico*. Venice: Marsilio.

Amalfitano, P., ed. 1986. *Il destino della Sibilla: Mito, scienza e storia dei Campi Flegrei*. Naples: Bibliopolis.

Amalia Scatozza Höricht, L. 2007. *Pithecusa: Materiali votivi da Monte Vico e dall'area di Santa Restituta*. Rome: Giorgio Bretschneider.

Amato, L., et al. 2001. "The Crypta Neapolitana: A Roman Tunnel of the Early Imperial Age." At http://www.unesco.org/archi2000/pdf/viggiani2.pdf

Amato, L., et al. 2009. "Ricostruzioni morfoevolutive nel territorio di Napoli: L'evoluzione tardo pleistocenica olocenica e le linee di riva di epoca storica." *Méditerrannée* 112:23–31.

Ambrasi, D. 1967a. "Il cristianesimo e la Chiesa nei primi secoli 1: I primordi del cristianesimo e la 'Campania Felix.'" In *SN*, 623–42.

Ambrasi, D. 1967b. "Il cristianesimo e la Chiesa nei primi secoli 2: Dalle origini alla pace di Costantino." In *SN*, 643–70.

Amodio, M. 2014. *Le sepolture a Neapolis dall'età imperiale al tardo-antico: Scelte insediative, tipologie sepolcrali e usi funerari tra III e VI secolo*. Naples: Giannini.

Amodio, M. 2015a. "Le basiliche cristiane e le trasformazioni dello spazio urbano di Neapolis tra IV e VI secolo." In *Realia Christianorum: Fonti e documenti per lo studio del cristianesimo antico. Atti*

BIBLIOGRAPHY

del Convegno, Napoli, 14 novembre 2014. A. Giudice and G. Rinaldi, ed. Bologna: Ante Quem, 153–88.

Amodio, M. 2015b. "Neapolis tardo-antica: La fondazione della basilica costantiniana e le trasformazioni del tessuto urbano." *Analysis Archaeologica* 1:7–39.

Amodio. M., et al. 2017. "Carta archeologica delle produzioni ceramiche a *Neapolis* (IV a.C.–VII d.C.): Uno strumento per la lettura e la fruizione del paesaggio culturale della città antica." In *La Baia di Napoli: Strategie integrate per la conservazione e la fruizione del paesaggio culturale 1. Per una connotazione del territorio, tra caratteri fisici e valenze culturali*. A. Aveta et al., ed. Naples: ArtStudioPaparo, 463–68.

Andreau, J. 1973. "Histoire des séismes et histoire économique: Le tremblement de terre de Pompéi, 62 ap. J.C." *Annales, Economies, Sociétés, Civilisations* 28:369–95.

Antonelli, F., et al. 2017. "Craftsmanship and Identity in the Hellenistic Funerary Reliefs of Naples: An Archaeological and Archaeometric Analysis." *Archaeometry* 59:1–12.

Aoyagi, M., et al. 2018. "The 'Villa of Augustus' at Somma Vesuviana." In *The Roman Villa in the Mediterranean Basin: Late Republic to Late Antiquity*. A. Marzano and G. Métraux, ed. Cambridge: Cambridge University Press, 141–56.

Armstrong, D. 2004a. "Horace's *Epistles* 1 and Philodemus." In *Vergil, Philodemus*, 267–98.

Armstrong, D. 2004b. "Introduction." In *Vergil, Philodemus*, 1–22.

Arthur, P. 1989a. "Archeologia e terremoti a Napoli." In *Terremoti*, 501–6.

Arthur, P., ed. 1994. *Il complesso archeologico di Carminiello ai Mannesi, Napoli (scavi 1983–1984)*. Galatina: Congedo.

Arthur, P. 1999. "The 'Byzantine' Baths at Santa Chiara, Naples." In *Roman Baths*, 135–46.

Arthur, P. 2002. *Naples: From Roman Town to City-State: An Archaeological Perspective*. London: British School at Rome, and Lecce: Dipartimento di Beni Culturali, Università degli Studi di Lecce.

Arthur, P., and G. Vecchio. 1985. "Il complesso di vico Carminiello ai Mannesi." In *Napoli antica*, 213–16.

Asheri, D. 1988. "Carthaginians and Greeks." In *CAH* 4: *Persia, Greece and the Western Mediterranean c. 525 to 479 B.C.*, 739–80.

Asheri, D. 1992. "Sicily, 478–431 B.C." In *CAH* 5: *The Fifth Century B.C.*, 147–70.

Atkinson, K.M.T. 1962. "The 'Constitutio' of Vedius Pollio at Ephesus and its Analogies." *Revue internationale des droits de l'antiquité* 9:261–89.

Aucelli, P., et al. 2017. "Late Holocene Landscape Evolution of the Gulf of Naples (Italy) Inferred from Geoarchaeological Data." *Journal of Maps* 13.2:300–310.

Aulinas, M., et al. 2008. "The 'Pomici di mercato' Plinian Eruption of Somma-Vesuvius: Magma Chamber Processes and Eruption Dynamics." *Bulletin of Volcanology* 70.7:825–40.

Bahrfeldt, M. 1899. "Le monete romano-campane." *Rivista italiana di numismatica* 12:387–446.

Baldassarre, I. 1985. "Napoli: problemi archeologici." In *Napoli antica*, 122–32.

Baldassarre, I. 1998. "Documenti di pittura ellenistica da Napoli." In *L'Italie méridionale et les premières expériences de la peinture hellénistique*. Rome: École Française de Rome, 95–159.

Baldassarre, I. 2010a. "Napoli ellenistica e la produzione pittorica campana." In *Atti del X Congresso Internazionale dell'AIPMA, Association Internationale pour la Peinture Murale Antique, Napoli 17–21 settembre 2007*. I. Bragantini, ed. 2 vols. Naples: Università degli Studi di Napoli "L'Orientale," 1:3–13.

Baldassarre, I. 2010b. *Il teatro di Neapolis: Scavo e recupero urbano*. Naples: n.p.

Barigazzi, A. 1951. "Un'orazione pronunziata a Napoli ai tempi di Adriano." *Athenaeum* n.s. 29:3–11.

Bellucci, A. 1961. "Gli archi dell'acquedotto Claudio ai Ponti Rossi." *Partenope* 2:81–94.

Beloch, K.I. 1989 [1890]. *Campania: Storia e topografia della Napoli antica e dei suoi dintorni*. C. Ferone et al., trans. Naples: Bibliopolis.

BIBLIOGRAPHY

Bérard, J. 1957. *La colonisation grecque de l'Italie méridionale et de la Sicile dans l'antiquité: L'histoire et la légende.* Paris: Presses Universitaires de France.

Berdowsky, P. 2017–2018. "Ex amicis Augusti: P. Vedius Pollio." *Palamedes* 12:93–140.

Berlan-Bajard, A. 2006. *Les spectacles aquatiques romains.* Rome: École Française de Rome.

Bernabò Brea, L. 1935. "Il tempio napoletano dei Dioscuri." *Bullettino della Commissione Archeologica Comunale di Roma* 6:61–76.

Bernard, S. 2018. "The Social History of Early Roman Coinage." *JRS* 108:1–26.

Bietti Sestieri, A.M. 1984. "Central and Southern Italy in the Late Bronze Age." In *Crossroads,* 55–122.

Boetto, G. 2005. "Le navi romane di Napoli." *Archaeologia Maritima Mediterranea* 2:63–76.

Boetto, G., et al. 2010. "I relitti di Napoli e il loro contesto portuale." In S. Medas, M. D'Agostino, and G. Caniato, ed. *Navis (4): Archeologia, storia e etnografia navale. Atti del I convegno nazionale.* Bari: Edipuglia, 115–22.

Boetto, G., et al. 2019. "Nuovi relitti dagli scavi del porto antico di Napoli." *Navis* 6:33-44.

Borriello, M.R., and A. De Simone. 1985. "Le stipe di S. Aniello." In *Napoli antica,* 159–70.

Borriello, M.R., et al. 1985a. "La necropoli di Castel Capuano." In *Napoli antica,* 232–74.

Borriello, M.R., et al. 1985b. "Le necropoli urbane." In *Napoli antica,* 228–30.

Bragantini, I., and P. Gastaldi, ed. 1985. *Palazzo Corigliano tra archeologia e storia.* Naples: Istituto Universitario Orientale.

Bragantini, I., et al. 2010. "Lo scavo di Piazza Nicola Amore a Napoli: Le fasi edilizie e decorative del complesso monumentale." In *Atti del X Congresso Internazionale dell'AIPMA* 2:607–21.

Brandt, J.R. 2006. "'The Warehouse of the World.' A Comment on Rome's Supply Chain during the Empire." *Orizzonti* 6:25–47.

Breglia, L. 1942. "Posizione della Campania nell'arte italica." *La critica d'arte,* 29–41.

Breglia, L. 1946–1948. "Le 'campano-tarentine' e la presunta lega monetale fra Napoli e Taranto." *RendNap* n.s. 23:225–47.

Breglia, L. 1952a. *La prima fase della coniazione romana dell'argento.* Rome: Santamaria.

Breglia, L. 1952b. "Vecchie notizie e nuove visioni nella monetazione di Napoli." *PP* 25–27:286–99.

Breglia Pulci Doria, L. 1983. *Oracoli sibillini tra rituali e propaganda (studi su Flegonte di Tralles)*. Naples: Liguori.

Breglia Pulci Doria, L. 1987. "Le Sirene: Il canto, la morte, la polis." *AION (archeol)* 9:65–98.

Bresson, A. 2013. "The *chorai* of Munatius Hilarianus or Neapolitan phratries as *collegia.*" *Mediterraneo antico: Economie, società, culture* 16:203–22.

Brillante, B. 2000. *Sebeto: Storia e mito di un fiume.* Naples: Massa.

Broneer, O. 1973. *Isthmia 2. Topography and Architecture.* Princeton, NJ: American School of Classical Studies at Athens.

Bruzelius, C., and W. Tronzo. 2011. *Medieval Naples: An Architectural and Urban History, 400–1400.* New York: Italica Press.

Buchner, G. 1975. "Nuovi aspetti e problemi posti dagli scavi di Pithecusa con particolari considerazioni sulle oreficerie di stile orientalizzante antico." In *Contribution à l'étude de la société et de la colonisation eubéennes.* Naples: Centre Jean Bérard, 59–86.

Buchner, G. 1977. "Cuma nell'VIII secolo a. C., osservata dalla prospettiva di Pithecusa." In *Campi Flegrei,* 131–48.

Buchner, G. 1985. "L'emporion di Pithecusa." In *Napoli antica,* 79–87.

Buchner, G. 1986. "Eruzioni vulcaniche e fenomeni volcano-tettonici nell'isola d'Ischia." In *Tremblements,* 145–88.

Buchner, G. 1987. "Pithecusa." In Zevi, *Campi,* 111–20.

Buchner, G., and C. Gialanella. 1994. *Museo archeologico di Pithecusae, Isola d'Ischia.* Rome: Istituto Poligrafico e Zecca dello Stato, Libreria dello Stato.

Buchner, G., and D. Ridgway. 1993. *Pithekoussai I: La necropoli. Tombe 1–723 scavate dal 1952 al 1961.* Rome: Giorgio Bretschneider.

Buchner, G., et al. 1952. "Fonti per la storia di Napoli antica." *PP* 25–27:370–419.

Buchner, G., et al. 1978. "L'isola di Vivara. Nuove ricerche." *PP* 33:197–237.

Buchner Niola, D. 1965. *L'isola d'Ischia: Studio geografico.* Naples: Istituto di geografia dell'Università.

Buchreiter, N. 1999a. "Un esempio di imprenditoria femminile in età imperiale. *Patavium* 13:99–106.

Buchreiter, N. 1999b. "Le iscrizioni del sepolcreto di via Cristallini a Napoli." *Patavium* 14:87–93.

Burnett, A.M. 1977. "The Coinages of Rome and Magna Graecia in the Late Fourth and Third Centuries B.C." *Schweizerische numismatische Rundschau* 56:92–121.

Burnett, A.M. 1986. "Naples and South Italy: Coinage and Prosperity, ca. 300 B.C." In *Monetazione di Neapolis,* 23–43.

Burnett, A.M. 1989. "The Beginnings of Roman Coinage." *AIIN* 36:33–64.

Burnett, A.M. 1998. "The Romano-Campanian Silver." In *Monetazione romano-campana,* 19–47.

Burnett, A.M., and M. Crawford. 1998. "Overstrikes at Neapolis and Coinage at Poseidonia–Paestum." In *Studies in Greek Numismatics in Memory of Martin Jessop Price.* R. Ashton and S. Hunter, ed. London: Spink, 55–57.

Burnett, A., and D.R. Hook. 1989. "The Fineness of Silver Coins in Italy and Rome during the Late Fourth and Third Centuries BC." *Numismatica e antichità classiche* 18:151–68.

Caccamo Caltabiano, M. 1981. "La serie PΩMAIΩN e la cronologia delle prime emissioni bronzee di Neapolis." *Rivista storica dell'antichità* 11:33–51.

Cairns, F. 1984. "IG XII 9,244 and the Demes and Districts of Eretria." *ZPE* 54:156–64.

Cairns, F. 1986. "IG Suppl. 555, Reinmuth No. 15 and the Demes and Tribes of Eretria." *ZPE* 64:149–58.

Caldelli, M.L. 1993. *L'Agon Capitolinus: Storia e protagonisti dall'istituzione domizianea al IV secolo.* Rome: Istituto Italiano per la Storia Antica.

Camodeca, G. 1977. "L'ordinamento in 'regiones' e i 'vici' di Puteoli." *Puteoli* 1:62–98.

Camodeca, G. 1980–1981. "Richerche su Puteoli tardo-romana (fine III–IV secolo)." *Puteoli* 4–5:59–128.

Camodeca, G. 1982. "Ascesa al senato e rapporti con i territori d'origine. Italia: Regio I, II, III." *Colloquio internazionale AIEGL su epigrapfia e ordine senatorio (Roma, 14–20 maggio 1981)* 2:101–63.

Camodeca, G. 1997. "Una ignorata galleria stradale d'età augustea fra 'Lucrinum' e 'Baiae' e la più antica iscrizione di un 'curator aquae Augustae' (10 d.C.)." *AION (archeol)* 4:191–99.

Camodeca, G. 2000–2001. "Lo *stadium* di Puteoli, il *sepulchrum* di Adriano in *villa Ciceroniana* e *l'Historia Augusta*." *RendPont* 73:147–75.

Camodeca, G. 2001. "I pagi di Nola." In *Modalità insediative*, 413–33.

Cangiano, L. 1843. *Sulle acque potabili pubbliche della città di Napoli*. Naples: Tipografia dell'Aquila di V. Puzziello.

Cantilena, R. 1985a. "La monetazione." In *Napoli antica*, 352–67.

Cantilena, R. 1985b. "Tre tesoretti con monete napoletane." In *Napoli antica*, 370–72.

Cantilena, R. 2004. "Presenza e funzioni della moneta nelle chorai delle colonie greche della Campania." In *Presenza e funzioni della moneta nelle chorai delle colonie greche dall'Iberia al Mar Nero: Atti del XII Convegno Organizzato dall'Università "Federico II" e del Centro Internazionale di Studi Numismatici, Napoli 16–17 giugno 2000*. Rome: Istituto Italiano della Numismatica, 171–93.

Cantilena, R. 2008. "Atene e l'area tirrenica: Questioni monetali." In *Atene e la Magna Grecia dall'età arcaica all'ellenismo, Atti Taranto* 47:519–34.

Cantilena, R. 2014. "La fine delle coniazioni in argento in campania e l'inizio dell'emissione del quadrigato." *AIIN* 60:195–203.

Cantilena, R., et al. 1986. "Didrammi e frazioni di argento." In *Monetazione di Neapolis*, 101–218.

Capasso, B. 1893. "Pianta della città di Napoli nel secolo XI." *ASPN* 18:104–25, 316–63.

🏛 BIBLIOGRAPHY

Capasso, B. 1978 [1905]. *Napoli greco-romana*. Naples: Berisio.

Capasso, M. 1983. *Il sepolcro di Virgilio*. Naples: Giannini.

Carafa, P. 2008. *Culti e santuari di Campania antica*. Rome: Libreria dello Stato, Istituto Poligrafico e Zecca dello Stato.

Carapezza, M., and M.L. Carapezza. 1986. "Energia eruttiva ed energia geotermica nei Campi Flegrei." In *Destino*, 183–89.

Cardona, M. 1880. *Delle origini della città di Napoli*. Naples: Estabilimento tipografico, Palazzo della corte di Cassazione.

Cardone, V. 1992. *Nisida: Storia di un mito dei Campi Flegrei*. Naples: Electa.

Carlsen, J. 1994. "*CIL* X 8217 and the Question of Temple Land in Roman Italy." In *Landuse in the Roman Empire*. J. Carlsen et al., ed. Rome: "L'Erma" di Bretschneider, 9–15.

Carsana, V., et al. 2009. "Evoluzione del paesaggio costiero tra Parthenope e Neapolis." *Méditerrannée* 112:14–22.

Cascella, S., and G. Vecchio. 2014. *La villa rustica di C. Olius Ampliatus: Suburbio sud-orientale di Napoli (Ponticelli)*. Oxford: BAR.

Càssola, F. 1986. "Problemi di storia neapolitana." In *Neapolis*, 37–81.

Castagna, R. 2003. *Ischia nella tradizione greca e latina*. Lacco Ameno: Imagaenaria.

Castagnoli, F. 1977. "Topografia dei Campi Flegrei." In *Campi Flegrei*, 41–79.

Castronuovo, S. 2000. *Posillipo imperiale: La villa di Vedio Pollione e poi di Augusto*. Naples: Altrastampa.

Castaldo, V. 1910. "Antichi teatri greci di Napoli." *AttiAccPontan* 40.2 v. 15:1–34.

Cavalieri Manasse, G., and C. Gialanella. 2016. "Il foro di Puteoli sul Regione Terra: nuove osservazioni." *RIA* 71:23–50.

Cavalieri Manasse, G., and H. von Hesberg. 2010. "Dalle decorazioni architettoniche ai monumenti romani." In *Napoli, la città e il mare*, 27–50.

Cavalieri Manasse, G., et al. 2017. "Nuove riflessioni sul complesso monumentale di Piazza Nicola Amore a Napoli." In *Complessi monumentali e arredo scultoreo nella Regio I Latium e Campania: Nuove scoperte e proposte di lettura in contesto. Atti del convegno internazionale (Napoli, 5 e 6 dicembre 2013).* C. Capaldi and C. Gasparrini, ed. Naples: Naus, 203–21.

Ceci, G. 1892. "Pizzofalcone." *NN* 1:60–62.

Celico, P., et al. 2001. "Acque termo-minerali." In *Ambiente geologico*, 237–52.

Cerchiai, L. 2010. "*Meta ton enchorion men enaumachesan:* Neapolis e la seconda battaglia di Cuma." *Incidenza dell'antico: Dialoghi di storia greca* 8:213–19.

Cerulli Irelli, G. 1965. "S. Sebastiano al Vesuvio: Villa rustica romana." *NSc* Suppl., 161–78.

Cervasio, S. 2007. "Napoli: A Sant'Andrea delle Dame, reperti di 8000 anni fà." *La repubblica*, Nov. 2.

Chambert, R. 2004. "Vergil's Epicureanism in His Early Poems." In *Vergil, Philodemus*, 43–60.

Chouquer, G., and F. Favory. 1987. "Reconnaissance morphologique des cadastres antiques de l'aire latio-campanienne." In *Structures agraires en Italie centro-méridionale. Cadastres et paysage ruraux.* G. Chouquer et al., ed. Rome: École Française de Rome, 81–231.

Chowen, R.H. 1956. "The Nature of Hadrian's Theatron at Daphne." *AJA* 60:275–77.

Ciaceri, E. 1966 [1924]. *Storia della Magna Grecia.* 3 vols. Rome: "L'Erma" di Bretschneider.

Ciavolino, N., and U. Dovere. 1991. *Corso di aggiornamento in archeologia cristiana e storia della chiesa: L'insula dell'episcopio di Napoli.* Naples: Archidiocesi di Napoli.

Cinquantaquattro, T.E. 2015. "Napoli: I cantieri della Metropolitana. Il teatro romano. *Atti Taranto* 52:865–79.

Cinquantaquattro, T.E. 2017. "Napoli." *Atti Taranto* 54:664–70.

Cinque, A., and P. Romano. 2001. "Evoluzione geomorfologica e caratterizzazione oro-idrografica della regione." In *Ambiente geologico*, 59–90.

Cinque, A., et al. 1991. "La successione di terreni di età post-romana delle Terme di Miseno (Napoli): Nuovi dati per la storia e la stratigrafia del bradisisma puteolano." *Bollettino della Società Geologica Italiana* 110:231–44.

Civitelli, G. 1893. "I nuovi frammenti di epigrafi greche relative ai ludi Augustali di Napoli." *AttiNap (=RendNap)* 17.2:1–82.

Clark, R.J. "Peter of Eboli and the Roman Baths of Puteoli." In *Roman Baths*, 147–51.

Cocchia, E. 1889. *La tomba di Virgilio: Contributo alla topografia dell'antica città di Napoli.* Turin: Loescher.

Cocchia, E. 1893. "Napoli e il Satyricon di Petronio Arbitro." *ASPN* 18:278–315.

Cocco, E. 2001. "La fascia costiera." In *Ambiente geologico*, 149–66.

Coldstream, N. 1994. "Prospectors and Pioneers: Pithekoussai, Kyme and Central Italy." In *The Archaeology of Greek Colonization*. G.R. Tsetskhladze and F. De Angelis, ed. Oxford: Oxford University, Institute of Archaeology, 47–60.

Coleman, K. 1993. "Launching into History: Aquatic Displays in the Early Empire." *JRS* 83:48–74.

Colonna, F. 1898. *Scoperte di antichità in Napoli, dal 1876 a tutto il 1897.* Naples: Giannini & figli.

Colucci Pescatori, G. 1986. "Fonti antiche relative alle eruzioni vesuviane ed altri fenomeni vulcanici successivi al 79 d.C." In *Tremblements*, 134–41.

Colussi, F., and C. Leggieri. 2009. "Ipogei greci ancora da scoprire: Il sito di Santa Maria Antesaecula." In *Sottosuoli*, 103–9.

Comparetti, D. 1997 [1872]. *Vergil in the Middle Ages*. E.F.M. Benecke, trans. Princeton, NJ: Princeton University Press.

Conedera, M., et al. 2004. "The Cultivation of *Castanea sativa* (Mill.) in Europe, from Its Origin to Its Diffusion on a Continental Scale." *Vegetation History and Archaeobotany* 13:161–79.

Correra, L. 1904. "Il tempio dei Dioscuri a Napoli." *AttiNap (=RendNap)* 23.2:210–28.

Cozzolino, A. 1960. "Del primo 'porto naturale di Napoli greca.'" *Partenope* 1.3:145–65.

Crawford, M. 1985. *Coinage and Money in the Roman Republic: Italy and the Mediterranean*. London: Methuen.

Cristilli, A. 2003. "Sculture neapolitane al Museo Archeologico Nazionale di Napoli." *RIA* 58: 7–35.

Cristilli, A. 2007. "Alcune osservazioni sulla Nike tipo Paionios da Napoli." *Oebalus* 2:187–201.

Cristilli, A. 2008. "L'arredo statuario del complesso archeologico di Agnano. Scultori a Napoli nel II sec. d.C." *BABesch* 83:155–69.

Cristilli, A. 2012. *Le sculture da Neapolis nelle collezioni del Museo Archeologico Nazionale di Napoli*. Naples: Giannini.

Cristilli, A. 2015. "Le evidenze greche e romane nell'*Insula Episcopalis* di Napoli: Una nuova ricostruzione storico-strutturale. *BABesch* 90:79–98.

Crowther, N.B. 1989. "The Sebastan Games in Naples." *ZPE* 79:100–2.

D'Agostino, B. 1979. "Il periodo del bronzo finale in Campania." In *Atti della XXI riunione scientifica: Il bronzo finale in Italia, in memoria di Ferrante Rittatore Vonwiller, Firenze, ottobre 21–23, 1977*. Florence: Istituto Italiano di Preistoria e Protostoria, 477–87.

D'Agostino, B. 1984. "Per un progetto di archeologia urbana a Napoli." In *Archeologia urbana a centro antico a Napoli:Atti del convegno*. S. Adamo Muscettola and Patrizia Gastaldi, ed. Taranto: Istituto per la Storia e l'Archeologia della Magna Grecia, 121–31.

D'Agostino, B. 1990. "Relations between Campania, Southern Etruria, and the Aegean in the Eighth Century. In *Greek Colonists*, 73–85.

D'Agostino, B. 1992. "Greci, Campani e Sanniti: Città e campagna nella regione Campania." In *La Campania fra il VI e il III secolo a.C.:Atti del XIV Convegno di Studi Etruschi e Italici*. Galatina: Congedo, 73–83.

D'Agostino, B. 2009. "Pithecusae e Cuma all'alba della colonizzazione." In *Cuma*, 169–96.

D'Agostino, B. 2011. "Pithecusae e Cuma nel quadro della Campania di età arcaica." *RM* 117: 35–53.

Dall'Osso, I. 1906. "Napoli trogloditica e preellenica." *NN* 15:33–51.

D'Ambrosio, A. 1972. "Una villa rustica a Qualiano di Napoli." *RendNap* n.s. 47:319–26.

Damiani, I., et al. 1985. "L'insediamento preistorico di Vivara: Gli scavi ed I contesti locali." In *Napoli antica*, 35–43.

D'Arms, J. 1974. "Puteoli in the Second Century of the Roman Empire: A Social and Economic Study." *JRS* 64:104–24.

D'Arms, J. 1981. *Commerce and Social Standing in Ancient Rome.* Cambridge, MA: Harvard University Press.

D'Arms, J. 2003 [1970]. *Romans on the Bay of Naples and Other Essays on Roman Campania.* Bari: Edipuglia.

De Caro, S. 1974. "La necropoli di Pizzofalcone in Napoli." *RendNap* 49:37–67.

De Caro, S. 1985. "Partenope – Paleopolis: La necropoli di Pizzofalcone." In *Napoli antica*, 99–102.

De Caro, S. 1994. "Appunti per la topografia della chora di Pithekoussai nella prima età coloniale." In *Apoikia*, 37–45.

De Caro, S. 2002. "Introduzione alle relazione sugli scavi in atto." In *Ager Campanus. Atti del convegno internazionale: "La storia dell'Ager Campanus, i problemi della* limitatio *e sua lettura attuale. Real sito di S. Leucio, 8–9 giugno 2001*. Naples: Jovene, 135–36.

De Caro, S., and D. Giampaola. 2008. "La circolazione stradale a Neapolis e nel suo territorio." In *Stadtverkehr in der antiken Welt*. D. Mertens, ed. Wiesbaden: Reichert, 107–24.

De Caro, S., and G. Vecchio. 1994. "Pausilypon: La villa imperiale." In Zevi, *Neapolis*, 83–94.

De Carolis, E. 1997. "Testimonianze archeologiche in area vesuviana posteriori al 79 d.C." *Archeologia, uomo, territorio* 16:17–32.

De Divitiis, B. 2015. "Memories from the Subsoil: Discovering Antiquities in Fifteenth-Century Naples and Campania." In *Remembering Parthenope*, 189–216.

De Feo, G., and R.M.A. Napoli. 2007. "Historical Development of the Augustan Aqueduct in Southern Italy: Twenty Centuries of Works from Serino to Naples." *Water Science & Technology: Water Supply* 7.1:131–38.

De Franciscis, A. 1954. "Le recenti scoperte in Santa Chiara e la topografia di Napoli romana." *ArchClas* 6:277–83.

De Franciscis, A. 1971. "Pozzuoli, *epineion ton Kumaion.*" *RendNap* n.s. 46:109–14.

Delile, H., et al. 2016. "A Lead Isotope Perspective on Urban Development in Ancient Naples." *PNAS* 113.22:6148–53.

Della Corte, M. 2009. "Augustus in His Last Visit to Campania: Capri and Apragopolis; Octavianum and Summa Villa." In *Apolline Project*, 144–56.

Della Valle, G. 1938. "La villa sillana e augustea Pausilypon." In *Campania romana*, 207–67.

De Marchi, A. 1913. "Sull'iscrizione della fratria degli Artemisi di Napoli." *Studi romani: Rivista di archeologia e storia* 1:326–28.

De Martino, F. 1952. "Le istituzioni di Napoli greco-romana." *PP* 25–27:333–43.

De Nardis, M. 2015. "Greek Magistrates in Roman Naples? Law and Memory from the Fourth Century BC to the Fourth Century AD." In *Remembering Parthenope*, 85–104.

Deniaux, E. 1981. "'Civitate donati': Naples, Héraclée, Cume." *Ktema* 6:133–36.

De Petra, G. 1891. "Napoli colonia romana." *AttiNap (=RendNap)* 16:57–79.

De Petra, G. 1884. "Nuove scoperte nell'antico teatro di Napoli." *AttiAccPontan* 16:51–56.

De Petra, G. 1895. "Sulle nuove scoverte dell'antico teatro di Napoli: Nota letta all'Accademia Pontaniana nella tornata 9 febbraio 1894." *AttiAccPontan* 16:51–56.

De Petra, G. 1898. "Di un antico ipogeo scoperto in Napoli." *MonAnt* 8:216–32.

De Petra, G. 1905. "Le origini di Napoli." *AttiNap (=RendNap)* 23:37–66.

De Petra, G. 1908. "Le sirene del Mar Tirreno." *AttiNap (=Rend Nap)* 25.1:1–36.

De Petra, G., and B. Capasso. 1912. *Le origini di Napoli Greco-romana.* Naples: Giannini.

De Polignac, F. 1995. *Cults, Territory, and the Origins of the Greek City-State*. J. Lloyd, trans. Chicago: University of Chicago Press.

De Sanctis, G. 1914. "Note sulla iscrizione degli Artemisi." *Revue épigraphique* 2:306–9.

De Sensi Sestito, G. 1981. "I Dinomenidi nel basso e medio Tirreno fra Imera e Cuma." *MÉFRA* 93:617–42.

De Simone, A. 1985. "Il complesso monumentale di San Lorenzo Maggiore. In *Napoli antica*, 185–95.

De Simone, A. 1986. "S. Lorenzo Maggiore in Napoli: Il monumento e l'area." In *Neapolis*, 233–53.

De Simone, A. 1987. "L'area archeologica di S. Lorenzo Maggiore in Napoli." In *Archeologia in Campania*, 189–94.

De Simone, A. 1995. "I terremoti precedenti l'eruzione: Nuove attestazioni da recenti scavi." In *Archäologie und Seismologie*, 37–43.

De Simone, A. 2009. "Ricerche e scavi a Somma Vesuviana." In *Apolline Project*, 157–71.

De Simone, G.F. 2008. "Il territorio nord-vesuviano e un sito dimenticato di Pollena Trocchia." *CronErcol* 38:329–49.

De Simone, G.F. 2009. "Pollena Trocchia: Archives and Field Survey Results." In *Apolline Project*, 191–206.

De Simone, G.F., et al. 2009. "Apolline Project 2007: Il sito romano di Pollena Trocchia in località Masseria de Carolis." In *Apolline Project*, 207–38.

De Stefano, P., and V. Carsana, ed. 1987. *Archeologia e trasformazione urbana: Catalogo della mostra "Napoli 1981–1986 città in trasformazione, 23 aprile–31 maggio 1987. Notiziario 12*. Naples: Sindaco Commissario Straordinario del Governo.

De Vita, P. 2001. "Clima." In *Ambiente geologico*, 167–74.

De Witt, N. 1922. "Virgil at Naples." *Classical Philology* 17:104–10.

D'Henry, G., et al. 1985. "La cultura materiale nelle aree limitrofe." *Napoli antica*, 300–32.

Diana, A. 1999. *Pausilypon e dintorni: Fatti, misfatti, personaggi e leggende*. Naples: Luciano.

Di Bonito, R., and R. Giamminelli. 1992. *Le terme dei Campi Flegrei: Topografia storica*. Milan and Rome: Jandi Sapi.

Di Donato, V., et al. 2018. "Development and Decline of the Ancient Harbor of Neapolis." *Geoarchaeology* 33.5:542–57.

Di Fraia, G. 1993. "Baia sommersa: Nuove evidenze topografiche e monumentali." *ASub* 1:21–48.

Di Nanni Durante, D. 2007–2008. "I *Sebastà* di *Neapolis:* Il regolamento e il programma." *Ludica* 13–14:7–22.

Di Nanni Durante, D. 2016. "Gli encomi per Augusto e Livia ai *Sebasta* di Napoli." *Maia* 68:399–411.

Di Nanni Durante, D. 2017a. "Le regine dello sport: Atlete e artiste in gara nel mondo Greco-romano." *Historika* 7:271–94.

Di Nanni Durante, D. 2017b. "Regolamento e programma dei Sebastà di Neapolis: I nuovi dati da Piazza Nicola Amore." In *Sebastà Isolympia*, 54–68.

Di Sandro, N. 1986. *Le anfore arcaiche dallo scarico Gosetti, Pithecusa*. Naples: Centre Jean Bérard.

Di Stefano, R. 1974. *La cattedrale di Napoli*. 2nd ed. Naples: Editoriale Scientifico.

Dittenberger, W., and K. Purgold. 1896. *Die Inschriften von Olympia*. Berlin: Asher.

D'Onofrio, A.M., and B. D'Agostino. 1985. "L'esplorazione a largo S. Aniello e a Villa Chiara." In *Napoli antica*, 147–56.

D'Onofrio, A.M., and B. D'Agostino, ed. 1987. *Ricerche archeologiche a Napoli: Lo scavo in Largo S. Aniello (1982–83)*. Naples: Arte tipografica.

D'Onofrio, A.M., et al. 1985. "Interventi di scavo a Napoli nell'area del Primo Policlinico: Il saggio D 1. Relazione preliminare." *AION (archeol)* 7:155–93.

Döring, M. 2007. *Römische Häfen, Aquädukte und Zisternen in Campanien*. Darmstadt: Institut für Wasserbau und Wasserwirtschaft.

Dougherty, C. 1993. *The Poetics of Colonization: From City to Text in Archaic Greece*. New York and Oxford: Oxford University Press.

Dougherty, C. 1998. "It's Murder to Found a Colony." In *Cultural*

Poetics in Archaic Greece: Cult, Performance, Politics. C. Dougherty and L. Kurke, ed. New York: Oxford University Press, 178–98.

Duhn, F.K. von. 1910. *Der Dioskurentempel in Neapel.* Heidelberg: Winter.

Dunbabin, K. 1989. "*Baiarum grata voluptas:* Pleasures and Dangers of the Baths." *BSR* 57:6–46.

Dunbabin, T.J. 1968. *The Western Greeks: The History of Sicily and South Italy from the Foundation of the Greek Colonies to 480 BC.* Oxford: Clarendon.

Ebanista, C., and I. Donnarumma. 2015. "La catacomba di S. Gennaro a Napoli: Nuovi dati sullo sviluppo del cimitero dagli inedita scavi del 1969–70." *Koinonia* 39:521–48.

Elia, O. 1938. "Un tratto dell'acquedotto detto 'Claudio' in territorio di Sarno." In *Campania romana: Studi e materiali editi a cura della Sezione Campana degli Studi Romani* 1. *Napoli, Rispoli.* A. Maiuri, ed. Milan: Università Cattolica del Sacro Cuore, 1:99–111.

Emmerson, A.L.C. 2017. "Beyond Continuity and Change: The *Columelle* of Southern Campania." *AJA* 121:345–68.

Emmerson, A. 2020. *Life and Death in the Roman Suburb.* Oxford: Oxford University Press.

Esposito, C. 1992. "Spaccanapoli: Il sottosuolo." In *Spaccanapoli: Centro storico.* U. Carughi, ed. Naples: Electa, 62–67.

Esposito, C. 2009. "La zona cimiteriale greca a Napoli." In *Sottosuoli,* 113–27.

Esposito, C. 2018. *Il sottosuolo di Napoli: Acquedotti e cavità in duemila anni di scavi.* Naples: Intra Moenia Edizioni.

Facenna, D. 1949. "Rappresentazione di negro nel Museo Nazionale di Napoli." *ArchClas* 1:188–95.

Faga, I. 2006. "Ceramica a pareti dal complesso archeologico di S. Lorenzo Maggiore." *ReiCretActa* 40:397–402.

Faga, I. 2010. "Vasi a pareti sottili dal porto di Neapolis: Tecnologia e archeometria." *Rivista di archeologia* 34:159–76.

Fagan, G. 1996. "Sergius Orata: Inventor of the Hypocaust?" *Phoenix* 50:56–66.

Fagan, G. 1999. *Bathing in Public in the Roman World*. Ann Arbor: University of Michigan Press.

Febbraro, S. 2005. "Merci e mercati: La circolazione dei beni e i consumi nel mercato di Neapolis tra I e IV secolo d.C." In *San Lorenzo Maggiore*, 26–34.

Febbraro, S., and D. Giampaola. 2012. "Ceramiche comuni e vernici nere dal quartiere artigianale di Piazza Nicola Amore a Napoli." *Facem* (version 06/12/2012). At http://facem.at/img/pdf/Febbraro_Giampaola_2012-12-06.pdf

Federico, E. 2004. "Sull'isola dei Teleboi: Nella preistoria scientifica di Giulio Beloch." In *Pompei, Capri*, 11–41.

Federico, E., and E. Miranda, ed. 1998. *Capri antica: Dalla preistoria alla fine dell'età romana*. Capri: La Conchiglia.

Fernández Murga, F. 1982. "Virgilio en Nápoles." In *Simposio Virgiliano: Conmemorativo del bimilenario de la muerte de Virgilio*. Murcia: Universidad de Murcia, 101–13.

Ferone, C. 1988. "Sull'iscrizione napoletana della fratria degli Artemisi: A.E. 1913, 134." *MGR* 13:167–80.

Ferrari, G., and R. Lamagna. 2016. "*Aqua Augusta* della Campania: Lo speco di Macrinus." In *Puteoli: Studi di storia ed archeologia dei Campi Flegrei*. G. Camodeca and M. Giglio, ed. Naples: Università degli Studi di Napoli "L'Orientale," 273–96.

Fishwick, D. 1989. "L. Munatius Hilarianus and the Inscription of the Artemisii." *ZPE* 79:175–83.

Flower, H. 2001. "A Tale of Two Monuments: Domitian, Trajan, and Some Praetorians at Puteoli." *AJA* 105:625–48.

Forti, L. 1951. "Rilievi dedicati alle ninfe Nitrodi." *RendNap* n.s. 26:161–91.

Foss, J.E., et al. 2002. "Paleosols of the Pompeii Area." In *Natural History*, 65–79.

Franciosi, G. 2002. "I Gracchi, Silla, e l'*Ager Campanus*." In *Romanizzazione*, 229–48.

Frederiksen, M. 1984. *Campania*. N. Purcell, ed. London: British School at Rome.

Frederiksen, M. 1986."Napoli e i greci d'occidente dal 450 al 350 a.C. circa: Vecchi problemi e nuove prospettive." In *Monetazione di Neapolis,* 3–20.

Gabrici, E. 1912."Tombe ellenistiche di S. Maria la Nuova in Napoli." *RM* 27:148–61.

Gabrici, E. 1951."Contributo archeologico alla topografia di Napoli della Campania." *MonAnt* 41:655–59.

Gabrici, E. 1959. *Problemi di numismatica greca della Sicilia e della Magna Grecia.* Naples: Macchiaroli.

Gais, R.M. 1978."Some Problems of River-God Iconography." *AJA* 82:355–70.

Gallottini, A. 1992. "Per la topografia dei Campi Flegrei: Una proposta di ricostruzione della Scuola di Virgilio." *Journal of Ancient Topography* 2:167–82.

Gebhard, E.R., and M.W. Dickie. 1999. "Melikertes–Palaimon, Hero of the Isthmian Games." In *Ancient Greek Hero Cult: Proceedings of the Fifth International Seminar on Ancient Greek Cult.* R. Hägg, ed. Stockholm: Swedish Institute in Athens, 159–65.

Gelis, C., et al. 2005. "Numerical Modeling of Surface Waves over Shallow Cavities." *Journal of Environmental and Engineering Geophysics* 10 (June): 111–21.

Geer, R.M. 1935."The Greek Games at Naples." *TAPA* 66:208–11.

Ghinatti, F. 1967. "Ricerche sui culti greci di Napoli in età romana imperiale." *Atene e Roma* 12:98–101, 592.

Gialanella, C. 2000. *"Puteoli.* Il Parco Archeologico della *via Puteolis– Neapolim."* In *Nova antiqua phlegraea: Nuovi tesori archeologici dai Campi Flegrei.* C. Gialanella, ed. Naples: Electa, 64–78.

Gialanella, C. 2012. "Le Terme Flegree da Pietro da Eboli ai giorni nostri." In *Aquae patavinae: Montegrotto Terme e il termalismo in Italia. Aggiornamenti e nuove prospettive di valorizzazione. Atti del 2º convegno nazionale, Padova, 4–5 giugno 2011.* M Bassani et al., ed. Padua: Padova University Press, 411–24.

Gialanella, C., and V. Di Giovanni. 2001. "La necropolis del suburbia orientale di Puteoli." In *Römischer Bestattungsbrauch und Beigabensitten in Rom, Norditalien und den Nordwestprovinzen von der späten Republik bis in die Kaiserzeit. Internationales Kolloquium (Rom, 1–3 April 1998).* M. Heinzelmann et al., ed. Wiesbaden: Reichert, 159–68.

Giampaola, D. 2004. "Dagli studi di Bartolommeo Capasso agli scavi della Metropolitana: Ricerche sulle mura di Napoli e sull'evoluzione del paesaggio costiero." *NN* ser. 5, 5:35-56.

Giampaola, D. 2005. "L'area archeologica di San Lorenzo nel quadro della topografia di Neapolis." In *San Lorenzo Maggiore*, 1–16.

Giampaola, D. 2009. "Napoli, museo sotterraneo: Alcuni spunti di riflessione." In *Sottosuoli*, 51–61.

Giampaola, D. 2013. "Dalle insulae di Neapolis all' 'isola conventuale.'" In *San Gregorio Armeno: Storia, architettura, arte e tradizioni.* N. Spinosa et al., ed. Naples: Fridericiana Editrice Universitaria, 87–102.

Giampaola, D. 2017. "Lo scavo della stazione Duomo ed il Santuario dei Giochi Isolimpici: Un progetto di conoscenza per la storia della città. In *Sebastà Isolympia*, 28–40.

Giampaola, D., and V. Carsana. 2007. "La fascia costiera di Napoli: dallo scavo al museo della città." In *Comunicare la memoria del Mediterraneo: Strumenti, esperienze e progetti di valorizzazione. Atti del Convegno Internazionale di Pisa organizzato dalla Regione Toscana.* Naples and Aix-en-Provence: Centre Jean Bérard and Centre Camille Jullian, 205–15.

Giampaola, D., and B. D'Agostino. 2005. "Osservazioni storiche e archeologiche sulla fondazione di Neapolis." In *Noctes Campanae: Studi di storia antica ed archeologia dell'Italia preromana e romana in memoria di Martin W. Frederiksen.* W.V. Harris and E. Lo Cascio, ed. Naples: Luciano, 49–80.

Giampaola, D., and G. D'Henry. 1986. "Il territorio." In *Neapolis*, 273–84.

Giampaola, D., and E. Felici. 2004. "Il mare torna a bagnare Neapolis." *ASub* 10.1:3–5.

Giampaola, D., et al. 2004. "Il mare torna a bagnare Neapolis 2. Dalla scoperta del porto al recupero dei relitti." *ASub* 10.3:15–19.

Giampaola, D., et al. 2005. "Napoli: Trasformazioni edilizie e funzionali della fascia costiera." In *Le città campane tra tarda antichità e alto medioevo*. G. Vitolo, ed. Salerno: Laveglia, 219–47.

Giampaola, D., et al. 2006. "La scoperta del porto di Neapolis: Dalla ricostruzione topografica allo scavo e al recupero dei relitti." *Marittima Mediterranea: An International Journal on Underwater Archaeology* 2 [2005]:48–91.

Giampaola, D., et al. 2017. "L'artigianato ceramico a Neapolis in età ellenistica: Topografia delle produzione." *Scienze dell'antichità: Storia, archeologia, antropologia* 23.2:415–35.

Gianfrotta, P.A. 1993. "Puteoli sommersa." In Zevi, *Puteoli*, 115–24.

Gianfrotta, P.A. 1998. "I porti dell'area flegrea." In *Porti, approdi e linee di rotta nel Mediterraneo antico*. G. Laudizi and C. Marangio, ed. Galatina: Congedo, 153–76.

Gianfrotta, P.A. 2010. "Le terme di M. Licinio Crasso Frugi a Baia." *ArchClas* 61:193–209.

Gianfrotta, P.A. 2011. "'…mare Tyrrhenum a Lucrino molibus seclusum." *ATTA* 21:69–80.

Gianfrotta, P.A. 2012a. "Da Baia agli horrea del Lucrino: Aggiornamenti." *ArchClas* 63:277–96.

Gianfrotta, P.A. 2012b. "Richerche nell'area sommersa del 'Portus Iulius' (1988–1990 e successive): Un riepilogo." *ATTA* 22: 1–20.

Giangiulio, M. 1986. "Appunti di storia dei culti." In *Neapolis*, 101–54.

Gigante, M. 1984. *Virgilio e la Campania*. Naples: Giannini.

Gigante, M. 1992. "Virgilio e i suoi amici tra Napoli e Ercolano." *Parnassos* 34:3–18.

Gigante, M. 1995. *Philodemus in Italy: The Books from Herculaneum*. D. Obbink, trans. Ann Arbor: University of Michigan Press.

Gigante, M. 2004. "Vergil in the Shadow of Vesuvius." In *Vergil, Philodemus*, 85–99.

Gigante, M., and M. Capasso. 1989. "Il ritorno di Virgilio a Ercolano." *SIFC* ser. 3, 7:3–6.

Giglio, M. 2014–2015. "Un santuario salutare dal territorio di Neapolis: Agnano." *AION (archeol)* 21–22:105–35.

Giglio, M. 2016. "Le terme ed il santuario ellenistico di Agnano: Nuovi dati dal territorio di Neapolis e Puteoli, tra il III a.C. ed il V d.C." *FastiOnline* 368:1–10. At http://www.fastionline.org/docs/FOLDER-it-2016-368.pdf

Giglio, M., and G. Camodeca. 2009. "Lo stadio e le sue trasformazioni." In *Cuma: Le fortificazioni 3. Lo scavo 2004–2006*. B. D'Agostino and M. Giglio, ed. Naples: Direzione Regionale per i Beni Culturali e Paesaggistici della Campania, 196–247.

Giove, T. 1985. "La circolazione della moneta napoletana." In *Napoli antica*, 367–70.

Girone, M. 1994. "Sui laucelarchi." *MGR* 18:81–87.

Graham, A.J. 1990. "Pre-colonial Contacts: Questions and Problems." In *Greek Colonists*, 45–60.

Greco, E. 1985a. "Forum Duplex: Appunti per lo studio delle agorai di Neapolis in Campania." *AION (archeol)* 7:125–35.

Greco, E. 1985b. "Problemi urbanistici." In *Napoli antica*, 132–39.

Greco, E. 1986. "L'impianto urbano di Neapolis greca: Aspetti e problemi." In *Neapolis*, 187–219.

Greco, E. 1992. "Nel golfo di Napoli: Tra Sirene, Sirenusse e Athena." *AION (archeol)* 14:161–70.

Greco, E. 1994. "L'urbanistica neapolitana: Continuità dell'antico." In Zevi, *Neapolis*, 35–53.

Greco, G. 2013. "Demetra-Cerere: Il culto tra continuità e discontinuità." In *San Gregorio Armeno: Storia, architettura, arte e tradizioni*. Naples: Fridericiana Editrice Universitaria, 61–73.

Gras, M. 1986. "Il golfo di Napoli e il Tirreno arcaico." In *Neapolis*, 11–35.

Greco Pontrandolfo, A., and N. Vecchio. 1985. "Gli ipogei funerari." In *Napoli antica*, 284–93.

Grüger, E., et al. 2002. "Environmental Changes in and around Lake Avernus in Greek and Roman Times: A Study of the Plant and Animal Remains Preserved in the Lake's Sediments." In *Natural History*, 240–73.

Guadagno, G. 1995. "Documenti epigrafi ercolanesi relativi ad un terremoto." In *Archäologie und Seismologie*, 119–28.

BIBLIOGRAPHY

Guarducci, M. 1938. "L'istituzione della Fratria nella Grecia antica e nelle colonie greche d'Italia." *MemLinc* ser. 6, 8:65–136.

Guidoboni, E. 1989a. "Catalogo delle epigrafi latine riguardanti terremoti." In *Terremoti*, 135–68.

Guidoboni, E. 1989b. "Pozzi e gallerie come rimedi antisismici: La fortuna di un pregiudizio sulle città antiche." In *Terremoti*, 127–35.

Guidoboni, E., et al., ed. 1994. *Catalogue of Ancient Earthquakes in the Mediterranean Area up to the 10th Century*. Rome: Istituto Nazionale di Geofisica.

Günther, R.W.T. 1913. *Pausilypon: The Imperial Villa near Naples*. Oxford: Oxford University Press.

Guzzo, P.-G. 2009. "Attività della Soprintendenza Speciale per i Beni Archeologici di Napoli e Pompei." *AttiTaranto* 48:1007–35.

Hackens, T. 1986. "Essai de métrologie comparée de Naples et des monnayages parallèles." In *Monetazione di Neapolis*, 429–41.

Hall, J. 1997. *Ethnic Identity in Greek Antiquity*. Cambridge: Cambridge University Press.

Hanslik, R. 1949. "Papirius 69: L. Papirius Paetus." *RE* 18:1071–72.

Hardie, A. 1983. *Statius and the Silvae: Poets, Patrons, and Epideixis in the Graeco-Roman World*. Liverpool: Cairns.

Hatzfeld, J. 1912. "Les Italiens residents à Délos mentionnés dans les inscriptions de l'île." *BCH* 36:5–218.

Higginbotham, J.A. 1997. *Piscinae: Artificial Fishponds in Roman Italy*. London and Chapel Hill: University of North Carolina Press.

Holloway, R.R. 1986. "Tipologia ed arte." In *Monetazione di Neapolis*, 407–12.

Holloway, R.R. 1992. "The Romano-Campanian Coinage." In *The Age of Pyrrhus: Proceedings of an International Conference Held at Brown University, April 8th–10th, 1988*. Providence, RI: Brown University, Center for Old World Archaeology, 225–35.

Hommel, P. 1954. *Studien zu den römischen Figurengiebeln der Kaiserzeit*. Berlin: Mann.

Iapino, S. 2003. "I rilievi votivi con dedica ad Apollo e alle ninfe Nitrodi." In *La rassegna d'Ischia* 24:23–37.

Imhoof-Blumer, F. 1923. Fluß- un Meergotter auf griechischen und römischen Münzen. *SchwNumRu* 23:173–421.

Ippolito, F. 1986. "I Campi Flegrei: Nascita e sviluppo." In *Destino*, 175–82.

Isler, H.P. 1970. *Acheloos: Eine Monographie*. Bern: Francke.

Isler, H.P. 1981. "Acheloos." *LIMC* 1.1:12–36.

Johannowsky, W. 1952. "Contributo alla topografia della Campania antica." *RendNap* n.s. 27:84–146.

Johannowsky, W. 1961a. "Recenti scoperte archeologiche in San Lorenzo Maggiore a Napoli." *NN* n.s. 1:8–12.

Johannowsky, W. 1961b. "Scavi e scoperte." *Fasti archaeologici* 16: no. 2112.

Johannowsky, W. 1975. "Problemi relativi a Cuma arcaica." In *Contribution à l'étude de la société et colonisation eubéennes*. Naples: Centre Jean Bérard, 98–105.

Johannowsky, W. 1978. "Importazioni greco-orientali in Campania." In *Les céramiques de la Grèce de l'est et leur diffusion en occident*. Paris: Éditions du Centre National de la Recherche Scientifique, 137–39.

Johannowsky, W. 1985a. "L'assetto del territorio." In *Napoli Antica*, 333–40.

Johannowsky, W. 1985b. "I teatri." In *Napoli Antica*, 209–13.

Kaufmann, Claus M. 1959. *The Baths of Pozzuoli: A Study of the Medieval Illuminations of Peter of Eboli's Poem*. Oxford: Cassirer.

Keenan-Jones, D. 2010. "The Aqua Augusta: Regional Water Supply in Roman and Late-Antique Campania." Ph.D. Diss. Macquarie University.

Keenan-Jones, D. 2015. "Somma-Vesuvian Ground Movements and the Water Supply of Pompeii and the Bay of Naples." *AJA* 119:191–215.

Knoepfler, D. 2017. "Trois nouvelles proxénies d'Érétrie: Contribution à la géographie historique de l'Eubée. Les dèmes de Phègoè, Ptéchai et Boudion." *REA* 119.2:395–484.

Lacerenza, G., and M. Morisco. 1994. "Il mitreo." In Arthur, ed. 1994, 47–49.

Lacerenza, G., and M. Morisco. 1998. "Sull'origine di un bassorilievo mitraico a Bruxelles." *AION (or)* 58: 528–32.

Lacroix, L. 1953. "Fleuves et nymphes eponymes sur les monnaies grecques." *RBNum* 99:5–21.

La Foresta, D., and F. Miele. 2017. "Gli Isolympia e la valorizzazione di un'eredità culturale: Analisi e prospettive." In *Sebastà Isolympia*, 128–57.

LaForgia, E. 1981. *Edificio termale romano di Fuorigrotta. Accademia di Archeologia, Lettere e Belle Arti di Napoli: Monumenti* 4.

LaForgia, E. 1985a. "Ceramica a vernice nera dallo scarico di fornace di Corso Umberto." In *Neapolis*, 362–66.

LaForgia, E. 1985b. "I complessi termali." In *Napoli antica*, 340–47.

Lambeck, K., et al. 2004. "Sea Level in Roman Time in the Central Mediterranean and Implications for Recent Change." *Earth and Planetary Science Letters* 224:563–75.

Lamboglia, N. 1950. *Per una classificazione preliminare della ceramica campana*. Bordighera: Istituto Internazionale di Studi Liguri.

Landi, A. 2004. "Note sulla persistenza della lingua greca d'uso a Neapolis." *Vichiana* ser. 4, 6.2:207–31.

La Rocca, E. 1974–75. "Due tombe dell'Esquilino: Alcune novità sul commercio euboico in Italia centrale nell'VIII secolo a. C." *Dialoghi di archeologia* 8:86–103.

Latte, K. 1941. "Phratrie." *RE* 20.1:746–58.

Lattimore, S. 1974. "A Greek Pediment on a Roman Temple." *AJA* 77:55–61.

Lehmann-Hartleben, K. 1941. "The *Imagines* of the Elder Philostratus." *ArtB* 23:16–44.

Leiwo, M. 1989. "Philostratus of Ascalon, His Bank, His Connections and Neapolis in c. 130–90 B.C." *Athenaeum* 77:575–84.

Leiwo, M. 1994. *Neapolitana: A Study of Population and Language in Graeco-Roman Naples*. Helsinki: Societas Scientiarum Fennica.

Leiwo, M. 1996. "Some Neapolitan families." In *Roman Onomastics in the Greek East: Social and Political Aspects. Proceedings of the International Colloquium Organized by the Finnish Institute and the Centre for Greek and Roman Antiquity, Athens, 7–9 September 1993*. D. Rizakes, ed.

Athens and Paris: Research Centre for Greek and Roman Antiquity and National Hellenic Research Foundation; De Boccard, 81–87.

Lenzo, F. 2011. *Architettura e antichità a Napoli dal XV al XVIII secolo: Le colonne del tempio dei Dioscuri e la chiesa di San Paolo Maggiore*. Rome: "L'Erma" di Bretschneider.

Lenzo, F. 2015. "The Theatines and the Columns of the Temple of the Dioscuri in Naples." In *Remembering Parthenope*, 242–65.

Lepore, E. 1952. "Per la storia economico-sociale di Neapolis." *PP* 25–27:300–32.

Lepore, E. 1967a. "Napoli greco-romana: La vita politica e sociale 1. Neapolis nel quinto secolo a.C." In *SN*, 139–92.

Lepore, E. 1967b. "Napoli greco-romana: La vita politica e sociale 2. La comunità cittadina del quarto secolo a.C. tra Sanniti e Romani." In *SN*, 193–240.

Lepore, E. 1967c. "Napoli greco-romana: La vita politica e sociale 3. Neapolis dalla 'societas' alla 'civitas' romana." In *SN*, 241–88.

Lepore, E. 1967d. "Napoli greco-romana: La vita politica e sociale. Neapolis città dell'impero romano." In *SN*, 289–346.

Lepore, E. 1985a. "La città tra Campani e Romani." In *Napoli antica*, 109–22.

Lepore, E. 1985b. "Napoli: La città romana." In *Napoli antica*, 115–22.

Lepore, E. 1990. "Gli avvenimenti del contesto Mediterraneo e l'Italia." In *Crise et transformation*, 289–97.

Letzner, W. 1990. *Römische Brunnen und Nymphäen in der westlichen Reichshälfte*. Münster: Lit.

Libertini, G., et al. 2017. "L'acquedotto augusteo del Serino nel contesto del sistema viario e delle centuriazioni del territorio attraversato e delle *civitates* servite." *Rassegna storica dei Comuni* n.s. 43:200–202.

Liccardo, G. 1992. "Lineamenti di epigrafia cristiana napoletana." *Rivista di archeologia cristiana* 68:259–70.

Liccardo, G. 2004. *Napoli sotterranea: Storia, arte, leggenda, curiosità*. Rome: Newton Compton.

Liddell, H.G., and G.E. Marindin. 1890. "Lampadodromia." In *A Dictionary of Greek and Roman Antiquities*. W. Smith et al., ed. 3rd ed., 2 vols. London: Murray, 2:4–6.

Lippi, R. 2002. "Le serie enee di Neapolis, fasi I–III: Aspetti ponderali e cronologia." *RIN* 103:21–47.

Lomas, K. 1993. *Rome and the Western Greeks*. New York and London: Routledge.

Lomas, K. 1995. "Urban Elites and Cultural Definition: Romanization in Southern Italy." In *Urban Society in Roman Italy*. T. Cornell and K. Lomas, ed. New York: St. Martin's, 107–20.

Lomas, K. 2015. "Colonizing the Past: Cultural Memory and Civic Identity in Hellenistic and Roman Naples." In *Remembering Parthenope*, 64–84.

Longo Auricchio, F. 2004. "Philosophy's Harbor." In *Vergil, Philodemus*, 37–42.

Longobardo, F. 2004. "Problemi di viabilità in Campania: La Via Domitiana." In *Viabilità e insediamenti nell'Italia antica*. L. Quilici and S. Quilici Gigli, ed. Rome: "L'Erma" di Bretschneider, 277–90.

Lucherini, V. 2009. *La cattedrale di Napoli: Storia, architettura, storiografia di un monumento medievale*. Rome: École Française de Rome.

Luongo, G. 2001. "Sismicità e vulcanismo." In *Ambiente geologico*, 91–109.

Luongo, G., et al. 1987. *Ischia: Storia di un'isola vulcanica*. Naples: Liguori.

Luraghi, N. 1994. *Tirannidi arcaiche in Sicilia e Magna Grecia: Da Panezio di Leontini alla caduta dei Dinomenidi*. Florence: Olschki.

Luschi, L. 1999. "Un rilievo della collezione Carpi e le ninfe Nitrodi a Roma." *Bollettino d'arte* 108:57–70.

Macchioro, V. 1912. "Le terme romane di Agnano." *MemLinc* 21:225–84.

Maddalo, S. 2003. *Il* De balneis puteolanis *di Pietro da Eboli: Realtà e simbolo della tradizione figurata*. Vatican City: Biblioteca Apostolica Vaticana.

Magaldi, E. 1932. "Il teatro antico di Napoli." *Dioniso* 3:63–78.

Malkin, I. 1987. *Religion and Colonization in Ancient Greece*. Leiden and New York: Brill.

Malkin, I. 1998. *The Returns of Odysseus: Colonization and Ethnicity*. Berkeley: University of California Press.

Malkin, I. 2002. "A Colonial Middle Ground: Greek, Etruscan, and Local Elites in the Bay of Naples." In *The Archaeology of Colonialism*. C.L. Lyons and J.K. Papadopoulos, ed. Los Angeles: Getty Research Institute, 151–81.

Mallardo, A. 1913. "Nuova epigrafe greco-latina della fratria napoletana degli Artemisi." *MemNap* 2.2:149–76.

Mancinetti Santamaria, G. 1982. "Filostrato di Ascalona, banchiere in Delo." In *Delo e l'Italia*. F. Coarelli et al., ed. Rome: Bardi, 79–89.

Marasco, G. 2001. "Aspetti sociali, economici e culturali del termalismo nel mondo romano." *Studi classici e orientali* 47:9–65.

Marazzi, M., and L. Re. 1985. "L'insediamento preistorico di Vivara: Le importazioni egeo-micenee." In *Napoli antica*, 43–49.

Marazzi, M., and S. Tusa, ed. 1991–1994. *Vivara: Centro commerciale mediterraneo dell'età del bronzo*. 2 vols. Rome: Bagatto.

Marchetti, P. 1986. "En guise d'épigraphie monétaire." In *Monetazione di Neapolis*, 443–68.

Maréchal, S. 2020. *Public Baths and Bathing Habits in Late Antiquity*. Boston: Brill.

Mariniello, A. 1981. "Il tracciato dell'acquedotto augusteo nel tratto Napoli–Miseno." *Mondo archeologico* 61:18–23.

Mariotta, G. 2003. "Riflessi della politica ateniese in Occidente nelle 'Eumenidi' (vv. 295–7)?" *SIFC* 4.1:129–35.

Marrone, R. 1996. *Le strade di Napoli*. 2 vols. Rome: Newton & Compton.

Martin, R. 1974. *L'urbanisme dans la Grèce antique*. 2nd ed. Paris: Picard.

Marturano, A., and V. Rinaldis. 1995. "Il terremoto vesuviano del 62 d.C: Un evento carico di responsabilità." In *Archäologie und Seismologie*, 131–35.

Marzano, A. 2015. "Sergio Orata e il Lago Lucrino: Alcune considerazioni sull'allevamento di ostriche nella Campania romana." *Oebalus* 10:131–49.

BIBLIOGRAPHY

Marzocchella, A. 1980. "Le tombe eneolitiche di Napoli Materdei." *Rivista di scienze preistoriche* 35:147–64.

Marzocchella, A. 1985. "Dalla preistoria all protostoria: L'eneolitico a Napoli." In *Napoli antica*, 27–29.

Mattingly, H.B. 1969. "Athens and the Western Greeks: c. 500–413 B.C." In *La circolazione della moneta ateniese in Sicilia e in Magna Grecia: Atti del Convegno del Centro Internazionale di Studi Numismatici*. Rome: Istituto Italiano di Numismatica, 201–22.

Maurizi, N. 1993–1995. "La presenza ateniese a Napoli: Aspetti mitici, culti, tradizione storica." *Annali della Facoltà di lettere e filosofia, Università degli Studi di Perugia* 31:287–309.

McDaniel, W.B. 1913. "Apragopolis, Island-Home of Ancient Lotos Eaters." *TAPA* 45:29–34.

Mele, A. 1985. "La città greca." In *Napoli antica*, 103–8.

Mele, A. 2007a. "Atene e la Magna Grecia." In *Atene e l'Occidente: I grandi temi. Le premesse, i protagonisti, le forme della comunicazione e dell'interazione, i modi dell'intervento ateniese in Occidente. Atti del Convegno Internazionale, Atene, 25–27 maggio 2006*. E. Greco and M. Lombardo, ed. Athens: Scuola archeologica italiana di Atene, 239–67.

Mele, A. 2007b. "La colonizzazione greca arcaica: Modi e forme." In *Eroi, eroismi, eroizzazioni: Dalla Grecia antica a Padova e Venezia*. A. Coppola, ed. Padua: Sargon, 155–62.

Mele, A. 2009a. "Cuma in Opicia tra Greci e Romani." In *Cuma*, 77–167.

Mele, A. 2009b. "Tra sub-colonia ed *epoikia:* Il caso di Neapolis." In *Colonie di colonie: Le fondazioni sub-coloniali greche tra colonizzazione e colonialismo. Atti del Convegno Internazionale (Lecce, 22–24 giugno 2006)*. M. Lombardo and F. Frisone, ed. Galatina: Congedo, 183–99.

Mele, A. 2014. *Greci in Campania*. Rome: Scienze e Lettere.

Melisurgo, G. 1889. *Napoli sotterranea: Topografia della rete di canali d'acqua profonda*. Naples: Giannini.

Melisurgo, G. 1997 [1889]. *Napoli sotterranea*. Naples: Edizioni scientifiche italiane.

Merkelbach, R. 1975. "Zu der Festordnung für die Sebasta in Neapel." *ZPE* 15:192–93.

Miccio, B., and U. Potenza. 1994. *Gli acquedotti di Napoli*. Naples: A.M.A.N.

Miletti, L. 2015. "Setting the Agenda: The Image of Classical Naples in Strabo's Geography and other Ancient Literary Sources." In *Remembering Parthenope*, 19–38.

Minieri, L. 2002. "La colonizzazione di Capua tra l'84 e il 59 a.C." In *Romanizzazione*, 249–67.

Miranda, E. 1982. "I cataloghi dei *Sebastà* di Napoli: Proposte ed osservazioni." *RendNap* n.s. 57:165–81.

Miranda, E. 1985a. "Istituzioni, agoni e culti: Le magistrature, gli agoni, I culti greci." In *Napoli antica*, 386–94.

Miranda, E. 1985b. "I rilievi funerari." In *Napoli antica*, 293–98.

Miranda, E. 1985c. "Testimonianze epigrafiche delle necropoli." In *Napoli antica*, 298–99.

Miranda, E. 1988a. "Due nuove fratrie napoletane." *MGR* 13:159–66.

Miranda, E. 1988b. "Tito a Napoli: Una nuova dedica onoraria." *Epigraphica* 50:222–26.

Miranda, E. 1990–1995. *Iscrizioni greche di Italia: Napoli*. 2 vols. Rome: Quasar.

Miranda, E. 1998. "Sacerdozi a Napoli in età romana." In *I culti della Campania antica: Atti del Convegno Internazionale di Studi in Ricordo di Nazarena Valenza Mele, Napoli 15–17 maggio 1995*. M. Cébeillac-Gervasoni, ed. Rome: Giorgio Bretschneider, 231–38.

Miranda de Martino, E. 2007. "Neapolis e gli imperatori: Nuovi dati dai cataloghi dei Sebastà." *Oebalus* 2:203–15.

Miranda de Martino, E. 2013. "Ritratti di campioni dai 'Sebastà' di Napoli." *Mediterraneo antico* 16.2:519–35.

Miranda de Martino, E. 2014. "Les *Sebasta* de Naples à l'époque de Domitien: Témoignages épigraphiques." *CRAI* 2014.3:1165–88.

Miranda de Martino, E. 2016. "Augusto e i Sebasta: L'identità greca nell'impero. *Maia* 68:389–98.

BIBLIOGRAPHY

Miranda de Martino, E. 2017a. "Augusto *ktistes* di *Neapolis.*" In *Come Aurora. Lieve, preziosa: Ergastai e philoi a Gabriella Bevilacqua. Giornata di studio – Roma 6 giugno 2012*. P. Lombardi, ed. Rome: Quasar, 155–61.

Miranda de Martino, E. 2017b. "I *Sebasta* dell'82 d.C.: Restauro delle lastre e aggiornamenti." *Historiká: Studi di storia greca e romana* 7:253–69.

Mitchell, R. 1966. "A New Chronology for the Romano-Campanian Coins." *NumChron* ser. 7, 6:65–70.

Mitchell, R. 1969. "The Fourth Century Origin of Roman Didrachms." *Museum Notes (American Numismatic Society)* 15:41–71.

Mitchell, R. 1973. "Hoard Evidence and Early Roman Coinage." *RIN* 75:89–110.

Monaco, L. 2002. "Centuriazioni e gestione delle acque: Considerazioni in tema delle assetti agrari *nell'Ager Campanus.*" In *Romanizzazione*, 87–123.

Molinari, N., and N. Sisci. 2016. ΠΟΤΑΜΙΚΟΝ: *Sinews of Acheloios. A Comprehensive Catalog of the Bronze Coinage of the Man-Faced Bull, with Essays on Origin and Identity.* Oxford: Archaeopress.

Monti, P. 1968. *Ischia: Preistorica, greca, romana, paleocristiana.* Naples: E.P.S.

Monti, P. 1980. *Ischia: Archeologia e storia.* Naples: Fratelli Porzio.

Montuono, G.M. 2002. "L'Acquedotto romano del Serino e la città di Napoli." In *Acqua e architettura*, 75-107.

Montuono, G.M. 2010. "L'approvvigionamento idrico della città di Napoli: L'acquedotto del Serino e il Formale Reale in un manoscritto della Biblioteca Nazionale di Madrid." In *Storia dell'ingegneria: Atti del 2° Convegno Nazionale, Napoli, 7–8–9 aprile 2008*. S. D'Agostino et al., ed. Naples: Cuzzolin, 1:1029–50. Archived at WebCite at http://www.webcitation.org/5qVks7IHP.

Morel, J.-P. 1981a. *Céramique campanienne: Les formes.* 2 vols. Rome: École Française de Rome.

Morel, J.-P. 1981b. "La produzione della ceramica campana: Aspetti economici e sociali." In *Società romana e produzione schiavistica 2.*

Merci, mercati e scambi nel Mediterraneo. A. Giardina and A. Schiavone, ed. Rome and Bari: Paterza, 81–97.

Morel, J.-P. 1985. "La ceramica campana A nell'economia della Campania." In *Napoli antica*, 372–78.

Morel, J.-P. 1986a. "Una grande produzione di Neapolis: La ceramica campana A." *Magna Graecia* 21.5–6:7–9.

Morel, J.-P. 1986b. "Remarques sur l'art et l'artisanat de Naples antique." In *Neapolis*, 305–56.

Moretti, L. 1953. *Iscrizioni agonistiche greche.* Rome: Signorelli.

Musto, R.G. 2013. *Medieval Naples: A Documentary History, 400–1400.* New York: Italica Press.

Napoli, M. 1952. "Realtà storica di Partenope." *PP* 25–27:269–85.

Napoli, M. 1960. "Una nuova fratria napoletana." *PP* 15:152–53.

Napoli, M. 1967a. "Le arti figurative." In *SN*, 593–622.

Napoli, M. 1967b. "Topografia e archeologia 1: La città." In *SN*, 375–416.

Napoli, M. 1967c. "Topografia e archeologia 2: I monumenti." In *SN*, 417–48.

Napoli, M. 1967d. "Topografia e archeologia 3: Il suburbio." In *SN*, 449–70.

Napoli, M. 1967e. "Topografia e archeologia 4: Le necropoli." In *SN*, 471–83.

Napoli, M. 1997 [1959]. *Napoli greco-romana.* 2nd ed. Naples: Colonnese.

Nasseri-Moghaddam, A., et al. 2007. "Effects of Underground Cavities on Rayleigh Waves: Field and Numerical Experiments." *Soil Dynamics and Earthquake Engineering* 27:4 (April): 300–313.

Nava, M.L. 2006a. "Napoli: Metropolitana, linea 6, Fuorigrotta – piazzale Tecchio." *Atti Taranto* 45:621–24.

Nava, M.L. 2006b. "Napoli, via S. Paolo: Scavi nel teatro antico." *Atti Taranto* 45:626–28.

Nava, M.L. 2007a. "Napoli, chiesa e convento di San Lorenzo Maggiore: Area del Foro." *Atti Taranto* 46:294–98.

Nava, M.L. 2007b. "Napoli, piazza Nicola Amore, stazione Duomo della linea 1 della Metropolitana: Santuario dei giochi isolimpici." *Atti Taranto* 46:304–7.

Nava, M.L. 2007c. "Napoli, via San Paolo 4 – via Anticaglia: Teatro romano." *Atti Taranto* 46:298–301.

Nava, M.L. 2008a. "Napoli, Museo Archeologico Nazionale: Scavo archeologico nel cantiere di ristrutturazione del 'Braccio Nuovo.' Necropolis Greco-romana." *Atti Taranto* 47:849–52.

Nava, M.L. 2008b. "Napoli, via San Paolo – via Anticaglia: Lo scavo e il restauro del teatro antico." *Atti Taranto* 47:852–55.

Nava, M.L. 2008c. "Piazza Nicola Amore – stazione Duomo: L'area del Tempio dei Giochi isolimpici." *Atti Taranto* 47:855–57.

Neuerburg, N. 1965. *L'architettura delle fontane e dei ninfei nell'Italia antica*. Naples: Macchiaroli.

Newby, Z. 2005. *Greek Athletics in the Roman World: Victory and Virtue*. Oxford and New York: Oxford University Press.

Newlands, C.E. 2012. *Statius, Poet between Rome and Naples*. Bristol: Bristol Classical Press.

Nichols, C., and J.H. McGregor. 2019. *Renaissance Naples: A Documentary History, 1400–1600*. New York: Italica Press.

Nielsen, I. 1993. *Thermae et balnea: The Architecture and Cultural History of Roman Public Baths*. 2 vols. Aarhus: Aarhus University Press.

Nijboer, A.J., et al. 1999–2000. "A High Chronology for the Early Iron Age in Central Italy." *Palaeohistoria*, 41–42, 163–76.

Nijboer, A.J., and J. van der Plicht. 2008. "The Iron Age in the Mediterranean: Recent Radiocarbon Research at the University of Groningen." In *A New Dawn for the Dark Age? Shifting Paradigms in Mediterranean Iron Age Chronology*. D. Brandherm and M. Trachsel, ed. Oxford: BAR, 103–18.

Ohlig, C. 2001. *De aquis Pompeiorum: Das Castellum Aquae in Pompeji. Herkunft, Zuleitung und Verteilung des Wassers*. Nijmegen: C. Ohlig.

Olcese, G. 2010. *Le anfore greco italiche di Ischia: Archeologia e archeometria. Artigianato ed economia nel Golfo di Napoli*. Rome: Quasar.

Olcese, G. 2011. "Produzione ceramica nel Golfo di Napoli e nella Campania settentrionale. Parte I: La ricerca archeometrica. Stato degli studi e prospettive di ricerca." *Immensa aequora* 3:35–49.

Olcese, G. 2017. "Wine and Amphorae in Campania in the Hellenistic Age: The Case of Ischia." In *The Economic Integration of Roman Italy: Rural Communities in a Globalizing World*. T.C.A. de Haas and G.W. Tol, ed. Leiden: Brill, 299–321.

Oosterhuis, D. 2007. "The Catalepton: Myths of Virgil." Ph.D. Diss., University of Minnesota.

Osborne, R. 1998. "Early Greek Colonisation? The Nature of Greek Settlement in the West." In *Archaic Greece: New Approaches to the Evidence*. N. Fisher and H. van Wees, ed. London: Duckworth, 251–69.

Ostrow, S.E. 1977. "Problems in the Topography of Roman Puteoli." Ph.D. Diss., University of Michigan.

Ostrow, S.E. 1979. "The Topography of Puteoli and Baiae on Eight Glass Flasks." *Puteoli* 3:77–140.

Pagano, M. 1980–1981. "Gli impianti marittimi della villa 'Pausilypon.'" *Puteoli* 4–5:245–55.

Pagano, M. 1983–1984. "Il lago Lucrino: Richerche storiche e archeologiche." *Puteoli* 7–8:113–226.

Pagano, M. 1995–1996. "L'area vesuviana dopo l'eruzione del 79 d.C." *RivStudPomp* 7:35–44.

Pagano, M., et al. 1982. "Recherches archéologiques et historiques sur la zone du lac d'Averne." *MÉFRA* 94:271–323.

Pagliaro, S. 2001. "Aspetti geologici." In *Ambiente geologico*, 39–57.

Pais, E. 1900–1901. "Per la storia di Napoli e Ischia nell'età sillana." *AttiNapoli (=MemNap)* 21:145–52.

Pais, E. 1908a. *Ancient Italy*. C.D. Curtis, trans. Chicago: University of Chicago Press.

Pais, E. 1908b. "Per la storia di Napoli, d'Ischia e di Pozzuoli nell'età sillana." In *Ricerche storiche e geografiche sull'Italia antica*. Turin: Società Tipografico-editrice Nazionale, 257–67.

Pais, E. 1908c. "Per la storia d'Ischia sull'antichità." In *Ricerche storiche e geografiche sull'Italia antica*. Turin: Società Tipografico-editrice Nazionale, 227–55.

Pais, E. 1922. *Italia antica: Ricerche di storia e di geografia storica*. Bologna: Zanichelli.

Pane, G. 1964."La villa Carafa e la storia urbanistica di Pizzofalcone." *NN* n.s. 4:133–48.

Pani Ermini, L. 1994."Città fortificate e fortificazione delle città italiane fra V e VI secolo." *Rivista di studi liguri* 59–60:193–206.

Paoli, P.A. 1768. *Antichità di Pozzuoli. Puteolanae antiquitates.* Naples: n.p.

Papadopoulos, J.K. 1985a."I culti orientali." In *Napoli antica,* 295–97.

Papadopoulos, J.K. 1985b."I rilievi funerari." In *Napoli antica,* 293–98.

Papadopoulos, J.K. 1997."Phantom Euboians." *Journal of Mediterranean Archaeology* 10:191–219.

Pappalardo, U. 1990. "L'eruzione pliniana del Vesuvio nel 79 d.C.: Ercolano." In *Volcanology and Archaeology,* 198–215.

Pappalardo, U. 1995."Osservazioni su un secondo grande terremoto a Pompei." In *Archäologie und Seismologie,* 191–94.

Pappalardo, U. 2001."Vesuvio: Grandi eruzioni e reinsediamenti." In *Modalità insediative,* 435–53.

Parma, A. 1992."Osservazioni sul patrimonio epigrafico flegreo con particolare riguardo a *Misenum.*" In *Civiltà dei Campi Flegrei:Atti del Convegno Internazionale.* M. Gigante, ed. Naples: Giannini, 201–25.

Parma, A. 2009."L'organizzazione del territorio rurale di Nola in età romana." In *Apolline Project,* 133–43.

Pedroni, L. 1996."Lo iato del IV secolo nella monetazione campana." *RIN* 97:11–28.

Peroni, R. 1985."Dalla preistoria alla protostoria: Il golfo di Napoli e la Campania." In *Napoli antica,* 23–27.

Perrotta, A., and C. Scarpati. 2009."Vulcani come distruttori e conservatori di habitat naturali ed antropici: Il Vesuvio e gli insediamenti romani." In *Apolline Project,* 279–86.

Perrotta, A., et al. 2006. "Volcaniclastic Resedimentation on the Northern Slope of Vesuvius as a Direct Response to Eruptive Activity." *Landslides* 3.4:295–301.

Pescatore, T., and H. Sigurdsson. 1993. "L'eruzione del Vesuvio del 79 d.C." In *Ercolano 1738–1988: 250 anni di ricerca archeologica.* L.F. Dell'Orto, ed. Rome:"L'Erma" di Bretschneider, 449–58.

Pesce, G. 1935. "La necropolis di Castel Capuano e di Via Cirillo." *NSc*, 257–93.

Peterson, R.M. 1919. *The Cults of Campania*. Rome: American Academy in Rome.

Pinsent, T. 1969. "The Magistracy at Naples." *PP* 24:368–72.

Pirro, A. 1905. *Le origini di Napoli: Studio storico-topografico*. Salerno: Fratelli Jovani.

Pisano, C. 2017. "Sulle 'tracce' di Strabone: La grecità di Neapolis in età imperiale." *Incidenza dell'antico* 15:133–53.

Pisapia, M.S. 1981. "L'area ercolanese dopo l'eruzione del 79." *RendNap* n.s. 56:63–74.

Pontrandolfo, A. 1986. "Le necropoli urbane di Neapolis." In *Neapolis*, 255–70.

Popkin, M. 2018. "Urban Images in Glass from the Late Roman Empire: The Souvenir Flasks of Puteoli and Baiae." *AJA* 122:427–62.

Potenza, U. 1996. "Gli acquedotti romani di Serino." In *Cura Aquarum in Campania: Proceedings of the Ninth International Congress on the History of Water Management and Hydraulic Engineering in the Mediterranean Region*. N. de Haan and G.C.M. Jansen, ed. Leiden: BABesch, 93–100.

Pozzi, E. 1986. "La monetazione di Neapolis nel IV e nel III secolo a.C." In *Monetazione di Neapolis*, 91–100.

Pugliese, L. 2005. "Le anfore d'allume dal complesso archeologico di San Lorenzo Maggiore." In *L'alun de Méditerranée: colloque international organisé par le Centre Camille Jullian, Naples, 4–5–6 juin 2003, Lipari, 7–8 juin 2003*. P. Borgard and J-P. Brun, ed. Naples and Aix-en-Provence: Centre Jean Bérard, 215–18.

Pugliese, L. 2014. *Anfore greco-italiche neapolitane (IV–III sec. a.C.)*. Rome: Scienze e lettere.

Pugliese Carratelli, G. 1952a. "Napoli antica." *PP* 25–27:243–68.

Pugliese Carratelli, G. 1952b. "Sul culto delle sirene nel golfo di Napoli." *PP* 25–27:420–26.

Pugliese Carratelli, G. 1967. "Il mondo mediterraneo e le origini di Napoli." In *SN*, 97–137.

Pugliese Carratelli, G. 1979. "Per la storia dei culti delle colonie euboiche d'Italia." *AttiTaranto* 18:221–29.

Purcell, N. 1990. "Mobility and the *Polis.*" In *The Greek City from Homer to Alexander*. O. Murray and S.R.F. Price, ed. Oxford: Clarendon, 29–58.

Rasulo, G., and M. Rasulo. 2009. "Il sottosuolo di Napoli e l'infrastrutturazione urbana: Il caso degli acquedotti storici." In *Sottosuoli*, 63–72.

Rasulo, M. 2002. "Bolla Aqueduct: A Two-Thousand-Year Lasting Service." *Hydraulic Information Management* 10:369–78.

Raviola, F. 1990. "La tradizione letteraria su Parthenope." *Hesperìa: Studi sulla grecità di occidente* 1:19–60.

Raviola, F. 1991. "La tradizione letteraria sulla fondazione di Neapolis." *Hesperìa: Studi sulla grecità di occidente* 2:19–40.

Raviola, F. 1993. "Tzetzes e la spedizione di Diotimo a Neapolis." *Hesperìa: Studi sulla grecità di occidente* 3:67–83.

Raviola, F. 1995. *Napoli origini*. Rome: "L'Erma" di Bretschneider.

Raviola, F. 1997. "Il mito di Phaleros, in quanto elemento di una convergenza e interferenza fra Atene e Neapolis nell'avanzato V secolo." *AttiTaranto* 36:347–57.

Renna, E. 1992. *Vesuvius Mons: Aspetti del Vesuvio nel mondo antico tra filologia, archeologia, vulcanologia*. Naples: Procaccini.

Riccio, A. 2002. "L'antico acquedotto della Bolla." In *Acqua e architettura*, 115–23.

Rickman, G. 1980. *The Corn Supply of Ancient Rome*. Oxford and NewYork: Oxford University Press.

Ridgway, D. 1979. "Fra oriente e occidente: La Pithecusa degli Eubei." *AttiTaranto* 18:65–81.

Ridgway, D. 1985. "Gli Eubei nel golfo." In *Napoli antica*, 76–79.

Ridgway, D. 1990. "The First Western Greeks and their Neighbors." In *Greek Colonists*, 61–72.

Ridgway, D. 1992. *The First Western Greeks*. Cambridge: Cambridge University Press.

Ridgway, D. 2004. "Euboeans and Others along the Tyrrhenian Seaboard in the 8th Century B.C." In *Greek Identity*, 15–34.

Rigsby, K.J. 2008. "Hauranus the Epicurean." *Classical Journal* 104:19–22.

Rittmann, A. and V. Gottini. 1981. "L'isola d'Ischia: Geologia." In *Bollettino del Servizio Geologico d'Italia* 101:131–274.

Robert, L. 1939. "Inscriptions grecques d'Asie Mineure." In *Anatolian Studies Presented to William Hepburn Buckler.* W.M. Calder and J. Keil, ed. Manchester: Manchester University Press, 230–48.

Rocco, A. 1942–1946. "Stele provenienti dal territorio dell'antica Neapolis." *RendNap* n.s. 22:77–92.

Rolandi, G., et al. 2007. "The 79 AD Eruption of Somma: The Relationship between the Date of the Eruption and the Southeast Tephra Dispersion." *Journal of Volcanology and Geothermal Research* 169:87–98.

Roncella, B. 2010. "I magazzini." In *Napoli, la città e il mare*, 63–68.

Rose, K.F.C. 1962. "Time and Place in the Satiricon." *TAPA* 93:402–9.

Rose, M. and S. Aydingün. 2007. "Under Istanbul." *Archaeology* 60.4 (July/August): 34–40.

Rossi, L. 2014. "Les frequentissimi mercatores de Pouzzoles et le blé égyptien à Rome." *MÉFRA* 126:469–86.

Rossi, L. 2016. " 'Horrea' et 'granaria' à Pouzzoles." In *Echanger en Méditerranée: Acteurs, pratiques et normes dans les mondes anciens.* A.-F. Baroni et al., ed. Rennes: Presses Universitaires de Rennes, 205–26.

Rostagni, A. 1952. "La cultura letteraria di Napoli antica nelle sue fasi culminanti." *PP* 25–27:344–57.

Roussel, D. 1976. *Tribu et cité: Études sur les groupes sociaux dans les cités grecques aux époques archaïque et classique.* Paris: Les Belles Lettres.

Ruggiero, M. 1883. "Napoli." *NSc*, 20–22.

Ruggiero, M. 1888. *Degli scavi di antichità nelle province di terraferma dell'antico regno di Napoli dal 1743 al 1876.* Naples: Morano.

Rutter, N.K. 1979. *Campanian Coinages 475–380 BC.* Edinburgh: Edinburgh University Press.

Rutter, N.K. 1986. "La monetazione di Neapolis fino al 380 a.C." In *Monetazione di Neapolis*, 67–84.

Rutter, N.K. 1997. *The Greek Coinages of Southern Italy and Sicily.* London: Spink.

Rutter, N.K., and A. Burnett, ed. 2001. *Historia numorum: Italy.* London: British Museum Press.

Salmon, E.T. 1967. *Samnium and the Samnites.* Cambridge: Cambridge University Press.

Salvatore, M.R., and M.L. Nava. 2011. "Napoli ed il suo centro storico." *Atti Taranto* 49 (2009):707–13.

Sambon, A. 1903. *Les monnaies antiques de l'Italie.* Paris: Bureau du "Musée."

Sampaolo, V. 2005. "L'attività archeologica a Napoli e Caserta nel 2004." *Atti Taranto* 44:663–705.

Sampaolo, V. 2012. "L'attività della Soprintendenza Speciale per i Beni Archeologici in Napoli e Pompei." *Atti Taranto* 50:1309–53.

Santore, J. 2001. *Modern Naples: A Documentary History, 1799–1999.* New York: Italica Press.

Santoro, L. 1984. "Le mura Greco-romane." In *Le mura di Napoli.* Rome: Istituto Italiano dei Castelli, 25–42.

Sartori, F. 1953. *Problemi di storia costituzionale italiota.* Rome: "L'Erma" di Bretschneider.

Savino, E. 2004a. "Considerazioni sulla data dell'eruzione vesuviana del 79 d.C." In *Pompei, Capri*, 369–75.

Savino, E. 2004b. "A proposito del numero e della cronologia delle eruzioni vesuviane tra V e VI sec. d.C." In *Pompei, Capri*, 511–21.

Savino, E. 2007. "Fra Campania e Roma: Note sulla cronologia del regno di Tito." *Oebalus* 2:239–47.

Savino, E. 2009. "Problemi della Guerra sociale in Campania nell'89 a.C." *Oebalus* 4:219–33.

Sbordone, F. 1967a. "La cultura 1: Uno sguardo alle origini." In *SN*, 511–20.

Sbordone, F. 1967b. "La cultura 2: Filosofi e letterati a Napoli verso il tramonto della repubblica." In *SN*, 521–42.

Sbordone, F. 1967c. "La cultura 3: 'Otiosa Neapolis.'" In *SN*, 543–48.

Sbordone, F. 1967d. "La cultura 4: Napoli e Stazio." In *SN*, 549–60.

Sbordone, F. 1967e. "La cultura 5: Gli spettacoli di Napoli antica." In *SN*, 561–70.

Sbordone, F. 1967f. "La cultura 6: Le pitture di una villa neapolitana." In *SN*, 571–82.

Scarpati, C., et al. 1996. "Neapolis: Le mura e la città: Indagini a S. Domenico Maggiore e a S. Marcellino." *AION (archeol)* 3: 115–38.

Scarpati, C., et al. 2009. "The History of Eruptions on the Northern Slope of Somma-Vesuvius." In *Apolline Project*, 271–78.

Scatozza Höricht, L.A. 2007. *Pithecusa: Materiali votivi da Monte Vico e dall'area di Santa Restituta*. Rome: Giorgio Bretschneider.

Scheidel, W. 2016. *The Great Leveler: Violence and the History of Inequality from the Stone Age to the Twenty-First Century*. Princeton: Princeton University Press.

Scherillo, A. 1977. "Vulcanismo e bradisismo nei Campi Flegrei." In *Campi Flegrei*, 33, 81–116.

Scherrer, P. 1990. "Augustus, die Mission des Vedius Pollio und die Artemis Ephesia." *Jahreshefte des Österreichischen Archäologischen Instituts in Wien* 60, *Hauptblatt*, 87–101.

Schraudolph, E. 1993. *Römische Götterweihungen mit Reliefschmuck aus Italien: Altäre, Basen und Reliefs*. Heidelberg: Archäologie und Geschichte.

Scognamiglio, E. 2009a. "Porto Giulio: Nuovi dati." *Archaeologia maritima mediterranea* 6:143–53.

Scognamiglio, E. 2009b. "La rada di Baia: Forma e frequentazione." *Archaeologia maritima mediterranea* 6:155–65.

Sear, F. 2006. *Roman Theatres: An Architectural Study*. Oxford: Oxford University Press.

Sgobbo, I. 1926. "Napoli: Il sepolcreto dei Fuficii ed un elogio di C. Duilio sulla via Puteolana." *NSc*, 233–41.

Sgobbo, I. 1929. "Terme flegree e origine delle terme romane." In *Atti del Congresso Nazionale di Studi Romani*. Rome: Istituto di Studi Romani, 186–94.

Sgobbo, I. 1938. "Serino: L'acquedotto romano della Campania: "Fontis Augustei Aquaeductus." *NSc*, 75–97.

Sherwin-White, A.N. 1973. *The Roman Citizenship.* 2nd ed. Oxford: Clarendon.

Sider, D. 1997. *The Epigrams of Philodemus.* New York: Oxford University Press.

Sigurdsson, H., et al. 1982. "The Eruption of Vesuvius in A.D. 79: Reconstruction from Historical and Volcanological Evidence." *AJA* 86:39–51.

Sigurdsson, H., et al. 1985. "The Eruption of Vesuvius in A.D. 79." *National Geographic Research* 1:332–87.

Sigurdsson, H., and S. Carey. 2002. "The Eruption of Vesuvius in A.D. 79." In *Natural History*, 37–64.

Smith, C. 1899. "The Torch Race of Bendis." *Classical Review* 13.4:230–32.

Snodgrass, A. 1994. "The Nature and Standing of the Early Western Colonies." In *The Archaeology of Greek Colonisation.* G.R. Tsetskhladze and F. De Angelis, ed. Oxford: Oxford University Committee for Archaeology, 1–10.

Sogliano, A. 1892. "Napoli: Scoperte epigrafiche." *NSc*, 479–81.

Sogliano, A. 1901. "Sorrento: Di una epigrafe latina recentemente scoperta." *NSc*, 363–64.

Soraci, R. 1982. "Note sull'opera legislativa ed amministrativa dell'imperatore Tito." *Quaderni catanesi di studi classici e medievali* 4:427–49.

Soricelli, G. 1987. "Appunti sulla produzione di terra sigillata nell'area flegreo-napoletana 1: Una produzione di terra sigillata a Napoli." *Puteoli* 11:107–12.

Soricelli, G. 1997. "La regione vesuviana dopo l'eruzione del 79 d.C." *Athenaeum* 85:139–54.

Soricelli, G. 2001. "La regione vesuviana tra secondo e sesto secolo d.C." In *Modalità insediative*, 456–72.

Soricelli, G., et al. 1994. "L'origine della 'tripolitanian sigillata'/'Produzione A della Baia di Napoli.'" In *Ceramica romana e archeometria: lo stato degli studi.* G. Olcese, ed. Florence: All'Insegna del Giglio, 67–88.

Spinazzola, V. 1893. "Un edificio della Napoli greco-romana." *NN* 2:90–92.

Stazio, A. 1986. "Il problema delle emissioni campano-tarentine." In *Monetazione di Neapolis*, 375–92.

Stefani, G. 2001–2002. "Intorno alla data dell'eruzione del 79 d.C." *RivStudPomp* 12–13:177–215.

Stefani, G. 2006. "La vera data dell'eruzione." *Archeo* 22.10:10–13.

Strandberg, R. 1961. "Il tempio dei Dioscuri a Napoli: Un disegno inedito di Andrea Palladio nel Museo Nazionale di Stoccolma." *Palladio* 11.1–2:31–40.

Strubbe, J.H.M. 1998. "Epigrams and Consolation Decrees for Deceased Youths." *L'antiquité classique* 67:45–75.

Sullivan, J.P. 1968. *The Satyricon of Petronius: A Literary Study*. Bloomington, IN: Indiana University Press.

Syme, R. 1961. "Who Was Vedius Pollio?" *JRS* 51:23–30.

Taliercio, M. 1986. "Il bronzo di Neapolis." In *Monetazione di Neapolis*, 219–373.

Taliercio Mensitieri, M. 1987. "Simboli, lettere, sigle sul bronzo di Neapolis." *Bollettino di numismatica* 4:161–78.

Taliercio Mensitieri, M. 1999. "Appunti sulla circolazione delle monete d'argento di Velia e di Neapolis tra la fine del IV e l'inizio del III secolo a.C." *RBNum* 145:69–82.

Tarpin, M. 2002. *Vici et pagi dans l'Occident romain*. Rome: École Française de Rome.

Taylor, R. 2009. "River Raptures: Containment and Control of Water in Greek and Roman Constructions of Identity." In *The Nature and Function of Water, Baths, and Hygiene from Antiquity through the Renaissance*. C. Kosso and A. Scott, ed. Leiden and Boston: Brill, 21–42.

Taylor, R. 2010. "Bread and Water: Septimius Severus and the Rise of the *Curator Aquarum et Miniciae.*" *Memoirs of the American Academy in Rome* 55:199–220.

Taylor, R. 2014a. "The Cult of Sirens and Greek Colonial Identity in Southern Italy." In *Attitudes Towards the Past in Antiquity: Creating*

Identities? B. Alroth and C. Scheffer, ed. Stockholm: Institutionen för Arkeologi och Antikens Kultur, 183–89.

Taylor, R. 2014b. "Movement, Vision, and Quotation in the Gardens of Herod the Great." In *Le jardin dans l'antiquité – The Garden in Antiquity.* K.M. Coleman, ed. Vandoeuvres: Fondation Hardt, 145–94.

Taylor, R. 2015a. "Roman Neapolis and the Landscape of Disaster." *Journal of Ancient History* 3:282–326.

Taylor, R. 2015b. "The Temple of the Dioscuri and the Origins of Neapolis." In *Remembering Parthenope,* 39–63.

Taylor, R. 2017. "Bath." *The Eerdmans Encyclopedia of Early Christian Art and Archaeology.* P.C. Finney, ed. 3 vols. Grand Rapids, MI: Eerdmans, 1:174–75.

Taylor, R. 2019. "Wheels, Keels, and Coins: Aquae Apollinares (Vicarello, Lazio) and Patterns of Pilgrimage in the Ancient Landscape." In *Waterlands in Antiquity (Terres de l'eau dans l'antiquité).* B.A. Robinson et al., ed. Aix-en-Provence: Presses Universitaires d'Aix-Marseille, 225–44.

Taylor, R. Forthcoming. "Naval Shows and Aquacades." In *The Oxford Handbook of Sport and Spectacle in the Ancient World.* A. Futrell and T. Scanlon, ed. Oxford: Oxford University Press.

Thiel, J.H. 1954. *A History of Roman Sea Power before the Second Punic War.* Amsterdam: North-Holland.

Thomsen, R. 1957–1961. *Early Roman Coinage.* 3 vols. Copenhagen: Nationalmuseet.

Tocco Sciarelli, G. 1985. "La fondazione di Cuma." In *Napoli antica,* 87–99.

Trapp, J.B. 1984. "The Grave of Vergil." *Journal of the Warburg and Courtauld Institutes* 47:1–31.

Trapp, J.B. 1986. "Virgil and the Monuments." *Proceedings of the Virgil Society* 18:1–17.

Traversari, G. 1960. *Gli spettacoli in acqua nel teatro tardo-antico.* Rome: "L'Erma" di Bretschneider.

Trendelenburg, A. 1911. "Der Dioskurentempel in Neapel." *Archäologischer Anzeiger,* 54–57.

Trowbridge, M.L. 1938. "Phaleros." *RE* 19:1664–66.

Trümper, M., et al. 2019. "Stabian Baths in Pompeii. New Research on the Development of Ancient Bathing Culture." *RM* 125:103–59.

Tuck, S.L. 2019. "Harbors of Refuge: Post-Vesuvian Population Shifts in Italian Harbor Communities." In *Reflections: Harbour City Deathscapes in Roman Italy and Beyond*. N. Bargfeldt and J.H. Petersen, ed. Rome: Quasar, 63–78.

Turner, B. 2013. "War Losses and Worldview: Re-viewing the Roman Funerary Altar at Adamclisi." *American Journal of Philology* 134.2:277–304.

Valenza Mele, N. 1993. "Napoli (1)." In *Bibliografia topografica della colonizzazione greca in Italia e nelle isole tirreniche*. G. Nenci et al., ed. Rome and Naples: École Française de Rome; Centre Jean Bérard, 12:165–239.

Valerio, V. 2007. "Observations sur le décor peint de la tombe C du complexe monumental des Cristallini, Naples." In *Peinture et couleur dans le monde grec antique: Actes du colloque, Musée du Louvre (10 et 27 mars 2004)*. Milan and Paris: 5 Continents editions; Musée du Louvre, 148–61.

Varriale, I. 2007. "La villa imperiale di Pausilypon." In *La villa romana*. R. Ciardello, ed. Naples: L'orientale, 147–66.

Varriale, I. 2015. "Pausilypon tra *otium* e potere imperiale." *RM* 121:227–68.

Vecchio, G. 1985a. "Il complesso archeologico di S. Chiara." In *Napoli antica*, 225–27.

Vecchio, G. 1985b. "Le mure di piazza Bellini." In *Napoli antica*, 156–59.

Vecchio, G. 1985c. "Le ville sul mare." In *Napoli antica*, 348–51.

Vecchio, G., et al. 2007. "Modifiche di un ambiente costiero: L'insediamento protoappenninico di Fuorigrotta – Piazzale Tecchio (Napoli)." Paper delivered at a workshop entitled "Environmental Crisis and Human Settlements in Campania from Latest Neolithic to the Iron Age." Centro Universitario Europeo per i Beni Culturali, Ravello, Sept. 3, 2007.

Vesperini, P. 2009. "Que faisaient dans la baie de Naples Pison,

Philodème, Virgile et autres Épicuriens?" *MÉFRA* 121:515–43.

Vezzoli, L., ed. 1988. *Island of Ischia.* Rome: Consiglio nazionale delle ricerche.

Viola, L. 1894. "Napoli: Nuove scoperte di antichità entro l'abitato." *NSc,* 171–75.

Viscardi, G.P. 2013. "*In limine:* Religious Speech, Sea Power, and Institutional Change. Athenian Identity Foundation and Cultural Memory in the Ephebic *Naumachia* at Piraeus." *Studi e materiali di storia delle religioni* 79:239–76.

Vitale, R. 1998. "I rinvenimenti di moneta romano-campana nell'Italia antica." In *Monetazione romano-campana,* 141–64.

Vitale, R. 2001. "Su rinvenimenti recenti di moneta romano-campana." *AIIN* 48:97–118.

Wallace, W. 1947. "The Demes of Eretria." *Hesperia* 16.2:115–46.

Wallace-Hadrill, A. 2011. *Herculaneum: Past and Future.* London and Los Altos, CA: Lincoln Limited; Packard Humanities Institute.

Weiler, I. 2018. "Überlegungen zum 'opsonion' bei den 'Sebasta' in Neapel." In *"Emas non quod opus est, sed quod necesse est": Beiträge zur Wirtschafts-, Sozial-, Rezeptions- und Wissenschaftsgeschichte der Antike. Festschrift für Hans-Joachim Drexhage zum 70. Geburtstag.* K. Ruffing and K. Dross-Krüpe, ed. Wiesbaden: Harrassowitz, 309–21.

Weiss, C. 1984. *Griechische Flußgottheiten in vorhellenistischer Zeit: Ikonographie und Bedeutung.* Würzburg: Triltsch.

Weiss, C. 1988. "Fluvii." *LIMC* 4.1:139–48.

Whitehead, D. 1986. *The Demes of Attica, 508/7–ca. 250 B.C.: A Political and Social Study.* Princeton: Princeton University Press.

Widemann, F. 1986. "Les effêts économiques de l'éruption de 79: Nouvelles données et nouvelle approche." In *Tremblements,* 107–12.

Widemann, F. 1990. "Implications économiques des désastres volcaniques: Le court et le long terme dans le cas de Pompéi." In *Volcanology and Archaeology,* 217–31.

Wijngaarden, G. J. van. 2002. "The Cultural Significance of Mycenaean Pottery in Italy." In *Use and Appreciation of Mycenaean*

Pottery in the Levant, Cyprus and Italy (1600–1200). Amsterdam: Amsterdam University Press, 249–59.

Wikander, Ö. 1996. "Senators and Equites VI: Caius Sergius Orata and the Invention of the Hypocaust." *Opuscula romana* 20:177–82.

Yegül, F. 1991. *Baths and Bathing in Classical Antiquity.* Cambridge, MA: MIT Press.

Yegül, F. 1996. "The Thermo-Mineral Complex at Baiae and *De Balneis Puteolanis.*" *Art Bulletin* 78:137–61.

Yegül, F. 2010. *Bathing in the Roman World.* Cambridge and New York: Cambridge University Press.

Yegül, F. 2013. "Development of Baths and Public Bathing during the Roman Republic." In *A Companion to the Archaeology of the Roman Republic.* J.D. Evans, ed. Malden, MA: Wiley-Blackwell, 13–32.

Zampino, G. 1995. *Le terme puteolane e Salerno nei codici miniati di Pietro da Eboli: Luoghi ed immagini a confronto.* Naples: Fiorentino.

Zevi, F. 1987. "Fra mito e storia." In Zevi, *Campi,* 11–72.

Zevi, F. 2004. "Inquadramento storico ai porti di Roma." In *Le strutture dei porti e degli approdi antichi: II seminario (Roma – Ostia Antica 16–17 aprile 2004).* A. Gallina-Zevi and R. Turchetti, ed. Soveria Mannelli: Rubbettino, 211–19.

Zevi, F., and G. Cavalieri Manasse. 2005. "Il tempio cosidetto di Augusto a Pozzuoli." In *Théorie et pratique d l'architecture romaine: Études offertes à Pierre Gros.* X. Lafor and G. Sauron, ed. Aix-en-Provence: Université de Provence, 269–94.

Zevi, F., and C. Valeri. 2008. "Cariatidi e clipei: Il foro di Pozzuoli." In *Le due patrie acquisite: Studi di archeologia dedicati a Walter Trillmich.* E. La Rocca et al., ed. Rome: "L'Erma" di Bretschneider, 443–64.

Ziolkowski, J.M., and M.C.J. Putnam, ed. 2008. *The Virgilian Tradition: The First Fifteen Hundred Years.* New Haven: Yale University Press.

INDEX

A

Abate, Felice 263
Abella 145
Acerrae (Acerra) 25, 58, 59; Roman prefecture 135; Serino Aqueduct 286, 365
Achaioi 80
Acheloös 42, 46, 91–96
Achilles 33
Acilius Strabo, Lucius 155
Acquaro-Pelosi Spring 262, 357
Acts of Peter 16, 367
Acts of Peter and Paul 16
Acts of the Apostles 366
Adamclisi 167
Aegeans 32–33
Aelius Antigenides, Publius, musician 169, 173, 343
Aemilia Rectina, athlete 322
Aenaria. *See* Ischia.
Aeneas 17, 19, 20, 28, 79, 250, 306
Afilae 369
Africa 138, 147, 230
Africa Proconsularis 230
Age of Heroes 33, 56, 76
Ager Campanus 22, 145. *See also* Capua.
Ager Falernus 22
Agnano 260, 261, 262, 268, 282
agriculture 21–22. *See also* Ager Campanus; Campania: agriculture and pastoralism; chestnuts; grain; Neapolis: agriculture, grain, olives and olive oil, wine; Neapolitanum.
Agrippa, Marcus Vipsanius 14, 16, 17, 18, 152, 186, 232, 241, 263, 266, 308, 339
Aidepsos (Aedepsus, Edipsos) 239, 241, 242
Ajax 33

Akragas 64
Aktia Games 315, 326
Aktion (Actium), battle of 307
Alba Longa 315, 318, 369
Alexander Severus, emperor 234, 243, 347-48
Alexander the Great 127
Alexandria 352
Amodio, Maria 7, 361, 362, 363
amphoras 6, 7, 54, 129, 137, 138, 149, 206, 217, 324, 325
Anatolians 33
Ancona 137, 179, 230
Annii, Campanian family 145
annona 230-36, 247, 355
Antinoös 176
Antioch 311, 344
Antium (Anzio) 250, 318, 341
Antonii 145
Antonines 169, 173, 235, 312, 351–52
Antoninus Pius, emperor 169, 184, 343
Antonius Julianus, orator 296
Antonius, Marcus, triumvir. 151, 218, 311, 326, 339
Antony: *See* Antonius, Marcus, triumvir.
Apennine culture 32
Aphrodite 316, 323; Euploia 75, 338-39
Apollo 48, 54, 78, 152, 202, 203, 248, 282, 283, 284, 339; cult 104, 252; Medicus 257–61; Phoebus 252, 316
Apostles 368
Appendix Virgiliana 302; Catalepton 5 334; Catalepton 8 334
Appian 143
Aqua Augusta. *See* Serino Aqueduct.
Aquae Sextiae (Aix-en-Provence) 249
aqueducts. *See* Bolla Aqueduct; Serino Aqueduct.
Aquileia 350

419

Arcadius, emperor 286
archaeology 89, 171, 236-37, 246-47, 369, 371; 20th century 4, 70-71, 142, 147-48, 189, 191, 205-11, 219-21, 232, 233, 241, 244, 262, 276, 280-82, 359, 360-64; 1880s-1890s (Risanamento) 4, 5, 221, 262, 265, 275-76, 286-87; 1980s 4, 5, 69-70, 189, 278, 351, 355; 2000s 6-7, 32, 36-37, 38, 49, 176, 185-86, 189, 194-95, 213-17, 223-25, 226-27, 275, 339, 355, 364; Collections 5, 7; early modern 3; evidence 1, 2, 35, 66-67, 69-73, 88, 109-10, 185, 355; Greek and Samnite Neapolis 37-38, 49, 52, 66-73, 109-10, 147-48, 233; Italian 5; lacunae and limitations of 2, 5, 66, 154, 185-86, 188-90, 194, 198, 238, 239, 241, 275, 347-49, 351, 352, 355, 357, 368; methodologies 5, 52, 66, 88; of Pizzofalcone (Parthenope) 38, 49, 52, 70; of prehistory and Iron Age 31-32, 33, 34, 35; of rural sites and villas 73, 158, 161-63; salvage 2, 3, 332; of suburbium 239; underwater 232; women in 5. *See also* Naples; Neapolis.
Archias, poet 299
Ardea 250
Argives 80, 81
Argo 43
Argos 80, 81
Aricia 135
Aristaios 80
Aristaioi, phratry 80, 175
Aristodemos 50, 51, 53, 54, 78
Armstrong, David 303
Artemis 80, 133, 181, 202, 325; Diana 133. *See also* Diana Tifatina.
Artemisioi, phratry 80, 133, 176, 181-82
Arthur, Paul 5, 277, 278, 349
Asklepiades of Bithynia 257

Asklepios 258, 262, 282
Astroni Crater (Lago Grande) 25
Atella 25, 73; Roman prefecture 135; Serino Aqueduct 286, 365
Athena 294; on coins 58, 99-101, 102, 108; sanctuary 12
Athens and Athenians: architecture 186; Brutus welcomed 152; coinage 100-1; demarchates 64; demes and demarchates 64, 84; diplomacy 57; Euboean kinship 293-94; games 322-27, 329 navy 42-43, 57-58, 64, 99-100, 101, 322-23, 338; at Neapolis 39, 40, 42-45, 47, 55-58, 63, 80, 96, 99-100, 203, 293-95; odeia 186; philosophy 301-2, 304, 336; Persian Wars 56; trade 62. *See also* pottery and ceramics: Attic.
Augustus, emperor (Octavian): *Augustales* and *vicomagistri*, patronage of 153; Capri and Ischia, ownership of 21, 77, 143-44, 292, 307, 327; final days 327-29; Kaisareion 214; local patronage of 154, Nesis villa, appropriation of 268; naval victories 217-18, 326, 337-39; Vedius Pollio and Pausilypon 242, 307-9, 336-37; Pax Augusta 187; Portus Julius 19, 263; *regiones* of Rome 177; Sebasta games in honor of 155, 186-87, 317, 320, 324, 326, 329, 337; Serino Aqueduct 262, 263, 273, 287, 357; Venus as ancestor 338; Virgil, companion of 305
Ausonius; *Moselle* 208-19, 337-39
Avella 271
Avellino 262; eruption of 1360 BCE 11
Avernus, Lake 14, 16-19, 28, 39, 162, 232, 260, 266, 337; Aeneas 250
Avianius Cilo, Aulus 255

INDEX

B

Bagnoli (Balneoli) 15, 238, 241, 260, 268, 269, 309

Baiae: 20th-century excavations 4; Alexander Severus' patronage 243, 347-48; baths and spas 18, 171, 241, 254-57, 258, 284, 285, 298, 316; bradyseism 16, 18; economy 23, 232; geology and geography 9, 13, 14, 20, 78, 284, 285, 316; Hadrian's presence 311; harbor 232, 247, 249; Lucrine Naiads 249; myrtle groves 257; mythical origins 14, 19, 250; *palatium (praetorium)* 164, 307, 308; Posidian waters 284; residences 239, 298; sculpture workshop 332; Serino Aqueduct 269, 286, 357; Severan period 347–56, 348; St. Paul's visit 16; Strabo's description 14; "Temple of Mercury" 282; tunnel to Lucrine Lake 266; Via Herculanea 92

Baios, hero 14, 19, 250

Balneum Bullae 260

Barigazzi, Adelmo 293

baths and bathing: Agnano 260-62, 268-69; bathing culture 171, 247, 253-62, 282-83, 288, 298, 330-32, 362-63, 365, 371; Bauli 311; Christian attitudes 260-61, 361-64; Herculaneum 16; Lake Avernus 18; Neapolis 138, 154, 171, 177-78, 186, 216, 217, 222, 224, 235-36, 238-39, 241-42, 249, 257-62, 269, 273, 275-83, 288, 289, 361-64, 365; Pausilypon 242, 281-82, 289, 309-10, 330-32; Pollena Trocchia 161; technology 18, 255-57, 273; western Bay of Naples 18, 138, 232, 284-85. *See also* Aidepsos; Baiae: baths and spas; Ischia: baths and spas; Pozzuoli: thermal baths; Sergius Orata, Gaius; Serino Aqueduct.

Battle of Cumae 49-50, 54-55

Bauli (Bacoli) 311; Serino Aqueduct 269

Bay of Naples: climate, agriculture, and pisciculture 9, 16, 21-23, 29, 37, 154, 245, 297, 298-99, 307, 316, 334-35; coastal road 10, 92, 169, 237; coastline and waterfront 9, 12, 13, 15-16, 18, 24, 26, 36, 38, 41, 42, 45, 46, 52, 72, 77-78, 82, 92, 97-98, 135, 157, 171, 215, 217-26, 230-31, 235, 241-42, 245-46, 250-51, 253, 255, 269-70, 297, 304-5, 309-11, 325, 334-35, 337-39; cultural appeal 1, 291-92, 297-98; early peoples 31-35; geography, geology, and hydrology 6, 9-23, 27-29, 253-62, 315-16; harbors 16, 38, 46-47, 78-79, 82, 131, 176, 218-26, 232-33, 247, 249, 316, 355-56, 357-58; Greek settlement 35-38; mythology 12, 13-14, 17-18, 19, 28-29, 32-33, 42-46, 79-81, 82, 90-96, 97-98, 250-53, 323-24, 322-27; navies and naval operations 2, 16, 19, 42-43, 49, 54-58, 64, 99-100, 101, 115, 131, 144, 149, 152, 249, 263, 291, 308, 322; shipping route 9, 32-33, 36, 77, 138, 230; villa culture 144, 297-303, 306-13, 334-35. *See also* Baiae; bathing and baths; bradyseism; Lucrine Lake; Portus Julius; villas.

Bay of Pozzuoli 13, 20, 255

Belisarius, general 274

Beloch, Julius 323, 324

Beneventum (Benevento) 71, 230, 308, 342

Boccaccio, Giovanni 305

Boeotia 80, 239

Boethius 334

Bolla Aqueduct 272-75, 288

Borriello, Rosaria 69

421

bradyseism 15-17, 18, 29, 215, 218-19, 222-25, 245, 313
Bragantini, Irene 215
Brandt, J. Rasmus 230, 231, 232
Bresson, Alain 181
Bromius 315
Brundisium (Brindisi) 143
Bruttium (Calabria) 96
Brutus, Marcus Junius, assassin of Caesar 15, 151-52, 153, 183, 192, 268, 317
Buchner, Giorgio 4
Burnett, Andrew 109, 124, 125, 126
Byzantines 2, 274, 330

C

Caccamo Caltabiano, Maria 124
cadastral grid 159, 160-61, 162-63, 164, 165, 183
Caedicia Victrix 175
Calatia 135
Calpurnius Piso Caesoninus, Lucius 301
Camodeca, Giuseppe 155, 358
Campani 24, 59-62, 65, 87-88, 293; Roman alliance during Samnite Wars 113-22. *See also* Osco-Samnites; Samnites.
Campania: agriculture and pastoralism 22-23, 31, 34, 94; Attic ceramics 24, 58; Augustan reorganization of towns 153; benefits from Constantine I 357; blood sport 186; borders 250; cavalry 131; chestnuts 177; Christian 366; coastal 24, 34, 52; coinage 86-87, 89, 100, 101-2, 108, 111; coin deposits 89; *Consularis Campaniae and Corrector Campaniae* 356, 357, 362, 364; cults 132-35, 153, 165; ethnic mix 60, 64, 72, 94, 101-2, 117, 121, 129, 144, 145, 153, 175, 293; Etruscans in 35, 46-47, 83;

geography and geology 9-29, 156-57, 231; Greek games 186; Greek–Samnite relations 60-63; Iron Age 34; Italiote ware 72; loss of privileges in late antiquity 356; military service and mercenaries 60, 102, 122, 129, 131; Neolithic 31; Opici in 60, 75; post-Vesuvius 163-65; prehistoric 31; prosperity of 58, 102 Protoapennine culture 32; Romano-Campanian coinage 122-26, 149; Roman involvement 85, 113, 114-22, 124, 132-36, 356; rural settlements and sanctuaries 73, 89, 133; Samnites in 52-53, 59-60, 72, 73, 75, 101, 114-22, 149, 293; Second Punic War 132-35, 146, 352; Severan period 347; Sulla in 144, 149, 165, 187; transport and trade 231, 141; Villanovan culture 34; wine 138. *See also* Ager Campanus; Capua.
Campi Phlegraei (Campi Flegrei, Phlegraean Fields) 13, 29, 32, 233, 253-54, 257, 258-60, 284, 337
Cangiano, Luigi 272
Cannae, battle of 131-32, 146
Cantilena, Renata 89, 105, 106
Canutius 192
Capasso, Bartolommeo 189, 279, 305, 326
Capo di Posillipo 14, 16, 238, 265, 287, 304, 307
Capo Licosa 251
Capo Miseno 19, 20, 253
Capri (Capreae, Kapreai): Augustus' dealings with 21, 144, 292, 307, 308, 327-29; Cumaean control of 77; Euboean 78; geography 12-13, 47; Greek 84; Neapolis' relations with 21, 24, 73, 77-78, 84; Roman acquisition 144, 307;

422

INDEX

Sirens' association with 43, 45; Villa Jovis 307. *See also* Teleboi; Telon.
Capua: agriculture 22, 171; amphitheater 319; Atella's alliance with 26; Attic ceramics 58; cavalry 131; cemeteries and tombs 237; Christian pilgrimage 366; coinage 86; commerce 176; Constantinian basilica 366, 368, 369; Cumaean exiles 50, 53–54, 60; Cup of Nestor, curation of 33; *deditio* of 338 BCE 124; demographics 172; Etruscan control 58, 60; Hannibal's dealings with 26, 132, 133, 146; Herakles cult 92; land grids 161; Octavian's colony 258; Osco-Samnite domination 59, 113; pottery 109; Roman alliance 113, 122; Roman conquest 133–35; Roman prefecture 135; Samnite seizure and control 59, 60–61, 73, 113; sanctuary of Diana Tifatina 133–35, 149, 166-67; Second Punic War 133–35, 149; Sullan land seizures 145, 165–66; Trimalchio's Feast, model for 179. *See also* Ager Campanus.
Capys 316
Caracalla, emperor 2, 170, 229, 230, 234-35, 347, 348
Carrara 137
Carsana, Vittoria 221, 224
Carthage 137, 138, 352
Casilinum 135
Cassandra 42, 42–45, 98
Cassino 31
Cassius Longinus, Gaius, assassin of Caesar 151
Càssola, Filippo 38, 44, 56, 75; Cumae 48, 49
Castellamare di Stabia 12

Castor and Pollux (Kastor and Polydeukes, Dioscuri, Dioskouroi): ancestry 77; coinage 134; cult 77, 79-80, 198, 205; iconography 202; sculpture 203-4; temple 191, 196–204
catacombs. *See* Neapolis: catacombs.
Catalepton of the *Appendix Vergiliana* 333–34
Caudini 59
Caudium 71
Cavalieri Manasse, Giuliana 228, 230
Ceionius Julianus 286, 357
Celsus 257
cemeteries, burials, and tombs. *See* Neapolis: cemeteries, burials, and tombs.
centuriation. *See* cadastral grid.
ceramics. *See* pottery and ceramics.
Ceres 153, 292. *See also* Demeter.
Chalkidians 20, 39, 40, 43, 47, 54, 55, 64, 80
Chalkis 40, 41, 43, 47
Charilaos (Charileos) 105, 106, 120-21
chestnuts 23, 138, 161–62, 177, 183
Chouquer, Gérard 159, 160, 165
Cicero: Bay cities' treatment of Pompey, reaction to 151; *"crater ille delicatus"* 298; *For Archias* 5, 10 299; *For Balbus* 21 142; *lex Iulia*, description 142; on *otium* and *luxuria* 299; Philodemos, reverence for 303; Siro, friendship with 302; villas on Bay of Naples 297
Cimitile 366
Circe 250
Civitas sine suffragio 113, 122, 142
Civitavecchia 233
Clanis. *See* Glanis (Clanis, Clanius) River.
Claudia, wife of Statius 315

423

Claudius, emperor 154, 257, 284, 294, 317
Clement VII, pope 2
Cleopatra, queen 218, 311, 326, 339
Clodii Nummi 155
Cocceius 18, 266
Cocchia, Enrico 179
Coelius Antipater 146
coinage 6, 254; Acheloös type 91–93, 94, 111, 253; agonistic 96; Alexandria 126; Allifae 86, 102; Alpheios 96; Antonine crisis and decline of 350; Apollo 104, 123, 133; archaeology 66, 88; archaeological contexts 88–89, 96, 110; Arethousa 90, 102; Artemis 108; Artemis (Diana) and cornucopia 133–34; Athena 58, 99–101, 102, 108, 111; bronze 88, 89, 100, 102-4, 105-6, 107, 109, 111, 123–24, 126, 132–33, 134, 135; bull-man 89–96, 99, 101, 102, 103, 105, 123, 250, 252–53; Cales 108; "Campani" 133; Campania 86, 87–88, 89, 100, 102, 108, 109, 111, 122; Capua 86, 102, 133; Carthaginian, minted by Capua 86; circle of dolphins 105, 125; circulation 103, 111, 124, 125, 135; collections 5; control marks 105–8, 111, 122, 125, 126; Corinth 105; cornucopia 133–34; Cumae 81, 86, 89, 90, 91, 99–100; De Luynes Collection 90; didrachms 89–90, 91, 93, 94, 95–96, 97, 99–100, 101, 102, 103, 104–6, 107, 124, 125; die studies 86–88; Dioscuri 133, 134, 198; drachms 106, 107; Elis 96; Erymanthian Boar 81; Fenserni 86, 102; Fisteli 86, 102; foundation myths 249; Gela 90, 93; Gelas River 93, 95; gold 88, 109, 125–26; Greek city-states 85;
Helios 108; Herakles 93; hoards 88–89, 110, 124–25; Hyria 86, 88, 100, 102, 103; iconography and symbols 90, 99–100, 101, 103–7, 108, 109, 111, 126, 132–35; Italy before the Romans 110; late Neapolitan 132–35; laurel 133; legends 86, 87, 90–91, 95, 99, 102, 105, 106, 123, 125; local cults 111; Magna Graecia 86, 91; Mars 125; Metapontion 125; military use 89, 99–100, 101, 109; mints and minting 87-88, 89, 94, 95, 100, 101-2, 102, 103, 106, 107, 108, 109, 111; Neapolis harbor excavations, finds 220; Nemean Lion 81, 92; Nike 91, 95-96, 97, 100, 101, 103, 105; Nola 86, 100, 102; obols 92, 100, 103, 104; October Horse 125; *omphalos* 133; owl 100; Parthenope 89–96, 99, 101, 102, 104, 105, 106, 250; Phocaean weight standard 89; Roma 123; Roman 89, 94, 107, 122-26; Romano-Campanian 89, 108, 109, 122–26, 149; Roma-Victoria 108; Samnite 86-88, 101-3; Sebethos River 26, 93, 94-96, 98-99, 101; Sicily 88, 90, 102-3, 253; silver 88, 89-90, 91, 92, 93, 94-95, 96, 97, 99, 100, 101, 102, 103, 104-7, 109, 122, 123, 124-26, 132, 350; Sirens 110; Syracusan 90, 101–2, 105; Taras (Tarentum, Tarantum) 105, 108, 125; Tereina 96–99, 101; Thourioi 90, 100, 101; Thourioi and Katane 90; triobols 104-5; water jug 97–98, 111; weight standards 89, 103, 111, 123, 125, 126; winged figure 111. *See also* mints.
Coldstream, Nicolas 34
collegia 175, 236

INDEX

Collis Leucogaeus (I Pisciarelli) 25, 258, 260
colonization 53
Colonna, Ferdinando 276
Commodus, emperor 234
Constantine I, emperor: ascendancy 330; Capua, basilica 366; Christianity, sanction of 347; church foundations and construction 347, 354, 358; Neapolis, dealings with 356–68; Neapolitan basilica and ecclesiastical compound 358-64, 365, 368–70; Serino Aqueduct restoration 262, 274, 285-86, 363-65; Via Antiniana restoration 358
Constantine I, emperor: 285
Constantinople: Christian basilicas 358; fora 362; Forum of Constantine 358; harbor 222, 247; Mese (main street) 358; Neapolis and Pozzuoli 358; Nika riots 358; spolia 365
Corellius 177
Coriglio 238, 241
Corinth 45, 105, 325
Cornelii 145
Cornelius, Gnaeus 254
Cornelius Lentulus, Lucius 116, 117
Corsica 138
Crawford, Michael 125
Crisis of the Third Century 348-49
Crispus, Flavius Julius, co-emperor 285
Cristilli, Armando 7
Crosby, H. Lamar 293
Croton. *See* Kroton.
Crypta Neapolitana 13, 18, 180, 234, 236–38, 265, 266–68, 280, 288, 305, 306, 355
Cumaean Gulf 46. *See also* Bay of Naples.
Cumae (Kyme): Aeneas at 250; amphitheater 319; Apollo cult 78, 81, 104, 152, 205; archaeology 4, 36, 185; Aristodemos' tyranny 49-51, 53-54, 61, 78, 83, 152; ascendancy 72; Athens 55–56; Baiae, control of 285; Battle of Cumae (474 BCE) 49-50, 54-55; excavations 4; borders 43, 98; Campani and Samnites at 24, 50, 59, 60–61, 62, 63, 73, 74, 104, 113, 116; Capri, control of 77; Capua, exiles at 50, 53-54, 60, 62; ceramics 37; Chalkidian (Euboean) founders 35, 36, 39, 40, 41, 47, 55, 104; city council *(boule)* 64; coinage 81, 86-87, 89, 90, 91, 99, 100; cultural life 300; decline 55, 62–63, 348; oligarchic dissidents and exiles 50-51, 52-54, 60, 61, 63-64, 66, 72, 78, 80-81, 116, 118, 152; early history 34-82 passim; economy 23; Etruscans, dealings with 3 5, 49, 58; Eumelos' arrival 79; excavations 3 6; fisheries, shellfish, and agriculture 23, 37, 58, 61–62; foundation and settlement 36-37, 46, 55; geography and geology 13, 14, 18, 20, 59; grain 58; Greek character in Roman era 151, 300; "Grotta di Cocceio" 266; harbor 36; Herakles cult 92; hill temples 205; intellectual life 300; Iron Age *(Fossakultur)* burials 34, 60; Ischia, control of 35, 36, 54; *Kymaioi* phratry at Neapolis 80; *municipium* status 118, 122; Neapolis, dealings with 24, 39, 40, 41; 46-54; oracle instructing foundation of Neapolis 39-40, 48, 53, 252; Opici, early residents of 60, 75; Parthenope (Palaepolis), dealings with 23-24, 39-40, 46-54, 75-77; plague 39-40, 48, 52-54, 67, 81; Pompeii diaspora to 172;

425

Rome, relations with 73, 113, 114, 116, 118, 122; Pompey, plaudits for 151; Pozzuoli (Dikaiarcheia), relationship to 14, 39, 46, 50, 78; roads 233; Roman prefecture of territories 135; Samnite Wars 118; Serino Aqueduct 262, 269, 286, 357; Severan period 348; Sibylline oracle 18, 48, 252, 316; stadium 186, 194, 211, 247; strategic outpost for Ischia 36–37; Syracuse, alliance with 49, 54; territory 24, 25, 53; theater 194; thermo-mineral baths 254–55, 285; trade and shipping 36, 46–47, 54, 58, 78; Trimalchio's Feast, model for 179; Vesuvius, refugees of 172; Via Domitiana 168; 233; wine 337
Curtius, Ernst 298
Cycladic people 33
Cyprian, bishop 352, 354

D

Dacian Wars 167, 184, 230
D'Agostino, Bruno 34, 49, 50, 51, 67, 351
D'Arms, John 5, 232, 300
De Caro, Stefano 31, 308, 312
Decius, emperor 354
De Franciscis, Alfonso 4
de Holanda, Francisco 199, 201
Deianeira 91
Delos 137, 149
Delphi 81
Demeter 51, 153, 202, 292, 294, 323, 339
De Polignac, François 51, 57
De Simone, Girolamo F. 160, 161
d'Henry, Gabriella 73
Diadochoi 127
Diana Tifatina 134-35, 149, 165, 166; sanctuary 135
Dikaiarcheia. *See* Pozzuoli (Dikaiarcheia, Puteoli).

Dio Cassius 159, 167, 320; *Roman History* 54.23.1–6 337; 66.22–23 28; 66.24.3 163
Dio Chrysostom 271, 293, 319; *Discourse* 28.1 213; *Discourse* 29.5–6 295; *Discourse* 64.11–13 294
Diocletian, emperor 347, 353
Diodoros of Sicily 17, 59; 4.21.1–2 18; 12.76.4 61; Second Punic War 131
Dion, philosopher 300
Dionysios of Halikarnassos 39, 59, 113; *Roman Antiquities* 15.5.1–15.6.5 116; 15.7.3–5 118; 15.8.3–5 119; Aristodemos 53; Cumae 50, 61, 118; Odysseus 250; Samnites at Palaepolis 117; Roman alliance 114; Samnite Wars 114, 115, 119
Dionysios Periegetes 23, 159
Dionysos 72, 312, 337
Dioscuri. *See* Castor and Pollux (Kastor and Polydeukes, Dioscuri, Dioskouroi).
Diotimos, admiral 40, 44, 55-57, 99, 101, 203, 323, 326
disasters 3–6, 155–67
Domitian, emperor 167, 168, 213, 229, 233, 314, 317, 320, 322, 340
Domitii 145
Domitius Ahenobarbus, Lucius 318
D'Onofrio, Anna Maria 5
Doriadai 80

E

earthquakes: 62/63 CE 155; 64 CE 156, 192, 341-42; 80-81 CE 168; 1688 191; 1980 4, 5, 185; collapse of Kaisareion 215; dynamics at Neapolis 176–77, 183, 215; Misenum, during eruption of Vesuvius 156–57, 168; motive for foundation

INDEX

of Sebasta 154; research 176;
Sorrento 168
Egyptomania 311
Elba 36
Elea. *See* Velia (Elea).
Elpenor 250
Emporion (Ampurias, Spain) 42, 72
Enipeos 42
Ephesos 307, 322
Epicureanism 300-3
Epidius, Gaius 250
Epikouros, philosopher 300, 302
Epilytos 153
Epitome de Caesaribus 347
Epopeus hill 20
Eratosthenes of Kyrene 39
Ercolano. *See* Herculaneum.
Eretria 20, 40, 64 84
eruptions 20-21, 22, 27, 31, 32, 47, 54, 155-68. *See also* earthquakes; Mt. Vesuvius.
Etruria 36, 71, 148
Etruscans: Battle of Cumae 48, 54; Campania, presence in 35, 46-47, 58, 60, 83; Capua, occupation of 58; family names 153; language 293; Neapolitan territory, presence in 72, 153; Pausanias 285; piracy 52; rise of 35; Samnites, relations with 60; silver 36; Syracuse 54; trade 36; Tyrrhenian Sea, dominion over 36, 48, 49.
Euboea and Euboeans: cults 104, 152, 249, 252, 338; ethnicity 43, 55, 65, 79-80; Etruscans, relations with 36, 48-49; identity of phratries 65, 79-80; mythology 46, 55, 293-94, 338; settlement and colonization 8, 12, 20, 34, 35, 36, 40, 41, 46, 47, 60, 75, 77, 80, 104, 239, 252, 293-94; strategic and commercial activity 34, 37, 78. *See also* Aidepsos; Capri; Chalkis;

Cumae; Eretria; Ischia.
Euereidai, phratry 79-80
Eueres 80
Eumachos, historian 134
Eumeleidai, phratry 79, 80
Eumelos 79
Eunostidai, phratry 79
Eunostos 80
Eurystheus 81
Eusebius of Caesarea 305

F
Fabius, Quintus 134
Falernian Plain 113, 114, 115
Fates 42, 251
Faustina, empress 307
Favorinus of Arles 293, 344
Favory, François 159, 160, 165
Fiorelli, Giuseppe 3
fisheries and shellfish farming 23, 37, 232, 245, 255, 298-99, 303, 306, 307, 311-12, 334-35, 344
Fiume dei Bagni 98. *See also* Okinaros.
Flavians 155, 191, 228, 271, 295, 339, 340. *See also* Domitian, emperor; Titus, emperor; Vespasian, emperor.
Flavia Thalassia, athlete 322
Flavius Claudius Constantinus. *See* Constantine II, emperor.
flora 6, 161
Flower, Harriet 229
foedus aequum 113, 122, 124, 127, 138, 142
Fons Augusteus 263
foodstuffs 136, 231
Fossakultur 34, 60
Frederiksen, Martin 5, 16, 59, 103, 110, 122
Fregellae 256
Fronto 170, 178, 296; *Correspondence* 2.6 179
Fuficii 145
Furies 97, 251

427

G

Gabrici, Ettore 4, 97
Gaiola 305, 313
Galen, physician 350
Galli, Li 251
games 152, 153, 192, 218, 307-8, 317, 325, 327. *See also* Olympia: Olympic Games; Neapolis: games; Pozzuoli: Eusebeia Games; Rome: Capitoline Games, Neronia Games.
garum 230
Gaudo *facies* 32, 33
Gauls 103, 138, 140, 318
Gaurus 9, 158, 316, 337
Gelas River 93
Gellius, Aulus 296
Gereonium 146
Germanicus, emperor 317
Germanus of Capua 260
Geryon 14
Gesta episcoporum neapolitanorum 358, 368
Giampaola, Daniela 6, 49, 67, 68, 73, 221, 224, 275
Giangiulio, Maurizio 45, 252
Gigante, Marcello 298
Gigantomachy 79
Giordano, Fabio 188, 189
Glanis (Clanis, Clanius) River, 25, 26, 42, 43, 98, 165
grain 23, 57, 58, 61, 62, 114, 125, 132, 133, 134, 136, 159-60, 174, 180, 22, 201, 230-36
Greco, Emanuele 4, 6, 7, 24, 68, 129, 171, 189, 191, 205, 206, 211, 217, 251
Greek family names 153
Gregory I, the Great, pope 178, 326; *Dialogue* 4.40 261
Gromatici veteres 1.235 164
"Grotta di Cocceio" 266
"Grotta di Seiano" 238, 240, 241, 266, 309-10, 312, 344
Grotta vecchia di Pozzuoli (Grotta di Posillipo). *See* Crypta Neapolitana.
Günther, R.T. 268, 281, 282, 297, 304

H

Hadrian, emperor 64, 169, 176, 282, 292, 311, 343
Hannibal 14, 26, 79, 132-35, 146-47
Hardie, Alex 292, 314
Harper, Kyle 350, 352
Harpies 97, 251
Hekataios of Miletos 8, 39
Helena, empress 358
Helle 45
Hellenism 291, 296, 317, 320
Hellespont 37, 45
Henry VI, emperor 303
Herakleia (Lucania) 142
Herakleidai (Heraklids) 80, 81
Herakles (Hercules) 8, 13, 14, 18, 79, 80, 81, 91, 92, 93, 271
Herculaneum (Ercolano): aqueducts 263, 271, 274, 365; arts 332; Bourbon excavations 3; bradyseism 16, 27-28, 29, 224, 247; cemeteries and tombs 237; College of the Augustales 93; cultural life 301; earthquakes 156; fountains 271; House of the Relief of Telephos 16; Maiuri's excavations 4; Neapolis' control of 26; papyri 302; philosophical circle 301; residences 186, 210; royal excavations 3; Suburban Baths 16; Sullan seizure of 143; Vesuvius, effects of 10, 28, 156, 158, 178, 263, 365; Via Herculanea 92; Villa of the Papyri 301, 302; walls 187; waterfront 16
Hercules. *See* Herakles.
Hermagoras, Marcus Aurelius, athlete 321, 343, 345

INDEX

Hermaioi, phratry 80
Hermes 80, 278
Hermitage Museum 284
Herodes Atticus 186, 296
Herodotus 56
Hesberg, Henner von 228, 230
Hieron I, tyrant of Syracuse (478-467 BCE) 20, 54
Hippodameian grid 2, 24, 66-67, 68, 83, 180, 205-6, 359
Hirpini 59
Historia Augusta: Septimius Severus 18.3; 23.2 233; *Severus Alexander* 347
Holloway, H. Ross 110
Homer 251; Homeric stories 33; *Odyssey* 5.377-78 293
Honorius, emperor 286
Horace 257, 303, 338, 344
Hortensius Hortalus, Quintus, orator 297, 299, 335
humanists, archeology 3
Hygieia 258, 262, 282

I

Iaia of Kyzikos, painter 332
Ino-Leukotheia 45; cult 83
inscriptions: Antigenides 345; Aqua Augusta 357; Capua 145; Chiaia 358; Christian 354, 371; Cup of Nestor 33; Epicurean funerary epigram 335-36; family names 137, 139, 145, 171-72; *Fasti Capitolini* 117; Greek 25, 33, 123, 126, 173, 174, 175, 198, 295, 320, 326, 335, 339-41, 352, 353-54; Herculanean district 167, 177-78; Hermagoras 342; honoring a prominent musician 343; Kos 64, 95, 173; Macrinus 286-87, 289; Nitrodes of Ischia 283-84; Olympia 214, 320-21; Oscan 87, 137, 173; phratries 79-81, 174-76, 181-82; Pompeii 172; Pozzuoli 172, 255, 263, 294-95, 357, 361-62; *Regio Thermensium* 273; restoration of Serino Aqueduct 262-63, 285-86, 364; Roman period, importance of 63; Rusticus 362; Sebasta Games 154, 218, 317, 319, 320-21, 322, 323, 326-27, 329, 338, 339-43; Sebethos 250; Septimius Severus and Caracalla 234, 221-23, 228-29, 234-35, 358; Serino Aqueduct 262, 286; temple of the Dioscuri 198
Irpina; earthquake 3
Irpinia 254
Ischia (Aenaria, Pithecusae, Pithekoussai): 1980s excavations 4; agriculture 36; Augustus 77, 143-44; baths and spas 138, 171, 248, 255, 258, 283-84; ceramics and clay 6-7, 29, 37, 38, 75, 137, 139, 141, 147; cults 152, 248, 255, 283-84; Cumae, control by 35, 36, 54; "Cup of Nestor" 33; early history 82; 79; earthquakes and eruptions 20, 47, 54-55, 79, 141, 142; Euboean occupation 34, 35, 36, 41; evacuations 47, 54-55, 66, 79; exchange for Capri 77; geography and geology 9, 19, 20-21, 29, 32, 33, 34, 288; harbor 36; inscriptions 288; Lacco Ameno 19, 283; Marius' evacuation to Africa 143; metalworking 20, 36; Nitroli 283; Neapolis, relationship to 20, 24, 39, 40, 41, 47, 54-55, 58, 66, 73, 77, 80, 89, 143-44; plague 54; Ptolemy 75; Roman era 143, 149, 152, 171; Sextus Pompey's occupation 152; strategic role 58; Sullan control 141; Syracusan occupation 20, 54-55, 83, 102; Terme Regina Isabella 283; trade 36, 54, 75; wine 138

429

Isthmia 44, 45, 327, 345
Isthmian Games 325
Isthmus of Corinth 45
Italiote ware 72. *See also* pottery and ceramics.
Italo-Geometric wares 38. *See also* pottery and ceramics.

J

Jewish War 164
Johannowsky, Werner 4, 24, 147, 189, 191, 196, 280, 305
John the Baptist 364, 368
John the Lydian, *On Powers* 3.70 358
Julia Mamaea 347
Julian port 19
Julianus, *consularis Campaniae* 364
Julio-Claudians 191, 214, 215, 225
Julius Caesar 137, 151, 152, 192, 337, 338
Julius Menecrates 314
Junii 145
Junius Silanus, Marcus 147

K

Kapreai. *See* Capri (Capreae, Kapreai).
Karos, sculptor 332
Kastor and Polydeukes. *See* Castor and Pollux (Kastor and Polydeukes, Dioscuri, Dioskouroi).
Keenan-Jones, Duncan 264, 268, 274, 287
Kos 64, 95, 173, 184, 362
Kretondai, phratry 79, 176
Kroton 78, 179
Kymaioi 80
Kyme. *See* Cumae (Kyme).

L

La Forgia, Elena 280
Lago d'Agnano (Lacus Anianus) 260
Lake Acherousia 14

Lake Trasimene, battle of 131
Lambeck, K. 245
Lamboglia, Nino 139, 147
land apportionment. *See* cadastral grid.
La Solfatara 25, 258
latifundia 136
Laurentius, antipope 261
Leiwo, Martti 151, 172, 292
Lepore, Ettore 57, 61, 62, 64, 73, 145, 170, 176, 179
Lettieri, Pietrantonio 263
Leukosia, Siren 42, 43, 98, 251
Liber coloniarum 163-67
Liber pontificalis 363, 368, 369-70
Licinius Crassus Frugi, Marcus 284
Licinius Lucullus, Lucius, consul of 74 BCE: Parthenope villa / Castrum Lucullanum 126-27, 144, 152, 164, 269-70, 297, 298, 306, 308, 309, 318-19, 330, 334-35, 370
Licinius Lucullus, Marcus, son of the consul of 74 BCE 151-52, 268
Licinius Murena, Lucius the Elder 335
Ligeia, siren 42, 98, 251, 253
Ligorio, Pirro 284
Lipara (Lipari) Islands 20, 152
Lippi, Roberto 107
Liternum 135
Livy: Charilaos (Charileos) 105, 106; Cumae 47; *History of Rome* 8.22.5-6 41-42; 8.22.7 115; 8.22.8-10 116-17; 8.23.25-26 121; 22.32.4-9 146; 23.1.5-10 147; 23.15.1-2 147; 35.16.8 130; fleet 130; Neapolis 47; Palaepolis 41-42, 47, 76, 115-17, 119-21; Roman alliance 114, 124; Samnite Wars 114-18, 119-22
Località Trinità (Piano di Sorrento) 43, 251
Lomas, Kathryn 121, 295

INDEX

L. Papirius Paetus 300, 344
Lucania 109, 142, 250
Lucherini, Vinni 367
Lucilius, Gaius, poet 319
Lucius Verus. *See* Verus, Lucius, emperor.
Lucretius (Titus Lucretius Carus), poet 333
Lucrine Gulf 13
Lucrine Naiads 249
Lucrinus (Lucrine Lake) 16–17, 19, 232, 255, 256, 266, 308, 339. *See also* Portus Julius.
Lucullus. *See* Licinius Lucullus, Lucius, consul of 74 BCE.
Luraghi, Nino 50
Lutatius 39, 40, 47, 48, 52, 62, 67; Parthenope 48
Lykophron, *Alexandra* 8, 40, 42, 43, 45, 56, 76, 98 251, 253, 283, 322, 323, 326

M

Macarus 369
Macedonia 110
Magna Graecia 38, 43, 46, 56, 58, 127, 153, 249
Maiuri, Amedeo 4
Malkin, Irad 36
Mark Antony. *See* Antonius, Marcus, triumvir.
Marcellus, praetor 132
Marchetti, Patrick 107, 108
Marcus Anterius 137
Marcus Antonius 297
Marcus Aurelius, emperor 170, 178, 307, 342, 350
Marcus Crassus. *See* Licinius Crassus, Marcus, triumvir.
Marechiaro 282, 289
Marii 145
marine equipment 220
Marii, Campanian family
Marius, Gaius 143, 144, 164, 181, 297

Massaliotes 75
Massilia (Marseilles) 179
Melankomas 295, 319, 322, 329
Mele, Alfonso 46, 52, 77
Melikertes 44, 325
Melpomene 42
Menippus 284
Mephitis 254
Messala, praetorian prefect 286
Messenians 81
Metronax 193, 194
Mevius Eutychus, Publius 250
Miletos 8, 39, 211
Minerva. *See* Athena.
mints: 4th century BCE 111; Magna Graecia 109; Neapolis 85–111, 123, 124; Suessa 108; Tarentum 108. *See also* coinage.
Miranda, Elena 80, 213
Misenos 250
Misenum 13, 14, 19, 23, 43, 78, 181, 250, 262; Lucullus' villa 306; Piscina Mirabile 271; Roman fleet 291, 308; Serino Aqueduct 269, 286; Severan period 348; Vesuvius 156-58, 168
Mithridatic War 143, 301
Molpe 250
Monacone 308, 328
Mons Tifata 133, 134
Monte Barbaro 158, 337
Monte Circeo 250
Monte Nuovo 15
Monte Olibano 269
Monte Spina 260, 262, 269
Mopsops 42, 322
Morel, J. Paul 139, 140, 148, 332
Morgantina, Sicily 96
Mt. Etna 20
Mt. Gaurus (Monte Barbaro) 158
Mt. Pinatubo 159
Mt. Vesuvius: agriculture 12; coastal deposits 15; environs 10, 26, 48,

431

94, 285, 337; eruptions 10, 12, 13, 15, 19, 22, 23, 26, 27–29, 31, 48, 94, 155–68, 170, 183, 194, 235, 274, 285, 337, 352, 364-65; 79 CE 19; geology 13, 22, 29; metaphors 28; refugees 167, 184; Statius 316; wine 23, 337
Munatius Concessianus, Lucius 177
Munatius Hilarianus, Lucius, to the Phrateres Artemisioi, *SEG* 39:1055 181–82
Muses 35, 145, 251, 291, 333, 334
Musonius Rufus 296
Mycenaeans 33, 34
Myron 332

N

Naples: Acquari 276; Archivio Storico of the Banco di Napoli 278; Balnei Novi 279; Capodimonte 264, 306; Caponapoli 5, 51, 66, 67, 68, 202; Cappella di S. Aspreno 275; Carminiello ai Mannesi 4, 247, 277, 278, 279, 355; Castel Capuano 70, 71, 73, 273, 278; Castel dell'Ovo 45, 370; Castel S. Elmo 68, 69; Centre Jean Bérard 6; Centro Internazionale di Studi Numismatici 6; Chiaia 238, 265, 358; Chiatamone 38, 46, 49, 57, 82; Chiesa della Sanità 335; cholera epidemic of 1884 4, 274, 369; climate 21–22; Colle S. Elmo 265; Corso Umberto 147, 148, 149; Donnaregina Vecchia 278; earthquake of 1980 3, 4, 185, 369; Fuorigrotta 31, 32, 238; Girolamini 141; Istituto Filangieri 189; Materdei 32; Megaride (Megaris) 45, 370; Mergellina 265, 312; Metropolitana (subway) excavations 6–7, 31, 142, 185, 219, 269, 275 (*See also* Naples: Piazza Nicola Amore excavations/Duomo Metropolitana station; Piazza Bovio excavations/Università Metropolitana station; Piazza Municipio excavations/Municipio Metropolitana station); Museo Archeologico Nazionale di Napoli 5, 6, 7, 203, 284, 312, 339, 342; Palazzo Carafa di Sta. Severina 269; Palazzo della Borsa 275–76; Palazzo Sansevero 271, 289; Parco Virgiliano 309; Piazza Amedeo 271, 289; Piazza Bellini 67, 276; Piazza Bovio 271, 275; Piazza Bovio excavations (Università Metropolitana station) 6, 31, 38, 219, 221, 226–30, 247; Piazza Cavour 6, 264; Piazza Municipio excavations (Municipio Metropolitana station) 6, 38, 139, 176, 218–21, 222, 223–25, 244, 275; Piazza Nicola Amore 147, 279, 321; Piazza Nicola Amore excavations (Duomo Metropolitana station) 6, 70, 72, 129, 212, 213–14, 215–18, 244, 247; Piazza Sta. Maria degli Angeli 31; Piazzale Tecchio 32; Piazzetta Trinità degli Spagnoli 265; Pizzofalcone 9, 23, 27, 37, 38, 41, 45, 47, 49, 70, 82, 109, 144, 164, 269, 308, 334; Policlinico 351, 371; Ponti Rossi 264, 269, 274, 275; "Porta dell'acquedotto" 273; Port'Alba 192, 264; prehistory 31–35, 82; Ramo Capodichino 263; Risanamento 4, 5, 8, 274; S. Agostino alla Zecca 279; S. Andrea delle Dame 31, 273; S. Aniello a Caponapoli 5, 51, 83; S. Gennaro at Capodimonte 353, 363; S. Gennaro (Duomo) 278, 355, 359, 360, 361, 363; S. Giovanni

INDEX

in Fonte 361; S. Gregorio Armeno 189; S. Lorenzo Maggiore 205, 205–11, 246; S. Marcellino e Festo 280; S. Paolo Maggiore 190, 197, 199, 203, 205 (*See also* Neapolis: Temple of the Dioscuri); S. Tomasso d'Aquino 70; Sta. Chiara 4, 276, 365; Sta. Maria ad Balneum 280; Sta. Maria Assunta (Duomo) 359; Sta. Maria del Carmine ai Mannesi 278; Sta. Maria Maggiore 141; Sta. Restituta 358, 359, 360, 361, 363, 371; Sta. Sofia 273; Spaccanapoli 68, 69, 191; Spanish Quarter 265, 275; underground 272–73, 288; universities 6; Via Anticaglia 188; Via Armando Díaz 31, 275; Via Capuana 278; Via Cirillo 71; Via Correra 192; Via Costantinopoli 264; Via Croce (Spaccanapoli) 68; Via dei Cristallini 127, 128; Via dei Tribunali 144, 190, 192, 278 359; Via del Cerriglio 270, 271; Via della Grotta Vecchia 266, 267; Via del Sole 351; Via Donnaregina 359; Via Duca di S. Donato 279; Via Duomo 213, 273, 278, 359–60; Via (Egiziaca a) Forcella (Spaccanapoli) 68, 178, 327; Via Enrico Pessina 192; Via Ferri Vecchi 279; Via Lanzieri 221; Via Medina 222; Via Monteoliveto 222; Via Nicola Nicolini 264; Via Nicotera 37, 38; Via Pisanelli 188; Via S. Biagio dei Librai (Spaccanapoli) 68, 191; Via S. Gregorio Armeno 280; Via Sta. Anna alle Paludi 342; Via Scura (Spaccanapoli) 68; Via Terracina 32, 280, 365; Via Toledo 222, 275; Vicolo Limoncello 276; Vico Sopramuro 67; Vico Sta.

Luciella 190; Villa Chiara 51
Napoli antica exhibit 69, 73
Napoli: La città e il mare 6
Napoli, Mario 4, 7, 66, 97, 189, 222, 266, 276, 305
Neapolis: *agora* (*See* Neapolis: forum); agriculture 21–23, 31, 32, 65, 144, 145, 147, 160–66, 169, 179–80, 183, 238–39, 297, 334, 344 (*See also* cadastral grid; Neapolis: chestnuts, grain, olives and olive oil, territory, wine); *annona* 230–35, 247; Antonine era 169, 349–51; aqueducts (*See* Bolla Aqueduct; Serino Aqueduct); archaeology 3–7, 8, 31–32, 34, 50–51, 59, 66–71, 84, 86, 88, 89, 109–10, 129, 139, 142, 147–48, 158, 161–63, 192–243, 280–81, 332, 347, 348–49, 351, 352 (*See also* baths and bathing; basilica of Constantine; coastline; complex at Carminiello ai Mannesi; forum; fountains and nymphaea; harbor; honorific arch; Kaisareion; Naples: Piazza Bovio excavations, Piazza Municipio excavations, Piazza Nicola Amore excavations; *Neapolitanum;* Temple of the Dioscuri; theaters, odeion, and performers; villas: Pausilypon, Ponticelli, Qualiano, S. Gennarello; walls); archons 63, 64, 173, 294, 323; Artists of Dionysos (Bacchic Artists) 218, 317, 343; Athenian settlers and influence 39–42, 43–45, 47, 55–58, 62, 63, 64–65, 80, 83–84, 96, 99–101, 111, 203, 293–94, 322–29; basilica of Constantine 358–59, 362–64, 365–68, 369–70; baths (*See* baths and bathing); bishops and bishopric 172, 280, 358–59, 360,

433

362, 367–68; *castrum Lucullanum* (*See* villas: Lucullan); cathedral of the Savior 358–59; cemeteries, burials, and tombs 66, 69–73, 84, 129, 136, 137, 149, 162, 175, 181, 185, 210, 216, 217, 247, 293, 335–36; cemeteries, burials, and tombs: catacombs 7, 236, 237–38, 353–54, 363, 371; cemeteries, burials, and tombs: Materdei 32; cemeteries, burials, and tombs: Pizzofalcone/Via Nicotera 37–38, 41, 49, 82, 109; cemeteries, burials, and tombs: Masgaba on Capri 328–29; cemeteries, burials, and tombs: of Parthenope 39, 40, 42, 52, 54, 98, 324, 327; cemeteries, burials, and tombs: of Virgil 236, 237, 304, 305–6, 344; cemeteries, burials, and tombs: Via Cristallini 127–29; chestnuts 23, 138, 161–62, 177, 183; Christians and Christianity 172, 260–61, 329–30, 347–71; city assembly *(ekklesia, populus)* 63–64, 115–18, 174, 196, 205, 356; city council *(boule, synkletos, ordo)* 63–64, 115–18, 117, 173, 174, 181, 196, 294, 320, 343, 356, 362; coastline 1, 6, 13, 14–15, 16, 39, 42, 52, 72–73, 82, 120–21, 169, 171, 215–16, 217–18, 219–20, 221, 222, 235, 237, 242–43, 245, 251, 265, 297, 304–5, 309–11, 325, 337–39 (*See also* harbor); Colonia Aurelia Augusta Antoniniana Felix Neapolis 169–70, 234–35; column donation to Constantinople 358; commerce, trade, and transport 9, 23, 77–78, 135–42, 145, 170–71, 176, 186, 196, 201, 205–9, 230–36, 243, 247, 348, 355 (*See also* Neapolis: coastline, grain, harbor, pottery and ceramics); complex at Carminiello ai Mannesi 4, 247, 277, 278, 279, 355; consolation decrees 294–95, 344; crisis of 216–211 BCE 132–35; crisis of 327/6 BCE 61–63, 85–86, 106, 114–22, 123–24, 142, 143, 144, 164, 175; Crisis of the Third Century 347–54; cults 57, 65, 72, 79–81, 83, 94, 111, 133, 152, 165–67, 184, 217, 249, 251–53; cults: founding heroes 327; cults: games 323–24; cults: healing 283–84; cults: Herakles 92; cults: imperial 175–76, 214; cults: *lares* 153; cults: saints 354; cults: Sebethos 250; cults: water and chthonic gods 254, 283 (*See also* Acheloös; Aphrodite; Artemis; Apollo: cult; Athena; Castor and Pollux: cult; Demeter; Mephitis; Mithras; Neapolis: Kaisareion; Nitrodes; Parthenope: Siren, tomb of Siren; Phaleros; Sirens: cult; Virgil, cult); demes *(demoi)* and demarchs *(demarchoi)* 62, 63, 155, 163, 168–69, 170, 173, 205, 294, 343, 353; demes *(demoi)* and demarchs *(demarchoi)*: Eretrian and Attic analogs 64–65, 84; demographics 171–72; ethnic and cultural hybridity 59–64, 70–74, 81, 83, 93–95, 114–22, 124, 129, 141, 142–3, 153, 173–4, 205; family names 62, 65, 86–87, 121, 136–37, 139–40, 145, 150, 153, 172, 174–75, 183, 293, 295, 325, 339–41 (*See also* Campani; Osco-Samnites; Samnites; Euboean founders; Neapolis: foundation); Exedra of Herakles 271; female athletes 322; *foedus aequum* 122, 124, 127, 138, 142; forum 2, 114, 168, 188–91, 194, 196, 205–6, 246; foundation

INDEX

of Neapolis 46–54; foundation of Parthenope 35–46, 75–77, 83; foundation myths 42–46, 48, 82, 90, 91–97, 101, 110–11, 249, 250–53, 288; 324, 325 (*See also* Neapolis: games, torch races; Parthenope: foundation, Siren; Sirens: cult, mythology); fountains and nymphaea 154, 186, 271, 269–71, 278, 279, 282, 289, 304, 309; funerary reliefs 136, 137, 149; games: Sebasta 73, 129, 154, 155, 163, 168, 171, 172, 185, 186–87, 193–94, 211–18, 271, 297, 314–15, 316–30, 332, 337–41, 342–43, 345, 348, 353, 365; games: torch races 40, 42–43, 44, 45, 56, 57, 95–96, 100–101, 129, 137, 203, 217, 321, 322–30, 345; government, administration, and magistracies 24, 45, 62–65, 77–78, 142–43, 173–76, 94, 184, 294, 295, 356; grain 22, 23, 57, 61–62, 114, 125, 132, 133, 134, 136, 159, 174, 180, 201, 230–36, 258; Greek language, customs, and culture in Roman period 25, 79–81, 82, 117–18, 119, 122–26, 127–29, 130, 137, 142–43, 144, 145, 151–53, 155, 166, 170, 171, 173–76, 178–80, 181–82, 185–87, 191–92, 193, 198, 201, 202–3, 205, 211–13, 218, 250–53, 254, 281–83, 291–346, 352–54, 371 (*See also* Neapolis: cults; ethnic and cultural hybridity, literary culture, music and musicians; philosophers and rhetoricians; theaters, odeion, and performers); Greek period 9–10, 23–26, 35–111; gymnasium 186, 212, 213, 217, 318, 326; harbor 9, 16, 38, 46, 47, 49, 82, 131, 169, 171, 176, 186, 213, 217, 218–25, 226, 229, 230, 232–36, 244, 245–46, 247, 249, 265, 271, 274, 275, 355–56, 357–58, 365 (*See also* Bay of Naples: coastline and waterfront; bradyseism; Neapolis: coastline; Neapolis: mole; villas); haven of *otium* 298–300, 317, 328, 333–34; Herculaneum gate 355; hippodrome 194, 212; honorific arch 186, 226–30, 234, 247; houses 114, 144, 156, 185, 186, 193, 209–10, 241, 255, 330, 349; *Insula episcopalis* 359–60; interactions with Rome, Samnites, and Carthage 113–42, 146–48; Jews 172; Kaisareion (Caesareum) 211–17, 218, 221, 223, 235, 244, 247, 326; land apportionment (centuriation, cadastration. *See* cadastral grid); *laukelarch* 63, 170, 174, 294; Levantines and Syrians 172, 301, 335–36; literary culture 178–79, 192, 287, 292–95, 299, 300, 301–3, 305–6, 313–16, 317, 319, 320, 326, 328, 329, 330, 333–34, 339–42, 344 (*See also* Statius, Publius Papinius;Virgil); *locus amoenus* 296–97, 299; *macellum* 186, 196, 206–7, 208; Materdei 32; mole (breakwater) 169, 218–19, 220, 221–23, 225, 230; Mithraea 278, 355, 371; music and musicians 169, 173, 192, 193, 218, 309, 317, 319, 320, 321–22, 326, 339–42, 343; navy and naval operations 85, 115, 116, 120–21, 130, 144, 149, 152, 249, 291, 322–23; navy and naval operations:Athenian 42–43, 56, 57–58, 64, 99–100, 101; navy and naval operations: Byzantine 2; navy and naval operations: Roman 131, 339; olives and olive oil 23, 90, 95, 100, 160, 161, 162,

435

230, 233; Peloponnesian mythological parallels 81; philosophers and rhetoricians 178–79, 193, 218, 292–93, 296–97, 300–3, 309, 313–14, 317, 330, 333–34, 344, 335–36; phratries 65, 79–81, 83, 133, 155, 174–76, 181–82, 184, 210, 236, 294, 325, 327, 348; plagues 39–40, 48, 52–54, 67, 350–52; population and demographics 2, 8, 50–54, 59, 61, 62–63, 65, 66, 70–73, 79, 145, 153, 167–68, 81, 94, 121, 152, 156, 167–69, 171–72, 177–78, 184, 211, 271, 274, 316, 348–53, 356 (*See also* Neapolis: ethnic and cultural hybridity); prehistory 31–35; *quattuorviri* 173; *Regio Furcillensis* 178; *Regio Herculanensium (Herculensis)* 177–78, 183, 326–27; *Regio Thermensium (Thermensis)* 177, 178, 214, 217, 273, 288; roads 29, 69, 92, 121, 146–47, 169, 187, 232, 235, 236, 237, 238, 241–42, 247, 305, 306, 309–10 (*See also* Crypta Neapolitana; Via Antiniana; Via Domitiana; Via Herculanea); Roman character of physical city 185–86; safe haven (*xenia, asylia*) 129–30, 143, 166, 192, 292, 317–18; Samnites (*See* Campani; Osco-Samnites; Samnites); sanctuary of Demeter at Caponapoli 5, 51–52, 67, 83, 202; *schola* of a guild or phratry 210; settlement and early history (*See* Parthenope); ships, fleets, and shipbuilding 64, 130, 131, 143, 147, 149, 231; ships, fleets, and shipbuilding: commercial 14, 45, 219, 220, 225, 226–27, 229, 230–32, 234, 244; ships, fleets, and shipbuilding: naval 85, 116, 120, 130–31, 219–20, 225, 235, 244, 339; ships, fleets, and shipbuilding: river barges 230–31 (*See also* Neapolis: navy and naval operations); Severan improvements 221–23, 225, 226–30, 233–35, 247, 347–56; stadium 186, 194, 212, 315; street grid (*See* Hippodameian grid); Street of the Torch 326–27; suburbs 10, 185, 187, 192–93, 211, 212, 236, 238–243, 246, 253, 258–62, 275, 279–82, 296, 301–2, 304–6, 307–13, 319, 330–32, 353–54 (*See also* baths and bathing; Crypta Neapolitana; "Grotta di Seiano"; Neapolis: cemeteries, burials, and tombs; Nesis; Serino aqueduct; villas); Sullan occupation and influence 77, 130, 141, 142–45, 149–50, 151, 164, 165–67, 170–71, 172, 173, 174, 187, 195–96, 225, 255, 292, 297, 300; Temple of the Dioscuri 95, 133, 190–91, 196–205, 246; temple of the imperial cult (*See* Neapolis: Kaisareion;) territory and boundaries (*chora,* Neapolitanum) 15, 21–26, 29, 43, 48, 50, 55, 58, 59, 62, 64–65, 71–72, 73, 83, 84, 110, 137–38, 145, 146, 151–52, 156, 158–67, 169, 171, 173, 177, 181–82, 183, 329 (*See also* cadastral grid; Capri; Ischia; Neapolis: demes and demarchs); theaters, odeion, and performers 153, 155, 156, 168, 178, 186, 189, 190–96, 205, 211–12, 218, 241, 246, 275, 276, 282, 309, 311–12, 314–17, 319, 320–22, 325–26, 330–32, 334, 339–42, 343, 344, 345 (*See also* Nero); tunnels (*See* Crypta Neapolitana; "Grotta di Seiano"); visual arts 2, 7, 129, 136, 137, 144, 146, 162, 177,

181–82, 185, 197–205, 212–15, 226–30, 238, 244, 247, 262, 281, 312–13, 319, 330–32, 344–45; visual arts: frescos 128, 209, 210–11, 278, 279–80, 342–43, 348, 358 (See also coinage; Nitrodes; villas: Pausilypon); Wall of Fame 129, 215–16, 218, 326, 339–40; walls 2, 6, 24, 66, 68, 69, 72, 74, 83, 114, 116, 147, 164, 171, 185, 191–92, 202, 212, 213, 218, 236, 246, 318, 324; walls: new foundation date 49, 50–51, 67, 70–71; walls: ring road 187; water resources 6, 249–90, 363–65 (See also Bolla aqueduct; Serino aqueduct; Neapolis: fountains and nymphaea); water spectacle 311–12, 319, 337–39; wine 7, 23, 110, 129, 136, 137–38, 149, 324. See also Augustus; baths and bathing; cadastral grid; coinage; Constantine I; earthquakes; Hippodameian grid; Mt. Vesuvius; Nero; pottery and ceramics; Sebasta Games; villas.

Neapolitanum (territory of Neapolis) 145, 160, 162, 169

Nereus 91

Nero, emperor 155, 156, 180, 192, 193, 194, 275, 276, 334; Ahenobarbus (family name) 317–18; performer 341–42, 345

Nerva, emperor 168, 229, 233

Nike (Victoria) 212, 214, 247

Nikopolis, Istria 326

Nesis (Nisida) 15, 75, 266; Brutus' sojourn 151, 183; Serino Aqueduct 268

Nitrodes 248, 255, 283, 284, 288

Nitroli 288

Nola: agriculture 12; amphitheater 319; Attic ceramics 58; Augustan reorganization 153; cemeteries and tombs 237; *chora* 26; Christian 366; commerce 155; geography 12; grain 134; Hannibal 132, 147; land grid 160, 165, 183; Oscans 59, 113; pottery 109; Samnite alliance 113; Samnite Wars 119, 120, 121; Serino Aqueduct 286, 365; Sulla 145, 165; Vesuvius 159

Notizie degli scavi di antichità 4

Nuceria (Nocera) 11, 12, 24, 58, 59, 85, 89, 250; Hannibal's approach 147

Numidians 146, 147

Nymfulae 369, 370

Nymphios 106

Nymphius 120, 121

O

Octavian 16, 152, 258, 266, 307, 311. See also Augustus.

Odysseus 12, 14, 17, 19, 28, 33, 42, 43, 79, 97, 250, 251

Oibalos 77, 250

oil 23, 54, 136, 137, 139, 162, 230, 233, 234, 235, 267

Okinaros 42, 98, 253

Olcese, Gloria 6, 217

Olius Ampliatus, Gaius 158

olives 23, 90, 95, 97, 100, 160, 161, 162, 230, 233

Olympia 213, 214, 320, 325, 345; Olympic Games 96

Olympics, modern 211

Olynthos 211

Opici 60, 75, 76

Opsii 145, 155

Oscans (Osci) 59, 74, 87, 113, 129, 137

Osco-Samnite peoples 72, 139, 144, 172, 293; family names 153. See also Campani; Opici; Samnites.

Ostia 78, 231, 235; Christian 366; Christian pilgrimage 366; commerce 171; commercial

architecture 208; Constantinian basilica 364, 368, 369, 371; Marine Gate 236; Mithraea 355; Portus 366; Vesuvius 172
Ovid 298, 308
oysters 16, 100, 222, 232, 245, 255, 335

P
Paccii 145
Paestum 32, 42, 98, 185, 251
Pagano, Mario 160
pagi (rural districts) 65, 166
Paionios 212
Pais, Ettore 144
Palaeopolis 38, 117
Palaepolis (Palaeopolis): alternative name for Parthenope 38, 41, 47, 76, 144; abandonment 126-27; name 41-42; Second Samnite War flashpoint 114-21, stronghold of Campani and anti-Roman faction 117, 144. *See also* Lucullus, Lucius Licinius; Naples: Pizzofalcone; Parthenope.
Palaimon 44, 45, 325, 327
Palazzo degli Spiriti 305
paleobotany 183
Palinurus 250
Paludi, Le 26
Pane, Roberto 189
Panathenaic Festival, Greater 324
Panhellenic games 317, 320, 329
Paoli, Paolo Antonio 256, 268, 304
Parma, Aniello 307
Paros 137
Parthenope (site and mythical Siren): 7th-6th centuries BCE 49; abandonment 38, 49, 51, 52, 54; classical sources 38-41, 47-49, 52-53, 56, 62, 67, 323; cult 40, 45, 55, 56, 57, 83, 94, 164, 166, 198, 251, 252, 283, 322, 339; Cumaeans 23, 40, 46, 50, 51, 52, 53, 54; decline 47, 66; 41, 358 foundation 31, 40, 41, 45, 46-53, 77, 101, 368 (*See also* Neapolis: games: torch races); geography and geology 9, 16, 23, 38, 46, 47, 238; harbor 47, 219; highway 70; Livy 114, 117; Lucullus 144, 152, 164, 330, 370; Ovid 298; Lutatius' foundation narrative (cited in Philargyrios, scholium on *Georgics* 4.564) 39-40, 47-49, 52-53, 62, 67; metonym for Neapolis or Naples in poetry 23, 159, 298, 305, 316, 333, metonym for Neapolis or Naples in prose; Nesis, identified as 75; plague and refoundation 52, 53, 57; Pliny, *Natural History* 3.62 39; Ptolemy 75; resettlement 49, 53, 57; Rhodian foundation 75, 76; roads 233; *Scholia Bernensia* (on *Georgics* 4.564, citing Suetonius) 39; Siren 23, 28, 39, 40, 48, 91, 92, 98, 203, 205, 316, 323, 325, 326; Strabo, *Geography* 5.4.7 39; tomb of Siren 39, 42-45, 52, 324, 325, 327, 329; torch races at 45, 57, 324-26; Tzetzes' scholium of Lykophron 732 40, 56, 323
Paschasius 260
Pasiteles, sculptor 332
Paul III, pope 2
Paulinus, bishop 366
Pausanias, *Description of Greece* 8.7.3 285
Pausilypon (Posillipo) 14, 238, 240, 297, 345; Augustus' appropriation 307-8, 336-37; baths 281-82, 289; building complex 241-43, 304-5, 308, 309-10; gardens 312; Hadrianic 169, 311; name 300-1, 308; plunder-hunting at 3; road to spa district and Pozzuoli 169, 241-42; Philostratus' art gallery (*Images*

INDEX

1.pr.) 330-31; Serino aqueduct 268, 281, 287, 289; theater 241, 311-12; Vedius Pollio 307, 337; 287, 300, 306-12, 344. *See also* "Grotta di Seiano."
Pedroni, Luigi 103
Peloponnesian War 58
pensiles balineae 255
Pentri 59
perfume 23, 138
Pergamon 179, 350
Persephone 18, 251
Persian War 55, 56
Peter of Eboli, *De balneis Puteolanis* 259, 260
Peterson, Roy Merle 324
petrographic analysis 137
Petronius, *Satyricon* 6–7, 170, 179, 180, 181, 184
Phaleros (Phaleron) 42, 43, 44, 45, 55, 82, 327
Pharos 9, 316
Pheidias 332
Philargyrios, Scholium on Virgil's *Georgics* 4.564, 40, 48
Philip II, king 127
Philippus 335
Philodemos of Gadara 301, 302, 303
Philodemos, philosopher 301, 302, 303, 333, 336, 344
Philostratos of Askalon 137, 242, 345; *Images* 1.pr. 330
Phlegraean Fields. *See* Campi Phlegraei (Campi Flegrei, Phlegraean Fields).
Phoebus 252, 316
Phoenicians 36
Pianura 25
Pindar 20
Pisano, Carmine 297
piscinae 245, 255, 299, 309
Piso. *See* Pupius Piso Frugi Calpurnianus, Marcus.

Pithekoussai. *See* Ischia.
Pizzofalcone. *See* Naples: Pizzofalcone.
plagues: Antonine 350, 371; Black Death 351, 352; Cyprianic 351, 352, 354, 371; Justinianic 351. *See also* Neapolis: plagues; Parthenope: plague and refoundation.
Pliny the Elder: agriculture 138; Claudius 154; Collis Leucogaeus 258, 260; earthquakes 156; Ischia 36, 283; *Natural History* 2.197 176–77; 3.62 39; 9.170 335; 15.94 177; 17.122 177; 31.4–5 249, 284; Vesuvius expedition 19, 158; excesses of villa pisciculture 299; wines 137
Pliny the Younger 297; *Epistle* 4.20 156-57, 168; witness of Vesuvius eruption 156–58, 168
Plotius Tucca 303
Plutarch 241, 242; *Sulla* 26.3 239; *Table Talk* 4.4.1 (667c) 239
Pollena Trocchia 169
Pollius Felix 252, 287, 314, 315
Polybios 24, 113, 129
Polykleitos 204, 278, 332
Polykrates 78
Pompeii: amphitheater 319; aqueducts 274, 365; arts 332; Augustan reorganization 153, 154; baths 273; cemeteries and tombs 237; controlled by various peoples 10; demographics 172; earthquake of 62/63 155, 156; excavations 3, 4; fountains 271; fourth style of painting 209, 280; Greek temple 185; *Insula Occidentalis* 187; *macellum* 206; population 171; refuse heaps 349; residences 186, 210; sanctuary of Apollo 68; Samnite control 59; Stabian Baths 273, 288; street grid 66; Sullan colonization 145, 165;

439

theater and odeion 186, 195-96; Triangular Forum 68; Trimalchio's Feast, model for 179; Vesuvius 28, 31, 156, 263; viticulture 22; walls 187; World War II bombing 4
Pompey, Sextus (Sextus Pompeius) 16, 152, 218, 241, 339
Pompey the Great (Gnaeus Pompeius Magnus) 16, 151, 292, 335, 337, 339
Pontianus 286, 364
Pontioli. *See* Pozzuoli (Dikaiarcheia, Puteoli).
Pontrandolfo, Angela 69
Poppaei 145
Portus (Ostia) 366
Portus Julius 232
Poseidonia (Paestum) 42, 109.
Poseidonios of Apamea, philosopher 300
pottery and ceramics 7, 33, 37, 57, 71, 73; Apulia 142; archaeology 8; Arretine red slipware 141, 162; Attic 24, 55, 58; black-gloss 141, 147; "Campana A" 139, 140, 141, 142, 143, 147, 149, 162, 206, 221; "Campana B" 147, 162; Campania 148; Carthage 140; Chiatamone 46; clinkers 148; control marks 137; diffusion 140; discard heaps 148, 225; Etruria 148; fourth-century BCE 109; *gutti* 139; interpretation 5, 66; Ischia 36; Latium 148; Neapolis harbor excavations 220; Neapolitan slipware 149; North Africa 140, 142; Piazza Municipio excavations 139; Protoapennine 32; Protocorinthian wares 38; red slipware 141; Rhodian 75; Sicily 142; sixth century BCE 49, 51, 66; Spain 142; tablewares 139; terracotta spacers 148; typology 148; workshops 147

Pozzuoli (Dikaiarcheia, Puteoli): amphitheater 180, 319; Antonine lull 351; *aquae Cumanae* 254-55; Attic ceramics 58; Augustan reorganization 153; blood sport 319; boundaries 24-25; bradyseism 15, 17, 18; cemeteries and tombs 247; cisterns 271; commerce and harbor 13, 16, 18, 23, 47, 58, 143, 155, 170-71, 176, 225, 230, 232, 235, 247, 291, 308, 348, 355, 357; commemorative arch 229, 247; control of Baiae 249; consolation decrees 294-95; Constantine I 357, 365, 368, 371; Constantinople 358; cults 249, 255, 288; Cumae 46, 78; demographics 172; Dicaearchus foundation myth 252, 316; early history as Dikaiarcheia 14, 15, 24, 78-79; economy 23; eruption and early abandonment 79; Eusebeia Games 169, 211, 319, 343, 353; food imports 230; forum 246; geography and geology 13, 14, 15, 20, 39, 79, 233, 285; Greek city 78-79, 84; Greek character in Roman era 151, 180; Greek roads 233; honorific arch 229, 247; inscriptions 172, 263; Jews 16; *macellum* 15, 206; marble temple on citadel 198, 205, 246; *marmorarii* district 332; origins 78; origins of Puteoli's name 14, 254; Pausilypon branch road 169, 309-10; politicians 155; Pollius Felix 314; Pompeii diaspora 172; Pompey, reception of 151; population 271; *pozzolana* sand 18; public buildings 154, 351; *regiones* 153; Rione Terra 232; Roman foundation 24, 79, 254; Roman prefecture

440

INDEX

135; Samian foundation 50, 78; sculptors' district 332; Serino Aqueduct 263, 269, 271, 286, 357; Severan period 348, 351; shellfish production 23; stadium 194, 212, 247; St. Paul 366–67; custody of Neapolitan triremes after Sullan siege 143, 165–66, 171; territory 24, 25; 135; theater 194; thermal springs and baths 249, 254, 255, 257, 259, 285; tombs 237–38; Trimalchio's Feast 179–80, 184; underwater archaeology 232; Vesuvius 172; Via Antiniana (Neapolis–Puteoli highway) 168, 183, 233, 234, 237, 265–66, 280, 358; Via Celle necropolis 237; Via Domitiana 168, 229, 231, 234; water resources 249
Pozzuoli-Neapolis road (Via Antiniana) 305, 309
Praeneste (Palestrina) 129
Praetorian Guard 230
Prochyte 20
Procida (Prochyta) 19, 32, 41, 75; Sextus Pompey's seizure 152
Procopius, historian 274
Proteus 91
Pseudo-Skymnos, Periegesis 39
Pterelaos 80
Ptolemy (Claudius Ptolemaeus), geographer 75, 76
Publilius Philo, Quintus 116–17, 119, 120
Pugliese Carratelli, Giovanni 34, 48, 75
Pugliese, Lydia 6, 324
Punic Wars 138; First 85, 89, 107, 130; Second 22, 24, 25, 86, 107, 109, 126, 129, 131–35, 149, 352
Pupius Piso Frugi Calpurnianus, Marcus 300
Pyrrhic War 109, 124, 126, 129, 146

Pyrrhus of Epirus 106
Pythagoras 78

Q

quinces 138
Quintilius Varius, Publius 303
Quintus Fabius Labeo 165

R

Raviola, Flavio 41, 49, 51, 54, 76
Regi Lagni system 25
Rhegion (Rhegium, Reggio Calabria) 64, 129, 130, 291, 299, 366
Rhenaia 137
Rhodes: amphoras 324; connection to Parthenope 75–77, 92
Rock of Hercules (Scoglio di Rovigliano) 92
Rome: Baths of Caracalla 2; Caelian Hill 179; Capitoline Games 211, 315, 320; Christian pilgrimage 366; Concordia 94, 125; Constantinian basilicas 364, 369; Dioscuri 203; fora 117, 125, 362; foundation myth 250; *lex Iulia* 142; medieval 2; Napoleonic 2; Neronian Games 211; Piazza del Campidoglio 203; Praetorian Guard 172; *regiones* 177; S. Agnese 366; S. Croce in Gerusalemme 366; Senate 115; S. Lorenzo fuori le Mura 366; S. Marcellino 366; S. Paolo fuori le Mura 366; St. John Lateran 366; St. Peter's 366; waterfront 235. *See also* Ostia; Portus.
Romulus Augustulus, emperor 334
roses 138
Rustica 178
Rusticus, *consularis Campaniae* 363, 364
Rutter, Keith 87, 96, 99, 102, 124

441

S

Sabelli 59
St. Aspren (Asprenus) 172, 367, 368
St. Candida 172
St. Jerome 78, 305
St. Nostrianus 280
St. Paul 16, 197, 364, 366-67, 368
St. Peter 172, 306, 364, 366-68, 371
Salamis, battle of 56, 338
Sambon, Arthur 106, 124
Samnites (Samniti): Campania 60; Cumae 62, 64; government 173; incursions 25, 35, 50, 52, 59-63, 78, 94, 101; Livy's and Dionysius' narratives of events of 327/6 114-22; mercenaries 102; dealings with Neapolis 62-65, 73, 83, 113-22; Samnite League 60, 113-14, 118; Sebethos River as ethnic symbol 94. *See also* Campania: Samnites in; Campani; Oscans; Osco-Samnite peoples; Neapolis: ethnic and cultural hybridity.
Samnite Wars 60, 73, 108, 149; First 103, 122, 343; Second 41, 61, 109, 114-21, 129; Third 109
Samos 50, 78
Samothrake 42
Sarmatians 167
Sarno River 11, 12, 23, 34, 58, 85, 231, 250
Sartori, Franco 173
Satrius Paconianus, Decimus 287
Scheidel, Walter 352
Scholia Bernensia, on Virgil's *Georgics* 4.564 39
Scipio the Younger 297
Sclina 369
Scoglio di Virgilio 304
Scuola di Virgilio 304
Sebethis 77, 96, 250
Sebethos (Sebeto) River 26, 46, 94-96, 98-99, 101, 160, 201, 222, 249, 250, 253
Seirenoussai (Mons Sirenianus) 46, 251
Seleukos, archon 173-174
Seneca, Lucius Annaeus 155, 194, 307; *Moral Epistles* 57.1-2 13; 76.3-4 193
Septimii 145
Septimius Severus, emperor 169, 228, 230, 233-35, 358
Sergius Orata 255-57, 273, 288, 335
Serino Aqueduct (Aqua Augusta) 288; Augustus 286, 357; Belisarius' incursion 274; Campania 286; commissioners 287; Constantinian restoration 274, 285-86, 370; construction 154; disruptions 263-64, 274, 286-87, 274-75; foundation 154; gradient and elevations 263-64, 269, 274-75; inscriptions 285, 286; length 263; Neapolis, service to 262-71, 272, 275, 276, 280; Pausilypon 281-82; Pompeii and Herculaneum 365; route 263-66; source 263, 285-86, 357; water volume 271
Severan dynasty 221-29, 233-36, 347, 364
Severus Alexander. *See* Alexander Severus.
Sextus Pompey. *See* Pompey, Sextus.
Sgobbo, Italo 269
Sherwin-White, A.N. 122
Sibyl, Cumaean and her oracles 18, 48, 252, 316
Sicily 20, 33, 46, 57, 58, 102, 130, 138, 152. *See also* Syracuse.
Sikels 56, 57, 323
Silius Italicus 145, 305; *Punica* 12.31-32 291
Simon Magus 367
Sinuessa 24, 168, 231

INDEX

Sirens 110-11, 288; Acheloös as father 91; cult 9, 12, 43, 45-46, 52, 75, 83, 97-99, 163-65, 250-53, 315; mythology 28, 42, 43, 91, 97, 251, 325; Odysseus' encounter 42, 97, 250, 251-52; tomb 39, 42-45, 52, 324, 325, 327, 329. *See also* Leukosia; Ligeia; Parthenope.
Siris. *See* Sybaris.
Siro, philosopher 302, 303, 304, 333, 334, 344
Sisyphos 44, 325, 327
Social War 130, 142, 144
Soloi 44
Somma 271
Somma Vesuviana, villa 161, 169
Soranos 283
Sorrentine Peninsula 12, 19, 43, 45, 99, 251, 287, 315
Spain 42, 92, 138; lead 274
Stabiae 9, 12, 23, 169, 316; royal excavations 3; Vesuvius 158. *See also* Castellamare di Stabia.
Stallius Hauranus, Gaius 335, 344
Staseas, philosopher 300
Statiellae (Acqui Terme) 249
Statius, Publius Papinius, poet 1, 158, 159, 172, 242, 270, 287, 326, 345; Capo Miseno, mythology 19; family 293, 294, 313; founding gods of Neapolis (Apollo Demeter, Dioscuri) 78-79, 80, 104, 202, 203, 252, 283-84, 323; imperial patronage 315; life 313-16; *Silvae* 314; 1.2.262-65 249; 2.2.1-13 314-15; 3.5.72-105 9, 315-16; theaters in Neapolis 195; Vesuvius aftermath 156; Virgil, reverence for 306
Stephen, bishop 359
Stertinius Xenophon, Gaius 154, 155, 257
Strabo's *Geography*: 5.4.3 22; 5.4.6 14; 5.4.7 39, 62, 257, 291, 325;

5.4.9 20-21, 54; 14.2.10 75; Athenians 39-44, 55; Baiae 20; baths 257; Campani 62-65; Campania 22; Chalkidians 39-41, 47, 80; Cumae 75; demarchates 65; descriptions 1; early settlements 36; Ischia and Capri 20-21, 36, 54, 143-44, 283; Lucrine Gulf 13-14; Lucrine Lake 16; Lucullan villa 270; Neapolis' foundation 39, 40, 47, 80; Neapolitan culture 291; Neapolitans as Romans 142-43; Odysseus 12; Parthenope 39, 40, 323, 325-26, 327; phratries 174; pre-Greek origins 10; Rhodians 75-76; Samnites 62; Trojan War 33; tunnels 266-67
Stufe di S. Germano 260
Suessula 113, 134; Roman prefecture 135; Sullan colonization 145
Suetonius (Gaius Tranquillus): Augustus and Capri 77, 327, 328, 329; Nero 276, 318, 341, 342; Parthenope 39; Titus 163; Virgil 305
Sulla, Lucius Cornelius, dictator 77, 130, 141, 142-45, 149-50, 151, 164, 165-67, 170-74, 187, 196, 225, 239, 241, 255, 292, 297
Sulla, Publius Cornelius, nephew of dictator 166, 300
Sullivan, J.P. 180
Surrentum (Sorrento) and Sorrentine Peninsula 59, 168, 251, 252, 263. *See also* Athena: sanctuary; Località Trinità.
Sybaris 56
Sylvester I, pope 364, 369
Symmachus, pope 261
Syracuse 49-50, 62, 83; assembly 64; coinage 90, 101, 102-3, 105; Ischia, dealings with 20, 47,

443

54-55, 83; tyrants 102. *See also* Battle of Cumae; Hieron I.

T

Tacitus, emperor 348
Tacitus, Publius Cornelius, *Annals* 15.34 342
Taliercio, Marina 123, 133, 134
Tanagra 80
Taras (Taranto, Tarentum): chestnuts 177; coinage 105; cultural life 299; fleet 130; Greek traditions 291; Roman domination 107, 130, 297; Samnite Wars 115, 119-20; Trimalchio's Feast 179
Teleboi 9, 77, 80, 316
Telon 77, 80
Telos 250
Tereina 42, 251, 253; coinage 96-99, 101
Tereus 177
Terracina 233
Tethys 42
Themistocles 56
Theodosian Code 286
Theon, Roman Christian 367
Theotadai, phratry 79, 175-76
Thermae Alinarum 260
Theseus, king 325
Thesmophorion 52
Thiel, J.H. 130, 131
Thomsen, Rudi 124
Tiberius, emperor 155, 198, 203, 307
Tiber River 114, 203, 230-31
Tibur (Tivoli) 129
Timaios of Tauromenion 20, 38, 39, 40, 76, 93, 251, 323, 324
Titans 28
Titus, emperor 163-65, 167-68, 295, 317, 322, 339-40, 345
Trajan, emperor 155, 167, 168, 169, 229, 230, 232, 233, 358
Trebius Loesius 137

tremors 15, 155; Campania 156. *See also* earthquakes.
Trimalchio's Feast 170, 179-80. *See also* Petronius, *Satyricon*.
Tritoli 256
Tronzo, William 364
Troy 19, 20, 33, 42
Tuck, Steven 172
tunnels. *See* Crypta Neapolitana; "Grotta di Cocceio"; "Grotta di Seiano."
Tyche 202
Typhon 20
Tzetzes 40, 56; Scholium of Lykophron, *Alexandra* 732 40; 733 323

U

Urania 313
Urbana 145

V

Valerii 145
Valle d'Ansanto 254
Varius Rufus, Lucius 303
Varro, Marcus Terentius 65, 174, 297, 298-99, 334
Vecchio, Giuseppe 5, 69, 308, 312
Vedius Pollio, Publius 14, 287, 300, 307-9, 311-12, 336, 344
Velia (Elea) 137, 153, 291, 292, 293
Velleius Paterculus 39, 73, 126, 335
Vergina 128
Verus, emperor. *See* Lucius Verus.
Vespasian, emperor 164, 295
Vesuvius. *See* Mt. Vesuvius.
Via Antiniana (Neapolis-Pozzuoli highway) 233, 234, 237, 247, 305, 309, 358
Via Appia 125, 168, 231
Via Domitiana 18, 168, 229, 231, 233, 247
Via Herculanea 92
Via Traiana 230

INDEX

Victoria. *See* Nike.
Villanovan culture 34
villas: Apragopolis 308, 328-29, 344; architecture 161; Baiae 255; Cicero 296; duke of Medina 312; Emperor Tacitus 348; Epicurean 301-2; Herculaneum 301; Limon (Epilimones) 242, 286; Lucullan 126-27, 144, 152, 164, 269-70, 297, 298, 308, 309, 318-19, 330, 334-35, 370; maritime 232, 255, 297, 298, 307-8; Neapolis 238; Oplontis 331; Pausilypon (Posillipo) 3, 14, 169, 238, 240, 241-43, 268, 281-82, 286-87, 289, 297, 300-1, 304-5, 306-12; political life 308; Pollena Trocchia 161, 169, 184; Pollius Felix 9, 286-87, 314-15, 316; Ponticelli 73, 158, 161, 162, 184; Qualiano 162, 183; San Sebastiano al Vesuvio 162, 183; S. Gennarello 161, 169; Siro and Virgil 302-3, 334; Somma Vesuviana 161, 169, 184; Tivoli 311; urbanization 309; Vesuvian 332; villa culture 296-303, 344; Villa Jovis 307
Vindex, Gaius Julius 318
Virgil (Publius Vergilius Maro), poet: *Aeneid* 33, 263; *Aeneid* 6.237-42 17; Avernus 17; cult 303-5, 344; death 305; *Eclogues* 303, 305, 333; Epicureanism 333; *Fourth Eclogue* 303; Garden of Naples 301-3, 333-34, ; *Georgics* 298, 305; *Georgics* 4.559-66 333; literary circle 301-3, 333; myths 303-5; Parthenias (nickname) 303; Naples (Parthenope) as his home 305, 316, 333; tomb 303-6, 344; Vesuvian villa 303
Vitruvius, *Ten Books on Architecture* 2.6.1-4 285
Vivara 19, 32, 33, 41
Volla (Bolla) region 26, 272
Volturnum 135
Volturno (Volturnus) River and Valley 22, 161, 231

W

wine 149; Ager Falernus 138, 315; Aminaean 138; bibliography 137; Cauline 138; Dionysos cult 72; export and trade 22, 54, 110, 136-38, 230; imports 230; Neapolis 7, 23, 110, 129, 136-38; Pompeii 22; Rhodian 324; storage 169; Sebasta Games 137, 324; Trebellian 137; Trifoline 138
World War II, bombing 4

Z

Zevi, Fausto 50, 78, 79, 152

*Production of This Book Was Completed
on 21 March 2021 at Italica Press,
Clifton, Bristol, United Kingdom.
It Was Set in Adobe Bembo,
Adobe Bembo Expert &
Carta Ornaments*

www.ingramcontent.com/pod-product-compliance
Lightning Source LLC
Chambersburg PA
CBHW021825220426
43663CB00005B/137